A Republic,
if You Can Keep It

A Republic, if You Can Keep It

Constitutional Politics and Public Policy

William L. Morrow

College of William and Mary

Prentice Hall
Upper Saddle River, New Jersey 07458

Library of Congress Cataloging-in-Publication Data

MORROW, WILLIAM LOCKHART, (date)
 A republic, if you can keep it: constitutional politics and
public policy/William L. Morrow.
  p. cm.
 Includes bibliographical references.
 ISBN 0–13–095067–X (pbk.)
  1. Political planning—United States. 2. Constitutional law—
United States. 3. United States—Politics and government.
I. Title.
JK468.P64M67 2000
320'.6'0973—dc21
                                                98–56094
                                                CIP

Editorial director: Charlyce Jones Owen
Editor-in-chief: Nancy Roberts
Senior acquisitions editor: Beth Gillett
Editorial assistant: Brian Prybella
Project manager: Joan Stone
Prepress and manufacturing buyer: Ben Smith
Cover director: Jayne Conte
Cover designer: Bruce Kenselaar
Marketing manager: Christopher DeJohn

This book was set in 10/12 New Baskerville by ElectraGraphics, Inc.,
and was printed and bound by Hamilton Printing Company.
The cover was printed by Phoenix Color Corp.

Printed in the United States of America

10 9 8 7 6 5 4 3 2 1

ISBN 0-13-095067-X

PRENTICE-HALL INTERNATIONAL (UK) LIMITED, *London*
PRENTICE-HALL OF AUSTRALIA PTY. LIMITED, *Sydney*
PRENTICE-HALL CANADA INC., *Toronto*
PRENTICE-HALL HISPANOAMERICANA, S.A., *Mexico*
PRENTICE-HALL OF INDIA PRIVATE LIMITED, *New Delhi*
PRENTICE-HALL OF JAPAN, INC., *Tokyo*
PEARSON EDUCATION ASIA PTE. LTD., *Singapore*
EDITORA PRENTICE-HALL DO BRASIL, LTDA., *Rio de Janeiro*

In memory of
Bruce Edward Morrow

Contents

chapter eleven

The Bureaucracy: Constitutional Politics and the Unelected Branch   *327*

chapter twelve

The Judiciary: Procedural Democracy and Policy Justice   *366*

Preface

As a student of American politics, I can best be described as a devout pluralist. In addition, for most of my academic career I have been constantly impressed by the existence of what I consider to be a distinct cause-and-effect relationship between the values and institutional structure sanctioned by the Constitution on the one hand and politics and policy on the other. Pluralist forces exploit these constitutional propensities to their advantage as they attempt to maximize their influence on policy. The result is a political condition that impairs the ability of the public and its representative institutions to deal effectively with the major policy problems of the late twentieth and early twenty-first centuries.

Existing literature on American politics and public policy does not, in my opinion, give enough credit to the leverage that constitutional inputs have on both politics and policymaking. Therefore, this book is my modest attempt to begin to fill that void. I have chosen to do so by drawing a good deal of the format for the analysis of the relationship between constitutional politics and public policy from analytical windows that are quite familiar to most students of American politics—Congress, the presidency, political parties, interest groups, federalism, the courts, and so on. I have also chosen to follow a distinct "input-transmission-output" sequence in the way in which I deal with the challenge. I begin with the role of the Constitution in shaping democratic theory in America and how that has affected public opinion. I then proceed to analyze how transition, or "intermediary," institutions gain policy salience by employing constitutional principles to amplify their role in both opinion formation and its translation into policy. Finally, I undertake to show how policymaking institutions flavor both the way they do business and the results of that business with constitutional doctrine.

I am indebted to many for their help on both the focus and the administration of this effort. A research grant from the College of William and Mary helped launch the project on sound footing. I would like to thank Eve Perkins, Alicia Jones, Karen Hammer, and Tess Owens, all of whom provided very helpful administrative assistance during my involvement in the project. From Prentice Hall, I would like to thank Dan Pellow, Beth Gillett, Darren Rich, Brian Prybella, and, especially, Joan Stone and Rene Lynch for their excellent work on the project as production manager and copy editor respectively. I also prof-

ited greatly from reviews by Roger Handberg, University of Central Florida; John J. Hindera, Texas Tech University; Albert J. Nelson, University of Wisconsin–La Crosse; and Ruth Ann Strickland, Appalachian State University. While I owe a debt of gratitude to all these individuals, all matters of fact and interpretation are exclusively my responsibility.

William L. Morrow
Williamsburg, Virginia

A Republic,
if You Can Keep It

chapter one

Public Policy

The Constitutional Cornerstone

This book is about the impact of the Constitution and what is herein termed "constitutional politics" on both the policy process and the character of public policy in the United States. Its major thesis is that the Constitution encourages a distinctive type of politics that has a direct and significant influence on public policy. As a source of the national government's basic authority to regulate individual, group, and institutional behavior, the Constitution apportions power in ways that affect the access of people to their government, the ways in which intermediary institutions such as the media, political parties, and interest groups impact on policy, and the ways in which our governing institutions interact to build consensus in support of options which eventually become public policy. Political forces are both intuitively and consciously aware of how the Constitution can bolster or restrain them in their efforts to maximize their leverage over policy decisions. They organize their efforts in ways that allow the Constitution either to help them, to be bypassed if its principles pose a danger, or to determine the arenas within which they conduct their campaigns to influence policy. When they do these things they are engaging in what can be branded "constitutional politics."

The nation faces policy challenges in the twenty-first century that will be unrivaled in both number and scope. Nonetheless, governments both national and subnational seem unable to muster the will, resources, and administrative capacity to address many of these problems with the proper perspective and determination necessary to cope with them adequately. Those cognizant of this condition, and of the warning it seems to be posing for the future vitality of the political system, might well be reminded of Dr. Benjamin Franklin's challenge to the nation following the adjournment of the Constitutional Convention in September 1787. When asked by a certain Mrs. Powell of Philadelphia what kind of government had been bestowed on the country as a result of the Convention's four-month effort, Dr. Franklin was reported to have said: "A republic, madam, if you can keep it." In all probability, in Franklin's opinion, the ability of the young nation to "keep the republic" was open to question. Although government has survived the social, economic, and political challenges confronting it for more than two centuries, the ability of the nation to "keep the republic" while responding logically to policy challenges that are growing increasingly complex is open to question.

A republic is a representative democracy, within which citizens elect policymakers to act on their behalf as they fashion public policy. It is one step detached from pure democracy. There are both practical and political reasons for a republic. On the practical side, it is unfeasible for a populace in all but the smallest of political jurisdictions to assemble and make policy directly. Elected representatives are virtually the only option. On the political side, elected representatives offer a way for citizens to protect themselves from their own policy obsessions, of which many may be irrational, destabilizing, and even dangerous. In the two centuries since Dr. Franklin's challenge we have managed the procedural part of the challenge very well. The control, or potential control, of citizens over who is elected to policymaking positions is perhaps greater today than at any time in our history. However, America has done better at preserving and expanding the institutions of electoral democracy than it has done at confronting and mastering the policymaking, or governing, challenge. While the formalities of electoral democracy have flourished, the challenge to produce, with consistency, public policies appropriate for the conditions they seek to alleviate has been far less noteworthy. Many policies are essentially politically derived assertions of moral intent, weak on both goal specificity and the necessary supportive resources.

Many identify problems adequately but delay or "backload" the commitment of resources necessary to solve them. Still others are the result of so many concessions and compromises among political forces that they bear little or no resemblance to policies that could address seriously the problems at hand.

Many factors underlie this public policy malaise. The Constitution is one of them, but certainly not the only one. The Constitution cannot stand alone as an independent force contributing to policy impotence or inadequacy. Instead, it serves as a structural factor that can amplify the mission, and facilitate the ability, of animate political forces to gain advantage in the policymaking process. Conscious of this, these forces execute a distinct type of politics, herein termed "constitutional politics," as they seek to leverage their position in the policy struggle. Such acumen on the part of political actors means that their strategies and tactics bring life to the Constitution as a policy force. Politicians are the energizers, the stimuli, and the catalysts. They enable the Constitution to impact on policy both directly and indirectly, but significantly in either way.

The Constitution assigns policy responsibilities to government institutions, but it does not assign policy incentives to political actors. Most political incentives are rooted in the self-interest of the individuals and groups that espouse them. The Constitution and its political use frequently amplify the expression of those incentives. The principles of government embodied by the Constitution can increase or limit the impact of those incentives on public policy. In addition, the fact that the Constitution apportions policy power among branches and levels of government often makes it difficult for citizens to determine precisely who or what is responsible for policy decisions, good or bad. Finally, because of its official diffusion of policy authority, the Constitution enhances the effect of special interests on both the development and administration of public policy.

Constitutions legitimize and structure the exercise of governmental power in societies. Each written constitution accomplishes this in its own way. Therefore, to say that the U.S. Constitution is unique is only to say that it has individuality, as do all constitutions in all representative democracies. Constitutions are unnecessary in authoritarian societies because in such systems all the legitimate coercive authority is held by a single entity, usually an individual or a clique. However, constitutions are essential in democratic societies because these communities are obligated to preserve a healthy balance between the rights of individuals on the one hand and the need for government to foster social and economic stability and protect people from harm induced by either internal or external forces on the other. In sum, in democracies constitutions both assign and limit the exercise of power. Constitutions, both written and unwritten, serve as charters or "rule books." A written constitution assigns power to government institutions with the expectation that the formal assignment of authority is, because of its written character, a reality that limits the potential of government to exceed its legitimate authority to act.

The Venerable Constitution

America was the first society in recorded history to empower and constrain its government by a written constitution. The written option was chosen because the Constitution's framers thought it the best way to avoid government impotence by empowering it sufficiently while, at the same time, minimizing the chances for majority tyranny. Recognizing that time and conditions may well make it necessary to change how the Constitution's provisions translate to the everyday world, the framers were deliberately vague in the conferral of some powers and offered two routes to formally amend the document.

Most Americans have come to worship the Constitution. They assume its principles and provisions are immutable. To them, the Constitution has become a form of "civic religion."[1] If things go wrong, they don't blame the Constitution. Instead, they blame the politicians. Most Americans believe current officeholders are not endowed with the moral purity and vision of the founders. However, such an interpretation is a mistake. While the framers were men of intelligence and wisdom, they were also pragmatists seeking to accommodate the growing popularity of democracy with their commitment to protecting property rights by making government more stable. Therefore, it is unreasonable to expect that they intended the Constitution to be a document relevant to all times and all conditions. Although not a member of the delegation that drafted the Constitution, Thomas Jefferson was very much a part of the founding period and, as president, was profoundly affected by its provisions. He once commented on the potential dangers of overexalting written constitutions produced by politicians of previous eras:

> Some men look at constitutions with sanctimonious reverence and deem them like the ark of the covenant, too sacred to be touched. They ascribe to men of the preceding age a wisdom more than human, and suppose what they did to be beyond amendment. I knew that age well; I belonged to it and labored with it. . . . We might as well require a man to wear the coat which fitted him when he was a boy, as civilized society to remain ever under the regimen of their barbarous ancestors.[2]

There is little doubt that it is potentially quite dangerous to cloak with a mantle of invulnerability a constitution authored by men seeking to both empower and restrain a government and its people on the one hand while attempting to protect the sanctity of property through a more stable regime on the other. Unfortunately, most Americans appear to do just that. They overlook, for example, that the nation's first constitution—the Articles of Confederation—was so inappropriate to the policy challenges facing the young country that it endured for only eight years. When the Constitution's provisions are stretched to accommodate changing conditions, we are inclined to attribute that flexibility to the wisdom of the framers, and not to the politics of the times. Without question, the framers do deserve credit for incorporating flexibility into the document, but probably not to the degree that politicians do when they seek to justify their policy quests as not just political crusades but constitutional crusades as well.

Nonetheless, the Constitution's flexible attributes, be they rooted in the design of the founders or in the strategies of politicians, potentially do make the document adaptable to changing conditions. It is this potential for flexibility, however inspired, that diminishes the potential problems warned of by Jefferson. On the other hand, it most certainly doesn't remove them. If the Constitution is employed politically to advance goals that are inimical to the nation's long-term well-being, Jefferson's argument is certainly germane.

Loyalty to the Constitution in principle is especially dangerous in America because our constitution arranged institutional structures and power assignments in ways that were, and remain, clearly antimajoritarian and with a decided disposition toward incremental, or very gradual, policy change. Most Americans would agree, in theory, that loyalty to one's country supersedes loyalty to its constitution. In reality, Americans generally do not distinguish between the two projections, assuming that constitutional standards and prescriptions would, if followed literally, accomplish things that are

in the nation's best interest. However, this is self-delusive. Constitutions, statutes, politicians, and citizens do not always prescribe and act on virtues that strengthen their country's chances for long-term survival and prosperity. Therefore, it is important to ask how these current institutional structures, and the politics and policies produced by these structures, are likely to affect those chances. Mark Twain expressed a comparable opinion rather firmly in a passage in *A Connecticut Yankee in King Arthur's Court*:

> My kind of loyalty was loyalty to one's country, not to its institutions or its officeholders. The country is the real thing, the substantial thing, the eternal thing; it is the thing to watch over and care for, and be loyal to; institutions are extraneous, they are its mere clothing, and clothing can wear out, become ragged, cease to be comfortable, cease to protect the body from winter, disease, and death. To be loyal to rags, to shout for rags, to worship rags, to die for rags—that is a loyalty of unreason; it is pure animal. . . .[3]

The U.S. Constitution has not yet reached the "rags" state insofar as its potential to help citizens and their government adapt to the policy requirements of the twenty-first century is concerned. However, the politics and policies often produced by what in this book is designated constitutional politics clearly do not embody the foresight and courage necessary to meet that challenge effectively.

Constitutional Politics: A Primer

Recognizing the public's reverence for the Constitution, politicians, interest groups, and individuals frequently cite the Constitution as an ally of their respective policy causes and as a defense of their behavior. This tendency, combined with the effects of the Constitution's assignment of policy power to separate institutions and to two distinct levels of government, together constitute constitutional politics. Politics is essentially a struggle among individuals and groups over the right to control government and dictate the character of public policy. If politicians can defend their choice of policy objectives, their selection of political strategies, and their overall public behavior as emanating from the Constitution, it mantles their crusades and strategies with a sense of legitimacy that often helps them leverage their influence over policy decisions. If individuals, groups, and policymakers sense that their quest to secure government support of their policy objectives can be advanced by exploiting the Constitution's structural mandates, how it assigns power to institutions that must share the policymaking responsibility, and its guarantee of fundamental communication freedoms to individuals and groups, not to do so would be politically irrational. As a result, the Constitution frequently is enlisted as a natural ally by politicians and groups in their attempts to influence the character of public policy.

The Constitution, Politics, and Public Policy

The U.S. Constitution is a seven-thousand-word document that is mostly devoted to assigning powers to institutions and mandating decision-making procedures. Most would likely find it rather uninspirational reading. Overall, the political use of only a few of its characteristics and provisions impact regularly and significantly on public policy. Most obvious are the policy-making conditions created by its deliberate fragmentation of institutional policy responsibilities. Included here are the separation of powers, checks and balances, federalism, and the guarantee of communication freedoms.

The influence of these realities is augmented by the fact that the assignment of power to institutions and actors impacted by these principles is often ambiguous and open to interpretation. The most significant policy-relevant provisions include Article I, Section 8 and the First, Ninth, Tenth, and Fourteenth Amendments.

The structures, processes, and guarantees contained in the Constitution do not function only as filters through which pass policy options on their way to legitimization. They also create their own distinct brand of politics. In social science parlance, the Constitution is a key independent variable in both the development and administration of public policy. The major purpose of this book is to describe and analyze that type of politics and its current and future influence on the nation. Three major hypotheses, or theses, will be explored. First, the Constitution encourages political behavior in ways that have clear and significant implications for the character and quality of public policy. Second, the politics encouraged by the Constitution often advantages the very forces the framers were attempting to constrain by the document itself. Third, assuming the first two hypotheses are accurate, the result has been a political and policy landscape that handicaps the public and its government in their efforts to cope effectively with contemporary policy problems.

Policy decisions are produced by the interaction of a host of factors, both political and institutional. This book incorporates a variation of the systems model as its principal methodological ally. The systems approach holds that host factors—social, economic, political, and structural—and often other unknown elements interact to produce policy decisions which, in turn, impact on the aforementioned factors to alter subsequent policy decisions. These factors include, but are not limited to, such items as historical-geographical conditions, socioeconomic circumstances, public opinion and behavior, government institutions, and elites or leaders. Major changes in any element within the interacting circles inevitably influence the other elements, usually reflecting a cause and effect pattern. The cause and effect relationship among the elements is not simply linear but circular and interdependent. Most applications of systems analysis to policymaking are inclined to consider constitutionally decreed government structure, and the institutions produced by it, as the conversion center, or "black box" dimension of the policy cycle. These institutions are usually regarded as transmission and conversion centers that weigh and synthesize policy options before they are formally converted into public policy. While their effect on policy is not necessarily neutral, systems analysts do not generally consider them independent variables in the policy process. An independent variable is one that affects institutional behavior and policy outputs without its behavior or structural integrity being changed in the process. This book attempts to isolate, insofar as is possible, the influence of constitutional provisions on political behavior as well as on the public policies and public attitudes produced by that behavior. In sum, it assumes that the Constitution encourages a distinct type of politics, and while that type of politics could in theory be overcome by a determined public and its leaders, the Constitution encourages the converse and, being the course of least resistance, that is the course that has been followed.

The Constitution: Past, Present, and Future

The Constitution is an eighteenth-century document attempting to cope with policy problems of the twentieth and twenty-first centuries. It was a political document drafted by society's economic elites who wanted to strengthen and stabilize government in order to protect property rights by discouraging majority rule while still committing themselves to popular sovereignty in principle. It was not a wholly undemocratic document, but it did seek to keep popular opinion at bay by minimizing its direct impact on policy institutions by filtering it through several separate policy stages. It did acknowledge that the fundamental authority for government to act was vested in the people. To that end, it established the House of Representatives as the major institution to receive and absorb public inputs directly. On the other hand, it ensured that pubic opinion would be filtered through, and tempered by, processes and institutions that would make American democracy a minorities-based, consensus-building exercise.

Contemporary policy problems bear little resemblance to those of the founding period. Today a democratic government's effectiveness rests on its ability to translate public demands into public policies that enable government to offer its citizens the necessary services, protection, and security they need to provide for themselves, their families, and their communities. Depending on the policy issue at hand, government is called on to subsidize individuals, families, and groups; to regulate institutional behavior in the interest of economic stability and the public's health and well-being; and (increasingly) to redistribute resources, activity, and wealth to accommodate the inescapable demands that humanitarianism places on democratic governments.

In light of these mandates, the Constitution of 1789, even as amended formally or by habit or judicial decision, is not up to the task if the framers' intentions remain intact. Today, the primary challenge of government is not to restrain majorities but to encourage their development. Government can be responsible and accountable only if the public makes its expectations known. Today we do not need to restrain, in principle, the exercise of power by government. Today we need to find ways to exercise that power flexibly and judiciously in ways that offer long-term solutions to escalating policy problems. In light of these challenges, the type of constitutional politics described above is an enemy, not an ally, to the cause. Constitutional politics can deter, deflect, even disengage government from its substantive policy challenges.

An assumption of this book is that the Constitution is adaptable to the policy challenges of the twenty-first century, but that this is heavily dependent on how its provisions are put to use. If its provisions are used as ways to rationalize obstruction and conflict of interest, and to leverage the impact of cohesive minorities on policy, then the Constitution is not up to the challenge. On the other hand, if it is used to encourage politicians and jurisdiction to experiment with policies, to debate the merits of proposals from constitutionally separate institutional perspectives, and to encourage the renewal of a healthy civic culture, then it can be an asset to those policy challenges.

Scholars are divided on the Constitution's prospects. Writers such as James Sundquist, Donald Robinson, Lloyd Cutler, Daniel Lazare, Charles Hardin, Daniel Hoffman, John Manley, and Kenneth Dolbeare argue that the Constitution has instituted too much of a policy "straightjacket" on public participation, institutional procedures and, therefore, on government policies.[4] While they believe that the Constitution did create avenues for individuals to participate in government, they do not believe the framers wanted a government that was genuinely democratic. Whatever dangers such a condition poses for the ability of government to respond to the policy essentials of today's society, the country still remains in the grip of the framers' mission. Constitutional problems have caused such things as unnecessary policy gridlock, careless presidential escapades in foreign policy, and increasing voter apathy. In general, these skeptics recommend major structural changes that will encourage political parties to unite behind coherent, balanced policy agendas and offer them the institutional structural harmony to enact them into law. On the other hand, scholars such as Arthur Schlesinger, Jr., James Ceaser, James Wilson, Nelson Polsby, Kathleen Sullivan, and Alan Brinkley maintain that, although the Constitution is by no means ideal, it is best to leave well enough alone.[5] They recognize that the American system has not produced the majoritarian-instilled policies that most parliamentary systems have, but they blame this condition less on the impact of constitutional structure on policy and more on the political structures and political habits that have developed beneath it, and on the inability of the American public, on its own, to develop into clear and cohesive majority and minority camps. What they slight somewhat is the cause and effect relationship between the Constitution and those dysfunctional structures and habits that have made our politics inadequate in the face of our policy challenges. Exploring such a relationship is a major objective of this book.

Constitutional Politics and the Policy Cycle

This book assumes that the content of public policy is heavily influenced by the processes that produce it, and that both those processes and the public policies themselves are marked significantly by constitutional inputs or expectations. The public's reverence for the Constitution encourages a reverence for the procedures it prescribes and the power assignments it makes. In short, both the means and ends of government in the United States regularly bear a constitutional mark. With the exception of some foreign policy decisions, American politics regularly embodies the constitutional syndrome. Several high-profile domestic issues regularly reflect constitutional inputs. Included are crime, abortion, pornography, and racial balance in education. Constitutional compliance is often more important than a critical assessment of the value of a policy proposal on its own merits.

What can be termed the policy "cycle" is essentially a linear sequence of stages through which policy proposals must tread as they are initiated, examined, modified, legitimized, and evaluated. Each of these stages is, in varying degrees, influenced by constitutional inputs. A description of these stages and a brief summary of some of the possible impact of constitutional inputs on them follows. Each stage is discussed in the order in which it impacts the policy-making process.

Issue Identification and Agenda-Building

Policy agendas are usually set by varying combinations of public opinion, pledges by officeholders and candidates for office, the media (especially television), interest groups, administrative agencies, and court decisions. Often agendas do not mirror the priorities of serious policy scholars who complain that policy agendas focus on modest short-term adjustments, thereby dodging the challenge of committing resources in ways that might deal with problems comprehensively and for the long term. This is because American politics is democratic politics. Democratic politics is multiconstituent in root and reactive in the way it addresses issues. We tend to wait for problems to fester before we address them seriously. The Constitution, via the principle of popular sovereignty, asks that government react to public opinion, not mold it. If that opinion is dispersed, policies produced in response to it are likely to incorporate attempts to please and/or appease as many interests as possible. Most public policy agendas are "service" in orientation, in that they seek to satisfy the public's requests for protection, security, employment, health care, housing, nutrition, and safety. Economic or international crises will often cloak agendas with overriding themes. However, that is not a regular event and, when it does occur, it occurs only with the public's approval. People have come to expect protection and service as a matter of right, not privilege. Such an interpretation is at odds with the Constitution's original treatment of rights as a way to keep government from interfering with an individual's right to communicate, worship, petition his or her government, and receive a fair trial. Nonetheless, it is a "spin" that politicians welcome as they seek to curry favor with those who elected them. Our democracy has evolved into one in which services offered by policies are dispensed to people who have a constitutionally rooted right to them. As a constitutionally designated nonelected independent branch of the national government, the federal judiciary has decreed that the rights of ethnic minorities include their right to attend integrated schools. Those decisions have had a significant influence on the policy agendas and budgets of the national, state, and local governments for nearly two generations. In addition, the rights phenomenon affects policy agendas when the media exploits its First Amendment right to select its policy menu and transmit it via television and newspapers, thereby mandating that officeholders deal with those questions under conditions that the media has, in essence, prescribed.

Americans are culturally suspicious of centralized power. This attitude has roots that predate the Constitution. Accordingly, the founders mandated a constitutional structure that disperses policy power widely among national government institutions and between the national and state governments. Therefore, policy agendas often incorporate proposals to reduce the national government's policy role and assign it, or return it, to states and localities. Often it appears that the main objective of the policy change is its procedural decentralization, or devolution, more than a concern for the policy consequences that are likely to result from those procedural changes. Education and welfare (entitlement) policies are particularly susceptible to such arguments, and most nationally imposed policies in these areas in the past half-century have incorporated these values.

These are a few of the ways in which the Constitution and constitutional "mindset" or "syndrome" have affected policy agendas in the United States. Usually the impact is indirect or cultural. Therefore, tracing a specific agenda item to a specific constitutional input is hazardous, if not impossible, because our reverence for the Constitution has conditioned us to view what is both good and bad about policy through a lens that has been culturally conditioned by our veneration of the document itself.

Policy Legitimation

Policy legitimation is likely the most high-profile stage of the policy cycle, and the one impacted most directly by the Constitution's deliberate fragmentation of policy power among three separate branches of government and between two levels of government. As a safeguard against arbitrary rule, and as a way to protect individual freedoms from unwarranted interference from government, the Constitution parcels out policy responsibilities among two legislative chambers, a president, and the courts. This condition, known as the separation of powers principle, means that both houses of Congress and the president must negotiate to find a common policy ground before policies can become law. Since each of these institutional entities performs an essential role in the legitimization of policy and since each

represents a different alignment of voters, all parties are encouraged to cling to their positions tenaciously and make concessions grudgingly because they know that their institution's consent is essential to the final policy product. Constitutional structure becomes an ally in the struggle to prevail, albeit relatively, in the policymaking process.

The constitutional division of power between the national government and the states impacts the policy process on a number of fronts. In the policymaking stage, federalism guarantees states equal representation in the Senate, thereby increasing the policy leverage of individuals and factions in the more thinly populated states and, by the same token, reducing the policy leverage of residents of the more heavily populated states. In the implementation stage, federalism influences the administration of policy by insisting that many nationally instituted policies be channeled through geographical entities (states) and their subunits (cities, counties, and special districts), most of which provide the policies with resources, geographical confines, and political alignments that are incongruent with efforts to maximize policy impact.

Policy Implementation

Policy implementation incorporates all efforts to administer a policy following its legitimation by a legislature or an executive order. Administrative agencies are the key implementation institutions, although their activities are often monitored carefully by legislatures. Presumably the main criterion or guideline for implementation efforts is that of efficiency, or the implementation of objectives by the most expeditious and economical means provided those procedures do not compromise the original intent of the legislation or executive order. However, Americans are not particularly fond of efficiency as an implementation guideline if such a standard interferes with procedures that are constitutionally prescribed or implied. Too high a stress on efficiency potentially can interfere with government's obligation to protect constitutionally guaranteed individual liberties.

The conflict between efficiency and constitutionally implied policymaking procedures was underscored by the late Chief Justice Warren Burger in *Immigration and Naturalization Service* v. *Chada* (1983). In speaking for the Court's majority, the Chief Justice wrote: "It is crystal clear from the records of the Convention, contemporaneous writings and debates, that the framers ranked other values higher than efficiency. . . . The choices we discern as having been made in the Constitutional Convention impose burdens on governmental processes that often seem clumsy, inefficient, and even unworkable, but those hard choices were consciously made by men who had lived under a form of government that permitted governmental acts to go unchecked."[6] The Court majority positioned itself in favor of some administrative routines (red tape) that citizens regularly, and appropriately, associate with a cumbersome and inefficient bureaucracy by noting that "with all the obvious flaws of delay, untidiness, and potential for abuse, we have not yet found a better way to preserve freedom than by making the exercise of power subject to the carefully crafted restraints spelled out in the Constitution."[7]

Therefore, what appears to be irrational to some can be very rational to others. Administrative agencies vested with the obligation to regulate a sector of the economy on behalf of the general public or the consumer are often obligated to follow procedural "due process" standards as they secure testimony from forces that would be affected by proposed regulations. Often agencies are required to explain their decisions before legislative committees. When the implementation challenge involves the dispensation of funds from national bureaucracies to constitutionally independent states and their localities, often agencies are asked to deal with jurisdictions that are not structured or staffed in ways that advance efficiency or, for that matter, even facilitate the objectives of the policies themselves very effectively. In sum, the Constitution mandates that governments preserve individual rights and follow decision procedures that are designed to protect the public from bad laws and bad administration. If the substantive integrity of policies is sacrificed or significantly modified as a result, so be it. The implementation challenge is, as a result of the legislative assignment of policy power to bureaucracies, becoming more critical to the determination of a policy's success or failure. Consequently, the implementation mandate itself can be expected to be affected increasingly by the very forces that impact legislatures and elected executives at the legitimization phase of the policy cycle.

Policy Evaluation

The influence of the Constitution on the evaluation phase of the policy cycle is somewhat more tenuous than it is in the other phases. This is because many policy evaluation efforts focus on optimal, or rational, solutions to problems regardless of constraints that could be placed on them by political or administrative norms. Such analyses are often very statistical, or quantitative, in cast and usually recommend actions that maximize results in light of available resources. Such evaluations are usually conducted by professional policy analysts, many of whom show little interest in the give and take atmosphere of the policy-making world. These analysts assume that policy problems can easily be identified and analyzed, that rational alternatives will be accepted because of their nature, that policy-makers will accept analytical procedures as both good politics and as a way to find agreement on what policies are best, and that policymakers can be converted into solicitors of objective policy truths.

These assumptions are far too idealistic. Rational studies often fail to consider how important it is to incorporate the expectations of politicians, interest groups, and administrators into policy recommendations, as well as how each of these entities attempts to exploit government structure in an attempt to leverage its position in policy decisions.

However, such analyses can be of some use to politicians and administrators because they can produce recommendations that establish policy standards to which politicians can turn once they decide their own ways of combating problems are obviously defective. The history of antipoverty policy since the mid-1960s offers an example. This is one policy field where problems seemed to worsen as governments spent more and more money to combat them. Frustration over these developments resulted in the Personal Responsibility and Work Opportunity Act of 1996, which converted traditional federally dominated welfare programs into state and locally dominated "workfare" programs. The expectation, and hope, was that state and local governments might combat poverty problems more comprehensively and adapt to situational differences better than could the federal government. Such a shift in procedure was politically astute because, by decentralizing policy responsibilities through the federalism format, it accommodated both the public's suspicion of centralized power and its veneration of constitutional principles. In addition, the hope that the jurisdictional transfer of antipoverty policy responsibilities to state and local governments might result in a more comprehensive approach to welfare problems meant, at least in this case, that there was no divergence between good politics and policy prescriptions bent on optimizing results.

While the rational comprehensive type of policy evaluation is the most undiluted type, evaluations that incorporate political and administrative reality into policy prescriptions are the norm. These evaluations examine and analyze the factors that contributed to the failure of earlier attempts to solve, or at least alleviate, the policy problem. Conclusions derived from this "feedback" analysis are then used to support fresh recommendations and strategies that accommodate those factors that disrupted the previous design. These include the attitudes of politicians, the impact of administrative agency norms, and the influence that formal structure may have had on decision making. If conducted appropriately such analyses will produce recommendations that modify the ideal to accommodate the real world, much of which is influenced by constitutional principles. Prescriptions for the federal government's involvement in education programs offer a good illustration of this. Education has always been considered almost exclusively a local government responsibility. Therefore, attempts by the federal government to subsidize education have had to accommodate such a reality. Accordingly, the Elementary and Secondary Education Act of 1965 targeted federal funds to school districts in the more economically deprived sections of the country, and defined them essentially as welfare monies, not funds to support education. Such a mission spin helped to deflect and dilute complaints that the federal government was intervening in a policy area that the Constitution, through the Tenth Amendment, had reserved for states and localities.

In conclusion, constitutional factors affect all stages of the policymaking cycle. Much of it is indirect, while much is very high profile, often being employed as a key reason to pursue a particular goal. The following chapters will offer more examples and implications of the pervasiveness of constitutional politics as an omnipresent factor in the development, administration, and evaluation of public policy in the United States.

The Format That Follows

The following chapters will explore the relationship between constitutional politics and public policy from, for want of a better expression, a "bottom up" perspective. First, beginning with the Constitutional Convention, Chapter 2 offers a brief analysis of the history of constitutional politics in America. This includes an analysis of the policy implications of the Constitution as intended by the framers and as interpreted by both descriptive and normative theorists. Chapter 3 offers a brief analysis of the relationship between constitutional doctrine and the types of policies produced by the political system. This analysis is presented at this point in the book so readers can relate subsequent analysis of the effect of institutions on decision making to the system's bias favoring some types of policies over others.

The focus then moves to an analysis of how constitutional politics affects our version of constitutional democracy from public opinion to policy actions taken by the public's representatives acting on the separate institutional "stages" mandated by the Constitution. Accordingly, Chapter 4 describes and analyzes the historical character of public opinion and how its registration on public policy is impacted by constitutional structure and political strategies impacted by that structure. Chapter 5 examines the influence of constitutional politics on how effectively public opinion is transmitted through two intermediary institutions—political parties and interest groups. Chapter 6 examines the reverberations of another intermediary institution—the media—on politics and policy. Chapters 7, 8, and 9 focus on how the two key constitutionally endowed policy institutions—the president and Congress—

have employed their institutional separatism to confront both historical and contemporary policy challenges. Chapter 10 focuses on how the constitutional principle of federalism affects public policy from both policymaking and policy implementation perspectives. Chapter 11 examines the highly significant impact of the public bureaucracy on politics and public policy, and on how that significance has been amplified by constitutional structure. An analysis of how the federal judiciary's constitutionally mandated institutional independence leverages its influence on public policy is examined in Chapter 12. As might well be expected, the focus will be on the Supreme Court. Chapter 13 highlights the consequences of constitutional politics for public policy and offers some suggestions for reform in light of contemporary political conditions. Its assumption is that the Constitution, at least for the foreseeable future, appears to be here to stay. Therefore, we should focus our attention on making the most of it.

A discerning observer of American politics once remarked that if the quest to explain and understand the causes for a complex phenomenon is undertaken in the right way it will become even more complicated. Examining and interpreting the impact of constitutional politics on public policy is certainly no exception to that. Therefore, if subsequent pages leave readers somewhat frustrated in their attempts to master the interdependent complexities of the historical, institutional, and political factors that have made constitutional politics so important to public policy in America, this book will have had its intended impact.

Endnotes

1. See Daniel Lazare, *The Frozen Republic: How the Constitution Is Paralyzing Democracy* (Fort Worth, Tex.: Harcourt Brace Jovanovich, 1996).

2. http://patriot.net/~cnc/nextrepublic.htm

3. As quoted in Jay M. Shafritz, *The Dorsey Dictionary of American Politics* (Chicago: Dorsey Press, 1988), p. 334.

4. See Robert A. Goldwin and Art Kaufman, eds., *Separation of Powers: Does It Still Work?* (Washington, D.C.: American Enterprise Institute, 1986) and John F. Manley and Kenneth M. Dolbeare, eds., *The Case Against the Constitution: From the Antifederalists to the Present* (Armonk, N.Y.: M. E. Sharpe, 1987), and Daniel M. Hoffman, *Our Elusive Constitution: Silences, Paradoxes, and Priorities* (Albany, N.Y.: SUNY Press, 1997).

5. See Lazare, *op. cit.,* and Alan Brinkley, Nelson W. Polsby, and Kathleen Sullivan, *The New Federalist Papers* (New York: 20th Century Fund, 1997).

6. 454 U.S. 812 (1983).

7. *Ibid.*

chapter two

The Constitution, Democracy, and Public Policy

The Historical Roots

On September 27, 1787 the Constitutional Convention approved the Constitution of the United States and dispatched it to Congress, then existing under the Articles of Confederation officially as the United States in Congress assembled, for further consideration and debate. Once that was completed, it was submitted to the states for ratification. After nearly two years of fervent debate in the states, it was ratified finally on June 21, 1788, when New Hampshire provided the ninth vote required for acceptance.

Formally amended twenty-seven times, and countless times by judicial and administrative judgment, the Constitution is striking in its impact on how Americans make decisions that affect their daily lives in very profound ways. This is because today, as in 1789, the Constitution is, as it has always been, a policy document. It is a policy document because it grants and restricts powers to the people and to those who make decisions on their behalf. It is a policy document because it mandates cooperation between and among sectors of government, each of which has definitive responsibilities for a part of the policy process. It is a policy document because it prescribes procedures for the adoption of policies and establishes a set, albeit a crude one, of policy priorities. Finally, and perhaps most importantly, it is a policy document because it allows those who contest over the specifics of policy to exploit its structural characteristics in an attempt to inflate their leverage in the enactment or defeat of policy proposals.

Social, economic, and technological conditions have changed dramatically since 1789. Two hundred years ago, in a notably simple and rustic society, the major challenge of government was to regulate behavior only to the extent necessary to provide for social and economic stability and unity in foreign policy. Decision-making procedures prescribed by the Constitution were geared toward preventing policy tyranny by either self-serving elites or a poorly informed and, in all likelihood, transient majority. By way of contrast, in today's society, the emphasis is upon how government distributes a variety of benefits and subsidies to individuals, groups, and institutions. The public remains concerned over how to keep public officials and public policy accountable to its wishes. In addition, a substantive mandate has been added. The public's concern for the character of substantive policy has grown in tandem with the democratization of the Constitution. In 1789, the House of Representatives was the only national institution subject to popular election. This represented only one half of one of the three co-equal branches of the national government. The others—the Supreme Court, the president, and the Senate as the other half of the legislative branch— were appointed by forces seeking to provide economic and intellectual elites an advantage in the control of government and its policies. Today, the Senate is popularly elected, as is the Electoral College, which registers state-based popular vote when it selects the president. While Supreme Court and other federal court judges are, as they were in 1789, nominated by the president and confirmed by the Senate, the fact that both the president and Senate have been heavily democratized means that these same democratic trends impact on the nomination and confirmation of judges.

The relationship between the democratization of the Constitution and the problems and promises this harbors for the processes and content of public policy will be explored further later in this chapter and throughout the book. However, before analyzing this phenomenon, it is best to examine what the Constitution's authors expected would be the document's impact on public policy. Analyzing the gap between original theory and contemporary policy offers students of public policy a way of judging how appropriate the Constitution is for today's policy challenges. Also, since the Constitution was not originally intended to be a democratic document in the current sense of

the term, such an analysis offers readers the opportunity to form judgments about what is both good and bad about the relationships that have developed between the Constitution and democratic theory since 1789.

Policy and Structure: The Constitutional Fundamentals

The Constitution was a controversial document in 1789 because of the implications it harbored for public policy. Its treatment of popular sovereignty and its structural character were illustrative of this. They remain so today. The founders were committed to vesting the public with the authority to direct the course of public policy, but not without structural and political checks on the possible misuse of that authority. What follows is a preliminary discussion and analysis of the impact of the Constitution's structural qualities on democracy and policymaking. It will be followed by a brief analysis of how the various schools or interpretations of democracy (and their spokespersons) have debated out and, in some cases, rationalized how the Constitution's structural character would, or could, serve their own policy crusades. Each of these topics will be resurrected regularly in subsequent chapters as the discussion turns to a more detailed analysis of the effect of structure on institutional policy performance and democracy in the American political system.

Separation of Powers

Simply stated, the Constitution assigns the three main functions of government—legislative, executive, and judicial—to three separate branches of government, each with a different source of selection, different term of office, and distinct roles assigned it by the Constitution. Congress is obligated to legitimize policy. It is divided into two houses—the House of Representatives and the Senate. The House members are apportioned to states on the basis of population and are popularly elected for two-year terms. The Senate represents each state equally regardless of population, with each state having two senators. The original Constitution provided for the appointment of senators by state legislatures. The Seventeenth Amendment, ratified on April 8, 1913, altered this and subjected senators to popular election by the people of their respective states.

The Constitution assigns what it terms "the executive power" to a President of the United States of America who is elected by an Electoral College for a period of four years. Members of the Electoral College are to be appointed by the state legislatures. Originally, these electors were so appointed without the influence of forces outside the confines of state legislatures. However, the development of political parties has encouraged state legislatures to subject the electors to popular election and, in most cases, mandate them to vote for the presidential candidate to whom the electors have pledged support. For all intents and purposes, this development has made the president a popularly elected public official and altered his policy incentive system dramatically.

The third function of government—the judicial—is assigned by the Constitution to a Supreme Court and other courts inferior to it that Congress may decide to establish. The Constitution does assign the Supreme Court original jurisdiction over certain types of cases, but does not give it the power of judicial review, or the right to declare actions of Congress, the president, or the states contrary to the provisions of the Constitution. That power was claimed by the Supreme Court, unilaterally, in the famous case of *Marbury* v. *Madison* (1803). As will be discussed in a later chapter, such a power provides the Supreme Court with a great deal of actual and potential policy leverage.

The separation of powers principle has many policy implications which will be discussed in ensuing chapters. However, two deserve brief mention at this point. First, originally the powers granted to each branch by the Constitution were presumed to be the only ones it could exercise. However, in truth, all three branches of government have legitimate constitutional claims over both the making of policy and its administration. Congress makes policy and can oversee the executive's implementation of it as a necessary prerequisite for making future adjustments. Courts are obligated to judge the constitutionality of the actions of Congress, the president, and the bureaucracy as they legitimize and implement policy.

Second, in the real world of policymaking, the two institutions that are routinely involved in public policymaking—Congress and the president—must cooperate with each other before policy can be officially legitimized. In other words, these two branches share policymaking responsibilities. Since Congress is bicameral (two houses), its two houses must agree. Since the president can veto legislation, his cooperation is necessary before policy decisions become law. Congressional overrides of presidential vetoes are infrequent. This sharing of the policy obligation is a very important procedural fact of life at the national level. It has major implications, not only for policy processes but also for the types of policies that are ultimately produced.

Checks and Balances

The constitutional principle of checks and balances allows each branch of government to check the other two by formal actions sanctioned by the Constitution. Presidents can veto legislation passed by Congress. Congress, by a two-thirds vote of both houses, can override a presidential veto. Presidents nominate federal judges, but the Senate must confirm the nominations before the appointments are official. Presidents initiate treaties, but the Senate must legitimize them. These are but a few of the structural "face-offs" allowed by the check and balance system. The major objective, however, was to control potential legislative excesses. Bicameralism and the presidential veto had this as their primary mission. As will be discussed later, the conservative democrats, most of whom were part of the Federalist movement, defended strenuously the check and balance idea because it offered a buffer against irresponsible congressional action, particularly that of the House of Representatives.

Federalism

Like separation of powers, federalism employs the notion of fragmented power to guard against majority tyranny. In the case of federalism, the fragmentation is areal or geographical, between two levels of government, whereas separation of powers disperses power among institutions within the national level. The Tenth Amendment to the Constitution, included in the Bill of Rights amendment package ratified in 1791, states that all powers not delegated to the national government or denied by the Constitution to the states are reserved for the states and the people. Like checks and balances, federalism was the result of a series of compromises at the Constitutional Convention between those who feared too much centralized power and those who felt the centralization of authority was necessary to protect property rights and privileges, and to provide for governmental stability. A totally centralized system would be a unitary one, with the central government possessing all the basic authority to govern the system. Under a unitary system, if the central government wanted to delegate policy power to subsidiary governments, it could do so at its discretion. The antithesis of this is a confederation, such as the Articles of Confederation, under which all, or nearly all, of the basic authority to

enact policy rests with the subsidiary governments. If they so wish, these governments can assign some powers to the central government. As the experiences with the Articles showed, this is very difficult to accomplish because our political culture nurtures a clear bias against centralized authority. Federalism represents a compromise between the unitary and confederal extremes.

Like separation of powers and checks and balances, federalism creates an area of controversy which influences both policy decisions and the amount of democracy present within the political system at any given time. Equal representation for each state in the Senate, regardless of population, provides some extra policy leverage for residents of sparsely populated states. The impact of this condition will increase as America becomes more urbanized and the migration of population from rural to urban areas makes population differences among the states more pronounced. In addition to population differences and differences in rural-urban makeup, states are not equal in their ability to meet the needs of their citizens, as is their challenge under the reserved powers grant in the Tenth Amendment. Some states are economically prosperous and have an asset-rich tax base from which to draw revenue to support their policy responsibilities. Others are comparatively poor economically and lack such a revenue base. Ironically, a greater percentage of the residents of the poorer states are more in need of welfare, health care, and housing assistance than are their counterparts in the wealthier states. Consequently, when the national government deals with this issue the inevitable result is policies that equalize benefits at the expense of taxpayers in the wealthier states. In sum, states with low federal tax contributions are heavily subsidized by taxpayers in the wealthier states. This makes the politics that precede such decisions more volatile and more ideological in cast. This is but one of the many effects of a constitutionally prescribed federalist structure on both policy procedures and policy outcomes that will be explored later.

Constitutionalism

The notion of constitutionalism, or limited government, is not a formal structural feature of the Constitution. Nonetheless, it influences policy in much the same way as does formal structure. A government impacted by constitutionalism is one that is not all powerful, but one that has specific or implied constraints placed on what it can control. Our constitution accomplishes this in two ways. First, since the national government is officially one of delegated powers, presumably it cannot enact policies that are outside its official jurisdiction. The same is true for reserved powers of the states, if the Tenth Amendment is taken literally. Rather flexible interpretations of the constitution's language by all three branches of government have altered this rather neat demarcation of authority over the past two centuries. Nevertheless, the delegated-reserved differential is still the official standard employed by some to judge the legitimacy of actions of both the national government and the states, and this point is raised rather often in debates over policies that involve national-state cooperation. A second way in which the Constitution shows deference to constitutionalism is in its treatment of civil rights. Almost by definition, if the people have rights, it means that governments cannot deprive them of their right to exercise those rights. They are civil rights, not privileges. Therefore, constitutionalism places restrictions on the scope of public policy, and fosters debate over whether certain actions involve the exercise of rights or privileges. It can complicate the definition of a policy issue and delay its consideration. These issues, along with others, will be examined in later chapters.

Judicial Review

Judicial review is perhaps a more tentative constitutional principle because it was not included officially in the document. Courts in many colonial governments were vested with such authority. However, the founders, fearing a power imbalance among the three branches, did not include it officially in the Supreme Court's delegated powers. The Supreme Court established the right of federal courts to exercise judicial review in the case of *Marbury* v. *Madison*. In essence, it consists of the right of federal courts to declare any law or action of any legislature, elected executive, or administrator at any level of government contrary to the language or intent of the U.S. Constitution. It deserves status as a constitutional principle because of its actual and potential policy impact. It puts the federal courts, especially the Supreme Court, in the position of "umpire" or "referee" over the executive and legislative policy players. It means the courts can determine what the often vague terminology in the Constitution means, and how congressional, presidential, and state powers are affected. Its significance cannot be overstressed: If there is no government institution assigned the power to do this, the Constitution as a governing force is meaningless. The policy implications of this are immense. This power potentially limits policy options. It certainly can be employed, as it has been many times, to update the meaning of constitutional language. The chapter on the courts and public policy will offer a more in-depth analysis of the impact of judicial review on public policy.

The Constitution in Transition: Policy Dialogues

The growth of population, urbanization, and technological advances introduced by the machine age have created major adaptation problems for governments of all types, especially those committed in whole or in part to the concept of self-government. As noted above, while the Constitution originally included comparatively little in the way of self-government or democracy, the passage of time and the amendment process have democratized the document considerably. However, there has been no correlation between the degree of self-government enjoyed by Americans and the ability of our constitutional system to respond adequately to our increasingly complicated and very demanding policy challenges. One of the results of such a crisis has been the resurrection of debate over how well our democratic institutions and traditions enable our government to respond, through the Constitution's structure, to the awesome policy challenges of today's world. Consequently, the debates over how democracy and constitutional structure should interact to produce legitimate public policies that occurred during, and immediately following, the Constitutional Convention continue to be relevant today. After all, in a democracy the basic challenge facing the people and their government remains essentially the same today as it was in 1789: If under a political system committed to at least a measure of self-government, how can popular sovereignty be exercised effectively so as to produce public policies that are adequate to the policy challenges confronting the nation?

James Madison examined this issue in the *Federalist Papers,* a series of eighty-five essays supporting the Constitution written for New York newspapers immediately following the adjournment of the Constitutional Convention in 1787. Joining Madison in the authorship of the *Papers* were John Jay and Alexander Hamilton. The purpose of the essays was to argue, in a debate format, for New York's ratification of the document. More than Hamilton or Jay, Madison confronted the potential policy problems associated with self-government. He argued that governments committed wholeheartedly to popular sovereignty are victimized by "mortal diseases" that lead to "instability, injustice, and confusion."[1] This is because self-government invites the "spirit of faction" to dominate the policymaking process. Such a spirit would surface regardless of whether or not the faction represented a majority or minority opinion. In either case, it would very often lead to policies that were adverse to the well-being of other citizens and the "aggregate interests of the community." Unfortunately, argued Madison, such a spirit would not embody the logic of reason but rather the "impulse of passion" conditioned by the self-interest of the members of all factions. An open and heterogeneous society promotes such a result. He concluded that "liberty is to faction what air is to fire." When the public is allowed a free hand in deciding how it is to represent itself, the natural result is for individuals to organize into groups, or factions, based on economic self-interest, and seek to convert public policy into a series of government actions that serve the best interests of group members. Therefore, public opinion usually reflects the self-interest of those invited to participate in governing themselves. Since self-interest is a genetic trait of man, it is mandatory that governments committed to the principle of popular sovereignty be structured to control the negative effects of factions. It does not matter whether the spirit of faction is parleyed by minorities or a majority. Public policies that respond directly to such a spirit can adopt tyrannical policies. Tyranny is tyranny, whether produced by a majority or a minority. Majorities can defeat tyrannical minorities at the ballot box. The major problem is majority tyranny, where popular control of factionalism is, by definition, impossible. Madison then posed what he considered to be the major challenge confronting representative government, that of guaranteeing "the public good and private rights" and thereby defying actual or potential tyrannical majorities, and to do it without forgoing "the spirit of and for popular government."[2] If Madison was correct, how is the dilemma to be solved? The answer to many, including Madison, Hamilton, and Jay, was to structure a constitutional government to control the negative effects of factionalism on government and public policy, while still maintaining a genuine commitment to the notion of popular sovereignty.

The control of the impulses of factions through government structure has been only one of several solutions advanced to deal with the problem of factionalism and self-government. Each theory, or school, that has focused on the issue has had to work within the framework of the Constitution, particularly its structural character. Each theory recognizes that the problem of factionalism is an actual, or potential, problem for democratic government. Furthermore, and perhaps most important for the thesis of this book, each theory finds the selective structural features of the Constitution to be an ally for its cause. This was the case in 1789, and it remains the case today. Insofar as the formative era was concerned, it was clear that the founding fathers did not share a common political theory. The Constitution was a product of compromise. Most of the founders agreed that factionalism represented a problem for self-government, and they concluded that the Constitution should pay more than passing attention to it, especially in light of the democratic spirit that prospered in the wake of the Revolutionary War. Divided over the extent to which factionalism would be a problem, and divided over how to structure a government that provided for popular input into policy while simultaneously controlling the excesses of factions, the founding fathers did not resolve the issue. It remains unresolved today.

Several theories of democracy that use the Constitution as a means to facilitate their goals have developed interesting prescriptions for dealing with the problem of factions. Two of these surfaced during the Constitutional Convention in 1787 and in the debates over ratification. Two developed subsequent to that time, but they are equally relevant. Proponents of each theory recognize either the tendency toward, or the virtual inevitability of, factions developing in democratic environments. Each employs the Constitution as its ally in an attempt to alleviate the impact of factions or to overcome the problem altogether. Some arguments will appear more relevant than others to the student of public policy in the America of today. However, they all recognize that democracy as a means of governing society in a coherent, selfless, rational fashion is not self-executing or natural. The two models that developed during the formative period will be discussed first, and the remaining two last.

The Jeffersonian, or Majority Rule Theory

This theory, ironically, questions many of the assumptions made by a majority of the delegates to the Constitutional Convention. The most important of these was the assumption that citizens are inclined by nature to parley their selfish side when they participate in politics. Although admitting that such a tendency exists, the Jeffersonian model argues that people can become selfless and acquire a common good point of view if given a chance to educate themselves and to debate issues in open forums. The hope is that the free exchange of ideas will result in reasoned choice. Clearly, this is a more optimistic view of human nature than Madison would have accepted. There is, of course, no guarantee that man's more altruistic side will dominate debates and provide the guidelines for the development of public policy, but the expectation of this persuasion was that it would. If that is the case, then commitment to the notion of government by an informed majority is possible. Public officials and public policy would reflect the views of the reasonable majority. Neither the constitution nor statutes should provide barriers to the will of the majority. In fact, so goes the argument, when reasonable and practical views of the public interest emerge from the free exchange of ideas, it should be easy to attract a majority of voters to support it.

Nonetheless, there is no guarantee that the will of the majority will always be reasonable and public spirited. Therefore, the right of minorities to criticize the majority is fundamental to this theory. There should always be a well-organized minority waiting in the wings to provide constructive criticism for the majority's policies. If the majority allows itself to be overrun by factionalism, then the minority takes its case to the people and in all likelihood will become the majority in the next election. Aware of this possibility, the majority should always adjust its policies to remain loyal to its original public interest commitment. If the majority is successful, the minority will remain the minority for an extended period.

Another important ingredient in the majority rule school is government's commitment to preserving man's natural rights. Since this, by definition, limits the policy power of government, it has roots in the principle of constitutionalism. It also is theoretically incompatible with majority rule. After all, if the nonfactious majority wants control in policy, why should there be limits to its authority? The majoritarians have a rather simple answer: Unless the citizen's basic rights are preserved, especially the communication rights of free speech, press, assembly, and petition, the ability of the people to uncover reasoned policy truths through the honest and open exchange of ideas is threatened. Furthermore, the political minority cannot perform its role as constructive critic of the majority unless these same communication rights are exempt from government control.

The majoritarian theory is a rather simplistic

theory, but its success rests on the development of, and effective use of, an institution which most of the founders, including Madison, thought was dysfunctional for politics and government—the political party. In Madison's view, the political party was but one example of the victory of factionalism over reason. However, to the majoritarians, strong, cohesive majority and minority parties represented the most logical route to the development, dissemination, and operationalization of policies that would serve the common good.

The political party was crucial to the majoritarians on another front—one that illustrated the problems this school had (and continues to have) with the Constitution. The original Constitution, as noted above, kept self-government at arms length, confining the direct input of citizens on government to the popular election of members of the House of Representatives. If, as the majoritarians expected, other institutions would eventually become democratized (as they have), it was nevertheless necessary to develop an institution to help overcome the potential policy paralysis that could result from fragmented government. Well-disciplined political parties committed to a policy agenda could accomplish this. Ideally, members of the majority party in the House and Senate would cooperate with a president of the same party to advance the party's will and thereby overcome the tendency of the separation of powers, check and balance system, and federalism to discourage the development of such a will.

As will be seen in subsequent chapters, the development of well-disciplined majority and minority parties has been difficult in America for a number of reasons, only one of which has been fragmented constitutional power. This condition has nourished the continued popularity of majoritarian theory as a corrective for government's seeming inability to legislate comprehensive policy changes. Scholar-theorists such as Woodrow Wilson, James

Thayer, Charles Beard, Oliver Wendell Holmes, Robert Jackson, Alexander Bickel, and John Ely have made the majoritarian model central to their reformist writings over the past century.[3] Their prescriptive rallying cry is simple, clear, and takes issue with the assumptions underlying the structural fragmentation of constitutional power. It is, in sum, that democracy requires that complete policymaking authority be awarded to the party that won the last election and all constitutional checks on the exercise of that authority are undemocratic and therefore unwise, if not illegitimate.

All this is not to say that the majoritarian school was, and is, totally at odds with the Constitution's structural atomization of power. Should the majority be overcome by the spirit of factionalism and not reflect reasoned concern for the public good, then even the majoritarian school would welcome the intervention of the check and balance mechanism to keep the majority in tow. By the same token, if the courts' exercise of judicial review had the effect of restraining the predatory wiles of a majority that had strayed from its public interest pledges, the Jeffersonian school would certainly applaud the decision. This has been the case occasionally in the past, despite the fact that Jefferson viewed the Supreme Court's declaration of its right to judicial review in *Marbury* v. *Madison* as inimical to the public interest because it was decreed by an institution almost totally divorced from public input and control.

The Madisonian, or Balanced Government Model

The majoritarian model was not popular at the Constitutional Convention. While there was a general endorsement of the spirit underlying consent theory, a majority of the delegates were too suspicious of majority rule to embrace it. They were more comfortable with a more conservative theory that could, if necessary, constrain the passions of a poorly informed majority. They found it in what can be termed the Madisonian, or balanced school. The structural characteristics of the Constitution reflect the delegates' sympathy with this point of view.

The Madisonians believed that the majoritarians were too optimistic about man's potential to work altruism systematically into the processes and politics of government. The history of societies and governments had shown beyond any doubt that man is instinctively egoistic and irrational. Therefore, it would be foolhardy to expect him, as an active member of one or more factions, to support any policies other than those which served his own interest. Therefore, it is necessary to include structural impediments to majority rule in any written constitution. In addition, this conservative response to the majoritarian school argued that constitutional structure should be employed to preserve society's social, economic, and political traditions. During the colonial period society was marked by a rather clear hierarchical distinction among social and economic classes. The Madisonians argued that it would be dangerous and destabilizing to ignore the experience of social and economic elites in the search for wise policies and government stability.

While there were marked differences between the Jeffersonian and Madisonian schools over whether man's altruistic or selfish instincts would dominate in the forums of democracy and over how to deal with man's frailties through constitutional structure, the two schools had several things in common. They agreed that the cardinal struggle in the mind of political man was between his desire to use government to help himself or his community. They agreed that the reason and public spiritedness instinct should prevail. They also agreed that the protection of civil liberties and property rights should be high policy priorities in any government. However, because of clear differences over which of man's instincts would win the struggle between selfishness and self-lessness, there were fundamental differences over how the Constitution should structure government to deal with the problem, or potential problem, of factions. The Madisonian solution was a constitution that balanced the needs of society for reasoned government with the public's need for self-government. If reason was to prevail consistently in policy decisions, it could best be realized by integrating democratic habits and allegiance to social and political institutions that have weathered the challenge of history. Constitutions should structure behavior so that policy decisions reflect caution and self-restraint. After all, it is better to be safe than sorry. If, for example, the preservation of rights is a high policy priority, it is dangerous to trust the preservation of those rights to the judgment of a majority. The preservation of man's rights is too important a goal of government to depend on an appeal to man's sense of reason and justice for its realization. If, as the conservative school argued, man's instinct for self-aggrandizement would result in the invasion or compromise in the freedoms of other men, then the right decision-making structures and a clear commitment to the principle of limited government could help prevent this. Although the Madisonian school assumed that the fusion of democracy with tradition and the need for stability and continuity in policy should be supervised by society's social and economic elites, these individuals could also succumb to the passions of self-interest. Accordingly, constitutional structure is as important in controlling elite excesses as it is in controlling these same instincts when voiced by the masses.

The Constitutional Convention and, ultimately, the Constitution itself, absorbed the Madisonian point of view. Separation of powers and federalism fragment power in order to make it difficult for the factious spirit of a majority, or an assemblage of minorities, to dominate. The check and balance system provides structurally induced ways to override the excesses of a faction or factions that might seize control of one or more institutions in the policymaking chain. Since the Constitution, in effect, requires the cooperation of several institutions that share the policymaking and implementation obligations, it is easy to veto or compromise factious excess at a number of points in the policy chain. These instruments of policy moderation were, in Madison's time, reinforced by the stabilizing influence of non-elected elites who were expected to hold key positions in policymaking institutions. For example, the Senate was not popularly elected but appointed by state legislatures. The president was not popularly elected but was selected by an Electoral College which was appointed by state legislatures. Although the policy role of judges was expected to be minimal in 1789, nonetheless they were nominated by a nonelected Senate. The gradual democratization of the Constitution has converted the Senate and the president into instruments of democracy. This would give members of the original Madisonian school some pause, to say the least.

Nevertheless, the Constitution's structural character is, for the most part, the result of the dominance of the Madisonian point of view during the Convention and during the debate over ratification. Despite the fact that more than two hundred years have passed since the debates between the Jeffersonian and Madisonian schools first surfaced, debates between advocates of the two theories continue. Policy debates over tax policies, civil rights policies, welfare policies, and law enforcement policies in such critical areas as gun control and drug control reflect this division. Modern day Madisonians fear that the democratization of the Senate and the presidency, together with the development of the social service state, are disturbing trends that threaten to break down the checks on majority rule and the necessary role of a responsible aristocracy as a stabilizing force in government. These contemporary conservative theorists cite the value of structure as a way to restrain this trend in much the same way as did Madison, Hamilton, and Jay in the *Federalist Papers.*

Broker Rule, or Pluralist Theory

The third major democratic model, that of broker or pluralist theory, was not a product of the country's formative period. It does, however, recognize as inevitable society's factious character. In contrast to Jefferson and Madison, pluralists do not consider factions genetically dangerous, but rather a natural phenomenon that can provide the basis for a viable theory of democracy. In sum, broker rule rationalizes, or justifies, politics as usual. Pluralism first emerged as a theory of democratic politics in the 1820s. Its champion was South Carolina senator John C. Calhoun. Calhoun first introduced the premises of what is now called pluralist theory when he developed his theory of the "concurrent majority." Regardless of the exact terminology employed, the terms concurrent majority, broker rule, and pluralism all share the same assumptions about people as political animals and government as a synthesizing force of vested interests.

The assumptions and prescriptions of pluralism can be summarized rather concisely: Abstract, *a priori* public interest standards do not exist. By its very nature, the concept of the "public interest" is a value judgment. Since it is subjectively derived it eludes verification by scientific methods. Theoretically, there can be as many views of the public interest as there are people who care to express an opinion on the question. Given people's genetic inclination to parley their own self-interest in politics, when such opinions are expressed they represent, in effect, individual self-interest, although they are often couched in public interest terminology. When forced to choose, people prefer their own interests over those of others and, if

given a chance to organize and influence public policy decisions, the self-interest syndrome predominates. Therefore, politics does not provide government with any way to prioritize, on any scale of morality, such opinion. Thus, all such opinions, by force of logic, should be treated equally. Consequently the dominance of any faction over others, be it in the majority or minority, is unjustifiable coercion. No one person, no single group, no political party has a right to rule either because of the "morality" of its cause or because it is a majority movement. Majority rule is meaningless to the pluralist because it presumes the right of a majority to coerce minorities. Coercion in any form in democratic governments is unjustified because it is impossible to prove the inherent sanctity of any value claiming to serve the public interest.

In theory, the only solution to this dilemma, according to the pluralist school, is to secure the universal consent of all parties affected by a policy decision to accept the decision. This means that all parties interested in the resolution of a policy issue must bargain with each other in the hope of reaching a compromise that is acceptable to all. Once that has been the policy result accomplished, it is by definition a legitimate decision because the problem of justifiable coercion has been eliminated and the unresolvable question of proving its inherent morality avoided. The compromise is, by its very nature, in the public interest because it was the result of a bargain struck by all the interested "equal" parties.

Pluralists accept the faction or group basis of politics and, in fact, hope that democratic systems become as factious as possible. The more groups in existence the greater is the chance for policy decisions to reflect social consensus in general. Furthermore, an abundance of factions means that policy compromises will reflect moderate, incremental changes as opposed to more sudden, dramatic, radical changes. That promotes social stability, which the pluralist school values for much the same reason as does the Madisonian school. Madison argued that heavily populated legislative districts had advantages over those more sparsely populated because the representative elected from a large district would have to represent so many factions that his final policy stand on key issues was bound to be moderate, and therefore safe. To Madison, this suppressed the potential radical effects of factions on government and policy. To the pluralists, such a broad representational base makes the policy system more legitimate because it is more representative of democracy's most natural forces of political expression—interest groups.

To the pluralist, self-interest and individual ambition explain nearly every policy result. Even in the case of government elites—those elected and appointed to key policy positions—ambition keeps the political system synchronized with the group basis of democracy. In most circumstances, such individuals are ambitious, or they would not have sought office in the first place. In order to be reelected or reappointed to their positions, they become very loyal to their constituencies. These constituencies are, in most cases, heavily fragmented by group differences. In order to represent their constituencies, these officials must do the best they can to represent all these groups, even those that were indifferent or opposed their original election or appointment. This is because the apathetic or disinterested can be moved to organize and oppose their reelection if decisions are made that work to their disadvantage. Consequently, to the pluralist school the ambition and self-interest of both leaders and followers serve to make the system more representative, and therefore more legitimate.

To be sure, when the pluralist model is transposed from theory to the real world of politics and policymaking, several imperfections quickly surface. Obviously, all factions do not have the same leverage in the policy process. Some groups are more wealthy, have better leadership, and have had better historical access to decision makers than have others. For example, business and professional groups have had, historically, more impact on the course of public policy than have groups representing the poor or ethnic minorities. Furthermore, it is obvious that the pluralist stress on incremental, moderate change as the essence of the public interest ignores the obvious need for society and its government to make quick, radical changes at times. Consensus-building does not always lead to rational policy changes in times of social or economic crisis. In addition, the pluralist model's comfort with the ambitious politician stands in stark contrast to the suspicion harbored by both the Jeffersonian and Madisonian toward such an individual. Also, pluralism advocates group conflict and intergroup conciliation as a substitute for participatory democracy. While the direct participation of citizens in policy decisions is rare in most democracies, it is nevertheless part of the mythology of democracy that citizens as individuals do impact directly on policy decisions. Therefore, a theory that advocates the employment of public officials as policy brokers between the people and their government appears to some observers to be countercultural.

Nevertheless, the pluralist model is important because it, more than the Jeffersonian and Madisonian models, attempts to exploit rather than harness man's self-interest orientation in politics. Ambition and avarice are not dangerous to the pluralist if such qualities surface regularly in large numbers within key institutions and at key stages of the policymaking process. The necessity of bargaining and compromise promises to temper the potential excesses that ambition could harbor for the political system. If ambition is institutionalized and allowed to run its course it will sow the seeds of its own self-control.

The official fragmentation of governmental power by the Constitution is tailor-made for the advocates of pluralist democracy. Separation of powers offers factions the chance to develop allies in several arenas, but officials in these arenas must ultimately agree on final policy decisions. This means that institutional separation encourages bargaining and compromise because cooperation among them must precede the legitimization of policy. Consequently, factions must forgo some of their demands in the interest of some sort of policy resolution. The check and balance system reinforces this by threatening to stymie policy efforts unless the president and Congress can agree on a policy solution. Federalism allows factions to compete within arenas subordinate to the national level, thereby relieving the national government of some policy challenges that can best be handled within the states. Although it is possible for some factions to dominate decision making at the state level, such an occurrence does not challenge the stability of the system in general because it is confined to decisions in one state, or, at best, a few.

Contemporary disillusionment with our political system and its policies is often explained by referring to the inflated impact of a few special interests on policymaking. If this is true, then it means that the assumptions of the pluralist school—that ambition and avarice explain most political action—are correct. However, it also means that pluralism has not been implemented very effectively. Group influence is too unequal. Some people who desperately need effective political representation have not been very well organized. In emphasizing equality of opportunity for factions to organize and express themselves, the system has allowed some groups much more political clout than others. Therefore, the healthy balance of group inputs so essential to the pluralists does not always play out on stage according to script.

This explains the popularity of models or theories of politics that challenge both the assumptions and results of pluralist politics in contemporary America. For example, Bruce Ackerman, while conceding that what he terms "normal" politics in America is that of interest groups attempting to influence elected representatives, says that these routines are challenged on occasion by what he calls "constitutional" politics, in which the people mobilize in force to make the system acquiesce to a new set of governing principles. This occurs very infrequently but is revolutionary in effect when it does occur. The Constitutional Convention and the debate over ratification was one such example. Others include acceptance of the efforts of the Reconstruction Republicans in the 1860s, and the political culture of the social service state introduced by the New Deal Democrats in the 1930s. Labeling our constitutional system a system of "dualist politics," Ackerman argues that Americans have historically placed a higher value on the results of constitutional politics than on normal politics.[4] In sum, the form of participatory democracy that produces constitutional politics is, according to Ackerman, a force that sets the stage for and puts limits on the effects of political pluralism. As long as Americans express dissatisfaction with the policy manifestations of pluralism, arguments such as that advanced by Ackerman, with its antifaction, popular sovereignty base, will remain popular.

The Foundationalist Model

The Jeffersonian model is based on the primacy of popular sovereignty and its linkage in spirit to the principles of parliamentary democracy, despite the fact that our government lacks a parliamentary structure. The Madisonian and pluralist schools are much less overwhelmed by the prospect and legitimacy of popular sovereignty than are the Jeffersonians. The final model examined here—the foundationalist model—is even more hostile to popular sovereignty than are the Madisonian and pluralist schools. The essence of foundationalism is its wholehearted commitment to the absolute protection of the fundamental rights of individuals. The foundationalists believe that democracy, if taken too seriously or literally, could result in policies that either deprive people of their natural rights or force major compromises in them.[5] For example, if a majority favors major restraints on the fundamental freedoms of speech, press, assembly, and religion, and elected officials respond accordingly, this would be the result of the democratic process but bad substantive policy. Consequently, the foundationalists consider the *content* of policy, especially in the area of natural rights, a more important measure of legitimate democracy than the processes that produced it. If democratic procedures have to be sacrificed in order to protect natural rights, so be it. The people have, over time and by engaging the Constitution as an ally, validated certain standards of government behavior which should restrain government from invading people's natural rights.

Rooted in the Lockean-based doctrine of natural rights that provided much of the inspiration for the Declaration of Independence, foundationalism relies heavily on the constitutional presence of the Bill of Rights and the process of judicial review. The fact that the Bill of Rights was appended to the original Constitution to appease antielitist, anti-Federalist forces in some states is important to the foundationalist school. Had this concession not been made, the Constitution might not have been ratified. That being the case, the contents of the Bill of Rights should be taken very seriously. Furthermore, they are quick to point out that the First Amendment begins with terminology that forbids, literally, any congressional action that compromises the peoples' rights to the freedoms of speech, press, religion, petition, and assembly. This is a significant restraint on the potential reach of policies that might even incidentally compromise these rights. Furthermore, the notion of judicial review enables the courts to serve as guardians of fundamental rights against any majoritarian-induced policies that may compromise them. The Jeffersonians were suspicious of judicial review because they considered it countermajoritarian. The foundationalists support it for the same reason.

Two obvious flaws in foundationalist thought involve the questions of to what extent should rights guarantees be considered absolute and uncompromisable and, even more important, what rights should be included on the roster of those that deserve protection at virtually any cost? Rights guarantees, when implemented by governments, clash with one another. They quickly lose their absolutist cast and, out of necessity, become relative. Even more significant is the issue of which rights are basic, which ones are a bit less so, and which ones should be considered privileges rather than rights. Scholars and politicians debate this issue regularly. There is little doubt that the First Amendment freedoms of speech, press, assembly, petition, and religion should be accorded high priority. However, there is much debate over how literally these freedoms should be applied by the courts. More important perhaps is the fact that scholars, groups, individuals, and elected public officials do not agree on how far this list should be expanded. What about the controversial alleged right to privacy? If it is a privilege and not a right, then policies outlawing all abortions would not violate the Constitution. If it is a fundamental right, then legislation can, and even should, authorize abortions under certain conditions regardless of how unpopular such policies might be in some circles. What about the claim of some individuals and groups for economic rights such as the right to a job and a living wage? What about the age-old claim by some of the right to own and use property for one's own economic benefit? Debates rage within judicial and legislative forums over whether such claims deserve classification as rights or privileges.

Elements of foundationalism influence public policy debates in legislative, judicial, and administrative forums in modern democracies. Whenever politicians, scholars, or citizens become frustrated over the policy impasses that are becoming more and more commonplace, attempts are often made to reclassify certain claims on government by citizens and groups as rights rather than privileges. The strategy is to extricate such claims from the normal routines and channels of politics and to reintroduce them as policies to be mandated by government as a matter of right. For example, it is clear that economic incentives of women and minorities often underlie official quests of these groups for equality or opportunity. They want jobs and decent wages, and to pursue them as a matter of right gives such crusades much more clout. Of course, this means that foundationalism can quickly be infiltrated by the ambition and self-interest incentives that concerned the Madisonians, and by the interest group forces that have provided the foundation for pluralist theory. For this reason, foundationalism, based on the Constitution's commitment to preserving the rights of individuals and classes of people, plays a major role in determining the nature of policy agenda, the ways in which policy debates are structured, and how policy outputs, or results, are defended.

Policy Dialogues and Public Policy: A Contemporary View

The Constitution incorporates assumptions and prescribes procedures that are often contradictory. These contradictions have been reflected in policy dialogues and processes over the past two centuries. Each of the postconvention policy dialogues offers a collection of preferences about what values and procedures should dominate policy debates and, ultimately, the content of policies themselves. The reverence shown by the public for any idea or process that is offered as constitutional in origin makes it comparatively easy for proponents of policies that reflect the assumptions or procedural preferences of the founders to gain leverage in the policy process. For example, the foundationalist argument that certain constitutional rights are virtually absolute encourages proponents of entitlement policies to add an economic or "income" rights spin to the Constitution's rights guarantees. This has been facilitated by the Ninth Amendment's acknowledgment that the enumerated rights should not be considered exclusive, and by the Supreme Court's mid-twentieth-century effort to interpret the Fourteenth Amendment's "equal protection" clause to consider granting educational and employment opportunities to racial minorities as a way to facilitate their quest for improved economic and social status. The Supreme Court, as a government elite force with the power of judicial review, could accomplish this, regardless of its short-term unpopularity. By ruling on rights issues in ways that contradict public opinion, the Supreme Court illustrates how important an elitist force can be in being servile to the foundationalist point of view at the expense of the pluralist or majoritarian perspective.

The assumptions of the pluralist and balanced government models assume that policies should embody compromise. Therefore, virtually all policies that involve hotly contested issues over the distribution of wealth and privilege illustrate these models. Examples include efforts to regulate the distribution and consumption of tobacco products, the production and marketing of food treated by insecticides, the regulation of corporate advertising, and minimum wage guarantees. These are but a few of the many policies that reflect balance and compromise induced by constitutional structure, constitutional guarantees of rights to petition government, and a public dominated by groups whose existence is dependent on these constitutional realities.

The Constitution, Public Policy, and the Democratic Paradox

The experiences of Americans with colonial governments, the Articles of Confederation, and the Constitution of 1789 illustrate how difficult it has been for Americans to deal with the twin issues of how to assign governments at both the national and state levels adequate policy powers while simultaneously attempting to ensure that the public's contribution to the character of those powers is of an acceptable moral cast. The public interest as a policy standard is impossible to determine scientifically or objectively. However, students of democratic theory do not need to agree on standards of policy morality in order for their prescriptions to have credibility. This is because they all share the assumption that it is best to guard against the possibility of public policies doing bad things rather than hoping policies will be universally good for society. Consequently, all schools seek to curb attempts by factions, actuated by the self-interest of their members, to register their uncompromised passions directly on public policy.

One way to accomplish such a goal is to insist that the basic source of government power—the Constitution—incorporates both a commitment to the theory of popular sovereignty and procedures, or structural obstacles, that help guard against its irrational application in the form of public policies. This enables government to reflect the best that popular sovereignty has to offer while simultaneously constraining its negatives. In some cases, this mission encourages theorists to question the assumptions that support majority rule. Indeed, what has made the Madisonian, pluralist, and foundationalist schools so controversial in some circles is the shared assumption that constitutionally grounded restraints on the exercise of majority rule are fundamental to creditable democratic theory. A sound model of democracy, they would argue, balances a concern for the need for public input with a concern for the quality of public policy. The ends and means of government are equally important.

Although the Constitution has been significantly democratized by time and formal amendments since 1789, these changes have served mainly to make the political system more susceptible to democracy's idiosyncrasies. This is a major paradox of democratic government as it has evolved in the United States. Simply stated, it is that the democratization of the political system has reinforced, not compromised, the impact of elites on public policy. Well-organized and well-endowed factions have exploited the Constitution's structural character to gain policy leverage that might well be relatively unavailable had not constitutional amendments and the passage of time subjected the Senate and the president to the faction-infested forces of representative democracy. The founders were not spiritual democrats. Most of them wanted to protect economic privilege. They did so by constraining the impact of popular sovereignty on government through the structural fragmentation of constitutional power.

Ironically, the democratization of government institutions such as the Senate and the presidency has not resulted in compromising the influence of economic elites on public policy. Elites are well organized and financially affluent. They use these advantages to become major players in elections by means of generous campaign contributions. They can afford to hire the best, most politically astute lobbyists. They control the major means of communication. While elections, the ability and opportunity to communicate positions on policy issues, and the right to contact the public's elected representatives can be clearly associated with a healthy procedural democracy, the conditions under which these democratic rights are exercised offer well-organized economic elites many strategic advantages over the relatively disorganized and asset-deprived majority. Consequently, the democratization of government institutions and elections has had the effect of reinforcing, not compromising, the policy objectives of the framers.

On the other hand, our commitment to the preservation of basic individual rights and to the principle of judicial review as a means of enforcing rights guarantees has helped overcome the inequitable exploitation of the weak and the unorganized by well-organized and well-financed minorities. One thing is certain: In the quest to make public policy responsive to both the wants and needs (not always the same) of the body politic, the Constitution is not a neutral force.

Endnotes

1. As quoted in John C. Livingston and Robert G. Thompson, *The Consent of the Governed,* 3rd ed. (New York: Macmillan, 1971), p. 84. This volume provides the student of public policy and theory with an excellent comparative analysis of the democratic policy implications of various theories of democracy.

2. *Ibid.,* p. 85.

3. See Woodrow Wilson, *Congressional Government* (1885); Woodrow Wilson, *Constitutional Government in the United States* (1907); James Thayer, "The Origin and Scope of the American Doctrine of Constitutional Law," 7 *Harv. L. Rev.* 129 (1893); Charles Beard, *An Economic Interpretation of the Constitution of the United States* (1913); *Lochner* v. *New York,* 336 U.S. 106, 111 (Jackson, J., concurring); Alexander Bickel, *The Least Dangerous Branch* (1962); and John Ely, *Democracy and Distrust: A Theory of Judicial Review* (1980).

4. Bruce Ackerman, *We the People: Foundations* (Cambridge, Mass.: The Belknap Press of Harvard University Press, 1991), especially Chapter 2.

5. *Ibid.,* pp. 10–16.

chapter three

Policy Objectives

Constitutional Politics and Issue Resolution

Public policies are rarely neutral in their impact. Policies are important to people, groups, and institutions because they marshal the coercive power of government in ways that affect them either favorably or unfavorably. For that reason, individuals and groups work to maximize their gains and minimize their losses in the policy process. Some policies advantage some individuals without disadvantaging others. Others advantage some people at the expense of others. Still others advantage classes of individuals (economic, ethnic, religious) while affecting other classes significantly, somewhat, or not at all. An individual's or group's stake, however defined, in a proposed rearrangement of the economic or social order will determine how he or she reacts to the proposal. An individual or group will welcome a policy proposal if there is perceived benefit, scorn it if it demands sacrifice, or ignore it if it appears that it will have no impact at all on how they live, work, or consume. In sum, certain types of policies encourage a distinct type of politics.

If one were to prioritize policy types according to the level of political conflict they engender, policies that distribute benefits would probably be the least controversial, policies that regulate some forces to benefit other forces would be considerably more controversial, and those that reallocate wealth, economic advantage, or social privileges between and among classes of individuals would be the most controversial. Two key questions surface from such trends. First, what kinds of policies does the body politic find the least controversial, moderately controversial, and the most controversial? Second, depending on the stakes they have in proposed policy changes, how do political forces use constitutional principles to leverage their influence in the resolution of those questions? The following discussion offers some tentative answers to these questions.

American Government: A Policy Typology

Before analyzing the role of constitutional politics in advancing, retarding, amending, or delaying the enactment of public policies, it is worthwhile to propose some tentative relationships between certain kinds of policy proposals and the distinctive kinds of political struggles that affect their resolution. The assumption is that each type of policy encourages a separate type of politics: i.e., differences in how proposals make their way to the policy agenda, how they are debated, who is involved in the debates and how intensive that involvement is, and how they are formally legitimated and implemented. The Constitution is certainly not a neutral factor in any of these stages. It can be used strategically to advance or defeat proposals. Furthermore, the way the Constitution apportions power among government institutions often encourages politicians to support or criticize policy proposals because of the impact they might have on the political integrity of their own institution: House, Senate, presidency, and the courts. Such roles develop from institutional affiliations, not from politics as we usually define it.

However, this distinctive kind of politics can be, and often has been, manipulated to facilitate established political objectives. For example, a legislator could declare his or her opposition to a presidential policy proposal because the proposal might undermine the historical role of Congress as the primary policy branch of government. In fact, the legislator's constituency, and ultimately his or her career, might also be advantaged by the same posture. If that is true, it is likely that the political incentive, not the institutional one, was what prompted the stand. The Constitution provides many opportunities for political actors to rationalize self-interest behind a smokescreen of constitutional doctrine. Regardless, if the Constitution triggers forthright conflict over the

legitimate role of separate institutions in the policy process, or if it serves as a disguise to lend legitimacy to base political motives, its role is significant.

A key question springs from this reality: How does the Constitution impact on the processes that produce these policies and, ultimately, on the nature of the policies themselves? A rather direct answer, offered at this point in the form of a hypothesis, is that the type of policy under question affects the ways in which policymakers pursue their goals, and the Constitution is frequently employed as an ally in those pursuits. Constitutional dictums are inputs which, when combined strategically with political calculations, create a distinct type of constitutional politics.

A convenient way to test the above hypothesis is through a typology window. A policy typology categorizes policies according to the kinds of objectives or results they seek, and then searches for differences or similarities in the political struggles that produce them. Although phraseology differs widely, scholars agree generally that public policies with domestic (as opposed to foreign) policy objectives seek to either *distribute* advantages; *regulate* the behavior of individuals and corporations; protect consumers; foster competition in the corporate marketplace; or *redistribute* wealth, property, legally prescribed advantages, or civil rights among classes of people or ethnic groups. These three types of policy—distributive, regulatory, and redistributive—encourage different decision-making procedures when they are debated and legislated and, in so doing, allow constitutional politics to impact on each differently.[1]

The Constitution and Distributive Policy

Distributive policies distribute wealth, advice, and authority to target groups that, presumably, will benefit directly from the decision. Ripley and Franklin describe a distributive policy landscape as one emphasizing the "decentralized award of federal largess to a seemingly unlimited number of recipients . . ."[2] Distributive policies are packaged in the form of such items as government contracts to corporations, tax loopholes, loans, price supports, and permission to harvest natural resources on federal properties. These policies, in essence, do things *for* individuals, groups, and corporations. They deny them little, if anything. They subsidize instead of restrict. Therefore, they are popular by nature. Their popularity is usually reinforced by the relative absence of heated competition for the money that funds them. For example, if farmers secure their price supports, cattlemen their grazing rights, and aerospace firms their contracts, each of these entities is relatively unconcerned about what subsidies or privileges the others are receiving. Of course, when financial resources become scarce and subsidies are cut back, then there is more competition among these forces for the limited resources that remain available. This makes distributive policy decisions somewhat more controversial.

For the time being, however, attention will be devoted to the norm itself and not to exceptions to it. More specifically, the focus will be on how the Constitution nourishes the incentives which underlie distributive policies, and how it serves as a catalyst to facilitate their enactment. The assumption underpinning the analysis is highly significant. It is that, owing to its democratic essence, *the American political system has a distributive policy bias.* The public and its elected and appointed agents naturally favor policies that distribute advantages more than they favor policies that regulate behavior or redistribute assets between and among classes of people. There is one cardinal reason for the system's distributive policy bias. As noted above, distributive policies function as the term indicates—they distribute monies, authority, rights, etc. that help individuals, institutions, and groups materially. Therefore,

distributive policies accommodate the self-interest incentive of both voters and their elected spokespersons.

These policies are the system's response to the public's factious tendencies. Being such, they attest to how realistic are the assumptions that underlie all four models of democracy discussed in the previous chapter, as well as to how practical is each theory's prescriptions for real world policymaking. Three of the models—the Madisonian, Jeffersonian, and foundationalist—all see danger in the influence of factions on policies. The pluralist model, while not accepting the untempered influence of factions on policy, argues that excessive factiousness can be controlled by representing as many factions as possible in the decision-making process, and by structuring decisions in such ways as to force compromises among them. If this proves nothing else, it proves that the issue of factions and their influence on policy decisions is probably inevitable in capitalist democracies. Furthermore, if democratic governments have written constitutions, it is likely that factions will attempt to exploit the character of these documents to their advantage. The United States is no exception. Just how well groups have succeeded in their mission to convert the U.S. Constitution's mission and structural character to their own policy advantage is, of course, subject to some debate. In politics all successes, as well as failures, are relative.

Nevertheless, the Constitution does bolster the influence of distributive forces on public policy, in several ways. First, as a result of the separation of powers principle, power tends to devolve or fragment with the executive and legislative branches, and interest group forces attempt to exploit this tendency to their advantage. As noted in Chapter 2, the separation of powers encourages a rivalry between Congress and the president which is rooted partly in politics and partly in institutional competition. The political reasons for the rivalry are most often explained by the differing voting alignments that presidents and legislators represent. Owing to his electoral base, the president's constituency is national in scope. House and Senate members represent subnational constituencies and therefore respond to different alignments of voters. For the time being, attention will be focused on the institutional roots of this rivalry and how that encourages structural arrangements within both branches that enhance the impact of distributive politics on policymaking.

Power is notably uncentralized in the House of Representatives, the Senate, and the national bureaucracy. The House and Senate have done this by design. Administrative agencies have followed suit, sometimes because the law requires it and sometimes because it is simply wise political strategy. Although the legislative chambers are constitutionally assigned different constituency bases and slightly different legislative priorities, the reason for specializing operations and fragmenting power in both houses is mainly political. In 1998, in the House there were twenty standing committees and more than eighty subcommittees. Each of these units has a highly specialized staff network upon which committee and subcommittee members depend for research and policy advice. Through their committee and (especially) subcommittee assignments, House and Senate members can influence policy decisions that affect their constituencies. In light of the importance of service to constituents, mostly via distributive policies, legislators thrive under organizational conditions that allow them to maximize their impact on subcommittee decisions. Hence, there is a clear bias toward organizational decentralization and committee and subcommittee autonomy. Fewer committees and subcommittees and a more centralized organizational structure would allow such policy claims much less identity. Subcommittees would forfeit some of their policy clout. Therefore, the base of atomized power in Congress is rather easy to understand.

The institutional mission of the two legislative houses reinforces the political one to help cement the uncentralized policy structure of Congress. The institutional factor clearly has constitutional roots. Since the Constitution separates the House and Senate from each other and from the executive branch, the members thereof have what might be termed a constitutional constituency. Consequently, legislators strive to maintain the policy integrity of their respective houses through an elaborate and fragmented subcommittee system that encourages the development of member expertise which can be employed in debates with rival institutions. The Senate Foreign Relations Committee has done this rather regularly since World War II, with investigations into the president's rationale for military intervention in Korea and Vietnam, and actual or suggested ventures into Somalia or Bosnia. On the domestic policy side, in 1977 President Carter asked Congress for the authority to initiate administrative reorganization proposals, subject to congressional veto, designed to cut costs and promote efficiency in the federal bureaucracy. The proposal was opposed by a fellow Democrat and political ally Jack Brooks, chairman of the House Government Operations Committee, on the grounds that the proposal constituted an unwarranted executive intrusion into a legislative prerogative—namely the legislative right to establish, fund, empower, and determine the organizational structure of administrative agencies. Although politics sometimes explains such a conflict, the differences between Brooks and Carter were not political. They were rooted in different constitutionally ingrained institutional perspectives that, in turn, owe their origin to the separation of powers. On many issues, executive-legislative differences are rooted in politics and defended institutionally. This was the case in 1993 and 1994 regarding President Clinton's proposal to reinvent government through reorganization and the elimination of unnecessary programs and the employees assigned to implement them.

Many chairmen of key congressional committees and subcommittees complained that a full compliance with the president's program would result in a congressional forfeiture of its constitutionally rooted historical right to create agencies and fund their programs. Control over an administrative agency's structure and budget means control over the policies administered by the agency. Arguments that presidential initiatives of this sort constitute an unwarranted intrusion of executive authority into legislative matters tend to cloak such arguments with some respectability. The constitutional cause serves as a smokescreen to hide the more predatory self-interest incentives of legislators and their allies in the bureaucracy.

In a very penetrating study of the effect of policy issues and institutional structure on public policy, Randall B. Ripley and Grace A. Franklin observed that subgovernments dominate the policy process when distributive issues are considered.[3] The term *subgovernment* is synonymous with the terms *iron triangle* and *triple alliance*. Collectively, these labels describe alliances that exist among congressional subcommittees, administrative bureaus, and interest groups, each of which supports the same policy objectives. For example, farm organizations that seek price supports for farmers align themselves with officials in the Department of Agriculture and members of the agricultural subcommittees with jurisdiction over such decisions. The purpose is the joint pursuit of policies that benefit them all. All three entities profit from distributing these rewards to the petitioning farmers. Similar policy networks exist to influence decisions in fields such as natural resources, business, labor, and national defense.

These are cooperative relationships that are, ironically, the result of the formal conflicts between and among institutions that often occur as a result of the separation of powers principle. Most of the founding fathers hoped that the separation of powers principle would serve to temper radicalism and foster government stability. Since distributive policy forces want government to support their quests for economic advantage, they are bothered by the prospect of institutional conflict that might compromise away or defeat their efforts to accomplish these objectives. As a result, these forces encourage the development of subgovernments as a way to bypass the otherwise disruptive effects of officially fragmented power on distributive policy decisions. They also welcome the development of other subgovernment networks because it means that other distributive policy forces have laid claim to their own policy fiefdoms and probably will not challenge other subgovernment domains. Consequently, institutions that are organizationally superior to subcommittees and administrative bureaus do not, as a matter of course, complain about the rather narrow policy objectives pursued by these alliances. These institutions—the full standing committees, the full House and Senate, and the executive departments—are, in reality, conglomerate-type organizations of many such policy enclaves. When all the enclaves are satisfied with how subgovernments respond to distributive claims, these "overhead" institutions are usually satisfied because many of their members are active in subgovernment networks. In these cases, the whole is rarely more than the sum of its parts. Ripley and Franklin have noted that subgovernment influence is the most salient characteristic of distributive politics at the national level.[4]

While subgovernments are institutionally the most significant force in distributive policymaking, their impact on the policymaking process marks a breakdown, or at least a major compromise, in how the Madisonian and pluralist theories of democracy hope to deal with the issue of factionalism in politics. It may be recalled that both these models seek to reduce the potential impact of a single faction or a few factions on policy by encouraging major compromises among factions before final policy decisions are made. While the subgovernment phenomenon has been faithful to both models in the representation of a wide array of factions through the alliance mechanism, genuine confrontations between and among subgovernments (and their component factions) have been the exception rather than the rule. So long as the members of each alliance are reasonably satisfied with the subsidies, grants, or loans they secure from the enactment of distributive policies, they are usually not concerned with what other alliances derive from the same process.[5] Consequently, the national government has permitted group access to decision arenas in ways that please the pluralists and Madisonians, but does not encourage the competition and compromises among them that would make for the successful implementation of either theory. Therefore, for the Madisonians the system does not allow constitutional structure or group competition to check potential group excesses. For much the same reason, pluralists are disappointed because the relative absence of the group competition and compromise they revere means the forfeiture of any realistic way of determining the public interest. Ironically, the fragmentation of governmental power mandated by the Constitution has encouraged the development of policy alliances that are significant mostly because they support policies that have bypassed the Constitution's structural hurdles.

The Constitution and Regulatory Policy

In contrast to distributive policies, regulatory policies focus on the regulation of behavior and on the denial or constraint of privileges or indulgences. Most regulatory policies focus on providing the general public with reasonably priced and safe products and services that it, the public, might not secure in the absence of such policies. Government regulatory policies

fall into one of two categories—protective and competitive. Protective regulatory policies stress the control of the conditions under which corporations can market goods and services. If businesses engage in activities that damage the environment, mislead the customer, discriminate against people on the basis of race or sex, or fail to disclose the underlying risks of an investment, often governments turn to protective regulatory policy as a solution. Competitive regulatory policies seek the protection of the public interest by controlling the number of firms that are allowed to enter the marketplace to provide products and services. The assumption is that higher-quality services will be offered the public if access to markets is limited, and if those who ultimately are allowed market entry agree to accept government-imposed quality standards. Policies that license television and radio stations, allocate routes for airline passenger services among competing airlines, assign trucking companies rights to haul designated types of goods over particular routes, or allow telecommunications companies to provide local and long-distance telephone service under specified conditions are all examples of competitive regulatory decisions. In recent years, national policy has stressed protective regulatory policy and deemphasized the competitive genre. As will be discussed later in this chapter, political conditions of the late 1970s and 1980s triggered a rather noteworthy move toward the deregulation of industries in a number of key economic areas.

Regulatory policy decisions are made in different arenas and are influenced by different considerations than are distributive policies. This arena contrast is very important, because it says something about how government policymakers deal with policy challenges that are more contentious in character than are distributive policies. Regulatory decisions, if implemented as promised in the law, affirm the claims of some economic forces and reject the claims of others. Since the forces making these claims compete with each other for licenses, access, or rights to markets, more people and their elected and appointed allies are interested in the decisions. Consequently, the policies that ultimately resolve these face-offs are usually produced by institutions located higher on the decision-making ladder than are those that resolve distributive policy issues. Insofar as Congress is concerned, regulatory policies are most heavily influenced by decisions of the full standing committees (instead of subcommittees), by floor debates in the House and Senate, and by conference committee resolutions of House and Senate differences.[6]

The impact of regulatory policy on the executive branch is even more significant. For reasons that are partly technical and partly political, Congress has decided to delegate many key regulatory policy decisions to the bureaucracy. Three types of agencies have been empowered with regulatory powers. Independent regulatory commissions were created expressly for this purpose, and are legally enfranchised to make regulatory decisions, implement them, and adjudicate any disputes that may arise during the implementation process. In sum, all three powers of government—legislative, executive, and judicial—that were assigned to three different institutions by the Constitution have by law been commissioned to regulatory agencies. Examples of such agencies are the Federal Trade Commission (FTC), the Securities and Exchange Commission (SEC), and the Federal Communications Commission (FCC). By way of a variation on a regulatory theme, Congress has established several independent agencies, such as the Environmental Protection Agency (EPA), and empowered them with regulatory powers very similar to those of regulatory commissions. Finally, cabinet-level agencies or executive departments such as the Departments of Health and Human Services (HHS), Housing and Urban Development (HUD), Agriculture (DOA), and Labor (DOL) have also been assigned regulatory policy responsibilities.

The propriety, as well as the constitutionality, of congressional decisions to delegate significant policymaking, administrative, and judicial responsibilities to administrative agencies has been debated frequently. Article I, Section 8, of the Constitution assigns Congress specific policy powers and grants it the right "to make all laws which shall be necessary and proper for carrying into execution the foregoing powers, and all other powers vested by this Constitution in the government of the United States, or in any department or officer thereof." Left unanswered is the question of precisely how general and unspecific laws can be before Congress can rightfully be accused of abdicating its legislative responsibilities by relocating them in the bureaucracy. Obviously, laws themselves cannot be so exacting as to prevent administrators from "fine tuning" them to meet different needs imposed by distinctive circumstances. Administrative expertise has to play some role in determining just how statutes should be applied on a case-by-case basis. By the same token, legislation that is so ambiguous that it seemingly expresses only the moral intent of Congress to address a policy question is, according to most observers, far too equivocal. Such legislation introduces questions of constitutionality (violating the separation of powers principle) and democratic accountability.

According to Theodore Lowi, the Economic Opportunity Act of 1964 (EOA) was a crowning example of how statutory ambiguity offered administrators a virtual policy "free hand." He concluded that the EOA made the delegation of legislative power to the bureaucracy the "order of the day." It was virtually impossible to find congressionally imposed operative rule-making or implementation standards anywhere in the statute. Administrative policy mandates were almost exclusively "end-oriented" sentiments of intent. For example, the director of the Office of Economic Opportunity (OEO) was authorized to provide for the "education" and "training" of VISTA (Volunteers in Service to America) participants, who were themselves charged by the statute to "combat poverty." The Community Action Program (CAP) was similarly charged and governed by the statute. Local CAP programs were to focus on antipoverty efforts, however recipient jurisdictions chose to define them, and to see that the administration of the programs included the "maximum feasible participation"of those targeted by the programs. Lowi concluded that such legislation assumed that laws are presumed good if they just start a process, that if laws provide the resources bargaining will provide the right policy answers, that it is undesirable to distinguish between public-sector and private-sector objectives in legislation, and that policies are not good unless they include broad delegations of policymaking power to administrative agencies.[7]

Such vast delegations of legislative authority to administrators had its roots in the Progressive movement of the late nineteenth and early twentieth century. Progressive era legislatures regularly employed open-ended statutory franchises to delegate policy discretion to administrative "experts" who could, presumably, be trusted to produce inherently "good" policy. The Progressive spirit remained a viable part of the legislative scene until the decade of the 1970s when statutes became increasingly detailed. By that time, administrative agency decisions had become so critical to the success or failure of programs dear to the reputations of legislators that they (legislators) assumed an increasing interest in statute specificity and oversight of agency operations. That trend, frequently labeled legislative "micromanagement" of administrative affairs, continues unabated today. In short, Congress began to relegislate for reasons that were essentially political. This renewed legislative concern for statutory detail was incorporated into such statutes as the Clean Air Act of 1970 and its 1977 and 1991 amendments, the Occupational

Safety and Health Act of 1970, the Employees Retirement Income and Security Act of 1974, and the Natural Gas Policy Act of 1974. In each of these laws, Congress demonstrated its interest in reclaiming much of its lost discretionary policy powers from the bureaucracy. This was because legislators had lost control over the ability to funnel policy favors to clients and constituents, and they wanted to recover at least some of it. This implies that legislators are more comfortable with regulatory policy objectives if they can be milked for a few distributive policy advantages.

Owing to the nation's distributive policy bias noted above, regulatory policies do indeed often have distributive policy consequences. When an individual, group, industry, or a sector of the economy is denied the privilege of controlling prices and markets, advertising goods or services in particular ways, or operating plants and factories that pollute lakes, rivers, and the atmosphere, some people benefit from these decisions. These benefits— whether they be for the consuming public in general or for small companies that have difficulty competing with larger ones—clearly have distributive policy overtones. However, because some forces or factions have been denied the legal rights to engage in certain behaviors, the route to the formal enactment of these policies is more controversial. In a sense, by their very nature, regulatory policies activate competition among factions or groups over the extent to which some groups will be advantaged and others disadvantaged by policy decisions.

The national government became concerned with regulatory policies only after it became evident that public policy could not forever allow well-organized, unrestrained, and often corrupt economic forces to exploit the consuming public without restriction. This became a serious policy issue when the instruments of production became mechanized, and waves of immigrants settled in cities to provide a cheap workforce for the newly mechanized factories. While these trends took several years to mature, they had become the foundation for a major revision in public policy theory by the 1880s.

The first statutory expression of the national government's concern for regulatory policy was the Interstate Commerce Act of 1887. This law created the first independent regulatory agency—the Interstate Commerce Commission—with the official mission of regulating the fares railroads charged passengers, and the fees they charged farmers and industries for the transportation of grain, livestock, and manufactured goods from locale to locale. The purpose was to provide the railroads with a decent return on their investment and the services they provided, while at the same time not allowing them to unreasonably exploit those who wanted to use their services. Since 1887, other regulatory agencies have been established to regulate corporate behavior on behalf of consumers. Regulatory agencies such as the Federal Trade Commission (1914), the Federal Communications Commission (1933), the Securities and Exchange Commission (1933), and the Environmental Protection Agency (1970) were all established to provide some sort of fair balance between the quests of industry for profit and the interest of the public in the fields of advertising, broadcasting, securities transactions, and the use of the environment.

Protective regulatory policies are not the result of an elitist exercise in creative thinking. They are policy responses to a public mandate demanding that government do something to counter the tendency of corporate America to exploit, unreasonably, the consuming public. One expectation behind the regulatory crusade was that, if legislation mandated regulatory agencies to develop regulations incorporating a balance between the interests of corporations and those of consumers, those policies would be, in essence, objective or neutral. Another assumption was that this presumed objectivity would more likely surface if regulatory commissions made the policy decisions with legislatively delegated policy authority, if commission membership was bipartisan, if members served for fixed, overlapping terms of office, and if members were removable only for cause and not for political reasons. This expectation was too optimistic. Many commission appointees had formerly been affiliated with the corporations and industries they were expected to regulate as commissioners, and their commission decisions reflected that.

In fact, the belief that legislation can mandate policy neutrality is naive. Attempts to depoliticize public policy decisions by statute are doomed to fail. Such statutory failures serve mainly to underscore the inescapable fact that policy decisions, be they legislative or administrative in origin, are intrinsically political. Changing the stage upon which policies are considered and legitimated does nothing, in the long run, to change the political nature of those policy decisions. Such has been the fate of statutory attempts to deal with regulatory problems by delegating policy authority to experts housed in structures outside the regular routes of political accountability.

Regulatory power has also been delegated to executive departments. Although key policy executives in departments such as Health and Human Services, Housing and Urban Development, Interior, Agriculture, Commerce, and Labor do not enjoy the security of fixed terms of office as do regulatory agency commissioners, they are nevertheless expected to balance the needs of consumers with those of corporations when they issue administrative orders that license certain products or approve certain practices. The controversial decisions of the Food and Drug Administration (Department of Health and Human Services) on whether to approve certain food additives, or to make certain controversial medicines available for prescriptions or over-the-counter sale, are examples of controversial regulatory decisions that emanate from executive departments.

Agency decisions either to not regulate or to deregulate are as political as are decisions to regulate. Groups that are disadvantaged by a regulatory decision will be advantaged by a decision to reverse it, and vice versa. Since the mid-1970s, the national government has responded favorably to pressures from the corporate and, in some cases, the consumer sectors to deregulate some industries. Usually the objective of these regulatory reversals has been to make U.S. corporations more competitive domestically and internationally. Policies enacted in the 1970s and 1980s that deregulated the airline industry, the savings and loan industry ("thrift" institutions), the trucking industry, and the telecommunications industry were key examples of such a trend.

Considering their objectives, regulatory policies stand in stark contrast to distributive policies. Constitutional politics impacts on each type of policy differently. It could be argued that the legislative delegation of policy authority to administrators was simply a legislative response to the increasing impact of technology and specialization on policy issues. After all, how can a body of a few hundred individuals make policy decisions that obviously require the expertise of engineers, physicists, chemists, lawyers, and physicians with any sense of assurance that their decisions will address the policy issue at hand? To be sure, legislators have personal and committee staff personnel to assist them with research and analysis, but their expertise cannot compete with that of a bureaucracy of nearly three million individuals, many of whom have spent their careers dealing with the complexities and frustrations that affect these policies. The logical answer is to delegate these policy responsibilities to administrators with the understanding that Congress can establish broad decisional standards and review and reject any decision at any time.

In fact, the federal courts have ruled that minimal legislature-prescribed standards or guidelines for administrative regulatory decisions must exist so that Congress cannot be accused of abdicating its legislative responsibility.[8] Therefore, it is not difficult to defend the practice of administrative agencies serving as policy agents for legislatures in fields where the intricate knowledge and application of scientific and other highly technical data are necessary.

Defending delegated authority on technological and scientific grounds is understandable. However, decisions to delegate also harbor major political advantages for legislators, and these advantages have roots in the Constitution. The principles of separation of powers and federalism encourage Congress to delegate policy responsibilities to the bureaucracy so that Congress can, for want of a better term, "wash its hands" of hotly contested, controversial issues that might undercut the popular support of its members. This might be termed the "hot potato" syndrome. If, for example, legislators conclude that it is a no win situation for them to deal with a controversial environmental, natural resource, trade, commercial drug, or pollution issue, what better solution is there than to reassign the responsibility to an executive department or regulatory agency, or to state regulatory institutions?

In sum, Congress can transfer the authority to act to another arena, claim that it is an executive branch or state responsibility, and take credit for resultant decisions that are popular and blame the other institution or jurisdiction (in case of the states) for decisions that are unpopular. If the recipient institutions move too aggressively to regulate industries or offend consumers whose support is basic to the political survival of legislators, the policy can be reclaimed as one that properly belongs to Congress.

The constitutional principles of separation

of powers and federalism invite such a strategy. Of course, problems of policy accountability ensue. Separate branches of government can each blame the other for abdicating their responsibilities or for faulty decision-making procedures. If the national government had a parliamentary or Westminster structure, under which the chief executive and his cabinet were selected by the legislature from its own membership, then a system of collective responsibility would exist, and accountability for the results of transferring policy responsibilities to nonlegislative arenas could not be avoided. By the same token, decisions by national institutions to decentralize power and assign responsibilities that were previously theirs to states and localities or, in many cases, to the competitive impact of the marketplace can be defended as attempts to reinvigorate the constitutional powers of the states as viable islands of policy power in the federal system or, as in the case of market competition, revitalize limited government as a viable constitutional principle.

There is yet another dimension of regulatory policy that, owing to the way in which Congress has decided to deal with it, illustrates the impact of the Constitution on both policy procedures and policy character. This involves the highly important role of a separate, independent judiciary on agency regulatory decisions. Congress does not want agencies to have unchecked regulatory responsibilities because such a condition could raise questions of constitutionality and, as noted above, might be politically inadvisable. If agencies were vested with regulatory discretion that was, from the legislative perspective, inappropriately exercised, Congress can control these excesses by new legislation or increased oversight. Also, Congress does not want to assign major agency oversight responsibilities to the president. That could challenge Congress's claim to policy primacy. Developments over the past two centuries have

made the president a substantial policy rival to Congress in any case. Therefore, Congress is unlikely, on its own volition, to vest the president with many more major sources of policy influence.

In addition to the political reasons for increased statutory exactness and legislative oversight mentioned above, Congress has attempted to check possible excesses in administrative agency use of policy discretion through two additional mechanisms that legislators consider politically safe. The first of these has involved designing the agency proceedings that precede official rule-making to encourage adversarial confrontations among all parties with a vested interest in proposed regulations. This sort of atmosphere encourages compromises and, true to the assumption of both the Madisonians and the pluralists, discourages decisions that vary significantly from the status quo. These procedures have their roots in the Administrative Procedure Act of 1946, but current rule-making procedures usually require many more steps than that law officially required.

These procedural requirements vary from agency to agency. Each agency has its own set representing the composite product of formal legislation, standards imposed by the courts, and those introduced internally within the agency. In sum, there are no decision-making procedures that apply to all agencies. A typical set of such requirements would include a formal announcement in the *Federal Register* of the agency's intention to consider a rule or policy change; maintaining a docket that includes all documents, recorded conversations, committee reports, meeting summaries, advisory opinions, and public commentary on any proposed action; the publication of any proposed rule in the *Federal Register* together with a notice of scheduled hearings on the proposal; conducting public hearings chaired by a hearings officer or a judge with expertise in administrative law and where arguments and cross-examinations are encouraged; allowing time for the public at large to submit data and commentary in support of or opposition to the proposal; and formal publication of the final regulation in the *Federal Register,* together with agency commentary on all the key issues raised by the public and the parties to the decision.[9] While these procedures encourage decisions that virtually force compromises among all interested parties, they are also very time consuming. It is not unusual for it to take up to four years for a final decision to surface from such a process. Nonetheless, such a process does serve the congressional drive to check potential excesses in regulatory policymaking.

The other key technique Congress uses to check potential agency excessivism is to empower courts to oversee agency activities. In contrast to the president, the courts are not regular policy rivals to Congress, and so Congress has been more comfortable with this option. Furthermore, since many appeals to agency decisions involve judgments as to the fairness of agency procedures, the courts are the most logical arena in which to resolve such issues. Presumably the judicial mind, by its very nature, encourages decisions that reflect equity and fairness in both procedures and results. Therefore, if agency hearings reflect consumer versus producer, industry versus industry, or company versus company confrontations, having such contentious face-offs resolved occasionally by appeals to the courts has the potential of moderating even further the impact of the open, adversarial nature of the required procedures described above.

In sum, the processes that precede the final promulgation of agency rules and regulations are all compatible with or, in some instances, specifically based on constitutional principles. Since independent regulatory commissions are formally assigned executive, legislative, and ju-

dicial responsibilities by statute, these actions officially violate the separation of powers principle. However, the balance that the founders expected the separation of powers to contribute to policy decision making is, in theory, very alive and well in the regulatory process because of mandated internal agency procedures and because the courts can review agency decisions. Furthermore, the objective of limited government is, in theory, served by the compromises and bargaining that precede final agency decisions.

All this rests on the assumption that the regulatory policy processes result in a genuine attempt by agencies to balance the interest of consumer with producer. However, given the political system's distributive policy bias, it is not surprising that often the industries targeted for regulatory constraints by agencies develop cozy relationships with agency personnel that result in policies that support, rather than restrain, those industries. The consumer clearly suffers as a result. This is sometimes called the "capture" theory because an industry presumably captures an agency's policy mindset and uses it for its own benefit. Sometimes Congress encourages this by voicing concern over how strict an agency has been with an industry. Agencies begin their existence with enthusiasm about their regulatory mission, only to find that political appointments to their ranks, the popularity of the marketplace economic ideology, and pressure from legislators make it more comfortable and far less controversial to assume a neutral or even proindustry policy stance.

Often, agencies easily succumb to industry's cooptation strategies. Cooptation is a strategy designed to convert an organization's opponents into allies or, at least, into forces that do not pose a threat to the organization's mission.[10] One way to accomplish this is to invite opponents to participate in the organization's decision processes. Also, it can be encouraged by persuading the opposition, the regulatory agency, that its best interests (long-term survival and growth) are best served by cooperating with industries that are, supposedly, regulatory targets. The history of regulatory policy is replete with examples of agencies that have, at one time or another, found it to be strategically astute to, as the expression goes, join the system rather than fight it. The Food and Drug Administration's relationship with the drug industry has, at times in the past, been accused of being too compliant with the drug industry's position when it came to authorizing the commercial sale of drugs. The Environmental Protection Agency has, in recent years, been criticized for its accommodation of agribusiness interests on the issue of the possible cancer hazard posed by certain chemicals used to control insect infestation on fruits and vegetables harvested for public sale. The Interstate Commerce Commission was, in its immediate postnatal period, accused of being too accommodative of the railroad industry when it came to setting charges for the transportation of individuals and commodities. In the 1970s and 1980s it was accused of being too much the handmaiden of the trucking industry, and opposed to the railroads, on key "right to route" decisions.

These are not universal tendencies in all regulatory enterprises. They tend to be cyclical in many cases. Nonetheless, when the capture strategy is successful, the result is often regulations that are more symbolic than actual. Industries use the agencies as protective shields or cocoons to avoid harsher regulatory decisions that would emanate from agencies more committed to their statutory mission. Public policy, instead of regulating industrial behavior in the consumer interest, becomes an ally to the corporate cause. Therefore, it is not surprising that, when a deregulation crusade took hold of American politics in the late 1970s and early 1980s, many industries did not welcome it with open arms. This movement,

and its significance for the impact of the Constitution on public policy, will be examined in the following section.

Constitutional Politics and Deregulation

The official deregulation of selected industries, begun during the Carter administration and continued through the Reagan and Bush administrations, had profound effects on most Americans. Affected were the railroads, airlines, truckers, banks and thrift institutions, bus companies, and the telecommunications industry. Restrictions were lifted on many activities that had been regulated by government for generations. The movement was notably bipartisan, with the Republicans supporting it because of their philosophical hostility toward government interference with business, and the Democrats supporting it because of their belief that deregulation would increase competition and therefore lower consumer prices.

Insofar as the constitution-policy thesis is concerned, the interesting part of the movement is how it resembled Ackerman's constitutional politics model, discussed in Chapter 2, in that it opposed the political system's bias toward distributive policy. While distributive politics is the type of politics most favored by the public and its elected representatives, conditions often demand that government do things other than distribute assets and privileges. In fact, to prove the system's overall distributive policy bias, some examples of conditions under which it succumbs to other forces can help the student of public policy to appreciate its primacy, but not monopoly. To borrow a time-worn analogy, sometimes exceptions to the rule help one appreciate the primacy of the rule (in this case, the tendency) itself.

The deregulation movement began in the mid-1970s, championed by such high-profile political figures as presidents Jimmy Carter and Ronald Reagan and Senator Edward Kennedy. They received key bipartisan support in both the House and Senate. The first statutory target was the railroads. The Railroad Revitalization and Regulatory Reform Act of 1976 offered railroads limited authority to set rates for their services. It was followed by the Airline Deregulation Act of 1978 which abolished the Civil Aeronautics Board (CAB) and canceled the government's authority to set passenger fares and control mergers in the airline industry. In 1980 the Motor Carrier Act relaxed restrictions on the trucking industry in a number of areas. Also in 1980, the Depository Institution Deregulation and Monetary Control Act eased restrictions on mutual savings banks, abolished ceilings on interest rates, and allowed banks to pay interest on checking accounts. Three deregulation actions occurred in 1982. The Bus Deregulatory Reform Act permitted bus companies to form without the Interstate Commerce Commission's approval. The Thrift Institutions Restructuring Act permitted savings and loan institutions to invest in nonresidential enterprises and make commercial loans. Finally, in 1982 the government and the American Telephone and Telegraph Company (AT&T) settled an eight-year dispute over AT&T's virtual monopoly over telecommunications services in many areas by announcing that AT&T had agreed to divest its twenty-two local operation companies, thereby disengaging the local monopolistic service operations from the competitive portions of its business.

There were several reasons why deregulation was so popular during this period. According to Martha Derthick and Paul Quirk, it took a curious and unusual series of events, together with a clear public mandate, for the movement to succeed.[11] First, there was the growing impression that the capture of agencies by industries had serious anticompetitive effects on business and negative effects on the

consumer. Second, academic elites, led by the economists, joined forces in support of reform. Armed with empirical evidence that, allegedly, supported the contention that the free market could be more self-regulatory and proconsumer than existing regulatory policies, these forces were virtually unanimous in their support of a deregulatory policy turn. Third, the public was becoming increasingly disenchanted with bureaucracy and big government. Deregulation seemed to be a logical way to appease this disenchantment. Fourth, political leaders joined forces to support deregulation.

The result was a rather substantial deregulatory movement. The results were not as favorable for all interested and affected parties as was originally hoped and expected. However, this should not detract from the fact that the deregulation movement did run counter to the normal routines and distributive bias of the policy process. The regulated industries that had successfully curried favors from regulatory agencies fought the deregulation movement, but lost the struggle. To be sure, Congress and the presidents that supported the movement were responding to public frustrations and so the crusade clearly was not conducted without public input. However, public input this time was not rooted in garden-variety pluralist politics, but was more sweeping in cast and, if classical democratic theory is the standard, perhaps more legitimate.

Consequently, this was constitutional politics played out successfully on a plane markedly different than the usual ones. It was, in Ackerman's term, an example of pure constitutional politics in which the general public represses the influence of special interests for the public good. As noted earlier in this chapter and in Chapter 1, factions usually exploit constitutionally fragmented institutional power for their own benefit, and often with much success. However, even when this strategy is unsuccessful, another constitutional input is perhaps even more evident. Beginning with the

Preamble, and surfacing intermittently throughout the document, the Constitution casts itself clearly on the side of government by consent, or popular sovereignty. Under this version of constitutional politics, the reader does not have to search behind the scenes to understand and appreciate how forces manipulate the Constitution's structural character for their own policy advantages. This kind of constitutional politics is more open, honorable, and, in a sense, refreshing.

The Constitution and Redistributive Policy

Redistributive policies seek to redistribute wealth, rights, opportunities, and other items of privilege among classes of people or racial groups.[12] Because they deal with the reassignment of advantages that Americans have traditionally valued highly, and because they affect large numbers of people simultaneously, redistributive policies are very controversial. Debates over how wealth and opportunity are to be redistributed, or if there should be any redistribution at all, are highly charged debates that often assume a "good guys" versus "bad guys" or a "winners" versus "losers" theme. They also have a clear ideological cast about them. They often involve debates over the proper role of government, as opposed to the private sector, in caring for society's underprivileged. Redistributive issues involve debate over such controversial questions as how equitable is a progressive income tax structure; is a sales tax too regressive; to what degree should younger generations subsidize the retired, aged, and infirm through publicly sponsored pension plans or medical care; should government have the right to require employers to select employees on the basis of affirmative action or equal employment opportunity standards; and should government have the right to require public schools to be balanced racially. These are ideological questions. They pit liberals against conservatives over what government should do *to* or *for* society or segments thereof.

Redistributive issues have a very high public profile. Sometimes they dominate presidential campaigns. They are often favorite subjects for newspaper editorials and television talk shows. They interest most people because they are affected by them economically and/or because they involve debates over the values we have cherished as a society historically. It is not unusual for terms such as "freedom," "liberty," "civil rights," and "property rights" to be employed by all sides in debates over redistributive issues. As a result of their high political profile and inherent controversy, redistributive questions are hotly contested and resolved in House and Senate floor debates, usually with a relatively high degree of presidential involvement. Congressional committees, subcommittees, and administrative bureaus, which dominate in distributive policy decisions, do not dominate in redistributive issue resolution.

Because of their controversial nature, redistributive questions are sometimes recast to reflect more of a distributive flavor before they are voted into law. Ripley and Franklin note that often House and Senate members must be convinced that the dispensation of funds under the redistributive format will be of direct economic benefit to key groups in their respective constituencies before they, the legislators, will support them.[13] This was clearly evident in the debates that preceded the enactment of the Model Cities program in 1966, and in the way in which funds were apportioned to the states after passage of the Comprehensive Employment Training Act of 1973 (CETA). In both instances, implementation standards were so flexible that key local groups were able to lobby federal administrators in the Office of Economic Opportunity (OEO) and benefit directly through awards of CETA contracts. From OEO's point of view it was important to disperse benefits to as many localities as possible so that it, OEO, could build up a broad base of support for the program's continuance. For example, Ripley and Franklin note that CETA dollars went to a notably large number of localities, and the alleged early success of the program was due to the geographic balance of fund dispersements and not based on how well individuals targeted for the fundings benefited from the program. The controversy in 1993 and 1994 over President Clinton's health care reform proposal reflected the same phenomenon. Physicians, hospitals, drug companies, insurance companies, and employers all reacted either favorably or unfavorably to the proposal according to how the proposed changes would affect their historic roles as providers of protection or dispensers of health benefits.

The distributive bias of the American policy system quickly surfaces in the debates over such controversial redistributive issues as employment policy and health care reform. Despite the fact that redistributive policies often assume a distributive cast when finally legitimized and administered, their character is impacted by the political use of constitutional principles. The Constitution is exploited politically by forces that both favor and object to redistributive proposals. Constitutional politics also affects the ways in which redistributive issues reach the policy agenda, and how such policies are implemented.

Constitutional politics affects the consideration and administration of redistributive policies in several ways. The first of these emanates from the Constitution's protection of civil rights on several fronts, the most important of which is the Fourteenth Amendment's provision that no state shall "deny to any person within its jurisdiction the equal protection of the laws." Although this restriction is targeted at states, the courts have ruled that the Fifth Amendment's due process clause requires the national government to guarantee citizens equal protection of the laws. In general, the equal protection standard means that governments in the United States cannot enact policies that treat people unequally. Policies that make unreasonable distinctions between categories of persons are unconstitutional. In effect, this means that public policy cannot sanction the unequal treatment of people on the basis of race, religion, or sex. The emphasis here is on government keeping policies from being formally discriminatory. However, to many groups and individuals it means that government can be petitioned to enact policies which afford them the opportunity to achieve prosperity equal to that of society's more affluent members. Government cannot legislate actual equality, but presumably it can, by legislation, create conditions that provide the opportunities that must precede such an event.

As a result, equality of opportunity campaigns manifest themselves in the form of civil rights legislation to erase discriminatory voting regulations, court decisions to integrate schools racially, job training programs for the economically disadvantaged, proposed constitutional amendments to eliminate discrimination on the basis of sex, affirmative action programs to guarantee that minorities and women are not subject to discrimination when applying for employment, campaigns to equalize pay between the sexes and among the races if job assignments require equal skills, public housing programs for the disadvantaged, and national health care reform proposals to insure the uninsured and provide for better access of the economically underprivileged to health care facilities. Proposals such as these, whether officially enacted or not, are controversial because they are redistributive proposals. As such, they germinate the ideological conflict and heated controversy generated by most redistributive proposals. The Constitution is their ally. Therefore, if the petitioners think that the Constitution will help them make up for any disadvantages they face in securing these opportunities through the normal routines of politics, they are inclined to "go public" with their grievances. Hopefully, the Constitution will help David slay Goliath.

The second impact of the Constitution on the consideration and administration of redistributive policies is derived from the first. In sum, it is that the Constitution's pro–civil rights posture encourages redistributive policies to be resolved by national action rather than by state or local action. Of course, state and local governments are deeply immersed in the administration of redistributive policies. In critical policy areas such as public housing, Medicaid, job training, and aid to the disadvantaged or underprivileged, states and localities make many significant decisions. However, most of these are in response to policies the national government has initiated. There are several reasons why the national government is the primary decision arena for redistributive policies. For example, if the purpose of an equal opportunity policy campaign is to provide for everyone's equality, these issues have to be resolved nationally because only the national government has jurisdiction over everyone. In addition, since the forces behind such policy campaigns tend to be those subject to discrimination, they seek to escalate or broaden the arena of conflict in order to escape the more discriminatory forces that were responsible for the alleged discrimination in the first place. Allies to the cause of equality are more likely to be found with presidents and federal courts because these institutions represent, or have jurisdiction over everyone, the politically strong as well as the weak, when they assume a policy position or make a judicial ruling. This is reminiscent of E. E. Schattschneider's "schoolyard analogy," in which he argued that when the school "bully" assaults another student, it is the latter who tells the teacher or the principal of the incident, and thereby escalates the arena of conflict. Since teachers and school administrators are responsible for the well-being of all students, the aggrieved student's complaints will likely receive a sympathetic hearing from these individuals. The bully would, of course, prefer to keep matters more localized.[14]

In sum, ethnic minorities, the disabled, and the economically underprivileged have used the Constitution as a symbol to champion their campaigns for antidiscriminatory policies. Even though the Constitution itself does not mention specifically the groups or classes to be targeted for equal rights efforts, any group that considers itself to have been disadvantaged by society's social, economic, or political structures rallies behind the Constitution in an effort to secure the rights to which they are entitled. Of course, since the Fourteenth Amendment was ratified in the immediate aftermath of the Civil War, it is clear that equality for Afro-Americans was the immediate goal of the equal protection clause. However, the Fourteenth Amendment outlaws laws and practices that make unreasonable distinctions among groups. It does not mandate that laws be passed to subsidize, train, or support in any way the crusades of the disadvantaged for economic, social, and educational equality. Nevertheless, groups that seek the rather subjective and elusive goal of equality today focus their efforts on securing these "rights." For example, Stephen L. Percy, in his study of the politics of implementing federal policies toward the disabled, notes that the incentive behind early legislation in this area was one of "good will." However, the strengthening of the civil rights movement in the late 1960s and early 1970s, led by ethnic and women's rights groups, encouraged groups representing the disabled to add a rights claim to their crusade. The result was several disability rights laws and aggressive pressures on the bureaucracy to implement the laws quickly and without compromise.[15]

A third effect of constitutional politics on the consideration and implementation of redistributive policies is an outgrowth of the symbolic strategy mentioned above. The tendency for redistributive issues to involve confrontations over how far the rights claim can, or should, be taken has drawn the courts into the process on a broad front. In short, redistributive issues tend to judicialize the policy process. Some of the reasons for this are rather obvious, and others a bit more elusive. Since society's disadvantaged seek to centralize decision making in the hope of finding allies to help them with their rights crusades, a logical institutional ally would be the court system. A key mission of the courts is both to define and oversee the implementation of civil rights policies. Therefore, civil rights forces are often encouraged to take their case to court. In addition, federal judges are not elected, but appointed for life. Consequently, and in contrast to elected officials, they are not as likely to respond to pressures from employers, labor unions, school officials, or any other group bothered by such movements because they, the judges, will not lose their position if they make unpopular decisions. For example, undoubtedly the single most important decision made by government in this century to advance educational opportunities for ethnic minorities was *Brown* v. *Board of Education.* This decision, which resulted in the gradual integration of the nation's public schools, would not have been made by Congress given the indifferent or hostile attitude that most members of the white majority had toward ethnic rights issues in 1954. In some cases it would have been political suicide for a congressman or senator to have supported such a policy. However, Supreme Court judges faced no such political risk, and were free therefore to decide this most critical of policy issues on the basis of the constitutional merits alone.

In addition, the policy implementation environment that confronts redistributive policies draws the courts further into the policy process. Since equality and rights are paramount goals of many redistributive policies, the courts are called on to establish standards, even quotas, to be met by agencies that administer such critical redistributive policies in areas such as affirmative action and equal employment opportunity. The courts must often rule on the fairness or appropriateness of such standards, and listen to appeals made by disappointed parties who complain that agencies have not complied with the standards, assuming they were fair in the first place. An excellent example of how and why the courts are asked to enter the redistributive policy scene was illustrated by the Supreme Court's decision in *City of Los Angeles, Department of Water and Power* v. *Manhart* (1978) in which the Court ruled that the city's requirement that female employees contribute a higher percentage of their salaries than males to the city's pension plan was a violation of Title VII of the Civil Rights Act of 1974. Title VII prohibited any sort of employment discrimination on the basis of race, color, sex, or national origin, and established the Equal Employment Opportunity Commission to enforce the provision. In the *Manhart* case, the Court ruled that despite the fact that women on average have a longer postretirement life expectancy than men, requiring women to contribute more to the city's retirement plan amounted to treating females as mere components of a sexual category, and was therefore in violation of Title VII.[16]

Appeals to the courts over practices such as this are virtually inevitable given the nature of the issue. In turn, this means that government agencies, foundations, large and small businesses, colleges and universities have to create their own in-house administrative operations (usually separate offices or bureaus) to oversee the implementation of Title VII standards. This, in turn, increases their overhead expenses and, in the case of commercial enterprises, can do battle with competitive advantages they may have enjoyed in the marketplace. In sum, the judicialization of public- and private-sector decision processes in issue areas that are fundamentally redistributive in character affects the way issues make the policy agenda, the way in which they are considered, and the way they are implemented.

It is clear that redistributive policy issues often have economic rights overtones. Such an orientation has, in turn, introduced a fifth impact of constitutional politics on redistributive policy. It has made constitutional principles a key part of the redistributive rhetoric and, presumably, the input that affects redistributive decisions. In addition to civil rights, debates over redistributive issues regularly involve disputations over how the Constitution's principles of limited government and federalism should be interpreted or altered to satisfy the political system's obvious need to resolve some policy challenges by redistributive means. Consequently, debates over whether to raise or lower taxes (particularly the former) inevitably spawn ideologically seeded confrontations over how far government should go in interfering with such emotionally charged concepts as "freedom," "liberty," and numerous "rights." Debates over President Johnson's War on Poverty in the mid-1960s, over President Reagan's supply-side-based quest for policy deregulation and government decentralization in the 1980s, and President Clinton's deficit reduction and health care reform proposals (both of which involved actual or potential tax increases) all illustrated how protagonists on both sides of these issues employ the concept of limited government as an ally to make their case.

Limited government is employed by conservatives to argue against tax increases, government intervention into the economy, and individuals' economic affairs. It is used by liberals as a way to justify government's support of policies that restrain the ability of entrepreneurial forces to exploit the politically weak. To conservatives, government should be limited in its ability to restrain economic growth and restrict entrepreneurial freedom by confiscatory policies. To liberals, society's more wealthy and entrepreneurial elements should be limited in their ability to exploit, for their own advantage, the resources and talents of the less privileged. Therefore, to liberals, rights of conservative forces to do these things should be limited, and public policies should incorporate such objectives. For a period of time late in the nineteenth century, the Supreme Court did accede to the conservatives' argument and ruled, on occasion, that laws which interfered too egregiously with a corporation's right to maximize the use of its property for economic advantage did constitute an unwarranted deprivation of property without due process of law. The Fifth Amendment's due process clause, originally designed to protect defendants in criminal proceedings, was employed to protect the rights of property owners to use their property for economic gain. However, for most of the twentieth century, the courts have rejected such an interpretation and ruled that legislation that taxes and regulates the use of property is justified because such policies are "affected with the public interest."[17]

The principle of federalism has been employed in a similar fashion. While a more detailed analysis of the impact of federalism on public policy will be found in a later chapter, a few comments on how it is used conceptually in redistributive policy debates is appropriate at this time. It may be recalled that the Constitutional Convention decided on a federal basis for allocating powers geographically in an attempt to placate both liberal and conservative delegates. Fearing concentrated power, the liberals emphasized the need for state sovereignty in most policy areas. Seeking to stabilize the political system and expressing doubts about the destabilizing effects of majority rule, the conservatives advocated a strong central government and limited state independence. The ultimate compromise, later termed a "federal" solution, delegated specific (but significant) powers to the national government and reserved any remaining powers that government could exercise legitimately to the states. This is a paraphrase of the Tenth Amendment's language, which is the only point at which the Constitution deals directly with how power is to be distributed under our version of federalism.

Federalism represented a political compromise between factions at the Constitutional Convention, and it is employed politically in redistributive policy debates today. Redistributive issues propose to redistribute wealth or other advantages, and it is commonplace for those who fear the national government's efforts to tax their assets or change their lifestyle for the specific benefit of another group or class to argue that such actions are the responsibility of the states, not the national government. For example, the early resistance by southern states to federal court orders to integrate public schools in the aftermath of the *Brown* decision was based on the argument that the states had exclusive jurisdiction over education policy as part of their reserved powers. The Fourteenth Amendment's equal protection clause, so went the argument, which was directed at state discriminatory practices, did not include education. Of course, most southern white politicians did not want integrated schools for social and cultural reasons at that time. It made their resistance to school integration more respectable to raise the jurisdictional issue spawned by federalism than to defend their position on grounds that suggested racial bias.

In the 1960s and 1970s the "new federalism" became politically popular. It proposed to return many significant policy initiatives to the states that had been gradually absorbed by the national government. Some support for the new federalism did come from individuals who were interested in restoring a healthy balance of policy responsibilities between the national government and the states. However, more support for the idea came from individuals and groups that did not think that the national government had any legal claim to certain types of regulatory or redistributive activity. Included here were assorted welfare programs, regulation of business, and education. The return, or reassignment, of policy responsibility in these areas to the states was the first step in a long-term campaign against what these forces thought were the negative effects of the regulatory and social service state. To claim that the national government's "usurpation" of state powers violated the spirit, if not the language, of the Constitution gave such an argument more symbolic legitimacy. Presumably, this would broaden support for the crusade.

In truth, the opponents of these programs were probably not very concerned about renewing the classical mission of federalism as a constitutional principle. Instead, they employed federalism as a smokescreen to obscure the actual purpose behind their campaign—that of killing or compromising national policies which they found objectionable. This represented an adaptation of what might be termed "states rights" politics. Since 1789 it has been commonplace for opponents of policies, or policy proposals, that have involved federal-state cooperation to argue that the policy is the constitutional responsibility of the states only. This has been true for controversial regulatory decisions, federal entitlement program subsidies, and civil rights policies promulgated by Congress or the Supreme Court. Again, opposition to such programs is usually personal and political in nature, but is framed or couched in constitutional terminology (in this case, federalism) to make it appear more honorable and therefore legitimate. Although never employing the states rights argument literally, President Reagan's 1981–1982 campaign to lower taxes, deregulate industry, and reassign some key national government policy responsibilities to state and local governments incorporated the same strategy. All of the Reagan reforms did not involve redistributive policies, but many of them did. In particular, the campaign to transfer some key responsibilities for funding and administering welfare and other entitlement programs from the national government to the states was defended on the grounds that the national government had grown too large and its agencies too bureaucratic. The states had suffered correspondingly by losing their ability to create policies and adapt them to the particular needs of their people. Therefore, it was time to restore some balance to our federal system.

Federalism has yet another impact on the consideration of redistributive policies. States have equal representation in the Senate because of federalism, and this gives disproportionately high weight to people in thinly populated states in all congressional policy decisions. However, because redistributive issues tend to be comparatively controversial, this disproportionately excessive weight of the smaller states weighs more heavily on their resolution. In an attempt to appease those forces who feared that a strengthened national government would enact policies that exploited the small-populated states, the Constitutional Convention agreed to represent states equally in one of the two legislative houses. This violated the "one man–one vote" idea, but the founding fathers as a lot were not overly enthusiastic about literal democracy anyway. Regardless, equal representation of states as geographic units in the Senate was a necessary prerequisite for acceptance of the Constitution. This did not have much policy significance in the republic's early years. Although there were population differences among the states, agricultural interests were important in

most of them. Similarly, although there were variations among states, manufacturing and trade interests were important in most states. Moreover, redistributive issues were not a part of the national government's agenda in the republic's immediate postnatal period.

However, times have changed. The industrialization and urbanization of America and the accompanying migration of population have changed the demographic profile of the states dramatically. West coast and sun-belt states have experienced major influxes of population and have been affected by the attendant policy problems that grow inevitably from rapid urbanization. By way of contrast, the Midwest and plains states have not been so impacted and, as a result, have become comparatively rural or nonurban in character. Nonetheless, the representation of each state in the Senate remains equal. Furthermore, redistributive issues are ones that tend to ignite controversies between urban and rural forces. Most of the nation's poor and underprivileged reside in urban areas. The same is true for ethnic minorities. These groups are usually the targets of wealth redistribution. Senators from less populated, more rural states that do not have large percentages of poor and underprivileged residents do not experience the same constituency pressures to redistribute wealth as do senators from the more highly populated, urbanized states. This means that senators from the less populated states must be assuaged more on redistributive questions. They can "drive harder bargains," as the saying goes. Furthermore, they can ask for distributive policy concessions that will build up good will in their own states in return for their support on key redistributive policies. For example, President Clinton's deficit reduction package passed the Senate by a one-vote margin in 1993, and only after Nebraska senator Robert Kerrey agreed at the last minute to support the president. Nebraska has a political culture rooted in agrarian conservatism. Consequently, Kerrey faced a comparatively high degree of ideologically grounded opposition to his support of a proposal that incorporated some significant tax increases. This was critical to his position on the issue because he faced a potentially tough reelection battle in 1994. Therefore, he needed to assuage Nebraska voters by appealing to their fiscal conservatism and cultural suspicion of big government. The senator's early opposition to the proposal was based on what he considered to be the proposal's relative deemphasis on spending cuts as a means to reduce the deficit. The popularity of spending cuts in politically conservative states such as Nebraska symbolized the people's opposition to big government, and was therefore a very popular position for the state's senators to assume. Kerrey finally supported the proposal, but only after extended and intense talks with the president. Clearly, Nebraska residents would not provide much of the revenue needed to conduct a major assault on the budget deficit. Nonetheless, the equal representation of the states in the Senate, induced by federalism, made Kerrey's vote just as critical to the bill's success as were the votes of senators from highly populated states such as New York and California.

As a rather outspoken senator and former candidate for president, Senator Kerrey was a high-profile senator, and the negotiations between him and President Clinton were well publicized in the press. However, relatively unknown senators, with the same voting leverage, can impact on policy decisions in much the same fashion. President Clinton's 1993 budget plan was controversial because it asked for major tax increases, including one on energy. The president originally requested a 10 cents per gallon increase in gasoline taxes. Senators appeared to be equally divided on the issue, and Clinton knew he could not afford to lose any support from Senate Democrats or the proposal faced certain defeat. Consequently,

when freshman senator Herbert Kohl, a Wisconsin Democrat, announced that he would vote for no proposal that included a gasoline tax increase of more than 4.3 cents per gallon, the president had no choice but to concede. What the president or the rest of Congress wanted was irrelevant. Clinton secured Kohl's support by agreeing to the 4.3-cent figure and a compromise budget plan was enacted. However, the policy costs were significant. Originally aimed at reducing the country's dependence on foreign oil, encouraging more efficient energy use, and assaulting a major source of environmental pollution, the concession forced major compromises in all these policy objectives. In addition, the revenue shortfall stemming from the reduced gasoline tax was estimated at $49 billion, forcing the president to look elsewhere for revenue and more program cuts.

This event illustrates the power of a relatively unknown senator to use federalism's representation base to leverage his own policy objectives in ways that affect the nation in significant ways. In effect, Kohl set a policy price for his support of the legislation. Kohl, facing a reelection battle of his own in 1994, wanted to limit the imposition of new taxes on the middle class, a position which was popular with Wisconsin voters.

Redistributive issues, by their nature, are very controversial, and it is not surprising that legislators will exploit whatever situational advantages they have to ameliorate the potentially negative effects of controversial legislation on their constituents. In that sense, Kohl's action was understandable. The fact remains, however, that the more controversial the issue, the more likely the Constitution's structural cast will be exploited to serve the political ambitions of individuals like Senator Kohl. Controversial redistributive questions targeting such goals as deficit reduction, racial equality, and comprehensive health care encourage senators from states whose populations are unrepresentative of the country as a whole to set a price for their votes and, in effect, determine policy for the entire nation.

It should be noted that redistributive proposals that involve tax increases or tax adjustments targeted for increased welfare, medical, and education benefits would often offer disproportionately high benefits to people in small, economically poor states, especially those with high percentages of rural poor. Such policies would redistribute wealth from the high-tax-base states to the low-tax-base states. Accordingly, and in contrast to the Kerrey and Kohl examples, senators from such states would be inclined to support many of these proposals, using their representational leverage to overcome the opposition of senators from larger and comparatively wealthier states whose taxpayers would be subsidizing residents of the poorer states. In any case, federalism's assault on the one person–one vote principle as manifested in the Senate's representation base affects how redistributive policy issues are framed, debated, and resolved.

Constitutional Politics and Policy Objectives: A Critique

The Constitution's provisions, principles, and norms impact directly on how domestic policy issues are posed, explained, discussed, and legitimized. The precise impact depends, in part, on what type of policy is under consideration. Although the categories are not mutually exclusive, in general policies either distribute, regulate, or redistribute resources, authority, and privilege. Each type of policy encourages a different type of policy debate within different levels or arenas of government. Distributive policies are the least controversial because these policies convey a variety of advantages to individuals and groups. The group basis of politics, acknowledged as inevitable by the pluralist and Madisonian schools, has contributed to

government's distributive policy bias. It is, pure and simple, easy for elected officials in quest of popularity and (ultimately) reelection, to vote for policies that build and reinforce this popularity. Regulatory programs are somewhat more controversial because key sources of political support for many of these elected officials are disadvantaged by decisions that regulate their market behavior on behalf of the relatively unorganized and less powerful consumer. Redistributive policies, because of their tendency to compromise the economic and social advantage of one "class" of people to the advantage of other, less privileged, classes are even more controversial.

In some cases, the Constitution generates a type of dialogue that makes the support or rejection of a policy proposal more likely. Opposition or support of this type is based, at least in form, on principle rather than self-interest. In fact, more often than not, dialogue based on principle serves as a masquerade for self-interest motives. This tends to be the case with redistributive and regulatory policies. Since distributive policies are more popular, constitutional politics affects their consideration in distinct ways. Separation of powers and checks and balances were designed to fragment the policy process to encourage compromises that would discourage irresponsible, or even tyrannical, policies. Because of the political system's bias toward the distributive option, forces seeking advantages for themselves through the public policy vehicle have created cooperative networks of support that unite interest groups, administrative bureaus, and congressional subcommittees in a cooperative quest for policies that mutually support each party to the alliance. These iron triangles, or triple alliances, exist as relatively hidden subsystems that operate beneath the pro-forma structural fragmentation of the policy process. If the United States had a constitutional system which united, politically, the powers and constituencies of the executive and legislative branches, such alliances would probably have a higher profile and would, therefore, be potentially more accountable to the public as a whole.

Endnotes

1. These categories were first introduced by Theodore J. Lowi in T. J. Lowi, "American Business, Public Policy, Case Studies and Political Theory," *World Politics*, vol. 16, pp. 677–715.

2. Randall B. Ripley and Grace A. Franklin, *Congress, the Bureaucracy, and Public Policy*, 5th ed. (Pacific Grove, Calif.: Brooks/Cole, 1991), p. 76.

3. *Ibid.*, pp. 82–90.

4. *Ibid.*, p. 73.

5. *Ibid.*, p. 76.

6. *Ibid.*, pp. 196–207.

7. Theodore J. Lowi, *The End of Liberalism* (New York: W. W. Norton, 1969), pp. 234–236.

8. See Gary C. Bryner, *Bureaucratic Discretion: Law and Policy in Federal Regulatory Agencies* (New York: Pergamon Press, 1987), Chapters 1 and 2.

9. *Ibid.*, p. 29.

10. A classic treatment of cooptation in the public sector can be found in Philip Selznick, *TVA and the Grass-Roots* (Berkeley and Los Angeles: University of California Press, 1949).

11. Martha Derthick and Paul J. Quirk, *The Politics of Deregulation* (Washington, D.C.: The Brookings Institution, 1985).

12. Ripley and Franklin, *op. cit.*, p. 21.

13. *Ibid.*, p. 141.

14. E. E. Schattschneider, *The Semi-Sovereign People: A Realist's View of Democracy in America* (New York: Holt, Rinehart & Wilson, 1960), Chapter 5.

15. Stephen L. Percy, *Disability, Civil Rights, and Public Policy: The Politics of Implementation* (Tuscaloosa and London: University of Alabama Press, 1989), pp. 240–241.

16. *City of Los Angeles, Department of Water and Power* v. *Manhart*, 435 U.S. 703 (1978).

17. See the discussion of the *Slaughter House Cases* and *Munn* v. *Illinois* in Gerald Gunther, *Constitutional Law*, 12th ed. (Westbury, N.Y.: The Foundation Press, 1991), pp. 436–442.

chapter four

Popular Consent

Constitutional Politics, Public Opinion, and Elections

Popular consent is most fundamental to the American system of government. It assumes that ultimate political authority resides in the people. This does not mean that the public should exercise direct control over the selection of all policymakers, or that citizens should constantly be directly involved in policy decision making. Rather, its most fundamental premise is that expressed in the *Declaration of Independence,* namely that should government stray from its primary mission of governing in the interest of the people and with their consent, the people reserve the right to replace the government with a regime that is committed to such purposes and practices. Presumably, this could be accomplished by ballots or by bullets, with the Revolutionary War being an example of the latter. Most delegates to the Constitutional Convention were suspicious of direct public involvement in both the selection of policymakers and in the policymaking process itself. However, even the founding fathers believed that the ultimate authority to replace a government that had strayed from its mandate rested with the body politic. In short, they were more committed to the notion of government *for the people* with their approval than to government *by the people.*

The democratization of the Constitution, both formally and informally, together with the development of political parties, changed all this. In contrast to the formative era, today the Senate is popularly elected. For all intents and purposes, owing to the way in which members of the Electoral College are selected, so is the president. In theory, the purpose of a political party is to increase the chances of a group of people, committed to the same philosophy of government and the same candidates for office, to win elections and control public policy decisions. As subsequent discussion will show, this portrayal is somewhat optimistic, especially in its assumption that party members share the same political philosophy and commitment to specific policies. Nonetheless, the acceptance of the political party by Americans as a legitimate vehicle of governance means that the concept of popular consent is interpreted more broadly today than in 1789. Today it incorporates more of a government *by the people* standard than it did in 1789. In fact, it assumes that the best decisions for the people are those that have been made with more involvement by the body politic. This occurs through the public's role in the selection of policymakers, through its participation in party primaries and conventions, and through public opinion polling. Popular consent has been taken more literally with the passage of time. Today, certainly more than in 1789, popular consent implies that the best decisions for the people are those that are made directly at the behest of the people.

This has major implications for both policy processes and policy content, and for the impact of the Constitution on each. The opportunity to participate in policy decisions encourages individuals, groups, and parties to seek ways to maximize their ultimate influence over such decisions. The structural atomization of power induced by the Constitution has fragmented arenas of political debate. As a result of its commitment to guaranteeing fundamental rights of opportunity and expression, the Constitution impacts on the ways candidates and their programs are presented to the public during election campaigns. Because the Constitution separates the power to govern among three separate branches at the national level, it introduces an accountability problem which, in turn, is exploited by both challengers and incumbents in their quest for election or reelection. Challengers allude to the gap between what the incumbent promised as a candidate and what the institution to which he or she was elected actually achieved during his or her tenure. Incumbents blame the gap between promise and performance on the irresponsibility of other branches of government or sister legislative chambers, and thereby attempt to absolve themselves of any blame for the lack of policy progress. All this translates into an environment in which candidates for office run against the record of the opponent, as opposed to one which emphasizes what candidates can do to change things for the better if elected. Finally, and most important for the thesis of this chapter, this contributes to a marked cynicism on the part of the electorate toward politicians, public officials, and government in general. This is occurring at a time when the people and their government need just the opposite.

Public Opinion and Electoral Politics

Any effort to determine how the Constitution impacts on the way public opinion is registered in public policy should begin with an examination of what issues are important to people when they decide to vote for or against candidates running for office. This is essential because elections are the most formal, regular, and consistent means available for citizens to tell their government what they want and what they don't want. Elections are, in essence, formalized conduits of opinion that flow between the governed and the governors. If the kinds of policies that governments adopt reflect the results of elections, either by way of changing who is elected or by altering the policy mandate for those who are reelected, then there is a clear cause and effect relationship between the electoral process and policy outputs. The Constitution impacts on how elections are structured, how candidates appeal to the electorate, and on how frequently and through what geographical bases the people are permitted to register their opinions. Therefore, its role is critical to the entire process. Just how critical is, of course, a judgment call, but some tentative propositions will be offered in subsequent discussion. For the time being, the analysis will focus on the nature of the public mindset when confronted with the election challenge, or obligation, as the case may be. It is impossible to assess the impact of the Constitution on both the conduct and results of elections unless we first determine what people think they are accomplishing when they vote. Only after addressing that can the Constitution be targeted as either an active or passive force both in determining what people, as voters, want and how elections deal with that challenge.

Over the past half-century, there have been many praiseworthy attempts by scholars to determine, by scientific means, what influences voters to vote as they do. Most of these studies, although not necessarily the most significant, have utilized a sociological approach, to uncover regularities in voting preferences. Sociologically oriented research stresses the impact of primary group relationships (friends, family, coworkers, place of residence, religion, and social status) on voting predispositions. The earliest systematic studies of voting behavior were sociological in genre because sociologists were the first in the social science family to utilize survey research techniques, and because the only data then available with which to compare the results of voter surveys was census data. Census data was organized into categories—income, religion, ethnic origin, area of residence—which sociologists found very compatible with their discipline base. The first major study stressing such an approach was by Berelson, Lazersfeld, and McPhee. It concluded that voting decisions had clear historical, primary group roots. As important as one's political beliefs were in shaping voting decisions, they concluded, historically rooted variables such as friends, class, family members, religion, and income were more important in drawing people sharing essentially the same demographic characteristics to a particular party and its candidates.[1] This made voting patterns very predictive.

While much voting behavior is quite predictive, often there are major shifts in voting patterns from election to election for which the sociological approach cannot account. The same year that Berelson, Lazersfeld, and McPhee published the results of their research, Campbell, Gruin, and Miller published another study which challenged the sociological focus and offered an explanation for shifts in voting behavior over time. Utilizing survey data collected by the University of Michigan Survey Research Center, they concluded that the shifts in voter preferences between 1948 and 1952 could not, almost by definition, be explained by previous voting patterns. Consequently, they offered a psychological explanation for voting preferences, stressing the individual's (as opposed to group) political party orientation and his or her reaction to the issues and the candidates.[2] This study was followed, in 1960, by a study by Campbell, Converse, and Miller which concluded that most votes could be explained by social and psychological factors. These included the individual's long-term predisposition to favor one party over others, and his or her resultant tendency to use party orientation as a convenient ideological framework or backdrop by which to judge candidates and issues.[3] This explanation, they argued, more directly relates to voting choices. It is more direct and proximate, whereas the sociological approach stresses factors that are more indirect and unattuned to voters' reactions to changes in the political climate which can cause shifts in party positions and, therefore, changes in voting behavior.

The sociological and psychological theories of voting behavior were challenged in 1957 by Anthony Downs's introduction of a nonempirical model which reexamined and reinterpreted the earlier theories in terms of their compatibility with the economic theory of rationality.[4] This theory argues that individuals act to maximize their self-interest when making decisions about jobs, investments, market strategies, and the like. When this model is applied to the political world, Downs argues that voters appear to make utilitarian distinctions between parties and candidates, and cast votes based on which party or individual will, in their opinion, provide them with more net economic benefit. This is a rational decision in that it incorporates past party promises and subsequent government performance as they relate to feeding the voter's quest for economic security and/or gain. In contrast to the sociological and psychological schools, this theory rejects explaining voter choices by group orientation or by party predisposition. Instead, it substitutes a rational choice criterion for voting. Individuals vote for the candidates and party that have taken positions on policy issues that will best serve their (the voters') economic self-interest. Furthermore, it reduces what might be termed the "issue workload" on the voters. Since they are concerned only with policy issues that affect their own interests, they can take shortcuts and ignore debates on issues which do not affect them thusly. Since most people are not consistently absorbed in politics regularly, owing to the stresses of life, the demands of their work, and the attention that must be paid to family matters, it is rational to withdraw from all political issues save those that impact in direct ways on their everyday lives. In essence, economic self-interest offers voters an issue shortcut. In sum, Downs rejected the thesis that voting is conditioned basically by either social group orientation or party affiliation, and substituted a more situationalist, opportunistic explanation—that voters judge every candidate and every policy issue according to how they or it will affect their best interest.

These three approaches to explaining voter incentives were the product of the 1950s. Since that time, the Downs theory has gained prestige in academic circles, and the sociological and partisan theories have lost influence. In reviewing the number of literature citations of the three works that brought each theory to

creditability—*The American Voter* (party identification), *Voting* (sociological), and *An Economic Theory of Democracy* (rational choice)—Martin Wattenberg has noted that, by the late 1980s, the Downs volume was cited over four times as frequently as *Voting* and more than twice as often as *The American Voter.* This contrasted markedly with the late 1960s, when Downs's work was cited a bit less frequently than *Voting,* and approximately half as often as *The American Voter.*[5] Wattenberg offers several explanations for this. First, since the Downs effort was theoretical and not empirical, it had applications beyond the political science discipline. Since it contributed to the development of public choice theory, it attracted interest from economists, psychologists, and sociologists. Second, the sociological and psychological models were more "time bound" than was rational choice theory. The former two theories drew their empirical support from historical data that might not be as relevant to explaining voter choices today as in the past. Since Downs's theory did not depend on such data for its creditability, it could be (and has been) applied to situations that even Downs did not anticipate when he developed the model.[6]

However, what appears to be by far the most important reason for the rise of public choice theory and the decline of the sociological and psychological models is that public choice theory is clearly more compatible with the development of what Wattenberg has termed "candidate-centered politics."[7] This represents an adaptation of V. O. Key's thesis in his seminal work *The Responsible Electorate,* in which he offered an "echo chamber" explanation for voting behavior. Key argued, in essence, that voters initiate very little in the way of policy alternatives which candidates and political party organizations take very seriously. Instead, voters react to the way issues are framed by parties and candidates and presented to them, the voters.[8] Voter surveys in the 1970s and 1980s revealed that voters were inclined to discuss their motives in public choice terms. This had not been as evident in earlier periods. Wattenberg argues that this change is rooted in the development of candidate-centered politics, which can be contrasted to the more political-party-centered politics of the past. A comparison of these two phenomena and the impact of constitutional politics on the candidate-centered strategy will be found in the next section.

The Constitution and Candidate-Centered Politics: The Policy Consequences

Probably the most striking difference between the electoral environment of the late twentieth and early twenty-first centuries and that of earlier generations is to be found in the ways in which elections are organized, strategized, and resolved. The pre-1980 period was marked by the dominance of party organizations, which exerted significant control over the selection of nominees through caucuses and conventions, over the finance of campaigns, and over policy agendas in the aftermath of elections. This was the era of the political boss, the smoke-filled room, and the patronage system which rewarded loyalists of the successful party and its candidates with lucrative jobs in government. It was a period when strong, well-disciplined party organizations could win elections from the county level to the White House by hard-nosed appeals to voters based on what the party could do for them. Policy agendas were set by party-based campaigns.

The rise of electronic journalism and its impact on the costs of campaigning for office are two new factors that have, in combination, changed all this, and changed it dramatically. Television provides people with most of the news they receive about policy issues, about campaign issues, and about candidates for office. More important, it does this by visual images and by thirty- or sixty-second sound bites.

It links elected officials with their constituents instantaneously and, in so doing, it effectively bypasses the political party as a policy and issue conduit between the people and their government. Strong party organizations offered the voters respectable vestiges of policy continuity. Television makes this seem much less essential to the officeholders and candidates seeking to unseat them because appeals for votes and campaign contributions can be made personally and directly through television. If candidates "appear" to be creditable or inspire voters on television, and if they say things that trigger favorable, quick, emotional reactions in their thirty-second commercials or in the coverage that networks and local television stations provide as part of the news, their chances for electoral success are greatly enhanced. In short, television is the catalyst that has changed the election game from one that used to be party centered to one that is candidate centered, and the policy implications of this change are profound.

The nature of V. O. Key's "echo chamber" has changed markedly. Ironically, this change serves to validate his theory. Voters are now reacting to candidate appeals to their emotions through a television sound-bite strategy. It makes Downs's theory more relevant to today's politics than that of earlier generations because it encourages candidates to promise voters short-term "quick fix" palliatives for their problems. In short, candidates adopt a voter self-interest campaign strategy. Voters have responded favorably. Voter surveys reveal a marked Downsian flavor to their attitudes about what they want from candidates and, ultimately, from government. Therefore, candidates emphasize appeals directly to voters and interest groups, thereby bypassing the party organizations.[9] Voters have developed a noticeable "What have you done for me lately?" evaluative frame, and candidates have responded in kind.

Although issue triviality has been a part

of presidential election campaigns for generations, trivialization has tended to dominate campaigns in the era of the candidate-centered campaign. For example, the presidential campaign of 1988 was noteworthy for its emphasis on visual appeals to voters that pictured the candidates visiting flag factories and riding in army tanks, and prisoners exiting prisons on furlough presumably to commit heinous crimes while on officially sanctioned prison leave programs. Issues focusing on the economy, foreign policy, the environment, health, education, and consumer protection often took a back seat to these "issues" during that campaign. It was a good illustration of how campaign strategists focus on appeals to the rather instantaneous, emotional reaction of voters to visual images in the era of the candidate-centered campaign.

Such strategies are introduced by campaign strategists who officially represent party organizations, thereby creating tensions between parties and voters. The voter's search for a Downsian or public choice backdrop to such campaign triviality often is found wanting. In 1988, for example, if a voter applied the "What have you done for me lately?" standard to the flag-burning and school prayer issues, most would have been unable to make a linkage. According to Wattenberg, such a tension between parties and voters is not unusual in the era of the candidate-centered campaign. Parties often sidestep or cloud the issues which interest the voter, and this further estranges the voter from the party. While political party officials are aware that Downsian incentives are important to voters, parties nonetheless focus campaigning efforts around rather trivial, ambivalent, symbolic, ideologically tinted appeals to voters in an attempt to appeal to as wide a range of the potential voting public as possible. As a result, issues such as equality, more or less government, higher or lower taxes, more or less regulation of industry have become the hallmarks of official party appeals to the electorate in recent

years. However, this has not been true for candidates. Individual candidates often find this of little use in their search for votes among an electorate that is increasingly influenced by a "What have you done for me lately?" attitude. While it is true that electronic journalism and the democratization of the nomination process have estranged candidates from their reliance on parties and encouraged them to appeal more to the economic incentives of voters, the fact that party organizations shy away from specific, meaningful policy stands further estranges both candidates and voters from parties. The increased costs of campaigning force candidates to seek campaign support from nonparty sources. Corporations, interest groups, and wealthy individuals are quick to respond.

Most often, these contributions are filtered through organizations known as political action committees (PACs), which are organizations created to raise and distribute contributions to individual candidates. Federal election laws restrict the amount of money individuals, corporations, labor unions, trade associations, and candidates themselves can donate to specific campaigns. PACs have multiplied in number to fill the gap. In the mid-1970s there were approximately 600 PACs in existence. By the early 1980s, that number had increased to well over 3,000. By the late 1980s, the number had increased to well over 4,000.[10] PACs are of two different casts. Some are the "segregated fund" type. These are the children of a parent organization, usually an interest group, corporation, union, or trade association. These PACs secure campaign funds from their parent organizations only, and not from public contributions. Others are of the noncommitted genre. These organizations solicit contributions from the public in general, usually by direct mail, to support candidates with funds that are independent of traditional interest group or corporation influence. An example of the segregated type of PAC is the National Rifle Association (NRA) Political Victory Fund. An example of the noncommitted type is the National Conservative Political Action Committee.

PACs have become the financial salvation of many candidates seeking sources of campaign support in the wake of the declining role of parties in campaign finance. They are the single most important source of funding for congressional campaigns, and their role in presidential campaigns is increasing. PACs tend to favor incumbents, feeling it is a better investment to "buy" access to an established winner than to risk making significant contributions to those who will likely lose elections. The result of this has been a heightening impact of incumbency on policy decisions. Supported by PAC contributions, well over 95 percent of House and Senate members are routinely returned to office. It is obvious that most PACs are actuated by Downsian-type incentives. Instead of a "What have you done for me lately?" orientation, the PAC variation would be something like "What have you done for our organization or cause lately?" It is also rather clear that the PAC phenomenon reinforces Schattschneider's observation that the pluralist political landscape is unevenly biased toward more well-organized, wealthy, and well-led political forces. For example, none of the top ten contributing PACs in the 1984 elections represented society's disadvantaged or ethnic minorities.[11]

Candidate-Centered Politics and Consent Theory: The Constitutional Roots

The Constitution's legitimacy as both fundamental law and a policy force is rooted in the popular sovereignty principle. Therefore, an analysis of its role in framing issues for the policy agenda and in influencing the way in which officeholders respond to public mandates is in order. Candidate-centered campaigns are vital to explaining each. The following discussion projects some connections, be they tentative, between the candidate-centered election process and the impact of the Constitution on both policy inputs and policy outputs.

Candidate-centered politics has introduced many changes to American politics. One of the most important has been in the ways in which policy issues are framed and discussed in campaigns. Party organizations, virtually deprived of their disciplinary influence over the nomination process and candidate campaign strategies, approach the campaign policy challenge by stressing general goals which they hope most voters will find symbolically appealing. The Constitution is replete with symbols available for use, and they are used without reservation. The Constitution's concern for freedom of expression; freedom of religion; the right to bear arms; due process, equal opportunity, and equal protection of the law guarantees; and (according to some) the right to privacy encourage party organizations and, if strategically appropriate, their candidates to focus on issues like the legalization of school prayer, the political and economic rights of minority groups and women, gun control legislation, and the freedom to terminate a pregnancy within a certain time frame. Some of these issues are critical to public safety and the economic well-being of many individuals. However, the Constitution's language encourages candidates to frame and debate them as rights that either exist or should exist, depending on one's point of view. This, in turn, encourages both candidates and voters to react to them emotionally and intensely, often in an "all or nothing" frame of mind. Such an approach sidetracks the inevitable, namely the ultimate need to compromise between and among forces with different ideas about what the rights universe contains and how those contents should be applied to society. In addition, it often consigns key economic issues such as employment, inflation, poverty, education, health, and employment security to low positions on issue agendas during campaigns.

Such strategies tend to reward candidates with appealing styles who do not necessarily offer voters the policy options they want or need. Nonetheless, especially since television has assumed an increasingly dominant role in campaigns, often the importance of a candidate's style is more important than his or her position on key policy issues. This means that campaigns and elections may not always function well as policy intermediaries between the people and their government as they once did. If candidates shrewdly exploit constitutional symbolism to make themselves more appealing during campaigns, the traditional model of the campaign as a policy issue enterprise is undermined. Excellent examples of the triumph of style over substance were the presidential elections of 1980 and 1984. President Reagan was elected by overwhelming margins in both elections, despite the fact that research revealed that the American electorate, in general, was not nearly as ideologically conservative as was candidate Reagan in 1980, and President Reagan in 1984.[12] Evidence suggests that voters were dissatisfied with the incumbent President Carter in 1980 and Walter Mondale, the 1984 Democratic Party nominee, for reasons that had little to do with either's policy positions. Nonetheless, Reagan initiated what came to be some of the most dramatic changes in public policy since the New Deal period. Wattenberg concludes that those two presidential elections illustrate the impact of candidate-centered politics on the electoral process, since voters wanted an alternative to Carter, and Reagan's personal appeal and shrewd campaign strategy made it easy to vote for the person rather than his policy agenda. In short, the size of Reagan victories, especially in 1980, was due in no small part to the tendency for voters to rationalize and thereby sidestep the policy issue factor.[13]

At the presidential level in the candidate-centered era, campaign foci have tended to shift from the party and toward the candidate. Reagan was elected primarily because he was not Carter, presumably with the hope that "things" would be better under Reagan. These "things" were, of course, policies. However, voters, as a rule, did not insist on policy specifics from Reagan during the 1980 campaign but apparently were satisfied to wait and cast a retroactive "performance" vote in the 1984 election. Satisfied in general with the condition of the economy and world affairs, voters reelected Reagan by an even greater margin in 1984. This suggests that, in the candidate-centered era, when candidates for president first run for office they can get away with portraying themselves as "do good" policy reformers, without having to be overly specific about what they want to accomplish. However, if they stand for reelection, they have no choice but to defend the specific policy changes they have wrought.

Therefore, the candidate-centered era seems to have inflated the role of performance voting at the expense of policy voting.[14] Performance voting is reactive voting. Instead of voters asking candidates to pledge themselves to a slate of policy reforms, they instead vote yes or no on policy conditions as they understand and experience them. If voters are satisfied, they tend to favor incumbents as they did Reagan in 1984 and Clinton in 1996. If they are dissatisfied, they usually reject incumbents, elect an alternative slate, and hope things will improve. The 1980 and 1992 presidential elections were good examples of this. If one examines the 1980 election exclusively through a policy reform window, it appeared to be a mandate for wholesale policy change. However, voter surveys contradicted that conclusion.[15] Voters seemed to prefer Reagan over Carter for reasons other than Reagan's policy conservatism.

This does not mean that presidential candidates can avoid policy issues in campaigns. It does mean that they are more at liberty to present themselves to the voters as individuals symbolizing the hope for change in broad policy areas, and as individuals who can deal with policy issues more effectively than their opponents. The 1992 presidential campaign offered another excellent illustration of this tendency. All three contenders—Bush, Clinton, and Perot—were long on promises to correct existing problems in the fields of budget deficits, health care reform, employment, and the environment. Each was notably short on the specifics of just *how* they would deal with each problem. Each pictured himself as a candidate that offered more hope for change than the other two. Some specific promises on the means of reform did creep into the campaign, but the successful candidate, Bill Clinton, quickly contradicted many of his pledges in the early months of his administration. The price he paid was an immediate plunge in his approval ratings. Obviously, he felt that the public would forgive him if, during the balance of his term, he could deliver on his substantive policy promises. No doubt Clinton had become sensitized to the need to perform rather than merely to promise.

Owing to the broad and diverse nature of their constituencies, candidates for president are encouraged to dodge specific pledges about how they plan to achieve the very general policy objectives they introduce in campaigns. Focusing too extensively on how policy reforms are to be facilitated often means discussing such controversial matters as higher taxes and spending cuts. On the other hand, candidates for the House and Senate often can afford to be more specific on these questions because their constituencies usually do not mirror in microcosm the president's constituency. Comparatively few factions are high profile in legislative districts. Consequently, these candidates can afford to be more servile to specific voter and group demands. If candidates appease these forces satisfactorily and gain major

PAC support, the chances for their election are enhanced. On the other hand, if candidates for president pursue the same strategy, they are likely to alienate more voters than they win over, and thereby undercut their chances for election. Ironically, both strategies illustrate the Downsian bias of the candidate-centered campaign, with each type of candidate employing a strategy and adopting a style that maximizes their appeal to voters long enough to gain election. In very few instances does such a strategy encourage campaigns to introduce and discuss policy issues in proportion to their actual significance for the nation and its people. In the case of congressional elections, this strategy reinforces the system's distributive policy bias. In the case of the presidency, it encourages candidates for the office to stress style at the expense of specifics and, once elected, to confront the distributive bias of House and Senate members with strategies that often lead to policy gridlock.

The ability of the president and Congress to work within the shared powers environment to develop meaningful policies has been seriously undermined by candidate-centered campaigns. Studies reveal that newly elected presidents faithfully attempt to implement their campaign pledges, and they usually offer Congress and the nation a policy agenda that is remarkably congruent with their campaign promises. However, many of these efforts are unsuccessful, because the president must work with, not in opposition to, Congress to develop purposeful policies. Since these two institutional forces do not share the same electoral incentives, their ability to share the policy responsibility effectively after the election process has been compromised by the demise of party discipline and the introduction of the candidate-centered campaign. The debate over the North American Free Trade Act in 1993 provided an excellent illustration of this. This, together with other effects of the Constitution on elections and on public policy, will be discussed in the following section.

The Constitution, Elections, and Public Policy in Perspective

The above discussion is by no means a comprehensive examination of how effective or ineffective are the linkages between elections and public policy in America. However, it does focus on the key characteristics of campaigns and elections that impact on public policy. The question remains: How significant is the Constitution and the political use of its principles to these effects? The discussion below offers some tentative conclusions.

First, the Constitution's role in impacting on electoral policy follow-through is rarely publicized, but nonetheless significant. For example, executive-legislative constituency differences are ordained by the Constitution. This means that the very forces responsible for decentralizing the nomination and election processes, weakening political parties as policy centers, and encouraging servile-oriented politicians have also made it more difficult for policy issues to be resolved purposefully and quickly after elections. The gridlock that has dominated president-Congress policy relations for the past half-century is rooted heavily in the separation of powers principle.

Second, a major impact of the Constitution on elections involves its embodiment of key features of American culture. A society's culture incorporates its value judgments about what actions are socially, economically, and politically right or wrong. It is a collective acceptance or rejection of certain norms of behavior and policy objectives. Americans have always revered such general (and often elusive) objectives as freedom, popular sovereignty, capitalism, decentralized government, natural rights, individualism, and limited government. Government intervention tends to be legitimate if that intervention synchronizes with these norms. For example, nationally instigated antipoverty programs such as community action legislation (1965) and a welfare reform act (1996) were well received by the public, in part because they empowered state and local jurisdictions to invest federal "seed money" in ways that allowed each jurisdiction to tailor programs to their own needs. In short, political culture establishes values which are eventually applied to policy problems. It makes some proposed solutions to problems very acceptable, and others alien to our cultural tradition. The Constitution's direct mandate for, or implied support of, these cultural norms tends to make it a friend to candidates and voters who seek institutional allies for their policy crusades. The Constitution has absorbed, and therefore reflects, most of our key cultural values in one way or another. For example, the Bill of Rights is dedicated to the preservation of natural rights and limited government. Federalism formalizes the norm or principle of uncentralized power. The popular election of members of Congress and, through the Electoral College, the president for overlapping terms of office illustrates the nation's allegiance to both popular sovereignty and limited government. While capitalism, or a marketplace economy, is not ordained by the Constitution, the fragmentation of power through federalism and the separation of powers provides capitalist forces with a very favorable political environment to leverage their influence on policy decisions.

Candidates for office are quick to exploit the Constitution's cultural symbolism. Constituent/voter demands for subsidies and for more, or less, government regulation often encourage candidates, if elected, to work for policy reforms that help voters attain what is theirs by "right," not by "privilege." The fact that the Constitution's focus is on communication and political rights matters very little. These rights serve principally as ways to help people realize their economic goals. Candidates and officeholders find it politically advantageous to make the transition.

In sum, kindled conclusively by politics, the concept of rights has been subjected to evolutionary pressures. For example, in their exhaustive study of the evolution of rights crusades in the United States, James MacGregor Burns and Stewart Burns concluded that campaigns for what came to be known as the right to an education were rather widespread by the end of the nineteenth century.[16] Some states included statements virtually guaranteeing such in their constitutions. This was the beginning of what they term the "reconstruction of rights" in the United States. The public considered a sound education a necessary intermediary step between the security of the home during childhood and the economic security necessary for a successful professional career. This crusade had flowered into the acceptance by most Americans of the idea of a set of economic rights by the New Deal period. Just how inclusive this concept should be has never been resolved. Nonetheless, a speech by President Roosevelt in January 1944 linked traditional civil liberties to eight specific economic and social rights. Referring to his new agenda as a "second Bill of Rights," Roosevelt included the right to a meaningful job, the right of farmers to grow and sell crops and produce at reasonable prices, the right of businessmen to competitive markets, the right of families to decent homes, the right to medical care and the chance to attain good health, the right to economic security in old age, and the right to a "good education."[17] Packaging each of these policy objectives as a right rather than an opportunity had the long-term effect of setting the economic and social policy agenda for the balance of the twentieth century. The Constitution's bias toward civil rights has made the transition to the economic sphere much

smoother because politicians and the public are less likely to question its legitimacy. If a policy objective is framed or packaged as a right, it gives it more legitimacy. In addition, it nurtures the distributive policy bias of the public and its elected officeholders. Political debates usually surface over precisely *how* to achieve the rights, but not over whether they deserve their place at or near the top of policy agendas.

However, to carry such claims to government packaged as rights instead of privileges or advantages makes compromises more difficult and the resolution of institutional and individual policy differences more time consuming and tedious. The same can be said for the politics of crime policy. Besides debating the role of entitlement programs on family stability and the ultimate effect of that on the crime problem, politicians have to deal with the gun control issue. This invariably introduces conflicts between those who want to control the availability and circulation of guns as a deterrent to crime, and those who want relatively unrestricted availability of weapons because of the Constitution's guarantee of the right to bear arms. The same holds true for campaign exchanges over the right to choice versus the right to life.

This tendency, in turn, introduces a third impact of the Constitution on elections and, ultimately, on public policy. There is a high degree of compatibility between what might be termed a "politics of symbolism" nurtured by the Constitution and the candidate-centered campaign. If voters are prepared to respond to symbolic appeals, then the impact of a candidate's style on the results of elections and, if elected, on the contour of public policy is inflated. In short, this condition is an open invitation for candidates to portray campaign rhetoric as eventual policy reality. This is especially true for presidential campaigns. The Reagan campaigns of 1980 and 1984 furnish excellent examples of this. Voter disenchantment with President Carter was key to the election of Ronald Reagan in 1980. However, reinforcing this was the unrivaled ability of candidate Ronald Reagan to effectively incorporate key American cultural values and habits into his campaign rhetoric, and therefore, strategy. So effective was this strategy that many voters subconsciously selected Reagan over Carter because Reagan was more effective in both his subtle and overt appeals to their cultural values than was Carter. Reagan argued with much success that big government was the big policy problem, most federal programs were bad, taxes were too high, and federal spending was too generous. A majority of voters found this comfortably compatible with their cultural and economic values, despite the fact that most of them, in one way or another, were markedly dependent on big government and generous spending financed by high taxes for their safety, security, and future (if not present) economic well-being.

Reagan did not have to distinguish between rhetoric and reality in his campaign. He asked voters to believe that rhetoric was reality. Rhetoric thrives on symbolism, and Reagan's campaign against big government had widespread appeal because it has been part of our political culture since the revolutionary period. More important, it is ensconced in the Constitution, primarily through the principles of limited government and federalism. In sum, in some cases the Constitution can lend a sort of symbolic legitimacy to presidential campaigns, and thereby encourages candidates to treat rhetoric as reality. Bill Clinton's 1992 campaign illustrated a variation on the same theme. In contrast to Reagan, Clinton preferred a larger role for government, but his campaign sidestepped as best it could the issue of tax increases as a way to support the increased role. Again, the cultural alienation of Americans to big government, reinforced by the same constitutional principles, encouraged a Clinton campaign long on rhetoric and short on facts. The Reagan and Clinton strategies were both

marked by hypocrisy. Reagan wanted a reduced role for government, but the political risks were too great to acknowledge the political costs of it. Many Americans were dependent on government entitlements and other subsidies that would be threatened by serious downsizing. Clinton, on the other hand, faced the same risks in confronting directly the issue of how to pay for his policy plans. More specifically, the question was clearly one of possible tax increases to support a larger role for government. In his case, he faced the possibility of alienating any potential voter who thought taxes were already too high—probably a majority of voters.

In Clinton's case, shortly after his election he faced the unpopular task of requesting new taxes to support his plans for new policies and his deficit reduction plan. This led to an early decline in his approval rating and, in some circles, renewed strength for Ross Perot who had exploited growing voter cynicism as a third candidate in the 1992 campaign. This suggests a very important conclusion that can be drawn from the domination of personalities, image-building, and rhetoric at the expense of serious policy debates in presidential campaigns. In short, it reinforces voter cynicism about politics and government. This, in turn, makes it difficult for elected presidents to become effective policy leaders once elected. The public takes on an anti-incumbent attitude, and legislators looking to ingratiate themselves with their constituents quickly identify with this hostility and, consequently, are reluctant to cooperate with the president as he seeks legislative confirmation of his policy agenda. This was evident in 1993 as President Clinton witnessed members of his own party in the House and Senate fail to support his jobs program, deficit reduction package, and the North American Free Trade Agreement.

Of course, it is true that not all campaign issues impacted by the divorce between rhetoric and reality are nurtured by cultural attitudes couched in constitutional language. Nonetheless, the Constitution's concern for rights in a variety of forms does, in all likelihood, encourage candidates to introduce proposals for new policies that promise jobs and personal and economic security. Rarely does such a campaign focus spring directly from candidates' or voters' efforts to make rights issues as such central to campaigns. However, it does spring from the realization that they are issues which many voters find easy to connect to their personal lives. They therefore find it easy to think of their solution as a solution the government should select for them as a matter of right. Furthermore, voters can rather easily connect the *right* of policy to exist, or a person to do something, to government action to fulfill that objective.

The procedures, or means to such an end, are comparatively simple, often decreed by the courts. For example, in 1989, when the Supreme Court in *Webster* v. *Reproductive Health Services* ruled that states could restrict abortion more than in the past, abortion quickly became a salient issue in state and local elections. Those who supported the *Webster* case could see a clear linkage between court action and policy, and the issue became the dominant one in gubernatorial elections held in 1989. In Virginia and New Jersey, the candidates for governor who campaigned to resist further restrictions on abortion were elected, in all likelihood because voters saw a clear link between the candidate and the change in state policies toward abortion. At the presidential level, President Bush responded to the *Webster* decision by announcing that he would veto any bill providing for public funding of abortions for victims of rape and incest. That action enabled voters to make a clear linkage between an officeholder or a candidate and his or her willingness and ability to influence a specific policy. In the case of Bush as the incumbent president, it was clear how his use of the veto would influence national policy on legal abortions. Voters responded, some favorably and some unfavorably, to his announcement, and it helped make the abortion issue a key one in the 1992 election when the president stood for reelection. Once a candidate makes it clear to the voters how he or she can influence policy in a way that they—the voters—understand, that policy issue, if controversial, will likely weigh heavily on the results of the election. In the case of abortion it was a Constitution-based contest between those who claimed that women should have a right to abortion and those who argued that an unborn fetus at any stage of development had a right to life.

Candidates seeking to exploit issues for their benefit face the challenge of showing voters how they, the candidates, if elected can do something about the issue that will affect voters in meaningful ways. To accomplish this, candidates search for what Samuel Popkin has termed "information shortcuts." Shortcuts encourage voters to focus on the issues and how they think the candidate can, if elected, influence them.[18] In short, candidates search for symbols that will attract support for their position from a broad base of voters. Depending on the issue, principles ensconced in the Constitution are a natural for such a strategy. Voters may disagree on many things, but virtually all of them support the Constitution, or their interpretation of it. Therefore, the direct or indirect linkage of a proposed resolution of a policy issue to the language or spirit of the Constitution can make the issue more meaningful to a wider voter base than would otherwise exist. Candidates are therefore attracted to it because voters seem interested. Often, these are not the issues that are of critical significance to voters across the board, but campaigns spend disproportionately large amounts of time on them nevertheless. For example, in the 1988 presidential campaign the issue of how compatible was flag burning with the First Amendment and whether the Constitution should be amended to allow school prayer were clearly not as significant substantively to voters as was the question of the national debt, a weak economy, and the future of many entitlement programs. Nonetheless, the two major party presidential candidates often debated school prayer and flag burning as if other problems were of little importance. It was much easier for voters to appreciate a potential performance linkage between a president's position on these matters and his impact on how they would be resolved. The linkage was much less clear on economic, deficit, and entitlement issues. Although voters recognize that the economy, education, unemployment, and the environment are critical issues, they clearly have more difficulty in understanding just how influential a president can be in dealing effectively with them, regardless of his campaign promises. Therefore, issues rooted in the Constitution can encourage candidates to dodge or deemphasize other, more critical issues, and emphasize comparatively unimportant issues if it can be determined that voters can make a clear "input-output" type linkage between those issues and the impact of an officeholder on them.

By way of illustrating such a linkage, it might pay to look at the history of the time-worn slogan "Mother, God, and Country" as it relates to willingness of candidates to use it effectively in campaigns. Popkin notes that this slogan was much criticized in the 1950s because it allegedly illustrated the vapidness of campaigns that were virtually devoid of policy content.[19] Regardless, many campaigns at all levels of government have emphasized variations on such a theme since that time. This is mainly because candidates know that most voters react either very favorably or quite unfavorably when such issues are introduced. In addition, all voters see rather clear means-ends linkages between what candidates say on such questions and how they can, once elected, influence results. These issues also have roots in the Constitution. For example, according to Popkin,

the motherhood issue has been resurrected in the campaign debates about abortion and the proposed Equal Rights Amendment. God, and the general role of religion in government and politics, have triggered heated exchanges over homosexuals in the military, school prayer, public support of private schools, and whether sex education programs in the schools could be restrained or eliminated without interfering with the First Amendment's free speech guarantee. The country issue surfaced often in the debates over the constitutionality of the Vietnam War and other actual or proposed peacekeeping actions that involved, or could have involved, U.S. military action. Constitutional politics, whether introduced directly or indirectly, has played a key role both in the way in which issues are raised in campaigns and in how they are discussed.

Americans have traditionally harbored suspicions about the use of government to solve, or attempt to solve, problems that appear to be rooted in man's unwillingness to help himself. This explains why policy problems in areas such as employment, poverty, and housing were so slow to make the national policy agenda. In fact, the entry of states and localities into these policy areas was delayed longer than conditions dictated, more than likely for the same reason. However, these issues did, of course, eventually make their way to the policy agendas of all governments, illustrating what Majone explained as the acknowledgment by government that the public interest and overall quality of life in America is affected by poverty, employment, and housing problems, and that appropriate government action might well help alleviate the situation.[20] In effect, the public's image of such issues was transferred from a mindset that considered them fundamentally private misfortunes to a situation in which they were clearly public policy issues.

Once the public stature of an issue gains voter acceptance, then its entry into the rhetoric of political campaigns quickly ensues.

Such issues are very critical in many campaigns because the ultimate solutions to be offered by government are either directly distributive in nature or have ultimate distributive overtones. In other words, candidates quickly recognize the inevitable connection between ways to deal with these problems on the one hand, and the potential for votes on the other. To be sure, all candidates do not recommend direct distributive solutions to such problems, as the Reagan example discussed earlier illustrates. However, they all explain their solutions as the most appropriate role for government as an activist force in these policy areas. In so doing, they are acknowledging the concern of government to confront and deal with such problems.

Candidates for office, as well as incumbents, tend to manipulate images in ways that will serve them most effectively. Competing images over how to deal with social and economic problems surface from the same set of social and economic conditions. Politicians as either candidates or as elected policy participants manipulate these images to serve their own needs. Constitutional politics is a great asset when it comes to applying these conversion strategies. Again the Constitution's actual and spiritual support of rights in a number of forms encourages politicians as either candidates or elected policymakers to promise constituents that their right to such things as respectable income, a good education, and decent housing can best be facilitated by the position they have taken on the issue.

As both candidates and officeholders, individuals are not regularly inclined to incorporate the Constitution's official language into the defense of their policy positions. Nonetheless, it serves as a psychological backdrop that conditions the policy positions for both candidates and policymakers. This enables the divorce between campaign rhetoric and political reality to endure, and reinforces growing voter cynicism about politicians and government in general. This, in turn, contributes to an anti-incumbent feeling within the body politic. Officeholders and candidates respond by attempting to assuage voters even more at a time when the policy challenges of the nation and world clearly demand that governments pay more attention to policy substance and less to process.

Symbolic Democracy and Public Policy

A final impact of constitutional politics on public policy rooted in the electoral process is a direct outgrowth of the triumph of image over substance in campaigns, especially presidential campaigns. In sum, it is that what can now be termed the public's willingness to accept image over substance in its choice of public officials encourages incoherence, corruption, and general disarray in a number of policy areas. When image prevails over substance in campaigns, it can carry over into government, and the results can be notably unsavory, if not dangerous.

Politicians can exploit the public's reverence for democracy by exploiting it for their (the politicians') self-interest. Campaigns stress symbolism, and it is not unusual for officeholders, elected or appointed, legislative or administrative, to employ symbols in much the same way as do candidates. To use symbolism effectively, elites must champion issues that have widespread public support. During the 1980s and 1990s, policies that focused on crackdowns on drug trafficking, the death penalty option for serious crimes, a "workfare" rather than "welfare" cast to antipoverty laws, revamping and "humanizing" the Internal Revenue Service, regenerating family values, and proposals for a constitutional amendment to prohibit flag desecration all garnered strong elite support because they were publicly popular.

Policy competence in authentic democracies is measured by the ability of those governments to manage their policy challenges in a responsive, efficient, accurate, professional, and accountable way. If American government is unable to consistently and meaningfully respond to its policy challenges, then the degree to which this is true is the degree to which its policy institutions are operating ineffectively and, in essence, undemocratically. If image and symbolism predominate in elections, then there is no guarantee that those elected to office will make accountable and responsible government a high-priority item. Translating public opinion into policies that often demand sacrifice as a price for meaningful change can be risky. Moreover, it also indicates that the public has accepted symbolism as an inevitable ingredient in campaigns, and chooses either to ignore it or to permit it to influence their choices. In either case, it introduces a potential, and often likely, gap between campaign promises and governing performance. Voters often expect campaign promises to go unfulfilled. Consequently, in the 1990s elites were quick to endorse such things as the need to reorganize Medicare, control health care costs, save the Social Security system from insolvency, and control the consumption of tobacco products. However, addressing these issues seriously meant taking on forces that were crucial to the support of legislative careers, namely the corporate forces that were key contributors to their campaigns. That explains why serious consideration of possible comprehensive solutions to all those problems was either abandoned, inordinately delayed, or dealt with in a peripheral or piecemeal fashion. An excellent example of the latter was the enactment, in 1998, of a patient "bill of rights" to deal with the managed care crisis in the health care industry. Patients whose illnesses were being overlooked or slighted by Health Maintenance Organizations (HMOs) asked for the imposition of strict regulations on physician behavior. The result was legislation enumerating patients' rights and a largely symbolic condemnation of HMOs that refused to honor them.

Several earlier experiences during the Reagan administration also illustrated this propensity. President Reagan, like all presidents, had his strong and weak points. However, most observers agree that he was a much more effective candidate than he was president. This is true of most presidents, but particularly true of Reagan. While some issues did surface and were carefully debated during the 1980 campaign, Reagan did not focus on them because he had a distinctive "stage presence" advantage over Carter. He turned out to be an excellent stage presence president, but a mediocre policy steward. Uncomfortable with the details of governing, he often took a hands-off approach to policy leadership. While he was very interested in staffing the executive office and the bureaucracy with partisans loyal to his "supply side" economic ideology, his assumption (or hope) was that this army of loyalists could organize and administer his policy reforms on their own without his continual involvement. This did not happen. The Iran-Contra affair was perhaps the best example. Although Reagan was chairman of the National Security Council, his virtual lack of concern for detail allowed staff members Oliver North and John Poindexter to organize a behind the scenes effort to secure release of American hostages in Iran through arms sales and to use the profits from such ventures to support an undercover operation to support the Contra forces in Nicaragua. Both efforts failed, and North and Poindexter were charged with violating both the Arms Export Control Act and the Boland Amendment respectively, each of which required congressional involvement in such decisions. Reagan's indifference toward the matter permitted his staff to make and conduct foreign policy outside the required formalities of government.

Similar problems were encountered in the early Reagan budgets, which were overly optimistic in their estimates of how projected revenues would meet the president's spending cuts promised in the campaign. Although periodically mired in problems of waste, abuse, and mismanagement since its creation, the Department of Housing and Urban Development was guilty of much more of the same during the Reagan years. An ideological opponent, in principle, of many HUD activities, Reagan did not insist on rigorous oversight of HUD's operations by the General Accounting Office or the Office of Management and Budget (OMB). The result was widespread abuse, waste, and poor management, resulting in millions of wasted taxpayer dollars and bungled programs. While Reagan was a near perfect image candidate, his disinterest in the management and oversight of government operations, such as those of HUD, aggravated an already existent problem. Symbolizing effectiveness as a candidate does not, on its own, help one to become an effective chief executive.

If the Constitution, because of the separation of powers and constituencies, did not afford candidates for president the chance to run for office against the records of Congress and the bureaucracy, image would play much less of a role in the nomination and election of a president. If our government incorporated the Westminster, or parliamentary, design, candidates for president would have to run for office as one member of a policy team, along with congressional candidates of their party. If their party was the incumbent party, it would be virtually impossible for the incumbent party to seek reelection by running against the government's record. Since the Constitution provides for different constituencies and overlapping terms of office for the president, the House of Representatives, and the Senate, we have had divided government most of the time since 1948, with different parties controlling the presidency and Congress. This permits presidential candidates from both parties to run against the record of the government, stressing their ability as leaders to

overcome the dysfunction of divided government. To portray themselves effectively as leaders, they pursue an image strategy to win votes. This in turn stresses personal qualities and policy promises, but not much in the way of in-depth policy analysis.

In order for voters to focus on the problems of divided government and the consequent need to vote for candidates as part of a party-based team, they clearly will have to acquire more of a sense of the impact of processes on policy and try to disassociate image with performance. The American people, in the era of electronic journalism, have had advertising's heavy hand placed upon them virtually from birth. As a result, they do not understand the consequences of symbolic politics very well. The linkage between image on the one hand and incompetence, inefficiency, and irresponsibility on the other will not be destroyed or compromised unless citizens come to understand the relationship and act to correct it. As things have evolved, the public is becoming more cynical about the inability of government to perform and many are withdrawing from an active interest in politics because their involvement appears to have little, if any, effect.

As discussed earlier, this condition has been aggravated by the Supreme Court's decision to disallow limitations on total campaign spending by, or on behalf of, candidates in elections. Activist, financially sound corporations and interest groups organize and sponsor virtually unlimited numbers of political action committees (PACs) that, in effect, subsidize the symbolism-infested strategies that dominate elections in contemporary America. According to the Court, the Constitution's First Amendment "denies government the power to determine that spending to promote one's own political views is . . . excessive. In the free society ordained by our Constitution, it is not the government by the people . . . who must retain control over the quantity and range of debate . . . in a political campaign."[21] The Constitution's support of free communication contributes to the gap between election promises and government policy performance. Society's more well-to-do forces usually profit from campaign strategies that sidestep hard policy questions and debates because addressing such questions often asks these forces to pay higher taxes or submit to more regulations. In effect, the First Amendment allows corporate elites to debase democracy by virtually "buying" unequal access to future and existing officeholders during campaigns. The masses are, in effect, left out. Ironically, free speech supports unequal access to the seats of power. The consideration of key policy issues is often avoided or dealt with in a notably token fashion.

Research has shown that elites often manipulate the public's policy preferences.[22] This has serious implications for democratic government because it makes public opinion "synthetic," in that the public ultimately conveys elite opinions as its own. Such a condition makes a mockery of democracy's canons of responsiveness and accountability, because what the public says it wants and what corporate elites say they want appear to be one and the same. The problem with the Constitution's stress on equality is that political equality is often cooptated by economic inequality. Candidates for office prefer to stress economic equality more than political equality. Therefore, the traditional defense of freedom of communication, or speech in particular, as something that serves democracy better if left relatively uncontrolled or supervised by government is defective. It assumes that all opinions have an equal chance of impacting on elections and government. In reality, such a "marketplace" where all opinions are voiced, transmitted, and considered equally simply does not exist. Elites representing corporate America have unequal leverage in campaigns and, ultimately, in policy decisions. These forces profit from symbolic politics. Symbolic politics enables elites to replace serious

consideration of difficult policy questions which, when resolved, would ask them to pay a significant economic price, with campaigns and a policymaking atmosphere that stresses image, symbolism, and rhetoric. The gap between policy need and the ability of the political system to respond to that need grows increasingly wider as a result.

The Rational, Frustrated Public

The American public finds itself in the unenviable and frustrating position of consenting to the policy products of a government that does not appear to be up to the task at hand. This would not be frustrating if the public's opinions on key policy questions or issues were uninformed, fickle, haphazard, and inconsistent. However, this appears not to be the case. Research has shown that public opinion, as it has responded to the major domestic and foreign policy issues of the past half-century, has been remarkably rational, stable, and adaptive.[23] All public opinion has not been transmitted regularly into public policy because government's intermediary institutions—political parties, legislatures, and elected executives—have faltered in their effort to register public opinion in public policy.

These institutions have, each in its own way, voluntarily or involuntarily, helped to compromise the direct transmission of public opinion into public policy. A few reasons for this have already been explored, and more will be discussed later. For the time being, the discussion will focus on how and why collective public opinion on most major policy issues can be considered rational, and has historically offered rather clearly definable, and defensible, options to policymakers. The term rational is employed here in the same way as do Page and Shapiro in their seminal work on public opinion and public policy. Rejecting the economists' view of rationality as the maximization of one's own self-interest, Page and Shapiro argue that public opinion reflects a surprising degree of rationality when considered collectively over time. This rationality is distinct from a definition popular among economists, and that offered by Downs in his democratic model. The economic and Downs models assume that people are largely ignorant of, and unconcerned about, policy issues because, most of the time, other matters are more important to them. They profess interest in policy matters only when issues clearly affect them, and then support policy options that will clearly maximize their self-interest. Page and Shapiro offer a more optimistic, albeit somewhat more fluid, view of rational public opinion. They argue that, considered on a collective plane over time, public opinion is coherent given the state of information available to the public, and is generally stable yet flexible enough to change when circumstances and events clearly point in that direction.[24] This view does not in any way assume that the average citizen/voter is well informed on most policy issues. This is why it is imperative to consider collective trends in opinion over extended periods of time. If this is done, irrational qualities tend to disappear or become suppressed.

Page and Shapiro examined historical trends in opinion about social issues, economic welfare, foreign policy, and military policy between the 1930s and 1990s, and found it to be remarkably rational when judged against their standards of rationality. They concluded that public opinion is usually very easily knowable by officeholders, is well rooted in available information, and often draws fine distinctions between various policy alternatives. In addition, they concluded that people show surprisingly good ability to define public interest and separate it from their own. Unfortunately, they also concluded that opportunities for people to secure an in-depth education on many

policy alternatives do not exist, and that government is out of touch or "phase" with public opinion about one-third of the time. They also agreed with Schattschneider's observation that elites often manipulate public opinion for their own benefit and, for the same reason, concluded that it is naive to assume that the marketplace idea of opinion formation will lead to an informed public. Political forces which have the most money, which have historical access to leaders, which own the major mediums of communication, and which contribute the most money to campaigns all have influence in policy decisions that is disproportionate to their numbers. In sum, political equality often falls victim to economic inequality.

All this can leave citizens very frustrated over the course of public policy and the receptiveness of public officials to their opinions. Cynicism about the value of voting and about the ability and/or willingness of government institutions to respond to public opinion is the result. While the Constitution and the politics it encourages did not cause such conditions, in all likelihood the breakdowns that have existed between discernable, rational public opinion and reasonable government responses have been exacerbated by constitutional politics. For example, general public suspicion of the U.S. role in the Vietnam War was evident for years before President Ford ordered our forces withdrawn. The insistence by presidents, especially President Johnson, that the Constitution's assignment of foreign policy leadership prerogatives to the president implied (to Johnson at least) that an operational policy divorce should exist between an informed president and a relatively uninformed public. On the domestic side, delays by government in responding to clear public mandates for more strict gun control measures, and policies to control air and water pollution and conserve natural resources are all good examples of situations where government fails to respond expeditiously to major, coherent waves of public opinion. In these cases opposition by forces that stand to profit from no government action at all—the National Rifle Association and many large corporations—has been successful in exploiting the separation of powers in ways which force major compromises in policy proposals or kill them altogether. As discussed earlier, the separation of powers system impacts on policy by forcing separate institutions with different incentives to cooperate nonetheless in the enactment of policy. Forces that oppose change can focus their efforts on only one link in the policy chain, perhaps on only one house of Congress, and if they are successful in getting that institution to reject change, the proposal is dead regardless of how overwhelming may be the support for the idea in other institutions. Since the Constitution indirectly mandates cooperation among several institutions before policy can be enacted, forces that want to stop, rather than start, new policies have a decided advantage.

Page and Shapiro conclude that the opinion of Americans on social issues such as abortion, gay rights, school prayer, pornography, women's rights, and communication rights has become more liberal over the past two generations. Liberalism in this sense signifies a growing public tolerance for the rights of individuals to adopt a lifestyle or work toward a policy goal that is not necessarily shared by the majority. Public opinion collectively displays more tolerance for social diversity than do most personal social attitudes. The same thing has been true for both domestic economic policy and foreign policy.

Political culture cultivated by the Constitution's stress on rights of individuals, be they part of the majority or a minority, might well help explain why public opinion has gradually reflected more tolerance for social and economic diversity. Loyalty to the Constitution might well engender a feeling of individual pride that results in a level of such tolerance that would be absent if the Constitution were

silent on the subject. Most Americans take a good deal of pride in being loyal to their Constitution. Unfortunately there are major differences among individuals and groups as to what is meant or implied by many constitutional objectives that are often rather nebulous. Rational public policies are often mere pipe dreams because of this.

Journalist E. J. Dionne has observed that opinion polls show Americans in general harbor conservative values but have liberal instincts, that they are eager for a political system that reflects this pattern, and that they think the existing state and character of campaigns and governance is growing more and more estranged from representing these twin concerns.[25] Dionne argues that politicians who call themselves conservatives do not really represent the public's wishes very effectively. The same can be said for liberals. The "coherence" in public opinion that Page and Shapiro mention is, according to Dionne, clearly evident in the opinion Americans voice about their government in the 1990s. Public opinion's most recent "cast" asks government to fuse the goal of social tolerance nurtured by the politics of the 1960s with what Dionne calls a conservative-based new sense of self-reliance.[26] Accordingly, Americans are becoming increasingly discouraged by the trend toward candidate-centered campaigns. Such campaigns too often slight public opinion as candidates seek to dramatize differences between themselves by simplifying, deflecting, or ignoring voter attitudes. For example, most Americans do not see a conflict between feminism as a political movement and the need for public policy to stress traditional family values. Nonetheless, campaigns and policy debates assume the two movements harbor incompatible goals.

According to Dionne, the American public seeks, simultaneously, to share policy burdens collectively through the selective and judicious application of government power while at the same time wanting to steer clear of any application of public power that might pose a threat to their liberties. The first goal reflects the impact of the liberalism of the 1960s (the sixties left), and the second accommodates the conservatism of the 1980s (the eighties right). These seemingly contradictory objectives reflect a not uncommon "Catch-22" syndrome that has affected public opinion throughout history. However, in fact, the objectives of the two movements are more similar than different. Each has sought to establish tolerant, benevolent communities through the liberation of individual potential. If they shared a common defect, it was that each movement assumed that politics and government policy, embodying their respective standards of morality, could do the job. The sixties left insisted on public policies that legislated tolerance and compassion. The eighties right insisted on policies that fostered individual initiative and responsibility.[27] Each movement embodied both of the seemingly contradictory impulses noted above, and the politics of both eras reflected it. The self-proclaimed "morality" of each movement has made its way into campaigns, agenda-setting, and policy debates since 1960. Campaigns have been conducted mainly as face-offs between what seem to be opposing ways to foster benevolent communitarianism through individual initiatives. The left has sought to empower individuals through the use of government, and the right seeks the same results by rejecting an enlarged role for government in social and economic affairs. Policy debates surface as either/or contentions between two diametrically opposed theories of how best to build individual initiative that would contribute to community justice.

The problem with such a political landscape is that it has virtually ignored public opinion. Liberals have failed to realize how much of a grudge the middle class has developed against the growth of government in general, and big bureaucracy in particular. Consequently, liberal elites have been wrong in assuming that opposition to welfare policies reflects racial

prejudice. Such opposition reflects, at least partially, a concern that welfare policies challenge the work ethic, namely that all should be taught to appreciate the value of work. Similarly, liberals probably misjudged the incentives that underlay the "family values" initiative of the early 1990s. Liberals considered this closet bigotry, when in fact it might well have reflected parental concern over how such a transition in social values might affect their children. Conservatives were guilty of the same sort of miscalculations on other issues. They tended to interpret the gay rights movement as an assault on heterosexuals, when it probably represented merely a quest by gays to be free from discrimination. Regarding economic policy, the conservatives' endorsement of supply side economics reduced taxes on the well-to-do by lowering taxes on savings and investment. However, the net result was to increase payroll and Social Security taxes on the middle class. Consequently, the middle class felt that it had become victims of the very movement that had pledged to exonerate them.[28]

According to Dionne, both the left and right have fallen victim to progressive political myopia, and the result is that neither movement has been a very effective representative of American public opinion. Campaigns and policy debates have been flavored by petty ideological battles over such issues as gay rights, flag burning, school prayer, big government versus small government, the death penalty, and racial quotas, while most Americans have been concerned about crime, the quality of education, the drug problem, the deficit and national debt, health care, and urban decay.[29] Note the constitutional roots of such issues as racial quotas, the death penalty, flag burning, and school prayer. Note also the public's *relative* unconcern for making these issues high-priority ones. The Constitution's support of rights in various forms has surely encouraged this "issue displacement" problem. Of course, the Constitution did not cause such issue displacement. A declining party system, the dominant role of the press (especially television) in campaigns and policy debate coverage, and an absence of legislation that places effective controls on the financial impact of corporate elites on political campaigns have been all more immediate causes of the displacement. However, constitutional principles made the displacement easier to introduce and accomplish and, regrettably, easier for the public to tolerate.

Americans, in general, think that policies can serve the public interest if government is serious in its search for policies that serve the common good. Americans, in general, have rejected the politics of the past generation because politicians, as both candidates and officeholders, have virtually abandoned the serious and consistent search for policies that benefit the public interest in the long term. People are frustrated with a politics that stresses political posturing, and one that sidesteps concern for long-term policy planning in the interest of short-term political benefits that advance politicians' political careers.[30] As discussed earlier, the Constitution, with its stress on rights and on the processes (as opposed to the substance) of government, helps facilitate such a politics of delay and opportunism. Since the separation of powers invites conflict between branches of government, as well as between and among factions seeking leverage over policy decisions, it is relatively easy for politicians to avoid the hard and sobering policy challenges of today's society and world. Politicians rationalize any unsatisfactory policy results and public frustration resulting from such conditions by blaming other branches of government, or perhaps by reiterating the intentions of the founding fathers to employ process as a check on ambition. After all, weak government is better than a strong government that is misdirected.

This does not mean that the public has an altruistic notion of the common good that

government has rejected. However, it does mean that most Americans know that the government should, and eventually must, advance solutions to problems that will help preserve the fabric of our social and economic systems for future generations. This involves sacrifice of short-term political expediency in the interest of long-term policy progress. The trend of politics since the 1960s has rejected what Robert Reich, as well as others, have termed an "enlightened self-interest."[31] Our policy responses to the Great Depression were not motivated by altruism, but by the realization that everyone had a long-term stake in helping American society as a whole recover from the economic collapse of 1929. Most of the New Deal policy reforms were, simultaneously, both rational and politically expedient. Government needed little or no externally imposed encouragement to make responsible decisions. Because of today's relatively prosperous economic conditions, in contemporary politics a marriage of the responsible with the politically astute is much more the exception than the rule. Policymakers usually need regular stimulation from external sources before they give serious thought to asking sacrifices of the current generation so that future generations might prosper. In recent years, such stimulation obligations have often been assumed by high-profile public and private figures, many of whom were new to the political mainstream. For example, when large annual deficits were a regular part of the political landscape, these individuals often entered politics and challenged policymakers to get the national government's fiscal house in order. The presidential candidacies of Ross Perot focused on this issue, as has the Concord Coalition, a public interest organization established by the late Senator Paul Tsongas and former Senator Warren Rudman. Such movements illustrate both the nature of and depth of the problem. Perot, Tsongas, and Rudman were all government outsiders who could afford to talk serious policy reform because they did not face the prospect of alienating voters and endangering their political careers by sponsoring such crusades. Most incumbent officeholders, with a few exceptions, felt that going beyond a passing, symbolic reference to the problem of the deficit was not cost-effective politically. The potential disadvantages outweighed the advantages of playing it safe.

Shortsighted Leadership and Public Policy: The Challenge

Americans collectively want more serious policy responsiveness and political vision than they receive from political leaders today. Subsequent chapters will describe and analyze how weak and ineffective our major policy institutions have become in facing this challenge. The weakness of three institutions is especially noteworthy—Congress, the presidency, and political parties. These institutions should focus on producing the rational, vision-grounded, coherent policies the public appears to want. However, they do not. Political parties do not unite majority factions in constitutionally separate branches as Thomas Jefferson and Woodrow Wilson advocated. Each candidate for office and each elected (and often appointed) officeholder has his or her own miniature constituency, or "party empire," that sustains the officeholder's career. The search for the policy coherence that would undergird an enlightened self-interest goes a-begging. House and Senate members have been, for the most part, the living embodiment of this problem, illustrating well what might be termed the problem of "career over country." Consequently, presidents find themselves imprisoned by such a system. With the entire country as a constituency, presidents very easily come to realize the need for policies that incorporate the need for an enlightened self-interest. However, since presidents need the cooperation of other institutions in their crusades for such objectives, they collide politically with politicians and administrators in these institutions who do not share the president's more inclusive views of the public interest. Instead, they ruthlessly equate their self-interest with the public interest. To secure any policy changes whatsoever, presidents must make deals with these forces, often compromising away any semblance of policy rationality to secure some sort of a deal that is paraded as serious policy reform.

The weakening of these three policy institutions has been accompanied by the strengthening of some nongovernment institutions which reinforce the move toward policy fragmentation by helping self-interest repress a serious search for the common good. Most noteworthy here is the growing strength of the press (especially television) and interest groups. Subsequent chapters will offer more in-depth analysis of the contribution of these institutions, making it easy to campaign for office, but difficult to govern. The role of the Constitution, and especially constitutional politics, in facilitating such conditions will also be analyzed.

The costs of such politics are great indeed. Government loses some of its moral authority, which may be hard to recover. The public becomes increasingly cynical as it witnesses a government mired in crude bargaining actuated by political self-interest, failing to realize perhaps that candidates and officeholders have convinced themselves that they have no other choice in a system where candidates and officeholders alike preside over their own miniature political parties.

Endnotes

1. Bernard R. Berelson, Paul F. Lazarsfeld, and William N. McPhee, *Voting: A Study of Opinion Formation in Presidential Campaign* (Chicago: University of Chicago Press, 1954).

2. Angus Campbell, Gerald Gruin, and Warren E. Miller, *The Voter Decides* (Evanston, Ill.: Row, Peterson, 1954).

3. Angus Campbell, Philip E. Converse, Warren E. Miller, and Donald E. Stokes, *The American Voter* (New York: Wiley, 1960).

4. Anthony Downs, *An Economic Theory of Democracy* (New York: Harper & Row, 1957).

5. Martin P. Wattenberg, *The Rise of Candidate-Centered Politics* (Cambridge, Mass.: Harvard University Press, 1991), p. 18.

6. *Ibid.*, pp. 19–20.

7. *Ibid.*, p. 20.

8. V. O. Key, Jr., *The Responsible Electorate: Rationality in Presidential Voting, 1936–1960* (New York: Random House, 1966).

9. Wattenberg, *op. cit.*, p. 21.

10. Jay M. Shafritz, *The Dorsey Dictionary of American Government and Politics* (Chicago: Dorsey Press, 1988), p. 412.

11. *National Journal*, vol. 16, November 11, 1984, p. 2698.

12. Wattenberg, *op. cit.*, Chapter 3.

13. *Ibid.*, pp. 4–11.

14. *Ibid.*, p. 93.

15. *Ibid.*, p. 110.

16. James MacGregor Burns and Stewart Burns, *The People's Charter: The Pursuit of Rights in America* (New York: Knopf, 1991), pp. 213–236.

17. *Ibid.*, pp. 263–264.

18. Samuel L. Popkin, *The Reasoning Voter: Communication and Persuasion in Presidential Campaigns* (Chicago: University of Chicago Press, 1991), Chapter 3.

19. *Ibid.*, p. 104.

20. Giandomenico Majone, *Evidence, Argument and Persuasion in the Policy Process* (New Haven, Conn.: Yale University Press, 1989), p. 24.

21. *Buckley* v. *Valeo*, 424 U.S. 1 (1976).

22. Benjamin I. Page and Robert Y. Shapiro, *The Rational Public: Fifty Years of Trends in Americans' Policy Preferences* (Chicago: University of Chicago Press, 1992), p. 394.

23. *Ibid.*, Chapters 1, 2, and 10.

24. *Ibid.*, p. 14.

25. E. J. Dionne, Jr., *Why Americans Hate Politics* (New York: Simon & Schuster, 1991).

26. *Ibid.*, pp. 9–28, 329–338.

27. *Ibid.*, p. 329.

28. *Ibid.*, pp. 330–331.

29. *Ibid.*, p. 331.

30. *Ibid.*, p. 332.

31. *Ibid.*, p. 333.

chapter five

Political Parties, Interest Groups, and Elections

Policy Intermediaries and the Constant Campaign

Intermediary institutions are extra-constitutional forces that impact on the development and administration of public policy by influencing the character of public opinion, how it is expressed, and the ways it is relayed to official arenas of decision making. They are extra-constitutional because they are not mentioned in the Constitution. Nonetheless, they impact on policy agendas and the ways in which issues are perceived, considered, and resolved. Their influence is profound, and cannot be underestimated.

In a republic, or representative democracy, how public attitudes are engendered, politicized, and transmitted to decision authorities is probably the most crucial gauge of the system's health and integrity. Democratic theorists, voters, and politicians have always stressed how important are the processes of our democracy to the development of sound policies. We assume that good processes will lead to good results. If government *by the people* is pursued faithfully, the result will be good policies *for the people*. Of course, what makes for good processes and good results is, fundamentally, a value judgment. What is one individual's salvation can be another's curse. Because there exists no general agreement on what good processes and good results are, the role of intermediary institutions on the development of public attitudes and on how they are transmitted and considered will always be controversial.

There are three major intermediary institutions that play critical roles in the development and implementation of public policy. They are political parties, interest groups, and the media, especially electronic journalism or television. Although the Constitution doesn't mention any of these institutions, it informally sanctions their existence as conduits of opinion to policymaking institutions. People can't govern themselves directly, and so these forces offer ways to absorb, organize, and channel public opinion to institutions that have been constitutionally endowed with policy responsibilities. Of course, politics is never a one-way street, and policymakers have found ways to use intermediary vehicles for their own political benefit. The following discussion and analysis will consider each intermediary institution as both a product of the Constitution and a crucial element in determining how the Constitution is employed for political and policy objectives.

Political Parties as Intermediaries: A Historical Perspective

The founding fathers thought factions were potentially dangerous, but nonetheless thought them inevitable. For that reason, institutional power assignments in the Constitution were deliberately fragmented to keep factions from dominating government. Political parties, together with interest groups and a more recent addition, the issue network, collectively constitute the factional universe in American politics. It is virtually impossible to gain an appreciation for the impact of factionalism on policymaking without considering all simultaneously, especially parties and groups. They are separated here only for purposes of analysis.

The classic party model stresses a party's ability to unite its members around a particular set of policy objectives. This has to be very difficult to accomplish in the United States. It is more likely to occur in societies with rather homogeneous economic, social, and religious institutions. It is also more likely to develop within political systems with more than two parties. The more parties there are, the more likely it is that an individual can find a party to match his or her specific political ideology and policy preferences. The United States is economically, religiously, culturally, and ethnically diverse. A multiparty system would seem well suited to such a demographic landscape, but it hasn't caught hold in the United States. Therefore, the American two-party system incurs the obligation of representing all major policy factions within a dual party framework. This condition impacts significantly on how well American parties function as intermediary institutions.

The U.S. Constitution has played a key role in the development and sustenance of our two-party system. Several constitutional contributions to party dualism can be cited. First, and perhaps most fundamental, is the support that political parties secure from the First Amendment's guarantee of free speech, a free press, and the right to petition government for a redress of grievances. In the *Federalist Papers* James Madison observed that "liberty is to faction as air is to fire." That observation references the close cause and effect ties between communication freedoms and the formation of political parties and interest groups. The freedom to speak and debate without fear of reprisal is a license for people and factions to petition government for policy favors. These favors can be defined as policies that advantage them economically, religiously, and socially, or policies that reflect their theory of "justice" or governance. Regardless of how communication rights translate into individual and group behavior, their existence has encouraged the development of factions, including political parties, which seek to leverage the impact of values on policymaking.

Constitutional guarantees of communication rights encourage the development of political parties, but why two parties? The First Amendment can explain the development of interest groups and parties, but why has a two-party system, instead of a multiparty system, been a regular part of the American political scene virtually since 1789? Because American society is so economically, socially, and ethnically diverse, factions are plentiful.

Nevertheless, with a few exceptions, such as the Progressive Party and the Socialist Party challenges to party dualism early in the twentieth century, the nation has stubbornly maintained a two-party structure. Tradition is no doubt important. Americans are accustomed to it. The Federalist versus Anti-Federalist struggle laid the base for the first two political parties—Federalists and Jeffersonian Republicans—which were organized shortly after the Constitution's ratification. In addition, most U.S. elections are held within single-member districts on a "winner take all" basis. Since only one official is elected from each district, losers get no representation. Therefore, factions are encouraged to merge in an attempt to develop coalitions large enough to win elections. There are no electoral rewards for factions that refuse to join one of the two major parties, and because the parties are faction-friendly, they have a very broad coalitional base. Consequently, American parties are a far cry from the ideologically homogeneous organizations suggested by the classic party model.

Tradition and single-member districts do encourage a two-party system. However, these factors are reinforced by two constitutional principles–a presidential system that requires an Electoral College majority to win a presidential election, and federalism, which assigns those electoral votes to states which, traditionally, cast them on a winner take all basis. In effect, the single-member district syndrome affects how Electoral College votes are cast. This means that presidential candidates seeking an Electoral College majority (not plurality) must try to placate as many interests in as many states as possible in the hope of winning elections. This, in turn, encourages the coalition strategies discussed above. Broad coalitions must be developed in the hope that the party will win a plurality of the popular vote in the state so that all that state's electoral votes will be cast for that party's presidential candidate.

In a sense, federalism brings a "confederal" cast to the organization and power structure within political parties. Confederations assign all basic policy authority to subnational jurisdictions. Since parties are extra-constitutional institutions, there is no constitutional assignment of power to any political party. Federalism takes care of that in a *de facto* sense. All U.S. senators and representatives represent either states or districts within states. States have their own officials to elect—governors, state assemblies, commissioners, and so on. Therefore, party efforts focus on how to win these elections. Consequently, it is imperative that national party organizations cement their strength within states, because all elections—presidential, congressional, state, and local—depend heavily upon how well a party does within states, in terms of raising money, developing sound campaign strategies, and getting out the vote to support its candidates. Therefore, the confederal, or "bottom up" structure of American parties is a by-product of the constitutional principles of federalism.

State party organizations do not need their national counterparts to succeed, but national organizations need their state affiliates. This encourages national party organizations to negotiate with state organizations in an attempt to develop a nationwide consensus on party principles and policy goals. This is a difficult order. It often results in party platforms that stress general platitudes that offend few, if any, of a party's rank-and-file, and hopefully attract independent voters and defectors from the other major party. This is why political party platforms developed at the presidential nominating conventions are often so inoffensive as to be meaningless. Parties cannot risk offending many people.

American political parties have been significantly democratized over the past two centuries, and that fact has further leveraged the impact of federalism on their behavior and electoral strategies. Party democratization began with Andrew Jackson's administration, but has been particularly important since 1960. Jackson instituted party-wide conventions for elite-based caucuses as the means of nominating party candidates for office. In the twentieth century, most conventions were replaced with party primaries as a means of nominating candidates. In effect, primaries are "nominating elections" that offer each member of a party the opportunity to participate in the selection of his or her party's nominees for political office. Presidential elections have been democratized as well, with electoral votes now being cast on the basis of which party candidate earned a plurality of a state's popular vote.

In effect, the democratization of American parties changed them from "top down" to "bottom up" organizations. There are advantages and disadvantages to both democracy as a bottom up process of decision making and hierarchy as a top down process. Hierarchical organizations can adapt to changing conditions more expeditiously than democratic ones because the development of a rank-and-file consensus is not a necessary prerequisite to a change in policy direction. Democracy is a much more time-consuming challenge, and it usually results in party positions that are incremental, marginal adjustments to the status quo. All, or most, rank-and-file opinions must be considered, and usually a safe, moderate position results from the negotiations that must inevitably transpire. Moving too far to the left or right threatens the party's core support, and this can be devastating in most elections. In sum, American political parties usually find it politically safe to be centrist and moderate, and usually very risky to be extremist and ideological.

The extent to which the two parties have been democratized over the past two centuries is directly associated with the inability of the nation to adapt quickly to the perceived need for changes in policy direction.

In short, there is an inverse correlation between the degree of democracy that exists within an organization and the ability of that organization to adapt to changing conditions. Democratic organizations with a very diverse rank-and-file base can be placed in a virtual policy straightjacket. Democratized political parties must keep as many members "in line" as possible to avoid voter defection, and that suggests a policy middle ground, even though conditions may not call for that kind of solution.

Democratization accentuates the centrifugal effects of federalism on political parties. This impacts on the ability of parties to provide their members and, ultimately, the voting public with clear-cut policy alternatives. Therefore, it is essential to examine, albeit briefly, the reasons behind the trend to democratize parties. As will be shown, the movement to democratize reflects the American tendency to favor devolution, or decentralization, as a "process" or "procedural" curative for what ails society, and if it's good for society it must be good for parties. Theory aside, democracy has evolved as a reactive theory of politics and government. Democratic governments tend not to pioneer major policy reforms until the perceived need for significant change is rather widespread. This is also true of political parties.

When parties first surfaced as conduits of representation they were dominated by elites. Nominations for elective offices were virtually dictated by party elders, and party platforms were essentially the formal expression of the policy positions of these aristocratic elements. Presidential nominees were the product of congressional party caucuses, and the election of presidents was conducted by elite-dominated party organizations in states. The majority party in the state legislature could determine, by its vote, how all that state's electoral votes would be cast in the Electoral College.

The exploration and settlement of the western frontier during the nineteenth century brought with it a notable spirit of egalitarianism, which was clearly antielite in cast. It rejected political aristocracy in favor of the common man. Its chief apostle was Andrew Jackson, who was first elected to the presidency in 1828 and reelected in 1832. Jackson's major goal was to make participatory democracy a fact of everyday life throughout society and government. The impact of Jacksonian democracy on government was especially profound. Key government institutions at all levels were significantly democratized. This included legislatures, executives, bureaucracies and, of course, political parties. Legislatures and executives became subject to universal manhood suffrage, popular election, and legally mandated short terms of office. Bureaucracies were introduced to the spoils system, wherein administrative appointments were made on the basis of party loyalty, without regard for experience or technical competence, as a reward for supporting the successful party's candidates in elections. Jackson believed that all men, particularly those who supported him and his party, should have an equal opportunity to serve in public office. An elite, patrician-based civil service had no preferential claim to public service.

Jackson's contribution to party democratization came in the form of the party convention, as an alternative to the party caucus, as a means to nominate party candidates for office. The first national party convention selected Jackson as the Democratic Party's presidential nominee in 1832. Conventions clearly were an attempt to involve the party's rank-and-file more systematically in the presidential nomination process because nominees were selected by formal convention votes and the delegates to conventions were elected by local and state party organizations. Party elites were, of course, often chosen to attend

conventions, but their influence was diminished somewhat by the more plebeian influence of party rank-and-file elements that were also in attendance.

The second major assault on party elitism was sponsored by the Progressive movement that surfaced in the 1880s in reaction to what became the spoils system's excesses. Spoils had emphasized loyalty to party and, ultimately, to its leaders, who dispensed favors to voters in return for their election support of the party's slate of candidates. This encouraged the development of party machines, headed by political "bosses" who used government power to serve and reinforce the interests of their parties, not the public in general. Progressives were successful in converting the federal civil service to a merit-based personnel system that rejected partisanship as the basis for personnel appointments. Regarding political parties, Progressives advocated replacing conventions with party primaries. Since primaries function as "nominating elections" they enshrined the parties' rank-and-file at the expense of their elites. The first party primary was held in Wisconsin in 1901, and the numbers of states to embrace the idea has expanded dramatically since that time. Since 1964, it has been possible for presidential candidates to secure enough delegate pledges in state presidential preference primaries to lock up their party's nomination well in advance of the party's national convention.

Both Jackson and the Progressives argued that the democratization of political party decision making would strengthen parties as conduits of public opinion. If democracy is the only evaluation standard, this is most certainly true. If participation, or the opportunity to participate, is an end unto itself, then both voters and policymakers must be prepared to accept the policy consequences of such a process. However, democratic procedures, pursued as a matter of principle, most certainly do exact their policy costs. In the case of party democratization there are several, many of which have a constitutional foundation. The fact that federalism anchors political power in states, and that presidents must secure a majority of electoral votes cast by states on a winner take all basis are, so to speak, constitutional "ghosts" at the party strategy "banquets." It is also important to remember that our two-party system is largely the product of the federal and presidential systems decreed by the Constitution. A two-party system encourages parties to consolidate and appease factions with party ranks before elections, whereas a multiparty system usually delays the factional accommodation challenge until after elections when legislatures are required to choose their leaders from among candidates offered by the various legislative parties.

Party Democracy in the Age of Television

The democratization of parties means that campaigns, both primary and general election, have also been democratized. This has been of particular significance since the advent of television, which has impacted significantly on the price of running for office. In short, television advertising takes money, and a lot of it. Party organizations can't raise the money, and so it is up to the candidates.

Consequently, campaigns have become increasingly candidate centered, with contenders being forced to find sources of funding for increasingly expensive campaigns by raising the funds themselves. Political Action Committees (PACs), as electioneering front organizations for interest groups, come to the rescue, but for a price. The price is the support of the interests' programs or issue positions should the candidate be elected. This

has made American democracy notably non-plebeian in cast. It means that most candidates for office, regardless of party, are becoming increasingly beholden to vested interests that can afford to contribute funds to candidates directly, and to their organizations in the form of "soft" money. Soft money is especially significant because it pays for personnel costs, mailing expenses, transportation, building rentals, and literature. Contributions of this type are not subject to federal campaign contribution expense limitations. Candidates soft-play or forfeit serious attention to campaign issues in the interest of raising money. A study conducted by the nonpartisan Committee for the Study of the American Electorate (CSAE) concluded that 30 percent of campaign budgets go for fundraising and the remainder for travel and staff expenses.[1] Three consequences for both public policy and democracy result. First, serious debate on issues is compromised. Second, candidates can easily become the *de facto* policy spokespersons for the vested interests that can afford to contribute large amounts to their campaigns. This occurs at the expense of those elements that cannot afford such contributions, raising serious questions of political equality. Third, it amplifies the role of the media, especially the broadcast media, in determining the strategy and (ultimately) the outcome of campaigns.

Television, especially, is becoming increasingly expensive, not only because the cost of television advertising time is increasing, but also because candidates are relying on television more and more to get their messages across. This is good in theory because television is an efficient way to reach voters. However, it is bad for several reasons. First, television campaign advertising is heavily negative in tone, stressing why the opponent should not be elected. Messages are usually conveyed in short "sound bites" that refer generally to a candidate's character, his or her experience or patriotism, and the like. Serious discussion and analysis of the issues is usually avoided. Voters become disgusted and disaffected. Public cynicism about government and the quality of individuals that run it sets in, and for good reason. American political dialogue has become decivilized. Campaigns often assume a "hard copy" quality, emphasizing candidates' personal defects, and deal with the serious business of governing only by happenstance. Candidates, if elected, often become too frightened as policymakers to do anything other than spend most of their time preparing for reelection, so that they can master the challenge better next time. Serious issues on the policy agenda go unattended or, if considered, are dealt with in a passing, relatively noncontroversial, incremental way.

The second reason to be disturbed about political campaigns' flight to television is even more serious. The costs of campaigning this way are so staggering that they compel candidates to seek campaign funds from any source and for any amount. The result is the increasing dominance of corporate "fat cats" in both the nomination and election processes, as well as in the character of public policies themselves. Accommodative public policies are, after all, the payoff for generous campaign contributions. As the saying goes: "He who pays the piper calls the tune." Definite policy tunes are being played, but increasingly they are being played for the few instead of the many. Between 1960 and 1996 the cost of all domestic political campaigns grew from $175 million to an estimated $4 billion. During that same period, the cost of presidential campaigns increased from $30 million to $700 million. In inflation-adjusted dollars, it cost 4.4 times as much to run a campaign in 1996 than it did in 1960. In the more confined period between 1976 and 1994, the average bill for a competitive Senate contest increased from $1,069,523 to $9,639,378. The total spent for television ads in those campaigns rose from $474,910 to $5,681,151. These figures represent a 249 percent increase adjusted for inflation. The total spent for television advertising rose by 364 percent.[2]

Televised political advertising is behind the staggering rise in campaign costs. That means more negative advertising in general, and attack ads in particular. Increased negative advertising means increasing voter cynicism. Increasing voter cynicism means lower voter turnout. In the period between 1960 and 1996, voter turnout in general elections declined by 25 percent, despite a five million increase in the number of registered voters, exceptional voter-turnout efforts, and the increase in candidate campaign spending noted above.[3] Low voter turnout inflates the electoral significance of the organized and financially secure minorities that virtually purchase candidate policy loyalties via campaign contributions. In a sense, the institutions constituting our version of representative democracy are being auctioned to the highest bidders.

A third effect of the campaign flight to television and its impact on campaign costs is on the type of candidates that find public office a realistic option. In short, these conditions encourage the rich to run and the modestly endowed to sidestep the challenge or obligation of public office. Recent Senate contests in heavily populated states such as California, Massachusetts, and Pennsylvania featured affluent candidates who can literally afford to buy their nominations and, in some cases, their election. With some major exceptions, a serious run for the presidency is increasingly becoming a rich person's game, attracting the likes of Steve Forbes and Ross Perot. Serious candidates who don't have the personal assets have to work for years to raise sufficient funds in order to purchase the necessary television exposure to become formidable candidates.

Theoretically, presidential primaries should be national debates about significant policy issues. In fact, they have degenerated into auctions open only to candidates with adequate financial muscle to bid. The Constitution does not make personal wealth a prerequisite for seeking the presidency or, for that matter, any elected office. Wealth should neither qualify or disqualify any person for any office. Unfortunately, the aberrations of federal election law have made both personal financial assets and shrewd fund-raising skills the two most important factors in the presidential nominating process. Candidates without wealth are handicapped from the beginning. They are confronted with the prospect of having to navigate an almost impossible financial obstacle course that only the most financially blest and politically adroit can survive.

Ironically, the founders' fears of increased democratization of the political system were unfounded. The democratization of our institutions and electoral processes has bolstered, not compromised, the impact of economic elites on politics and policymaking. The exercise of the Constitution's guarantee of communication freedoms has meant that economic power can virtually control elections and buy policy favors. For this reason, the political system doesn't deal effectively with the health challenge posed by tobacco consumption, with the need to systematically conserve our natural resources, with the need to attack air and water pollution methodologically, with the need to equalize the availability of adequate and fairly priced health care, or (and most important) with the need to legislate significant campaign finance reform.

Therefore, the costs of political party democratization in principle are significant, even ironic. Democratization assumes concomitant interest on the part of voters to participate and take advantage of their new opportunities. However, the opposite is often the case. In some party primaries, voter turnout percentages are in the single digits. In general elections, it is often under 50 percent. This means that organized minorities within parties, by controlling campaign agendas and organizing voting turnout efforts from within their ranks, can control the outcome of primary elections. Organized minorities can defeat disorganized majorities at any juncture, and party primaries are certainly no exception. Right wing or left wing elements within parties can control nominations and present voters with uninviting choices in general elections, thereby reinforcing voter cynicism and disaffection.

Party Democracy and Public Policy

Before examining the impact of political parties on public policy, a summary of how constitutional politics has contributed to the current state of parties as conduits of opinion is warranted. Democracy encourages the development of factions, one form of which is the political party. Parties are distinguished from other factions because their composition is broader and they are organized for the purpose of electing candidates and running government. Parties tend toward a confederal power distribution pattern because federalism as a constitutional principle affords states political autonomy, and states are the geographic basis of all elections, even elections to Congress and the presidency. The Constitution assigns states equal representation in the Senate and requires presidents to secure a majority of Electoral College votes, all of which are assigned to the states based on the total number of elected legislators (House and Senate) it sends to Congress. Since Electoral College votes are cast on a winner take all basis by state, a two-party system is encouraged because the electoral stakes are so high that factions of all sorts are encouraged to organize around two major political movements (ultimately, political parties) in order to maximize their leverage in elections. To do otherwise likely would guarantee an election loss.

The constitutional principle of popular sovereignty encourages reformers to seek democracy and the devolution of power as process, or procedural, cures for such maladies as organization elitism, corruption, and the perceived inability of party organizations to reflect the policy positions of their members. The ultimate tool of devolution and democratization—the party primary—is an intra-party election to determine the party's nominees for office. Because potential nominees must reach out to party rank-and-file for votes in primary elections, candidates turn to broadcast journalism, especially television, as the most efficient way to reach voters. This can be costly, virtually forcing contenders to solicit financial support from corporations and other well-endowed sources, with the expectation that they will be treated very favorably in the policy process. It also encourages a sound bite quality to campaigning that is virtually devoid of serious issue analysis. This alienates voters, causing apathy, disaffection, and cynicism.

If political parties are to be effective intermediary forces in American politics and government, they must be effective both in transmitting public opinion in a balanced, accurate, and efficient way to decision arenas and in impacting responsibly on public policy decisions within those arenas. Effective impacts are defined as policy decisions that incorporate diverse points of view in the ways that make public policy a meaningful response to changing social and economic conditions. If public policy merely mirrors the various points of view via distributive policies that subsidize various sectors of the economy, the challenge has not been met. Nor has it been met if regulations applied to all or some of those sectors are relaxed in response to pressure. The purpose of public policy, indeed, is not to support group indulgences. It is to govern society effectively. This means that laws must not equate the public interest with the policy objectives of vested interests. While the "public interest" is a very subjective concept, it certainly implies that all people, through interest groups or acting as individuals, have a stake in supporting policies that demand the temporary forfeiture of private indulgences in favor of programs that will be of net benefit to all individuals and groups over the long term. Political parties in America, as currently constituted and engineered, do not fare well either as representative institutions or as institutions which work for meaningful, long-term policy change. They are too confederal, too decentralized, too devoid of the necessary will and the necessary resources to serve either as effective representatives of opinions or as stages upon which the nation's unfinished policy business can be articulated and debated in a meaningful way. In classical terms, political parties are "weak." They are undisciplined. They are far more committed to winning elections than they are to governing by any set of meaningful principles. In reference to the analysis offered in Chapter 2, they are too heavily Madisonian and not sufficiently Jeffersonian. They have been democratized to the point that fear of voter rejection encourages policymakers to equate good policies with policies that protect them from defeat at the next election. Policies made on a stage with such a backdrop are rarely the bold, decisive, meaningful answers the public has a right to expect of its government.

The following discussion will discuss the impact of political parties, as they currently function, on public policy. Some of the impacts are procedural in nature—i.e., influencing the ways in which institutions and their members make decisions. Others are substantive—i.e., focusing on the kinds of policies that result from these conditions, and how relevant or irrelevant they are to meeting the challenge of government as a publicly endowed and publicly supported coercive force in society.

First, voters are allowed, even encouraged, to apply a policy double standard when they vote for candidates in both primary and general elections. Presidential candidates try to attract voters by selling their talents as helmsmen, or inspirational leaders who are above the trench warfare of routine politics. Presidential candidates can be effective without being specific if they are charismatic and inspirational. Ronald Reagan and Franklin Roosevelt were probably the best twentieth-century examples of this type of candidate. On the other hand voters want legislators who have a good bedside manner, people who will take care of them both as individuals and as members of families. People expect legislators to support policies that will help them secure and keep jobs, educate their children, provide them with income and health care security, and keep the streets in their neighborhood safe. Political parties often do not bridge this potential "appeal gap" between their presidential candidate and their congressional candidates, and voters see no special reason to vote a straight party ticket. Attempting to make the linkages between presidential and congressional candidate strategies may reveal contradictions and inconsistencies and undercut voter support for all party candidates at all levels. Therefore, voters see nothing wrong in voting for the person, not the party. Split-ticket voting becomes commonplace. While parties do appeal to voters to elect the party slate of candidates, the slate is usually bound by the fact that they are all Republicans or Democrats, and not because they all have pledged themselves to work for a package of specific policies that logically synchronize into an overall change of direction for government. Sometimes voters will respond favorably to such symbolic appeals and elect a president and a Congress of the same party, only to be

disappointed when that symbolic unity doesn't result in the policy reforms that should rightfully be expected from unified government. Eventually, voters choose not to ignore such appeals and choose to vote the candidate instead of the party. With increasing regularity, this results in divided government and policy gridlock. Divided government and policy gridlock provide excuses for policymakers to play the interbranch and interparty "blame game" for policy failures. Accountability is compromised and legislative incumbency is reinforced.

If incumbency grows to the point of virtually guaranteeing legislators reelection, they are said to have "safe" seats. This means that their continued, uninterrupted service virtually guarantees them key committee, subcommittee, and party leadership positions. Virtually ensured of reelection, these individuals can advance policy alternatives that are clearly too far to the right or left of the party mainstream and not fear voter rejection. Such positions, when articulated by a party's legislative leaders, can leave the impression that the entire party is becoming more ideological and program oriented, as was the case with House Speaker Gingrich after the 1994 elections. However, this is usually not the case. The fate of the Republican Party's Contract with America, developed by its House and Senate leadership in the aftermath of the 1994 elections, provides an excellent illustration. The 1994 elections swept many Democrats from office and gave the Republicans control of both houses of Congress for the first time in forty years. The Republican leadership interpreted the election results as a voter mandate to renew conservative government. In fact, the results were more a reflection of voter pessimism with government in general. Voters had Ross Perot as a protest alternative in the 1992 presidential election. They had no such option in 1994, and therefore vented their antisystem frustrations on the incumbent party—President Clinton and the Democratic majorities in the House and Senate. The Republican congressional leadership did not read the election results the same way, and the Contract with America was the result. It offered general policy endorsements of term limits, a balanced budget, school prayer, tax and spending cuts, devolution of federal power to state and localities, and major cuts in entitlement programs. Most of these items as objectives resonate well with most people. The rub comes in their translation into reality. As will be discussed at some length below, Republicans have been victimized nearly as much by the politics of dependency as have Democrats. Therefore, when gestures toward an ideological reaffirmation of conservative principles are translated into specific policy proposals that ask people, Republicans as well as Democrats, to sacrifice, the response is less than overwhelming. The Republicans learned this very quickly. President Clinton was reelected in 1996 and, while Republican majorities were returned to both the House and Senate, voters were asking both parties to eschew ideology and seek meaningful, workable policy reforms within the compass of divided government. The Contract's key ideological zealot, House Speaker Newt Gingrich, was also forced into a comparatively low-profile role in the wake of the 1996 election. In sum, it is clear that the recent tendency for party leaders in both the House and Senate to advance ideology (in this case, classic conservatism) as a panacea for problems does not mean that party grass-roots elements agree. Therefore, the problem of weak, relatively undisciplined, electorally conscious political parties is still a serious one. The incentive gap between party leadership and the rank-and-file illustrates that problem.

A second effect of weak political parties on the policymaking process is an extension of the first. It can be summarized as follows:

Weak political parties leverage the impact of the separation of powers and federalism on policymaking. The impact of these two constitutionally mandated principles on policymaking will be discussed at length later in the book, and so it will only be summarized briefly here. A well-disciplined political party that commits its members and candidates for office to a specific package of policy reforms can overcome the institutional estrangement encouraged by the separation of powers and federalism, provided that party's candidates hold both the presidency and both houses of Congress. If party control is divided, that advantage is lost. Even if it is unified and the party is not ideologically and programmatically homogeneous, the advantage is also lost, as was the case with President Clinton and the Democratic congressional majority between 1993 and 1995. If the party discipline advantage is lost, then structural matters surface to affect both the processes and character of policy. When congressional parties permit ideology to frame their policy options the effects of structure are exacerbated even further, especially under conditions of divided government. During the 105th Congress (1997–1999), the differences between House Speaker Newt Gingrich and House Minority Leader Richard Gephardt were rooted in ideology, or principle. Gingrich was, at least rhetorically, the ideological conservative advancing the marketplace and fiscal austerity as the solution to most social and economic problems. Gephardt was the old-line Democrat, advancing the principles of the Rooseveltian-rooted social service state as the only pragmatic guideline for the pursuit of social and economic justice. When party leaders are actuated by principle, as in these cases, compromises are difficult to hone, and when they come they are usually too accommodative of current stakeholders to be meaningful for the long term. The separation of powers necessitates, in fact, that separate institutions cooperate to produce policy. However, when the party leaders within the separate institutions are engaged in a war over what ideology or principle should be embraced by all policy proposals, cooperation is long in coming and the final results are often less than appropriate for the long haul.

As with the separation of powers, the impact of federalism on public policy is accentuated by weak, overly democratized political parties. In the case of federalism, the results are perhaps more ominous. Strong political parties, whose entire membership is committed to a package of policy reforms developed as practical solutions to the problems at hand would be able to discipline their rank-and-file members to fall into line. However, weak parties whose leaders are obsessed with winning elections are by and large unable to accomplish this. The result is the unabated continuation of "pork barrel" politics with all of its negative repercussions for the nation's long-term well-being. The pork barrel is historically well entrenched on the congressional scene. Legislators seek to shore up voter support in their state or district by incorporating projects into authorizations and appropriations legislation that will be of benefit to a specific representative from a specific district or the two senators from a specific state. Bridges, dams, highways, office buildings, and research projects allocated to key universities with a state or district are but a few examples of pork barrel legislation. All 535 members of Congress want their fair share. The costs can be significant, and the results marginal, if not meaningless. None of this legislation is undertaken with the national interest in mind. Furthermore, it can be very costly, especially during periods when deficits are expanding. Finally, it is a bipartisan phenomenon, with Republicans as well as Democrats profiting equally from the practice. When Democrats were in the majority in both houses of Congress, then Republican House Minority Whip

Newt Gingrich complained about the Democrats' propensity to wallow at the pork barrel trough. Most pork barrel money goes to districts of legislative leaders because of their influence over funding. However, the ascension of the Republicans to congressional power in 1994 did nothing to reverse the tide. In fact, the Republicans exploited their House and Senate leadership positions to secure pork for their districts at a more alarming rate than had the Democrats. A study conducted by the group Citizens Against Government Waste (CAGW) discovered a 16 percent increase in pork expenditures (as that group defined it) during the second session of the 104th Congress, the first controlled by a Republican majority in forty years. Commenting on the irrelevance of party politics to spending issues, CAGW president Tom Schatz observed that the advantages of the pork barrel had merely "shifted from one set of barons to another."[4] Republican senators Richard Shelby (Alabama), Ted Stevens (Alaska), and Mark Hatfield (Oregon) were very successful at delivering monies to their states, as were Democratic senators Bennett Johnson (Louisiana) and Robert Byrd (West Virginia), despite their minority status.[5]

Once portrayed by Brian Kelly as the "Pope of Pork," Byrd is probably the best example of how legislators work overtime to deliver projects to their constituencies, regardless of cost, impact on deficits, or economic need. In a congressional career that approached fifty years, Byrd managed to place such facilities as a U.S. Fish and Wildlife Service office in a small community in the West Virginia Panhandle, and a major Coast Guard computer operation in the small community of Martinsburg. He literally "showered" West Virginia University, located in Morgantown, with federal funds to support research on coal technology, wood products, Alzheimer's disease, occupational safety, and veterans' medical care. He managed to direct NASA research funds and funds to design the "classroom of the future" to Wheeling Jesuit University. He succeeded in relocating the FBI's fingerprint center, a "pork chop" that includes a $250 million structure, from Washington to Clarksburg, West Virginia, a community of approximately 18,000. Clarksburg also was blessed with the $250 million Stonewall Jackson Dam, and also received money to upgrade its airport and organize an aviation training center. The choice to name a recently constructed high school in Clarksburg the Robert C. Byrd High School was made for reasons that are obvious to all who are familiar with Byrd's impact on the community.[6] Byrd was one of the senators most avidly opposed to the Line Item Veto Act of 1996, which permitted the president to eliminate pork barrel items from legislation before signing it. The Supreme Court's decision to declare that law unconstitutional in 1998 elated Byrd, and for obvious reasons. He had fought its enactment on constitutional grounds—that it gave the president too much authority over legislative affairs. The constitutional argument was, of course, essentially a smokescreen, or a way to afford the continuation of pork barrel politics an air of constitutional legitimacy.

Federalism offers state-rooted inputs into public policy. All House members represent districts within states. Senators represent states as geographic areas and, most important, that representation is equal, with no allowances made for population differences among states. Therefore, states have equal policy leverage in the Senate, at least insofar as voting weight is concerned. Furthermore, senators for the more thinly populated states are often the ones to build up the seniority necessary to secure key positions on the significant spending committees and subcommittees. This is because the thinly populated states tend to be more homogeneous politically, and their elected legislators tend to have the inside track for regular reelection pro-

vided they remain loyal to the state's political profile as legislators. The result is that pork is dispensed to the smaller states at disproportionately high levels. A glance at the Fiscal Year 1997 state per-capita pork barrel spending levels provides an illustration. Comparatively small-populated states such as Alaska ($114.23), Montana ($49.29), South Carolina ($23.65), and Nevada ($31.66) received high per-capita pork barrel allotments. On the other hand, highly populated states like New York ($4.61), Illinois ($4.24), New Jersey ($3.05), and Michigan ($0.96) received drastically lower per-person amounts.[7] Therefore, not only is pork barrel legislation often wasteful, deficit aggravating, and nonpublic interest in tone, but it also does battle with the democratic notion of procedural and benefit equality. Clearly, this would not be the case were it not for the constitutional principle of federalism.

A fourth effect of a weak, undisciplined, hyperdemocratized system of political parties on public policy is well illustrated by the salience of pork barrel politics. In short, it is that weak parties are unable to cope with the "entitlement mentality," or "culture of dependency," that has become an institutionalized part of the policy culture in the past generation. In fact, because parties have been unable to muster the necessary courage to resist dependency politics, they devote much of their time and energy during campaigns and while governing actually encouraging it. Political parties, as presently constituted, do little to overcome the divisiveness of the separation of powers and federalism. Campaigns are candidate centered, not party centered. Some candidates approach voters with an appeal that is cast in principle, or ideology. Often this is successful. If it is successful, however, it is because candidates conclude that it best suits the culture and demography of the district, and not because it was decreed by the party. More often, campaigns are organized around a "What can I do for you?" approach to voters. The emphasis is on distributive policies, or entitlements—a better road, school, office building, a federal contract that will bring employment possibilities, more effective crime control, cheaper and better health care, increases in assistance to families on poverty, and so on. This is, above all, a relationship cultivated between a candidate and the voters in the district he or she hopes to represent. While some of the promises may have merit on the "micro" scale in the districts within which they are represented, any contribution they make to the ability of the nation as a whole to address key policy questions is, by and large, coincidental.

Candidates for office, running in name as Democrats and Republicans, run candidate-centered campaigns financed heavily by their own fund-raising efforts. Candidates promise things that will encourage voters to depend on them for the continuation of services and subsidies—workers on Social Security and Medicare, the poor on Medicaid and family assistance, industries on protective regulations, minorities on affirmative action, and farmers on crop subsidies. American politics currently is not party politics. It has become dependency politics. Most groups are so dependent on government for the continuation of the support or legal advantages afforded them by public policy that they find it difficult to think of themselves as part of an interdependent national "whole." However, such a perspective is imperative if parties are to reassume their classic role of policy stewards and government its role of mandating occasional individual and group sacrifices in the interest of long-term societal gain. As matters stand now, there is no reward for sacrifice or self-restraint on the part of any single group because others don't follow suit. When the Democrats were the congressional majority, they used their committee and subcommittee leadership positions to secure incumbency

through the incremental growth of entitlements, and they were roundly criticized by the Republicans—roundly criticized, that is, until the Republicans became the congressional majority and quickly realized how lucrative the same sort of politics could become. For example, Congressional Republicans and Democrats alike were alerted early on to the dependency potential of the 1997 proposal to reauthorize the Intermodal Surface and Transportation Efficiency Act of 1991. The House Transportation and Infrastructure Committee, which considered the reauthorization proposal, received nearly 1,500 proposals from House members to earmark special transit projects for their districts. While many of these project requests did not survive committee scrutiny, it is the incentive behind them that is important.[8] It illustrates that the pork barrel and its dependency politics of either variation is certainly not a monopoly of either of the two major parties. It is a political and policy inevitability of a political system whose political parties have lost the healthy balance between top down and bottom up governance.

In a real sense, the public's affinity for the politics of dependency is responsible for the government stagnation that it, the public, has come to despise. One of the best recent illustrations of how dependency politics encourages systemwide decisions that are too accommodative of dependency politics was the 1997 agreement between President Clinton and Republican congressional leaders on how to achieve a balanced budget. This was to be accomplished by cutting taxes and doing virtually nothing to constrain the progressive growth of entitlements. It was a good, short-term political decision for both Clinton and the Republican leadership. Although deficits were eliminated by 1998, the 1997 deal virtually ignored the long-term structural problems that will surely ensue if the problem of ballooning entitlements, especially Social

Security and Medicare, is not addressed before matters reach the crisis stage. Furthermore, the effect of the tax cuts will more than likely start to affect revenue significantly around 2005, at a time when entitlement spending is poised to surge because of the influx of retiring "baby boomers." Moreover, the fact that such a short-term, "quick-fix" agreement was hashed out in 1997 may delay a return to the issues raised by the agreement until it is far too late to handle the problem without extensive fiscal pain. Optimists would argue that the fact that there was an agreement is a good omen, in that it sets the psychological stage for further agreements in the future. One matter is indisputable: The closer the nation gets to the baby boomer retirement era without dealing with the problem more systematically, the more difficult it will be to do anything at all about it. Statistics do not lie. The influx of new retirees will be met with a situation in which the ratio of workers supporting these entitlements to those claiming them will be at a historical low. If that problem goes unattended, the federal government's main financial obligation will be to write checks that transfer a rising share of the middle-class worker's income to the growing percentage of middle-class retirees.

A more disciplined political party system might well encourage more proactive, sacrificial thinking and policymaking at this point in time, and make the political timetable a bit less ominous. Potentially, stronger political parties could provide current incentives for more long-term structural entitlement reform. Politicians are unlikely to do it on their own because it requires making the idea of sacrifice politically appealing, and that is a risky proposition. The public in general tends to support the idea of mandated sacrifice and austerity in theory, but individuals and groups tend to balk when they understand how it will affect them specifically. Illustrative of the NIMBY ("Not in my back yard!") syndrome,

when push comes to shove people want to transfer the obligation to sacrifice to others. Nonetheless, political party–instilled policy leadership that teaches the long-term advantages of sacrifice could set the stage for more futurist action on the portending entitlement crisis. Current political trends do not forecast that, and the surprise appearance (Fiscal Year 1998) of the first annual budget surplus in a generation makes a focus on austerity even less likely for the foreseeable future. A turn-of-the-century Democratic president would want to please the party's traditional clientele, and these groups decidedly favor spending instead of austerity. A Republican president would know that entitlement reform has historically been a dead-end issue for the party, and therefore likely would not push the issue. In both cases, the temptation would be to postpone consideration of the problem until the president's second term. By that time, the first surge of baby boomers would have begun to retire, and major sacrifices might well be required. Then the problem would no longer be a prospective one.

A fifth effect of weak, excessively democratized political parties on public policy involves the effect on the quality of policy leadership. In short, weak parties mean weak policy leadership. Candidate-centered campaigns and the fear of losing elections make officeholders and their challengers so beholden to voter vicissitudes that they can do little more than react to and appease public opinion. The job of officeholder and policymaker has been converted into a *de facto* continuous campaign for reelection.[9] In comparison to most democracies, elections occur rather frequently in the United States, and we fill nearly half a million public positions by popular election. Party primaries merely exacerbate the problem by adding an additional election challenge to the demands of frequent general elections. Because of the number and frequency of U.S. elections, policymakers are notably unprotected from public opinion fluctuations. They respond by spending more and more time electioneering, and less and less time with the challenge of governing. The policy agenda suffers. Ultimately, the public suffers.

The Constitution requires that all members of the House of Representatives be elected every two years. In no other major democracy is a legislative term so short, with the average being four or five years. Senators serve for what appear to be relatively comfortable six-year terms. However, one-third of the Senate is elected every two years. This means that one-third of the senators are under constant electoral pressure, even if the Senate as a whole is not. The founders did not provide for popular election of the Senate. That had to await the ratification of the Seventeenth Amendment. With popular election of the Senate a fact of political life, the Senate's political demeanor has become increasingly like that of the House.

Although intended as the ultimate in political party democracy, primaries have not delivered what they promised. The primary is an institution unique to U.S. parties and their politics. Parties in no other democracies use the party primary as a way to select nominees for office. Between 15 and 40 percent of House and Senate incumbents face opposition in primaries. Even in cases where no primary opposition materializes, there is no way to anticipate it very far in advance. Accordingly, incumbents plan for primary challenges just in case they materialize.[10]

Therefore, U.S. political parties fail to encompass the cause of their candidates effectively. In most democratic countries, such as Great Britain, candidates win or lose depending on the national popularity of their party and (of course) its policy agenda. The fate of each candidate is tied to the fate of his or her party. This is not true in the United States. While the popularity of a party and its presidential candidate can be of considerable help to a candidate, it is of less help in the United States than it is to candidates in most democracies. In the United States, legislators seeking election or reelection must sponsor their own advertising and publicity campaigns, compile their own records of public service, raise most of their campaign funds, and fight it out with their opponents on their own.

It might be expected that these conditions would lead to a high rate of turnover in Congress. However, the opposite is the case. Congressional turnover is noticeably low in comparison to rates in other democracies. This raises an interesting question: How can the threat of defeat lead, in effect, to the securing of incumbency? The answer is that threats, or potential threats, to one's incumbency encourage an "insurance" strategy and style to politics. Because incumbents are vulnerable to defeat, they will do virtually anything to protect themselves politically, even if polls show incumbents to hold safe seats. The result is a constant campaign mentality. Such protective strategies usually work. Accordingly, incumbents protect themselves in any way they can, even if the probability of defeat is slim or zero, for it would be impetuous to assume that seats are completely safe.[11]

Reinforcing all the above is the reality that, in contrast to publics in most other democracies, Americans in general are obsessive democrats. They are committed to democracy in principle and use it as a procedural curative for many organizational and institutional problems. We are not spiritually committed to Edmund Burke's "indirect" theory of representation, although we must accept it as a pro-forma necessity. Burke argued that representatives are elected to exercise their best judgment on behalf of constituents. If that judgment collides with constituent views, then the representative should follow his or her own conscience and judgment. This interpretation of democracy considers public opinion to be only one of a number of factors that should be incorporated into policy decisions. By this view, legislators should be rewarded for judgment and courage, constituency opinion to the contrary notwithstanding. The role of constituents in such a system is significant, but constrained. Constituents do not give direct orders to those whom they have elected. Rather, constituents make retroactive judgments about how well legislators are doing. If that judgment is unfavorable then a new set of leaders can be elected. This is not unlike the relationship between a patient and his or her doctor. The patient chooses the doctor but usually does not prescribe the treatment for a medical problem. If the physician does not appear to be treating the problem to the patient's satisfaction, then the patient has the option to change physicians, and often does.[12]

The theory of representation that is most popular with Americans is the Rousseau, or "direct democracy," theory. According to this school, representatives are direct agents of the electorate. They must go to great lengths to monitor public opinion in their constituencies. Having determined that, then they are obligated to reflect that opinion in policy decisions as best they can. There is little if any judgmental discretion vested in the representative. If the representative's opinion is at odds with the opinion of the constituency, the representative is obliged to follow the dictates of the constituency. His or her judgment should not intervene and influence inputs into policy decisions. Ideally, under such a theory, there would be no role for the representative as liaison between the people and policy decisions. But most societies are too large to make literal direct democracy of the Greek city-state or New England town meeting a reality. Therefore, representatives are necessary as conduits of public opinion. They monitor it, digest and distill it, and transmit it to decision forums in as close to its natural state as is feasible.

However, this theory can lead to considerable frustration. Culturally committed to democracy as a panacea, citizens fail to realize that obsession with democratic procedures can virtually paralyze decision processes and can offer activist minorities opportunities to defeat disorganized majorities. Officeholders feel compelled to accommodate their constituents and, because of the imperatives and expenses of the constant campaign, find it necessary to appease activist minorities for financial and strategic reasons. Citizens become frustrated with these conditions and ask for even more democratization in the form of term limits, balanced budget amendments, and campaign finance legislation.

Having adjusted to a constant campaign mentality, House and Senate members have responded by organizing congressional structure and staff assignments to serve the new imperative. The number of standing subcommittees has nearly tripled since 1965, allowing junior as well as senior members the opportunity to leverage their policy influence formally within the legislative process. In 1957 the total number of House- and Senate-appointed staff stood at 3,556. In 1996 the total was 32,820, a number which included all individuals supporting Congress in any capacity—office staff, committee and subcommittee staffs, and support agency staffs.[13] Of course, much of this growth has been in response to the growth of government's policy responsibilities and to the increasing technical nature of policy issues. However, much of it is also due to member interest in shoring up support within their constituencies. The number of House staff assigned to home district offices doubled between 1972 and 1992. On the Senate side, it quadrupled during the same period. This trend is in response to the growing importance of constituency service—sometimes known as casework—to senators and representatives. It has been estimated that at least half of congressional staff time is spent on constituency service rather than on policymaking matters.[14] In short, Congress has become structurally subservient to the bedside manner, and the bedside manner is strategically congruent with the imperatives of the constant campaign.

The political and structural results of the constant campaign mentality have been gradually instituted during a period when both Congress and the president should be spending more, not less, time on substantive policy matters. Political parties must win as many elections as possible, so goes the argument, so that the parties' programs can be adopted. However, to institute major policy changes, some people and groups are going to have to forgo at least some of the indulgences of dependency politics. But sacrifice is countercultural to the constant campaign imperative. Therefore, promises of change through sacrifice are made, elections are won, the contradictions between sacrifice and indulgence become apparent, legislators and presidents succumb to the campaign imperative, and little gets accomplished. Hard choices are postponed and factions are appeased. After all, another election is just around the corner.

This suggests another policy result of a weak political party structure: Weak political parties, and the conditions that have created them, have converted much of the public dialogue to a dialogue of symbols from a dialogue of debates over how to deal with specific policy problems by mostly instrumental means. Rhetoric takes the place of action. Promises substitute for deeds. The right ideology or doctrine, if reflected in policy as an objective, will be self-executing. If, for example, we can instill economic growth through tax and spending cuts, capitalism for the marketplace will take care of everything. Reduced taxes will trigger more spending. More spending spurs employment. More employment means people have more money to spend. This, in turn, triggers more demand for goods and services. This creates the need for even more jobs, which means that more and more poor people will be employed. Perhaps that means that the problem of poverty will be dealt with effectively, and so on. We can get schools back on a moral course with a school prayer amendment. A balanced budget amendment will take care of deficit spending. The nation can reenergize its sense of patriotism and unified sense of purpose if an amendment is adopted that outlaws flag desecration.

In short, the Constitution has become a symbolic outlet for policy frustrations. It's a justifiably revered document, but it isn't the last word. It's best to consider it just a "rough draft." Statutes that legislate simplistic "solutions" to difficult problems accomplish the same objective. Legalize the death penalty and it will prevent crime. Deal with the problem of youth crime by trying juveniles as adults. In sum, easily understood moral imperatives, if reflected in speeches and ensconced in the Constitution or in statutes, will take care of everything.

Of course, in reality, they usually do not. Moreover, politicians know they do not. However, the realities of the constant campaign make it much easier to make promises that resonate well with voters symbolically and, in effect, buy more time. Officeholders appear to be attacking problems head on. In fact, they are not, and most of them know it. When the gap between pretense and reality finally becomes clear, reputations suffer, and public cynicism increases. Austerity, for example, makes for effective symbolic politics, but it contradicts the realities of political Darwinism, which equates survival with the effective deployment of dependency politics. However, that tends to exacerbate the budget deficit problem. When this becomes apparent, public cynicism increases. The public equates legislation with deception and politicians with lying and dishonesty. Politicians are not genetically dishonest. The system has made them such. The potential costs of not being deceptive are simply too great.[15]

Finally, weak political structures strengthen the impact of interest groups in the policy process. Parties as superstructures can mitigate the impact of specific interests. There is an inverse relationship between the relative strength of parties as superstructures and the strength of factions in American politics. The stronger the parties, the weaker the factions, and vice versa. Madison argued that large constituencies were preferable to small ones because more factions would have to be accommodated in large districts before policies were finally legitimized. This decreased the opportunity for one faction, or a comparatively few factions, to dominate in policy decisions. This makes policies safer, more stabilizing, and therefore less dangerous. Although Madison did not advocate the development of political parties, he would most certainly conclude that strong parties are much preferable to powerful interest groups for the same reason that he supported highly populated constituencies. They offer the same advantages to extra-constitutional politics that they do to politics played out in institutions established by the Constitution.

The constant campaign mentality also increases the impact of interest groups on policy. Legislators and presidents need inordinate amounts of money to run for office. Groups are the source of most major contributions, especially increasingly critical soft money contributions. Since group salience and financial assets are grossly uneven, the more well-heeled groups are the major campaign players. Candidates know this, and become increasingly dependent on these groups for support. If elected, the former candidates turned policymakers are more beholden to these groups in the policy process. He who pays the piper calls the tune. If groups are represented unevenly in politics,

they are often represented unevenly in policy. This is a particular problem for Congress because many constituencies, including states, are dominated by comparatively few factions. In light of the constant campaign's financial imperatives, it would be political suicide to ignore, or even slight, these interests regularly in policy decisions. Consequently, the problem of a biased interest group system is accentuated by the inability of political parties to mitigate the effects of the constant campaign.

Political Parties as Intermediaries: A Critique

A responsible critique of parties as intermediaries must be a cautious one. The intermediary role is a liaison role, a conduit role, one which transmits citizen attitudes to policymakers in ways that both minimize opinion distortion and yet provide decision makers with meaningful ways to translate that opinion into positions they assume on policy issues.

This is difficult. First, ours is a very diversified society. It could be argued that there are as many publics as there are factions. To be sure, some legislative districts are more demographically homogeneous than are others, in which case clear opinion trends can be more easily discerned than in more diversified, competitive districts. Second, more and more districts are becoming competitive, owing to the influences of urbanization, industrialization, immigration, and population migration. For example, the South was a Democratic stronghold between the 1930s and 1980s. That is no longer the case. Since the Reagan era the South has been decidedly Republican in presidential elections, and most southern congressional districts are now very competitive, with many showing signs of becoming Republican strongholds. Third, individuals are by nature reactive. They tend not to have strong opinions about policy issues until an event triggers a highly favorable or unfavorable reaction on their part. Most are neutral about military engagements until troops are committed. Americans generally were indifferent about school integration until the *Brown* decision. Crime control and traffic safety tend not to be priority issues with some people until they, or a member of their family, are involved in an automobile accident or become the victim of a crime. Therefore, if policymakers are trying to deal with an issue proactively, in anticipation of more serious problems in the future, public opinion may not be very helpful. Nonetheless, most contemporary policy problems—entitlements, the solvency of Social Security and Medicare, quality education, family stability, adequate health care, environmental protection, and urban decay—are problems that demand futurist solutions. Fourth, and finally, the ways in which many issues are framed and discussed by politicians as both candidates and officeholders infer that problems can be resolved by ideology rather than pragmatism. If it is either conservative or liberal, it is either good or bad. If it centralizes or decentralizes government power, it is either good or bad. If it requires governments to increase or decrease public spending it is either good or bad. If it unleashes the forces of the marketplace or controls the predatory wiles of corporate America, it is either good or bad. To the extent that simplistic, ideologically framed rhetoric can inspire the public's interest in an issue, the results are beneficial.

However, usually the opposite is the case. Usually it adds to citizen estrangement from government. Politicians don't seem to be talking about issues in ways that connect to the real world that voters face daily at home, at work, in the streets, or in school. Interest in issues fades, citizens become increasingly cynical, and voter turnout wanes. This makes it very difficult for any intermediary institution,

especially political parties, to perform effectively as an opinion conduit. The raw material just isn't there.

The above analysis has depicted the American two-party system as a "weak" system. It is weak because the parties lack the ability to deliver, on a regular basis, support for a set of policy options that the parties have clearly articulated as being better than those articulated by the other party. The important terms here are clearly articulated options, rank-and-file support, and *regular* delivery. Voting in Congress is often highly partisan, as was the case with the Deficit Reduction Act of 1993. At other times it is notably bipartisan, as in the case of the 1996 welfare reform legislation and the 1997 balanced budget agreement. Given the realities of hyperdemocratized parties; the constant campaign; a diverse, non-ideological, and often indifferent public; the impact of federalism as a representation venue; and the separation of powers as a structural fact of life, political parties cannot cultivate policy loyalties and deliver disciplined votes on legislation over time. In sum, the fact that parties are relatively weak means that they reflect the nature of the political world. They have not created it.

In this sense, perhaps political parties are too effective as conduits. If American politics is, by its nature, structurally and politically diffused, nonprogrammatic, accommodative, and power averse, why shouldn't political parties embody and reflect these realities as they respond to the intermediary challenge? If Americans are culturally obsessed with democratic procedures as universal correctives, or panaceas, for policy dysfunctions, why shouldn't political parties function more as mirrors of public opinion and indifference than as policy tutors and instigators of policy change? Should not their major mission be to register citizen opinion and/or indifference rather than mold it? If democracy is defined exclusively as the registration of opinion, whatever its character or nature, in representative arenas, then the current role of the American party system can be defended.

However, there may be more at stake here than meets the eye. If representation is allowed to pursue its natural course through the faction, or interest group, venue, representation of opinion becomes unequal, or biased, in favor of those factions that are better funded, better led, better organized, and historically have had better access to decision arenas. Some factions are more equal than others. Furthermore, the democratization of parties via primaries has invited well-organized factions to control the nomination process and heavily influence the campaign policy positions of nominees in ways that run contrary to rank-and-file member opinion. All too often, democracy provides an opportunity for an organized minority to defeat a disorganized majority.

Furthermore, the realities of "running scared" make party incumbents beholden to financially well-heeled special interests. This directly contradicts the notion of political equality as a democratic standard. The fact that more House districts and states are becoming electorally competitive exacerbates this problem. The more competitive the district, the more necessary it is to raise inordinate amounts of money to mount a serious campaign. Therefore, the more beholden are candidates to the special interests that have the funds to contribute, at a price of course.

The two-party system, as currently constituted, does not represent the diversity of opinion that it should. Federalism and the separation of powers (especially the requirements for presidential selection) have clearly contributed to its continuance. Because parties have such inclusive voter strategies, it is difficult for them to represent all their rank-and-file components equally. The nod goes to those elements with the resources to help candidates gain and continue in office. This ac-

centuates the representational problem, encourages member defections, and increases the number of independent voters. Some voters become apathetic and disinterested in politics because they cannot find a comfortable party home. Independent or third-party candidates do little to satisfy defectors because they rarely garner enough votes to encourage the two major parties to reinventory their strategies. Ross Perot's presidential candidacy in 1992 and 1996 did alert the two major parties to the degree of citizen discontent, but the response was not to search for more innovative policies as much as it was to find ways to lure the defectors back into the established party ranks. Americans are culturally competitive and interested in using politics and government to better themselves and their communities. The two major parties, as currently constituted, do not serve these purposes well.

Above all, most Americans are pragmatists. They believe that a progressive political center can be both representative and innovative. They very much dislike the increasing polarization of political rhetoric that emanates from party spokespersons on both sides. They are disgusted with scandal-mongering and the personalization of political dialogue. They have grown to dislike politicians as a lot because they seem to be playing different roles on different stages than they were expected to do when elected. They do not like partisan gridlock and useless finger-pointing. Indeed, voters have brought on divided government and gridlock by their votes. However , they expect such conditions to lead to innovative, but also accommodative, agreements between the two major parties. But too often accommodation means postponing difficult choices, reaching decisions that are clearly too marginal or incremental in character, or taking unnecessary risks with established programs in the hope that another level of government or a different set of administrative procedures will improve matters. In sum, the two-party system spawns a breed of divisive and irrelevant rhetoric and patterns of decision making which are largely irrelevant to the policy crisis that government desperately needs to address.

Irrelevant partisanship extends from the White House to the states' houses, and it doesn't seem to be abating. Its growth and sustenance can be explained, in part, by the fact that policymakers may well understand that they do not have the time, the resources, or the political courage to address policy problems effectively. Attempting to outmaneuver the other party with a thought-stultifying cliché or an empty platitude buys a temporary respite from the inevitable. It is especially noticeable during election years, when the focus is almost exclusively on raising the funds to win elections. Both the print and broadcast media have fallen victim to these strategies. They favor "horse race" type reporting during campaigns, focusing on who is ahead and why. Between elections they like to report on gridlock, partisan-inspired investigations, court cases involving civil suits against the president, the role of the first lady as policy counselor, and who are likely future presidential candidates. They do not, by and large, focus on why public officials are not addressing our serious problems. The media like the "side show" side of free government, and the distractive side of party politics satisfies that craving. An uncivil political circus makes for good tabloid journalism, and by no means do media forces resist it.

The nation needs party-induced partisanship of another sort, and it is not getting it. Party leaders have failed to organize their troops around a specific policy agenda supported by realistic ways to achieve it that stands in stark contrast to the agenda of the other party. Partisanship needs to be expressed in ways that force policymakers to deal pragmatically with the complexities of policy issues. It is true that the founders considered parties a form of faction that might well interfere with creative discourse. However, they realized all too soon that the lack of a party-based majority and a well-organized minority made it very difficult to examine issues thoroughly and settle policy disputes with formal votes. Ours was the first experiment any government in the world had with political parties, and it worked. Differences were resolved by dialogue rather than by bullets. It was a healthy form of partisanship—one directed at seriously dealing with the nation's policy agenda—not the destructive variety that has been so commonplace in recent years.

The road to party-based partisan renewal will not be easy. President Clinton was elected as an "in name only" Democrat who deliberately blurred the more traditional distinction between Democrats and Republicans in order to strike major compromises on welfare reform, deficit reduction, and a balanced budget. Although he was elected to the presidency twice, the Democrats lost control of Congress during his presidency and his 1998 impeachment further eroded his influence. Clinton was an accommodator who reached out to different groups as a matter of both strategy and style, and frequently other politicians began to imitate him. Former Republican House Speaker Newt Gingrich held steadfastly to his position in the wake of the Republican "revolution" of 1994, but tilted clearly toward the Clinton position after Clinton's 1996 reelection, and then resumed a confrontational strategy when he concluded that the president's affair with Monica Lewinsky made Clinton more politically vulnerable. Gingrich miscalculated and resigned the speakership and his House seat as a result. The middle ground appears safer. Many congressional leaders on both sides of the political fence have risen to power by being bipartisan and accommodative and are not likely to change. Congressional party caucuses do not reflect the honest partisanship of past years. Furthermore, since elections are so costly and the constant campaign mentality has a virtual lock on congressional incumbents, members of both parties seek campaign support from the same special interests. If incumbents from both parties drink from the same "financial fountain" it is very difficult to expect partisan gestures that will cause them to lose favor with these vested interests.

Nonetheless, the public is more comfortable with healthy partisanship, and it will come sooner or later. Party leaders in the style of Jefferson, Jackson, and Van Buren will have to make it happen in response to growing public frustration. A healthy overhaul will eventually arise from the destructive ashes of bipartisanship. The nation, indeed the political parties themselves, cannot afford any other alternative.

Interest Groups as Intermediaries

Interest groups are the most prevalent and significant expression of the impact of factionalism on public policy. Their significance to politics and policy has been recognized for over two thousand years. Aristotle wrote of the advantages of collective action over individual action. James Madison wrote of the inevitability of factions in a democracy, and of their potential danger, in *Federalist No. 10,* where he commented that "liberty is to faction as air is to fire."[16] Originally, the Constitution confined exercise of direct popular sovereignty to the House of Representatives. Senators were appointed by state legislators, and presidents were selected by an Electoral College whose members were appointed by state legislatures. However, like other political and social institutions, the Constitution fell prey to the rising tide of democracy. The Seventeenth Amendment provided for the direct election of senators. Decisions to popularly elect members of the Electoral College were made by state legislatures. In an effort to maximize their leverage within political parties, states decided to appoint electors pledged to vote for the presidential candidate who won a plurality of their state's popular vote. To maximize their state's leverage in the selection of the president, the appointed electors were expected to vote unanimously for the state winner. The net effect of these changes was to enhance the role of popular sovereignty in politics and policy.

Madison's explanation of the inevitability of factions was based on his understanding of human nature. His assumptions were those of Thomas Hobbes, i.e., people are by nature motivated by self-interest and ego satisfaction. They are not, by disposition, charitable, magnanimous, selfless, and interested in promoting the common good unless, of course, their own interests would be advanced by such gestures. People of a common persuasion could be expected to organize into groups in the hope of leveraging their impact on policy decisions.

Accordingly, factions actuated by economic self-interest, religious convictions, the quest for protection or security, and philanthropy were inevitable but nonetheless potentially dangerous. If one or a few factions came to dominate policy decisions, it/they could enact policies that would dominate, even oppress, other factions. This could be defended only if power were equated with legitimacy. Even if an alliance of groups would produce a statistical majority, that fact alone would not mean its public policies were inherently right. Majorities can be just as oppressive as minorities. In short, factions are inevitable and unremovable, and their effects potentially very dangerous unless government can be organized to control their possible excesses.

The founders' solution to factional excesses was constitutional structure. If the

Constitution could fragment power in ways that controlled factional intemperances, everyone would profit. Government would be stable, irrational policies would be discouraged, and popular sovereignty would be preserved. The result was the separation of powers principle, the check and balance principle, and the principle of federalism. Separation of powers brings to the policy table different alignments of factions impacting on a two-house Congress, the presidency, and (on occasion) the courts. Each house of Congress is constitutionally independent of the other. Therefore, compromises from among these independent institutional perspectives must precede the enactment of policy. Moreover, the president can veto a bill. The mere possibility of this impacts on Congress when it considers legislation. The president's point of view can be carefully incorporated into a bill even before it is sent to the Oval Office for signature. Of course, if a president is popular, that fact alone encourages legislators to take him seriously. If both the House and Senate can muster a two-thirds vote to override a presidential veto, a bill becomes law without the president's signature. However, in order to do this, more factions have to be accommodated to secure the required override supermajority in both houses. This further dilutes the impact of a single group on policy. In addition federalism, by dividing powers between the central government and the states, moderates the impact of groups in two ways. First, by assigning states equal representation in the Senate, the influence of the more radical movements in highly populated states is reduced. Second, constitutionally guaranteed state political sovereignty means that one or a few groups can dominate state politics, and that may be all they need to accomplish their objectives. Under such conditions, they would waste little time with national politics.

The Madisonian argument was essentially that the best government is the one that accommodates all factions, since factions were likely to be the political channels through which public opinion would be funneled. John C. Calhoun agreed, arguing that no opinion held by an individual or group can be proved to be inherently just, moral, or ethical. Therefore, the only option for government is to invite and digest as many opinions as possible, and to enact policies that reflect a synthesis of them all. Absent universal agreement on a single policy option, the only practical definition of the public interest is a policy that accommodates all the interested groups. To Calhoun, democratic politics was "lowest common denominator" politics.

However, what if a responsible point of view doesn't have an interest group sponsor? What about potential groups that are not yet organized? What about the smaller groups with resources so limited that they cannot afford to buy publicity and gain access to decision-making forums? Should their values be ignored because they are, for one reason or another, constrained in their ability to compete equally with established groups? Each of these questions alludes to a problem with the pluralist, or group, theory of democracy that Madison did not address. More so today than in Madison's time, it questions the legitimacy of groups as effective conduits of public opinion.

Several factors act in concert to compromise the democratic legitimacy of interest group politics. First, and perhaps most important, the interest group system is biased toward the comparatively well-to-do groups. It is these groups—the labor unions, trade associations, professional groups, retired citizens, and business organizations—that can afford to spend money and, in effect, buy access to decision-making forums. Others can't count on it, and some may be denied access altogether. Schattschneider's observation that the "flaw in the pluralist heaven is that the heavenly chorus sings with a strong upper class accent" is particularly relevant.[17] It is the well-to-do groups that have the funds to sponsor Political Action Committees during election campaigns, and who make major soft money contributions to parties and to candidates. Without them, candidates and their respective parties would be forever handicapped in their attempts to win office. They are the ones that can increase their leverage by exploiting federalism's guarantee of equal state representation in the Senate by spurring local chapters and affiliates into action in both campaigns and legislative debates. Smaller affiliates in the smaller states have the same potential leverage as do the larger affiliates in the larger states.

A second flaw in the Madison (pluralist) prescription is that some key values go unrepresented for want of interest group sponsors. This is the problem of the potential group, or the group that should be organized and active but, for any number of reasons, is not yet that way. Usually people holding these opinions do not consider organizing themselves until they have been seriously disadvantaged by events or policy trends. Conservation groups don't organize until resources or species are threatened. Antitobacco lobbies don't organize until increasing numbers of people acquire lung cancer and research shows an undisputable correlation between smoking and lung cancer. Labor unions did not organize until low wages became economically threatening and children were inhumanely exploited in the workplace. Diehard pluralists argue that politicians take the unorganized into account because they fear that they will organize to oppose them if they (the politicians) don't absorb and act on their views. These potential groups are significant to explaining how both legislators and administrators make decisions. Representing them is inevitable, given the career consciousness of public officials. Politicians are actuated by self-interest, as are all individuals. Therefore, this self-interest results in all of so-

ciety's interests being considered in one way or another by all government institutions.[18]

Another problem with the impact of interest groups on public policy not anticipated by Madison is the problem of "interest group liberalism" and its impact on the policy bias of administrative agencies.[19] For well over half a century administrative agencies have been assigned considerable policy discretion by legislatures. Agencies are also sources of new policy ideas. Consequently, the policy premises that agencies bring to these two responsibilities are critical to determining the character of policy outputs. Interest groups respond to the vesture of policy discretion in agencies by, in essence, lobbying them in much the same way they do Congress. Administrative agencies, especially those with jurisdiction over distributive policies, have the same interest in the success of policy proposals as do the interest groups and, for that matter, so do congressional subcommittees with jurisdiction over the same programs. This trio of interests comprises the iron triangle networks that have been so much a part of the policy scene for the last half-century. When Congress enacts a law, or when an administrative agency issues an executive order that supplements a law, such actions often incorporate the policy positions of friendly interest groups. Under these conditions, public policy becomes, in essence, the legal registration of interest group opinions. There is little or no distinction between laws and interest group opinions. Government becomes, in essence, a series of atomized enclaves of public officials exercising power at the behest of private-sector forces. For example, there are a few differences between what the Department of Agriculture supports and what the American Farm Bureau Federation and the House and Senate Agriculture Committees support. The Department of Education, the National Education Association (NEA), the House Committee on Education and the Workforce, and the Senate Committee on Labor and Human Resources are all on the same general policy wavelength. The Departments of Army, Navy, and Air Force, along with members of the House and Senate Armed Services Committees, align themselves with defense contractors in the pursuit of weapons contracts that will mutually benefit all three parties.

Interest group liberalism is dysfunctional to the group model of democracy for several reasons, none of which Madison himself could have forecasted. First, compromise among groups is not guaranteed. Spending may be cut on occasion in some areas, but often programs that subsidize groups are not cut seriously from budget to budget. Most often, they are increased and this suits other members of other iron triangle networks so long as they get their fair share of concessions elsewhere in appropriations legislation. Second, this condition entrenches powerful vested interests in the institutional framework of government— the very thing the founders were trying to discourage. Madison wanted government to make hard choices among conflicting values. Instead government becomes a holding company for vested interests, and the difficult issues are not placed on the policy agenda. Finally, the founders wanted in the Constitution a government with more power and one that could plan more systematically than could the government under the Articles of Confederation. Instead, interest group liberalism has provided a government that is, in fact, too fragmented and decentralized to engage seriously in long-range planning.

Finally, Madison and the other framers could not possibly have anticipated the impact of technology on politics and public policy. Fast data gathering makes it easy for vested interests to back up their positions with facts that are difficult to dispute, and they gain policy leverage as a result. Nor could the founders have foreseen the advent of modern campaigning and its reliance on the electronic media to frame the nature of policy discourse. Television makes campaigning extremely expensive, and candidates are virtually forced to depend on the same well-to-do forces that dominate the policy process in other areas (discussed above) for campaign support. This reinforces the bias of the interest group system, making some forces far more equal than others. This, in turn, compromises the factional balance that the founders considered so essential to making the system serve, simultaneously, the demands of both popular sovereignty and the need to control faction excesses.

Interest Groups and Constitutional Politics

The impact that interest groups have in public policy is heavily influenced by constitutional structure. Group strategists are conscious of this, and develop strategies to influence policy with the institutional results of constitutionally fragmented power in mind. What are these constitutionally friendly conditions and how do they play out in public policy?

First, the legitimacy of interest groups is based on the communications guarantees of the First Amendment—i.e., the guarantees of free speech, press, assembly, and petition. While laws do require that interest groups report costs of direct lobbying efforts and the amount of campaign contributions, the purpose is disclosure, not the constraint of group activities. Group campaign contributions are limited to $5,000 per candidate, but this can be easily circumvented by establishing as many election "front" organizations—known as Political Action Committees (PACs)—as are necessary to subsidize campaigns to levels that groups think strategically appropriate. In addition, there are no legal limits on the amount of soft money that can be contributed to a candidate's campaign organization or party organization. Soft money is spent by parties on overhead and administrative expenses such as facility rentals, utilities, transportation, personnel, and printing costs, thereby freeing other donations for electioneering use. In short, this is how groups use elections to petition government. It is growing in importance because of the rising cost of campaigning, which makes parties and candidates more dependent on large contributions. In turn, it increases the policy leverage of large, financially secure groups. Candidates, if elected, know that large contributions were not given out of philanthropy for the democratic process. Contributing groups expect, and receive, a sympathetic ear for policy causes once the successful candidates assume office.

Second, interest groups exploit the fragmented government structure manufactured by the Constitution's separation of powers, check and balance, and federal principles. Some groups seek government subsidies, others seek favorable investment environments, while others seek to prevent, delay, or compromise what they consider to be oppressive government-induced constraints on their activities. Large groups representing the corporate sector often seek to defeat moves to regulate their activities. The Constitution is particularly friendly to this strategy. It is easy to defeat a bill or proposal by getting one house of Congress or, for that matter, a key subcommittee in that chamber, to disapprove it. Group energies can be concentrated on that one chamber and the relevant committees and subcommittees. Lobbying the House, the Senate, and the president only spreads resources more thinly and lessens the chance of success. However, because of bicameralism (a two-house legislature) groups seeking to defeat legislation can concentrate on severing only one link in the policy process chain, either the House or the Senate, and

the proposal dies. If different versions of a bill are passed by the House and Senate, a bichamber consensus must be developed. This offers groups an opportunity to exploit the "separate institutions sharing (policy) power" reality of constitutional politics. Separate institutions must agree before anything is done. Their institutional separation enhances their bargaining leverage. This, in turn, makes for very low common denominators in public policy. Results tend to be marginal, or incremental in nature. Otherwise, no legislation at all is a distinct possibility. To groups fighting government regulations, a bland result produced by the separate institutions fact of life is much preferred to something far more coercive that could be produced by a more integrated constitutional structure.

By the same token, groups with a relatively weak power base can leverage their claims to policy justice by exploiting the separation of powers principle. They can always take the "oppressive" and/or "exploitive" groups to court in the search for justice. No federal judge is popularly elected, and comparatively few state and local judges are. Therefore, judges can afford to decide cases based on the law and the Constitution. Power and convention can be suppressed or reversed by courts, acting as an independent branch, based on authority granted them by the Constitution and statutes. Accordingly, comparatively weak groups go to court without hesitation. For example, school racial integration on a national scale was decreed by the Supreme Court in 1954. Afro-Americans, then a very weak political force, could not have achieved integration as quickly or on as broad a scale had not they called on the courts to help them. Environmental groups do the same thing with regularity in an attempt to constrain what they consider to be the environmentally exploitive practices of cohesive, well-financed corporate lobbies.

Federalism can be used in much the same way. If the national government decides regulation is necessary, it is usually because of the sweeping, inclusive nature of the problem, and probably because it has the consumer, the worker, the young, or the under-privileged in mind as the policy beneficiary. If the case can be made for the policy being a state, not national, responsibility, groups can lobby for the devolution, or decentralization, of power. Energy companies were successful with such a campaign during the Eisenhower administration. The deregulation of the savings and loan industry during the Reagan administration was based, in part, on the same argument. The case for a major devolution of family-targeted welfare policies was behind the Personal Responsibility and Work Opportunity Act of 1996—the most significant since the New Deal era.

Third, interest groups exploit the growth of administrative policy discretion—a phenomenon encouraged by the separation of powers—to advance their policy causes. The Constitution divides supervision of the bureaucracy between Congress and the president. Congress creates agencies, funds them, and establishes their jurisdiction. However, the president, as chief executive, is responsible for supervising their activities and through the budget power recommending changes in their budgets. Therefore, because of the separation of powers, administrative agencies do not have a single boss. Both Congress and the president supervise them. This gives agencies the opportunity to find security for their policy causes elsewhere. Like all individuals, bureaucrats seek security and the organizations for which they work seek permanency. As assemblages of career and security-conscious employees, agencies want a power base that will offer continual support for their policies, and one which promises more longevity than the support they can expect from either the president or Congress, both of which can have their government careers altered dramatically by elections.

Therefore, agencies seek interest group allies, and they find them without much trouble. Since most policies are very complex, Congress allows administrative agencies to issue executive orders that fill in the policy details to make specific what formal legislation often leaves deliberately obscure. Congress also finds this strategy politically advantageous because regulatory issues are usually controversial issues. If agency regulations anger constituents, legislators can always blame the bureaucracy and take the political heat off themselves. Executive orders have the force of law. Accordingly, the vesture of policy responsibilities in administrative agencies is welcomed by the interest group community because it invites groups to lobby and befriend bureaucrats. By establishing and cementing such relationships, groups gain a "lock" on administrative government, usually for the intermediate to long term. The career incentives of bureaucrats invite such a lock. Most administrative personnel are careerists, and many have spent their professional lives with the same department or bureau. Therefore, they are professionally bonded to the "sanctity" of what they do, and are unlikely to alter that commitment substantially. Interest groups find these agencies and their personnel welcome allies because of their relative permanency on the government scene. The notion of interest group liberalism, discussed above, offers a long-term illustration of the policy results of successful interest group lobbying of the public bureaucracy. Illustrations of this phenomenon will be found later in this chapter.

Fourth, and perhaps most important, interest groups have filled the policy and electoral vacuum left by weakening political parties. As noted above, American political parties, although extra-constitutional in origin, have a two-party bias that has been encouraged, at least in part, by the constitutional principles of separation of powers and federalism. Because we have only two major parties, the rank-and-file composition of each is rather diverse in comparison to that of parties in a multiparty system. This means that parties have two options as intermediary institutions. They can either develop policy positions that consolidate and accommodate their diverse bases, or they can persuade their members to support ideas that the party hierarchy deems are in the best long-term interest of both the party and the country. Parties are weak because they do too much of the former and not enough of the latter. Often, rank-and-file members become increasingly discouraged by the parties' lack of effective stewardship and withdraw from active support of the parties. On the other hand, this endangers the parties' electoral chances unless other forces can step in and do, in the name of the parties, what they could not do for themselves. More often than not, interest groups come to rescue and fill the vacuum. This is especially true for groups that are large, cohesive, well financed, and well led, and whose members are geographically dispersed in ways that make it strategically wise for parties to pay them heed.

Interest groups have, in effect, colonized political parties, remade their agendas, and now determine how party organizations and their candidates for office run their campaigns. For example, it is very difficult to distinguish between what the Republican party supports and what the active interest groups that identify with the party support. This is why the Christian Coalition, the National Rifle Association (NRA), major defense contracting firms, as well as other business and trade groups, have so much leverage in determining the position of Republican candidates on key tax spending, welfare, family, and civil liberty issues. By the same token, Democrats are heavily influenced by organizations such as the National Education Association (NEA), the AFL-CIO, the AARP, and various environ-

mental, women's rights, and consumer groups. It is difficult for the Democrats, as a party, and their candidates for office to take stands in opposition to the policy crusades of these groups. The financial and voting costs are, for the most part, too great.

The virtual impossibility of separating parties as intermediaries from the activist interest group clusters that comprise them means that parties have been forced to prefer policy positions that assuage these groups as singular movements. This is done at the expense of serious party concerns for the big policy issues—those that have multiple causes and that require energy and sacrifice from multiple sources to be addressed effectively. Included here are questions of urban infrastructure, neighborhood blight, quality education, family stability, the environment, the costs of health care, and the long-term integrity of the Social Security system. To be sure, political parties devote much rhetoric to the need to combat these problems, and occasionally policymakers enact laws which joust with them in peripheral ways. However, history has shown that it takes a crisis to get policymakers to focus on them seriously.

One of the most serious problems confronting American government is the decline in the power of political parties and the concomitant growth in the power of interest groups. Political parties were born during the Constitution's first decade as institutions dedicated to the mobilization of public support to overcome the atomizing effects of separation of powers and checks and balances. History shows clearly that it has been the policy mandates generated by strong party organizations through elections that have brought about America's major social and economic reforms. Obvious examples are the New Deal and Great Society reforms. More fleeting ones include the Reagan Revolution and, on a much lesser scale, the Republican Revolution of 1994.

In general, political parties have lost their traditional appeal, and to some perhaps even their legitimacy. Owing to the impact of television on campaigns, parties have lost their role as contact points between candidates and voters. This trend has been gradual, extending back perhaps half a century. However, it reached a peak that would be difficult to surpass in the 1996 elections when the national committees of both political parties became the direct sources of subsidy for interest groups. In effect, this was a direct reversal of the traditional party–group campaign relationship. The Republican National Committee sent more than $5 million to organizations such as Americans for Tax Reform and the National Right to Life Committee. The Democratic National Committee sent smaller amounts to numerous minority groups to be spent in voter registration efforts.[20] Sometimes labeled the "astroturf" strategy, this is but one example of how interest group efforts have turned dramatically to grass-roots maneuvers in an effort to engender spontaneous constituent support for items on the groups' agendas. Most groups have hopped on the grass-roots bandwagon for fear of losing the policy clout they so treasure. Borrowing political party strategies, they build up grass-roots good will for their programs and expect votes for candidates who support their causes. In terms of "support for the cause" strategies, interest groups are behaving much like political parties have traditionally behaved.

Group agendas, in contrast to those traditionally presented by political parties, are distinctly self-serving in cast. They seek to protect themselves and advance their policy causes through the sanctity of the law. They want subsidies, licenses, tax breaks, economic security, insurance, and regulatory relief. They want to blur the distinction between the public and private sectors. In short, they want to institutionalize the politics of dependency, discussed earlier in this chapter. They do not have the immobilization of government in mind when they adopt these strategies and make these claims, but all too often that is the result. Governments become so committed to nourishing group agendas that they cannot afford to do much else. In the meantime, the big issues receive little serious attention in the law. They require sacrifice and planning, and the benefits are mostly long term. In sum, the kinds of policy changes the nation needs are the very kinds of changes that interest groups resist. While career-conscious policymakers may well realize this, they cannot muster the courage to do much about it. Their response is to pay lip service to the need to do something, postpone serious consideration of the problems, and occasionally enact token, piecemeal legislation that has little but symbolic value. In short, political leaders dodge and evade, lest they antagonize key vested interests upon which they have grown to depend.

Interest Groups as Intermediaries: The Policy Consequences

Interest groups provide policy leverage for individuals who share a common goal. In theory, they transpose the notion of political equality from a focus on the individual to a focus on the group. Democratic theory assumes that individuals are equal as voters and before the law. Insofar as the transmission of opinions from their source to decision arenas is concerned, the political system should not play favorites. Only after legislatures and administrative agencies have received and interpreted all opinion transmissions should policy decisions be made. At that point the qualitative, or judgmental, factor enters the picture, because policymakers will, for several reasons, consider some opinions to be more relevant than others to the policy issue at hand.

As conduits of public opinion, what do interest groups do to the notion of political equality? In short, they distort it. By registering opinion collectively through the group mechanism, some opinions become more equal than others. A representational edge goes to individuals who are affiliated with highly cohesive, well-financed, and well-organized groups. Schattschneider was correct. There is a bias to the pressure system. That bias plays itself out in campaign finance strategies, appointments to key administrative and legislative staff positions, and in the development of group policy allies within government. Therefore, if classic democratic theory is the standard, interest groups are not effective intermediaries. If leveraging a situationally advantaged interest group's point of view in the most effective way is the standard, then interest groups are very effective. However, democratic theory enshrines representational equality. By this measure, groups do not fare well. Consider the following case examples. Each offers an opportunity to appreciate how organized minorities (groups) can defeat unorganized majorities. It is the unorganized majorities whose opinions are denied the access and fair consideration assumed by democratic theory. For that reason, the credibility of the interest group system as an effective intermediary should be questioned.

The Government "Chain-Saw Massacre"

Established in 1995, the Emergency Salvage Timber Sale Program became law as a rider to an appropriations bill. It received no committee consideration whatsoever in either the House or the Senate. It was attached to the appropriations bill during floor debate in the House. The program authorized logging companies to cut and process salvage timber located in national forests. Salvageable timber is presumed to be below average in quality,

and therefore to harvest it would do little, if any, damage to the forest and the ecosystem. However, the law is so nebulous on the definition of salvage timber, that timber companies have, in effect, the authority to harvest most trees located on federal lands if they so choose. The law's definition of salvageable timber includes that timber located in parts of a forest that are "lacking the characteristics of a healthy and viable ecosystem."[21] This is a very amorphous definition and, in effect, could make most sections of a forest open to harvesting if the terms "healthy" and "viable" were interpreted liberally. The law then proceeded to suspend the application of six environmentally conscious laws that sought to protect all sections of forests from uncensored logging, and made them inapplicable to salvageable sections of forests. Included were the National Environmental Policy Act, the Multiple Use Sustained Yield Act, and the Endangered Species Act. It also denied citizens the right to sue the U.S. Forest Service for careless logging decisions in the salvageable sections. Finally, it declared earlier court decisions outlawing timber sales in the newly designated areas to be null and void.[22]

The new effect of this rider was to open sections of forests to logging that were previously off-limits because of the potential threat it would pose to the environment. The rider, in effect, released the timber companies from any effective constraint they would face from environmental interests or from proenvironment laws, provided that the companies could secure Forest Service permission to harvest timber in liberally defined salvageable areas. This is usually not difficult because of the close relationship that has developed between the Forest Service and the timber companies over time. The Forest Service is simply doing its job—that of providing permits for companies to log trees in national forests. Looking at the question in context, and thereby considering the public interest, is not part of the agency's official mission. It finds it strategically unwise to do so. Of course, so do the timber companies.

This case is just one example of a trend that Paul Roberts has termed the federal "chain-saw massacre." The close ties between the Forest Service and the timber companies has allowed the Forest Service to use its policy discretion to license the logging of U.S. forests under the pretense of preserving them. In addition to the ultra-generous "spin" it places on the term "salvageable," the Forest Service has legal authorization to remove diseased or "sick" trees in order to reduce or prevent the spread of diseases to surrounding trees. According to Roberts, the effect of such an empowerment has been to permit the Service to "treat" diseased trees (the official term) by categorizing virtually any section of any forest, regardless of its condition, as sick and therefore available for logging privileges. It has done exactly that, virtually with reckless abandon, all officially in the name of conservation and disease-free trees. In effect, it is virtually impossible to distinguish between the interests of the logging industry and the proclamations of the Forest Service. Paul argues that the Forest Service "is essentially a timber bureaucracy . . . whose budget is tied to the number of trees it can 'harvest' and whose managers have long been rewarded for keeping those harvests high—even if it means selling trees at a loss or breaking environmental laws."[23] All this is done with the blessing of House and Senate members whose political fortunes are closely tied to their support of the timber industry. The model of a classic iron triangle, such an alliance has, according to Roberts, "put the Forest Service, Congress, and industry in a mutually beneficial trinity."[24]

It is important to note that the general public, by paying taxes, has subsidized the timber industry by making it convenient for the companies to gain access to forest areas.

Tax dollars have built roads to provide access to timber, and other laws have allowed major equipment expense tax write-offs for the companies. However, unless laws restrain resource exploitation, long-term ecological damage could be the result. For example, the removal of trees from watershed areas interferes with the ability of fish to breed effectively. The natural beauty and recreation potential of some areas could be seriously threatened. Logging interferes with water table levels and the ability of various forms of wildlife to survive. In short, the general public is likely to be unsympathetic with the immediate and long-term results of the 1995 rider. It became law nonetheless.

These events offer excellent illustrations of how vested interests privatize public policy to serve their own ends—not by contract, but by cooptation and by politics. The timber lobby is strongest in the West, an area of sparsely populated states. These states, nonetheless, have representation in the Senate (due to federalism) equal to much more highly populated states. This offers vested interests in these states policy leverage they would not have were their strength concentrated in the highly populated states. It also illustrates how the ideologically based argument against "big government" in principle is more effective as a symbolic political ploy than as a guideline for constraining government functions and reducing costs. In this case, group forces that had traditionally complained about the invasive powers of big government were employing the power of the national government to serve their own ends. In effect, there was no real distinction between what the law provided and what the timber companies and the Forest Service wanted. However, it is unlikely that most citizens and taxpayers wanted it.

Often House and Senate members attach group friendly riders to major bills, knowing that the chances of their inclusion in law is slim. During the 104th Congress (1995–1997), several attempts were made to exempt industries from the Environmental Protection Agency's clean-up efforts in specific congressional districts. Expecting to lose the ultimate struggle, legislators introduced the riders anyway, and for sound political reasons. Any official favor currying by legislators, especially committee and subcommittee chairs, is likely to result in continued support by industry-sponsored Political Action Committees (PACs) in future elections. All that is necessary is to show the PACs that you are on their side, whether your crusade on their behalf is successful or not.

"Wise Use" Politics

Another example of interest groups targeting resource exploitation and development is framed very clearly by the constitutional principle of federalism. The wise use movement is a coalition of grazing, mining, oil, and timber interests based in the American West that seeks to open government-regulated land to resource exploitation and development. As a coalition of developmental activists, it seeks to unravel many of the gains made by the environmental movement since the 1970s. The term "wise use" was first introduced by the nation's first head of the Forest Service, who employed it to argue for a balance between exploitation and conservation on undeveloped land. The land had to be put to wise use or it should not be subject to development. The wise use movement seeks to reverse Pinchot's standard and give the edge to development over conservation.[25]

Environmentalism's gains during the 1970s were at both the national and state levels. Nationally, the Environmental Protection Agency was created, and clean air and water legislation was enacted. Within states and the court systems, many environmental advocates were successful in efforts to hold corporations responsible for pollution and in efforts to restrict the unrestrained development of wetlands and forest areas. The recent wise use movement represents, so to speak, a counterrevolution to the environmental revolution of the 1970s. Although effectively challenged by grass-roots environmentalists on some fronts in some states, it has enjoyed considerable success, in part because it has effectively exploited the jurisdiction of states over key developmental decisions. Since other regions of the country are more likely to be proenvironment, it is advantageous for these efforts to be sponsored in states in the West, where the mood is decidedly more developmental. The West is more dependent on the development of natural resources for economic growth. Other sections of the country are much less so. Consequently, many westerners viewed the environmental revolution of the 1970s as the work of easterners who were totally insensitive to western community quests for local prosperity.

The result has been the creation of scores of antienvironment organizations spread throughout the West. They target state legislatures for prodevelopment alterations to existing environmental policies. They adopt populist-sounding names such as People for the West, and describe themselves as grass roots in origin. In effect, the grass-roots ploy is merely a smokescreen to make corporate lobbying appear more symbolically respectable. In the case of People for the West, in 1992 nearly all its total budget ($1.7 million) was donated by resource-based firms such as Cyprus Minerals, Chevron, Hecla Mining, and NERCO Minerals. Its corporate membership included companies such as Boise Cascade and Pacific Power and Light. ASARCO's coordinator of state legislative affairs was its chairman.[26] These organizations have used their corporate funding to sponsor petitions, produce antienvironment bumper stickers, and hold rallies. One of their primary concerns, pursued successfully to this point, is the preservation of a century-old law that allows cheap corporate access to mineral resources on federal property. Other groups and their crusades include the Idaho Association of Commerce and Industry's successful campaign to enact an "audit privilege" statute for Idaho which permits companies to audit environmental violations for which they were responsible, and grants companies penalty immunity.[27] Wyoming enacted a similar law, and similar bills have been introduced in most states. In Idaho, nearly one-fourth of all campaign contributions came from developmental firms. The results speak for themselves. In addition to the audit privilege law, the Idaho legislature passed laws which established a heavily endowed "constitutional defense fund" to support efforts by the state to challenge the federal government's right to control the exploitation of mineral resources on its own land. In an effort to prevent environmentalists from purchasing land leases, the Idaho legislature passed a law allowing leases to go only to ranchers.[28]

The wise use movement has not gone unchallenged. Environmentalists have also used well-organized, group-coalition campaigns to defeat many developmental campaigns in the state of Washington, where a dispute between environmentalists and the timber industry has been underway for years. Environmentalists joined with labor unions, women's groups, and civic organizations to defeat key developmental initiatives in the 1996 elections. In sum, both industry and environmental groups have found it strategically advantageous to fight for their causes at the state, rather than the federal, level. The lines are rather clearly drawn, the stakes are clear, the enemy is easy to identify, and the ability to win is enhanced by the subnational nature of the jurisdiction.

The two case examples discussed above illustrate the relatively unrestrained impact of vested interest on forests, water, and mineral resources and how the principle of federalism

can be an ally to groups seeking such advantages. However, such successes can do irreparable long-term damage to both the public interest and the interest of groups exploiting the resources. It is often to the long-term benefit of private interests to collaborate with government and forces representing the environment as they—the private interests—seek to maximize their long-term economic potential. Failure to do so could significantly compromise group goals, or even lead to disaster. What economists call the "tragedy of the commons" could well be relevant. Consider the hypothetical situation of a forest that is made available to several companies for logging purposes with virtually no harvesting limitations. Since each firm is in the business of maximizing profits, each sees no utilitarian value in collaborating with other firms to limit the number of trees harvested. Furthermore, each firm believes that government regulation of the free market is bad in principle. After a time, the companies realize that there are fewer and fewer healthy trees to harvest. They then increase logging activities until the tree supply is exhausted. Firms then find themselves either out of business or forced to relocate at considerable cost. In addition, the depletion of the forest has a negative impact on area wildlife, the soil, the attractiveness of the area to tourists, and property values. In short, everyone, including the vested interests, loses. This is called the "tragedy of the commons."

Hard Choices on Hold

The public interest is usually advanced if government enacts policies that deal with problems proactively. To be proactive in stance is to, so to speak, head major problems off at the pass. Enact legislation now that will prevent a potential problem from reaching crisis proportion in the future. However, such a posture has little immediate reward, and politicians are inclined to delay serious consideration of critical problems in ways that permit them to have the best of both worlds. They deal with the problem symbolically by authorizing studies of it, thereby postponing the agonizing experience of legislating sacrifice until sometime in the future. Such a strategy is encouraged further if government has a weak underlying party structure, as has been the case since the mid-1970s.

Interest groups often profit by political strategies designed to delay consideration of a problem by researching and studying it. An excellent case in point is the role of interest groups in encouraging the Clinton administration and Congress to delay consideration of how to deal with the projected health and retirement expenses of an increasingly aging society faced with a diminishing income base to provide for those expenses. The United States will be faced with an unprecedented demographic crisis if government doesn't approach this problem more proactively. The first wave of the so-called baby boomers will reach age 65 in the year 2011 and, unless steps are taken well in advance of that date, Social Security and Medicare expenses, together with the revenue necessary to service the national debt, threaten to consume all the anticipated revenue for that year and, of course, subsequent years. The way to avoid such a crisis is to act proactively to reduce the current drain on these budgets and provide for an increase in future revenue. However, policies that require a reduction of payouts, a delay in the retirement age, and tightening of eligibility requirements for medical assistance and retirement age are very unpopular with that segment of the public that would be forced to sacrifice now or in the not too distant future. Therefore, groups representing these interests enter the political fray on the side of delay. In 1995 a government study commission recommended changes such as those mentioned above, and the report was

ignored. Subsequently, a commission of distinguished economists argued for a reduction of inflation-adjusted Social Security increases after concluding that the Consumer Price Index had overprojected inflation by about 1 percent per year. A 1 percent reduction in Social Security, to bring payments more in line with the true inflation rate, would save the government approximately a trillion dollars over a twelve-year period.[29]

Such a cut, although obviously modest, was more of a sacrifice than the AARP would be willing to tolerate. With membership of over 33 million, its political base was indeed widespread, affecting many people in all constituencies, presidential and congressional. Soon after the commission published its report, AARP executive director Horace Deets announced the group's opposition to it, arguing that the net result would be to subject all people on Social Security or other benefit and pension plans to the ravages of inflation, thereby destroying the advantages they then enjoyed. AFL-CIO president John Sweeney and Teamsters president Ron Carey argued that the idea amounted to, in essence, a tax increase on workers, poor people, and the elderly.[30]

With such widespread, formidable opposition as this, it is not surprising that the response of policymakers, from the president on down, was to sidestep the issue. The White House suggested that President Clinton had reservations about the proposal and wanted to study the issue further. The Republican congressional majority leadership indicated they would consider the idea only if President Clinton endorsed it first. Both sides were reluctant to ask for sacrifice from such powerful groups with such widespread political bases. A few legislators, such as Senator Bob Kerrey (D–Nebraska), supported the suggestion, primarily because facts simply don't lie.

The Social Security dilemma is a good example of a current policy problem that has been slowed or paralyzed by the symbolism of study and analysis. Many pressing issues have been subject to the same strategies successfully in the past, and they continue today. Many of them have constitutional politics as a source of procedural legitimacy. The issue of carcinogens in food is an excellent example. For years the agribusiness industry has insisted that the constitutional guarantee of due process of the law be applied to chemicals as well as to people. Therefore, a food additive or chemical applied to fruits and vegetables during the growing cycle should not be banned as a carcinogen (possibly cancer-inducing) until it has undergone multiple, rigorous tests on laboratory animals over a long period of time, with some of the studies being conducted by the industries themselves. If the results are negative for the industry, then begins another long-term process of appeal. In the meantime, foods that have absorbed possible cancer-inducing chemicals into their genetic construct are still being consumed by people, to the economic benefit of the growers and marketers. If a cancer epidemic develops as a result of this, then the costs of dealing with it will be prohibitive, not unlike the costs of waiting to deal with the Social Security issue until the first of the baby boomer generation begins to retire. In short, unaddressed major policy challenges ultimately become major policy crises.

Government desperately needs institutional support from strong political parties that can make austerity, sacrifice, and proactive policies seem logical, and therefore politically astute. The net result of this would be to weaken the policy influence of interest groups. It is difficult to weaken the policy influence of interest groups in any way other than by suppression by party. The Constitution's First Amendment affords them a situational advantage that is reinforced by the dedication of their members to their causes. Sacrifice as a policy option must at least be

brought to equilibrium status with indulgence. This can be accomplished only if political parties and their leaders begin to sell sacrifice as an advantage rather than a disadvantage. This can only be done if political parties renew the roles they played during the Jefferson, Franklin Roosevelt, Lyndon Johnson, and (for a brief period) Reagan administrations. The experiences with the Social Security issue discussed above illustrate how important strong interest groups are to virtually guaranteeing leadership timidity under weak government conditions. Columnist David Broder summarized it well in observing that weak governments produce bad policy, and weak parties produce weak governments.[31]

Corporate Welfare

What reformists have termed corporate welfare is probably the best example of the invidious cooptation of public authority by vested interests. It can best be illustrated by describing the condition, along with illustrations, than by focusing on how one or a few vested interests succeeded in gaining it for their company or industry. It is one condition that, by its very nature, scorns taxpayer interests by securing government handouts for interest groups. Because of the special interests' role in political campaigns, these programs were on the increase during the 1980s and 1990s, while programs such as education, child nutrition, and health care were being threatened with budget cuts.

Handouts come in assorted packages. The most direct form is a subsidy to market a product, as has been the case with government subsidies of large California wineries' programs to market their products abroad. The official defense of such a policy is that it helps promote domestic employment by the wine industry if foreign advertising is successful. However, subsidies have not been available to small wineries which could also employ more people if their markets were to expand. The large wineries have very active PAC operations. The small ones do not. Several giant food and restaurant corporations, such as McDonald's, Pillsbury, Tyson Foods, and Conagra, have received subsidies to advertise their products overseas. Products such as pet food, frozen french fries, fast foods, and oranges have been targeted for foreign advertising subsidies.

The cost to taxpayers of these programs has been estimated at over $6 billion a year. Corporations that profit from such subsidies contributed an estimated $53 million to congressional campaigns between 1986 and 1996. Commercial shipping firms that agree to permit the military services to use their vessels during wartime receive hefty annual subsidies in return for the government option. Although such a program is obsolete and of no use to the government in today's world of high-tech warfare, Congress has been very reluctant to modify the policy. Some vessels receive up to $2 million a year in subsidies. Congress is reluctant to abandon the policy outright because the maritime industry contributed approximately $18 million to congressional campaigns between 1986 and 1996.[32]

Another type of corporate handout at the public's expense is the indirect subsidy. Indirect subsidies allow corporations to use government land and other resources at very attractive prices or contract terms, often after public money has made the resources accessible. The logging rider case discussed above is one example of an indirect subsidy policy. Another example, perhaps more outrageous, has been the virtually free resource exploitation that has occurred by virtue of the General Mining Law of 1872. This law was passed at a time when business activity desperately needed priming. It allowed, and still allows, business to extract minerals on federal lands

without paying any royalties whatsoever. Since 1872, the federal government has been compelled to sell land containing upwards of $15 billion worth of reserves for less than $20 thousand. Congress has found it strategically advantageous to leave the law untouched. Had the law insisted on the fair value of the extracted minerals, it could yield up to $200 million a year in federal revenue. PAC organizations representing oil, gas, coal, and the utility industries were the third largest contributors to congressional campaigns between 1981 and 1996.[33]

Interest Groups and the Parasite Culture

As the federal government's policy responsibilities have grown, so have the costs of campaigning for office. Interest groups realized early on that the growth of government's policy responsibilities meant that they, the groups, had a growing stake in how those responsibilities were translated into policy. In essence, two choices were available. Groups could have taken their chances, been relatively uninvolved, and hoped that policies would not restrict their quests for markets and profits too greatly. Or, they could have worked actively to prevent restrictive government controls and, even better, colonize government power and convert it to their own use. Needless to say, the latter option is the most natural, considering the incentives underpinning capitalist ideology. Groups came to Washington in droves to lobby Congress and a bureaucracy that was being awarded increasing amounts of policy discretion. They came in the form of lawyers and lobbyists, to try to leverage their influence by impacting on statutory language directly, by interpreting vague legal phraseology in ways that served their interests, and by insisting on a long list of procedures that guaranteed firm due process of the law before agencies could issue regulations constricting their rights to markets or products. They came for concessions, licenses, tax breaks, subsidies, and regulatory relief. They came to make friends with legislators and administrators and to show these policymakers how much they had in common with the interest group community. In short, interest groups came to Washington in peace to help out.

What better way available to help career-conscious legislators or presidents than to help them secure their careers or, in the case of presidents, their niche in history? One obvious way to accomplish this was to help these officials gain reelection so that they had a chance to make their political and policy marks. Therefore, financial contributions to campaigns appeared to be a cost-effective strategy. Campaigns were becoming increasingly expensive, primarily because of the cost of television advertising, and so these offers were well received. The Federal Election Campaign Act of 1974 restricted organizational contributions to campaigns to $5 thousand per organization per campaign. Therefore, the logical choice was for each group to establish several separate campaign-focused organizations, each of which would have the right to contribute the maximum to a campaign.

Thus, Political Action Committees (PACs) were born, and politics and policy have been marked indelibly by them. They have made legislators and presidents dependent on them for vital campaign support and, like it or not, the public has to accept the policy fallout. A premium is placed on legislative incumbency because once you have an ally, it is best to keep him/her in office for as long as possible. Therefore, most PAC contributions go to incumbents. A heavy majority (upwards of 90 percent) are usually returned to office. As a result intelligent, energetic, challengers to incumbents usually have little chance of gaining

office, depriving the public and policy of the chance to fresh approaches into policies.

Most important, however, these events have created what Kevin Phillips has called a "parasite" culture in Washington.[34] The bias of the interest group, or pluralist, system has become ensconced inside the capital beltway. By exploiting the fragmented power conditions established by the separation of powers, well-to-do lobbies have succeeded in converting government to their own use by putting their expertise, the law, and election strategies to good use. They use the Constitution's fragmentation of policy power to defeat or heavily mitigate legislation they find oppressive to their interest. They offer administrative agencies impacted by a "dual boss" problem that is encouraged, in effect, by the Constitution's separation of powers system, vital long-term support for policies that are of mutual interest to them. They employ the constitutionally rooted guarantee of due process of the law to instill a "paralysis by analysis" state of affairs within Congress and, especially, administrative agencies. The politics of delay has several rewards. It usually favors compromise. It permits public concern over a policy imperative to dissipate and become, therefore, much less of an imperative. Most important, it permits the policy status quo to continue to the group's advantage as long as the decision process takes.

In conclusion, if balance, fairness, equity, and an overriding concern for the common good are the criteria for effective intermediary performance in the American political system (and they should be), the interest group complex does not fare well. Constitutional politics amplifies the negative effects of a system that has, due to what might be termed "political Darwinism," come to be very unrepresentative of people or the interest group complex as a whole. This, of course, is a reflection of more fundamental problems in the political system. Voter apathy and weak political parties have created a government too weak at its roots to suppress the excesses of the interest group system described and analyzed above. The job of government is to govern, not to register and support the indulgences of the parasite culture.

Endnotes

1. Committee for the Study of the American Electorate, "Use of Media Principal Reason Campaign Costs Skyrocket" (http://www.Tap.epn.org/csae.media.htm). The committee drew its conclusions from data supplied it by the Public Records Division of the Federal Election Commission.

2. Curtis Gans, "Stop the Madness!" *The Washington Monthly*, vol. 29, no. 5 (May 1997), p. 21.

3. *Ibid.*

4. R. Morris Barrett, "The Price of Pork," *CNN/Time* (http://www.allpolitics.com/1997/gen/resources/pork/), (June 9, 1997), p. 2.

5. *Ibid.*, p. 3.

6. Brian Kelly, *Adventures in Porkland: How Washington Wastes Your Money and Why They Won't Stop* (New York: Villard Books, 1992), pp. 131–133.

7. Citizens Against Government Waste. As reported in "Fiscal 1997 Per Capita Pork Spending, Plus State Totals" (http://www.allpolitics.com/1997/gen/resources/pork/percapita/).

8. Ben Wildavsky, "Pigging Out," *National Journal*, vol. 29, no. 16 (April 19, 1997), p. 757.

9. Anthony King, "Running Scared," *The Atlantic Monthly*, vol. 279, no. 1 (January 1997), pp. 41–61. This essay offers an exellent overview of the causes and costs of the constant campaign mentality.

10. *Ibid.*, p. 44.

11. *Ibid.*

12. *Ibid.*, p. 47.

13. *Ibid.*

14. *Ibid.*, p. 48.

15. *Ibid.* For an assessment of how constitutional structure and electoral pressures encourage the same response from presidents, see Bruce Buchanan, *The Presidential Experience: What the Office Does to the Man* (Englewood Cliffs, N.J.: Prentice Hall, 1978).

16. *The Federalist Papers.*

17. E. E. Schattschneider, *The Semi-Sovereign People: A Realist's View of Democracy in America* (New York: Holt, Rinehart & Winston, 1960), p. 40.

18. This thesis is explored thoroughly in David B. Truman, *The Governmental Process* (New York: Knopf, 1951).

19. See Theodore J. Lowi, *The End of Liberalism: The Second Republic of the United States,* 2nd ed. (New York: W. W. Norton, 1979).

20. David S. Broder, "News of the Weak," *Washington Post National Weekly Edition,* (January 31, 1997), p. 21.

21. Ralph Nader, "Logging Without Laws," *Liberal Opinion Week*, vol. 7, no.7 (April 22, 1996), p. 1.

22. *Ibid.*

23. Paul Roberts, "The Federal Chain-Saw Massacre: Clinton's Forest Service and Clear-Cut Corruption," *Harper's Magazine*, vol. 294, no. 1765 (June 1996), p. 38.

24. *Ibid.*, p. 41.

25. Samantha Sanchez, "How the West Is Won: Astroturf Lobbying and the Wise Use Movement," *The American Prospect*, no. 25 (March-April 1996), pp. 37–42.

26. *Ibid.*

27. *Ibid.*

28. *Ibid.*

29. Broder, *op. cit.*

30. *Ibid.*, p. 22.

31. *Ibid.*

32. Common Cause, *The Costs of Corporate Welfare*, 1997.

33. *Ibid.*

34. Kevin Phillips, *Arrogant Capital* (Boston: Little, Brown, 1994).

chapter six

The Media

Policy Intermediaries, Technology, and Marketplace Politics

The mass media are of three genres: print journalism, radio, and television. Each seeks both to inform and entertain. Presumably, there exists a clear line of demarcation between the information and entertainment roles. Individuals either read newspapers and magazines, listen to or view programs that inform them about public affairs and public policy, or they do the same while searching for entertainment. In the past, rather clear distinctions could be drawn between news, the analysis of news, and entertainment. That is much less the case today.

The Media and the News: The Post-Watergate Era

The media are essential to a healthy democracy, but they are not elected. Therefore, presumably their role responsibilities as businesses will be congruent with the transmission and analysis of news in ways that contribute to an informed public. Another presumption is that they, as well as the public, will agree generally on the definition of what constitutes news. Both of these presumptions have been brought into question in light of the media's behavior since the Watergate crisis. While journalism has always responded to the attack instinct, since the Watergate incident it has increasingly become more of a media standard than an exception. In addition, the definition of news has also been altered significantly, with sensationalism and scandal becoming more the norm than the exception.

Cognizant of this, politicians—both candidates and incumbents—respond accordingly. They search for the notorious and unusual in events and in their opponents' backgrounds and increasingly frame their campaign and policy agenda priorities around them. Politics and policymaking have increasingly become a blood sport in response to changing press standards. It is easy to attack ideas or individuals because of their genetically unsavory qualities or to assault a political opponent's background because of a questionable event, public or private.

It hasn't always been this way. Before Watergate, especially during periods of crisis, the press, politicians, and the public were usually allies in the search for the truth about what caused a government problem or crisis, as well as on how to deal with it sensibly and expeditiously. If politicians were rumored to be involved in questionable relationships with members of the opposite sex, the media usually ignored the subject because it was unethical to report on and analyze events that apparently had nothing to do with the challenge of governing. The Vietnam War began to change this. Television brought the war directly into homes. As casualties mounted and progress seemed to be slow in coming, reporters began to question the rationale behind the commitment in the first place. Having lost most of the public's support for the war, President Johnson decided not to seek reelection in 1968.

However, the shift was cemented half a decade later with the Watergate crisis and President Nixon's resignation in the face of a House impeachment inquiry. The work of two *Washington Post* investigative reporters, Bob Woodward and Carl Bernstein, successfully exposed the crisis and, in so doing, changed the standards of journalism for an indeterminate future. Woodward and Bernstein did the public, the Constitution, perhaps even our democracy a major service, and the media's reputation probably never stood taller than in the immediate wake of the Watergate incident. The media's subscription to the old rule of not questioning authority no longer held. Watergate changed the way journalists viewed themselves and defined a new norm for the entire profession. Suddenly it became the media's moral obligation to question authority, as well as the personal lives

of politicians, especially presidents. The "gate" standard became the window through which the media's skepticism impacted the presidency. Watergate was succeeded by Iran-Contragate, Whitewatergate, Filegate, and Monicagate. The media began to look for conflict, controversy, and unbecoming events in the private lives of presidents as well as other politicians. Moreover, these events became news. Not only were they different, they were all sensationalist in cast, and many had a tabloid flavor to them.

The advent of cable television increased the number of news networks, news programs, and talk shows. There was not enough traditional news to fill the time available, so the vacuum was filled by items production staffs thought would interest the viewing public. The norm gradually became to select something interesting and make it news, instead of uncovering the news and finding ways to make it interesting. The news and talk shows needed to make the news significant. Audiences are attracted by adding a bit of speculation and spice to the stories under discussion. Allegations about sex or money scandals do not have to be verified to make air time and, in effect, become news. Furthermore, improvements in technology make it easier to research individuals' backgrounds in the hope of finding something possibly unseemly and therefore newsworthy. In short, forget about making something important interesting; concentrate instead on making something interesting important. Moreover, call it the "news."

This has been the media's response to the Watergate incident. Since Watergate, politicians have had to perform on a stage conditioned by these new media norms. The implications for politics, policy, and democracy are significant indeed. They have muddled the difference between the public and private lives of politicians. Private events have become legitimate and significant political issues. Furthermore, the trust that had been built up among the people, their government, and the press in the pre-Watergate period has been compromised. Such trust is essential during periods of stress and crisis, and government may not be able to rely on it in future crises. Furthermore, these events have contributed to public cynicism about the integrity of the press and politicians and, ultimately, about government. In turn, this reduces citizen interest in politics, cuts into voter turnout in elections, and allows the organized few to make public policy for the disorganized and disinterested many. In short, it is a prescription for minority rule in a system that presumably defines democracy as majority rule.

News as Entertainment

Most people have been drawn to electronic journalism, or television, as their primary source of both news and home-centered entertainment. The average American adult watches almost 1,500 hours of television programming a year.[1] Television was introduced as an entertainment medium and it has grown in response to viewer (consumer) demand for more of the same. Private firms own and operate most television stations, most of which have network affiliations. Competition for the viewing audience is keen. Each network and its local affiliates want to offer the most appealing program menu in the hope of capturing as large a percentage of the viewing audience as possible. Consequently, there is a tendency for television programming to blur the distinction between news and entertainment. The more of an entertainment flavor a program has, regardless of its true purpose, the more likely for it to attract a respectable percentage of the viewing public. Disasters, sex, and crime play well in fiction, and they play well as the news. Policy issues get a few seconds' coverage as a transition to the coverage of such items as the sex lives of public figures, including the president, or the trial of an ex football player accused of murder. The main criterion for public service broadcasting is what the public needs to know. The principle underlying the entertainment criterion is how much fun or diversion viewers enjoy and/or experience.

Two key events in the 1980s encouraged television news programs to go "show business" in format. Competition for audiences increased dramatically with the advent of cable television and local stations' acquisition of technologies that permitted them to cover events first hand. The three major commercial networks appointed new directors, each of whom attempted to prove his worth by adopting audience-friendly programming strategies. The networks' news divisions were expected to be profitable for the parent company, and therefore were encouraged to adopt a "bottom line" approach to programming—if it sells, go with it; if it doesn't, drop it. Television news magazines such as *Dateline* (NBC), *A Current Affair, Twenty-Twenty* (ABC), *Hardball* (CNBC), and *Turning Point* (ABC) were introduced in the 1990s as a way to feed on viewer craving for the dramatic. Even the modestly successful news magazines can be profitable because they cost much less to produce than do dramatic shows. Both network and local stations found that they could do well financially without public service news compromising their viewer appeal. In response to increasing competitive pressure, any way to make the news profitable is good. News magazines make the news entertaining, are very cost-effective, and can compete effectively for viewers with prime-time entertainment programs. The same sort of logic is behind decisions to offer talk shows and tabloid specials.[2]

Therefore, the presentation of television news and news analysis is often impacted by the entertainment syndrome in ways that significantly influence television's ability to be an effective intermediary between the people and their government. The following section will focus on the character and significance of television, as the public's primary source of information on politics and public affairs, as an intermediary force in the American political system. In addition, it will analyze the role of the Constitution in affording all media venues the opportunity to influence politics and public policy, as well as the role of constitutional politics in determining how those opportunities have been cultivated by media representatives.

The media's mandate as an essential intermediary is found in the First Amendment, which guarantees freedom of the press, freedom of speech, and the right to petition the government for a redress of grievances. The concept of democracy assumes, indeed rests on, the existence of these rights. Classic democracy assumes the existence of an informed public that has studied and debated all sides of an issue before it transmits its opinion to its elected representatives. Furthermore, it assumes that the constructive criticism of all policy options is a necessary prerequisite to citizens becoming informed and government enacting policies appropriate to the problems it seeks to address. The "truth" or, in effect, the most "practical"policy alternative will not be chosen unless these things happen in advance of policy decisions.

These conditions place significant obligations on the press. Reporting and analysis of news is expected to be both high priority and thorough. If the press misrepresents the truth deliberately, the accused perpetrator can be taken to court and sued for libel. The mere existence of this possibility should make news analysis more accurate. In the search for the facts, or the truth, the media can often be intrusive and annoying. However, if the results are the elucidation of facts that have been hidden or forgotten, the analysis of an issue in its historical context, or even the elevation of a theretofore ignored or slighted problem to a spot on the policy agenda, then a free press has served its role as policy intermediary effectively. The press can present and analyze policy options, sponsor debates, and produce editorials or commentaries which trigger responses and debates on issues.

The same is true for elections. Media elements can analyze candidates' records and experiences and the way in which candidates debate issues, and they can help voters and potential voters understand the electoral process. The media has the potential to make the public either optimistic or pessimistic about leaders, policies, and the nation's future. All this is true if, and only if, the media and its spokespersons constantly link what they do and how they do it to the democratic mandate. If they fail to do this, or compromise it significantly, then the results may even be counterproductive. People could become relatively uninformed as to the facts. They could become discouraged, rather than encouraged, about the country's future and the quality of its leaders. They could become apathetic and disinterested in government as a meaningful positive force in their lives and in their communities.

In short, if the media—especially television—blends entertainment and news together and presents them, in effect, as one and the same, its obligation to be democracy's servant has been tainted. Poor or superficial presentation and analysis of news lead to a misinformed public. A misinformed public is subject to manipulation by those who understand how misinformation can be an ally to a cause that would otherwise atrophy. That, in turn, helps put government in the hands of the wrong leaders who make the wrong decisions on the public's behalf. Once realizing this, the public could become pessimistic and cynical and withdraw from civic activity. The result is a major compromise in the foundation of democratic government.

The following discussion will describe and analyze the extent to which the media—

especially television—have fulfilled their intermediary obligations. The hypothesis is that the media have not met their responsibilities, and that they have not done so because they have permitted the politics of the marketplace to interfere with their obligation to be a responsible conduit of information that links, constructively, the public with its policy leaders. This is not because media executives, reporters, and news analysts have forgotten the distinction between news and entertainment. It is because the imperatives of the marketplace and the resultant competition for audiences are so much a part of the media culture that a homogenization of the two is considered to be the only way to compete effectively. This is not to say that some journalism isn't dedicated to the classic role of the media in a democracy. National Public Radio and the Public Broadcasting System, its television counterpart, are dedicated by charter to in-depth news coverage and news analysis. In the form of issue analysis programs such as *Frontline* and *The American Experience* they have regularly offered the public a chance to understand and analyze key political, social, and economic issues. The commercial networks and their local affiliates occasionally offer the same opportunities. However, the viewing audience for these programs is relatively small. Most viewers get their news from the local and network evening and late night news programs. The advent of cable television has cut into these audiences, encouraging commercial television executives to add more of an entertainment flavor to news coverage than existed before cable television became seriously competitive.

The Media's "Competitive Pit"

Television viewers experience regularly the results of what is herein labeled television's "competitive pit"environment. Its roots lie in

the assumption, by television executives and programmers, that drama, sensationalism, and "unusual" stories attract viewers. Furthermore, since news programs must reserve time for commercial advertising, coverage has to be brief and to the point. Neither networks nor local stations can afford not to cover what the competition considers to be a "hot" story. Therefore, brevity of coverage permits programs to keep up with the competition while still maintaining the essential advertising support line. In addition, audience attention can be secured by dramatic, sensationalist spins to regular news stories, and by covering stories that have a violent, scandalous, or hard copy quality. In fact, much of the competition faced by network and local newscasts comes from what might be termed "tabloid" competitors. These are programs that devote entire programs to the coverage of scandals, unsolved crimes, the social and sex lives of public figures, and so on. If newscasts appear to be tainted, or even consumed, by entertainment values, market competition is the reason.

The presentation and analysis of news has been rendered even more competitive by the impact of technology. Communications satellites allow the virtual instant transmission of news events visually around the world within seconds. Rewards go to those networks with the most correspondents and reporters assigned to the world's economic and political "hot spots." In recent years, such competition has become even more keen, because many local stations now have contracts or other agreements with foreign communications firms to transmit news events directly to them, thereby bypassing the major networks. This means that the networks compete with local stations, including their affiliates. A good example of how a network rushed into coverage of an unverified story due to such competition was the experience of the American Broadcasting Company (ABC) and its evening news anchor, Peter Jennings, of presidential candidate Bill Clinton's alleged affair with Gennifer Flowers. Local news sources in Arkansas reported the alleged liaisons and went public with them. ABC decided not to cover the story until more verification could be secured. However, when NBC, CBS, and CNN went with the story on their network newscasts, ABC executives threw caution to the wind and did the same, even though no news source had yet discussed the alleged incidents with either Flowers or Clinton. In a similar vein, all four commercial networks reported that President Clinton's infamous "runway haircut" provided him aboard his plane on a runway at the Los Angeles Airport cost $200 and delayed incoming and outgoing commercial flights. All networks reported both the cost and the traffic confusion as facts when, in effect, neither was true. The haircut did not cost $200 and no airport traffic was inconvenienced.[3]

Because tabloid-like stories increasingly set news agendas, the notion of the press as a news "gatekeeper" has been abandoned or compromised. A free press should be a responsible press, and unless there is a conscious attempt to separate real news from rumors and scandal, along with an attempt to cover stories that truly affect people as citizens and voters, the role of the media as an effective intermediary is compromised. Stories must be verified as best they can before they are aired or published. Increasingly, the "check it out" standard is, itself, out. The "sleaze syndrome" has been brought to mainstream. Tabloids tend to set news agendas. Policy players who are often the subject of the alleged stories become alienated from the press and are less likely to cooperate with reporters on matters of genuine public significance.

As with the tragedy of the commons principle discussed in the previous chapter, when sensationalism becomes cultural, a herd mentality takes over, and reporters representing all media venues compete to see who can be the first to report the most, verified or not. Under these conditions it is important to be first with judgments, not with facts. The field of investigative reporting, such as that undertaken by Woodward and Bernstein during the Watergate incident, has been tainted by the tabloid mentality. Watchdog journalism now has to share the investigative stage with negative reporting and sensationalism. In terms of media attention, President Clinton's association with the Whitewater affair, his questionable 1996 campaign fund-raising efforts, and his affair with Monica Lewinsky were often of higher priority to both print and broadcast journalism than was coverage and analysis of his proposals to reform health care, clean up the environment, "reinvent" government, expand volunteerism, reform welfare, and improve race relations.

The Scandal Scramble: The Media and the Presidency

To illustrate how the media's spin on an event can convert a key policy issue into a somewhat more dramatic and therefore more marketable issue, consider the early stages of the media's treatment of the Clinton administration's 1996 campaign fund-raising activities. In early March 1997, a Sunday edition of the *Washington Post* featured an article by investigative reporter Bob Woodward which focused on Vice-President Al Gore's fund-raising role in the 1996 presidential campaign. The article stressed Gore's role as a "shakedown" figure in his requests for contributions to the Democratic Party. It is common for Sunday morning talk shows to use the *Post* articles as the focus of discussion, and that Sunday was no exception. High-profile Democrats were questioned about the ethics of Gore's work—where it took place, on whose time, and if government facilities or resources were used. In each case the response was no, even though Gore did make some calls from the White House on a private phone line paid for by the Democrats. The following Tuesday, the *Post* headline reported, in essence, that, in Gore's opinion, he had broken no law.[4]

A further examination of Gore's 1996 fund-raising activities did, by mid-1998, raise major questions of propriety, if not legality. However, no such evidence existed when the *Post* article appeared. At that juncture, it was clear that the media were attempting to milk a scandal out of what then appeared to be a serious, concerted party effort to raise campaign funds in a critical election year. No doubt it had taken too much time and involved too much money, and certainly solicitations were made from parties whose legitimate right to involve themselves directly in American elections was questionable.

However, the Clinton-Gore 1996 fund-raising efforts were not the true problem, only a manifestation of it. The real problem was the overextended role of money in elections. However, the talk shows and newspapers chose not to focus on that, at least not in March 1997. Campaigns are so expensive that candidates feel compelled to seek support from nearly every source they can. No doubt, the peripheries of the law are often tested, if not broken. However, the key issue is: What is wrong with the current system of campaign financing that encourages such behavior, and what can be legally done to change it? Clinton was certainly actively involved in raising money, but so had been George Bush and Ronald Reagan before him. He did reward contributors with overnight stays in the Lincoln bedroom, but that could be considered a fringe benefit of incumbency. That practice certainly broke no law. Nor should Clinton's active involvement in the enterprise have been surprising. In effect, he was raising money for what looked to be a formidable Republican challenge in the wake of the 1994 election results. Apparently grappling to

make as much press mileage out of the Clinton-Gore fund-raising activities as possible, one columnist compared Clinton's effort to the Watergate scandal—an event that involved felonies such as breaking and entering, wiretapping, theft, and presidential obstruction of justice.[5]

The key point of this episode is straightforward: What were symptoms of a very serious political problem were infected by the scandal syndrome and sold by the media as the problem itself. Clinton and Gore were certainly not the embodiment of fund-raising ethics in doing what they did the way they did it. However, they did it out of what appeared to be a desperate attempt to level the contributory playing ground which had usually favored the Republicans because of the historical advantages they have had in fund-raising. The most significant "scandal" in this episode was a political process so heavily driven by money that it essentially forced an incumbent president and vice-president to become virtual influence-peddlers in the search for funds. Second, and perhaps most important, the results of those efforts might well have influenced the Clinton administration's position on key policies. If, for example, it could have been firmly established that the administration was allowing contributions from multinational corporations to influence its decisions on international trade policies, that would indeed have been a scandal. The overriding fact of life is that money can buy political access and policy favors. This makes the case for a policy imperative of a different sort—one that limits the role of money in campaigning so that the chances for it to taint policy decisions are diminished. However, that was not the scandal upon which the press focused after the *Post* article appeared. With citizens already desensitized to the "scandal as news" strategy, the media's rather consistent tendency to overplay the nongermane serves mostly to reinforce that paralysis.[6]

Another illustration of how the media's thirst for sensationalist stories undermines its obligation to develop stories from facts rather than hope, and how that hope can become contagious, was its treatment of President Clinton's alleged illegal role in the Whitewater scandal. According to Gene Lyons and the editors of *Harpers Magazine,* the Whitewater episode offered an excellent illustration of how the "status and effrontery of the accuser" encourages reporting accuracy to yield to "semi- or uninformed speculations."[7] According to Lyons, the entire Whitewater affair was introduced in 1992 through a series of articles and editorials by *New York Times* investigative reporter Jeff Gerth. These pieces ignored many of the real facts pertaining to then presidential candidate Clinton's involvement in the failed real estate venture. Instead, the articles pieced together selected events and, in effect, constructed them as an alleged full-blown scandal. Similar to events that led to press exploitation of Clinton's affair with Gennifer Flowers and his badly timed haircut at the Los Angeles airport, reporters' competition for news quickly turned into a highly competitive, pressing search for any fact or rumor that could be converted into a news story. Most major newspapers, including the *Washington Post,* were quick to the scene, many dispatching reporters to Arkansas in an attempt to be the first with the latest on the alleged scandal. According to Lyons, when it became apparent that there was much less there than had originally been expected (and hoped), the media then attempted to restore its credibility by, in effect, joining forces with political opponents of the president by highlighting opponents' statements and extensively covering congressional hearings into the affair. To quote Lyons: "It is always safest to run with the pack, and editors who invest thousands on a scandal don't want to hear that there's no scandal to be found. In the post-Watergate culture, few reporters wish to appear insufficiently prosecutorial—particularly not when the suspects are the president and his wife. By definition they've got to be guilty of something, it may as well be Whitewater."[8]

Probably the most significant example in recent history of the media's exploitation of scandal was its coverage of the Clinton-Lewinsky sex scandal and the congressional reaction to the now infamous Starr report. Serious coverage of public policy issues was virtually abandoned to examine and interpret the details of the relationship, how Congress would treat the Starr report, and if impeachment of the president would follow, which it did. To be sure, the impeachment and trial of a president is a newsworthy item. However, judging by the way the major television networks treated the case, the incident was more about sex and how sexual relationships are defined than it was about the potential price the nation and the world may well have paid because Congress, the president, and the media were so absorbed with the case that major policy issues went unattended. For weeks the affair and the impeachment issue was the lead story on network newscasts and the major subject, often the only subject, discussed on every major television and radio talk show. "Sex sells" is an accepted truism of the media trade, and sex at the Oval Office level sells even better. Despite data that showed the public to be growing increasingly tired of the media's exploitation of the incident, the network and news moguls clung tenaciously to making it the number one global news item. Networks and talk shows attempted to outposition one another with new scoops and spins on the incident. To some it seemed as though there was a race afoot to see which network and which shows could most completely saturate their programming with news and interpretations of the event. Reporters and talk show hosts seemed to be unable to raise any other subject. In short, the Fourth Estate was in the grip of a sex scandal–impeachment frenzy, and trivia, opinions, rumors, and projections of future events were multiplied, embellished, and discussed to death. There is little doubt that the House decision to impeach the president was encouraged by the way the media highlighted the scandal.

The Clinton-Lewinsky episode proved once and for all that the media had become a major, if not *the* major, player in the scandal industry's far-reaching negative impact on politics and government. The scandal industry—an agglomeration of new organizations, networks, reporters, and talk show hosts, along with a few high-profile politicians and (in the Clinton-Lewinsky case) an aggressive special prosecutor—collectively were on a high-pitched, high-speed feeding frenzy without regard to the impact it presaged for media standards and the reputation of future official investigations. The momentum was so high speed that it was virtually impossible for even the most sober minds to recollect that, for this scandal as with all previous scandals, the passage of time would help put the event in a fair perspective, much as it did the Iran-Contra affair a decade earlier. The latter event, treated at its height by the scandal industry as a major constitutional crisis, turned out to be essentially a political event triggered by a bizarre running-amok of the national security bureaucracy. Political historians have not portrayed it as the major criminal incident the scandal industry first pictured it to be. In short, the scandal industry is allowed to feed unabated on the hysteria it generates and, most important, is allowed to equate the degree of effort it invests in the coverage of a scandal with the significance of that event for politics and government. If that effort assumes a hard copy or an "opinion as news" tone, so be it. The media's treatment of the Clinton-Lewinsky episode and the president's impeachment provided one of the best examples of this trend in recent history. Although

the nation's and world's political and economic problems did not wane and the future of the Clinton presidency was at stake, the media continued to highlight the details and interpretations of the scandal and the impeachment proceedings rather than focus on the significance of these events for the presidency, the administration of justice, and how they impacted on the way both the president and Congress were fulfilling, or failing to fulfill, their constitutional policy mandates.

Degeneration at the Hub

All politics, it has been said, is local. In increasing numbers, citizens appear to think that most of the important news is local, or that if any item is newsworthy it will be aired on local newscasts. Research conducted by the Pew Research Center in 1996 showed that 65 percent of adults regularly watched local news programs, and only 42 percent regularly watched network news programs.[9] Often local programs are aired for an hour, and people lose interest in news by the time national newscasts are aired. Networks cannot present local sports and weather forecasts or, of course, local news items. In times past, local news programs were balanced in content and usually delivered in an efficient, responsible way. However, in the early 1970s, some local stations began to recognize that the addition of an entertainment flare to the newscasts was economically profitable because it attracted viewers and was easier and cheaper to produce than a dramatic program. The trend caught on quickly. Local programs expanded from a half-hour in length to up to as much as ninety minutes. Additional programs sometimes appear during the day.

Recognizing that viewers are drawn to shows with a low-keyed, family atmosphere, and to individuals they come to know via the screen, they staffed local reporting and anchor crews with appealing personalities who brought the news to them with a person-to-person flavor. News anchors engage in informal "happy talk" to highlight the newscasters instead of the news.[10] If the news is disturbing, if it is reported by their newscaster friends, it will appear more palatable. Another approach is to emphasize the drama of local events by selecting items that are sensationalist in flavor—murders, lost children, abused women, tornados, mudslides, explosions, insect infestation, and activities of local cult organizations. A 1990 content study of fifty local news programs in the Rocky Mountain area reported that disaster items constituted 53 percent of news content, the more terrible the event the more the coverage. A 1993 *Washington Post* survey found that between 46 and 72 percent of news items carried by area stations dealt with either crime, sex, accidents, public fears, or disasters. Furthermore, a 1990 study conducted by the *Columbia Journalism Review* concluded that, of the thirty-two stories aired on local channels and analyzed by the *Review,* eighteen were either misleading or incorrect. Other research has shown that local news reporters are more likely to accept the interpretations of their interviewees than are newspaper reporters.[11]

The arrival of satellites has made it easier for local reporters to go to the field and transmit live reports, even of nonlocal events. The Cable News Network (CNN) began the practice of feeding some of their footage to local stations, in return for reciprocity of course, and the three other commercial networks (CBS, NBC, ABC) quickly followed suit. The result has been that local stations can now lay claim to being the only news source viewers need. To compete, the national networks became more sensationalist oriented in response. In recent years, even presidential candidates have recognized the advantages of "going local." It improves the odds of a favorable presidential spin. More local than national newscasters are likely to stand in awe of the president, owing to their infrequent contacts with the presidency and relative inexperience with national politics. As a candidate, President Clinton pursued the same course during the New Hampshire primary, largely because the network reporters wanted to concentrate on his alleged affair with Gennifer Flowers. House and Senate members can usually get their commentaries on policy issues videotaped and aired on local channels without editing or criticism. That may well be very effective communication, but it is very poor journalism on the locals' part.[12] Legislators, as well as presidents, are not as likely to get as free a ride with the networks as they do with local stations. In sum, according to Steven Stark, when the obligation of a free press in a democracy is taken into account, local news gives viewers what they want, but definitely not what they need.[13]

Episodic News Bias

Both networks and local stations compete for audiences with what Shanto Iyengar has called an "episodic" news bias.[14] This supplements the penchant for the dramatic as discussed above. However, it is considerably broader in context, encompassing news items that are not dramatic or sensationalist in nature. The episodic bias, or frame, is an episode in a continuing event or part of a larger story. In effect, it is a case example or illustration of a problem. Examples include the devastation a flood has brought to one family, the effect of drug addiction on a single individual, a murder or an attempted murder, or the bombing of a building. This can be compared to another type of news event—one that incorporates a "thematic" bias. Thematic news frames the news in the context of a larger problem. In effect it uses cases to illustrate a larger trend or an overall condition. Examples include the effects of an increase or decrease in the level of spending for welfare, health, education, drug enforcement, and housing. Other examples include the meaning behind terrorist acts, why the education system is producing students without adequate communication skills, or why there will be a squeeze on the Social Security system unless legislation demanding sacrifice is enacted to avoid it. In sum, episodic news presents cases, and thematic news presents a problem in context. Episodes make good pictures, while thematic news encourages good thoughts.[15]

With thirty-minute news programs allowing approximately twenty-one minutes for news presentations, the bias obviously favors episodic news . It is more dramatic, it is covered quickly, and it tells the entire story, in light of the objective. However, it doesn't tell the viewer much that he or she needs to know in order to make a critical judgment about the pros and cons of a given policy. Many news stories are a fusion of the two types. For example, a news story can briefly survey the problem of the homeless in a given city, and then proceed to focus on the plight of one homeless person. However, the bias is to prefer the latter focus to the former. The former is more time consuming, and it encourages reporters or analysts to editorialize. They hesitate to do this for fear of offending key segments of the viewing audience. Reporters would rather cover picketing by striking workers at a work site rather than analyze the causes of the strike. They would rather cover how long individuals have been held hostage and how they are being treated than analyze the events that led up to the taking of the hostages in the first place. This applies to both domestic and international news events, and to election campaigns.

Many analyses of the media's impact on society and government stress the negative results for quality news reporting of the short, sound bite cast to the way reporters cover the news. Iyengar's study of the impact of television on issue framing carries this one step further and focuses on how such coverage affects viewers' political choices. The results are interesting indeed. He examined television audience reaction to both episodic- and thematic-oriented coverage of six key political issues—crime, international terrorism, unemployment, poverty, racial inequality, and the Iran-Contra episode. His purpose was to correlate the audience's attribution of political responsibility for problems with the type of coverage that dominated each issue. He concluded that an episodic bias tends to invoke responses that blame individuals for their own problems, while a thematic focus elicits responses that blame social or economic conditions for the problem. Since television news programming is clearly biased toward the episodic, its ultimate effect is proestablishment, or status quo. It does not encourage citizens to become civic activists who crusade to change conditions that produce such situations as poverty, poor education, delapidated housing, and drug addiction.[16]

The significance of this for the health of a democracy is high, because theoretical democracy assumes an activated, optimistic, community-oriented public. If the episodic bias encourages citizen pessimism and a withdrawal from community activism and political participation, its effect on the health of our democracy is decidedly negative.

Abuse of Professionalism

Journalists like to consider themselves professionals. They are trained to cover and analyze the news objectively with an informed public being the ultimate objective. However, as discussed above, competition among networks and stations interferes, because the trivialization of news content and reporting often does not seem very professional by any standard. Media professionalism can be, and has been, compromised for two other reasons. These were exposed and analyzed by James

Fallows in a 1995 book. Fallows attributed public pessimism toward the media to two conditions. The first is the tendency of some reporters and analysts to be overly committed to being objective in principle when it comes to reporting and analysis. The second is the tendency for some high-level journalist-commentators to garner generous salaries with the expectation that they will dissect politicians and public policies on camera and before lecture audiences.[17]

The first part of the problem is the reporters' preference for analyzing the political backdrop of an issue as opposed to the issue itself. For example, when President Clinton proposed renewing diplomatic relations with Vietnam, most major newspapers focused on the trouble he would probably encounter because he avoided the draft during the Vietnam War. The same approach was taken in the analysis of Clinton's proposals to fund programs for more street-level police, the debates over immigration policy, proposals to reform Medicare, and the debates over how to reform entitlement policies. Projecting possible political fallout from policies is something in which reporters think they excel, and this kind of reporting can be undertaken with a semblance of impartiality. In short, reporters and analysts can be professional when they do this. They have the experience, and it offers them a chance to be neutral as they go about their work. Should they decide to assess the merits and demerits of a policy proposal, a degree of professional impartiality is much more difficult to maintain. In sum, the net effect of such an approach is to evade the real journalistic challenge—that of weighing all sides of the issue as a service to the public. Journalists would rather speculate about whether a medical breakthrough will qualify its originator for the Nobel Prize rather than what it means to the field of medicine. Reporters representing both print and electronic journalism can maintain their objectivity by pursuing scandals

and exposing contradictions in politicians' positions, more than they can if they focus on analyzing the issues. The result is a race, among journalists of all types, to be the best at degrading politics and politicians.

Fallows's second complaint about the present role of the media is the corrupting effect of journalists' demanding and receiving huge fees to address major interest groups and corporations. Politicians are legally prevented from doing this, but media representatives are not. However, much more serious is the practice of some journalists of seeking high fees for appearing on television shows that deliberately incite arguments and shoutfests. This tends to convert reporters into performers, and the prestige of the entire profession suffers. Competition to gain public "one-upmanship" over one's peers turns the profession into a sporting event, thereby debasing its intended mission. The mission of many high-profile journalists has changed from one of healthy skepticism about politicians and government to one of corrosive cynicism about both. It is time to rework the media's priorities.

Fallows is optimistic that this state of affairs can be reversed. He points to the increasing popularity of National Public Radio (NPR) as a source for news. Programs such as ABC's *Nightline* began as experiments and have become popular. In addition, the increasing use of the Internet offers individuals the opportunity to consult sites that, by nature of the venue, must necessarily deal with policy and political substance rather than with their more flamboyant, and dysfunctional, by-products.[18]

The Media as Intermediaries: The Election Connection

Elections are the major dynamic linking the people have with their government. Whether one subscribes to the notion that elections represent referenda on how existing leaders are performing, or whether they represent ways to transmit public opinion directly to decision arenas, elections are crucial. Elections offer candidates the opportunity to present their policy priorities and defend them. They offer voters the chance to judge a candidate's character and leadership qualities. They offer voters opportunities to insist that candidates show serious allegiance to the party as a center of policy doctrine, or to insist that candidates be their own person, representing them only, and be demonstrably unattached to policy appeals from the party hierarchy. In sum, elections periodically unite leaders with followers for reasons that are central to the democratic process.

The media are, without question, the most critical factors in elections as currently constituted. Newspapers and (especially) television determine the nature of communications between candidates and voters, how those communications are transmitted, how often they are transmitted, and, to a significant degree, how potential voters are likely to react to them. Therefore, any analysis of the role of the media in elections should appropriately begin with the expectation that many, if not all, of the major problems with the media as conveyors of news also apply to the media in democracy's electoral phase. To be more specific and interrogatory: Are the same factors that have trivialized and introduced a tabloid flavor to news reporting present during elections? The answer is yes, and for essentially the same reason. The following analysis will explore both the effect of this truth on campaigns and why, given the nature of the modern campaign challenge, the transplantation has been so easy to accomplish.

First, some summary statements about what modern campaigns are like. These should be rather easily appreciated because virtually all citizens have had the opportunity to witness, view, and hear aspects of cam-

paigns that illustrate the phenomenon. Many of them were explored in earlier chapters. Therefore, this discussion will be brief and to the point. First, campaigns rarely involve serious efforts to explore issues in-depth. They are approached in general, symbolic ways that point out ideological differences between candidates as either liberal or conservative, favoring a large or a reduced role for government, or supporting the centralization or the decentralization of government power. The hope is to appeal to voters' emotions without being very specific about how these symbolic commitments might translate into distinct policies that might demand sacrifice.

Second, factors that trigger the above strategy make the use of twenty- or thirty-second television sound bites a natural way to visually convey campaign messages. Pictures showing a candidate surrounded by American flags imply the candidate is patriotic, and therefore good. Scenes showing a candidate at a military installation are intended to imply that he or she is strong on defense and recognizes the critical role of the military in the modern world. Short visuals of candidates in grammar schools or ones showing them interacting with a group of underprivileged or handicapped people are intended to convey that the candidate has a passion for the well-being of society's young or disadvantaged. Scenes cement impressions. Pictures are worth a thousand words. However, often pictures can be worth a thousand facts, because often they do not convey a candidate's true position on the issue at hand. However, that is not important during a campaign, provided that visuals and their accompanying sound bites do their image-building job.

Third, during campaigns both print and electronic journalism are preoccupied with the factors attendant to candidates' character, family, political, and (if relevant) military careers, and any alleged current or past scandals that may be plaguing them. Investment ventures gone wrong, sexual escapades, and associations with society's shady elements (however defined) are all fair game. Often they don't have to be substantiated in fact, for rumors can be news items unto themselves and can be identified as only rumors. Such an approach has the dual advantage of not placing reporters on the "issue-analysis block," and helps to make an item newsworthy exclusively because of its dramatic or sensationalist quality.

Fourth, journalists like to stress the horse race side of campaigns. They like to report on who is ahead, by how much, and why. This keeps campaign reporting objective, and therefore safe for the journalists. Again, the messages are simple, the statistics do not lie, and it holds the potential of fomenting some viewer interest in the campaign.

It is important to note that candidates' campaign strategies, including how they advertise, synchronize totally with how television wants to cover news. That is to say, they want to emphasize the visual, do it quickly, and do it dramatically. Therefore, when candidates make appearances they do it with television coverage in mind. They speak in generalities, they choose supportive audiences, and they choose scenes or backdrops which play to viewers' emotions instead of judgments. Both network and local television will cover only brief segments of the event. If candidates and their staff set the appearance stage carefully, viewers often will be unable to distinguish between purchased advertising and actual television coverage of the event. The latter certainly has a better impact on the campaign budget. The commonality between news and advertising even extends to the media's horse race bias. Often candidates will pay for special polls in areas that seem to favor the candidate in order to "stack" the results, hoping that the results will be reported as news by both the print and electronic media. To be reported as the leader can provide the campaign with some momentum.

In sum, campaigning and news reporting have a common incentive. They both seek to sell their product in ways that lure the viewer/voter into their web of influence. The strategies employed by each are remarkably the same. In both cases the target of the strategy, the viewer/voter, is shortchanged, particularly if the evaluative standard is how well the results of the strategies prepare the voter to assume his or her obligation as an informed citizen-participant in a democratic system.

The Media, Democracy, and Public Policy

An analysis of how the contemporary media, especially television, impacts on public policy should begin with a reminder of how crucial intermediary institutions with a communication mission are to the health and functions of a democratic system. Secondly, because of this, both media representatives and policymakers attempt to use communications technology to realize their goals. In the case of electronic and print journalism, it is a large listening, viewing, and reading clientele. In the case of politicians and policymakers, it is election to and maintaining office. It is this reality that steers the impact of journalism on policy in the directions it does.

Therefore, if the evaluation of the media's impact on elections is based on how well they inform and educate voters, the record is patchy at best. Consequently, the windows, offered below, through which the media are evaluated do not paint an appealing picture. Advances in communications technology have contributed significantly to this state of affairs. On the other hand, that same technology has the potential to be focused in ways that are far more functional to both democracy and public policy than it has been in the past quarter-century. It is also important to note that the media (especially television) are not the exclusive cause of the following problems. Journalism has contributed significantly to each, but journalism acts in conjunction with other intermediary institutions, political forces, and cultural realities to impact on politics and public policy in the following ways.

Constant Campaign Mentality

The constant campaign is a fact of life in modern politics. The president, House and Senate members, and, in varying degrees, elected state and local officials permit the constant campaign mentality to impact both on the policy positions they assume and on how they spend their time. Politicians need money for campaigns, and lots of it. They cannot afford to alienate potential donors, especially potentially generous ones. In short, politicians become timid, very accommodative, and inclined to view compromise and consensus development as ends unto themselves. The quality of the policy product is secondary to the need to reach some sort of decision. In effect, processes have priority over policy substance.

Television offers the conditions that encourage this. Communication via satellite to television stations in home districts is instantaneous. It can be brief, couched in an appeal to principle, and conveyed enthusiastically and personally. It is a way to bank votes for the next election. A sense of concern, and deference to constituents of all types, are of the highest priority. It becomes all-encompassing. It is important both to fund-raising and gaining newspaper endorsements. In short, it is genetically connected to campaign strategies. Moreover, it makes news reporting and citizen reaction to one's labors focus on how well the officeholder is taking care of people and industries within the constituency.

This is the enshrinement of technique and process, not policy substance. However, this is where the rewards are. The constant campaign mentality becomes the essence of the office, from the presidency on down. It means hiring staff assistants that specialize in public relations and fund-raising and, in the case of legislators, it often means assigning these individuals to district offices so that voters can have more direct access to the legislator. It means organizing appearances to obtain maximum media exposure, and making statements that are media appropriate, in that they are short, on topics that concern constituents, and general in tone so as to maximize political fallout. In sum, television makes the constant campaign easier to manage and it has gradually become an assumed part of an elected policymaker's job description. At a time when policymakers should be spending more, not less, time on policy content, television as a medium encourages the opposite.

Tyranny of the Visual

The term "tyranny of the visual" was introduced by Kathleen Hall Jamieson.[19] Her research on the perceptive impacts of television has been exemplary. The term should be interpreted and applied literally. In essence, it means that people are far more inclined to be impressed and won over by visual images than they are by words or voice. If facts contradict images, images virtually always win. Politicians gain far more public approval by looking like leaders than they do by actually being good leaders. Of course, sometimes they do both very well. However, in modern politics it is not necessary to be good at both. An appealing style and a bit of charisma are major personal assets in both campaigning and in (symbolizing) governance.

Obviously, television leverages the impact of image and style in politics, policy processes, and policy content. It was often said that President Reagan was the best "acting" president in the nation's history. An actor by profession, he acted out the presidential role to perfection. Even his detractors reluctantly conceded that. They were quick to point out, however, that he may have lulled the country into a false sense of confidence about the state of the country and the world because of his ability to use the television camera to comfort and inspire people. Reagan often would be caught on camera championing the needs of the underprivileged, while at the same time requesting budget cuts in programs designed to help them. He and Michael Deaver, his communications assistant, knew that pictures not only meant a thousand words, they could mean a thousand facts.

Both incumbents and challengers know this, and they act accordingly. It makes the use of television a natural course for those who have even a modicum of ability to tap its potential. However, the results are distributing, if not ominous. Style is of higher priority than is a serious concern for policy content. It reinforces the advantages of the constant campaign which, by itself, sacrifices substance to process. In cases where television images mask contradictions or deceptions, it is even more disturbing. Policy problems can fester while public officials on camera offer assurances that things aren't as bad as they seem. Public officials appear to be dishonest. When the public becomes aware of the discrepancy between rhetoric and reality, its pessimism about government, politics, and politicians is reinforced. In turn, this undercuts the very foundation of democratic government.

Michael J. O'Neill has applied Jamieson's thesis to societies worldwide, and he shares her pessimism about the impact of images on public attitudes. Noting that television has brought citizens and their governments closer together, he concludes that public affairs have now been democratized in most societies as a result. Elites used to have the upper hand, but now image-empowered citizens have it. The poor in many countries have come to believe that they can improve their economic status by hard work and political activities. However, as in the United States, the collapse or compromise of elite rule in countries is a mixed blessing, be-

cause usually special interests, not the body politic, have stepped in to fill the leadership vacuum left by the collapse of elite rule. Elites use television to manipulate opinion through symbols and citizens react accordingly. The result is not creative thought, but cultural and political superficiality. According to O'Neill, television "transforms all of life into moving images and sensory stimuli. It creates impressions instead of ideas and emotions instead of thought."[20] Democratization and people empowerment are appealing in theory, but power without cognizance and consciousness may mean that the democratic curative is worse than the condition it seeks to remedy.

Deinstitutionalized Politics

Before the Watergate episode, one of the twentieth century's most high-profile media events, public policies at the federal level were the result of agreements struck among politicians representing institutions whose members had considerable loyalty to both the institution itself and the ability of its leaders to represent it effectively in negotiations with representatives of other institutions. Speakers of the House, House Majority and Minority Floor Leaders, the Majority and Minority Floor Leaders of the Senate, chairs of key congressional committees, and cabinet secretaries could count on considerable support from their own organizational ranks when they negotiated with the president to reach policy agreements. In return, these leaders dispensed favors to the institutional rank-and-file–favorable committee and subcommittee assignments, priority status for their proposed legislation when debated on the floor of the House or Senate, and speeches in their districts to help them gain reelection. In short, significant prestige and potential policy clout accompanied the position of institutional leader.

In their negotiations with each other and with the president, these leaders could

insulate themselves against short-term vacil-
lations in public opinion. This gave them
time to focus their attention on the job at
hand. As the spokespersons for separate institutions that had to cooperate with each other
to produce policy agreements (rooted in the
separation of powers doctrine), they were
temporarily minimizing the impact of short-
term variations in public opinion on policies.
This was an effective extension, or supplement, to what the founders had in mind when
they created staggered elections and different
constituency bases for all government institutions and assigned each institution a different
policy prerogative. The purpose was to grant
minority elites enough of an institutional toe-
hold so they could resist attempts by temporary majorities to dominate policy decisions.
Conditions within these institutional networks were very conducive to discussing the
true merits and demerits of policy proposals.
Negotiators were inclined to present and
defend their own best judgments, with constituency opinion of secondary consideration.

Watergate, together with the frustrations of
the Vietnam War, greatly altered this environment. Institutions became more suspicious
of each other. Laws were enacted limiting
presidential influence over public budgeting
and finance and reducing his flexibility to engage troops in extended foreign operations
without congressional consent. Other legislation placed formal restrictions on campaign
contributions, opened congressional and
agency files to public scrutiny, established independent counsels to investigate alleged illegal
activities, and created codes of ethics for
elected and appointed government employees.
Most significant for this analysis, it brought a
new breed of policymakers to Washington—
ones dedicated to constituent servitude and
ones hostile to institutional attempts to influence their policy positions. Efforts by congressional party leaders to unite them behind common party objectives were resisted. They were

the servants of the people back home who had
revolted against the misuse of presidential
power by insisting on more democracy. These
legislators and, for that matter, presidents, were
inclined to make their own cases with their own
constituencies on their own time with funds
that they themselves raised. They revolted
against the relatively closed, institutionalized
character of policy negotiations in favor of a
more individualized system in which the significance of the traditional bargaining networks
was compromised in favor of a more open, free-
for-all system within which each legislator could
make his or her case within committees and in
floor debates.

The mass media, especially television, made
this transition rather easy. Satellite transmission of legislators' opinions on pending policy
debates could be easily transmitted to television stations back home as well as to national
networks. Furthermore, journalists from all
media venues found the change exciting and
began covering it as a news item unto itself.
They found new television-adept personalities,
many of them relatively junior in rank, in key
subcommittee assignments and having significant leverage on public policy. The devolution
of power may have introduced a more *ad hoc,*
chaotic flavor to policy discussions and debates, but that offered the drama and sensationalism that news media were seeking. Television's exploitation of the new conditions fed
on itself. Both presidents and legislators could
readily appreciate the publicity advantages accruing to them if they "went public" with policy positions, thereby inviting press coverage
and helping them cement their relationships
with their constituents.

However, this deinstitutionalization of the
national policy process was not without its
problems. The open publicity, via the press, of
policy differences between legislators and
groups made compromises that involved major
actor concessions much less likely. Once a
policy figure has gone public with his or her

position, making concessions is much less likely, because the person might appear to be without principle. All public officials want to be thought of as people of principle. This, in turn, encourages policy resolutions that reflect the lowest common value denominator, because an agreement is unlikely to be reached unless all parties to the debate salvage something from the experience. Processes tend to displace a serious concern for content under such conditions. This was occurring at the very time when the nature of policy problems demanded that more, not less, time be spent on the content of policy solutions. The mass media, especially television, helped facilitate the reorientation.

Weak Political Parties

The Watergate-inspired devolution of politics and policy power has had negative results for the role of parties as policy forces in the United States. Interest groups, especially the more high-profile, well-to-do ones, have stepped in to fill the vacuum. This has had negative results for political campaigns. Again, television is the root of the problem, not only because of the sound bite nature of campaign advertising, but also because of the high cost of the advertising itself. This makes candidates, and future policymakers, more beholden to the interests from which they secure most of their campaign contributions. It means that representing the public, and the policies produced by that representation, are becoming increasingly more elitist and less representative of the body politic as a whole. This increases public cynicism about government, encourages citizen disinterest and withdrawal, and thereby compromises the foundation of democratic government itself.

Consumer Culture

A healthy slice of the American public has become slowly addicted to television and its menu of entertainment options. Television networks, cable companies, and local stations pursue viewers by attempting to sell them entertainment. By deluging the market with entertainment in the form of drama, situation comedy, and even in selecting and reporting the news, television diverts the public's attention away from a sober confrontation with the key policy issues of the day. Television viewers are the consumers of all this. The products offered must appeal to viewers before they buy the product with the viewing time they spend. Many programs and films popularize characters who, by and large, are self-interested but not avaricious and who generally conform to accepted social norms. Characters in vintage family-oriented television programs played by performers such as Dick Van Dyke, Robert Young, and Mary Tyler Moore were replaced by popular actors like Jerry Seinfeld, Tim Allen, Drew Carey, Cybil Shepard, Craig Nelson, Fran Drescher, and Bill Cosby. These actors portrayed people who, although often idiosyncratic, nonetheless sought professional, social, and personal goals that were clearly mainstream in cast.

Newscasters, both network and local, almost invariably appear as prototypes of mainstream suburbanites. Over time, viewers have come to accept the personal attributes and (especially) the goal orientation of many of these characters, who influence their own personal, social, and professional norms. These are people who are not especially inspired, but individuals who want their lives to move along safe and culturally acceptable courses. According to Mark Edmundson, television "is inhospitable to inspiration, improvisation, failures, [and] slipups."[21] Since viewers gradually adopt the norms demonstrated on television, they gradually come to act like them and want much of the same things of life as they do. One such person norm is that of conformity, or the goal to blend in and be accepted.

As consumers of television, Americans

have become notably reactive and uninnovative in demeanor. Moreover, and the significance of this cannot be understressed, they are becoming increasingly accustomed to having entertainment served them for consumption with no feedback expected, except perhaps for the Neilson ratings. Such a media-cultivated consumer culture carries over into the public's attitude toward politics and policy. Americans want to be entertained by politicians as both candidates and officeholders. They are comfortable with reactive, bystander roles rather than those that expect them to initiate and debate policy alternatives. In general, they do not challenge themselves to think about the crucial policy issues of the day from either causal or remedial perspectives. Civic citizenship does not mean the careful examination and forceful debate of policy options. It is more comfortable to adopt a wait and see attitude. If policies are enacted that affect them negatively, then they protest, often too late for major government commitments to change course. Once aware of this, often they become cynical toward politics and withdraw even further from their civic obligations. In sum, the market forces that drive the electronic entertainment industry have helped to create both an entertainment consumer culture and a political consumer culture. All of this is rooted, ultimately, in the First Amendment's guarantee of communication freedoms. However, this is not the kind of result the framers had in mind.

Decline of Social Capital and Civic Engagement

Finally, and rooted significantly in the consumer culture condition, is the negative effect of television on one of democracy's most valuable cultural resources—that of social capital. Social capital refers to the attitudes, feelings of trust, and norms that people acquire as the result of working together to solve problems.

The problem-solving efforts are more successful because of these conditions. It is a particularly useful condition if its impact on people encourages them to become involved in civic engagement enterprises, or to connect with community life in a number of ways. These could include political organizations, volunteer organizations, discussion groups, church activities, and recreation groups and activities. Writing in the 1830s, Alexis de Tocqueville concluded that what he considered to be a healthy American democracy was due in no small part to the peoples' commitment to civic participation. Such involvements develop attitudes of "civility" in people—the appreciation of the role of tolerance, compassion, and understanding and the rewards of self-sacrifice for community well-being.

Robert D. Putnam has conducted extensive historical research that shows a high correlation between high levels of social capital and civic engagement on the one hand, and stable governments and economic prosperity on the other.[22] Societies with high levels of both tend to have high moral standards and a willingness to sacrifice indulgences in the interest of overall societal betterment. In societies with low levels of each, the opposite tends to be the case. Societies of "joiners" do better than societies within which individualism has been culturally dominant.

Americans used to be high on the social capital and civic engagement scales, but this is no longer the case. Americans who reached maturity during the Depression and World War II periods were, and continue to be, far more community-engagement-oriented than have been subsequent generations. "Time-budget" surveys of middle-class Americans in 1965, 1975, and 1985 revealed a marked, regular decline in civic engagement. Adults were asked to record all their daily activities, and the results were tallied. Between 1956 and 1985, the time devoted to visiting and socializing dropped by approximately 25 percent.

The amount of time spent with clubs and associations was down by about 50 percent. Memberships in such varied organizations as labor unions, the Red Cross, parent-teachers associations (PTA), the League of Women Voters, fraternal, and many voluntary associations declined between 25 and 50 percent. Other surveys revealed a marked decline in political activities, including rallies (down 36 percent), volunteer political party work (down 56 percent), and school affairs and town meetings (down 39 percent).[23]

Many explanations have been advanced to explain this indisputable trend. Included are residential mobility, a decline in living standards, suburbanization, on-the-job time pressure, the civil rights movement, an overall disillusionment with civic life triggered by events such as the Vietnam War and Watergate, the expansion of the social service state, and the drug and sex cultural manifestations of the antiauthority movement of the 1960s and 1970s.[24]

However, Putnam challenges all these explanations and offers persuasive evidence to substantiate his conclusions. For example, surveys show that people experiencing work-time pressures are more engaged civically than are people who are not. The more affluent are less civically engaged than are low and middle-income individuals. The civil rights revolution did trigger a "white flight" away from central cities and a corresponding civic disengagement. However, the civic disengagement trend has been more evident within black communities.[25]

By the process of elimination, Putnam concludes that the decline in social capital and civic engagement is due primarily to one culprit—television. He offers substantial evidence to substantiate his conclusion. Civic engagement began to decline at the very time when most American homes acquired television sets. It accelerated along with the increasing number of hours people spent watching television. Television viewing was approximately 50 percent higher in 1995 than in the 1950s. In addition, most homes had acquired multiple sets by that time, reinforcing the addiction. To prove that the correlation is not simply circumstantial, and that television is the major problem, Putnam notes that newspaper reading became increasingly popular along with television. Those addicted to newspapers have become more, not less, civically conscious. Furthermore, this trend has virtually nothing to do with race, economic status, age, or the level of education. Newspaper readers of all demographic types are joiners. In contrast, television addicts are much more likely to be loners.[26]

Why is television so destructive to social capital and civic engagement? Putnam offers two reasons. For one, television creates a "time displacement" problem. People sacrifice other activity options to watch television. Among these options are, of course, organizational activities that might well cultivate more of a sense of civic responsibility. Second, owing to the dramatic and often negative content of television programs, heavy television viewers tend to become skeptical of others' qualities of benevolence. That being the case, efforts at civic engagement would likely appear futile to people who have been so socialized.

The role of television in undermining social capital and civic responsibility is clear. In order for such a condition not to have negative impacts on public policy, Tocqueville's correlation between public civility and a healthy democracy would have to be rejected, as would the research evidence offered by Putnam. That would be foolhardy. Furthermore, in this case, television has not damaged political and policy discourse by the way in which it covers public figures and public events, or by the theory it adopts to determine news hour menus. It does it by simply being there, conveniently available at little cost, with a marketplace-induced fetish for the dramatic and the unusual.

The ability of the political system to produce cohesive, meaningful solutions to policy problems declined as political parties weakened, as interest groups strengthened, and as technology through television made civic engagement less inviting. The social fragmentation spawned by television finds counterpart trends within and among the government's constitutional and extra-constitutional institutions. When individuals abandon others and retreat to the privacy of the home to watch the "good guys" beat the "bad guys" or to become intimate with the horrors of worldwide atrocities in every way but to smell the gunpowder, they are forfeiting more than they realize. Gradually they will come to realize that a fragmented society means a government fragmented more seriously than even the founders would have found advisable. Sooner or later it will be necessary to relearn the forgotten craft of sociability.

This is not to say that privacy is bad, for it most certainly is not. However, borrowing from defenses often made of the separation of powers principle, there are inherent advantages to balance. Both society and government would profit from a social state in which individuals voluntarily compromise between privacy and sociability. The useful pleasures of dialogue can be mixed with the fixation to electric monologue. In the process of doing so, the advantages of both will be appreciated for what they have to offer, and both politics and society will be the better for it.

The Internet as a News Medium

In theory, the mass media can help bind the country together by offering people the chance to absorb, share, and discuss information. The rival perspective, and the one more

dominant in recent years, is that the media are so powerful and money driven that they have poisoned politics and culture by overstressing the coverage of scandal and other sensationalist events at the expense of key policy issues. However, even as the media are being castigated for their excessive power and influence, computer technology is gradually threatening its social importance and political influence. Whether the new technology will reverse or intensify recent trends is irrelevant. It will continue to grow in importance and we can only hope that its potential civic benefits will outweigh its downside. Cable, computers, and fiber optics deliver special detailed information on everything from finance to diseases to a constantly expanding number of users. The threat to the economic health and influence of the television networks and their affiliates with their more generally pitched news and entertainment menus is real. If the television and newspaper industries begin to lose advertising revenue to the Internet, then they won't be able to afford the programs and news personnel to attract audiences. While newspapers, magazines, and books have the advantage of portability over both television and computers, if habits change even these forums could be in trouble. After all, the mid-century appearance of television did great harm to the demand for evening newspapers.

In the early 1990s, well over half of Americans depended on television for the news. By 1998, that figure had shrunk to well under 50 percent. Some of this withdrawal was due to growing disinterest in the news, but much of it was due to viewing cable news during the daytime. Regarding the Internet, in 1995, 4 percent of adults over eighteen went on line once a week to get the news. By 1998, that figure had risen to 20 percent.[27] The bottom line is that more and more people can get more and more news, information, opinion, and entertainment from more and more sources that are relatively accessible and inexpensive. Such a proliferation of access points could well make the economic, social, and political impact of each one of them incrementally less as time passes. Furthermore, this condition harbors the potential of further distracting the public away from news and toward entertainment as a high-priority communication item. The television industry's fear of losing more and more of its audiences explains why it rewards television news "star" personalities such as Jane Pauley, Katie Couric, and Sam Donaldson with huge, multimillion-dollar contracts.[28]

Americans are becoming more and more dependent on their computers for, among other things, information about health, medical care, investments, business opportunities, and entertainment. They are increasingly using the Internet as a source of news and opinion. This offers several advantages. With only a modicum of effort, computer users can get news and opinion at any time and at any level of depth and sophistication they seek. National and local newscasts, as well as many major newspapers, have, for a considerable period of time, recognized this potential threat to their audiences and subscribers. In many cases networks, their local affiliates, and newspapers have developed their own Web sites to keep viewers and readers part of the established news family. In short, citizens can use the Internet to keep up with government and communicate with legislators more often and more effectively. The potential for the development of a more serious, responsible, and active body politic is indeed offered by the Internet.

However, there are very significant potential limitations to employing the Internet as the primary source of news and opinion. It may isolate people even further from one another, amplifying the civic culture problem introduced by television. If that becomes the case, then the likelihood of developing a strong civic culture has been dealt another serious, if not fatal, blow. A two-year research project sponsored by Carnegie-Mellon University concluded that people who use the Internet as little as one hour a week are slightly more likely to be lonely and depressed than nonusers. If true, this condition could well reinforce the growing sense of pessimism that people harbor toward their government and its leaders. Whether the Internet becomes a bane or boon to the nation's quest for a more effective and accountable government will depend almost exclusively on the willingness of users to recognize its potential and use it to build a sense of civic virtue. It could go either way. David Thorburn eloquently summarized both sides of the issue by noting that "the computer encourages joining, interaction, sharing, the creation of communities of interest; yet it is also congenial to our uncivic preferences for isolation, the avoidance of human contact, solipsism, 'lurking,' voyeurism. Through its power to confer anonymity, it feeds instincts for scandal, revenge, name-calling, pornography. It is the best of Webs, the worst of Webs. It promises, simultaneously, to become the Agora, True Democracy, but also, Big Brother."[29]

Intermediary Institutions and Constitutional Politics: The Policy Challenges

Intermediary institutions in the American political system do not serve the people or their government well. The classic roles of political parties, interest groups, and the mass media as generators of ideas and conduits of opinion have been altered by the natural contours of a politics that has turned democracy's theoretical strengths into its operational weaknesses. Political parties have been negatively impacted by structural decentralization to the point of allowing well-organized and cohesive minorities to dominate a comparatively inactive majority party base. Well-organized and well-financed interest groups have exploited the Constitution's communications guarantees to acquire disproportionate leverage in both the election and governing processes. The mass media, especially television, in the quest for an audience, has dramatized, simplified, repressed, and, on occasion, even ignored the public affairs agenda. The public has grown cynical over the inability of the three intermediary forces to deliver what it needs by way of policy options and analysis. All three seem to function in ways that are adverse to original intent.

The Constitution, by guaranteeing fundamental communications rights and championing popular sovereignty, offers individuals, groups, and corporations the opportunity to make self-interest appear respectable, if not honorable. The decentralization of nominations procedures within parties is procedurally democratic, but it invites minority control of parties, which is undemocratic. Factions are an inevitability, but if open competition among factions leads to the dominance of the fittest, the democratic notion of representational equality has been compromised. If television, in its quest for citizen markets, sensationalizes and simplifies issues and, in the process, produces a citizenry that is addicted to the medium, the civic underpinnings of democracy have been seriously tainted.

American politics in the late twentieth century was impacted heavily by public reaction to the Watergate crisis and the Vietnam War, most directly the former. Without a doubt, the most significant lesson of Watergate was that the Constitution worked, and the country was relieved of a president who had abused the public trust. However, Watergate left scar tissue. The public grew suspicious of government authority, and fond of democratization as a matter of principle. Much of what weak parties have permitted to happen to

their ability to be a formidable governing force, or what strong, activist factions claim by right, is a product of the belief that procedural decentralization of decision making is a long-term curative for what ails the country. This is part of the Watergate legacy, and it is counterproductive. The fondness of journalism for scandal and "pack attacks" on public officials is clearly a product of the Watergate incident. However, this approach weakens government and weakens the media's ability to choose programming, listening, and reading menus which inform and interest people in public affairs.

Proportionality in politics and government has become dangerously unbalanced and desperately needs reorientation. The analyses of the effectiveness of government's major policy institutions that appear in subsequent chapters will reflect the weaknesses of the intermediary institutions discussed in this and the previous chapter. Any effort to refurbish and strengthen institutional policy roles must incorporate, simultaneously, efforts to alert and reorient intermediary institutions to their responsibilities. Unless reforms occur in tandem, neither will succeed.

Endnotes

1. Gary C. Woodward, *The Veronis, Shuler and Associates Communication Industry Forecast* (privately printed, 1991), p. 55, as referenced in Gary C. Woodward, *Perspectives on American Political Media* (Boston: Allyn & Bacon, 1997), p. 2.

2. John Gamson, "Incredible News," *The American Prospect*, no. 19 (Fall 1994), pp. 28–35.

3. Hedrick Smith, narrator, *The People and the Power Game*, PBS Video, 1996.

4. Jonathon Cohn, "Scandals for Dummies," *The American Prospect*, no. 32 (May-June 1997), pp. 17–19.

5. *Ibid.*

6. *Ibid.*

7. Gene Lyons, et al., *Fools for Scandal: How the Media Invented Whitewater* (New York: Franklin Square Press, 1996), p. 25.

8. *Ibid.*, p. 56.

9. Steven D. Stark, "Local News: The Biggest Scandal on TV," *The Washington Monthly*, vol. 29, no. 6 (June 1997), p. 38.

10. *Ibid.*, p. 39.

11. *Ibid.*, pp. 38–39.

12. *Ibid.*, p. 41.

13. *Ibid.*

14. Shanto Iyengar, *Is Anyone Responsible?: How Television Frames Political Issues* (Chicago: University of Chicago Press, 1987), pp. 13–16.

15. *Ibid.*

16. *Ibid.*, pp. 127–143.

17. James Fallows, *Breaking the News: How the Media Undermine American Democracy* (New York: Pantheon, 1996).

18. This phenomenon is explored by way of contrasting "institutionalized pluralism" with "individualized pluralism" as it applies to presidential bargaining strategies in Samuel J. Kernell, *Going Public: New Strategies of Presidential Leadership* (Washington, D.C.: CQ Press, 1986), pp. 10–39.

19. See Kathleen Hall Jamieson, *Packaging the Presidency: A History of Presidential Campaign Advertising* (New York: Oxford University Press, 1996) for an example of how the author pursues this theme.

20. Michael J. O'Neill, *The Roar of the Crowd: How Television and People Power Are Changing the World* (New York: Times Books, 1993), as quoted in Jonathon Yardley, "The Media's World Revolution," *Washington Post National Weekly Edition* (September 6–12, 1993), p. 36.

21. Mark Edmundson, "On the Uses of a Liberal Education as Lite Entertainment," *Harpers* (September 1997), p. 41.

22. Robert D. Putnam, "Bowling Alone: America's Declining Social Capital," *Journal of Democracy*, vol. 6, no. 1 (January 1995), pp.65–78.

23. Robert D. Putnam, "The Strange Disappearance of Civic America," *The American Prospect*, no. 24 (Winter 1995).

24. *Ibid.*

25. *Ibid.*

26. *Ibid.*

27. Robert J. Samuelson, "No More Media Elite," *Washington Post National Weekly Edition* (July 13, 1998), p. 26.

28. *Ibid.*

29. David Thorburn, "Web of Paradox," *The American Prospect*, no. 40 (September-October 1998), p. 80.

chapter seven

Congress

Constitutional Politics and the People's Branch

The Constitution's political reverberations affect Congress perhaps more than any other government institution. In all probability, the founders expected the Constitution's institutional role assignments to deploy more literally than they have. They expected that policymaking would be confined almost exclusively to Congress and that the president would devote most of his attention to policy implementation. Madison declared this clearly in *Federalist No. 51* when he stated decisively that "in republican government the legislative authority necessarily predominates."[1] Therefore, the founders wanted to ensure, insofar as was possible, that separated powers and checks on those powers would impact directly and continually on the branch assigned policymaking authority. As a result, they fashioned Congress to be a bicameral or two-house chamber. In addition, they gave each house different responsibilities. For example, revenue bills must originate in the House. Only the Senate is involved in confirming presidential appointments, and treaties. Only the House is involved in the impeachment of the president, but only the Senate can convict an impeached president. To discourage irresponsible policies, the founders required that majorities in both houses approve bills before they are sent to the president for signature. Since each house has a different constituency base, with the Senate representing states equally and House districts determined by population, different constituency-rooted incentives would have to be accommodated before Congress could enact policies. If the president vetoes a bill, a two-thirds supermajority in both houses is necessary to override the veto. In sum, the Constitution's structural arrangements and role assignments virtually compel Congress to accommodate the political by-products of fragmented structure and policy assignments at virtually every turn in the policy process.

The Constitution conferred a constrained

policymaking system on the national government. The policy power of any one institution constitutes only one part of the policy puzzle which, only when assembled, becomes official public policy. Richard Neustadt's observation that our government is one of "separated institutions sharing powers" applies not only to presidential-congressional relations, but also to relations between the House and the Senate.[2] In other words, the founders mandated a system which has resulted in both houses developing a system of interaction that accommodates the power balance decreed by the Constitution. Anytime the parameters of an institution's policy powers affect how it interacts with other institutions in the development of policy, the Constitution and its political progeny are impacting on that policy. While the Constitution may not be omnipresent, it is very often present at very critical times. This is as the founders wished. If policy power deliberately fragmented could not impact on how legislatures make decisions, it was probably useless as a constraint against potential policy tyranny.

The Constitution's vesture of formal policymaking power in Congress is formidable, and it explains the founders' insistence on a bicameral legislature with bounded policy assignments. In Article I, Section 8, Congress is assigned the power to collect taxes, borrow money on the credit of the United States, regulate interstate commerce, coin money, establish a postal system, establish naturalization and patent policies, create a federal judicial system, raise and support an army and navy, declare war, and (perhaps most important) "make all Laws which shall be necessary and proper for carrying into Execution the foregoing Powers, and all other Powers vested by this Constitution in the Government of the United States, or in any Department or Officer thereof." In addition, Congress was assigned certain negative and appointment confirmation roles, such as the power to impeach

and try a president and federal judges, power to ratify treaties, and the responsibility to confirm presidential nominees for ambassadorships, judgeships, and cabinet positions. In short, the powers are formidable, and it is little wonder that the founders wanted the execution of most of these assignments to be impacted by fragmented constitutional power.

It is crucial to bear in mind that the founders submitted a governmental system that was more effective than that offered by the Articles of Confederation, but yet significantly constrained in what it could do. That was during a different day and time. More than two hundred years of population growth, technological change, wars, urbanization, and economic development have created policy challenges that no doubt would dwarf anything the founders could have imagined. Under these conditions, a constitutional system that fragments power in the interest of societal stability and safety may well seem ill-suited to the times. Ill-suited it may well be unless, of course, ways can be found to unify political power and overcome the barriers that constitutionally fragmented power poses for cohesive, yet representative, policy development. If this cannot be achieved, then constitutional politics will reinforce the effects of an already fragmented society on politics and policy. This is why the conditions affecting the ability of the nation's intermediary institutions to meet their challenges, discussed in the previous chapter, are so critical to determining whether Congress can meet the policy challenges of the twenty-first century in ways that make constitutional politics relevant, rather than irrelevant, to those challenges.

The analysis of intermediary institutions in Chapters 5 and 6 found that each of them— political parties, interest groups, and the media—have been ineffective in meeting the intermediary challenge. Political parties and interest groups have not provided equal access to all forces that need, indeed are entitled to, representation. Political parties have not performed their role as teachers, tutors, and faction unifiers at all well. The interest group medium advantages the well-organized, well-to-do groups at the expense of those that are poorly organized and poorly financed. In the interest of audience expansion as a prelude to financial gain, television has made public service news virtually a necessary evil, and has often replaced it with, or converted it into, programming with a sensationalist, tabloid flavor. In sum, current conditions impacting on political intermediaries favor the centrifugal over the centripetal. This does not help Congress deal effectively with policy issues that require sober thought and public sacrifice. In fact, it encourages the opposite. Therefore, it is important to bear the following point in mind during the discussion of congressional decision processes that follows: The structure, politics, and policies produced by Congress are continually impacted by conditions that compromise the effectiveness of intermediary institutions in American politics and government. Furthermore, this has not been a strict cause-effect, zero-sum phenomenon. Congress did not suddenly discover weak intermediary institutions and respond in kind, although there is often a clear condition-response pattern to the relationship between intermediary institutions and congressional behavior. Nonetheless, the same societal and economic forces which weakened intermediary institutions simultaneously weakened the ability of Congress to respond to its policy challenges effectively. Once in a weakened state, they both feed on each other's deficiencies and compound what is mostly a negative impact of constitutional politics on public policy.

Before analyzing how the major congressional decision-making forces—committees, leaders, staffs, and parties—have responded to changing social, economic, and political conditions, it is advisable to summarize briefly what those conditions have been and how Congress has responded to them in both structure and behavior.

Congress as a Responsive Institution

The founders intended for Congress to be the governmental institution most responsive to public opinion. Congress has taken that responsibility seriously in the course of the past two centuries. When public opinion decidedly favors a particular course of action or theory of government involvement in society or the economy—as was the case during the Jacksonian era, the New Deal, the Great Society, and both world wars—Congress, as well as the presidency and courts, have usually responded quickly and in kind. These are exceptions to the normal conditions. Usually the nation is not facing a crisis and the public is not actively providing policy institutions with policy inputs that demand major changes from the status quo. This trend is broken on occasion by events that affect public opinion positively or negatively. However, that opinion is reactive, or after the fact, and is often conveyed as an attitude about such matters as government power, spending, crime, poverty, deficits, or the apparent misuse of military power. Usually, its effect is to set a cultural stage upon which Congress enacts policies which conform to the new or adjusted cultural norms. Page and Shapiro's study of public opinion, discussed in Chapter 4, concluded that the public offers policymakers rather stable, yet flexible, suggestions as to what types of policies are preferred.[3] The opinion-rooted cultural stage discussed here is congruent with that.

However, it is important to note that the more segments of the public become accustomed to government's providing them with such things as subsidies, protective regulations, educational opportunities, and law enforcement, the more unlikely it is that these segments will want to forgo the advantages received from them. To that extent, public opinion is stable in its support of policies that offer these advantages. Nonetheless, the public reacts favorably or unfavorably to events that have nothing whatsoever to do with its dependency on government, and yet by its reactions can place policy options on the legislative agenda which would, if enacted, do battle with those dependencies. For example, more often than not in recent years, the public has viewed Congress unfavorably, believing that its members are too self-serving and not in tune with contemporary policy challenges, including the increasingly obvious need to insist on sacrifice as a prerequisite for meaningful policy change. On the other hand, most Americans support their own House and Senate members, ostensibly because they have a good political bedside manner. They listen attentively to their requests and complaints, and do what they can to take care of their needs. The ugly option of sacrifice does not invade these relationships. Sacrifice is for others who, obviously, are clearly taking advantage of government and contributing to public waste and large deficits.

Therefore, Congress is increasingly facing a public that asks legislators to be profiles in courage on the one hand, and servile to their constituencies on the other. Americans support the idea of planned, long-term change, but are not interested in big cuts in governmental services to which they have become accustomed. It is not a case of Congress being unable to gauge what the public wants. That is rather clear. However, because the cultural stage has served up clear operational inconsistencies, Congress is much less certain of how to respond. The public wants Congress to be both responsive and responsible. In an era increasingly influenced by budget cutbacks and fiscal austerity, Congress finds it im-

possible to do both. As the following discussion will show, Congress's institutional effectiveness, at least in the public's mind, has suffered as a result. The discussion will focus on how Congress, as an institution charged "by the people" to enact effective policies "for the people," has responded to both public opinion and changes in the political and economic landscape over the past half-century.

The Protective Pluralist Period

This period extended from approximately the mid-1930s to the early 1970s. It was the era of the congressional barons, or elites, whose safe-district-rooted congressional longevity had placed them in key committee and party positions in their respective houses. These elites consisted of committee chairs, ranking minority committee members, and other "players" whose congressional tenure, willingness to serve a time as junior "apprentices" to the more senior elites, and willingness to accept committee work obligations qualified them for acceptance into the ranks of the influential. Committee chairs were vested with significant formal powers over committee activities and floor debates. Regardless of which party controlled the respective houses, these coalitions dominated both policy agendas and policy content. For the most part, they were conservative in political cast. If the Democrats were in the majority, a conservative southern coalition was in control. If the Republicans were in power, conservatives from the Midwest and New England were in charge. Therefore, the policy bias of the committees, and of Congress, was toward marginal, or incremental change. Reciprocity, or "quid pro quo" politics, was a dominant norm. Committee members exchanged potential leverage in other policy areas for the right to control their own. Alliances among committee and subcommittee members, administrative bureaus, and interest groups (iron triangles) were an accepted part of the policy scene. Although these coalitions made trouble for activist, liberal presidents, public opinion accepted executive-legislative conflict induced by these differences as being a healthy manifestation of the separation of powers principle. Congressional structure nurtured efforts by these elements to stabilize government, and protect the public from the policy's most radical elements. These conditions reflected a variation on the "conservative democracy" theme explored in Chapter 2. Individual rights, especially property rights, were best preserved by a system under which elites were called on to make policy judgments on behalf of the public.[4] The public, in general, saw no reason to challenge the traditional dominance of congressional affairs by elite networks. Congressional elitism was a cultural fact of political life. Struggles between the president and Congress, and between the houses of Congress, induced in part by these legislative barons, served mostly to preserve individual political and property rights.

One major assumption dominated Congress-public relationships during the protective pluralist period: Effective policymaking mandates that representative institutions be somewhat insulated from popular democratic forces. Only under these conditions can legislators exercise their best policy judgments. If popular pressures are too intense and too regular, legislators are compelled to relinquish the compromises that must be struck to engineer the public interest effectively. The public good is best preserved if left in the hands of elites whose work will eventually be judged by the people in the election process. Ironically, keeping the people "at bay" during governance helps, rather than hinders, the democratic process. Too much participation constrains government effectiveness. In sum, the protective pluralist period adapted the founders' affinity for structurally restrained

elitist government to the needs of the mid twentieth century. The results of protective pluralist politics were ones with which, by and large, the founding fathers would have been comfortable. In all likelihood, they would have preferred more competition-induced checks on the iron triangle networks than the system offered. However, the overall conservative tone of the policies produced during the period likely would have allayed their concern. Therefore, for the most part, during this period, the Constitution played out in legislation essentially as Madison, Hamilton, and Jay had intended.

The protective pluralist period was, as the label indicates, pluralist as well as protective in cast. Pluralism as a theory of democracy was discussed in Chapter 2, so its components will not be recounted here, except to note that legislative elites function as representatives of and liaisons between groups as they go about the challenge of developing a policy consensus. Group inputs are preferred over citizen inputs because they are more identifiable and stable in root. In addition, group leaders can become de facto members of the bargaining groups, depending upon the issue at hand. Campaigns and elections are distractions to these elites. Even legislators from competitive districts are not good members of the elite networks. Forthcoming election challenges limit the bargaining ability of the member. He or she is therefore more interested in receiving credit for something than in extending it, which the policy barons prefer. Unless one is prepared to extend credit and assume some good will and trust on the part of other team members, there is little common ground available to do business. Consequently, direct public pressure was a nuisance. Meaningful public opinion was relayed through interest groups that had salience in the barons' districts, as well as in other districts. If a legislator knew his or her district well, it was represented well in legislation. Heads of administrative agencies who know their policies well represent the causes of people who profit from those policies when they are invited into the bargaining networks. A lobbyist who is in tune with his or her clients' interests will represent the interest of everybody who is affected favorably by those policies. The acceptance of these assumptions made grass-roots inputs unnecessary. In commenting on the Senate of the 1940s and 1950s, William S. White observed that "Constituent pressure . . . is rarely the *cause* of any Senator's action." He noted that the late Senator Theodore Green of Rhode Island once referred to a stack of postcards from constituents as "disgusting little things" as he threw them in the wastebasket.[5]

In sum, the public condoned this indirect democracy theory of representation during the protective pluralist period. Its acceptance was rooted in the political culture of the times, which was notably trustful of political leadership. Presidents Franklin Roosevelt, Harry Truman, Dwight Eisenhower, and John Kennedy were, for the most part, inspirational leaders whose administrations were comparatively free of scandal. In addition, with some major exceptions, domestic legislative challenges were dwarfed by international challenges during this period, including two major wars and postwar recovery efforts. Furthermore, much of the domestic focus was on rather routine legislative matters—immigration policies, private bills and resolutions, land claims, and the extension of already instituted New Deal programs. However, pressure was building for government to address major substantive policy challenges that would trigger the public's interest, including civil rights issues and issues affecting urban and suburban life. In addition, the public's faith in leadership was challenged by the Vietnam War and the Watergate incident. The result was the development of a participation and accountability "chic" on the part of the public which challenged the assumptions and practices of the protective pluralist era.

The Individualized Pluralist Period

The period characterized by individualized pluralism began in the mid- to late 1960s, and was firmly entrenched by the mid-1970s. The term originated with Samuel Kernell in his analysis of presidential leadership, but it is also notably helpful in explaining how the changes in the climate of public opinion change congressional electoral and policy behavior.[6] Individualized pluralism changed congressional culture from a workhorse to a show horse atmosphere. Under the former, rewards go to those who develop policy expertise as team players. Under the latter, rewards go to those who go it on their own with a high-profile, flamboyant style in an effort to secure their legislative careers. Several factors were behind the change. One was the growing public cynicism about the integrity and judgment of political leaders in the wake of Vietnam and Watergate. Another was the growing frustration on the part of blocks of urban voters over Congress's virtual ignoring of policy problems affecting urban areas, even though activist presidents had been pushing them. On another front, protests against the Vietnam War kindled interest in citizen activism in many other policy areas, including consumerism, the environment, campaign financing, and civil rights. In addition, court-induced congressional redistricting brought a level of cosmopolitanism to some districts, and along with it more citizen activism to be felt by more legislators. Population growth and migration made many sections of the South and West more demographically diverse, thereby encouraging legislators from these regions to be more attentive to the needs of their more politically balanced constituencies. Finally, the technological revolution was making major inroads into broadcast journalism, especially television. By the late 1960s, it had become easy to transmit news events and commentaries instantly to constituencies and to the country generally. This made it convenient to bypass the networks of congressional barons to gain legislative clout.

Legislators affected by the individualized pluralism syndrome are, in short, their own people. They are not beholden to bargaining networks, nor are they especially loyal to the norms of camaraderie in any context. The public opinion that is important to them is the public opinion of their constituency only. They are independent individuals with few personal and institutional loyalties. Moreover, they are little interested in forgoing short-term advantages for the long-term gains that often result from bargaining. They tend to be egocentric people who are reluctant to commit themselves to institutional arrangements that might compromise the virtual one-on-one relationship between them and their constituents. Instead, according to Kernell, they "prefer immediate, explicit, and tangible exchanges."[7]

Legislators during the individualized pluralism period have become demonstrably career conscious and constant-campaign-oriented. To quote Thomas Mann, they "are in business for themselves . . . and are likely to view themselves first and foremost as individuals, not as members of a party. . . ."[8] In contrasting the House of Representatives "classes" of 1958 and 1978, Michael Robinson found that the 1978 class was three times more prone to use congressional recording and transmission facilities than was the 1958 comparison group. Although his research applied to the use of these facilities for campaign purposes, he noted an increasing difficulty in distinguishing between the use of technology for campaigning on the one hand, and governing on the other. The increasing use of communications technology was creating, in Robinson's terms, House members who were "more dynamic, egocentric, immoderate and, perhaps, intemperate."[9] Individualized pluralism's early seeds were sown as early as the 1958 elections, which brought several northern liberal Democrats to Congress who quickly became impatient with the more conservative committee elites. However, neither House Speaker Sam Rayburn or Senate Majority Leader Lyndon Johnson was willing to embrace their cause, mostly because any successes likely would have been repressed by the incumbent Republican president, Dwight Eisenhower. However, the elections of Democrats Kennedy and Johnson to the presidency brought with them significant increases in the number of liberal Democrats in both houses of Congress. As a result, a few House and Senate practices were liberalized. In the House, the Rules Committee was enlarged to include more liberal legislators. In the Senate, a rule was adopted to make it easier to invoke cloture and defeat a conservative filibuster. These changes were minor in comparison with what was to come. However, they were enough to remind defenders of the old system that the new breed of legislator was soon going to be a major force with which to be reckoned. By the mid-1970s the new breed, together with its cultural by-products, were the dominant forces in both the House and the Senate.

The new breed of congressman and senator is much less prone to consider negotiations an essential part of the policy process than were their earlier counterparts. They tend not to be married to institutional networking as a route to success. Their main loyalty is to those who elected them, and their choice of staff, committee and subcommittee assignments, and work schedules reflects that. Trips to their districts are so frequent that the House and Senate often have to schedule serious floor debates and critical votes between

Tuesday mornings and Wednesday evenings to guarantee that quorums are present. In short, the individualized pluralism period has been marked by a revolt against hierarchy and institutional influence on legislators' behavior. The protection against excessive interest group influence offered by the protective period has been replaced by a system which rewards individual legislators for dealing with groups directly, especially those which dominate in their constituencies. Cultivating such relationships means votes and campaign finance support. It also means that these group interests are not viewed unfavorably when these legislators cast votes on policies.

While the protective period adapted Madisonianism to the realities of mid-twentieth-century politics, the individualized period offers an environment that encourages the opposite. The impact of groups is always tempered somewhat by committee deliberations and floor votes. However, since the individualized environment bypasses or reduces the impact of negotiations on policy decisions, one key moderating force is eliminated from the process. This is very significant, because individual group positions remain intact for a longer period of time, making their ultimate impact on final policy decisions more direct. When interest group pressures are too great, attempts to examine proposals for their intrinsic merit are lost or compromised. This is not what the founders wanted or expected. However, it is the environment which molds the public opinion to which modern House and Senate members respond.

The impact of these conditions on congressional processes and policy products has been profound, and they will be discussed in some depth later in the chapter. However, before proceeding with that, it is necessary to describe and briefly discuss several basic realities about Congress and how it has traditionally organized itself to conduct its legislative business. Once these are understood, then an analysis of the impact of individualized pluralism on those realities will be more meaningful.

Congress: The Policy Fundamentals

Understanding how Congress conducts its business means comprehending four basic truths about congressional organization and operations. The first of these is that *most of the basic legislative work is accomplished by the standing committees and subcommittees in both houses.* During the 105th Congress, the House and the Senate each had twenty standing committees. Committees are composed of several subcommittees that allow the committees to examine legislative proposals with a degree of specialization. Subcommittees also offer legislators the opportunity to develop expertise in one or more policy areas, as well as the chance to serve key elements in their constituencies by leveraging their influence on subcommittee and, ultimately, full committee decisions. The number of subcommittees has grown rapidly over the years. In 1945, there were 97 subcommittees in the House and 35 in the Senate. By 1967, the number had risen to 101 and 80 respectively.[10] The number of subcommittees changes with regularity in response to both policy conditions and legislator demands. Approaching the end of the twentieth century, the total number of House and Senate subcommittees seems to be firmly fixed at well above 200. Part of this increase is due to the growing technical nature of policy challenges. However, as will be discussed later, much of it is due to the efforts of congressional party organizations to give their members as many key job assignments as possible.

All organizations must parcel out job assignments to subunits. In this sense, congressional committees and subcommittees do for their parent houses what, for example, the

Chevrolet or Pontiac automobile subdivisions do for General Motors. In addition to the obvious mission of helping Congress conduct its legislative business effectively, congressional committees have an additional constitutional role—that of helping Congress maintain a competitive policy balance with the executive branch. The separation of powers principle encourages interbranch rivalries, and one of the best ways for both the House and Senate to become competitive equals with the president and the bureaucracy is through an independent and specialized committee and subcommittee system. Therefore, committees take on special significance in a constitutionally separated system of government. This can be contrasted with conditions in most parliamentary systems, within which legislative committees are mostly organizers and conduits for policy packages presented them by legislative majorities. Also, in separated systems strong committees and (especially) subcommittees are encouraged by administrative agencies and interest groups that want to develop and nourish iron triangle networks to advance mutual policy causes. Independent committees and subcommittees that can be befriended provide ways for these forces to bypass potential threats posed by the separation of powers to their policy quests. In sum, a strong and independent congressional committee and subcommittee system is encouraged by the Constitution and its political by-products.

A second key to understanding the organization and operation of Congress is that *partisanship determines how it organizes to conduct its business*. With the exception of the vice-president, whom the Constitution designates as the Senate's presiding officer, all House and Senate officers are selected by member votes cast along strict party lines. The Speaker of the House is elected by a unanimous vote of the majority party, as are the respective majority and minority floor leaders, as well as the party whips. Since the vice-president officially presides over the Senate, the Senate counterpart to the House Speaker is the Majority Floor Leader who is voted in by a unanimous vote of the majority party. He or she coordinates the Senate's business with the Minority Floor Leader who is elected by a unanimous vote of his or her party membership. In addition, committee membership is divided proportionally between parties, with each committee reflecting approximately the same party membership percentages as exist in the parent house.

A third fundamental reality affecting the way Congress conducts its affairs is that *the rules under which the House and Senate conduct their business are not neutral in use or effect*. Since the basis of organization is partisan, rules are often applied in a partisan fashion. For example, the House Rules Committee is officially charged with the responsibility of making a qualitative assessment of the relative importance of bills reported by committees. Presumably this means giving significant bills more favorable floor status and debate time. However, if the Committee's majority finds the bill repugnant, it can report it with an open rule that allows for it to be amended on the floor, in the hope that amendments will compromise or defeat its core purpose.

The filibuster, or unlimited debate, rule in the Senate is often employed for the same purpose. In fact there is no such thing as a filibuster "rule." The filibuster option exists because there are no Senate rules prohibiting unlimited debate. Small, well-organized minorities, as well as majorities, can employ the filibuster to delay consideration of a bill in order to force compromises of its contents or, in some cases, to actually kill it. Filibusters can be stopped by a successful vote of cloture, requiring a three-fifths vote of the entire Senate. However, senators are reluctant to invoke cloture for two reasons. First, they take pride in preserving the Senate as a forum which encourages unencumbered debate. Second, although a heavy majority of senators may oppose a filibuster, they are reluctant to support a cloture vote because sometime they may be part of a small minority that seeks to affect policy by the same means. If they tolerate others' filibuster strategies, they can expect reciprocity when it comes their turn. For this reason, as well as a minority's adept use of floor amendment strategies, a cohesive majority party or coalition has much more difficulty in imposing its will in the Senate, as compared to the House. The result is that Senate majority leaders must work more closely with minority leaders to enact legislation.

Filibusters can be used to thwart confirmation of presidential appointees, as was the case in 1993 when President Clinton withdrew his nomination of Dr. Henry Foster, a pro-choice advocate on the abortion issue, as U.S. Surgeon General because Foster's supporters could not defeat a Senate filibuster. In the wake of that defeat and hoping to avoid repeated confrontations, Clinton tended to nominate less ideological, more middle-of-the-road candidates for cabinet, subcabinet, and judicial positions.

By threatening to sponsor filibusters, senators can often gain major policy concessions from their colleagues. Frequently, they employ a "hold" strategy. Holds are unwritten privileges or understandings that permit senators to block floor consideration of policies by asking their party chieftains not to schedule them for floor debate. The power of the hold rests in the implicit threat of a filibuster unless concessions are made in advance of floor debate. For example, in 1995 former Senator Bill Bradley (D–New Jersey) advanced a hold on every bill reported by the Senate Energy and Natural Resources Committee to encourage the committee to consider and report legislation that protected a tract of privately owned land in New Jersey from commercial development.[11] Former senator William Cohen (R–Maine) once employed the same strategy on the Senate's consideration of five nominees for Agriculture Department positions, asking that floor consideration of their nominations be delayed until the Secretary of Agriculture addressed the potato problem in Maine.[12]

A fourth reality that affects the organization and operation of Congress is that *the seniority norm significantly influences the choice of committee and institutional leaders.* It has been more important in influencing the choice of committee chairs and ranking minority members than in influencing the choice of institutional leaders. Insofar as committees are concerned, the chair position usually goes to the individual who has the longest uninterrupted tenure on the committee, and whose party is the majority party in the parent house. Seniority is usually not critical in making initial committee assignments. Party leaders consider member wishes, geographic balance, and demonstrated commitment to the party's leaders and programs when making initial assignments. With infrequent exceptions, however, seniority is the only factor affecting a member's retention on a committee.

Because of the seniority norm, or principle, the majority party's most senior members have the inside track for committee chair positions, and most senior figures will more than likely chair the most powerful committees. Therefore, committee chairs tend to be older individuals, and represent states or districts that are relatively safe for the party. These constituencies are likely to be politically conservative, and therefore often at odds with the more liberal trends that often surface nationally and affect, of course, the selection of the president. In addition to this tendency to encourage executive-legislative conflict, the seniority principle often encourages conflict between chairs and parent house leadership, because the latter are often chosen for their ability to represent all factions of the majority party and, in reality, the parent houses in general. However, seniority does have its advantages. It discourages intra-party struggles over who should chair committees, and it keeps committees more independent and powerful than would be the case if chairs were selected by majority party vote or a vote of committee members, or, in the case of the House, appointed by the House Speaker.

The Watergate scandal had a direct impact on congressional committees. Committees' decisions were democratized, thereby diminishing the influence of committee chairs. Nevertheless, shrewd and forceful committee chairs were able to maintain significant power and influence over committee affairs and, ultimately, over public policy. Congressman John Dingell (D–Michigan) and Congressman Bud Shuster (R–Pennsylvania) were two such examples. Once labeled the "most feared man in Washington," Dingell used his position as chair of the House Committee on Energy and Commerce to leverage his championing of proconsumer and proregulatory interests in regulatory policy, especially the production, transmission, and distributional pricing of natural gas.[13] Dingell used his knowledge of the gas industry to launch major legislative oversight investigations into the pricing practices of the entire natural gas industry. Dingell's approach toward industry representatives was forceful and often confrontational, making his inquiries more successful than would have been the case had a less intense and focused person chaired the committee.

Another powerful post-Watergate committee chair was Representative Bud Shuster (R–Pennsylavania). In contrast to Dingell, who was an across-the-board advocate for the consumer, Shuster used his chairmanship of the House Committee on Transportation and Infrastructure to channel vast amounts of pork barrel money back to his constituency and to the constituencies of his close political associates in the House. Working closely with Ann Eppard, a former staff employee turned lobbyist, Shuster allied himself closely with agents of the construction, chemical, railroad, and advertising industries who profited from his passion for the pork barrel. Hundreds of millions of dollars of project money made their way back to his district, virtually revitalizing it economically. A fifty-three-mile stretch of U.S. Highway 220 was made into a four-lane highway, appropriately named the "Bud Shuster Highway." Numerous other highway, interchange, sewer, recreation, and hydroelectric projects were funneled to the district as a result of his influence. Shuster's strategy was to reward his friends and punish his political opponents. The House version of the 1991 highway bill was so replete with Shuster's pet projects that many of his fellow legislators protested. One senator, Daniel Moynihan (D–New York), referred to Shuster's home district as the "state of Altoona," a city in his (Shuster's) district that had profited significantly from pork barrel projects. In 1994 when Senator Bob Graham (D–Florida) complained about Shuster's practices, Shuster threatened to cancel nearly $500 million in demonstration projects earmarked for Florida. Friendly industries contributed generously to Shuster's campaign war chest, despite the fact that he was unopposed in most of his campaigns for reelection. Sizeable campaign war chests are often used to discourage reelection challenges.[14]

Finally, a fifth reality of the congressional policy landscape, and one that has taken on more importance in recent years, is that *the House and Senate members are becoming increasingly dependent on office and committee staffs for policy ideas, legislative strategies, and campaign assistance.* As legislative and campaign requirements gradually consume more and more of a legislator's time, he or she naturally turns to the staff complex for support. This poses a significant threat to the representation challenge, because it substitutes the judgment of the expert for the instincts of the elected politician. In Ross K. Baker's terms, it is essentially a case of "the unelected leading the overburdened."[15] At the beginning of the nineteenth century, there were more House and Senate members than there were staff. By 1985 House rules permitted eighteen full-time and four part-time staff per member. Senators averaged thirty-one per office, with larger staffs being assigned to senators from highly populated states. In addition, all committees and subcommittees have staff assigned to members of both the majority and minority parties.[16] Although both the House and Senate handle the same policy and oversight challenges, the House has four and one-half times the manpower to do it—435 members as opposed to 100. This means that House members have fewer committee assignments, and can therefore develop more policy expertise which, in turn, makes them less dependent on staff for policy cues. With less than one-fourth the manpower of the House, senators have more committee assignments and, in general, do not develop the expertise of their House counterparts. Therefore, they are more dependent on staff, and there exists the possibility of delegating too much authority to both their personal and committee staffs.[17] In addition to the questions such a condition poses for representative government—the delegation of policy power to the unaccountable—it can also undercut the interpersonal networks that have been so much a part of the Senate's tradition and, in turn, make senators less loyal to the Senate as an institution than they have been historically.

In addition to these five rather universal realities of congressional life and politics, there are several by-products of bicameralism that have historically influenced the ways in which Congress conducts its business. Some of these have been referenced in earlier discussion, while others are noted here for the first time. One of these is the manpower differential, discussed above, that encourages senators to be more deferent to staff and, on occasion, to the president and bureaucracy. Another involves differences in constituency pressures. Senatorial districts—the states—are more heterogeneous in character. In all but the most thinly populated states, where both Senate and House members represent the entire state, House districts are smaller and more homogeneous. This means that there are more constituency pressures on senators than on House members. This condition contributes to a third by-product of bicameralism. The Senate has molded its rules system to accommodate senators' constituency pressures, making it easier for senators to press the case for constituents than can House members. Senate rules allow a senator to introduce and pursue an issue at nearly any point in the legislative process, and virtually force the entire Senate to consider it. Furthermore, the senator need not be a member of the standing committee to which the relevant bill was assigned. The House has little tolerance for such *ad hoc* strategies, and offers few opportunities for its members to do the same. In fact, senators don't often conduct special policy crusades for causes that affect a relatively small population in their state. It isn't cost-effective, and may be poor political strategy.[18] Finally, the Senate has historically been considered more of a "club," where mutual respect and comity have won out over what senators considered to be the more plebeian and pedestrian environment of the House. Therefore, the Senate is presumed to be more prestigious than the House. Members respect one another because they are fellow ambassadors from their respective states, irrespective of the political differences that divide them. Presumably, this makes the Senate more stable, more reliable, and more responsible politically. Furthermore, during the protective pluralist period discussed above, such a condition encouraged compromises among the Senate's "barons" that produced the kind of temperate, moderate policies favored by the founding fathers.

Each of these by-products of bicameralism has had an impact on policy processes and policy outcomes and, to the extent they have not been altered by the by-products of individualized pluralism (discussed in the next section), they will continue to do so. Their roots are, of course, in the Constitution's principle of federalism which, along with the separation of powers principle, are structural "ghosts" at many policy banquets.

Individualized Pluralism: The Policy Fundamentals

Congress is considerably different now than it was during the protective pluralist era, and much of this difference can be explained by the impact of individualized pluralism on both the attitude of its members and on its decision processes. The following discussion revisits the policy fundamentals analyzed above through the individualized pluralism window, and attempts to describe how Congress has been changed, the effects of those changes on both policy content and policy processes, and the extent to which constitutional politics has played a role in the entire transition. Two points should be kept in mind. First, the overall effect of individualized pluralism on congressional decision making has been to atomize and decentralize power. Second, presented in the form of a hypothesis, the more power is fragmented and decentralized within institutions, the more likely it is for constitutional politics to impact on the decision processes and policy products of those institutions.

Committees and Seniority

Both Congress generally and its committees in particular have always had to struggle with tensions introduced by the imperatives of constituency representation on the one hand, and national policymaking on the other. During protective pluralism's zenith (the 1940s and 1950s) a relatively healthy equilibrium existed between the two, and the standing committees were mostly responsible for that equilibrium. The division of labor that existed among committees was considered rational, and their work and recommendations were respected. Committee chairs were, by and large, individuals of prominence and prestige. Membership on committees helped House and Senate members realize their ambitions as both politicians and as policy experts. The reward system within Congress valued hard work, and committees offered the most obvious arena for that. Other important norms included those of apprenticeship (working with and learning from elders), specialization, institutional loyalty, mutual respect, and courtesy. To be sure, committees were bastions of partisanship that rewarded majority party members far more than they did minority party members with such benefits and larger budgets and larger staffs. However, it was a rather healthy polarization, with each party respecting the other's values and accepting, philosophically, decisions that embodied them. Junior members of Congress and of committees depended on the institutional party leaders for help in securing their legislative careers. This was offered in the form of party financial assistance for election campaigns, speeches, advice, and acceptance as part of the "club," or "team." Committees were a functional, vital part of a benevolent hierarchy that served both leaders and apprentices.

Then came the revolution, the causes of which were discussed earlier in this chapter. Legislators, especially those elected in the late 1960s and early 1970s, no longer considered the traditional committee structure and sociology to be of use to them as they sought to secure their legislative careers. Constituencies had become more competitive because of their increasing demographic diversity. Relying more and more on television in campaigns, the high costs of television advertising necessitated looking beyond party coffers for adequate financing. Traditional institutional structures and loyalties gave way to quests to secure incumbency by committing office resources, time, and energy to constituency service. The representation and policymaking imperatives were thrown out of balance in favor of the former.

The overall effect of the revolution on congressional committees was to compromise their power, invade their stability, undercut the camaraderie of their membership, and decentralize their authority. Congressional politics during the protective pluralism period was, in essence, committee politics. Policies were molded by committed policy masters who controlled committee positions and agendas in ways that nursed their constituency interests. Most conflicts were resolved within committees, thereby significantly reducing the number of floor amendments. Bills already bore the imprint of committee members before they reached the floor. Legislators not assigned to the committees found it difficult to develop the expertise to "take on the system" during floor debates, and consequently found it difficult to attract support for major floor challenges to committee recommendations.[19] Strong subgovernments, or iron triangles, nourished by the reciprocity of baron-sponsored logrolling, were the result.

However, beginning in the late 1960s, new and recently elected members of Congress began frontal assaults on this system. They were averse to the institutional game, and sought key assignments and recognition quickly. Many subcommittees were established to provide junior members with opportunities to serve as chairs, thereby gaining leadership experience and publicity that would advantage

them politically in their districts. Party organizations retreated to the background as the old-line barons, still serving as committee chairs, struggled with junior members to control committee agendas and decision processes. Junior members were successful in several quests to formally democratize committees. In addition to increasing the number of subcommittees, reforms were instituted that modified the seniority rule to allow committee members to select or dismiss committee chairs. Several chairs lost their positions shortly after these reforms were instituted in the mid-1970s. Three House committee chairs were removed in 1975, and one in 1977. In the Senate, the Armed Services Committee's ranking minority member lost his position in 1985. Chairs lost their power to set, unilaterally, committee meeting times and meeting agendas. Committees were permitted to meet without the chair present. Once terms had been set for floor debates on bills, limits were placed on how long chairs could delay their consideration. If floor debates were delayed for more than seven legislative days, a majority vote of the committee could vote to begin floor consideration of a bill without the chair's approval.

Other reforms impacted the structural focus and internal management of the standing committees. A major objective of the reformists was to make Congress more of a co-equal partner with the president in both policy and finance. As a result, Congress enacted the Budget and Impoundment Control Act in 1974. This law established procedures to help Congress free itself from committee and subcommittee structures which examined the budget in a piecemeal fashion, and to examine it from more of an integrated point of view. It established a budget timetable that mandated the establishment of expenditure limits in each functional area of the budget, and then encouraged Congress to work within those limits when deciding how to appropriate money.

Separate House and Senate budget committees were created to help prepare budget resolutions that incorporated these efforts. The act also created the Congressional Budget Office (CBO), which was to provide well-researched, current, and multiyear projections of income and expenditures which Congress could use as it established budget priorities. The purpose was to challenge the then existing dominance of the president and his budget agency—the Office of Management and Budget (OMB)—over the budget. The law also put limits on the president's ability to impound appropriated funds, making them unavailable for expenditure. The law required Congress to honor a presidential request to impound funds within forty-five days. If permission was not granted, then the president could not impound money and it had to be spent as the law directed. The budget committees created by the 1974 act were superstructures that were layered over the existing appropriations and authorizations committees in an effort to gain for Congress a more comprehensive approach to the budget process. A second purpose of the law was to restore more executive-legislative equilibrium in budgeting and finance. Ironically, it also forced Congress to make planning and priority decisions that many of the "new breed" culture found uncomfortable. Prioritizing means making hard choices, many of which demand sacrifice. This is countercultural to the new breed's constituency service orientation, especially during periods of economic hardship. This may help explain why the 1974 law has not delivered the rationality to budgeting and the coordination to long-term financial planning that it promised. In all likelihood, disappointments with the law may well represent just how difficult it is for Congress to master competently the challenges of effective representation on the one hand, and effective governance on the other.

Attempts to improve policy coordination among committees proceeded along other fronts during the individualized pluralism period. In 1974 the House altered the policy jurisdiction of many standing committees and, for the first time, introduced a rule allowing bills to be referred to several committees. Called the "multiple referral" principle, its purpose was to increase the amount of scrutiny to which a bill is subjected, to afford multiple-committee review of policy questions that clearly fall under more than one committee's jurisdiction, and to inspire committees to cooperate with each other, thereby reducing the effects of formal jurisdictional differences on how proposed legislation is interpreted and examined. The practice also has the advantage of bringing the House leadership into the management of bills because of the need to develop ways to bring committees together.[20] Bills can either be referred to two or more committees simultaneously (most common), or they can be split into sections and each section sent to separate committees, or they can be examined by one committee and then sent to a second committee. The proportional use of multiple referrals gradually expanded from a low of 6 percent of all referred bills in 1975 to 14 percent in 1986.[21] In addition, the multiple review is often employed voluntarily. Davidson and Oleszek estimate that approximately one-quarter of the House committee work and one-tenth of Senate committee work is impacted by the multiple referral principle.[22] The multiple referral rule was adopted to accommodate the new breed's desire for increased involvement in legislative matters, because multiple reviews offer more legislators the opportunity for policy input. It has, simultaneously, encouraged intercommittee appreciation of the multiple effects, or domino character, of most policies. However, since several committees have their chance at bat, so to speak, under a multiple referral system, fewer of these bills become law than do bills that are referred to only one committee.[23]

Other moves during the 1970s, most of

them rooted in House or Senate party actions, compromised the salience of the old committee structure in legislation. In 1973 the House Democrats created a committee caucus that was authorized to choose subcommittee chairs and determine subcommittee budgets. That same year, the House Democratic Caucus enacted a Subcommittee Bill of Rights which required that bills be sent to subcommittees, that subcommittees have adequate staff and financial support, and that they be allowed complete control over their agendas. In 1974 House Democrats passed a rule that all committees had to have a minimum of four subcommittees, thereby forcing such a structure on the House Ways and Means Committee. In 1976 party caucuses were authorized to establish the number of subcommittees along with their jurisdiction. In 1977 party resolutions were passed allowing party caucuses to select committee chairs.[24]

Floor alterations to committee recommendation became more common in the 1970s. The tradition of casting House floor votes anonymously was abandoned in favor of roll-call votes in 1971. That action had the effect of stimulating floor debates and votes on legislative details, thereby compromising even further the influence of committees on policy. The trend of these actions is clear: The antisystem, antiauthority, antielite, participatory nature of the reform era ushered in a new way of confronting policy challenges that virtually equated the open representation of policy views in multiple forums with effective governing.

Partisanship and Rules

Reform era changes in the application of Congress's partisan organization base and in its political use of rules occurred simultaneously. Often the changing nature of the first (partisanship) directly impacted on the use of the second (rules). Therefore they will be analyzed together.

At first, it may appear to be somewhat ironic that the role of partisanship, the role of party leaders, and the application of House and Senate rules were all bolstered by the reforms of the 1970s. However, if the antiestablishment nature of the revolution is borne in mind, such effects may not appear to be so strange. The assault on the committee-anchored traditions of the protective pluralist period had as its objective the compromise of committee power, and that assault was conducted from both a power devolution perspective and a power centralization perspective. Congressional party organizations were the source of both attacks. The devolution, or decentralization, assault came in the form of enhanced subcommittee power and control of subcommittee jurisdictions and budgets by party sources outside the committee. That was discussed in the previous section. The second attack came from party-based hierarchical sources, including House and Senate leaders as well as the party caucuses. Altering the rules to increase the chances of the attack's success was, in essence, a natural course of action.

There are several ways to measure the role of partisanship on congressional decision making, One is to evaluate the role of institutional leaders and party organizations on how Congress is organized and energized. Another is to evaluate the effect of party-line votes on policy. The first is more valuable than the second. This is because party voting doesn't tell us much about how cohesive party organizations are. It may reveal something significant about how popular party leaders are, or how nonpartisan an issue is. That will be examined more in depth below. For the time being the focus will be on the impact of the reform era on the roles of party leaders and party organizations in adapting Congress to the realities of the reform era. Since the Democrats were the majority party during the

1970s, the focus will be on the altered roles of the House speaker and of the House Democratic Caucus, an organization composed of all House Democrats.

Before the 1970s the major role of the Democratic Caucus was to select the speaker and to make a few decisions regarding assignments of Democrats to standing committees. However, in response to the demands of newly elected Democrats, in 1971 the caucus directed its Committee on Committees—responsible for selecting Democratic members of standing committees—to consider factors other than seniority when selecting committee chairs. Although nothing was done immediately to change the lineup of chairs, this move had the effect of placing them all on notice that their disrespect for the party line could eventually cost them their positions. By 1974 some caucus members were able to force caucuswide votes on some controversial chairs, and three were denied reappointment. A fourth, Ways and Means Committee chairman Wilbur Mills, resigned under pressure before a formal vote was taken. In 1975, the caucus assumed the right to choose the subcommittee chairs of the House Appropriations Committee. Using the House Rules Committees's control over the rules of floor debate, the caucus voted to permit revenue bills reported by the Ways and Means Committee to be reported to the floor with an open rule, thereby permitting the legislation to be amended on the floor. This was a major break with tradition. The Ways and Means Committee had, by tradition, an understanding with the Rules Committee that its bills would be reported with a closed rule that would permit no amendments from the floor. This was a major compromise in the ability of the committee to virtually dictate the final House version of a bill in its report.

Coinciding with these changes were reforms that increased the power of the House speaker and the Democratic caucus. During 1973 and 1974 all House Democratic leaders (speaker, majority leader, whip) were assigned to the party's Committee on Committees (providing them leverage over committee assignments), the speaker was made chair of a newly created Steering and Policy Committee; he was also assigned the right to appoint and remove a majority of the members of the Committee on Committees, and to appoint all the Democratic members of the House Rules Committee. In 1974 he was granted the multiple committee referral option (discussed above), and the authority to establish special, *ad hoc* committees to consider legislation if he thought the standing committees were politically or jurisdictionally inappropriate. In addition the role of the Democratic caucus was strengthened. As noted, it was assigned the responsibility of electing committee chairs irrespective of seniority, and meetings could be called quickly by only a few of its members so that policy questions could be thoroughly examined as soon as those members thought it necessary.

In sum, the House reforms of the early to mid-1970s strengthened the position of individual members and subcommittees, rejuvenated the position of House speaker, and increased the policy role of the Democratic Caucus. Some of the changes were devolutionary in direction, while others centralized power. However, all of them were directed at opening congressional decision arenas and processes to the rekindled forces of democracy that were surfacing in society and employing electronic journalism to make their points quickly and directly. The standing committees and their chairs, bastions of power and stability during the 1940s, 1950s, and early 1960s, were attacked and weakened by both the decentralizing and centralizing forces of reform. The major beneficiaries were the party organizations, voters in areas represented by legislators who had by the early 1970s gained enough electoral security to champion reform, and voters in constituencies of recently elected legislators who were elected because of their antisystem, prorepresentation stances and consequently were unwilling to make a real world difference between the challenge of campaigning and the challenge of governing.

Reforms in the Senate were similar to those in the House, although less comprehensive. In 1970, Senate rules were altered to allow a senator to sit on only one of the top four prestige committees—Appropriations, Finance, Armed Services, and Foreign Relations. Shortly thereafter, the Democratic Caucus (then the majority party caucus) ruled that a secret caucus vote on committee chairs would be held if 20 percent of Senate Democrats requested it. In 1975, junior senators petitioned for more staff assistance, and received it. In 1976 and 1977 rules were adopted that limited any senator to one full-committee chairmanship and two subcommittee chairmanships. This action offered more senators the chance to chair a committee or subcommittee. Following the House example, in 1975 the Senate amended its rules to require that most standing committee markup sessions and conference committee sessions be opened to the public and to the press. Finally, in 1975 a contingent of liberal senators succeeded in breaking a filibuster on a proposal to change the cloture rule—the rule that, if invoked, defeats a filibuster. The new rule specified that a vote of 60 percent of the entire Senate, as opposed to two-thirds of those present, was sufficient to invoke cloture and defeat a filibuster.[25]

In fact, the net result of these reforms for Congress was the accommodation of the electoral and representative missions at the expense of the governing mission. Not only were congressional internal procedures democratized, but members also gradually began to devote more of their time and resources to gaining reelection in the hope of securing their legislative careers. The decentralization and fragmentation of legislative institutions and processes was a logical way to feed the political results of these reshuffled imperatives. However, that created problems of coordination, and so party mechanisms were strengthened to lend some hierarchical coherence to the fragmented institutional landscape. However, those changes also served the reformers' goals, because they offered ways to bypass or compromise the impact of the "democracy insensitive" standing committees.

Government Parties and Electoral Parties

One of the legacies of the postreform Congress has been the tendency to associate the policy positions of congressional leaders with party positions that are notably ideological or doctrinaire in cast. In a sense, this represents Congress's embodiment of the increasingly ideological and symbolic character of political dialogue and rhetoric in general. The net effect of such dialogue is to make the solutions to perplexing policy problems appear to be relatively simple in concept and procedural in focus. For example, many politicians argue that problems can be dealt with effectively if power is either centralized or decentralized in principle, if taxes are either reduced or increased, or if industry is either heavily regulated or deregulated. However, few, if any, complex policy problems will be resolved by policies produced primarily because they embody any of these precepts as a matter of principle. Good policy solutions blend the pragmatic with the ideological. Nonetheless, one of the legacies of the post-1970 congressional reforms has been to simplify policy discourse and to encourage congressional rhetoric and voting to be more ideological in tone.

It is certainly true that there has been a generation-long trend toward more pro-forma party unity in Congress. A "party vote" occurs when a majority of each party's membership votes together in opposition to the other party. A "party unity" score measures the percentage of party members voting together. In 1984, the percentage of party vote frequency was 47 percent for the House and 40 percent for the Senate. That same year the House-Senate party unity percentages were 74 percent for the Democrats and 72 percent for the Republicans. These figures can be compared to those a decade later in 1994, the year of the so-called "Republican Revolution." In 1994 the House party vote percentage was 62, while the Senate's was 52. Party unity percentages for 1994 were 83 percent for both parties.[26] This increased polarization was occurring at the very time that the strength of the general public's commitment to political parties, other than symbolically, was on the wane. This was due to several factors, including a rising level of education and a growing importance of the news media as a source of political information. The number of committed party identifiers was shrinking and the number of independents was rising. Even strong party identifiers were becoming less willing to vote a straight party ticket.[27] These conditions suggest continued party decline rather than resurgent strength.

Congressional trends suggest that political parties are regaining their ideological, tutorial, and programmatic character and, in effect, perhaps becoming more disciplined. This observation, of course, appears to contradict the above observation and those made in the previous chapter. In that chapter, political parties were pictured as very disjointed and undisciplined. How can this apparent inconsistency be explained? The answer is that the recently renewed ideological cast to American political parties, especially the Republican Party, has been largely confined to the congressional arena. It has not spread to the party rank-and-file. Despite the fact that

most voters tend to side with one of the two major parties, they are not becoming more ideologically homogeneous. They do not divide surgically into liberal and conservative camps, however those terms are defined. If anything, the opposite appears to be the case. Americans are a diverse lot and, due to migration patterns, immigration, and population growth, congressional constituencies are becoming more heterogeneous, not homogeneous. Ideological rhetoric is more advantageous politically to politicians representing homogeneous, not diverse districts. However, even if districts are demographically diverse, that does not mean that those who vote necessarily are. In other words, those who vote are becoming more ideologically homogeneous while, at the same time, the general population is not.

There are several reasons for the discernable gap between ideology-inspired congressional rhetoric and the political facts of constituency life. First, senators and representatives, especially Republicans, are in fact more ideological than at any time in recent memory. They secure their party's nomination and are often elected because they are supported by well-organized, well-financed, cohesive minorities that sponsor and respond to voter turnout campaigns in an era when voters in general are becoming increasingly apathetic. The gradual decline in voter turnout has several causes—post-Watergate skepticism about politics and government, negative campaign advertising, and the public's growing realization that solutions to key problems lie in pragmatism and not ideology. Consequently, candidates with clear ideological messages encourage voters to think that politicians are becoming increasingly irrelevant to their lives. Party organizations and their candidates focus their fund-raising efforts on well-to-do potential donors and on corporations. Regular linkage with party rank-and-file seems increasingly irrelevant to financing campaigns. As a result, political parties have allowed their local organizations to degenerate, leaving them without a core base of voters who can be relied on to vote for the party slate with any degree of regularity. An increasing percentage of those who do vote regularly represent cohesive, ideologically homogeneous minority movements within the party. The role of the Christian conservatives within the Republican Party in recent years is a case in point. The growing apathy among other party regulars makes these factions more significant in determining party nominees via direct primaries and conventions, as well as how well the party's candidates fare in general elections. Organized minorities have considerable advantages over disorganized and apathetic majorities. Recognizing the need to increase rank-and-file electoral participation, in recent years parties have sponsored major "get-out-the-vote" (GOTV) campaigns. In a sense, these campaigns illustrate the problem of faction dominance parties. This is because the major party voter mobilization efforts are often conducted by the organized minorities that dominate the parties—the Christian conservatives for the Republicans and the labor unions for the Democrats. In addition, professional pollsters and political operatives hired by the parties to study what types of issue positions are likely to appeal to voters usually focus on how to appeal to groups whose members are likely to turn out in greater numbers once a candidate's issue position becomes clear. This is often called an "astroturf" instead of a grassroots strategy. While it may win elections for candidates in close races, the result is a campaign focus on an increasingly smaller percentage of the electorate, making it increasingly difficult to stem the deterioration in voter turnout.

A second reason for the developing ideology/pragmatism schism within political parties is rooted in the increasing trend toward divided government. Voters often elect presidents and congresses of a different party, thereby creating a divided government condition which encourages the congressional majority and the president to blame each other for policy impasses. Therefore, policies incorporating an ideological switch of direction are often defeated because of this disharmony. Each branch blames the other for the stalemate, and both either escape or postpone being held responsible for it. Consequently, legislators often don't have to explain why their policies are so unrepresentative of their constituency majorities. Executive-legislative conflict often leaves the issue unresolved. Even if it is resolved by compromise, the final result represents neither party's original position, so therefore neither party nor the president is responsible. Conflict introduced by the political repercussions of the separation of powers buys time and postpones the inevitable.

Third, and very important, the policy agenda has been subjected to what Kenneth Shepsle has called "fiscalization" since the late 1960s.[28] This means, in effect, that matters involving budgets, deficits, inflation, entitlements, health care, and retirement benefits have been taking on increasing policy significance. Since most of these issues impact on one another, coordinating how they are discussed and analyzed within Congress is critical. However, this also means that bargains have to be struck among various points of view before any type of agreement at all can be reached. In turn, this means that firm, ideological positions can fall victim to compromise and, in effect, become virtually unidentifiable in the final legislative product. Therefore, if constituency majorities do not experience firsthand the downside of their representatives' ideological crusade, they are much more likely to tolerate it. Furthermore, the public has become accustomed to, and therefore is more likely to tolerate, ideological exchanges over how money is to be raised and expended. These are questions that seem to naturally trigger "either/or" exchanges among political adversaries. For example, either big government is bad because it is inefficient, insensitive, and wastes money, or it is good because it protects the underprivileged from the predatory wolves of the marketplace economy, and therefore major expenditures for such purposes are a moral necessity. Tax reductions directed toward the higher income brackets are either a way to free capital for investment to spur economic growth, or they are an elite-engineered scheme to subsidize the wealthy at the expense of the middle and lower income groups.

Finally, legislation that mandates sacrifice can very often have its effect without those who avidly support it being held accountable for it. This is because many laws enacted by Congress are legitimized via what might be termed omnibus legislation. Omnibus bills are bills that contain several items, most of them controversial, but which are passed as a "package," usually in the form of a *continuing resolution* or a *reconciliation bill*. Legislators can support them because sacrifice is dispersed, with everybody sharing the pain. If Congress and the president must cut spending and/or raise taxes to deal with the deficit, presenting sacrifice in the form of a bill that asks all to sacrifice has a better chance of passage than if the same proposals were presented separately. Multiprovision bills demanding sacrifice are easier for Congress to pass and difficult for a president to veto.[29] Democrats were very successful with such a strategy during the Reagan administration. Reagan signed several multiprovision continuing resolutions into law that, more than likely, would have been vetoed had they been sent to him as freestanding legislation.[30]

Therefore, rather than finding themselves between the proverbial "rock and a hard place," congressional ideologues often find themselves in the envious position of being able to have their cake and eat it too. This offers at least a partial explanation for the gap between what might be termed the government parties and the electoral parties. If roll-call votes are a measure of congressional partisanship, Congress has indeed become more partisan since the 1970s reforms. This has occurred despite the fact that the electoral parties seem to have weakened during the same period. Ticket splitting has become almost habitual, and voters chose either to initiate or retain divided government over unified government in eight of the national elections held between 1976 and 1996. Weak electoral parties are clearly associated with divided government results.[31] Logic would seemingly dictate that weak electorate parties would lead to weak government parties.

However, divided government conditions appear to fortify government parties rather than weaken them. Historically, this has been the case, but the reform era apparently has introduced a countertrend. Reason would dictate that strong electoral parties would mean strong government parties. If voters reflect a party orientation in elections, then legislators would be inclined to assign party organizations in Congress the leverage they need to establish policy agendas and work for their enactment (majority party), or to constructively criticize proposals and offer alternative agendas (minority). On the other hand, if voters show indifference to parties in elections, then the inclination would be to slight party organizations and their leaders at the governing stage. However, the reform period brought with it the election of a number of policy zealots who were committed to policy reform for its own sake. These individuals understood the potential value of strong congressional parties to their cause. Therefore, they worked to strengthen governing parties at the same time the electoral parties' strength was declining. Moreover, governing parties have never been very helpful to legislators in reelection campaigns. Furthermore, the omnibus character of legislation, discussed above, helped shield members from potential constituency retribution. In short, congressional policy enthusiasts saw no policy or career reason to link government party strength to electoral party strength, and therefore did nothing about the latter. In fact, the divergence between the two may well have served to further weaken the electoral party because legislators were not concerned about its health.

The discussion above focused on efforts undertaken by House Democrats to strengthen the impact of party on policy in the 1970s. Congressional Republicans did the same during the Reagan and Bush administrations. When the 1992 elections briefly returned unified government to the stage temporarily, this time with the Democrats in charge, the congressional Republicans quickly rallied around alternative, and clearly conservative, policy principles. When the Democrats lost their majority control of both houses in 1994, thereby reintroducing divided government conditions, they quickly became more party conscious in order to offer an effective policy challenge to the new majority. When members of the opposition party suddenly find themselves confronting a hostile president who is attempting to undermine their most fundamental policy assumptions, they tend to feel threatened. They respond by repressing any free-lance tendencies they might have and do their best to organize a loyal opposition. In short, divided government encourages strong legislative parties.

Party voting indeed has increased since the beginning of the reform era. It was especially apparent during the Reagan presidency, a period marked by a clear ideological cleavage between the president and the congressional Democratic majority.[32] Party voting on an issue occurs when more than half the members of one party vote differently than more than half the members of the other party. Some of

this reflects the homogenization of voter activists in districts. For example, David Rohde has argued that the voting liberation of black voters in the South has converted southern Democratic legislators into spokespersons for minority causes, and thereby they vote essentially the same ways as their northern Democratic counterparts. The northeastern liberal wing of the Republican Party has lost strength in the past generation, to be replaced by a large number of conservative western and southern representatives and senators. This trend explains some of the party unity voting.[33] This, of course, shows some linkage between the electoral and governing parties. However, it does not say that party factors are important to voters when they cast their votes. As noted above, voters are increasingly engaging in split-ticket voting at the very time that the legislative parties appear to be gaining more cohesion.

The fact is that party unity voting statistics do not reveal much about actual ideological cohesion within legislative parties. For example, although the percentage of congressional party unity votes has increased since the beginning of the reform era, especially since the Reagan administration, the total number of roll-call votes has decreased dramatically. This has permitted approximately the same number of unity votes to dominate a smaller voting universe, thereby producing higher percentages of party unity voting. For example, during the 95th Congress (1977–1978, Carter administration), there were 1,540 role-call votes in the House, 37 percent of which were party votes. By way of contrast, during the 100th Congress (1987–1988, Reagan administration), there were only 847 roll-call votes, 52 percent of which were party unity votes.[34]

Therefore, the base number of bipartisan votes declined in the 1980s as contrasted to the 1970s. In addition, another key party-based factor was at play. It may be recalled that the Democratic majority had, in the mid-1970s, assigned the speaker more control over the composition and procedures of the Rules Committee. This resulted in an increasing number of bills being reported to the House floor with a "closed" rule, a rule that prohibited floor amendments to committee reports. In turn, this prohibited the introduction of many potentially damaging amendments that might have compromised the fundamental nature of the proposed legislation, thereby encouraging bipartisan voting.[35]

Before divided government became, for want of a better term, a relatively "normal" condition, its problems often would be resolved in a future election, and the succeeding government would be unified. This was certainly the case in the elections of 1954 and 1976. However, things have changed and divided government seems more of a rule, not an exception, in the postreform period. Voter-initiated policy changes have not been a part of the political scene for some time. Careers in Congress are not secured or lost by keen party competition in congressional districts. Instead, they rely more on the abilities of incumbents to free-lance their way to success with constituents via candidate-centered campaigns.

As a result of these realities, the partisanship of congressional decision making since the 1980s, particularly in the House, has not been primarily the result of electoral inputs, although factors such as the nationalization of southern politics do explain some of it. However, the most plausible explanation lies in the tendency for legislators of both parties to unite behind their congressional party organizations and party leaders in the hope of maximizing their policy leverage in the face of divided government. Therefore, conditions of divided government that assume the existence of weak electoral parties were in fact the very conditions that prompted the development of stronger, more cohesive legislative parties.[36] Divided government can only occur in political systems impacted by a constitutionally specified separation of powers system, as in the United States. The character and quality of politics and policy have been heavily influenced by the repercussions of divided government in the past generation. Regardless of whether one considers these effects to be good, bad, or neutral, the Constitution is not an innocent bystander when it comes to searching out forces to applaud or condemn for the condition.

By-Products of Bicameralism

Analyses of the political and policy effects of constitutionally fragmented government usually focus on executive-legislative relations or on nation-state relations. Comparatively little is done with House-Senate relationships. This is unfortunate, because the *de facto* constitutional mandate for separate institutions to share policy obligations applies as strongly to House-Senate relations as it does to other networks bound by the same expectations.

According to Steven Smith, the distinct institutional positions of both houses affect how each develops a policy agenda, how its members allow it to align its policy positions, and how each develops strategies to leverage its influence.[37] How each chamber deals with these challenges is influenced by its constitutional status and representational base. The Senate is smaller, represents states equally, and is more collegial, more dependent on staff, more individualistic, and, as a result, less efficient than the House. Senators are proud of their institution and its ability to operate by self-imposed, unwritten norms. Therefore, the Senate is understandably more a prisoner of tradition than is the House. Therefore, the era of individualized pluralism has impacted the Senate much less than the House. The House did indeed become more partisan, more hierarchical, and more influenced by altered rules and procedures than did the Senate. On the other hand the Senate has, since the confirmation of the Seventeenth Amendment in 1914, been a body directly responsive to voters. In all probability, its democratization saved it as a co-equal policy arm of Congress, but it had the effect of making it responsive to swings in public opinion. In turn, that reduced its value as a source of stability in government and politics. However, since senators serve for six-year terms, with only one-third of them elected every two years, one might expect the Senate to be considerably less prone than the House to embody and reflect public-engendered partisan swings. While the Senate has been somewhat less responsive to partisan fluctuations than has the House since 1914, the Seventeenth Amendment closed the gap considerably.[38] In a sense, the democratization of the Senate has made its membership more vulnerable to opinion swings than the House because state-based constituencies are more diverse than the substate districts of House members. President Reagan's popularity with the electorate was registered more enthusiastically in the Senate than in the House. The Senate was quicker to adopt and to sustain support for Reagan's economic reforms than was the House. Therefore, it has been the Senate's democratization or, in Charles Stewart's term, its "popularization," that has preserved its integrity as a co-equal part of the legislative equation.[39] This has been accomplished at the price of compromising the founders' hope that the Senate would distinguish itself by adding to the legislative process a "permanency to provide for such objects as require a continued attention and a train of measures."[40]

Policy agendas, by force of circumstance, do not vary much between the House and Senate. Policy issues confront both houses with essentially the same overall priority cast and degree of intensity. Since the Senate has a constitutional role in ratifying treaties and in confirming executive appointments, its agenda can occasionally become more congested than that of the House, despite the fact that it has less than one-fourth the manpower. In addition, the larger and more demographically balanced character of senators' constituencies encourages the Senate to give some problems, such as those impacting urban areas, higher priority than the House is willing to grant. Strategies are determined by the positions other institutions have taken on matters the Senate gives high priority. Divided government makes this more of an issue because it is likely to reveal major president-Senate differences in many policy fields.

According to Smith, the label "postreform" is far more applicable to the House than the Senate.[41] The House did strengthen party influence far more than the Senate. Committee power was compromised more in the House than the Senate for two principal reasons. First, the Senate is more married to tradition in principle than is the House. Second, because of their comparative manpower disadvantage, senators are very much dependent on a strong committee network to do the necessary legislative work. Because it champions individualism, senators are reluctant to give party leaders and organizations powers and status that would threaten individual senators' quests for recognition and policy leverage. Only in the increasingly important policy field of budgeting have Senate rules been modified to the point of compromising senators' individualism.[42] In the case of budget issues, in a few instances since the 1970s, party leaders and budget specialists have been allowed to speak for the entire Senate.

Since the Senate rules and procedures have not been as impacted by the reform period as have those of the House, the potential exists for the Senate's role as an institutional "filter" to be even more marked than it was during the protective pluralist era. Tempering such a potential is the fact that the Senate has been at least as impacted by the reform period's stress on constituency and electoral politics as has the House, if not more so.

Generally, House districts are less competitive politically than are Senate districts which, because of their statewide compass, are more cosmopolitan. Both houses are expected to be responsive to public opinion. A constant stress on constituency and electoral affairs is a significant norm, or role system equalizer. Nonetheless, all legislation must pass through the Senate "filter," and that filter becomes potentially more important if the two houses accommodate the norms of the reform period differently. Reportedly Thomas Jefferson, when serving as President George Washington's Secretary of State, once asked the president why he poured hot coffee from a cup into a saucer. Washington replied he had done it for the same reason legislation is sent to the Senate, namely to "cool it off." Of course, at that time the Senate was selected by state legislatures. It is now popularly elected and therefore subject to the same public opinion directives as is the House, although on a different scale. However, that scale can be important. Since Senate districts are larger and more cosmopolitan than are House districts, senators can be expected to reflect a more balanced political perspective than can most House members. The fact that the Senate's practices have not been altered significantly by the new era reforms potentially makes that even more important. These differences were clearly demonstrated during the impeachment and trial of President Clinton.

That importance can perhaps best be appreciated by examining policy issues which don't divide the public appreciably and therefore offer the Senate an opportunity to make a judgment on the intrinsic merits of a proposal, such as its constitutionality. Such circumstances offer the Senate a chance to exercise its judgment and serve, in effect, as an assembly of learned elders that uses its constitutionally separate institutional position to temper the potentially more passionate and predatory instincts of the House. Ross Baker's analysis of House-Senate differences over a 1986 legislative proposal to deal with the international drug traffic problem offers such an opportunity.[43] Public opinion was virtually unanimous in its support of government efforts to do something. Therefore, the question was not if something should be done, but what should be done. Both the House and Senate wanted strict laws providing serious penalties for convicted drug dealers. However, many Senators from both parties voiced concern that what was clearly a more aggressive and punitive House bill was "constitutionally suspect," because it authorized military forces to administer policies outside its constitutional mandate, approved a change in the Fourth Amendment's guarantee against unreasonable searches (the exclusionary rule) by legislation, and authorized a federally imposed death penalty for a crime that didn't involve treason or a capital offense. Senator Daniel Evans (R–Washington) called the House bill an "election year stampede that will trample the Constitution in the process."[44] Of course, only one-third of the Senate was standing for reelection in 1986, as opposed to the entire House. That made a stance in principle more feasible politically for the Senate than the House. However, that is precisely what the founders had in mind. The issue was finally resolved after a liberal-conservative coalition of senators proposed a solution that provided very generous funding for the antidrug campaign, but eliminated the House requirements for the death penalty, modification of the exclusionary rule, and that military forces be used to seize drug smugglers. In this case, although the House was able to respond immediately to public demand for an antidrug effort, it was the sobriety of the Senate that cooled it off and allowed it to dodge the constitutional issue altogether. This was a classic case of the Senate functioning as a safeguard against what it considered to be ill-considered and hasty action by the House. In effect, the Senate was functioning as Madison had suggested in *Federalist No. 63,* as a "temperate and respectable body of citizens" who mediate and allay passions until such time as "reason, justice, and truth can regain their authority over the public mind."[45]

Therefore, policy issues of the late twentieth and early twenty-first centuries often invite House-Senate institutional differences to have their impact on policy decisions. Even highly partisan issues are often impacted. The all-encompassing nature of many policy challenges that surfaced as major issues during the 1980s offers a good illustration of this. Because dealing with deficits effectively requires unpopular policy choices, including spending cuts and tax increases, the House was unwilling to take the initiative on these matters during the Reagan and Bush presidencies. The House has always had primacy in revenue and appropriations legislation because of the constitutional requirement that all revenue bills originate in the House. Eager to cooperate with President Reagan's policy reform proposals as a package, in 1981 the Senate endorsed the entire package, including provisions for a tax cut, before the House had a chance to act on it. The same thing occurred in 1982 on a tax increase proposal. In this instance, the House didn't voice reservations because tax increases are, by definition, unpopular politically. On the foreign policy front, the Senate is supposed to dominate because of its role in treaty ratification and ambassadorial appointments. Nonetheless, during the 1980s and 1990s the House made high-profile, aggressive moves to achieve equal partnership with the Senate in foreign policy. This was not done at the Senate's expense, for its importance was not compromised. The importance of the House was, in effect, elevated. Along with members of the Senate Foreign Relations Committee, members of the House International Relations Committee attended Strategic Arms Limitations talks (SALT), monitored elections in the Philippines, and met privately with foreign leaders. Both houses conducted a joint investigation of the Iran-Contra episode in 1987. The same was true in the emerging field of "intermestic" policy, or those policies which naturally affect the economies of several nations and world regions simultaneously. Both House and Senate members invite and bring many foreign corporate and government executives to their states and districts to assess the possibilities for foreign business investment in the United States. Walter Oleszek calls the House-Senate institutional changes triggered by these events examples of why "adaptability, participation, and innovation" are major contributions of bicameralism to the policy challenges of the postreform period.[46]

The Crest of Post-Watergate Politics: The Clinton Impeachment

Perhaps the most high-profile example of how subject Congress had become to the forces of post-Watergate politics and individualized pluralism was illustrated by the House of Representatives impeachment of President Clinton in December 1998. The imperatives of the constant campaign, its contribution to the politics of personal destruction as a substitute for the politics of party and institutional governance, and the role of a scandal-hungry media all encouraged the president's political opponents to employ impeachment in their effort to embarrass and weaken him politically and to tarnish his reputation historically. The destructive politics of the post-Watergate period had, with the Clinton impeachment, reached its zenith.

There exists perhaps no better illustration than the way in which the House Judiciary Committee developed and considered the impeachment issue. The Committee was sharply divided along party lines—Republicans supporting impeachment and Democrats opposed to it. Since the Republicans held a majority of committee appointments, they closed ranks and approved four articles of impeachment against the president. Committee Democrats, to a member, opposed each article on the grounds that accusations that the president had lied before a grand jury and had acted to obstruct justice had not been proven, and that the alleged crime—being less than forthcoming to an independent counsel and a grand jury investigating a presidential sexual liaison—did not constitute a "high crime and misdemeanor" as demanded by the Constitution as a basis for impeachment.

Debate within the Judiciary Committee was highly partisan and acrimonious at times, reminiscent of hotly contested election campaigns that turn into negative, name-calling exercises with the character assassination of the opponent seemingly the main objective. Republicans chastised Democrats for not performing their constitutional duty. Democrats charged Republicans with lowering the bar for impeachment to conduct a political vendetta against the president, using the Constitution as a political hammer. Highly offended by the turn of events, one committee Democrat commented that to "call the Judiciary Committee a kangaroo court would be an insult to marsupials everywhere." What had become the post-Watergate norm for campaigning had infected congressional deliberations as well. The Congressional responsibility to do the "right" thing through reasoned deliberations had fallen victim to post-Watergate campaigning norms. No longer could any clear distinction be made between campaigning and legislating. They had become merely different stages of the same destructive political crusade.

By a highly partisan vote, the full House voted to impeach the president on two of the four articles reported by the Judiciary Committee. The president was subsequently tried on the approved articles in the Senate, where

his conviction and removal by a two-thirds vote was a virtual impossibility. Ultimately, the Senate voted against convicting the president on both charges by very convincing margins. That predictable reality may have influenced the demeanor of the Senate during the Clinton trial because, on some issues, the Senate proceedings did indeed reflect more of a bipartisan tone than it had in the House. However, those incidents were refreshing exceptions to the tone of the impeachment crusade overall. As a body whose members represented significantly broader constituency bases than its House counterpart, the Senate was more in tune with public opinion on the impeachment issue. In addition, the founders' hope and expectation that the Senate would be more stately, bipartisan, temperate, and stable in both demeanor and action was clearly evident during the impeachment trial. By the same token, issues such as whether to hear witnesses during the trial did generally divide the Senate along party lines, indicating that post-Watergate politics had impacted the Senate as well as the House, albeit on a less persistent and somewhat less salient basis.

From the beginning to the end of the Clinton impeachment crisis, opinion polls showed the public to be decidedly against the president's impeachment and removal from office. Despite this reality, Republican House Speaker Newt Gingrich had made the president's suitability for office a high-profile issue in the 1998 elections. The strategy clearly backfired. For the first time in sixty-four years, the presidential party actually gained seats in the House of Representatives in a midterm election, explained in part by Gingrich's decision to stress the impeachment issue in the campaign. However, at least as important was that, because of the Republican policy pledges in the 1994 Contract with America (many of which had been unfulfilled by 1998), congressional Republicans, not the president and the Democratic party, had become the party of policy change. Many of those policy promises had not been realized, and voters retaliated by reelecting the president in 1996 and more Democrats to the House in 1998.

The result of all this was the de facto "impeachment" of Speaker Gingrich, who resigned both the speakership and his seat in the House in the wake of the 1998 election results. However, the Republican leadership crisis did not end with that event. The House Republican Caucus selected Louisiana Representative Bob Livingston to replace Gingrich at the beginning of the 106th Congress. True to the tabloid-drenched, soap opera definition of news and the "character assassination" nature of post-Watergate politics, the magazine *Hustler* reported that Speaker-designate Livingston had, like President Clinton, engaged in extra-marital affairs. Livingston confessed to same and resigned as a candidate for Speaker, pledging to resign from Congress later in 1999. Like Gingrich, Livingston had, in effect, been "impeached" by the Republican crusade to impeach President Clinton. The Republican Caucus then turned to Illinois Representative Dennis Hastert as their choice for Speaker, and Hastert was elected Speaker when the 106th Congress convened in January 1999.

House Republicans persisted with the impeachment process despite the fact that more than 60 percent of the public declared their opposition to it throughout the entire process. Such a course stands in obvious disregard for the principle of popular sovereignty. Moreover, it does not seem to be sound politics. One obvious answer is political backbone, but that directly contradicts the political calculus of the constant campaign mentality that has become so pervasive in American politics. A more careful examination of the turn-of-the-century political terrain yields a more plausible explanation. The

highly partisan committee and floor votes were well-rooted in the opportunistic politics of the time. For many Republicans, a vote to impeach was not fraught with risk. A large proportion of both House parties, including all members of the Judiciary Committee, were from relatively safe congressional districts. Numerous Republicans represented districts in which polls favored the president's impeachment. It could be argued that these members were merely being responsive and accountable to their constituents.

However, many Republicans who voted to impeach hailed from competitive districts, some of which cast a majority of their votes for Clinton in the 1996 election. In these instances, Republicans voted against their constituents on the impeachment question. Why did they think it worth the risk? Two possibilities stand out. First, many likely concluded that, since it was nearly two years until the next election, the voters' proclivity for short-term memories would mean that the issue's salience would dissipate well in advance of the next election and therefore would not handicap the members' quest for reelection. Second, they were well aware of the clear intensity gap that existed between the groups that avidly favored impeachment (religious groups and secular Clinton-averse groups) and the public's comparatively placid stand against impeachment. It was easier to be intensely against President Clinton than it was to intensely support him, and these Republicans were well aware of that. Therefore, unless these Republicans voted to impeach, so went the argument, the zealous anti-Clinton forces could sponsor well-financed candidates to challenge them in the 2000 elections. Well-organized minorities can usually defeat challenges from disorganized or relatively apathetic majorities, as this case illustrates. Thus a course of action that appears to be irrational to an outside observer can be very logical or rational to members of an organization who, for political reasons, tend to define problems and their solutions from more of a contextual point of view. Nonetheless, a continued disconnect between the public and its representatives can be dangerous in the long term for all parties. Such a ridiculing of responsiveness and accountability increases public cynicism toward government and its leaders, and that flouts the concept of popular sovereignty. Furthermore, while intensity usually wins over moderation in the short term, over the long term the reverse is usually the case. Either the purists become moderates or voters eventually choose to elect moderates to replace them.

President Clinton was only the second president in history to be formally impeached by the House of Representatives and the first popularly elected president to experience that fate. However, the significance of that event must be considered carefully in light of the politics of the era. The fractionalization of politics that occurred in Watergate's wake resulted ultimately in the destructive, inquisitorial type of politics that led to Clinton's impeachment. During other political eras, it is unlikely that a president's unsavory sexual escapades would have been exploited by the press and by partisan opponents like Clinton's were in the aftermath of Watergate. In short, Clinton's impeachment probably represented the ultimate expression of the politics of destruction on the way Congress defined (and redefined) its mandate and conducted its business at the close of the twentieth century.

Constitutional politics were clearly evident throughout the impeachment process. Impeachment was available as a political option because it was a constitutional option. Giving it a destructive politics "spin" in the pursuit of constitutional "justice" served largely to make a political crusade more legitimate and, presumably, ultimately more politically acceptable. This helped the devout supporters of Clinton's impeachment and removal rationalize the pursuit of impeachment despite significant public opposition. During most of the impeachment ordeal, Clinton's performance approval rating remained well above 60 percent. Ironically, within a week after his official impeachment, a poll showed Clinton to be the person most admired by most Americans. These realities were ignored by impeachment zealots. After all, they were being responsive to a "constitutional constituency," and that must certainly be of a higher priority than a "political constituency." Besides, since it was nearly two years until the election of 2000, they assumed that any voters disenchanted with their stand on impeachment would likely forget about differences they had with their representatives on the question by that time. In sum, the impeachment vote was presumably a free vote.

History will be the judge of just how significant President Clinton's impeachment was to his reputation as president, to the role of the presidency as a policy institution, and to the role of Congress as a responsive, responsible, and deliberative body. In the case of Congress, the assessment is bound to be considerably less than salutary. The Clinton impeachment placed the political polarity that was the essence of destructive politics clearly in the spotlight. Regardless of how one stood on the impeachment question, the way it was considered by the House should have left no doubt that the days of reasoned, seriously deliberative House discussions and debates were, at least for the time being, a thing of the past. At both the committee and floor stages of consideration, members of both parties appeared to be uninterested in a balanced analysis of the facts. Their minds seemed to be made up before the first witness was called or the first colleague spoke. The way the debates and discussions were conducted at both committee and floor stages undermined both the legitimacy and credibility of the impeachment process. There was virtually no attempt to allow a consensus about the legitimacy of the four articles to emerge from a careful discussion and analysis of the credibility of each. Genuine deliberation assumes that participants are open to the introduction and interpretation of new facts and, most important, that these participants are open to changing their minds in view of new facts and arguments. The impeachment process embodied virtually no such fairness of perspective.

Were the Clinton impeachment an isolated case of the absence of congressional deliberation during turn-of-the-century House politics, then it would have been of little significance. However, it was not. It was essentially a very high-profile example of a cancer that had gradually eaten away at congressional responsibility in the post-Watergate period. Congressional parties were more ideologically polarized than they had been since the New Deal period, making true deliberation on most issues, impeachment, or policy questions a virtual impossibility. Congressional Republicans, becoming a majority and assuming legislative leadership in 1994 for the first time in nearly half a century, were inexperienced and not up to the challenge. In selecting Gingrich as House Speaker in 1995, they chose an ideologue with a confrontational demeanor at the very time they needed just the opposite. This increased the polarity between the parties and reduced the number of House members in both parties willing to identify themselves as moderates. The new speaker, Dennis Hastert, assumed office with a reputation as a distinctly less confrontational and more accommodating conservative than Gingrich. Hastert pledged to work overtime to bring the warring factions of the House together, to rekindle the spirit of mutual respect for honest differences, and, in essence, to restore respect for serious deliberation as the only practical route to meaningful policy progress.

It is easy to promise such a turnaround but difficult to achieve it. Political positions nourished by conditions that reward a politics of personal destruction are not altered significantly by rhetoric that underscores the need to legislate and investigate from a more accommodative set of premises. Rather, change will more likely ensue when politicians conclude that it is simply good political judgment to revise their behavior. In the meantime, the unhealthy political environment that both produced and resolved the Clinton impeachment issue will continue to take its institutional and policy tolls. The Clinton impeachment certainly weakened Clinton as a president and perhaps even the presidency as a policy institution for an undetermined period. It also weakened Congress as a policy institution. During the impeachment struggle, House Republicans saw their majority trimmed, their public reputation undermined, and a speaker and speaker-designate forced into resignation. In addition, their legislative agenda had suffered at the hands of the president. In 1998, Clinton thwarted most major Republican policy proposals, including several social initiatives, proposals to use the budget surplus to cut taxes, efforts to enact a school voucher program, and an attempt to place major restrictions on abortions. However, the Republicans did the same to many key Clinton proposals including a major anti-tobacco program, an HMO patient's bill of rights, an expansion of Medicare eligibility, campaign finance reform, an increase in the federal minimum wage, and presidential fast-track trade negotiation authority.

In short, a weakened presidency does not necessarily mean a stronger Congress. The result can be a standoff between a weakened president and a feeble congressional majority of the opposite party. That the nation probably did not suffer irreparably from such conditions at century's end was largely because, on a relative scale, both the domestic and international policy climates were relatively subdued. Nonetheless, such a caretaker policy ambience extracts its policy costs by delaying government's ability to address serious long-term policy problems. Such a situation is a far cry from what both Clinton, as a candidate for president in 1992, and the Republicans, in their 1994 Contract with America, had promised the public.

Congress and Constitutional Politics: The Policy Consequences

The career incentives of House and Senate members have adapted to the political realities of the post-Watergate period in ways that impact directly both policy processes and content. Most of the adaptations reflect the same exigencies that have impacted on intermediary institutions, discussed in Chapters 5 and 6. Therefore, the following analysis will highlight the role of Congress in exploiting, exacerbating, and, perhaps in a few instances, actually causing the type of politics and policies that have impacted on the intermediary institutions. It must be remembered that ambition, self-service, and economic gain as sources of political motivation are virtually universal. Therefore, a politician seeking a legislative career, an interest group working for the well-being of its members, a political party official working to elect party candidates to office, and a television network or a newspaper seeking to enlarge institutional profits may all pursue their objectives in ways that make them both strategic and policy bedfellows. Bearing that in mind, some of the policy consequences, both procedural and substantive, of the current congressional incentive system will be examined.

Divided Government and Policy Incrementalism

The policy consequences of the divided government phenomenon will be explored in depth in Chapter 9. However, it deserves mention here in passing, not only because it is encouraged by the current congressional incentive system, but also because the divided government condition, together with its cousin the "divided institution" condition, frequently provide the seeds, soil, and fertilizer for other policy problems. If the majorities in both houses of Congress are of a different party persuasion than is the president, a divided government condition exists. This has been the rule rather than the exception since 1954, and especially since 1968. However, even when a *de facto* divided government condition does not exist, the same party's hold on the presidency and Congress is often very tenuous. This means that concessions are often made to the minority party out of fear of threatening the majority party's fragile hold on its majority coalition. As a result, policies produced by the two scenarios may not, in matter of fact, be very different.

Voters have shown ambivalence toward political parties, pessimism toward politics, and cynicism toward politicians and government institutions since the early 1970s. Split-ticket voting is common, and divided or institutionally tenuous government has been the result. In turn, this has encouraged the legislative parties to focus more on the ideological, or theoretical, differences that divide them. This increases friction between the president and the congressional majorities, often resulting in petty "grudge matches" that take time, dislodge the serious policy agenda, and further alienate the public. Policies produced by such a political scenario are often marginal adjustments to the status quo, despite the fact that many long-term policy problems desperately need to be addressed with a rational, comprehensive, long-term frame of mind. The separation of powers provides the adversaries to such a contest with a solid, independent platform from which to make their case. Since each institution needs to cooperate before policy agreements can emerge, parties to policy disputations ask for major concessions before agreeing to cooperate. Most likely, at that point the inventive policy options that might have made a genuine difference have been strategically discarded in the interest of finding a policy common denominator. Policies resulting from such conditions are often modest, marginal, incremental changes from the status quo and, most likely, grossly inadequate responses to the policy task at hand.

Breakdown of Political Parties

Despite the fact that the post-Watergate period brought with it an increase in legislative party discipline, that reality served to weaken further an already degenerating political party condition. It did so because it permitted the congressional party members to identify with ideological, principled solutions to policy problems that were often at odds with public opinion, but survived politically nonetheless. Multiple committee referral practices and the omnibus nature of many legislative bills enabled legislators to dodge accountability for legislation demanding sacrifice. Aware of the growing divorce between themselves and the congressional party ideologues, the public grew increasingly pessimistic about parties, leaders, and institutions. To function well as intermediaries, political parties must be strong from the bottom up. There should be both a strategic and policy common ground that unites government parties with electoral parties. If cynicism and apathy eat away at a party's base, any strength it shows in its upper echelons simply illustrates the party problem, and does nothing to correct it. This can have serious long-term policy consequences.

An excellent example of how a gap between the public on the one hand and congressional policy zealots on the other can undermine and ultimately defeat an effort to deal with a serious policy problem by more than incremental means can be found in the defeat, in 1995, of President Clinton's health care reform proposal. In a book length work, former political reporter Haynes Johnson and political reporter and columnist David Broder adroitly explain how congenital problems afflicting the American political system were largely responsible for the proposal's failure.[47] However, a close reading between the lines reveals that the bifurcation between the public and legislative zealots contributed heavily to the proposal's defeat. The authors noted that the first two years of Clinton's first term ignited nationwide debates over the proper role of government in the lives of both people and the corporate world. The focus of the debate was health care reform. The public accepted the president's assessment of the state of health care. It consumed about one-seventh of the gross national product. Nearly 37 million people were without any form of health insurance. Millions more faced the prospect of losing their health coverage due to unemployment. The need to repair the system was obvious. As divided as the nation was in 1992, there appeared to be a public consensus in support of health care reform. Clinton had made it a major issue in his 1992 campaign. He had Democratic majorities in both houses of Congress. Everything seemed to be on line politically for reform, and the timing appeared to be optimal.

Despite these favorable circumstances, a proposal for a comprehensive overhaul of a system that nearly everyone—legislators, the president, the public, and some sectors of the health care industry—agreed needed an overhaul was never subjected to formal, open, informed debate. In short, the system failed the people. Part of the fault lay in Clinton's strategy. A task force appointed to examine the problem and recommend a solution held its discussions secretly, prompting suspicion on the part of some legislators and the press. The group's cochairs, Hillary Clinton and Ira Magaziner, had disadvantaged the president early in his term, and continued to do so on this project, primarily by not communicating regularly with Congress, relevant administrative agencies, the press, and the public. In addition, the president probably had too many other items on his policy agenda, thereby draining interest away from the health care issue. In addition, the recommendation was a notably complicated one that asked, in essence, that employers be responsible for their workers' health care costs. The public's reaction to that was negative, thinking that it went too far in the direction of "undeserving entitlement" status. However, the party system failed the mission as well. Many congressional Democratic enthusiasts introduced their own pet bills that accommodated their own pet reform theories. Some of these bills stressed market competition. Others advocated government-managed health care. Others wanted a combination of the two, along with increased payroll taxes. In essence, it was a family feud within the Democratic Party, with the "new" Democrats facing off against the old line, New Deal element of the party. Republicans, especially the conservative element, were avid in their ideological opposition to the proposal. In anticipation of the Clinton proposal, Republican House Speaker Newt Gingrich was plotting the Republican seizure of Congress in the 1994 elections by opposing all versions of what he labeled "Clintoncare." This obviated any chances for a bipartisan agreement on the issue. Senate Majority Leader Bob Dole also was opposed in principle to any agreement, in part because he planned to run for the presidency against Clinton in 1996.

In addition, interest groups opposed to the plan mounted one of the most costly, and effective, campaigns in history. The focus was on the grass roots. Mail and television advertising reached a fever pitch. The famous "Harry and Louise" commercial, depicting a middle-class couple discussing the dangers of the equivalent of socialized medicine, was particularly effective. Other commercials, lobbyists, and demonstrators all raised the specter of a potential bureaucratic nightmare and socialized medicine if the proposal was approved. The base-line public consensus that had originally supported the plan, in effect, dissipated. The proposal was doomed.

Johnson and Broder explain the proposal's defeat by naming the conventional villains—interest groups, the system's credibility gap, partisan politics, and weak political parties. They do not rank those in any priority order. However, it is interesting to speculate that, had our political parties shown grass-roots strength that was reflected within congressional circles, most of the system's problems might well have been overcome. Had legislators listened to the people instead of to themselves, legislative opposition would have been more practical and less ideological. Had there been a clear linkage joining the electoral and governmental parties on both sides, congressional consideration would have been more reflective of an honest division between two factions over how best to deal with a policy problem that can only worsen if neglected. Consider the potential for strong parties to repress the excesses of credibility, partisanship, and interest groups in the interest of effective, long-term, health care reform. However, that was not the case. The realities of the politics of the "new" Congress, and its effect on the health of the party system, would not permit it.

The Bipartisan Middle

Conventional opinion argues that for a system victimized by avid partisanship, weak political parties, strong interest groups, a government credibility gap, and a proclivity for divided government, the only solution is the politics of the possible or what is herein termed the "bipartisan middle." Policy solutions honed to reflect the lowest common denominator among political adversaries operating within institutions impacted by these forces are not the best way to deal with policy problems, but they may be, according to some, the only way. The North American Free Trade Agreement (NAFTA) and the Personal Responsibility and Work Opportunity Act of 1996 were both the result of negotiated agreements between President Clinton and bipartisan majorities in both the House and Senate. These were very significant statutes that necessitated major compromises in the hardline positions assumed by the liberal wings of both congressional parties. To some observers, they may well have sacrificed too much principle in the interest of political expediency. On the other hand, it could be argued that the factors incorporated into the final products were essential if government was to be loyal to its representative mandate.

However, history has shown that major changes in policy direction come only during times when parties are strong and solutions are partisan. Only strong parties can develop clear policy alternatives, educate the public, and develop and hold majorities in line to effect significant policy change. The New Deal of the 1930s and the Great Society of the mid-1960s are two twentieth-century examples. While today's policy problems are among the most challenging in our nation's history, today's politics is inappropriately suited for the challenge. Having surrendered to the realities of the free-lance, constant campaign culture of the post-Watergate Congress, congressional party leaders on both sides of the aisle have not attempted to rally their party ranks around a consistent policy agenda that suggests a clear contrast to the agenda of the other party. To be sure, there are occasional flashes of policy coherency, such as that advanced by former Republican House Speaker Newt Gingrich during the 104th Congress when he alerted the Republicans and the na-

tion to the pitfalls of bipartisanship. That was followed by an energized effort on the part of congressional Republicans to enact pledges made as part of the Contract with America. However, President Clinton's reelection reminded Gingrich and his party that the nation as a whole was not ready for such radical reforms. Until Clinton became vulnerable to impeachment, Gingrich's leadership style during the 105th Congress incorporated a clear bias for the bipartisan solution.[48] President Clinton's leadership on the 1993 deficit reduction legislation sharply divided Democrats and Republicans. His 1997 agreement with Republicans reflected just the opposite—a triumph of bipartisanship. After President Reagan's election to the presidency in 1980, a long-term political marriage between the president and congressional Republicans ensued, but it dissipated early in his second term in office.

Both the Reagan and Clinton crusades fell victim to the imperatives of individualized pluralism. When Gingrich turned bipartisan, so did the House Republicans. When Republicans gained control of both the House and Senate in the 1994 elections, so did Clinton turn more moderate. To be sure, a form of partisanship remains alive and well on capitol hill. However, it is a "petty" partisanship, not the "party" partisanship that the system so desperately needs. It is the partisanship of individual legislators appealing to their constituents in their own ways with financial resources that they have raised mostly on their own. It is a partisanship that stresses rhetorical gestures against or in support of such matters as big government, the marketplace, and government bureaucracy. However, this sort of partisanship serves only to ignite constituent emotions and offer legislators temporary political mileage, not to organize serious debates and discussions over major policy issues.

As president, Bill Clinton was a man of the policy middle ground, and that made it difficult for congressional legislators to move much beyond a strategic commitment to compromise. In addition, the realities of divided government in an age impacted by economic dislocation and cultural anxiety may well point to the politics of the pragmatic as the only procedural alternative. House and Senate members who have acquired a good deal of institutional power over time, such as that of committee chair, are reluctant to forfeit that power to leadership requests for party policy coherence. However, a new age and its new policy do not synchronize with Congress's inclination to conduct business as usual. The public wants leadership, and the nature of policy problems virtually demands leadership. Bipartisanship produces agreements, but not often the necessary policy solutions. As Matthew Spalding has noted: "Bipartisanship masks a necessary discussion of issues that need to be resolved."[49]

The record of the 105th Congress (1997–1999) illustrates Spalding's observation very well. Divided government conditions were present. However, in stark contrast to the historical trends, the trend toward widening annual deficits was not. This was not because President Clinton and the Republican-controlled Congress had seen the error of historical fiscal trends (deficits) and had decided, finally, to cooperate in efforts to combat the deficit problem. It was the result of a booming domestic economy that had dramatically increased employment levels, and a roaring stock market that had significantly increased the assets and taxable capital gains of millions of Americans and hundreds of corporations. These conditions increased federal tax revenues dramatically, so much so that annual deficits were (at least temporarily) eliminated by Fiscal Year 1998, four years before President Clinton's targeted year of 2002. This offered a rare opportunity for Congress to respond to the president's appeal for investing the surplus to deal with long-term problems such as the pending Social Se-

curity crisis, the integrity of the Medicare program, and problems affecting public education. Congress defaulted in 1998. Instead of dealing seriously with several long-term policy problems proactively, congressional majorities chose to increase the level of pork barrel spending, to postpone indefinitely action on campaign finance reform, and to kill legislation establishing national liability standards obligating tobacco companies to compensate individuals for smoking-induced illnesses. Since the long-term "crisis" implications of a festering deficit problem were, at least temporarily, removed from high-priority status, pettiness and partisanship surfaced to deflect Congress and, ultimately, the nation from a necessary focus on enduring critical issues.

Most of these questions involved confronting and demanding sacrifice from some of the nation's largest corporations. Too many legislators were too dependent on these corporations, and their affiliated lobbies, for campaign support. Instead of exploiting economic prosperity for the long-term benefit of the public in general, legislative majorities chose to exploit that very prosperity to benefit the career aspirations of their own ranks. In preparing for the 1998 elections, members of both parties in both houses regularly engaged in a very discernable form of "me-too" politics. Me-too politics concentrates on copying or exploiting slices of the opposition's programs in the hope of winning elections. Republicans clearly adopted this strategy in 1998. Knowing that the public supported the Democrats' concern over Social Security, they chose to postpone debate on it despite the fact that most Republican leaders favored some form of privatization of the system. Health Maintenance Organizations (HMOs) were under fire in 1998, and Democrats sought to legislate major HMO reforms. The Republican majority threw its support behind an HMO patient bill of rights which offered no formal change in how HMOs were organized or managed. The Democrats' support of major legislation regulating tobacco companies was killed by the Republican majority in both houses, and justified by arguing that the problem could best be handled by the states.

The Fiscal Year 1999 budget agreement, struck just three weeks before the 1998 elections, reflected more election-year positioning. The $500 billion package included the president's education proposals, emergency defense funds, an emergency bailout fund for economically hard-hit farmers, new funds for fighting drug trafficking, a summer jobs for youths program, research funds for medical research, new funds to fight global warming, and a graduated tax cut for businesses, the self-employed, and farmers. It was a typical resolution to fiscal impasses that often develop in election years under divided government conditions: If party adversaries can't agree on a rational budget plan, give each party most of what it wants, allow each to claim victory, and hope that your side does a better job of selling its version of the victory to the voters. Regarding the Fiscal Year 1999 agreement, the Democratic president got his education program, summer jobs program, and farm relief program. The Republican congressional majority got its defense spending money, its anti-drug-trafficking funding increases, and its graduated tax cuts for businesses and the self-employed. In addition, both parties voted to fund a "piñata-like" package stuffed with special spending pork barrel projects that stood to benefit both sides. It was traditional election year divided government politics. The price was the abandonment of the spending ceiling agreed to in the Balanced Budget Agreement of 1997. No existing programs were trimmed back or eliminated. The new expenditures were financed by the Fiscal Year 1998 budget surplus, funds the president originally wanted to commit to restore financial integrity to the Social Security program.

Elections are won both by mobilizing your own party and doing what you can to demobilize the opposition party by denying its ability to develop its message and mobilize its supporters. By stressing electoral strategies over policy substance, each of these activities veered Congress and the country away from the concern that could, and should, have been shown for addressing long-term policy problems. More disciplined national and congressional party organizations would discourage such delay and exploitation. Governments organized around cohesive majority and minority parties that synchronize the opinions of party elites with party rank-and-file tend to confront policy issues head-on. Ideological confrontations between party leaders within institutions are meaningless if ideological positions are sacrificed in the interest of winning elections. Party-organized debates under such conditions tend to focus more on the intrinsic merit of policy alternatives than on political posturing and assuaging constituents. It is essential that both the majority and minority party be both numerically strong and cohesive. One of the ironies of the Clinton administration was that President Clinton's bipartisan leadership approach served to weaken the Democratic Party rather than strengthen it. Although it didn't hold the presidency during this period, the Republican Party's grass-roots support actually grew and so did its numbers in Congress and in the statehouses. When President Clinton was first elected in 1992, there were 58 Democratic senators. After the 1996 election, there were 45. After the 1992 election, there were 259 Democrats in the House. After 1996 there were 208. When Clinton was inaugurated in 1992, there were 28 Democratic governors. After the 1996 elections, there were 17, and those presided over states whose populations totaled only about a quarter of the nation's total.[50] While the degree of these losses cannot be totally blamed on President Clinton, much of it most certainly can. His bipartisan approach to governing divided the old Democrats from the new. As a congressional party, the Democrats found it very difficult to present a united front to support the president's policies and oppose those of the Republicans. Consequently, the raw material necessary to build both strong majority and minority parties as a prelude to effective governance was compromised during the Clinton administration, even though Clinton himself was elected by a safe voting plurality in both 1992 and 1996.

Scandal as Political Agenda

Congressional investigations, advertised as impartial fact-finding enterprises, have become the modern version of the "witch hunt" in the post-Watergate period.[51] Before Watergate, intensive investigations into the personal and political lives of presidents, legislators, and judges were undertaken only in the most unusual of situations. Watergate, with its exposure of criminality at the highest circles of the presidency, changed all that. Ostensibly, in an effort to purify a system gone wrong, several pieces of legislation designed to expose alleged corruption and punish the offenders, including the 1978 Ethics in Government Act, were enacted. However, the purpose of this legislation was, at least in part, political. According to Robert Bennett, it "taught both parties that scandal could serve as a shortcut to political success."[52] Encouraged by the political fallout from divided government, congressional investigations have increased both in number and character. The potential payoff is significant. The Democrats scored impressive gains in the 1974 elections following Watergate, and attained the presidency in 1976.

In a similar vein, Republican attempts to defeat President Clinton in 1996 were based in part on their exploitation of questions raised about his possible illegal involvement in an Arkansas land deal (Whitewater) that had

taken place and terminated before his election to the presidency. It became rather clear from the investigation's outset that it was anything but a neutral inquiry. The office of independent counsel, created by the 1978 legislation and reauthorized in 1994, authorized the appointment of a person to investigate alleged scandal within the executive branch. While this may be sound in theory, it has, in effect, resulted in individuals with partisan-charged agendas attempting to find excuses to investigate and/or indict high-profile executive branch officials, including the president. Both parties are equally guilty of partisanizing justice by these means. Republicans thought that the appointment of an independent counsel to investigate a Republican Secretary of Defense was a bad idea. But it was a good idea if the investigation target was President Clinton. Democrats, on the other hand, who complained about the investigatory tactics of Whitewater independent counsel Kenneth Starr, found nothing wrong with the idea when the target was a Republican Secretary of Defense. Republicans thought the 1997 investigation into alleged fund-raising improprieties during the 1996 campaign was a good idea provided they focused on Democratic fund-raising efforts. They were less enthusiastic when the investigation was expanded to include Republican fund-raising efforts.

Immediately after Starr submitted his report to the House Judiciary Committee suggesting possible grounds for impeaching Clinton for perjury and obstruction of justice in the investigation of the Lewinsky affair, Republicans were divided on how to proceed. Responding to pressures from House Republican leaders, nearly all quickly fell into line and closed ranks in support of the impeachment alternative rather than some form of censure. That decision sealed the president's fate in the House. Following the Judiciary Committee's recommendations, the House impeached Clinton by a vote that broke almost completely along party lines. Committee and floor debates on the issue were almost totally partisan. Politics, not constitutional principle, dominated from the outset. The Senate trial of the president began in a spirit of bipartisanship, but then disintegrated into open party conflict on key procedural issues, the most significant of which was a witness issue—should there be any and, if so, who should they be? If there is any doubt about whether impeachment is fundamentally a political, as opposed to a constitutional issue, a review of the Clinton impeachment and trial events should remove all doubt. With more diverse constituencies and a reputation for being more deliberative and somewhat aloof from the more predatory type of politics that surfaces regularly in the House, the Senate appeared to be, as the framers intended, a more appropriate place to determine the president's fate. Nonetheless, the political roots of the Clinton impeachment also influenced proceedings significantly in the upper house.

The Constitution obligates Congress to oversee the executive branch. In theory it is one of the beneficial by-products of the separation of powers that can help protect democratic accountability. However, oversight was intended to be primarily an interinstitutional relationship, not a political one. Compromising the policy objectives of oversight and replacing those with political missions can have unsettling and unjust effects on both people and the policy agenda. Some officeholders can literally face potential bankruptcy by hiring counsel to defend themselves. Talented individuals are discouraged from seeking public office. It increases public cynicism about government institutions and their leaders. It develops feelings of animosity between and among executives and legislators who ultimately have to cooperate to produce legislation. Finally, it skews the attention of the press, Congress, and the president away from the pressing substantive policy issues of the day at a time when the nation cannot afford

it. An example of such misuse surfaced in 1998 during the Starr-Clinton conflict and, because of that, did not receive the attention it deserved. During this period, Senator Orrin Hatch (R–Utah), as chairman of the Senate Judiciary Committee, placed intensive pressure on Attorney General Janet Reno to request the appointment of an independent counsel to investigate questionable Democratic campaign fund-raising tactics during the 1996 election campaign. Hatch asked specifically that any such investigation not include Republican fund-raising strategies, despite the fact that documentary evidence uncovered earlier had shown that former Republican Party national chairman Haley Barbour had illegally solicited foreign contributions in Hong Kong during the 1996 campaign. Only Democrats were to be included in the Hatch mandate. Hatch pressured Reno to the point of asking her to resign if she did not comply or, if she refused, threatening her with a contempt of Congress citation unless she conceded to him on his terms. As Judiciary Committee chairman, Hatch had jurisdiction over the Justice Department's budget, over its personnel policies, and over the confirmation of judgeship appointments to federal courts. That gave Hatch more leverage over both the department and the White House than he deserved, considering the highly partisan use of his position in this case. It is indeed remarkable to witness a partisan politician ordering government to prosecute his political enemies. However, that was essentially what Hatch was doing. It was clearly an abuse of his authority as committee chairman.

The message is rather clear: Partisan politics has no place in the investigation of alleged crimes or ethics violations. The public recognizes this, and when enough people inform Congress that it is time to departisanize the quest for justice, it will stop. Once an ethics of procedure becomes viable politically, the congressional predatory instinct can be corralled. Most government servants do not deserve what these investigations do to their personal lives and careers. Most important, the public and the policy agenda deserve much better from those who equate personal attacks and character assassination with effective public service.

Issue Networks

Issue networks are associations of individuals and groups that seek to influence policy for the same reason as do iron triangles, or subgovernments. In contrast to iron triangles—which are rather permanent, well-defined, autonomous alliances among congressional subcommittees, interest groups, and administrative bureaus—issue networks are decidedly more short term in duration, fluid in composition, and slipshod in strategy and tactics. However, often they can be very intense in focus. A large network can be made up of numerous interest groups, government officials, administrative agencies, and individual citizens. They organize to support or oppose a policy proposition, and tend to dissipate once government has ruled on the issue. Network members do not always agree on strategies and tactics. They are much less stable than are iron triangles. They have not replaced iron triangles in the policy process. Instead, their growing significance means that they deserve an increasingly larger share of the policy stage. Hugh Heclo argues that an exclusive focus on iron triangles, or subgovernments, is misleading because it ignores "the fairly open networks of people that increasingly impinge upon government."[53]

Issue networks have existed as long as has lobbying, but their presence and significance was amplified considerably by the politics of the post-1970 reform era. Many issue groups arise in opposition to what they consider the excessive influence of the corporate world in

politics and government, and the reform period was well suited to such a crusade. Its stress on democracy and liberalism was accompanied by a distrust of what its advocates considered to be the excessive influence of capitalism and its special interest by-products on public policy. In short, the reform period was a promising time to "take on the system," and this translated into efforts to liberate ethnic minorities, the underprivileged, and the consumer from the predatory and exploitative grasp of the corporate world and the special interests that represented it. Many issue network participants are interested in their policy crusades out of principle, with material rewards clearly being secondary. They often stress the need to make policy more fair or more moral in content. Consequently, some networks (or components thereof) approach their challenges with fervor and passion. As a result, they are often unamenable to compromise.

This, in effect, meant more of an emphasis on regulatory policies that would bring corporations to heel. Similar to the congressional revolt against the standing committee barons, outside Congress business corporations were the "bad guys," and they needed to be made more accountable to the public and to their employees. It may be recalled from Chapter 3 that regulatory policies are more controversial than distributive policies because they require some entities to sacrifice in favor of the benefit of other entities. Consequently, regulatory policies are usually more politically controversial. Forces enter the policy fray both in support and in opposition to regulation. Such conditions invite the formation of issue networks working both sides of the issues in question. Once issues such as the environment, automobile and product safety, civil rights, misleading advertising, and the availability and cost of energy are elevated to the policy agenda, issue networks quickly organize in an attempt to influence the results. This is mostly because the public in general is affected by how the issues are resolved. Everyone is a consumer. Nearly everyone owns and operates an automobile, and has to pay for energy to heat and cool their residence. Consequently, when policy proposals surface that could potentially improve the lot of the consuming public, *ad hoc* alliances of existing groups, individuals, public interest organizations, legislators, and executive officials are not uncommon.

Social regulatory legislation enacted between 1969 and 1977 offers an excellent illustration of how policy during this period, at least officially, was public or consumer oriented. Examples include the National Environmental Policy Act (1969), the Water Quality Improvement Act (1970), the Occupational Safety and Health Act (1970), the Consumer Product Safety Act (1972), the Federal Water Pollution Control Act (1972), the Clean Air Amendments Act (1974), the Energy Policy and Conservation Act (1974), the School Bus Safety Act (1976), and the Surface Mining Control and Reclamation Act (1977). In addition, during this same period, twelve new regulatory agencies were established to administer the public interest according to standards specified in these as well as other laws. Included were agencies assigned regulatory jurisdiction over environmental protection, railroad administration, highway and traffic safety, postal rates, consumer product safety, occupational safety, and the safe use of nuclear fuel.

Issue networks were active in supporting and opposing these regulatory policy initiatives and the agencies that administered them. Because these types of issues have continued to be rather salient ones, issue networks have continued to be key policy players on the policy scene. The founders probably would consider them more healthy to a balanced democracy than are iron triangles, primarily because issue networks, almost by definition, are not likely to gain (as do iron triangles) institutionalized permanence within government and use that position to stake claims on major slices of the public budget.

Issue networks affect policy processes and content in other ways, not all of them favorable. They make policy processes considerably more intricate. Some issues may be, on the surface, rather simple to resolve. However, in an attempt to monopolize processes and control results, members of issue networks often refuse to bargain, thereby complicating a process that would otherwise be comparatively simple. They are not, by nature, consensus oriented. They often work to preserve the pureness of their opinions at the expense of consensus development. Many of their members become zealots, who crusade for a single solution or point of view while pointing out how policy compromises lead ultimately to an abandonment of mission. Many issue networks seem allergic to the notion of issue closure. They revel in debating issues, and are therefore inclined to keep issues alive well beyond their logical termination point.[54]

Presidents, as policy spokespersons for the entire body politic, often find the fluidity and unpredictability of issue networks even more frustrating than iron triangles. Although few iron triangles find a wholehearted ally in the president, at least they offer a high degree of predictability and tend to reflect society's larger factions and more high-profile values. If the president is at odds with any or all of these value constructs, he can at least clearly identify the enemy. However, in the changing, friction-laden, relatively open world of the issue network, authority and power are transient and notably unfixed. Conflict can arise in policy areas that have been stabilized for years, only to be assaulted frontally by issue networks, often with success. Recalling the discussion and analysis in Chapter 3, iron triangles, or subgovernments, are so firmly anchored to their own historical policy advantages, most of them distributive in nature, that they only welcome changes that reinforce or amplify those policy advantages. In the more amorphous world of the issue network, many of these embedded, policy-privileged alliances are fair game for policy regulation or redistribution. Moves to change the status quo can originate anywhere—the president, a public interest group, an ambitious first-term Senate or House member, or an activist group or individual. Although this development has definitely democratized the policy processes, it has also complicated them. According to Gais, Peterson, and Walker, although subgovernments are still a key part of the policy scene, "their influence is less pervasive than in the 1940s and 1950s, and the system can no longer be accurately characterized as a loose collection of subgovernments."[55]

The era of individualized pluralism began, in part, because policy issues were beginning to become both regulatory and redistributive in nature. Issues became more ideological in nature, resurrecting questions introduced, and resolved temporarily, during the New Deal period. Included were questions over the proper role of government in ensuring worker health and safety, in ensuring a clean environment, and in protecting consumers against corporate fraud. Subgovernments flower during periods when people are comfortable with, or at least not bothered frequently by, distributive policies. However, little short of a regulatory and redistributive "revolution" transpired during the Kennedy, Johnson, Nixon, Ford , and Carter administrations. To be sure, there have been selected deregulatory and antiredistributive policy backlashes since 1980. However, the regulatory and redistributive policy legacy of that period is still very much a fixed part of the federal government's value commitments and, most certainly, its budget. The salient niches of such policies as Medicare, Medicaid, environmental protection, racial equality, and consumer protection attest to this exigency. These policies have produced a notably different system

of conflict resolution than that offered by the iron triangle, or subgovernment, phenomenon. Redistributive and regulatory questions invite ideological confrontations among interests that coalesce in support of, or in opposition to, regulatory and redistributive policy proposals. Fewer key congressional decisions are made in subcommittees and in administrative bureaus. More people are affected by these decisions and more fundamental values are brought into question. Therefore, the full Congress and, increasingly, the president, are more actively involved.

"Going Public" Policy Mentality

A major legacy of the individualized pluralism period on Congress and public policy has been what can be termed the "going public" policy mentality. Since the 1970s, most House and Senate members equate both electoral and policymaking success with a good constituency-based bedside manner. Certainly the constant campaign mentality is an excellent illustration of this, as is the tendency for legislators, regardless of party persuasion, to want to reward constituencies with generous servings of policy pork, or public spending in districts for projects that increase employment and commerce. Although traditionally Republicans have accused the Democrats of being the "party of pork," statistics show that pork barrel politics is both omnipresent and bipartisan.[56] Both biases encourage legislators to spend the bulk of their time with constituency service in one form or another. The obligation to govern in a way that requires occasional sacrifice in return for a better future is not high priority under the current scheme of things.

The policy manifestations of the constant campaign mentality are an excellent case in point. One of the policy legacies of the reform era was the 1972 Federal Election Campaign Act. This law introduced a system of public support of presidential campaigns, as well as placing legal limits on the amount of money individuals and organizations could contribute to any campaign. The limit was placed at $5,000 per organization per candidate, and at $1,000 per individual per candidate. The fact that contributions were to go to candidates directly, instead of parties, clearly encourages candidate-centered campaigns. Furthermore, there was no indexing for inflation, so as time passed each such contribution meant less to the candidates. This meant that they had to scurry more seriously for funds to pay for television advertising. The meager size of contribution limits meant that party and corporate "fat cats" could not support individual campaigns as they had in the past. Therefore, candidates had to solicit very small sums from a very large assortment of individuals, making candidates and (ultimately) officeholders more beholden to their constituencies. Both parties and candidates can and do receive large soft money contributions from fat cat elements. This makes them more beholden as policymakers (if elected) to these interests. Increasing voter apathy increases the political leverage of these interests even further. Ironically, a reform that was designed to expunge, or at least constrain, the impact of vested interests on politics and policy (the Federal Election Campaign Act) served ultimately to increase the leverage of vested interests over policy decisions.

As party identification and its impact on voter behavior declined during the 1970s and 1980s, legislators' political party affiliations gradually became less significant than their voting records. Supporting the president or the House or Senate party leaders on a close vote on a critical bill had to be weighed against the possibility that the vote could come back to haunt the legislator come the next election campaign. Therefore, electoral calculations began to affect legislative behavior. Consequently, beginning in the 1970s,

there were many fewer bills introduced and roll-call votes taken. Furthermore, in pursuance of member electoral security, the ratio of bills enacted into law to those introduced declined significantly.[57] Legislating less frequently reduced electoral vulnerability.

Another impact of the constituency orientation was on how legislation was framed in advance of voting. Many reform era policy challenges involved austerity, or sacrifice, in terms of reduced benefits or higher taxes. Legislators sought ways to obscure the linkage between their votes and unpopular policy decisions. Multiple referral practices as well as omnibus bills, discussed above, helped significantly in this respect. Voting only one time on budget resolutions and continuing resolutions made it difficult for voters to pin an unpopular policy on their senator or representative. In addition, the Deficit Reduction Act of 1986, popularly known as the Gramm-Rudmann-Hollings Act, virtually cleared legislators of any responsibility of voting on budget cuts. This law specified that budget cuts were to apply to all programs across the board if Congress could not agree to cut programs by pretargeted amounts. Therefore, the system dictated austerity, not legislators themselves. This permitted legislators to play both sides of the issue for political gain. They could claim they had voted for austerity and sacrifice by endorsing Gramm-Rudmann-Hollings, while at the same time absolving themselves of any responsibility of voting against any specific program that did damage to their constituencies. Consequently, the reform period's constituency-centered bias seriously undercut the ability of voters to hold legislators accountable, while at the same time permitting the most serious policy problems to drift, victimized by symbolic politics.

Pundits and Policy

A final effect of the reform period on congressional decision making involves the increased role of staff experts, or pundits, on both the policy process and policy content. Legislators primarily focused on assuaging constituents and planning for campaigns simply do not have the time to develop in-depth policy expertise on their own. This trend has impacted both houses but, due to the Senate's comparative manpower disadvantage, it impacts on the upper house more than on the lower. The Senate is less than one-fourth the size of the House, and yet has essentially the same policy responsibilities. According to Ross Baker, the Senate workload encourages senators to function at a "cosmic" policy level, where they are "superficial in their grasp of policy," while leaving the policy details to their staffs.[58]

The delegation of policy prerogatives to nonelected experts introduces accountability problems in a democracy. In a sense, it converts legislators into administrators responsible for delegating power to experts who make policy decisions in their behalf. To be sure, Congress retains its right to legitimize policies officially, but the source and defense of policy options has gravitated, by force of circumstance, to personal and committee staffs. Of course, staff decisions have to serve the career ambitions of the legislators. Once that is on line, and legislators grow to depend on it, it serves to fragment decision making further. In a sense, staff expertise becomes the new system's substitute for the role that seniority played under the old system.[59] However, unlike seniority, expertise serves to disperse, not centralize and coordinate, the policymaking process. Consequently, this introduces yet another variation of the irony of the reform period, namely that a reform geared toward making Congress more informed and responsive functions instead to enable those ultimately responsible for decisions to remain uninformed and dependent upon experts, isolated from the real world of politics, for policy cues.

Congress at the Crossroads

Insofar as congressional politics is concerned, the twentieth century closed on a distinctively ominous note. The policy challenges of the twenty-first century will be profound, demanding sacrifice and commitment to uncovering and endorsing rational solutions to festering policy problems in fields such as health care, Social Security, education, disease prevention and control, poverty, resource management, and campaign finance. Ironically, the post-Watergate trends in congressional decision making have created conditions which both encourage and reward legislators for delaying the serious consideration of long-term solutions to these problems. At a time when legislation should be long term and comprehensive in focus, it nonetheless reflects frustrating tendencies to be piecemeal, "me-too," and often "do nothing" in character.

The record of the 105th Congress (1997–1999), the twentieth century's last full-term Congress, offers an excellent case in point. Partisanship and electoral politics saturated that Congress at virtually every policy turn, undermining a golden opportunity to set the nation's long-term policy house in order. It served during a period of unprecedented economic prosperity—a period that brought years of sustained low inflation, high employment, and corporate prosperity. Annual cash budget deficits disappeared years ahead of even the most optimistic projections. This era offered politicians the chance to set their sights on the needs of future generations and to commit fiscal and human resources in ways that could well serve those needs. However, it chose not to do so. It was dominated by bitter partisan haggling over legislation that would have controlled excesses of the tobacco industry, placed reasonable restraints on campaign finance excesses, improved the accessibility of more people to reasonably priced medical care, and dealt proactively with the approaching possibility of a bankrupt Social Security system. These were but a few of the long-term policy challenges shelved by the 105th Congress in favor of bitter partisan infighting over how to deal with the implications of the Starr report on the possible impeachment or forced resignation of President Clinton, how to assuage key corporate interests and secure their financial support for the 1998 elections, and how to link education reform to increased family stability, anticrime programs, and the reduction of poverty. The politics of survival suppressed any suggestion of a politics of accomplishment.

The legislative history of antitobacco legislation in 1998 offers an excellent illustration of how Congress fiddled while the long-term health interests of both the country and the world burned. The long-term effects of unchecked consumption of tobacco on the health of people worldwide could be catastrophic. If 1998 consumption levels go unchecked, by the year 2025 nearly 500 million people are likely to die as the result of tobacco-related diseases. That equates to a Vietnam War death total every day for twenty-two years, a Titanic death toll every twenty-seven minutes for twenty-seven years, or a single death every 1.2 seconds. Despite these ominous predictions, Congress refused to enact President Clinton's proposal to levy a heavy per-pack tax on cigarette sales, and earmark the revenue for the health care of those suffering from tobacco-related diseases. Those opposing the proposal, mostly conservatives, did so on the grounds that it was too much of a "tax and spend" proposal, and enthusiastically supported the idea that each individual state sue the tobacco companies for compensation for Medicaid expenses expended by the states to treat those with tobacco-related illnesses. Such a position was taken despite the fact that tobacco-related diseases impacted directly and negatively on goals that conservatives were then championing—child health,

the right-to-life position on abortion, and welfare and health care spending controls. Nonetheless, a state-based solution was finally adopted. Clearly a convenient "pass the buck" strategy employing a constitutional smokescreen, this strategy exploited the constitutional principle of federalism and the devolutionary trends in government to the benefit of those who, for political reasons, could not stand up to the tobacco companies. The tobacco companies had spent over $30 million in lobbying in 1998 and had contributed funds to nearly half of the House and Senate races in 1996, and those who voted against the legislation expected more of the same in 1998, prompting former U.S. Surgeon General Leonard Koop to observe that "Congress was trading public health for PAC money."[60]

Despite the fact that the public appeared to favor moderation and pragmatism in party politics and public policy, congressional Democrats and Republicans were sharply divided on philosophical grounds during the 105th Congress. Party agendas were ideologically firm, and compromises were difficult to achieve, especially as the 1998 elections drew closer. As was the case on the tobacco issue, the constant campaign mentality drew members of both parties toward intransigent positions on policy issues so that clear policy lines could be drawn between themselves and their opponents in the upcoming campaign. Dependency on PAC money and a major dependency on large soft money contributions resulted in the defeat of a major campaign finance reform proposal, although one did pass the House only to be defeated in the Senate. Deferring to the political clout of physicians and the health care industry in general, Congress failed to enact a proposal to empower dissatisfied patients to challenge managed health care plans. Considering the president to have been irreparably weakened politically by the Lewinsky scandal and by his lame-duck status, the Republican majority did everything it could to block most of President Clinton's initiatives. The Democrats, bolstered by the president's occasional veto, retaliated with an in-kind counterattack. With an election soon approaching, members of both parties concluded that they would rather run for reelection on their favorite issues than on a legislative record drenched with compromises.

The president attempted to overcome the legislative impasse by issuing executive orders to accomplish a bit of what was lost by the stalemate. However, these efforts were generally long on symbolism and short on content. Nonetheless, they did beget an illusion of action, however limited. After Congress failed to fully fund the president's proposal to find and eliminate tainted food from the marketplace, Clinton unilaterally commanded that warning labels be placed on unpasteurized vegetable and fruit juices. Following the Senate's rejection of antismoking legislation, the president ordered that research be conducted into which brands of cigarettes were most popular with teenagers. After Congress refused to enact his health care reform package, the president ordered federal agencies to provide Medicaid coverage for millions of additional children. None of these actions were momentous by any definition of the term. However, they were at least more than was generated by the legislative process.

Most of the 1998 legislative accomplishments were of an election year political "slam dunk" type. While they were significant in their own right, they were also genetically nonpartisan in cast. That made them good election year fodder. Few defend the tax collector, so a major Internal Revenue Service reform bill easily secured strong bipartisan support and was enacted, as was a generously funded highway construction bill. For the same reasons the Senate found it easy to support a treaty expanding the North Atlantic Treaty Organization (NATO). Few enemies were made by these decisions. Regarding the more con-

tentious and highly partisan budget decisions, the Republican Congress and the president resolved their differences not by compromise but by legislated indulgences. The Fiscal Year 1999 budget agreement, discussed earlier, illustrates how easy it is to allow election year political positioning to result in spending more and planning less. On balance, bitter partisanship was the order of the legislative times in 1998, and the 1999 agreement (October 1998) reflected that. Failing to compromise on most key budget items, the president and the Republican congressional majority agreed to support most of what both camps wanted without cutting or reducing funding for any existing programs, with each side hoping that its version of the budget "victory" would win the most voters in the 1998 election.

The Politics of Demography: Congress and the Census

An example of how the 105th Congress politicized a constitutional mandate in preparation for the new century's policy challenges can be found in the way legislators handled the question of how to count people for the year 2000 census. The Constitution requires a census to be taken every ten years. To some, this may seem like a pro-forma, essentially ministerial exercise in counting and record-keeping. However, it became a hotly contested political issue during the 105th Congress, and for good reason. How to count people for representational purposes has been a contentious issue since the founding of the republic. It was the issue at stake in negotiations that led to the famous three-fifths compromise during the Constitutional Convention, whereby all native-born and naturalized citizens and three-fifths of "other persons" (referring to the slave population) were to be included in census counts. At issue then, and still today, was/is the following: How should political power be officially apportioned among jurisdictions, especially states, that contain widely different numbers of people? The solution in 1789 was a two-house national legislature, one representing states based on their population (House of Representatives) and one representing them equally regardless of population (Senate). Figures for representation in the House were to be based on census figures, and reapportioned every ten years to allow for population growth, decline, and migration.

Although census taking has been a political issue historically, it has been especially heated since the 1960s. At stake is essentially how the nation's political power shall be distributed. More specifically involved are questions such as the role of race and ethnicity in public policy and, ultimately, how far government can be trusted when it comes to counting people. The U.S. Constitution was the first written document that established a dependency of political power on an official head count. Therefore, it is essential that such a count be accurate and not subject to political manipulation. Politics should not falsify the truth. It found a way to do so nonetheless.

The official census count was to determine the number of House seats assigned to each state, but it was up to the legislatures in each state to determine how individual district lines were to be drawn. Shrewd state-based politicos soon discovered that district lines could be drawn to political benefit. In 1812, Massachusetts governor Eldridge Gerry successfully engineered a very partisan district-drawing scheme through his state's legislature. One district was so geographically distorted to meet Gerry's goals that it reminded a political cartoonist of a salamander. Hence, the term "gerrymandering" has been employed ever since to refer to the practice of drawing legislative district lines for partisan advantage. Public ridicule and judicial revocations rendered gerrymandering obsolete for an extended period, but it surfaced again in the

late-1960s, 1970s, and 1980s in response to pressures to increase the representation of minorities in government. The liberalization of immigration policy and various civil rights and voting rights acts gave the Justice Department the right to examine the propriety of legislative districting to determine if state legislatures had deliberately discriminated against minorities by scattering their political impact via districting decisions. The result was, in some cases, a reversal of the discrimination trend. In an attempt to maximize minority leverage in some districts, district lines resembled caricatures of spiders and snakes, thereby relegating Gerry's salamander to symbolic ridicule. Following a lengthy litigation process, the Supreme Court in 1995 and 1996 ruled that it was unconstitutional to create districts primarily for the purpose of increasing the political impact of minorities in Congress.

While these court challenges were developing, concern was being voiced over how accurately minorities were being counted in the census. President Clinton and congressional Democrats joined the Bureau of the Census in contending that a literal count of people is impossible, and that millions were going uncounted in every census. Obviously, the president and his congressional allies had concluded that a more accurate count would be politically advantageous to them. The weight of the argument was decidedly on their side. It was estimated that the 1990 census missed between eight and nine million individuals, and perhaps had double-counted nearly five million others. This was because the counting method relied on mailed questionnaires and a detachment of enumerators to track down as many nonresponders as possible. Armed with the support of a private study that concluded the same, the Census Bureau contended that, once 90 percent of the people had been contacted, a statistical sample of the uncounted be interviewed and the survey results be used to close out the totals.

The Bureau conceded that its recent counts of economically disadvantaged blacks had probably underestimated their numbers significantly more than it had for whites, probably by about a three-to-one ratio. Accordingly, the Bureau argued that the best way to get control of the problem was to introduce a sampling process, whereby nose counters would extrapolate national figures from samples collected from specific districts. Without controversy, Congress had authorized the Census Bureau to employ sampling to gather data on the economic and social characteristics of households. However, it had specifically prohibited the use of sampling data to determine the basis for assigning House districts to states. Few people care about the number of households that heat and cook with natural gas, but Congress cares very much about how many people are counted in each state. For example, if sampling projected an additional 700,000 residents for New York, some state would lose a House seat to accommodate that alleged reality.

What appeared to be a scientific attempt to get at the demographic truth became a hotly contested political issue, and for good reason. No one argued with the assumption that most of the uncounted population was black, Hispanic, homeless, and relatively impoverished. In short, these were potentially Democratic Party voters. In addition, the advent of affirmative action programs and racial identity policies in the 1970s and 1980s increased the political importance of these undercounts rather dramatically, primarily because minority employment goals were usually based on pro-rated census figures. With so much at stake, minority groups and their political allies began to push for more accurate census counts.

The undercount issue was important to many nonminority groups as well, for reasons that had little to do with race. As census taking moved from the technical, statistical challenge arena to the political domain in the 1970s, court decisions were mandating that states reapportion both congressional and state legislative districts to conform to the one man–one vote principle. This meant that rural areas could no longer be overrepresented in state assemblies. More important, it meant that urban districts profiting from this change could gain more leverage in federal grant-in-aid decisions, many of which were allocated on the basis of census data. More than any time in history, the census count, or undercount, became associated directly with money and, ultimately, with political power. Consequently, in 1980 urban officials representing sizeable minority populations insisted that the 1980 census count be calibrated to accommodate the estimated minority group undercount. These requests raised a plethora of technical and legal issues in political, professional, and legal circles. There was no guarantee that such adjustments would challenge the ratios of the actual count. In addition, it seemed unfair to some that national projections should be applied across the board to all communities where the minority-nonminority ratio would often be very incongruent with the national figures. Consequently, the Census Bureau refused to incorporate projected minority group undercounts in the 1980 census, thereby generating a barrage of lawsuits by officials in the nation's largest urban areas. Ultimately, the Supreme Court determined that the Census Bureau acted within the law by not incorporating projected undercounts in the 1980 census. Bolstered by the court decision, the Bureau announced the same policy in 1990, and again ran into several lawsuits sponsored by the nation's largest cities, led by New York, Chicago, and Los Angeles. Although the Secretary of Commerce confessed to a likely undercount of minorities in 1990, he was unconvinced that using undercount projections in the census would have made the count more proportionally accurate. In 1996 the Supreme Court rejected the cities' claims, letting the actual census count stand as the official one.

As the year 2000 census approached, the debate over the possible role of projected minority undercounts made its way to Congress. Those likely to profit from such projections were the liberals, most of them Democrats. Those likely to be disadvantaged by the same were the conservatives, most of them Republicans. It came as no surprise that the congressional parties were divided on the issue. Politics impacts on the principle of equity in very predictable ways, much the same as it did on the use of the Starr report. At stake in the debate over how the year 2000 census was to be conducted, and if any undercount projections were to be incorporated in the final official figures, was the issue of constitutional legitimacy. Politics aside, the census must be creditable in order for our political system to function with any degree of democratic integrity. Although the temptations to use it politically may seem overwhelming, the governmental system must find some means to reject or override the temptation. The political proponents of sampling, both congressional and urban, argue that modern scientific sampling methods would lead to a more accurate, and politically legitimate, census enterprise. Opponents contend that the Constitution mandates an actual head count only for House-seat apportionment, and that the certification of a sampling plan would invite Census Bureau administrators to manipulate sampling formulas and impact on census data in ways that affect the assignment of political power.

In January 1999, by a split 5–4 decision, the Supreme Court rejected the statistical sampling plan for the 2000 census, with the court majority arguing that the Census Act prohibited such a supplement to a direct head count. The majority's position was based on its interpretation of the Census Act, not on whether sampling actually violates the Constitution's requirement that an "actual enumeration" of the American public be made each decade. The court's four most liberal justices challenged the five-member conservative majority, arguing that the law clearly allowed sampling as a means to ascertain a more accurate count because census takers are often denied access to crowded housing complexes and must therefore record zero occupancy. Because of the political implications of the ruling, it was one of the most significant of the court's 1998–1999 term. The decision was a defeat for President Clinton and the Democrats, and a corresponding victory for congressional Republicans. Since the decision affected only how people are counted for legislative apportionment purposes, a more liberal Congress could, in the future, alter the law to allow sampling for apportionment purposes. The constitutionality of such a law would likely be challenged, and the courts would again be called on to unearth a judicial solution to a fundamentally political issue. It may indeed be the case, as Michael Teitelbaum and Jay Winter have observed, that "we have allowed the political stakes riding on census counts to rise too high to expect politically committed groups to restrain themselves from attempting to control the collection and tabulation of data. In demography, all numbers count. But in politics some numbers count more than others."[61]

Congress and Constitutional Politics: A Critique

Kenneth Shepsle has offered a sound paradigm for judging the impact of reform movements on congressional behavior. His thesis is that the strains Congress encounters in its attempt to satisfy, concurrently, the role demands of constituency representation and policymaking are anchored in three competing obligations—to represent constituencies, to organize itself to do its legislative job, and to respond to the partisan appeals of political parties.[62] These existed in a comparatively healthy state of symmetry during the protective pluralist period. Especially stable and significant was the jurisdictional mandate, which played out in a strong standing committee system, strong committee chairs, and an institutionalized structure which offered legislators ways to develop expertise and to use that to develop credibility with their constituents. Beginning in the late 1950s, that committee prominence was subject to increasing challenges by new and recently elected liberals who saw the system as a roadblock to their realizing their policy goals. By the 1970s, the rebellion had gone full course. Committee salience had been compromised. Party consent requirements modified the seniority principle. The rules systems, especially in the House, had been modified to allow majority rule to impact on legislation. In short, the balanced system of the protective pluralist period gave way to a system in which the constituency imperative dominated the committee and partisan imperatives. High priority constituency service and decentralized committee power introduced problems of policy coordination, and therefore party organizations were strengthened to lend some coherence to a notably atomized congressional landscape.

While direct cause-effect relationships between the formalities of the Constitution and these events most likely do not exist, constitutional principles have facilitated their development and have been used by political adversaries to leverage arguments against one another. The relationship between the separation of powers and federalism on the one hand and an uncentralized two-party system was explored in Chapter 5. It is the two-party system, with only two parties appealing to all society's elements, that virtually mandates parties to be bottom up organizations that

consider votes for their candidates to be more important than coherent party policy objectives. Both major political parties are, in fact, fifty state-rooted organizations. During the protective pluralist period, congressional party leaders were often successful in persuading legislators to adopt common policy positions. This has been the case less frequently during the individualized pluralism period. Once the wave of institutional reforms caught on, legislators found it rather easy to adopt the principles of federalism, separation of powers, and checks and balances as a way to justify their reborn allegiances to constituencies.

In the interest of safety and stability, the Constitution deliberately disperses power among several institutional forces, each with its own constitutionally assigned right to represent people (and factions) in the policy process. Decentralization and the consequent representation of social and political diversity is spiritually conformist to the founders' objectives. The Constitution's framework permits all the diversities of all states and all localities to work their way up through uncentralized party mechanisms to congressional party organizations with few, if any, alterations. A highly decentralized committee and subcommittee system offers a convenient outlet for the registration of these diversities in the formal makeup of the two houses. The constitutional and cultural stress on conditions of equality of people and, in effect, equality of constituencies limits the ability of both houses to sustain attempts to organize their affairs on a hierarchical basis. All legislators have equal rights to serve on committees and subcommittees, introduce bills, be equally represented in party caucuses, and so on. In short, all legislators have the same assortment of rights to influence legislation at several stages of the policy process. For good measure, include the impact of bicameralism, which mandates that these accommodations be played out on two independent legislative stages, the second one representing the states as geographic entities equally. The effect of all this is to slow the policy process and to stimulate compromise. Both sluggishness and compromise encourage marginal, or incremental, solutions to policy problems. All of this is as the founders intended, and is very acquiescent to the norms of the individualized pluralism or reform period in American politics.

However, the founders also sought to balance policy inputs among both factions and institutions in the policy process. While the notion of "separate institutions sharing (policy) powers" is a modern operational adaptation of the impact of separation of powers on policy, most of the founders would likely endorse it as a necessary transformation of their ideas to meet the challenges of a society far larger and more complicated than theirs. In all probability, the 1970s "representational revolt" within Congress has undermined the ability of Congress to function as well as a separate policy force as it did during the pre-1970 period. The proliferation and strengthening of subcommittees has elevated relatively inexperienced politicians to key policy positions. Many of these individuals do not have the experience that affords them the ability to manage subcommittee staffs effectively, to draft legislation, and to develop coalitions. Their predecessors during the protective pluralist period were, in general, better able to meet these challenges effectively. In all organizations power can be proliferated and decentralized too greatly and the effectiveness of the entire organization can suffer as a result. Congress is no exception to this. Since the 1970s, full committees have been more active in revising the work of their subcommittees, and the full houses have spent more time redoing the work of the full committees. Legislation since the 1970s has been less the result of committee and subcommittee expertise and more the result of efforts by skilled floor leaders in assembling majority coalitions in support of policies. To quote Shepsle: "Extreme decentralization, in effect, threatens to destroy legislative independence without substituting compensating safeguards."[63] According to Shepsle, the role of Congress as a policy force within the "separate institutions" framework has been compromised by the negative results of the renewed stress on the representation norm. In sum, "representative impulses inside the legislature conflict with the legislature's ability to maintain its separateness, its independence, and hence its influence in the larger political system."[64]

Nearly all of the policy consequences of the reform period's impact on Congress have clear constitutional roots. Divided government cannot exist in a parliamentary system, but it has become the rule rather than the exception in our separated system over the past generation or so. Divided government encourages a politics of ideology, symbolism, and interbranch scandal-mongering that deflects the energies of government away from the serious policy issues of the times, and aggravates an already dangerously high level of public cynicism about government and its leaders. It also encourages bipartisan responses to policy problems and appears to consider compromises ends unto themselves. Bipartisanship eschews parties as a source of policy coherence and honest debates over how best to approach policy problems that often appear unsolvable. Consequently, parties have come to mean little more than historically accepted labels upon which candidates for office hang their political hats in the hope of winning elections. The Constitution's check and balance principle translates logically into a congressional mandate to oversee activities of the executive branch. However, the legitimacy of that mandate has been seriously compromised by investigations that put politics, character assassination, and personal attacks ahead of serious attempts to keep the government accountable to its people.

The overpowering misfortune of the Clinton-Lewinsky scandal and President Clinton's impeachment was that it dominated Washington politics for more than a year over the protest of a clear majority of the people. Most Americans believed that the president did wrong, but also thought that impeachment was too serious a penalty for his indiscretions. Despite that reality, the House Republican majority persisted in its preoccupation with the issue, ultimately securing Clinton's impeachment. That preoccupation did not come without its costs to the nation. It offended public taste, devalued national dialogue, and turned Congress into antagonistic, caustic, partisan camps. Most important, it relegated a host of national and international problems to the policy "back burner." The repetitive prattle that clogged the nightly television news and discussion shows overshadowed an increasing backlog of unattended policy business.

All systems need reform-induced transfusions from time to time. To the extent that the reforms of the 1960s and 1970s encouraged Congress to reevaluate how effectively it was pursuing its democratic mandate, the results were favorable. The reforms, however, were democratic in root, and while that is good in principle, they must be implemented with care to be effective. While the notion of effectiveness is admittedly subjective, it is almost universally accepted that democracy has two components—the procedural and the substantive. If substance suppresses procedures, government runs the danger of becoming authoritarian. However, if Congress, as in the Clinton-Lewinsky case, allows a

ratings-conscious media to determine its agenda while the nation's policy business goes virtually unattended, then its excessive concern for procedures suppresses a serious concern for solid substantive policies, and government runs the risk of becoming impotent. Unfortunately, the legacy of the reform period for both Congress and the nation has been mostly the latter.

Endnotes

1. Roy P. Fairfield, ed., *The Federalist Papers* (Garden City, N.Y.: Anchor Books, 1961), p. 160.

2. Richard M. Neustadt, *Presidential Power: The Politics of Leadership* (New York: Wiley, 1960), p. 33.

3. Benjamin I. Page and Robert Y. Shapiro, *The Rational Public: Fifty Years of Trends in Americans' Policy Preferences* (Chicago: University of Chicago Press, 1992), p. 14.

4. William E. Hudson, *American Democracy in Peril*, 2nd ed. (Chatham, N.J.: Chatham House, 1998), p. 15.

5. William S. White, *The Citadel* (New York: Harper and Brothers, 1956), pp. 135–153.

6. Samuel D. Kernell, *Going Public: New Strategies of Presidential Leadership*, 3rd ed. (Washington, D.C.: CQ Press, 1997), pp. 27–33.

7. *Ibid.*, p. 27.

8. Thomas E. Mann, "Elections and Change in Congress," in Thomas E. Mann and Norman J. Ornstein, eds., *The New Congress* (Washington, D.C.: American Enterprise Institute, 1981), p. 53.

9. Michael Robinson, "Three Faces of Congressional Media," in *Ibid.*, p. 93.

10. William L. Morrow, *Congressional Committees* (New York: Scribner's, 1969), p. 39.

11. Roger H. Davidson and Walter J. Oleszek, *Congress and Its Members*, 5th ed. (Washington, D.C.: CQ Press, 1996), p. 253.

12. *Ibid.*, p. 322.

13. P. Weiss, "Conduct Unbecoming?" *New York Times Magazine* (Oct. 29, 1989), p. 41, as quoted in Gerald Garvey, *Facing the Bureaucracy: Living and Dying in a Public Agency* (San Francisco: Jossey-Bass, 1993), p. 68.

14. See Eric Painin and Charles R. Babcock, "Working the System," *Washington Post National Weekly Edition* (April 13, 1998), pp. 6–9.

15. Ross K. Baker, *House and Senate* (New York: W. W. Norton, 1989), p. 89.

16. *Ibid.*, pp. 89–90.

17. See Michael J. Malbin, *Unelected Representatives* (New York: Basic Books, 1980).

18. David J. Vogler and Sidney R. Waldman, *Congress and Democracy* (Washington, D.C.: CQ Press, 1985), p. 87.

19. J. Leiper Freeman, *The Political Process: Executive Bureau-Legislative Committee Relations* (New York: Doubleday, 1955); David B. Truman, *The Governmental Process* (New York: Alfred Knopf, 1951); and Theodore J. Lowi, *The End of Liberalism* (New York: W. W. Norton, 1969).

20. Roger H. Davidson and Walter J. Oleszek, "From Monopoly to Management: Changing Patterns of Committee Deliberations," in Roger H. Davidson, ed., *The Postreform Congress* (New York: St. Martin's Press, 1992), p. 130.

21. *Ibid.*, p 133.

22. *Ibid.*, p. 140.

23. *Ibid.*

24. Kenneth A. Shepsle, "The Changing Textbook Congress," in John E. Chubb and Paul E. Peterson, *The Changing Textbook Congress* (Washington, D.C.: The Brookings Institution, 1989), pp. 252–253.

25. Norman J. Ornstein, Robert L. Peabody, and David W. Rohde, "The Changing Senate: From the 1950s to the 1970s," in Lawrence C. Dodd and Bruce I. Oppenheimer, eds., *Congress Reconsidered*, 3rd ed. (Washington, D.C.: CQ Press, 1985).

26. *Congressional Quarterly Weekly Report* (December 31, 1994), pp. 3658–3659.

27. David Broder, *Behind the Front Page* (New York: Touchstone Press, 1987), p. 202.

28. *Ibid.*, pp. 259–262.

29. Barbara Sinclair, "House Majority Party Leadership in an Era of Legislative Constraint," in Roger H. Davidson, *op. cit.*, pp. 95–96.

30. *Ibid.*, p. 96.

31. See Norman Ornstein, Thomas Mann, and Michael Malbin, *Vital Statistics on Congress, 1992* (Washington, D.C.: CQ Press, 1992), pp. 64, 67. These data were compiled from the Survey Research Center/Center for Political Studies, *National Election Studies.*

32. *Ibid.*, pp. 199–200. Data gathered to support these conclusions were based on statistics provided by *Congressional Quarterly.*

33. David Rohde, *Party Leaders in the Post Reform House* (Chicago: University of Chicago Press, 1991).

34. David Rohde, "Electoral Forces, Political Agendas, and Partisanship in Congress," in Roger H. Davidson, *op. cit.*, p. 34.

35. Davidson and Oleszek, *op. cit.*, p. 34.

36. Michael J. Malbin, "Political Parties Across the Separation of Powers," in Peter W. Schramm and Bradford P. Wilson, *American Political Parties and Constitutional Politics* (Lanham, Md.: Rowman and Littlefield, 1993), p. 85.

37. Steven S. Smith, "The Senate in the Postreform Era," in Roger H. Davidson, *op. cit.*, pp. 171–176.

38. Charles Stewart III, "Responsiveness in the Upper Chamber: The Constitution and the Institutional Development of the Senate," in Peter F. Narduli, *The Constitution and American Political Development* (Urbana: University of Illinois Press, 1992), p. 77.

39. *Ibid.*, p. 91.

40. *Federalist No. 63*, as quoted in *Ibid.*, p. 81.

41. *Ibid.*, pp. 190–191.

42. *Ibid.*, p. 191.

43. Ross K. Baker, *House and Senate, op. cit.*, pp. 212–223.

44. *Ibid.*, p. 215.

45. *Federalist No. 63*, as quoted in *Ibid.*, p. 77.

46. Walter J. Oleszek, "House-Senate Relations: A Perspective on Bicameralism," in Roger H. Davidson, *op. cit.*, pp. 193–204, 208.

47. Haynes Johnson and David Broder, *The System: The American Way of Politics at the Breaking Point* (Boston: Little, Brown, 1996).

48. Paul Starobin, "Dare to Bicker," *National Journal,* vol. 29, no. 12 (March 22, 1997), p. 559. Starobin's essay offers a keen insight into the issues surrounding the partisanship debate.

49. As quoted in *Ibid.*, p. 558.

50. Michael Barone, "Divide and Rule," *National Journal,* vol. 29, no. 28 (July 12, 1997), p. 1412.

51. Robert S. Bennett, "We Should Scuttle the Partisan Ship," *Washington Post National Weekly Edition* (March 21, 1997), p. 21.

52. *Ibid.*

53. Hugh Heclo, "Issue Networks and the Executive Establishment," in Anthony King, ed., *The New American Political System* (Washington, D.C.: American Enterprise Institute, 1978), p. 88.

54. *Ibid.*

55. Thomas L. Gais, Mark A. Peterson, and Jack L. Walker, "Interest Groups, Iron Triangles, and Representative Institutions in American National Government," *British Journal of Political Science*, vol. 14 (April 1985), p. 163.

56. Ben Wildavsky, "Pigging Out," *National Journal,* vol. 29, no. 16 (April 19, 1997), pp. 754–757.

57. H. W. Stanley and R. G. Niemi, *Vital Statistics on American Politics* (Washington, D.C.: CQ Press, 1988), p. 172.

58. Ross K. Baker, *op. cit.*, p. 158.

59. Lawrence C. Dodd, "The Rise of the Technocratic Congress," in Richard A. Harris and Sidney M. Milkis, eds., *Remaking American Politics, op. cit.*, p. 108.

60. Address to the National Press Club, September 10, 1998.

61. Michael Teitelbaum and Jay Winter, "The 2000 Census May Be a Lose-Lose Situation," *Washington Post National Weekly Edition* (September 21, 1998), p. 23. Much

of the material and line of argument in this section was derived from this essay.

62. Chubb and Peterson, eds., *Can the Government Govern?*, *op. cit.*, p. 239.

63. Kenneth A. Shepsle, "Representation and Governance: The Great Legislative Tradeoff." Paper prepared for presentation at the Constitutional Bicentennial Conference, Nelson A. Rockefeller Center, Dartmouth College, May 5, 1987, p. 39. This paper, with minor modifications, appeared in the *Political Science Quarterly* 103 (Fall 1988), pp. 461–481.

64. *Ibid.*, p. 43.

chapter eight

The Presidency

Policy Stewardship in a Separated System

The president is the focus of the nation's policy agenda. Responding to nationwide electoral mandates, presidents develop policy priorities and work diligently to convince forces within and outside government that their agendas embody the true national interest. Despite the fact that the Constitution assigns very little official policy responsibility to the president directly—mentioning only the power to negotiate treaties, apprise Congress periodically on the "state of the union," and veto legislation passed by Congress—the president and his cabinet and staff (collectively termed the "presidency") have become the major source of policy stewardship in American government.

There are multiple causes for the emergence of the president as the nation's policy leader. Two reasons predominate, and both have constitutional roots. First, government institutions established by the Constitution have been heavily democratized over the past two centuries. The public has considerably more electoral and policy input into the selection of legislative and executive leaders today than it did in 1789. The more beholden leaders are to the people for their offices, the more they are inclined to consider the public's policy agenda if it is expressed clearly and if it appears to be of significant concern to a large number of voters or potential voters. The presidency has been subjected to more institutional democratization than have its sister national institutions—Congress and the federal judiciary. The Electoral College still formally selects the president, but electors' votes are cast state by state for the candidate who won a plurality of the vote in each state. The framers did not intend for electors to be so selected, preferring instead for them to be selected by a vote of each state's legislature. The framers intended to insulate the president from irresponsible factions and the public's vicissitudes.

This is definitely not the case today. Today,

members of the Electoral College are appointed by state legislators from rosters of party elites whose presidential candidate won a plurality of votes cast within each state. The expectation is that electors will vote unanimously for that candidate. The implications of this for presidential policy leadership are profound, and they will be examined later. Suffice it to say here that the democratization of the presidential office carried with it the assumption that the president would no longer be primarily an elitist, institutional check on potential congressional policy excessivism as the framers intended, but a torch bearer for the president's version of the public's policy agenda.

The second constitutionally rooted reason for the emergence of the president as the nation's chief legislator can be found in the separation of powers principle. The separation of powers apportions policy responsibilities among several institutions of national government, but such an apportionment means that each of these institutions must ultimately cooperate with the others to produce policy decisions. Each of these institutions—the president, the Senate, and the House of Representatives—has a different constituency base. House members represent districts within states, senators represent the interests of states as a whole, and presidents represent, presumably, the interests of the entire nation. In the wake of the democratization of the presidency, the president is the only official who has political incentives to articulate and work the policy interests of the entire nation. The democratization of the presidential office has introduced such an imperative, and because the president is now the only policy spokesperson for the people in composite, a president's historical reputation rests on his ability to shepherd as much of this agenda as possible through institutions that don't share either his political or institutional perspectives. We now elect presidents with the expec-

tation that their major role is that of policy steward. This reality stands in stark contrast to the Constitution's bias toward the more staid executive, administrative, and Madison-like "guardian" expectations of the office. This role as the nation's policy steward would not be as important as it has become if our national government had a parliamentary constitutional structure. Parliamentary governments obligate the chief executive and the legislative majority to develop and enact the nation's policy agenda as a team. Minus a parliamentary structure but nonetheless responding to the forces of democratization, the American political system foists the most of the policy agenda-building responsibility on the president, and trusts that somehow he and Congress will be able to work things out.

The causes for and effects of the expansion of the president's policy responsibilities over time have been subjected to extensive scholarly examination. Three of the most prominent analyses were undertaken by Clinton Rossiter, Thomas Cronin, and Aaron Wildavsky.[1] Rossiter identified the expansion of presidential policy and political responsibilities with the corresponding genesis of new presidential roles—those he labeled as "extra-constitutional" in root because the Constitution fails to recognize their reality. Rossiter's thesis was first introduced in 1956 but has sustained its authenticity over the past half century. Cronin and Wildavsky offered more modernized, policy-focused versions of the Rossiter thesis. Cronin organized the president's policy obligations into three policy subpresidencies— foreign policy and national security, macroeconomics, and domestic policy and programs. Each requires the president to actively pursue seven different activities to fulfill the policy demands of each subpresidency: political and legislative coalition building, crisis management, administrative oversight of government routines, oversight of policy implementation, priority setting and program design, recruitment of leaders, and symbolic and morale building leadership. Wildavsky's version of the president's role obligations is considerably simpler, dividing the president's responsibilities into domestic and foreign policy obligations. During the Kennedy administration, Wildavsky noted a clear difference in the ability of the president to muster the necessary resources to meet his role responsibilities in domestic, as opposed to foreign, policy. Presidents encountered constant opposition to the realization of their goals on the domestic scene but were considerably more successful on the foreign front. However, by the 1980s the situation was notably different. Presidents continued to encounter difficulty with domestic policy stewardship, but the same problems were beginning to surface on the foreign stage as well. Foreign policy issues had become more cosmopolitan in cast, affecting both U.S. and foreign politics simultaneously. In addition, the politics of the constant campaign had made foreign policy fair game for issue-hungry politicians seeking office. The result was a foreign policy stage significantly influenced by the same types of inputs that had theretofore been largely confined to the domestic scene.

The Presidency and the Authority-Responsibility Gap

The president's policy responsibilities are a composite of formal obligations found in the Constitution and ones annexed by time and circumstances. Most of these circumstances consist of social, economic, and political problems that have developed both domestically and worldwide that demand government policy responses. Virtually all important presidential roles are significant because they are policy roles. Being that, they involve the president in regular political combat. It makes little or no difference whether these roles are rooted in the Constitution directly or whether they have accrued to the office over time.

Rossiter's classification of presidential roles, although nearly half a century old, provides an excellent anchor for analyzing the growth of presidential policy responsibilities. Some roles have clear roots in the Constitution. Others have evolved outside its language. According to Rossiter, the Constitution makes the president chief of state, chief legislator, chief diplomat, chief executive, and commander-in-chief of the armed forces. As chief executive, the president nominates top administrative officials and oversees the faithful execution or implementation of the law. As chief diplomat, the president appoints and receives ambassadors, and negotiates treaties. As commander-in-chief, the president directs the military in foreign conflicts where U.S. interests are at stake and the use of military force seems warranted. As chief legislator, he submits messages to Congress on the state of the union, which include major policy recommendations, and he has the authority to veto legislation passed by Congress if he judges it contrary to the public interest.

In addition to the president's constitutional powers, Rossiter offered a series of extra-constitutional role responsibilities. Each is rooted in American government's need to respond to changing domestic and foreign social, economic, and political events. Included are the president's role as leader of the world's free nations, chief of party, manager of prosperity, protector of the peace, and voice of the people. The first refers to the United States post–World War II primacy as a steward to lead the world's underdeveloped nations toward economic prosperity and political democracy. This new role also carried with it the obligation of leading the West's efforts to stave off Communist military challenges to the more mature democracies in Europe and the Far East. The party chieftainship is bestowed on the president as the result of leading his political party to victory in a presidential election. As his party's *de facto* leader, the president is obligated to develop and orchestrate his party's efforts to instigate policy change. The manager of prosperity role was the result of the economic challenges brought on by the New Deal and the demobilization of the military effort following World War II. Included were such challenges as worker retraining, conservation of resources, the recovery and revitalization of businesses, and analyzing the effects of government spending and interest rates on inflation and employment. The Employment Act of 1946 established the three-person Council of Economic Advisors to help the president with this new responsibility.

The voice of the people role is a natural outgrowth of the democratization of the presidential office. As the country's only public official elected by the entire body politic, the president is expected to sponsor policy crusades that serve the long-term interests and well-being of everyone. This is, of course, impossible. The public is simply too diverse economically, ethnically, socially, and religiously to expect one office to represent every individual and faction in a balanced fashion. On some issues, such as emergency economic recovery policies, or ones responding to clear military aggression against the United States, presidents expect, and usually receive, strong and widespread bipartisan support. However, regarding issues such as welfare reform, environmental regulation, health care, pollution control, education, consumer protection, and foreign trade, the public is often very divided, and strong bipartisan support is usually missing. In these policy fields, deciding on a clear course of action that is both effective and popular is very difficult, if not impossible. Most of these policies are regulatory or redistributive in character. As such, they are more controversial by nature than are distributive policies. They demand that some people

forgo indulgences or privileges in the long-term interest of everyone. Distributive policies dispense advantages, but regulatory and redistributive policies advantage some at the expense of others.

The growing significance of the president's constitutional and extra-constitutional powers means that a president's niche in history is determined by how well his presidency mastered those challenges. However, the Constitution, a political culture suspicious of centralized power, weak political parties, strong interest groups, and the globalization of political and economic issues all work against presidential attempts to master these challenges. It means, in effect, that the president, in order to become a successful policy steward, must overcome what can be termed a very formidable "authority-responsibility gap."

For purposes of the following analysis, an authority-responsibility gap exists under conditions where the president has an understood *responsibility* for promising and delivering policy results, but legal and political circumstances do not provide him with the necessary formal or legal *authority* to do so. The Constitution assigns the president very few specific policy powers, and is completely silent on the matter of policy staff assistance. The founding fathers did not expect the president to perform many direct, major policy roles. Of course, there are numerous federal statutes existing today that assign modern presidents significant policy responsibilities. Laws also provide presidents with staff assistance to help develop policy proposals, budgets, and administrative regulations, as well as with machinery to help oversee the implementation of policies. Regardless, the president's policy responsibilities have expanded more rapidly than has the constitutional and statutory authority for him to deal with them satisfactorily. This, in essence, is the authority-responsibility gap. Presidents have far more policy responsibilities than they have resources to deal with them, and the gap is widening.

The Constitution laid the foundation for the authority-responsibility gap. It dissipates policymaking and policy implementation responsibilities among two houses of Congress and a president. As a result, all three institutions share the obligation to develop and implement policies despite the fact that the constituencies and, therefore, the policy incentives of each are markedly different. The fact that Congress has conceded to the president a major role in policy agenda development means, ironically, that these constituency differences usually aggravate deliberations when the two legislative chambers and the president attempt to resolve their policy differences. More presidential policy responsibilities mean more clashes. The democratization of the presidential office has both created and fueled some of the more intense conflicts. The problem has been aggravated by weakening parties, a scandal-hungry media, and the imperatives of the constant campaign. What Lowi calls the democratized, "plebiscitary" presidency has made presidents the public's policy stewards and brought them into conflict with legislators whose constituency obligations are notably different from their own.[2] In light of these circumstances, the presidential policy challenge is so awesome that one scholar has termed it an impossible job, and today's presidency the "impossible presidency."[3]

Since the New Deal period, presidents have attempted to bridge the authority-responsibility gap in two distinct ways. They have done it either by bargaining with their adversaries or by asking the public directly for support in the hope that presidential adversaries get the message and begin cooperating. Usually, presidents work on both fronts simultaneously. The task is formidable, because the adversaries are often well organized, well funded, and scattered throughout both the public and private sectors. Included are many members of both houses of Congress, interest groups, career bureaucrats, and representatives of the media, especially television. These forces are obliged to serve constituencies and professional norms in ways that often clash with presidential policy incentives. While both the bargaining and public appeal strategies usually are conducted simultaneously, the following discussion will treat them separately.

Bargaining and the Authority-Responsibility Gap: The Neustadt Solution

The intellectual father of bargaining as a solution to the presidential authority-responsibility dilemma was Richard Neustadt.[4] His book, *Presidential Power: The Politics of Leadership,* was heralded as both a descriptive and prescriptive breakthrough in the study of presidential power. Although it now shares the analytical stage with other descriptive and prescriptive models, it remains nonetheless a very relevant theory.

According to Neustadt, anyone who is president has some significant formal and informal power. Some of it can be traced directly to the Constitution, and some of it comes to the president from just occupying the office. However, these powers are by no means enough for the job at hand. The president performs many important services for politicians and other officeholders, but this alone does not guarantee sufficient influence over the political forces from whom he needs cooperation—legislators, interest groups, the media, state and local officials. These entities do not automatically support him even though he regularly provides them with information, political support, friendly administrative and judicial appointments, and the like. The reason is obvious—they do not share his policy/constituent obligation or his outlook on policy priorities.

Presidents usually lack the formal power to order these officials to endorse and implement their policy agendas. Therefore, they must try to *influence* them in ways that will bring them around to their position. A president's official command authority is usually confined to a rather thin range of policy issues that affect very few people. That is usually of little value. The system of shared policy powers implies that members of each institution should not risk offending members of the other institutions with orders or commands. Even when the president's formal command authority is sufficient to ensure compliance, it is often not wise to employ it. When President Truman dismissed General MacArthur as head of the U.N. forces in Korea, he suffered a significant loss of prestige that severely constrained his ability to influence many key policy decisions affecting the economy, trade, and labor-management relations. When President Eisenhower ordered troops into Little Rock, Arkansas in 1957 to enforce court-ordered school desegregation, he succeeded in the immediate task at hand, only to find that he too suffered a subsequent loss of prestige, and influence, in key national policy decisions. Therefore, the exercise of formal power, while sometimes inevitable, should be considered a last resort. A persuasion strategy is far preferable. Therefore, the essence of presidential power is, according to Neustadt, the "power to persuade."[5]

Since the democratization of the presidential office has forced the president into an incentive conflict with other political forces that do not share his political perspective, the persuasion challenge is a formidable one. This means that a president must frame his policy arguments in ways that encourage his adversaries to think that the presidential solution is also their solution. One way to encourage this is for the president to offer them political assistance in return for their support of his policy agenda. For example, the president can make campaign appearances in their districts, or be photographed with them. His status and authority afford him a significant advantage here. Most of those he seeks to persuade can use his support for their own political advantage. In sum, presidential power rests on the president's ability to trade advantages with those from whom he needs cooperation. Power accrues from his success at persuasion which, in turn, is the result of effective bargaining.

Neustadt argues that a president must know how to bargain effectively. If he cannot bargain effectively, all the status of his office, his formal powers, his charm, and his ability to reason will be of little or no use in his attempt to gain policy influence. The desire to attain such influence must also be present. If a person does not want power, he or she is unfit for the contemporary presidency. No other official in the country, or the world for that matter, occupies a position that necessitates such an exercise of leadership. However, that leadership is ineffective if presidents can't acquire the influence necessary to exercise it effectively. Regardless of the nature or ideological direction of a president's policy commitments, to attain them a president must want power and therefore must be able to bargain effectively.

Effective bargaining and, ultimately, the attainment of the necessary influence to succeed, results from the president's ability to guard his power prospects. That is accomplished by minimizing controversy as a route to maximizing leverage over others. A president's professional reputation is very important. If the public, congresspersons, senators, interest group leaders, and representatives of the media are swayed by a president's ability to explain and defend his policy positions convincingly, they become his allies and not his opponents. A president can employ personal charisma, charm, policy expertise, and good television presence to create these favorable conditions. In short, presidents should do what they can to enhance their personal prestige and the perceptions among members of the Washington community that they are doing a good job.

Most members of the Washington community represent force fields from which the president needs cooperation in order to bargain effectively. Between the early 1930s and the mid-1970s, these forces, particularly those in Congress, had considerable political leeway to engage in bargaining without offending their "constituencies" or "clients." They were elites possessive of discretionary authority delegated them by their constituents on the understanding that such discretion would usually be employed on the constituents' behalf. From a president's perspective, these elites were the basis for coalition-building through bargaining. Once established, these coalitions could be counted on to provide the president a reservoir of political support that transcended many policy issues, and not impact on just one issue at one point in time.

The bargaining and coalition-building challenge is particularly suited to a scenario in which elites furnish more policy inputs than does the public in general. Citizens can participate in policy decision making by electing those who speak for them, so the public is certainly not ignored. However, once elected, under this scenario the officeholders are vested with significant *de facto* discretion to strike agreements with politicos in other institutions. Samuel Kernell has called this condition one of *institutionalized pluralism*.[6] Its effect on Congress was explored in Chapter 7. It is pluralistic because a multitude of elites representing various group and constituency perspectives enter the bargaining process in an attempt to secure the best policy outcome for their constituents or clients. It is institutionalized for two reasons. First, each party to

the bargaining process secured his or her legitimacy, and therefore status, as a bargaining force from an affiliation with a policymaking institution. Included here are congressional committees, subcommittees, party caucuses, party leaders in both houses of Congress, and spokespersons for interest groups. In contemporary parlance, most of these are "inside the (Washington) beltway" forces. Second, these networks work because their members trust one another. They have worked together on many policy issues and members develop impressions of what to expect from each other. Ideological positions and bargaining styles become well known. Once bargains are struck, all members support them even though some may have reservations. Mutual respect develops within these coalitions in respect for tolerance displayed during discussions and for postdecision unity.

Presidential bargaining strategies within an institutionalized pluralism network is a two-tiered coalition-building enterprise. The first of these is what Kernell calls the presidential coalition. It consists of groups, individuals, presidential cabinet and staff members, and a few bureaucrats who rally to the president's support. Since these coalitions are single issue in orientation, they are temporary and usually dissipate once it becomes clear that the policy effort was either a success or a failure. Kernell labels the second type a protocoalition.[7] These are networks of officials organized to coordinate or orchestrate the president's proposal through, within, or around policy networks. They are staff and cabinet officials who work closely with committee, subcommittee, and party leaders in Congress, as well as with interest groups and political leaders in states and cities. Often protocoalitions and iron triangle networks are one and the same. These alliances of interest groups, congressional subcommittees, and administrative bureaus are united by their common support of the same policy objective or objectives. If the president shares these objectives, he and his staff exploit these networks enthusiastically. If they oppose the president, then they constitute an obstacle which other, more *ad hoc,* protocoalition networks must control or circumvent as they work to actualize the president's policy goals.

Functioning effectively between the 1940s and 1970s, institutionalized pluralism offered presidents very favorable bargaining conditions. Friends and adversaries were rather easily identifiable, and presidents could approach them knowing that if they were won over to the presidential point of view, presidents could count on their support for awhile even if some coalition members faced possible constituency-induced reprisals for positions they had taken.

The processes decreed by institutionalized pluralism were not very democratic in the classical sense of the term. However, the bargaining process does not function well if the negotiators are too beholden to shifts in public opinion. The founders certainly would have endorsed it as a reasonable way to constrain the dangers of literal democracy within a system of constitutionally separated powers. The Constitution provides for staggered House, Senate, and presidential terms. It also assigns members of each of these institutions a different constituency base. Staggered terms virtually ensure that the passions, crusades, and vicissitudes of public opinion must be well rooted and prolonged to have a policy impact on government. By assigning senators and representatives state and substate constituency bases, the Constitution virtually guarantees that various minority points of view will be aired institutionally in House, Senate, and even presidential forums in ways that guard against an ill-informed majority's opinion being incorporated into public policy without amendment. Institutionalized pluralism's endorsement of a strong elitist influence in bargaining served mainly to add

another filter between public input into government and ultimate policy decisions.

Neustadt's theory seemed particularly relevant during the heyday of institutionalized pluralism. Presidents such as Franklin Roosevelt, John F. Kennedy, and Lyndon Johnson used it effectively. Roosevelt was particularly effective. However, nothing is forever, and changes in the American political climate triggered by the Vietnam War, Watergate, and the growing role of the media in covering elections and policy debates began to undercut the foundation of institutionalized pluralism in the early 1970s. Since that time, the presidents have not found conditions regularly conducive to its use. The entire political system has become more democratized, and elites have become far more beholden to the norms of plebiscitary democracy. While presidents have not abandoned the Neustadt prescription for successful power-building, they have had to deal with it in a much larger universe, a universe that has changed dramatically the way in which presidents seek to gain leverage over institutions with which they must share the policymaking obligation.

Presidential Power and Individualized Pluralism

According to Kernell, in the mid-1970s *individualized pluralism* displaced institutionalized pluralism as the key cultural input influencing the president's bargaining and coalition-building strategies. Individualized pluralism describes a condition under which parties to the bargaining process are less bound by loyalties to institutions of which they are members and to bargaining as culturally accepted behavior, and more bound to strategies that stress short-term political gain in the interest of securing individual political careers. Decision makers, under these conditions, are more inclined to register immediate and clearly discernable fluctuations of constituent opinion in their bargaining strategies than they would be under the institutionalized alternative. Under conditions of individualized pluralism, policy players, or "traders" as Kernell calls them, prefer policy exchanges that are quick, clear, and tangible.[8] When politicians sensed that protocoalitions were weakening as independent bargaining forces, they quickly switched strategies. Politicians became more politically egocentric, working directly for themselves, forgoing attempts to realign the crumbling protocoalition solidarity that had characterized institutionalized pluralism. They were freed to pursue their careers on their own, a strategy that promised as much insecurity as it did freedom. Responding to these uncertainties, politicians were quick to cultivate more close and continuous contacts with constituents. This strategy had a clear "continuous campaign" flavor. Developing close political relationships with "inside the beltway" persona was no longer as important as was cultivating well-anchored, close political ties with constituents and clients.[9] In short, players on the individualized pluralism scene were more inclined to go public on a regular basis than they were prior to the mid-1970s. Going public undermines the norms that sustained the comparatively productive bargaining networks of the institutionalized pluralism era.

Kernell offers at least three reasons for the advent of individualized pluralism. First, the growth of the social service state and its dependent clientele has created widespread demand for entitlement programs and the subsidies that support them. Illustrative of the policy system's bias toward distributive policies, politicians are inclined to respond with assorted and expensive entitlement policies. Politicians naturally understand the clear linkage that exists between such policies and constituent contentment. Second, modern means of communication and travel have provided politicians with easier access to their con-

stituencies, and vice versa. According to Kernell, this potentially contaminates the bargaining environment by increasing the number of forces to be accommodated in policy decisions.[10] Third, the weakening of political parties has permitted politicians to establish their own "miniature political parties" devoted exclusively to sustaining their political careers. The decline in party strength has also undercut the policy camaraderie that politicians in different institutions once had for each other, a condition which bolstered the impact of bargaining and coalition development. The Vietnam War and the Watergate crisis also served to hasten the decline of institutionalized pluralism. Because of these two disheartening events, the public became increasingly cynical toward government, and even toward the exercise of authority of any type. This was manifested in moves to renew direct citizen participation in government, and in the election of candidates pledged to champion the cause of the "citizen against the system."

This latter phenomenon was well illustrated by the House of Representatives' "Class of '74." Perhaps more than any newly elected freshman class up to that time, new House members elected in 1974 embraced the individualistic spirit that had triggered the drive for individualized pluralism. Subsequent classes reflected that same attitude. In a study comparing the political priorities of the House Class of 1958 with that of the Class of 1978, Michael Robinson observed that the latter group was far more inclined to use television in their campaigns, in their effort to acquire status and prestige in the House, and in their quest for reelection. Arguing that the seeds of a new congressional character were being sown by such changes, Robinson noted that, in comparison to their counterparts in 1958, the Class of 1978 was clearly more "egocentric" and "immoderate" in attitude and demeanor.[11] Instead of being encouraged to go public by circumstances they encountered after being elected, these individuals came to Congress as public animals and, in effect, stayed public in both their attitude and legislative demeanor.

What about the effects of individualized pluralism on the president? The answer is clear: Presidents have had to adapt to the political facts of life. They have had no choice but to go public with their own policy crusades. The implications of individualized pluralism for a president's coalition-building strategies are very significant indeed. Presidents find fewer distinctions to be made between new legislators and the "old guard." The basing points for forming potential coalitions are far less clear than they once were. New members of the House and Senate want a piece of the policy action quickly, and many secure subcommittee chairmanships during their first terms. Instead of a few strong leaders that are readily identifiable, the president finds a myriad of leaders with comparatively weak power bases. Most of these new leaders do not have much influence over other legislators. Few consider themselves subordinate, in fact, to anybody. There are many more actors with which to deal and few, if any, can guarantee the president any follow-through on the promises they make to him. The power base with which the president has to deal has expanded almost geometrically, increasing exponentially the chances of bargaining failure.[12] Presidents, in sum, have no choice but to go public themselves. While not obsolete, Neustadt's model must adapt to the new exigencies and share the stage with a more inclusive strategy that virtually compels the president to present his case directly to the people in the hope that they will instruct their senators and representatives to "go president" with their policy pledges.

There are both advantages and disadvantages to a going public strategy. Presidents can exploit the advantage they have over Congress when it comes to media coverage. That is certainly a plus. If presidents are good at invigorating public opinion, that is also a plus, because the emancipated legislators have gone public themselves clearly because they are very sensitive to public opinion. In addition, if a president is successful with a going public strategy, it can be much more efficient than building coalitions through a bargaining strategy. However, there are also disadvantages. Presidents may find the public rather apathetic about their policy reforms. Furthermore, people have been so saturated with drama and sensationalism on television that they may well have developed an immunity to being moved much by a presidential speech dramatizing the need for policy change. However, probably the most serious danger of a presidential going public strategy is its tendency to substitute what may appear to some to be coercion or command for compromise. Successful bargaining depends on, and rewards, compromise. However, when a president takes his policy case directly to the people there is a tendency to simplify it, dramatize it, and frame it in what might appear to be "all or nothing" terms. In such forums, presidents tend to frame arguments in terms of principle, not compromise. Furthermore, they are on the record as having framed it that way. It is very difficult, although not impossible, to compromise on emotionally charged and notably firm positions that were taken before a nationwide television audience. Bargaining thrives under conditions in which the participants do not have to sacrifice principle to make concessions. Public forums do not contribute such advantages, and they make subsequent efforts to bargain over differences in principle very difficult.

Policy Coalitions and the Presidency: A Strategy Synthesis

To become successful policy leaders, presidents must build coalitions to support their policies and, if possible, exploit existing political networks that may be favorably disposed toward presidential programs. The two approaches to coalition-building discussed above—bargaining and going public—do not compete with one another in the real world of policy network construction. The popularity of a president, and public enthusiasm for his policies, certainly contributes to a president's prestige, professional reputation, and his status within the Washington political community. Favorable marks in each of these categories certainly enhance a president's bargaining leverage under conditions of institutionalized pluralism—conditions which Neustadt considers favorable for a president's success in bargaining. If a president goes public in response to the subjugation of protocoalitions to the enticements of individualized pluralism, it does not necessarily mean that the results of such a strategy will undercut his influence within the weakened, although still existent, protocoalition networks. Presidents still need the support of protocoalition forces to gain the legitimization of their policies, even though these forces no longer provide as much internally generated support for his policies as they once did. Although Neustadt concedes that strong public support for a president translates into significant bargaining leverage, he feels that a deliberate going public strategy is unwise because public apathy may make the president appear to have failed, and because, as noted above, going public can appear to be too unilateral and coercive in nature. This also encourages the conclusion that efforts at bargaining have failed.[13] Neustadt argues that a president's election provides enough of a public opinion support base, making a resort to a postelection going public follow-through unnecessary. Advocates of the going public strategy could possibly counter with the argument that the popular election of a president is just the first step in a long-term relationship with the public. A presi-

dent's election, in this context, is just an invitation to continue regular contacts with the public after the election. Presidents know that Washington politicians, from whom they ultimately need support, are also very sensitive to public opinion. If a president's going public strategy is successful, these same politicians certainly would not want to be known as his adversaries so long as public approval for his policies was relatively high.

Some efforts at going public have indeed come in the wake of the failure of a president to gain congressional support for his policies. President Wilson's public campaign for his version of a League of Nations occurred after the plan had been rejected by the Senate. His subsequent effort to rally public support to coerce the Senate into changing its vote also failed. President Franklin Roosevelt's attempt to rally public support for his court packing plan after Congress rejected it also failed. Publicity of the earlier failures of both the Wilson and Roosevelt plans in Congress may well have contributed to the public's lack of enthusiasm about direct presidential appeals to them. However, President Truman's going public strategy to secure public support for what came to be known as the Truman Doctrine was a resounding success, as was President Clinton's effort to rally public support for the North American Free Trade Agreement (NAFTA), despite the fact that most of the members of the president's own party in the House and Senate had announced their opposition to the pact. Truman and Clinton both succeeded, at least in part, because in each case it was clear that the public was either uninformed about, or suspicious of, the policy proposal, and both presidents adopted a preemptive, proactive strategy that helped to change the supportive climate before a formal vote was taken.

The case of Clinton and NAFTA is particularly interesting because it illustrates the compatibility of the bargaining and going public strategies in the era of individualized pluralism. Clinton did not carry much political capital away from his rather narrow victory by a plurality vote in 1992. Therefore, the popular support base acknowledged by Neustadt to be so vital to a president's bargaining leverage was, by and large, unavailable to the new president. That was illustrated by very close congressional votes on many of his early policy proposals. Concluding that a going public strategy was his only option in an effort to gain public support for NAFTA, a crime bill, gun control legislation, and health care reform, Mr. Clinton embarked on such a course in the fall of 1993. He convened former presidents Carter, Ford, and Bush together in the White House for nationally televised statements in support of the free trade pact. At that same gathering, Clinton made an impassioned plea for its acceptance, an appeal so emotionally charged that it convinced even the skeptics that the president's heart was truly committed to the agreement.

Later in 1993 Clinton delivered to a group of black ministers an even more emotionally charged appeal for the restoration of family values as a first step in combating the problems of crime, education, and poverty. The speech was reminiscent of many of Martin Luther King's speeches in its stress on the values of work, family, self-discipline, and respect for human dignity. Mr. Clinton's effective use of rhetoric in these cases reminded many observers of the rhetorical skills of presidents Franklin Roosevelt and Ronald Reagan who were extremely effective in connecting values to policies, and in explaining to the public why their policies were more compatible with traditional American values than were the policies they proposed to reject. Clinton's late 1993 campaign appeared to follow the same pattern, and it helped bring success to his efforts to gain approval for NAFTA. It showed beyond any reasonable doubt that Clinton was beginning to realize that significant presidential influence

can result from the linkage, through rhetoric, of values broadly shared by the public on the one hand, and specific policy reforms on the other. Facing an intense and prolonged debate over health care reform, Mr. Clinton learned this lesson none too early in his presidency. However, since his health care reform campaign was unsuccessful, perhaps he didn't learn the lesson well enough.

If successful coalition-building virtually mandates a systematic going public strategy by presidents, does this mean that careful consideration of bargaining strategies is irrelevant, or virtually so? No, it does not. The basic premises and prescriptions of Neustadt's model remain very relevant to presidential policy success, and the NAFTA case offers an excellent illustration of just how necessary it is. In a sense, the opposition within Congress to NAFTA illustrated individualized pluralism carried to the extreme. Opposition forces were led by key Democrats such as the majority leader and majority whip in the House. Two of the top three Democratic party leaders in the Senate opposed the president. Officials such as these have traditionally provided critical, essential support on a wide range of issues for presidents such as Franklin Roosevelt and Lyndon Johnson. The traditional bonds of party loyalty that cemented such coalitions for Roosevelt and Johnson had all but vanished by the time of Clinton's election. Undisciplined parties make coalition-building difficult. Therefore, presidents must look to the opposition party for support, as Clinton did. While he succeeded in developing a bipartisan coalition that was sufficient for the president to win the NAFTA struggle by a very few votes, that coalition was very fragile, owing to its heterogeneous base. It certainly was not a coalition that was available to help the president on subsequent policy crusades. Nonetheless, the fact that Clinton was able to construct a coalition durable enough to win victory on the NAFTA issue illustrates that, at least in some cases, bargaining is still a necessary strategy for presidential policy success. To be sure, it is played out on a different stage and with different actors than were the bargaining games of the institutionalized pluralism era.

Much of what Clinton did to secure the necessary votes for NAFTA was vintage Neustadt. He defined the critical votes and engaged in old-fashioned "horse trading" to lure the undecided and some who originally opposed him into his camp. Clinton, like all presidents, brought a resource advantage to the bargaining table on the NAFTA issue. He cut deals with wavering legislators, pledging money for public works, industrial development projects, government contracts, and job programs in their districts. It was pork barrel politics in its most obvious form. All successful presidents have used all their resources and advantages of the office in attempting to win critical policy struggles. Lyndon Johnson followed the same strategy in winning the struggle for voting rights legislation in 1964 and 1965. President Reagan did the same before succeeding with a tax reform package in 1986. Johnson was president during the heyday of institutionalized pluralism. Reagan and Clinton were presidents when individualized pluralism was center stage. Nonetheless, all had to call on Neustadt's assumptions about the importance of bargaining to presidential policy success. Clearly, individualized pluralism makes the challenge more difficult. In the case of NAFTA, the winning coalition was one in which the opposition party support outnumbered support from the president's party by better than a two-to-one margin. This is highly unusual, if not unique. That aside, the NAFTA experience illustrates how high the bargaining stakes remain in presidential policy strategies, and how much more difficult the bargaining challenge has become in the era of individualized pluralism.

In analyzing the impact of coalitional politics on the presidency, Lester Seligman and Cary Covington have concluded that major differences exist between the composition of coalitions that elect presidents and those the president must mold to enjoy success as a policy leader. By label, these are the electoral and governing coalitions. Presidential candidates must appeal to a very broad-based, inclusive coalition of voters to win the presidency. However, once in office presidents find that the electoral coalition is often of very little use as a network from which they can build strength within government to predominate in policy struggles.[14] Electoral coalitions appear in two stages—the nomination phase and the general election phase. The political party forces that are often essential to a candidate's securing nomination may represent the party's right or left wing. In such instances the nominee must assume a more centrist position in the general election in order to attract support from as many party members as possible. Once elected, the president usually finds that the constellation of party factions, interest groups, and the demographic classes of people that supported his election may be too unorganized and diffused ideologically to be of much assistance in developing governing coalitions.

Governing coalitions consist of committee and subcommittee leaders in Congress, members of the president's staff, cabinet officials, spokespersons for interest groups, and sometimes members of the media. All such officials have incentives that are clearly tied to serving clients or constituencies. Therefore, it would be very unusual for any governing coalition to be a virtual mirror of the president's rather loose and amorphous electoral coalition. In response, presidents seek to add to the core of the governing coalition what Seligman and Covington call "issue-specific peripheral supporters" that give the coalition more of a politically inclusive tone.[15] This can weaken the president's impact on policy by consuming an inordinate amount of time, and also encourage a president to moderate a few of his ambitious policy goals so that the coalition can be kept intact. As a result, the art of governing becomes very similar to the art of campaigning.

In essence, Seligman and Covington agree with Lowi, Neustadt, and Kernell on their assessment of the impact of the democratization of the presidential office on the policy posture and coalition-building strategies of presidents. While the president's public exposure has increased dramatically since the advent of individualized pluralism, successful coalition-building remains essential to presidential policy success. Individualized pluralism has dictated that the process be more situational and *ad hoc* in character, and that it be conducted on a different stage with more actors.

Constitutional Politics and the Presidency: The Policy Consequences

Politics is a struggle between and among competing forces for the right to develop and administer public policy. The Constitution *per se* is not one of those competing forces. Rather, it is a document whose structural mandates and rather amorphous assignments of power and rights guarantees are often exploited by political forces in the hope that it will gain them more leverage over public policy. Presidents have been thrust onto the policy scene because Congress has delegated them large amounts of discretionary policy power, and because the office has been significantly democratized over the past two centuries. This democratization has made the president, with his national constituency, a policy crusader for the entire body politic. A president's constituency base, constitutionally mandated, is different from those assigned to the House and the Senate. Such an arrangement often results in "divided government," or a situation in which the president represents one political party and the House or the

Senate, or both, are controlled by the other party. The policy consequences of this phenomenon will be analyzed in depth in the next chapter. For the time being, the analysis will focus on how the different political incentives of key Washington policy figures affect the president as he attempts to respond to his perceived policy mandates, and how struggles between the president and these forces has been, and continues to be, exacerbated by constitutional politics.

The "Quick Fix" Policy Mentality

The president, House, and Senate are elected for different, overlapping terms of office. The presidential four-year term is midway between the two-year term for House members and the six-year term for senators. This reality, along with the different constituencies represented by each institution, serves the framers' check and balance mission very effectively. Ironically, it has been the democratization of the Senate and the presidency that has made clashes over policies among the three institutions more intense. Originally, the president and the Senate served more as elite-based checks on the potential election-engendered, populist-rooted excesses of the House. Now that the president and senators are popularly elected, constituency differences, if anything, intensify conflict among these institutions.

Constituency variations, interest group pressures, weak political parties, and a pluralist-political atmosphere combine to make presidential coalition-building very difficult. The president's four-year term does not afford him much time to prove his worth to the public as a policy leader. Bargaining and coalition-building difficulties add even more pressure. Presidents want to accomplish things rather quickly. They want a policy "brag sheet" to present to the public if they seek a second term. If they are serving their second term, they want the same for their party's new nominee for the presidency. In light of the constitutionally mandated four-year term, they respond in several ways. They can take credit for policy successes whose seeds were sown by the previous president. They can pay selective inattention to policy results that contradict or compromise their claim that things have improved due to their policy initiatives, as did President Clinton when he claimed, in 1994, that the economic recovery was due almost exclusively to low interest rates engendered by his deficit-reduction program. During periods of divided government when party control of Congress and the presidency is divided, they can blame the lack of policy progress on the "other" party that controls Congress. Such strategies are not uncommon for presidents of either party.

However, voters insist on something concrete upon which to judge the policy performance of presidents, and presidents realize this. Therefore, sometimes they may make more concessions than they should in order to claim credit for some policy progress, albeit modest progress, before the voters. They may settle, as did presidents Bush and Clinton, for budget and deficit reduction agreements that pare spending far less than they had promised or had hoped. Presumably, any agreement is better than no agreement at all. In addition, after experiencing repeated frustrations on domestic policy struggles, presidents may suddenly stress foreign policy issues, and begin to arrange summit meetings and find excuses to take foreign junkets. After all, the president is chief diplomat, and when he functions in that capacity he does not confront the deep-seated political opposition to his policy crusades on many (but not all) foreign policy issues as he does on domestic issues. Television coverage, instantly piped to television screens throughout the country, has the effect of portraying the president as the country's "man in Tokyo"

or "man in Moscow." Such strategies are usually targeted at significant policy issues. An increasing number of policies are "intermestic" in character, involving formal and informal economic and political relationships with other countries. Nonetheless, for a president to assume a higher profile in foreign policy as his domestic policy frustrations grow, has political advantages for him as he seeks to establish some vestige of policy credibility within the narrow time frame of a brief four-year term. In sum, often there is more than just a little political expediency involved in the decision to "go foreign." Presidents Nixon, Carter, and Bush adopted such a strategy not early in their terms, but later on as their domestic agenda fell victim to the delays, roadblocks, and compromises introduced by pluralist polities and fragmented constitutional power. In sum, a president's decision to go foreign, to compromise away policy principles, to take credit for policy successes that should, by right, be shared, and to pay selective inattention to facts that contradict a quest to claim exclusive credit for policy successes reflects the president's conclusion that policy quick fixes are better than no policies at all.

The results of such strategies are not, of course, always detrimental. However, such efforts do suggest that presidents are not always as attentive to the serious nature of some policy challenges as they perhaps should be. Of course, these same games are played on different stages by congressmen and senators, and even bureaucrats. Unfortunately, each time they are played, it means that the nation's festering social and economic problems are made hostage to strategies reflecting short-term political expediency.

Cognitive Dissonance

Policy pressures on the president, together with the unwillingness of other institutional actors to accept presidential policy options without intense bargaining and compromises, often place the president under a great deal of psychological stress. In turn, this can lead to frustration and attempts to deal with the problem in ways that are unhealthy for both the quality of public policy, and even democracy itself. Because of the separation of powers principle, legislators often find it convenient politically to blame policy impasses or policy failures on the president. Had the president, so goes the argument, been more effective as a policy steward, the results would have been different, and all who participated could be proud of the result. By the same token, the president can argue that political opportunism and ideological myopia on the part of legislators was responsible for the result. However, since the president has become the focus of national policy leadership winning office promising major policy changes, he cannot escape being held accountable for policy crusades that fail or which, if enacted, do not deliver what was promised. Since well before President Truman uttered the oft-quoted phrase "the buck stops here," the policy "buck" was well anchored in the presidency.

The psychologically rooted strains that the policy demands of the presidency place on the president as an individual cannot ever be measured precisely, and they certainly cannot be anticipated by an individual before he becomes president. Several political scientists have attempted to analyze how the pressures of the office impact on the president psychologically, with undesirable policy results. Two of the most creditable efforts have been made by James D. Barber and Bruce Buchanan.[16] Their work can best be described as research which fuses political science with psychology, making them "political psychologists" of a sort. Barber classifies presidential behavior using two psychological variables. An *active-passive* variable rates both incumbent presidents and candidates according to how much energy they invest, or promise to invest, in

policy reform crusades. Some are simply more committed to policy reform than are others. A *positive-negative* variable tries to measure how presidents feel about the results of their policy efforts. Some accept policy defeats philosophically and remain optimistic, while others take defeat personally and consider it a sign of how inadequately they have responded to the challenges of the office. Presidents who react positively have high self-esteem, and those who react negatively have low self-esteem.

There are four possible character combinations: active-positive, active-negative, passive-positive, and passive-negative. Active-positive presidents have ambitious policy agendas and emerge from combat with other policy actors with comparatively healthy and realistic views of the presidency's strengths and weaknesses in the agenda-building, bargaining, and coalition-development games. Active-negatives want to gain and hold on to power as an end unto itself, and one of their self-imposed standards of success is how often they think they have won and lost policy struggles. Active-negatives tend to be insecure, and the exercise of their power of command and enjoying their policy victories are ways in which they compensate for their insecurity and low self-esteem. They do not live well with failure and are sometimes prone to react irrationally and irresponsibly. Passive-positives seek approval and affection from their peers and are less likely to get it if they are too bold in crusading for controversial policies. Passive-negatives harbor an innate dislike for politics, and enter it out of what they say is a sense of obligation. No president embodies the qualities of one character type exclusively. Barber argues that twentieth-century presidents such as Franklin Roosevelt, Harry Truman, John Kennedy, and Jimmy Carter were, by and large, presidents who demonstrated qualities that were preponderantly active-positive. Richard Nixon and Lyndon Johnson demonstrated active-negative qualities much of the time. Warren Harding and Ronald Reagan were predominately passive-positives, and Calvin Coolidge and Dwight Eisenhower were passive-negatives.

In light of the policy challenges that face a president, it is clear that the active-positive character type is best suited to handle the inevitable frustrations that befall a president as he wrestles with the political forces actuated by individualized pluralism. Active-positives are much less likely to embark on irresponsible, unaccountable, or even illegal actions when their policy strategies fail. Assuming that Barber's categories are generally reliable in making a causal link between character and decision behavior, the nation might well have been spared the nearly relentless escalation of the Vietnam War by the active-negative Johnson, or the Watergate scandal instigated, presumably, by a presidential staff working to secure the reelection of the insecure, active-negative Nixon, or the Iran-Contra affair engineered by the staff of the passive-positive Reagan whose aloofness from the trench warfare of politics was encouraged by his drive for acceptance and to be in tune with those around him. It is, of course, impossible to establish a definite cause-effect relationship between character and decisions, and any effort to do so will always be met with challenges that the analyst has been selectively inattentive to other, equally plausible, explanations for the same policy decisions. Nevertheless, it is certainly safe to conclude that a president's frustrations with the opposition he encounters in his policy crusades does encourage him and his staff to develop compensatory strategies. Such strategies can have negative consequences for the nature of public policy and for the quality of American democracy.

Bruce Buchanan's *The Presidential Experience: What the Office Does to the Man* offers a systematic analysis of the negative impact of the role demands of the presidency on the presi-

dent, and the potentially ominous repercussions of those for policy and democracy in the United States.[17] In contrast to Rossiter, Buchanan does not link the president's expanding role obligations specifically to new policy roles. Instead, he offers four generic functions of the presidency that include, by implication, the Rossiter roles. They are *policy advocate, symbol, mediator,* and *crisis manager.* Three of these—policy advocate, mediator, and crisis manager—can be associated with the democratization of the office and the extra-constitutional roles offered by Rossiter. This lends further support to the proposition that the growth of the national government's policy responsibilities has been shouldered by the president, especially in agenda-setting and coalition-building. His official independence from Congress means he has to shoulder more of an independent policy role than would be the case if the Constitution had mandated a parliamentary structure.

However, according to Buchanan, more important than the generic functions of the president are the recurring exposures that result from the performance of the functions. These exposures are dysfunctional to the office in many ways, most of which have potentially negative results for public policy. They are *frustration, deference, dissonance,* and *stress.* Frustration is the direct result of the policy advocate function which, as has been noted above at length, forced the president into confrontations with legislators, groups, and individuals who do not share his policy priorities. Deference is the direct result of the symbolic function, which results from the president's ceremonial responsibilities and is very similar to Rossiter's extra-constitutional "voice of the people" role. Deference (to the president) develops when people with whom the president consults or converses defer to his opinion, or what they infer as his opinion. Because he is the president, they tend to hold him in awe. They want his approval, and are disinclined to tell him the truth if they think he would not approve. A negative reaction might, in turn, do damage to their relationship with him. Stress is the outgrowth of the mediator and crisis management functions. According to Buchanan, these obligations are characterized by "unpredictability" and "episodic intensity," and are "turbulent" by nature.[18] A series of such experiences wears on most presidents both physically and emotionally. Dissonance results from a fusion of the symbolic and policy advocate roles. This suggests that presidents, serving as both symbols and policy advocates, are inclined to distort reality to their advantage when they go public and develop coalitions. The hope is that the nation as a whole will be inspired and that parties to bargaining negotiations will respond by accepting the core of the president's policy position. In attempting to gain the upper hand with a going public strategy and in coalition-building, presidents are encouraged to frame their arguments in ways that make their policy options seem the most logical. If they have doubts personally, they keep them to themselves. Any facts that might contradict the case they are making are selectively shelved, and only those facts that reinforce their position are introduced. They interpret events in ways that make their position seem the most plausible. In sum, it is "rosy scenario" politics in its most obvious form. It makes distortion, or lying, politically expedient. The fact that the people look to presidents for moral leadership gives them additional leverage in this "game" because most people want to believe what presidents tell them. According to Buchanan, very few presidents can resist the temptation to employ such a strategy.[19]

Most presidents become victimized by what Buchanan and psychologists have termed *cognitive dissonance*.[20] A president's resort to dissonance, or "expedient misrepresentation," as a weapon in policy struggles is an inevitable result of the policy advocate and symbolic roles. The president symbolizes the nation's highest moral standards and policy aspirations. If citizens want to think of him as a Prince Valiant or hero who is positioned above the pettiness of routine politics, he is inclined to speak and act the role. He tends to portray himself as a statesman, who is spiritually divorced from political "trench warfare." Most often, such a portrayal misrepresents the president's instincts and experiences as a political figure. Most presidents have many of the same failings as other individuals. In fact, more often than not, they are products of the "trench warfare" that their symbolic role asks them to reject. Therefore, misrepresentation of the true self to accommodate the public's role expectations appears to be the only way to be faithful to these role expectations. Unfortunately, this does not carry much leverage in negotiations with adversaries over policies. Therefore, since the symbolic role has conditioned presidents to deceive, misrepresenting reality in a going public effort, or in bargaining, or in coalition-building is not difficult for most presidents. They quickly get used to it. The more they function as symbols and policy advocates, the more accustomed they become to deception as a strategy. Such an attitude regularly permeates presidential advisory circles, the members of which often consider themselves policy "elites."[21] They often defend their right, and the right of the president, to lie in order to increase the president's policy influence. Such an attitude is rooted in the assumption that the president and his advisors know more about the character of, and consequent need for, the policies they advocate than does the public and do most members of Congress. Aware of the leverage disadvantage of telling the truth, deception becomes a necessary means to the appropriate end. The temptation to lie overcomes any personal scruples the president or his staff may have against such a strategy. Dissonance then becomes "cognitive" or deliberate. The long-term impact of such behavior could be the gradual destruction of a president's ability to distinguish truth from lies. In other words, self-delusion can become so habitual that it becomes part of one's routine decision-making pattern.

The question might well be asked: Is such deception, when it occurs, necessarily detrimental to the president and his role as policy advocate and policy engineer? After all, he faces so many obstacles to the realization of his policy objectives, it may seem altogether appropriate to employ such a strategy. The authority-responsibility gap is often so wide that the president can easily drift into an "end justifies the means" frame of mind. Certainly the president usually has his interpretation of the nation's interest in mind when he establishes a policy agenda. Therefore, his sincere commitment to such an end might make him feel that some deception is a small price to pay to increase the odds of a presidential victory.

There is no definitive answer to this question. However, it is clear that when the deceptive practices of presidents and/or their staff have been exposed, it usually results in an undermining of both the legitimacy of the presidency and the future policy leverage of the guilty president. The damage has not always been fatal, but the United States no longer is in a position to afford presidential policy impotency given the scope and depth of the policy problems that face both the nation and world.

A few examples of the causal relationship between presidential deception and policy leverage are in order. Not all of these have involved deception employed to gain leverage directly over public policy. However, even in cases where policy was not directly involved, the president's subsequent influence over policy suffered measurably. Lyndon Johnson's self-deception and rationalization of the facts as he increased the nation's commitment to the Vietnam War damaged his professional reputation, status, and prestige so greatly that he decided not to stand for reelection in 1968. Once Richard Nixon's involvement in the Watergate coverup was exposed and impeachment proceedings commenced by Congress, his public approval rating and reputation within the Washington political community plummeted. This left his presidency so weakened that he cited this, not possible impeachment, as the official reason for his resignation. Ronald Reagan's OMB director, David Stockman, revealed in a magazine interview that neither the president nor the key members of his staff were aware of the inconsistencies that existed between their optimistic public statements about plans to reduce the deficit and the actual possibilities for doing so. Once their naivety was exposed, the presumptions the press and the public had made about Reagan being a decisive, independent-minded, factual person were brought into question and his prestige and professional reputation suffered a temporary setback. Astute management of the event by the president's communications advisors resulted in a public apology by Stockman, and the president's status as a creditable leader was rather quickly restored. Recovery is usually not that easily managed. Finally, Lieutenant Colonel Oliver North, a key member of Reagan's National Security staff, admitted in congressional hearings that he had deliberately lied to Congress about the administration's role in arranging "out of budget," non-government support for the Contra effort in Nicaragua. He asserted he did so because of the imperative of the mission, an imperative clearly not shared by most members of Congress. In short, he laid claim to a "right to lie" based on an "end justifies the means" rationale. Although the president was never officially implicated in the Contra aid effort, his professional reputation and status were dealt significant setbacks from which it took the administration considerable time to recover.

The message from all this is rather clear: When deception is disclosed it tends to do major, perhaps irreparable, damage to the ability of the president to gain the policy leverage he needs in order to faithfully fulfill his role as the nation's chief legislator. This is true for both the situational circumstances which allow the president to utilize the Neustadt strategy effectively, and for the going public strategy. If a presidential deception is exposed, whatever the issue, there is a serious danger of a credibility gap developing between the people and their president. In an era where presidential appeals to the public for policy support are growing increasingly essential, it would appear that presidents can hardly afford the risk. On the other hand, playing it straight and avoiding all traces of deception may put them at such a disadvantage that they have no other choice. If this is indeed the case, then it certainly underscores the negative effects of the constitutional independence of the presidency as an institution on the president as a person, and how that affects what he does as the nation's chief policy advocate and, in reality, its chief policy engineer.

The Heroic Presidency

Constitutional factors encourage presidents to portray themselves as heros, and use any personal charisma, public popularity, and professional reputation they have developed to seek support from any sector of society or government that will help them in their quest for policy leverage. This is understandable, given the leadership problems associated with the authority-responsibility gap. It underscores the opportunistic nature of a president's policy strategies. It explains why both the Neustadt and going public strategies have been praised for their prescience. To paraphrase Neustadt's observation, insofar as the production of public policy is concerned, our system is one in which separate institutions with constitutionally decreed different sources of office share the policymaking obligation. The president is the chief orchestrator

of the sharing enterprise. As such he must be flexible, shrewd, alert to opportunities, willing to concede, persistent, and sympathetic with the incentives of other political actors.

Presidents with high self-esteem are likely to fare better than those with pronounced insecurities in such an environment. It would be comforting if individuals who approached the challenge optimistically and philosophically were guaranteed election to the presidency. They are not, of course, and therein lies a serious problem.

A president who must base his search for policy support upon such a strategy will certainly be more successful than one who lacks such an instinct, given the current state of U.S. politics. The problem is that there is simply no guarantee that such individuals will be elected on a regular basis. Presidents with an active-positive character bent, with clear charismatic qualities, and who enjoy the give-and-take environment that bargaining demands will clearly perform better than ones who lack these qualities, or those who have them but who are unwilling or unable to utilize them effectively. Most recent presidents, including Johnson, Carter, Eisenhower, Reagan, and Bush, lacked either the necessary qualities to be regularly successful, or the ability to use them consistently and effectively. There would be more consistent and, presumably, effective presidential leadership if the president were the head of a strong political party organization that had a majority in both houses of Congress. Policy crusades would then be more "collegial" in nature, and much less responsibility would be placed on the president individually to deliver on policy promises. Under such conditions, the president's character, charisma (or relative lack thereof), and aptitude for bargaining and coalition-building would be less critical. It would be a team effort, and the president would be only one member of the team, although a very important one. Such conditions would reward party discipline, and parties would be known more for the policies they support than for the attractiveness of the candidates they nominate and elect.

Unfortunately, such conditions do not exist. As a result, more pressure, both actual and psychological, is placed on the president to develop and shepherd a policy agenda through the quagmires of pluralist politics. While it could be argued that some of the same qualities it takes to be elected president serve the president well in the coalition-building game, not all of them necessarily do. While an incumbent president might be well advised to apply his election strategy to his plans to go public after assuming office, this will probably not be of much use to him as he attempts to put the finishing touches on the governing coalitions he so desperately needs. Our system today rewards the Hamiltonian type president—one who separates himself from the political trenches, stresses his symbolic role as spokesman for the people, exploits his charisma to develop a following, and undermines the classic function of political parties by seeking policy support from members of the opposition party. This latter strategy compromises the ability of the opposition party to function as a constructive critic of presidential policies. This stands in stark contrast to the strategy of a Jeffersonian type president who is dedicated to developing a package of policies through his party organization, and who invites the opposition party to be critical of such efforts. Only by welcoming such criticisms can the majority party fine tune its policy package to make it more compliant with the public's wishes and, in all likelihood, more relevant as a potential solution to the policy problems it addresses.

Today's political atmosphere, with its stress on candidate-centered campaigns and individualized pluralism, makes the Hamiltonian strategy virtually the only presidential option. Some are good at it, and others are clearly not

so good. However, the nation desperately needs political conditions which produce political resources which are supportive of presidential policy leadership regardless of who occupies the office. Under such conditions, where parties play more of a policy role, presidential character, temperament, political experience, and charisma would be less important. A continuity base would be established to the pattern of public policy, and executive and legislative officeholders would be assigned the critical task of shepherding programs faithful to that base through the policy process. If the next president represented the same party, he could draw on the policy foundation already in place. If a passive-positive type president replaced an active-positive type with these conditions in place, the change would presumably have much less of a potential impact on the results of the party's (not the president's) plans for policy reform. In sum, under such conditions it would be less important *who* the president is, and *what* party and programs he espouses would be more important.

In conclusion, the president's separate constituency and separate four-year term, mandated by the Constitution, encourage a Hamiltonian (and Neustadt) approach to presidential policy leadership with all the potential inconsistency and uncertainty that accompany it. It will take a more Jeffersonian, party-based atmosphere that is geared toward overcoming the political divisiveness encouraged by the separation of powers and variation in constituencies to extricate the nation from such a condition. Until that time, constitutional politics will continue to hold the country hostage to a "luck of the draw" syndrome and all the policy uncertainties that accompany it.

Enhanced Presidential Bureaucracy

A fourth effect of constitutional politics on the president's management of his policy challenges has been the growth and expansion of the presidential staff complex. The growth of the size and responsibility of the president's staff has paralleled the growth of the president's policy responsibilities. In simple terms, staffs exist to help executives manage their policy and administrative responsibilities. The more responsibilities that are assigned to, or accrue to, an executive, the more the need for staff to help ease the executive's workload. The growth of the president's staff has accompanied both the amplification of his constitutional roles and the addition of his extra-constitutional roles. Staff assistants can be a godsend in some circumstances, and a clear liability in others. Since most members of the president's staff are concerned with policy in one way or another, the astute management of their resources, expertise, and judgment certainly facilitates the president's ability to place workable policy reforms on the agenda and to oversee their implementation once they have been enacted. However, ineffective or misguided use of staff can be counterproductive, both for the president's reputation and for the quality of public policy. Presidents have had staff assistants since the beginning of the republic. For most of the first century and a half, staff assistants were few in number, and most of their time was spent helping the president manage his office, correspondence, and time. They were only occasionally concerned with policy matters. This was the norm until the New Deal period, when the president began to use his staff for policy advice and administrative oversight. The New Deal drastically altered the scope and number of public policies for which the national government was responsible. What has since been labeled the "social service state" was the ultimate result of the New Deal policy revolution. Through a widely applied grant-in-aid strategy, the national government became involved in subsidizing state and local programs through the grant mechanism. Usu-

ally, the law required states and localities to supplement the national offering by contributing a certain percentage of the total program costs. Funding policies for housing, highways, welfare, and urban redevelopment are examples of the types of policies that have been impacted by federal grants-in-aid. In addition, the national government sponsored several public works projects unilaterally during the New Deal period. Federally chartered agencies such as the Tennessee Valley Authority (TVA), the Works Progress Administration (WPA), and the Civilian Conservation Corps (CCC) were examples of such agencies. Finally, federal legislation granted broad policy discretion to both Congress and the president to do what was feasible within the broad confines of the law to help American businesses recover from the devastating effects of the depression.

The significance of this for the presidency was that it provided momentum for a vast increase in the size and role of the president's staff. The president had, for decades, been gradually establishing himself as the country's policy advocate. The New Deal cemented this role. In addition, in a variety of ways it also placed the presidency, as an institution, stage center in both the development and administration of policy. The constitutional roles as chief executive and chief legislator took on added importance. The seeds were sown for what became the quick acceptance of the manager of prosperity role. Since President Franklin Roosevelt was a major catalytic force behind the New Deal reform policies, the voice of the people role took on added significance. Most people credited Roosevelt with the New Deal policy revolution. Since that time, presidents have had no choice but to take credit, willingly, for national policy reforms that succeed, and assume the blame for those crusades the public considers failures.

During even the early stages of the New Deal it became clear that the president, as chief executive, needed assistance in the management of the national government's new responsibilities. The pre–New Deal presidency was simply not structurally able to handle the increased workload. Consequently, in March 1936, President Roosevelt appointed a three-member commission to study the organization and operations of the executive branch including, of course, the presidency. Its primary mission was to address the coordinating problem of managing the implementation of New Deal programs. Established officially as the President's Committee on Administrative Management, it became known as the Brownlow Committee in honor of its chairman, Louis Brownlow. Since the committee's major focus was management, its final report concentrated on how to make the administration of the new programs more expeditious and efficient. It recommended additional presidential staff to help in the coordination effort, the expansion of the government's budgeting and planning capacities, a major reorganization of the executive departments, and an expansion of the merit system to draw more competent administrators into the federal bureaucracy.[22]

Insofar as the official impact on presidential staffing was concerned, the Committee recommended the creation of an Executive Office of the President (EOP). The Reorganization Act of 1939 authorized the president to establish such an office, and President Roosevelt did so very quickly via an executive order in September, 1939. Thus began the institutionalization of the presidential staff complex, a complex that has grown and adapted to changes in the government's, and hence the president's, policy responsibilities over the past sixty years. The original EOP consisted of a White House Office to help the president manage the routines of the White House, the Bureau of the Budget, the National Resources Planning Board, the Liaison Office for Personnel Management, and the

Office of Government Reports. Except for the White House Office, the overriding objective of these agencies was the improvement of government planning, quality, coordination, and accountability. Each had a notable supervisory or integrative flavor to its mission. For example, the Bureau of the Budget, located since 1921 in the Treasury Department, was transferred to EOP to provide the president a formal role in coordination budget requests from the various agencies and commissions. This is illustrative of the political environment within which the president's staff has functioned since 1939. It is an inclusive, macroscopic, overviewlike environment that can be traced to the president's nationwide constituency and his constitutional role as chief executive. No other elected official in government has the same role-based incentive. Since other national government institutions, especially Congress and the bureaucracy, reflect political incentives that service subnational constituencies or specific clients, only the president can be expected to assume such an integrative approach to his staff structure.

This strategy has continued since 1939. In 1946 the Council of Economic Advisors was added to EOP. Its purpose was to coordinate thinking and advise the president on ways to foster economic prosperity. In 1947 the National Security Council was added. Consisting of the president as chairman, the Secretaries of State and Defense, the director of the Central Intelligence Agency, and any other official the president wants to include, the NSC has the responsibility of coordinating thinking on military and foreign policy matters and advising the president accordingly. Since 1950 various staff agencies have entered, and some have exited, the EOP complex. In response to the Soviet space challenge in the late 1950s, a National Aeronautics and Space Council was added to the staff operation. A Council on Environmental Quality was added in the late 1960s. An Office of Science and

Technology Policy was included in 1976. An Office of Administration was added in 1977 to help other EOP units with budgeting, record-keeping, data processing, and financial management. President Nixon expanded the Bureau of the Budget's responsibilities to include studying and recommending changes in administrative management and organization. He appropriately renamed it the Office of Management and Budget (OMB).

Insofar as the management of domestic policy is concerned, perhaps the most significant addition to EOP has been a domestic advisory complex. Between 1939 and 1970, the president sought and received advice on domestic policy from senior aides in the White House Office and from staff members of the Bureau of the Budget. In 1970 President Nixon expanded and, in effect, institutionalized this activity by creating the Domestic Council. This unit has been renamed several times since the Nixon administration, but its major function has remained essentially the same. The original Domestic Council was intended to function in domestic policy as the National Security Council functions in foreign and military policy. All domestic-policy-focused cabinet secretaries were official members of the Council, but most of the work was accomplished by small task forces formed from among the Council's membership. The Council rarely convened as a unit. President Carter removed the cabinet secretaries from official membership, and it has continued to function with special presidential appointees serving as policy coordinators and research supervisors since the Carter administration. Since most policy problems extend beyond the official jurisdiction of one cabinet department, the domestic policy group can go about its work by developing study, research, and advisory groups with a "problem," or "issue," focus. The president finds this very helpful because his nationwide policy perspective is at variance with policy options that carry the

stamp of one cabinet or subcabinet agency or one or two congressional subcommittees. Most problems are more inclusive in nature than such organizations are inclined to think they are. For example, problems of education in urban areas are tied to welfare policies, transportation policies, housing policies, business policies, and health and nutrition policies. If standing executive agencies or legislative subcommittees are asked to recommend ways to deal with urban education problems, each unit is inclined to recommend a solution that considers its own policy focus central to the resolution of the issue. In all probability, the efforts of several agencies will have to be coordinated to deal with the problem. The president is very aware of this, not necessarily because he brings any special insights to the job that have somehow bypassed others, but because his policy incentives are molded by his nationwide constituency. To assume such a policy perspective does not mean that the president is any less of a politician than are the other actors who have a much more limited definition of the public interest. It means only that the president's constituency perspective coincides more naturally with what an outside observer would equate with a public interest solution.

A large and institutionalized presidential staff system is here to stay. What are its implications for the processes and quality of public policy? Equally important, to what extent does the staff's existence and relationship to the president reflect a type of politics that has been honed, at least in part, by what has been labeled in these pages as constitutional politics? Politics is a struggle among individuals, groups, and organizations over the right to make and administer public policy. The president's staff is a key presidential ally in his policy struggles with congressional committees and subcommittees, administrative agencies, and interest groups as each attempts to predominate in official policy decisions. In a sense, the president's staff is his army in such a struggle.

One impact of constitutional politics on the president's staff is that its growing prominence is due, in part, to the type of politics induced by the separation of powers. The president needs help in his struggle with forces who oppose him for term duration and constituency-variance reasons. He needs data and research that support his point of view. Therefore, the larger, the more specialized and propresident the staff, the better. The staff complex functions somewhat like a "countergovernment" or a "counterbureaucracy" dedicated to defending the president's policy perspective. Such a structure "counters" what the president considers the comparatively myopic policy perspectives of Congress, the bureaucracy, and interest groups. Political forces whose incentive differences are solidified by constitutional mandates naturally seek to arm themselves with all the political and data power available to them to help them fare well in the policy struggle. This applies to all interested policy players, including the president.

A second potential impact of presidential staff activities, clearly dysfunctional, is the possibility that the president might rely on staff judgments so heavily that he becomes isolated from political, economic, and social reality. The White House is a very palatial place, and the president often is treated by his staff with a degree of reverence that virtually precludes disclosure of not only the true facts affecting economic and social life in America, but it can also result in the suppression of valuable staff opinions that are simply not aired for fear of offending the president. In his book, *Victims of Groupthink,* Irving Janis reflects on how four key foreign policy errors were either inaugurated or allowed to worsen because the president's staff was victimized by a condition Janis and other psychologists have labeled *groupthink*.[23] The decisions that led to

our vulnerability at Pearl Harbor in the months preceding our entry into World War II, the escalation of both the Korean and Vietnam wars, and the planning that preceded the Bay of Pigs invasion in 1961 were all bad decisions largely because a groupthink environment pervaded staff meetings as staff members discussed the various policy options available. They were concerned about possible ostracism from the group if they spoke against an option they thought the president might prefer. They were also victimized by the illusion that they were virtually invulnerable to error because of their inclusion in the group. After all, these were meetings of the president's own advisors, chosen for their sound judgment and expertise. As a result, many staff members suppressed their own reservations about many options discussed. Fearing ostracism from other staff members and fearing that they would displease the president if they voted against what appeared to be a developing consensus during the meetings, many staff members actually voted to support policy recommendations that they privately thought were faulty. Only in cases where the president recognized the potential for groupthink to infiltrate and influence staff were presidents able to preempt the problem by realigning staff structure, and insisting on constructive criticism of all options discussed. Janis argues that President Truman's actions during staff talks preceding the recommendation of the Marshall Plan and President Kennedy's staff use strategy during the Cuban Missile Crisis were examples of presidents successfully preempting the groupthink problem. The institutional separation of the presidency from other branches of government, together with weak political party organizations, cause the president's status to impact on the type of advice he receives. It encourages staff advice to be less constructively critical than it would be if our parties were more disciplined and the president a part of a political party based governing team.

Of course, groupthink is not inevitable. Presidents with active-positive character inclinations can promote and reward staff candidness by demonstrating that they are individuals who can stand the controversial political heat that goes with the office. In addition, and in contrast to foreign policy advice, advice on domestic policy options is bound by its very nature to reflect the forces of political pluralism. Cabinet members, bureau chiefs, members of congressional committees and subcommittees, and interest group leaders all are prone to reflect constituency and client pressures when their opinions on policy are solicited, or when the president attempts to lure them into his governing coalition. In other words, there are both political and structural reasons for advice to the president on domestic policy matters to discourage the development of groupthink.

Although it is true that domestic economic, religious, and racial factors impact on foreign policy decisions much more regularly than in time past, the president still finds that staff advice on foreign policy issues is much less impacted by the forces of political pluralism than is the case with domestic issues. This leads to a third effect of constitutional politics on the development and policy use of presidential staffs. Facing more estranged and entrenched opposition to their domestic programs, presidents have, since the 1970s, converted the missions of some staff components from ones originally created to serve the *institution* of the presidency over the longer term to ones designed to serve the *immediate* policy goals of the incumbent president. The Office of Management and Budget (OMB) has been particularly impacted by this transition. The Brownlow Committee's recommendations focused on controlling and organizing the budget and improving policy management. The committee expected the former Bureau of the Budget (now OMB) to function as a unit that integrated agency budget requests with the president's program, and that evaluated agency programs with an eye to recommending organization and management changes that would increase efficiency and planning effectiveness. The goal was to make the Bureau an objective, nonpartisan enterprise run mostly by career executives, not political employees. The Bureau was faithful to this mandate for the better part of a decade (1939–1949), after which its reputation as a nonpartisan arbiter of budget questions began to suffer, albeit very, very gradually. Its management mission was never as successful as was its early record in budgeting.[24] Even in the area of budgeting, the Bureau's early success depended on the willingness of the president to accept its established routines and reporting deadlines. If a president wanted to alter or reprioritize his policy strategy after submitting his budget to Congress, clashes with the Bureau's timetable and routines became inevitable. President Truman voiced some annoyance with the Bureau's routines, but it was President Kennedy who first displayed clear dissatisfaction with the Bureau's procedures. President Johnson's frustrations were similar, as were President Nixon's. Finally, Nixon took action to formalize changes in the Bureau's makeup and mission in 1970 by reorienting its mission and renaming it the Office of Management and Budget (OMB). By that time, presidents had come to realize that their formal impact on policy through the budget *per se* was quite limited, recognizing that the resolution of budget issues always reflected the impact of competition among interest groups seeking to secure as many distributive and regulatory policy advantages from government as possible.

President Nixon recognized this, and the formal addition of a management mission to the agency's role obligations was no accident. In a sense, it marked the formalization of a change that had been in the offing for years. Management, insofar as OMB's new role is concerned, means management to help the president in his policy crusades. It does not stress administrative management that focuses on supervising and coordinating the implementation of legislation, although it can involve that. Since the Nixon administration, OMB has become a partisan spokesman for the incumbent president's policy agenda. This was particularly true during the Reagan administration when the president made it his main organizational arm and its director, David Stockman, the chief spokesman for the president's drive to cut federal spending and to reduce what Reagan thought were overly burdensome regulations on the business community. Presidents Bush and Clinton showed no inclination to change OMB's newly bestowed partisan role.

The reason for this is clear, and there is an undisputable constitutional input into it: Occupying an office that is constitutionally separate from other branches of government, with growing policy responsibilities, the president must muster help for his effort from any source he can. The forces with which he must struggle and, hopefully, win over to his side are forces which use the constitutional independence of the House, Senate, and the states to their advantage. The natural response to the formal polarization of power by the Constitution is for the forces that hope to win the policy struggle to use the formal proliferation of power to their advantage. The president's national constituency puts him on the catbird's seat in such a struggle because he can fulfill his policy mission only by bringing enough of these other disparate forces together long enough to forge a governing coalition in support of his policy agenda. Other political actors do not experience such an imperative. The partisanship of staff operations, no doubt an evolutionary inevitability under the most nonpartisan of conditions, is

accelerated and accentuated in the unique policy environment under which the president is expected to function.

Whether the effect of this particular manifestation of constitutional politics on policy is mostly positive or negative is subject to debate. Anytime elected officials increase their reliance on staff for policy advice, especially for representing them as policy spokespersons, they run the risk of being misrepresented and embarrassed. Since presidents need to sustain as much bargaining leverage as possible by keeping their prestige and professional reputation high, a staff member who overstates, understates, or misrepresents the president's opinion on an issue places the president's status and professional reputation in peril, at least temporarily. The Stockman case discussed earlier illustrates such a danger. Furthermore, the increasing partisanship of staff operations can lure staff advisors, as policy spokespersons for the president, into a "cognitive dissonant" frame of mind. Many staff members in the White House Office and elsewhere in EOP serve as presidential "alter egos." Their political persuasions and policy commitments, coupled with their close personal relationship with the president, make it virtually inevitable that they will find it as convenient as has he to practice strategically deceptive tactics if they think it in the president's best interest to do so. White House chiefs of staff, press secretaries, and some WHO key policy advisors are particularly prone to this. Carter's press secretary, Jody Powell, readily admitted he deliberately lied to the press on several occasions to give the president more time to deal with a crisis. Reagan's national security advisor, John Poindexter, admitted he lied to Congress about the specifics of an "arms for hostages" agreement with Iran and plans to redeploy some of the profits that arms contractors made from the deal to support the Contras in Nicaragua.

Often deception induced by the politicalization of staff operations extends beyond the confines of the White House Office. Although the alter ego syndrome is less applicable to other EOP components than for WHO, their growing role as avowed presidential partisans encourages the same results. For example, when Reagan's OMB director David Stockman assumed office he ordered a computer simulation to project the effects on the budget deficit of the president's plans to increase defense spending while simultaneously reducing taxes. The projection of unprecedented deficits accompanied by higher interest rates and the possible erosion of confidence in the financial markets alarmed Stockman, whose partisan mission was to make the president's linkage of available revenue to policy objectives appear logical. His response was to alter the assumptions fed into the computer system to change the projected results, making the president's plans appear more reasonable and therefore more politically acceptable.[25] This, coupled with the fact that the plan did not ask for sacrifice, undoubtedly made it much easier for Reagan to develop a governing coalition in support of his budget. However, for reasons that appear obvious in retrospect, the results were not as projected. After leaving the presidency, Reagan's popularity as an ex-president was regularly overshadowed by the growing realization that he, assisted by a highly partisan OMB and WHO, had lulled the nation into a false sense of optimism about the effects of tax cuts on generating a level of economic growth that would accommodate higher defense expenditures via a wider tax base.

A highly partisan staff can also encourage presidential decisions that fail to reflect the necessary technical and political diversity that is necessary for their long-term success. Reagan's idea for a "Star Wars" defense system, although hatched by the president, was supported by only a few select advisors who were largely unaware of the proposal's technical

problems, but were nonetheless very sensitive to the president's desire to take credit for the idea. Poindexter and a few handpicked members of the National Security Council staff engineered the Iran-Contra coverup without consulting with others, including (so they argued) the president, about the feasibility of the project's success as well as the legality of the undertaking itself. Had President Nixon's intimate WHO advisors—especially Haldeman, Ehrlichman, and Dean—deliberately widened the advisory field and solicited opinions as to how best to deal with what the president considered to be a serious Democratic challenge in 1972, perhaps the entire Watergate tragedy could have been avoided.

From the president's perspective, it is obvious that he needs an active and specialized staff to combat and negotiate with other forces whose political differences with him are reinforced by constitutionally mandated constituency differences and different term of office pressures. The constitutionality of the staff is unquestioned. Its growth has reinforced the impact of the separation of powers and checks and balances on government. It has no real power aside from what the president wants to assign it. However, its growing partisanship, especially in the wake of Watergate, has encouraged some observers to recommend a presidential strategy that rekindles the spirit and purpose of the Brownlow Committee's recommendations. In a nutshell, these recommendations suggest that a staff operation directed toward neutral, long-term service to the presidency as an institution is much more preferable to one that is openly partisan and dedicated to the service of the sitting president. As a result, recommendations for reform have included the reinvigoration of the staff's role in administrative management and policy implementation, a presidential advisory network that systematically incorporates the opinions of cabinet secretaries, and the appointment of staff officials who are assigned the task of deliberately fostering a wide variety of policy inputs into the presidential advisory system, both in foreign and domestic policy.[26]

However, formal organizational correctives to take politics out of staff operations or to reduce its political role simply serve to illustrate how genetically political are staff operations. Formal organizational changes do nothing to change the president's policy incentives. To presidents, as well as other politicians, organization is not the systematic orchestration of labor to accomplish a task efficiently. To politicians, organization is a variation of Schattschneider's observation that "organization is the mobilization of bias."[27] It is something to be used to advance the political mission of those it serves. Consequently, despite the flurry of post-Watergate recommendations to reorganize and reorient the president's staff, presidents of both parties have not taken them seriously. To do so would be, in their opinion, to place them at a disadvantage in the struggle to predominate in the policy struggles that are an inevitable by-product of the constitutional fragmentation of policymaking power.

Urban Policy Bias

A fourth effect of constitutional politics on the president's policy role is related to the structure of the Electoral College, and how that structure has been impacted by party politics. The Constitution assigns each state the total number of electoral votes that it has senators and representatives. Since each state is assigned two senators and a minimum of one representative, the minimum number of electoral votes even the smallest populated state can have is three. The more heavily populated states have increased electoral representation in proportion to the size of their delegation in the House of Representatives. In the 1992 presidential election California, the largest state, had forty-seven electoral votes.

North and South Dakota, Wyoming, and Alaska had the minimum of three. Only in the smaller states does a state's equal representation in the Senate weigh what might be termed nonurban elements disproportionately high vis-à-vis urban population. Even in these states, most of the population lives in what the Bureau of the Census would classify officially as an "urban" area. It makes little difference, however, because such states' proportional weight in the 538 electoral vote total is relatively small. Most candidates for the presidency spend little campaign time in these states for obvious reasons.

Once political parties became an acceptable part of the American political scene, during the early nineteenth century, they quickly moved to maximize their leverage in elections at all levels of government. An early target was the Electoral College. State legislatures quickly succumbed to party pressures to have each state's electors chosen by popular vote instead of by the state's legislature. Furthermore, slates of electors then ran for selection as electors pledged to support the candidate for president selected by (depending on the era) a caucus of national party leaders, national party conventions, or, as has been the case in most states since the 1960s, party primary elections. If the party's candidate won a plurality of votes in any state, all that state's electors were instructed to vote unanimously for the successful candidate. Appointment as an elector became, in effect, an honorary position with no voting discretion. It remains the same today.

The significance of these developments for the president and his policy focus has been profound. Presidential candidates from both parties must focus their campaigns on voters in what have been termed the "big swing" states. These are the heavily populated states with large blocks of electoral votes. If a candidate wins one of these states by a plurality vote of one or more, all that state's electoral votes go to that candidate. This, of course, makes candidates very attentive to voter opinion in those states. However, it does much more than that. These states all have heavily populated urban centers and many of them contain potentially cohesive blocs of votes which could swing the entire state's electoral vote into either candidate's column if this cohesion were cemented by an event, an issue, or a candidate's personal appeal. This not only makes presidential candidates attentive to the entire state, but political events could make them overly attentive and servile to the opinions of minority groups, labor unions, or religious sects in these large states during the course of a campaign.

Therefore, candidates and incumbent presidents from both parties tend toward what might be termed "urban policy bias." Urban policy is not a single policy but a conglomeration of various policies targeted at both central cities and suburbs. Included are policies affecting urban education, welfare, housing, transportation, health, sanitation, infrastructure, law enforcement, and the distribution of drugs. Of course, nonurban areas face many of the same problems, but usually on a much smaller scale. Presidents as both incumbents and candidates must address these issues or face either electoral defeat or significant erosion of the actual or potential bases for governing coalitions. To be sure, Democrats and Republicans have developed different strategies to appeal to urban voters in heavily populated states. Historically, Democrats have stressed distributive policies such as entitlements, grants, job training programs, unemployment insurance, and education subsidies. Republicans have stressed less dependence on government and more on policies that free market forces in the hope that economic growth can provide employment opportunities and overall economic security for all, even the economically disadvantaged. Therefore, the parties differ in their choice of means, but not ends.

Political events could change the tenacity of the hold the big swing states have on the pres-

ident's policy agenda. Recent elections have shown it to be more tenuous than it has been historically. Voter apathy is increasing because some people feel estranged from their government and have concluded that voting is a useless exercise that only leads to disappointment and frustration. Low-income voters and racial minorities are among the first to withdraw from politics when apathy becomes increasingly widespread. These individuals are among those who profit most from the president's urban policy bias. If voter apathy progresses to the point where these groups appear to be forfeiting their potential electoral leverage over the president, then presidents may begin to alter their campaign and governing strategies. They will never, however, have second thoughts about the significance of the large states to their election and presidential success.

The president's urban policy bias reinforces the impact of the separation of powers on American government and policymaking. The urban orientation of the president stands in contrast to the *comparatively* less urban orientation of Congress. Equal state representation provides rural America with disproportionately high representation in the Senate. In addition, representatives from either party from the more rural, thinly populated states tend to assume a conservative policy posture that often conflicts with a president's more liberal orientation. Before 1960, a president-Congress, urban-rural contrast was more apparent than it is today. Today, owing to the overall increase in population and the migration of people from rural areas to the cities and from the urban north to the sunbelt states, the urban population weight is larger in proportion to rural areas than it ever has been. However, much of this population shift has been from central city to the suburbs, and from rural areas to the suburbs. The political culture and policy priorities of most suburban areas are notably different from the central city. Consequently, the historical rural-urban contrast is gradually being replaced by a central city–suburban contrast. This, together with the tendency for central city voters to be less interested and active in politics, has made the policy orientation of today's urban areas more conservative in composite than has been the case historically. Presidents will undoubtedly respond with a different urban strategy to reflect these differences. Such a change will be tempered, in all likelihood, by the fact that the central cities and the suburbs must coexist. Problems of one ultimately affect the other. The realization of such an inevitability means that the politics of urban areas in the heavily populated states will continue to be of prime concern for both presidential candidates and incumbent presidents. The president's alleged liberal policy orientation as contrasted historically to the comparatively conservative cast of Congress is no longer as apparent as it once was. Nevertheless, rural America maintains an inflated representation in the Senate because states are represented equally in that body, and some House districts are demographically still predominantly rural in cast. Therefore, even if presidents continue to find it politically expedient to maintain the attentiveness they have shown to the policy problems of urban areas in heavily populated states, it is very difficult to argue that the policy issues that get their attention as a result are not the ones that should be high on the nation's priority list anyway.

Constitutional Politics and the Presidency: The Post-Watergate Legacy

The Watergate incident, together with the Vietnam War, changed the political landscape upon which policymakers seek office and develop policy. Policymakers inevitably reflect the attitudes and incentives of those who elect them to office. Because Watergate and Vietnam involved the inappropriate use of presidential power, either illegal or unwise, Americans grew increasingly suspicious of the vestiture of significant discretionary policy power in the presidency and, for that matter, in government in general. The discussion and analysis of the impact of individualized pluralism on Congress since the early 1970s in Chapter 7 illustrates very well the impact of the post-Watergate public mindset on congressional politics. Presidents have had to respond to the same changes. The breakdown of institutionalized pluralism and the resultant going public strategy illustrate the impact of these same changes on presidential policy leadership. In short, both the president and Congress, as institutions mandated by the Constitution to share the national policymaking obligation jointly, must deal with changes in the public's attitude toward power as they attempt to perform effectively as policy players.

Politics is not simply a progression of electoral and policymaking struggles. It is also a way to express the public's values and habits during struggles both to win office and to govern. Americans have always been suspicious of concentrated power. The Constitution formally institutionalized that suspicion. Watergate and Vietnam simply made people more suspicious of centralized power. Presidents have responded in kind, even though many policy problems demand more, not less, centralized management. In other words, at the very time the nation needs more top down policy planning and administration, its elected leaders, especially the president, are being asked to adopt more of a bottom up approach to both challenges.

The Reagan and Clinton presidencies offer excellent illustrations of this trend. The Reagan presidency is often sold as one that changed the nation's political climate from one of dependency on the social service state to one that was suspicious of government power in principle. That is a myth. Reagan didn't create such a mood, for it has always been there. He personalized it and used the presidency to give it respectability. However, if Reagan hadn't done this, others would have. Reagan was a master at substituting rhetoric for reality. Despite the way the Reagan era was (and is) treated by the media, there was, in fact, no Reagan policy "revolution" that changed government in any dramatic way. His administration saw no lowering of the overall tax burden. He didn't terminate any major government function. His administration saw no wholesale return of national government power to states and localities. He wanted to do all these things, but didn't pursue many of them much beyond the rhetorical stage. He found a welcome ally in the media which, as discussed in Chapter 6, is all too willing to pursue the dramatic and superficial at the expense of the real. The result is a major distortion of reality and, in effect, a major misjudgment of the effect of the Reagan administration on the contours of public policy.

The same was true for the Clinton presidency. Although President Clinton may well have been a spiritual New Deal and Great Society Democrat, the public's post-Watergate mindset would not permit him to parley "big government" solutions to policy problems. Instead, he became a "new Democrat" who advanced adjustive, pragmatic policy options. Many of these involved tax cuts and a reassignment of federal power to the states in many policy fields, especially entitlements. Like President Reagan, when faced with a Congress that appeared less than sympathetic to his proposals, he readily went public with his crusades to sell his programs to people first, in the hope that the result of successful salesmanship eventually would work its way back to Congress. Faced with divided government for all but two years of his presidency, Clinton's approach to policy leadership was clearly bipartisan in tone. The 1996 welfare reform legislation and the 1997 balanced budget agreement were both very conservative, if not reactionary, laws by New Deal and Great Society standards. The welfare reform act, analyzed in depth in Chapters 10 and 11, transferred the federal government's role in family entitlement policies to states and localities. The budget agreement used tax cuts and tax breaks to encourage economic growth and ease financial burdens on families with children, with special tax breaks going to families with children attending college. These laws were popular not only because they didn't demand financial sacrifice (quite the opposite in the case of the budget agreement), but also because they played to the traditional tides of public opinion that had been reinvigorated, but not established, by President Reagan.

The legacies of Watergate and Vietnam made the "bully pulpit" presidency a logical strategy for presidents able to do it well, and both Presidents Reagan and Clinton responded well to the challenge. Reagan's reputation as a persuasive speaker served him well as president, at least in terms of his ability to inculcate loyalty through rhetoric. However, Clinton's successes were no less impressive. Aware of the constraints placed on his institutional leverage by less-than-majority election victories and by divided government, President Clinton used the presidential bully pulpit to nudge people into policy activity in the absence of official public policy that directly supported his policy initiatives. He went public in the name of volunteerism as a way to deal with serious problems outside the institutions of official government and public policy. He sponsored a bipartisan-backed volunteer "summit" in 1997 to give the volunteer approach a high-profile sendoff. Later that same year he called for a national dialogue on race relations that sought to cultivate more tolerance and understanding among people of different national origins. In 1996 President Clinton approached the problem of obscenity and violence on television in much the same fashion when he appealed to the broadcasting and film industries for more wholesome programming and film making.

The more liberal elements of the Democratic Party interpreted Clinton's actions as symbolic, comparatively painless substitutes for official public policy. However, the public in general appeared to like them. The president's approval rating rose in tandem with these appeals. The reason is clear. The president was asking for action, not action mandated by policy but action to deal with problems that wasn't supported by the policy "crutch" of government. Although of a much different political cast than President Reagan, President Clinton came to realize that rhetoric which links accepted American values to policy offers a way for the president to compensate for the constitutionally rooted formal policy weaknesses of the presidency. For presidents to focus their rhetoric on the linkages between broadly shared values and specific policy options is a natural, if not inevitable, result of the impact of the post-Watergate period on the presidency.

Perhaps more than any time in history, the post-Watergate period has both illustrated and tested the policy limitations of the presidency. The president can go public to embarrass entrepreneurs, to highlight issues, and to energize people. The Constitution often precludes his doing more. Presidents want to make things happen in areas that Congress would often rather ignore or slight. The resort to a "preacher-in-chief" strategy carries the Neustadt prescription for persuasion to a much more inclusive arena. This may be all to the good, because the underlying strength of a society may well be measured by the ability of its leaders to persuade than by the ability of its laws to coerce. If a constitutionally independent Congress blocks presidential policy initiatives or the public seems indifferent to them, the bully pulpit may well perform a valuable function.

Few would argue that what President Clinton wanted to accomplish by his bully pulpit strategy was not worthwhile. Asking people to volunteer their time for worthy causes and to come together to discuss what they have in common as human beings rather than what divides them because of race may appear pallid and useless to some, but it is difficult to argue that they are not commendable things for people to undertake. Moreover, they may yield favorable results. American society needs to recharge its social capital networks, and presidential involvement in the crusade is certainly not a negative.

President Clinton's increasing use of the presidential bully pulpit during his second term was a response to the public's post-Watergate antiestablishment mood, to the political and policy realities of divided government, and to political weaknesses brought on by his impeachment. To some observers this illustrated the growing weakness of the presidency as a policy force in American government. However, it could be viewed as a strength rather than a weakness. A government often threatened with budget deficits and increasing demands on its resources needs to look for alternative ways to cope with its policy problems. Such a dilemma affects legislators as well as presidents. Therefore, it could be argued that Clinton's leadership strategy was more of an adjustment that accommodated new political and economic realities than it was a surrender to policy uncontrollables. The roles of the president as chief legislator, chief executive, chief diplomat, and voice of the people remained unchallenged. Clinton merely attempted to apply them to altered political, social, and economic conditions. What, during Clinton's first term, appeared to be a series of notably modest policy initiatives was, at least according to the president, essentially a reanimation of the presidential office and a definitive reaffirmation of presidential power.

Although they certainly were not "mail

order" conditions, Clinton used the political constraints of the time as an opportunity to develop less expensive yet innovative ways to meet his policy leadership challenge. Although history will be the final judge, and his impeachment diminished his policy leverage, Clinton may well have used the constraints of the times to expand the long-term power of the presidency. Seeking a favorable niche in history, all presidents attempt to leave their mark on the office, usually by way of increasing its influence. Clinton was no exception.

In addition to the bully pulpit strategy, Clinton efforts to increase presidential influence were asserted on four fronts. First, he reasserted the unilateral policy powers of the presidency in several areas. Perhaps the most controversial of these was his use of authority vested in the president by the Antiquities Act of 1906 to, by executive order, create the 1.7-million-acre Grand Staircase-Escalante National Monument in Utah in order to preserve the area's natural resources from exploitation by developers. The impact of Clinton's action was compromised somewhat by a subsequent decision of the Bureau of Land Management to permit limited oil and gas exploration on the reserve by firms that had existing rights to exploration privileges. However, that does not detract from the significance of the president's decision. His action was undertaken unilaterally, thereby circumventing the legal requirements for public hearings and environmental assessments. It was an unusual assertion of presidential power that took on special significance because it was exercised at a time when it was more popular to bash the assertion of presidential power than to welcome it. Second, the president expanded the application of claims for presidential executive privilege (a strategy to protect the confidentiality of decision making) to include not only communications between the president and other officials, but also communications between presidential subordinates.

Some of this was an attempt to save the president from personal embarrassment. However, much of it, such as the refusal to surrender a 1995 memo from Justice Department officials criticizing the president's antidrug campaign, represented an effort to keep a presidential policy on line and in focus. Third, Clinton sought, although unsuccessfully, presidential immunity from a civil suit brought by a former Arkansas civil servant (Paula Jones) claiming sexual harassment. Fourth, the president virtually ignored provisions of the War Powers Resolution, passed over President Nixon's veto in 1973, when he refused to secure official congressional approval of his decisions to send troops to Haiti, Bosnia, and Somalia, and to intervene briefly in Iraq. All of these unilateral actions were defended on the grounds that America's role as global peacemaker can be used efficiently and effectively only if the president acts with dispatch and with firmness.

Therefore, President Clinton's response to the political and economic constraints of the post-Watergate period was the use of both the bully pulpit and a reinvigoration of what he believed to be the inherent constitutional prerogatives of the presidency in areas where he believed public and congressional approval was not necessary. In essence, he refocused presidential leadership challenges to meet altered conditions. Responding to public opinion, he became a new Democrat, committing government to affording people the opportunity to do something worthwhile with their lives, but working to stabilize or reduce its role in the economy and culture.

The Watergate Legacy and Presidential Policy Leverage: The Clinton Experience

In 1978, in the wake of the Watergate scandal, Congress enacted, and renewed in 1994, the Ethics in Government Act, a law providing for the appointment of independent counsels to investigate irregularities in the behavior and activities of administrative officials, including the president. At the request of the Attorney General, counsels were appointed by panels of federal judges. The theory behind the law was to provide for independent, objective investigations of alleged actions that may have violated statutory or constitutional law. The purpose was to avoid an incumbent administration's own Department of Justice investigation of charges levied against other members of the same administration.

While sound in theory, between 1978 and 1998, independent counsel investigations were usually anything but nonpartisan. Appointments usually went to lawyers with clear records of political and judicial partisanship. Of the counsels appointed during the Reagan, Bush, and Clinton administrations, only James McKay, who investigated the Reagan Justice Department, was clearly a political independent. Donald Pearson, who investigated the activities of the late Commerce Secretary Ron Brown, was a registered Democrat. The remaining counsels who supervised high-profile investigations were Republicans. These included Whitney North Seymour, who investigated Reagan staff assistant Michael Deaver; Iran-Contra prosecutor Lawrence Walsh; Arlin Adams, who investigated a housing scandal; Joseph DiGenova, who investigated the charges that President Clinton's opponents had improperly gained access to his passport records; Robert Fiske, who inaugurated the Whitewater investigation; Donald Smaltz, who investigated and brought charges against President Clinton's Agriculture Secretary Mike Epsy; and Kenneth Starr, who replaced Fiske in the Whitewater inquiry and pursued it until it led to an inquiry into Clinton's sexual indiscretions, a matter that had absolutely nothing to do with the Whitewater inquiry. Investigations conducted under such circumstances can hardly be conducted ob-

jectively. Partisanship was inevitable. It is virtually impossible to separate the political from the neutral in very high-profile cases. Regarding the Whitewater-Jones-Lewinsky investigation, at times it appeared to many observers that Starr was possessed by a mission not only to defeat a political opponent, but to humiliate and criminalize him. Starr was an avowed conservative Republican. Clinton was a center to left-of-center Democrat. Under such conditions, it is virtually impossible to expect such an investigation to be conducted objectively, despite the fact that counsels always find legal justification to invoke certain procedures during the investigation.

Finding little to suggest that Clinton was guilty of any wrongdoing in the Whitewater matter Starr, in an effort to establish that Clinton was less than trustworthy, maneuvered the inquiry into an investigation of the president's Oval Office extra-marital sex escapades. The investigation concentrated on the president's relationship with a White House intern, Monica Lewinsky. Clinton first denied the affair, but later recanted and admitted to a sexual relationship with the intern. In attempting to deflect Starr's investigation, Clinton argued that a lawyer-client privilege existed between him and his White House counsel. The Supreme Court rejected that argument, and compelled the counsel to testify before a grand jury convened by Starr. The Court also mandated that members of the president's Secret Service detachment be compelled to testify about what they knew of the relationship between the president and Lewinsky. Starr's investigation led to a report to Congress that resulted in impeachment proceedings against the president, charging that he had perjured himself and obstructed justice. He was subsequently impeached by the House.

Clinton's actions, both personal and official, were unfortunate for him as a person, as a family man, and as an incumbent president.

His presidency was crippled significantly by the scandal and his impeachment. He wanted to make a significant mark on history, and that is very hard to accomplish if the president serves, as did Clinton, during a noncrisis era of relative peace and tranquility. The post-Watergate public distrust of government and its leaders, encouraged by a sensationalist-hungry media, compounded his problems. The cultural deference that shielded his predecessors from such hypervigilance did not protect Clinton. Unlike the failings of his predecessors, Clinton's moral failings became the news. The press, and ultimately the public and rival politicians, were looking for failings. They found them and they exploited them.

Clinton's presidential heroes were Abraham Lincoln, Theodore Roosevelt, Franklin Roosevelt, and his boyhood idol John F. Kennedy. In varying degrees, these presidents were leaders who put their stamp on history not merely by being successful policy stewards, but by being presidents who embodied successfully the country's values and its consciousness. As a second-term, lame duck president, Clinton knew that his best hope for a respectable niche in history was to stress the reconciliation of differences and to promote a values agenda. He publicly aligned himself with some religious crusades, he constantly stressed the importance of personal responsibility and the commitment to family as ways to constrain the growth of crime and poverty in America. He talked eloquently about eliminating religious prejudice, the importance of the community to long-term social and economic prosperity, and the need to reach out to political opponents in a search for a common political ground on which all could labor intensively for the betterment of society in general. In sum, he sought to be a significant force of national unification. That was a realistic agenda for a second-term president facing a pessimistic public and divided government conditions.

However, the president jeopardized, if not destroyed, the realization of those objectives when he became inappropriately involved with Monica Lewinsky and attempted to hide it by being less than truthful with the public in the early stages of the Starr investigation, and by adopting a questionable legal defense strategy. It is virtually impossible to unify a country when the lead stories on the evening news concern Oval Office sexual liaisons, and when the opposition party and a special prosecutor appear to be on a "search and destroy" mission to discredit, if not destroy you. President Clinton's personal indiscretions, as unsavory as they were, did not legitimize the tactics of his opponents as they sought to undermine his presidency. However, the president's recklessness opened the door to a culturally newsworthy event that fed on itself, and therefore he had only himself to blame. The result was a second term that began with much promise but which ended with the president attempting to dodge his problems by trying to compartmentalize them, and by blaming his accusers' strategies for the media's preoccupation with the matter. By engaging in such reckless behavior and in defending it the way he did, the president was doing the very things he had earlier warned were undercutting the nation's civic morality.

At first Clinton dodged responsibility for his actions by denying any involvement with Lewinsky, but confessed later to a relationship. Rather than doing battle with politicians' growing sense of paranoia he, Mrs. Clinton, and White House aide Sidney Blumenthal accused the Starr team of being a part of a "right wing conspiracy" and one of Starr's assistants of being a religious fanatic. Instead of trying to erase the growing sense of political paranoia, the president and his allies exploited it. The purpose of these tactics was to undercut the opposition by generating so much disgust over its tactics that any formal charges levied against the president would be received with public approbation, and therefore delegitimized. The cost of such tactics was the displacement of his values agenda and the acceleration of the impeachment campaign against him. The bully pulpit strategy, discussed above, that Clinton had inaugurated so successfully in 1997 was relaxed somewhat in 1998 following the disclosure of the Lewinsky incident. If a president does not embody and live by the very norms he asks the public to assume, why should a bully pulpit strategy be taken seriously, especially if the president's behavior illustrates the very things that crusade sought to eliminate?

However, the major long-term impact of the Clinton-Starr conflict was not Clinton's personal indiscretions, how he fought the investigation of them, how they were exploited by the media and his political opponents, or even the trauma of his impeachment, but its long-term effect on the presidency as a policy institution. The repercussions of the president's personal carelessness were exacerbated by hypercoverage of both the affair and the investigation by a scandal-obsessed media in what had become a media-dominated society. The scandal dominated the media like the oft-cited plague. For months the news and the talk shows were dominated by the event. The scandal was discussed and analyzed to death. Had it happened during an earlier era, the president likely would have escaped much of the negative publicity and the focus of his presidency would have remained a policy focus, not a scandal obsession, and it is unlikely he would have been impeached. However, Watergate's contribution to fragmented governmental and political power and a scandal-obsessed media made Clinton pay a heavy price. Divided government conditions exacerbated the problem. For months, the lead story on most news and panel programs was the Clinton-Lewinsky-Starr matter, not more pressing policy issues such as world famine, international terrorism, nuclear prolifera-

tion, education, medical care, and entitlement reform. Even on days when there was no fresh news to report on either the scandal or the Starr investigation, television anchors, reporters, and talk-show hosts would interview each other or new guests who would repeatedly discuss existing evidence and events and speculate on what was likely to happen next and what that could mean for the Clinton presidency. Once Clinton was impeached, the focus turned to the chances of his being convicted by the Senate and removed from office. In short, the tone of the coverage throughout was little short of orgiastic.

The major issue surrounding the Starr inquiry was not the effect of the investigation, with its prurient overtones, on Clinton the person and his historical reputation as an impeached president, but its long-term impact on the institution of the presidency as an institution of significant policy leverage. President Clinton, Congress, the media, and the Supreme Court may have compromised that in very significant ways for the intermediate to long term. The presidency as a significant policy force may never be the same. What potential negative fallout does the impeachment incident harbor for the presidency? First, and perhaps most important, it may well have compromised the value of presidential policy staff to the development and oversight of public policy. Seeking advice on sensitive issues, presidents may not be willing or able to consult their senior aides, their own counsel, or perhaps even ex-presidents like they were able to do before the Starr investigation. For example, a president's private discussions with White House attorneys are no longer protected from grand jury questioning because, according to the courts, these attorneys are employed by the people, not the president. Should presidents hire private attorneys at exorbitant hourly fees to advise them on the same issues, conversational confidentiality presumably would be preserved.

Such a strategy, even if a president could afford it, would further isolate the office from the American people. Of course, Clinton's litigation strategy in challenging Starr contributed to their confrontations being handled in court, with the president losing most of the time. Had he not selected such a strategy, the courts would not have been called on to resolve the issues. In a sense, Clinton's strategy was one that, in effect, compromised the privileges of the office in a significant way.

Second, the courts ruled that Clinton could not invoke executive privilege in an attempt to limit grand jury interrogation of his staff. Historically, presidents have used the executive privilege successfully to keep certain information off limits to the public, legislatures, the media, and the courts. Most of the time they have been successful. However, the strategy failed President Nixon in the Watergate scandal, as it did Clinton in the Starr investigation. Future presidents will still be able to invoke the executive privilege, but each time the courts honor a challenge to its use, its future utility is very likely compromised.

Third, and significantly encouraged by media coverage, the impeachment saga served to institutionalize the right of an adversarial political culture to prey on the president as a target upon which to vent its values and realize its goals. This has the effect of compromising, if not eliminating, the presidency as a moral force in establishing policy agendas and working to facilitate them. Public life has become more of a soap opera than an exercise in statesmanship. As bad as they were, President Clinton's personal inadequacies were probably not any worse than many of his predecessors. However, due largely to the predatory culture of his age, both he and the nation paid a higher price for them. Public deference to the presidency had virtually disappeared even before he assumed the office. What the media ignored before, they exploited during his term. The toleration politi-cians once ignored in each other before the age of scandal, they had begun to exploit well before Clinton assumed office. The vigor and zealousness with which Independent Counsel Starr pursued the president may well have had political roots. However, its methods were also very compliant with an adversarial political culture whose seeds were sown in the Watergate scandal. The independent counsel law was a direct result of Watergate. Therefore, as personally vulnerable as was President Clinton, the seriousness of the crisis in which he found himself was due at least as much to the "signs of the cultural times" as it was to his personal failings.

Independent Counsels and Presidential Power: The Constitutional Dimension

The Starr investigation was, by most accounts, not only one of the more zealous legal assaults on an incumbent president, but also an assault on the presidency itself. The political dimensions of the conflict obscured what was, in essence, an attack on the presidency as an institution. Like all presidents, Clinton considered his mission to be that of policy "caretaker" for the entire body politic. That obligation alone, so goes the argument, should exempt the president from the normal routines of judicial inquiry because such inquiries can distract him from this most important constitutional policy mission, one that he was elected to pursue. President Clinton reacted to Kenneth Starr's subpoena to testify in the Lewinsky investigation much as President Thomas Jefferson did when Supreme Court chief justice John Marshall subpoenaed him to testify in the trial of his (Jefferson's) protagonist, Aaron Burr. Jefferson told Marshall he would not comply and Marshall withdrew the subpoena.

The doctrine of judicial supremacy,

introduced by Marshall in *Marbury* v. *Madison*, raises key questions about both the legality and practicality of subjecting an incumbent president to the normal routines of the judicial process. It is one thing to argue that "no person is above the law" and quite another to apply that principle in ways that distract presidents from pursuing their policy agendas. That is precisely what happened in the Clinton-Starr conflict. If judges apply the "no person is above the law" regularly to standard court cases, few would object. However, when the structural power, and policy, balance between the three coordinate branches of government is at stake, more serious questions are raised about the universality of the principle.

According to Edwin M. Yoder, Jr., the anti-authority culture of the post-Watergate era has tended to relegate the structural implications of judicial action to the background. The Clinton-Starr conflict is a case in point. Yoder argues that no government can perform effectively without some structurally grounded protections from judicial intrusion. For example, the Constitution (Article I, Section 6) states that members of Congress "for any speech or debate in either house . . . shall not be questioned in any other place." The Supreme Court has consistently ruled that this means that legislators cannot be sued for unsubstantiated or libelous statements made during floor debates or for statements made during committee hearings. This protection has been used by the Court to include statements made by congressional staff in the course of conducting legislative business, but it does not include statements made by legislators or staff members during press conferences. The Court does not consider the latter an integral part of the legislative process. This partial legislative immunity is a logical translation of the separation of powers principle to the real world of policymaking. In addition, Congress has, by statute, exempted itself from the same ethical standards it imposes on the executive branch, as well as from investigations by a special prosecutor. Neither the Constitution or statutes offer presidents the same privileges and, by ruling that President Clinton was not immune from a civil suit instigated by Paula Jones because it would not interfere with his official presidential responsibilities, the Court decided that the immunity principle did not apply to the presidency. As a result, Clinton spent considerable time on his defense of the charge, taking valuable time away from his presidential responsibilities.

Yoder argues that presidents deserve the same immunity shield as the Constitution and the Supreme Court have awarded Congress.[28] He maintains that Starr's tactics harbored more long-term collateral damage to the notions of "sound precedent, custom, comity, common sense, and constitutional balance" than did the congressional investigations of Senator Joseph McCarthy and Richard Nixon in the early 1950s. He notes that "on a strict view of the separation of powers, it is less than obvious why a judge—or derivatively, a special prosecutor—may haul a president before a grand jury. Why is this any more consistent with the separation of powers than if Bill Clinton sought to summon Chief Justice Rehnquist to the Oval Office to explain by what secretive process of reasoning his court allowed Paula Jones's frivolous law suit to proceed?"[29]

The assumption here is, of course, that the nature of the controversy is key to whether a president should be immune from judicial inquiry. President Clinton never claimed to be above the law, only that the issue was one involving a personal indiscretion, not one involving "high crimes and misdemeanors," which could subject a president to impeachment charges. According to Yoder, the Starr investigation cloaked a rather trivial issue with the protection of the Constitution and it was allowed to proceed on those grounds. President Clinton agreed to testify before the grand jury via a video hookup from the Oval

Office. Aware of his political vulnerability on the issue and of the post-Watergate antiauthority culture, Clinton chose to comply with the subpoena, thereby allowing, according to Yoder, "pettifogging legalism" to win out over "constitutional considerations."[30]

Finally, Kenneth Starr's application of the independent counsel mandate did battle with probably the most legitimate constitutional source of presidential policy power—that of popular sovereignty. According to the Preamble to the Constitution, the legitimacy for all government action is vested in the people. In effect, it is the engine and the fuel that provides legitimacy for government action. One of the public's most significant inputs into public policy is its right to select, through the formal mechanism of the Electoral College, the president of the United States. It elected President Clinton twice—in 1992 and 1996—and, despite Clinton's personal indiscretions, gave him a very high job approval rating throughout the Starr investigation and the impeachment proceedings. The fact that the public approved of the president in spite of the Lewinsky episode had no effect on either the focus or pace of the Starr investigation or the impeachment process. A case can be made for ignoring public opinion in such cases. The character and dispensation of justice, it could be argued, should not result from a popularity contest. On the other hand, the president was not being investigated for "high crimes and misdemeanors" committed against the public. At stake was the possible illegal way in which the president fought charges that sexual encounters with Lewinsky had actually occurred. For purposes of argument, assume that Starr was engaged essentially in conducting a political vendetta against the president under the smokescreen of an independent counsel inquiry. If that was the case, then his flouting of public opinion during the course of the investigation raises serious constitutional questions. Under such

conditions, the powers of a special prosecutor exceed those that the three independent branches have over each other. The president is the public's magistrate. That is his most significant constitutional and policy obligation. Therefore, if he is forced to shelve such an obligation in an effort to defend himself against criminal charges, those charges should focus on very, very serious alleged crimes. Otherwise, he should be immune from fighting the charges, at least during his term of office.

The Lewinsky episode by itself did not, by any measure, constitute an event that impacted on the affairs of state. It did so only indirectly by obligating the president to neglect his official policy responsibilities as he defended himself against both the charges and the way the independent counsel was investigating them. The relationship with Lewinsky itself did not, according to key constitutional law scholars, meet the "high crime" criterion established by the Constitution as a basis for bringing impeachment charges against a sitting president. Deceiving a grand jury under oath and suborning perjury are indeed criminal offenses. However, to do these things to cover up the details of a sexual adventure are hardly "high crimes and misdemeanors," given the subject of the coverup. Moreover, had any semblance of the "let the punishment fit the crime" maxim been applied to the Lewinsky case, there would have been no investigation because the episode under investigation did not involve criminal activity. Therefore, an independent counsel's investigation of it had to be rooted in something other than alleged illegal presidential actions that threatened the ship of state.

President Clinton's personal misconduct was the product of his poor judgment, but it never should have become a government issue. It did because politics was allowed to misdirect a loosely drawn special prosecutor law into a political crusade against the president.

Republicans were surprised and angered by Clinton's 1992 victory and his reelection in 1996. Many had come to consider the presidency as theirs by right. Accordingly, many Republicans did not appear content to debate Clinton over policy matters, but sought to question the worthiness of the man himself to hold the office. This translated into examining and exposing Clinton the person, as well as Clinton the politician and president. The appointment of a Clinton protagonist as special prosecutor gave the permanent investigation crusade the legitimacy it needed. Originally targeted for extraordinary situations, the independent counsel statute was employed to investigate the president's activities on any front that promised, potentially, to embarrass him or to question his legitimate claim to the presidency. While comparatively few party members were actively involved in efforts to discredit the president, many more benefited from efforts to do so and therefore made no attempts to discourage Starr as he wandered from event to event in an attempt to uncover something that might subject the president to criminal charges. Starr began with the infamous Whitewater inquiry, proceeded to the "Travelgate" investigation, then exhaustively examined events leading to the suicide of a Clinton advisor (Vincent Foster), examined possible presidential involvement in the questionable scrutiny, by White House staff, of FBI and CIA personnel files. After nearly four years of investigation, Starr found nothing to implicate Clinton directly in any of these events. The president was finally caught committing, not the crime of larceny or murder or grand theft, but a very inadvisable and terribly executed crime of the heart.

Perhaps the president's behavior was so inappropriate that he genuinely deserved the treatment he ultimately received from the special prosecutor, Congress, and the media. However, was the resultant cost in policy shunting and increased public cynicism worth it? Of course, there is no universal definition of morality. It is intrinsically a subjective term. However, it is reasonable to conclude that it was equally, if not more, immoral for government and the media to neglect critical public policy issues such as health care and the growing gap between the wealthy and the poor while focusing on the president's sexual recklessness. Considering the president's high job approval ratings during the impeachment crisis, a clear-cut public majority had concluded that the true moral question was not: "Did the president have an inappropriate relationship with Lewinsky and, if so, did he lie about it under oath and apologize appropriately for it?" Rather, it seemed to be more like: "Why has the public and its government been sullied by a political, legal, and media system that has concentrated public attention on the president's personal life rather than on the country's and the world's major policy problems?" The many who did not support the impeachment of the president were not defending his libidinous behavior. They simply concluded that such behavior, repugnant as it was, should not be the target of a costly investigation and ravenous media coverage.

The special prosecutor law was poorly conceived and even more poorly implemented. Insofar as the Constitution and its political fallout are concerned, it raised many questions that can be laid to rest only by its rejection or significant modification. The Constitution carefully separates the three branches of government. In spite of this, the independent counsel statute assigned the appointment of counsels to judges, fortified the office with imposing inquisitorial powers, and instructed counsels to report their findings to Congress. This clearly doesn't square with the founders' intentions. The framers obviously would not have endorsed a law that allows the judicial branch to choose an independent counsel who exercises executive branch powers and reports to the legislative branch. The founders specifically banned judges from the impeachment process, and yet the law made the selection of special counsels the responsibility of a panel of three federal judges.

In Kenneth Starr's case, the independent counsel became an impeachment advisor to Congress. Although Starr appeared to be comfortable with this role, the law was more at fault than he. In effect, the independent counsel statute directed prosecutors not to decide cases legally but to deal with inherently political and policy questions. When judges decide who should investigate a president, they are performing political, not judicial functions. In the course of their consideration of possible nominees, they are free to consult anyone they choose, including legislators and other politicians who could be political opponents of the president, or whoever is under investigation. Perhaps Congress by law assigned judges such a partisan task because they (the legislators) expected to be consulted on potential nominees. Should that be the case, then senators some day may find themselves evaluating a report from a special prosecutor whose appointment may have incorporated their opinions. In fact, probably neither judges nor legislators should have any formal or behind-the-scenes role in selecting special prosecutors. Since a special prosecutor's role is essentially an executive one, both the spirit and intent of the separation of powers was violated by the special prosecutor law.

Special prosecutor laws should limit inquiries to specific, significant government issues, otherwise the future of the presidency may well be in jeopardy. If independent prosecutors remain a part of the government scene under the borderless conditions of the 1978 law, future presidents will automatically assume that gossip, hearsay, and media attention alone could spark an independent counsel investigation. Once ignited, the process has the potential of spreading like a firestorm into any part of the president's political or social

past that the original charge even remotely touches. Future presidents will possibly have to mistrust their most loyal staff members, for they might be compelled to become witnesses against their boss. In the wake of the Starr investigation and report, presidents will be encouraged to hire a private law firm to advise them because conversations between the president and White House counsels may not be guaranteed confidentiality. If a president's Secret Service detachment can be called on to tattle on small matters, the president will be forced to weigh the advantages of protection against the need for privacy.

The key question for the long term is: Does the nation want to continue to legitimate the right of special prosecutors to conduct unbridled "whodunit" campaigns against incumbent presidents for reasons that have little, if anything, to do with their (the presidents') official public responsibilities? Should future presidents, out of fear of possible independent counsel probes that have nothing to do with government or politics, be expected to adopt a "bunker" mentality upon assumption of the presidential office? The answer to both questions is no. Accordingly the special prosecutor law should be allowed to expire without renewal or be significantly modified to prevent a repeat of the events leading up to the Starr report. Otherwise, not only will the long-term power of the presidency be in jeopardy, but the sanctity of the popular sovereignty also will be brought into question.

Endnotes

1. See Clinton Rossiter, *The American Presidency*, rev. ed. (New York: Harcourt, Brace and World, 1960), pp. 15–43; Thomas A. Cronin and Michael A. Genovese, *The Paradoxes of the American Presidency* (New York: Oxford University Press, 1998), pp. 142–169; and Aaron Wildavsky, *The Beleaguered Presidency* (New Brunswick, N.J.: Transaction Publishers, 1991), pp. 29–66.

2. Theodore J. Lowi, *The Personal President: Power Invested, Promise Unfulfilled* (Ithaca, N.Y.: Cornell University Press, 1985).

3. Harold M. Barger, *The Impossible Presidency: Illusions and Realities of Executive Power* (Glenview, Ill.: Scott, Foresman, 1984).

4. Richard M. Neustadt, *Presidential Power and the Modern Presidents: The Politics of Leadership from Roosevelt to Reagan* (New York: Free Press, 1990).

5. *Ibid.*, pp. 29–50.

6. Samuel J. Kernell, *Going Public: New Strategies of Presidential Leadership*, 3rd ed. (Washington, D.C.: CQ Press, 1997), pp. 12–20.

7. *Ibid.*, pp. 16–17.

8. *Ibid.*, pp. 27–33.

9. *Ibid.*, pp. 34–38.

10. *Ibid.*

11. Michael Robinson, "Three Faces of Congressional Media," in Thomas E. Mann and Norman J. Ornstein, *The New Congress* (Washington, D.C.: American Enterprise Institute, 1981), p. 93, as cited in *Ibid.*, p. 29.

12. Kernell, *op. cit.*, pp. 34–37.

13. Lester G. Seligman and Cary R. Covington, *The Coalitional Presidency* (Chicago: Dorsey Press, 1989), pp. 14–15.

14. Neustadt, *op. cit.*, pp. 64–68.

15. *Ibid.*, p. 15.

16. James D. Barber, *The Presidential Character: Predicting Performance in the White House*, 3rd ed. (Englewood Cliffs N.J.: Prentice Hall, 1985), and Bruce Buchanan, *The Presidential Experience: What the Office Does to the Man* (Englewood Cliffs, N.J.: Prentice Hall, 1978).

17. *Ibid.*, Buchanan.

18. *Ibid.*, p. 23.

19. *Ibid.*, p. 24.

20. *Ibid.*, p. 80.

21. David Wise, *The Politics of Lying: Government Deception, Secrecy and Power* (New York: Vantage Press, 1973), as quoted in *Ibid.*, p. 79.

22. President's Committee on Administrative Management, *Administrative Management in the Government of the United States* (Washington, D.C.: U.S. Government Printing Office, 1937).

23. Irving Janis, *Victims of Groupthink: A Psychological Study of Foreign Policy Decisions and Fiascos*, 2nd ed. (Boston: Houghton Mifflin, 1982).

24. John Hart, *The Presidential Branch* (New York: Pergamon Press, 1987), p. 76.

25. *Ibid.*, pp. 81–82.

26. *Ibid.*, pp. 188–190.

27. E. E. Schattschneider, *The Semi-Sovereign People* (New York: Holt, Rinehart & Winston, 1960), pp. 20-46.

28. Edwin M. Yoder, Jr., "Politics Is Obscuring an Historical Constitutional Confrontation," *Washington Post National Weekly Edition* (August 10, 1998), p. 23.

29. *Ibid.*

30. *Ibid.*, p. 22.

chapter nine

Executive-Legislative Relations

Post-Watergate Politics and Public Policy

In the United States the challenge of governing involves, at a minimum, the development of policy coalitions from among separate institutions, the members of which have different constitutionally anchored constituency bases. The challenge of governing *effectively* is for those coalitions to produce policies that forgo marginal, incremental policy changes, and replace them with policy decisions that are coherent, farsighted, and stable. America has had considerable difficulty in accomplishing the latter because the institutions that must cooperate—the president, Congress, the bureaucracy, and often the states—usually harbor different constituency-based views of the public interest.

History reveals that the president and Congress have usually been able to overcome tensions induced by the separation of powers and produce public policies that have been, by and large, appropriate to the problem or condition they were designed to address. Two reasons for this stand out: First, the existence of comparatively strong, well-disciplined political parties for the first 150 years of our constitutional history and, second, the ability of those parties to attract enough voter support to elect a president and a Congress of the same political party. This was generally the case between the time that parties had established themselves as a permanent part of American politics (Andrew Jackson's administration) until the mid-1950s. During that period, only the administrations of Zachary Taylor (1848) and Rutherford B. Hayes (1876) were faced with problems of "divided government." In each of these cases, the newly inaugurated presidents were faced with a House controlled by a majority of the opposition party. In addition, for the first fifty years, the majority party had virtual plenary control over the bureaucracy due to a very strong patronage system, under which the majority party appointed party loyalists to key administrative positions. Bureaucrats had little opportunity to develop a constituency base or client ties that clashed with that of the party in power.

Relations between the president and Congress were not always harmonious during this period, despite the predominance of party government. Congress and presidents of the same party fought over the introduction and expansion of the civil service system in the late nineteenth and early twentieth centuries. Many of President Franklin Roosevelt's late New Deal policy initiatives and administrative reorganization plans, including the infamous court packing plan, were rejected by an overwhelmingly Democratic Congress. Nonetheless, most of the time executive-legislative relations were notably harmonious, bolstered by a high degree of partisan loyalty to party ideology, the availability of a generous amount of presidential patronage power, and the regular existence of a "coat-tails" effect in presidential elections.

During the nation's first 150 years, political parties were able to overcome the intended effects of the separation of powers on national government. During most of that period, the country was rather homogeneous in character. Labor unions were in the formative stages for most of this period. Urbanization and industrialization had not displaced the rustic culture of rural America as the nation's dominant way of life. Religious sects did not regularly play major roles in politics and elections. Court decisions had not yet freed ethnic minorities from legalized racial discrimination in employment and education. In short, economic, cultural, ethnic, and religious forces did not carry enough political weight to invade and dislodge the major parties' ideological hold on their voters. This began to change in the mid-1950s and politics has not been the same since.

The Politics of Divided Government

American national politics, since the mid-1950s, has been significantly impacted by divided government. The century and a half

bias toward unified government was uprooted in the 1950s and replaced by a clear (albeit irregular) pattern of presidential-congressional conflict triggered by each branch being controlled by a different party. Such has been the case for a majority of the time since 1954, usually with the Democrats controlling Congress and Republicans dominating the presidency. This pattern was reversed by the congressional elections of 1994 which placed Republicans in control of both houses of Congress to face-off against a Democratic president, Bill Clinton. The roots of the struggle remain virtually the same, because they are institutional in cast, regardless of which party controls which branch. The politics of party-based cooperation has been replaced by a clear pattern of intensified institutional and partisan conflict between the president and Congress. Policy disputes between the two branches have become a regular part of American national politics and, in effect, one of today's prominent issues of governance.

Politics is fundamentally a struggle for power to control government institutions and control policy decisions produced by those institutions. Accordingly, because they have usually controlled the presidency for the past generation, Republicans have usually championed increased presidential power, and Democrats an increase in Congressional power. This may well change if Democrats continue to control the presidency, and Republicans the Congress.

Once the divided government pattern became clear, each party began to champion the cause of the branch in which it dominated. Republicans have supported such reforms as a presidential item veto, a balanced budget amendment to curb what they consider the reckless habits of a Democratic-dominated Congress, and repeal of the Twenty-Second Amendment, which limits a president to two elected terms in office. In addition to these proposals to amend the Constitution to help the president win his policy disputes with Congress, Republicans have also supported efforts to centralize more power in the Executive Office, or in agencies which have a clear presidential policy bias. The efforts of presidents Nixon and Reagan to both partisanize and strengthen the role of the Office of Management and Budget (OMB) in both budgeting and management are examples of this. Presidents Reagan and Bush instituted broad-scale efforts to have regulations proposed by administrative agencies reviewed by OMB before being officially promulgated. In order to prevent corporations from being saddled with what he thought were unreasonable antipollution regulations, President Bush required that all Environmental Protection Agency (EPA) regulatory proposals be cleared by the President's Council on Competitiveness, an independent agency dedicated to preserving and expanding the competitive edge of American corporations in foreign trade.

When Democrats control the presidency, they too have worked to increase the president's policy leverage. Although Republicans won control of Congress in 1994 for the balance of the century, Democrats have had congressional majorities for most of the divided government era. Under those conditions, the Democrats' focus was on increasing congressional influence in the policy process. In an ironic, but politically understandable, change of strategy, Democrats become suspicious of the expansion of executive authority when Republicans control the presidency. They respond by working to enhance the leverage of Congress under such conditions.

Democratic congresses have succeeded in legislating restrictions on the ability of the president to impound (refuse to spend) funds already appropriated, and have restricted OMB's authority to provide unilateral estimates of federal revenues and outlays without first coordinating such estimates with the Congressional Budget Office (CBO).

CBO is the congressional response to OMB, conducting its own research on budget and financial issues. In addition, congressional Democrats have subjected the president and his staff to "freedom of information" reporting requirements, sunshine laws, codes of ethics standards, and the inquiries conducted by special prosecutors, as was the case in the Iran-Contra episode. By the way of illustrating just how critical is a party's control of an institution to its (the party's) position on how powerful the institution should be, when Democrat Bill Clinton became president, it was the Republicans who championed a special prosecutor as one way to investigate the Clinton family's role in a failed real estate enterprise while he was governor of Arkansas, an incident labeled the Whitewater scandal.

Some of this interparty jockeying for institutional advantage undoubtedly has been beneficial for both public policy and government accountability. In a sense, it has rekindled the spirit and intention of the separation of powers principle. To the extent that it has limited or negated bad decisions because it has forced the exposure of illegal actions or faulty decision making, such as in the Watergate crisis or the Iran-Contra incident, the public has been the beneficiary. Both Democrats and Republicans have employed their House and Senate party majorities to make both houses key institutional forces in the policymaking process. If these institutions were not constitutionally separate, such a game would not be as intense because each party to the conflict could not claim the Constitution as an ally in its crusade. In short, the Constitution encourages a politics of rivalry and confrontation when divided government exists, and often when it doesn't. For example, even though the Republicans were the congressional minority party when the Whitewater episode surfaced, their demand for a special prosecutor was successful primarily because they raised the same sort of question that Democrats did before a special prosecutor was authorized for the Iran-Contra investigation. They argued that comprehensive and fair investigations would be enhanced if conducted by a neutral third party. The prosecutor was appointed. However, this did not deter congressional Republicans from sponsoring a congressional investigation of the incident. Although the official reason cited for the investigation was the congressional right to oversee the bureaucracy, party rivalry undoubtedly played a major role. When the issue of the Democrats' 1996 campaign fund-raising strategies arose in 1997, President Clinton, a Democrat, was the focus of the probe. Again, the Republican-controlled Congress supported a special prosecutor investigation of those allegations against the president. Predictably, the White House opposed it.

Such a cast to executive-legislative politics has a long history. Conflicts between the president and Congress escalated along with the tightening grip that Democrats developed on Congress in the 1960s and 1970s. This grip was especially strong in the House where, until 1994, it has been interrupted only twice, for two-year periods, since the New Deal era. The Democratic hold on the Senate had not been as strong, but still very formidable. Republicans controlled the Senate for a six-year period shortly after World War II, and for another six-year-period stint during the Reagan administration. During these two periods, tensions between the House and Senate increased markedly. Occasional Republican majorities in the Senate did little to convince the Republican Party that Congress was their institutional policy ally. Between 1954 and 1994, if congressional Republicans had been pressed to choose between the presidency or Congress as the institution most likely to reward them with significant policy leverage, they probably would have chosen the presidency. If the post-1994 Republican control of Congress continues, that attitude is likely to change.

The election of Republican majorities in both houses of Congress in 1994 may have hailed the dawn of a new era in both congressional politics and in executive-legislative relations. If a new era is upon us, then the conditions that produced the former dominance by the Democrats must necessarily lose their salience. They may indeed do just that. However, before dismissing them, they should be identified. There are several reasons for the Democratic dominance of Congress for most of the past half-century. First, Republicans held the White House when the Great Depression began, during the serious recession of 1958, and during the Watergate scandal. Voter backlashes to all these events brought heavy Democratic majorities to Congress. Once in control of both houses, the Democrats quickly exploited the advantages of incumbency. Since these Democrats were more populist-oriented than were their Republican counterparts, they worked to patronize their constituents with a long-term and steady barrage of distributive policies. This strategy lured such diverse elements as blacks, labor unions, Jews, environmentalists, feminists, Hispanics, and the urban poor into the Democratic fold. Each of these groups or movements found at least a few congressional Democrats who enthusiastically support its cause.

While such a politics of dependency did not make congressional Democrats a very cohesive block of partisans, it did perpetuate the identification of each of those groups with the Democrats for an extended period. Between 1954 and 1994 voters became accustomed to returning Democrats to Congress. Democrats developed a very appealing bedside manner, and responded to constituent inquiries and needs quickly and effectively. Finally, Republican successes in presidential elections helped Democrats muster a good deal of the protest vote directed against presidential incumbents in off-year elections during that period.

The Democratic advantage in Congress was offset somewhat by Republican dominance of the presidency between 1952 and 1992. Independent voters tend to vote for Republican presidential candidates. The Republicans have been less permeated by factions than have the Democrats, allowing them (the Republicans) to cater more to the opinions of independents and conservative Democrats during election campaigns. The party heterogeneity that helped Democrats maintain control of Congress tended to damage the party's efforts to win the presidency. Democratic presidential candidates must hold the party's diverse group base together during presidential election campaigns, or face certain defeat. This means that Democratic candidates are prone to make conflicting and contradictory statements on issues in order to keep the party unified. This can undercut their credibility. In addition, as the Republican Party turned somewhat to the political right in the 1980s, it adopted policy positions that had a good deal of symbolic appeal to voters. Stressing such objectives as the decentralization of significant national policy power to states and localities, the deregulation of business, and lower income taxes, the Republicans exploited the cultural affinity Americans have always had for limited government and a focus on individual initiative.

Republicans have been advantaged somewhat by Electoral College politics, another constitutional input into the growing conflict between the president and Congress. Each state, regardless of population, has two Electoral College votes reflecting the state's Senate delegation. This provides voters in small-populated states with inflated leverage in presidential elections. The total state electoral vote is equal to the total number of House and Senate members it has, so state population differences are reflected by electoral votes that reflect the size of a state's House delegation. Nonetheless, the Senate electoral element violates the one man–one vote principle to the advantage of the thinly populated states. The smaller states have been, historically, heavily Republican in orientation.

Such an advantage is of little value to Republicans in elections in which the Democratic candidate is more successful than the Republican in appealing to the political mainstream, as was the case with Lyndon Johnson's defeat of Barry Goldwater in 1964. In addition, unpopular events such as Watergate and Gerald Ford's pardon of former president Nixon, or a shaky economy during a Republican incumbency, can bring Democrats to the presidency, as was the case in 1976 and 1992. Consequently, the Republicans did not have as solid a lock on the presidency as the Democrats had on the Congress (especially the House) between 1954 and 1994.

Nonetheless, the political trends in place since the 1950s have encouraged the two major parties to identify their interests with one of the two national policy branches—the Republicans with the presidency, the Democrats with Congress. During most of this period, Republicans have sought to strengthen the power and autonomy of the presidency, and the Democrats have sought to preserve and enlarge congressional power. These trends have served to exacerbate executive-legislative conflict. The separation of powers has provided formal, institution-based platforms that have encouraged each party to use its control of a separate institution in an attempt to increase its leverage over policy decisions. As a result, conflict between the two branches has become more partisan since the mid-1950s. Democrats in Congress have assaulted Republican presidents for the Watergate and Iran-Contra incidents, and for making controversial, political nominations to the Supreme Court in the likes of Robert Bork and Clarence Thomas. Republican presidents, such as Reagan, Nixon, and Bush, regularly denounced the Democratically controlled Congress for wasteful, spendthrift legislation, and policies that (in their opinion) suffocated business with burdensome regulations. In addition, both sides seek other organizational and institutional support for these crusades. Presidents expand their policy staffs and rely on them increasingly for research and advice on both domestic and foreign policy. Presidents "partisanize" agencies such as the Office of Management and Budget (OMB) by converting them from neutral research and management organizations into partisan institutions that speak for, and lobby for, the president's policies. Congress has reacted with legislation such as the War Powers Act (1973), which restricts presidential flexibility in military commitments, and with its own answer to OMB, the Congressional Budget Office (CBO), which carries the congressional case on the budget into battle with OMB and the president. Inherent tensions between the two branches, intended by the separation of powers, have been exacerbated by conflicts between the two parties speaking from power bases they have established in these constituency-separated institutions.

Institutional Conflict and Divided Government

For the first 158 years (1796–1954) of our constitutional history, strong political parties enabled the political system to respond rather effectively to its policy challenges. The same political party controlled both houses of Congress and the presidency 78 percent of the time during this period. Presidents elected to office carried a majority of their party's House and Senate candidates into office 92 percent of the time during this same period.[1] The only presidents who failed to do so were Millard Fillmore, Rutherford Hayes, and Grover Cleveland during his first term. By way

of contrast, in only four of the last eleven presidential elections has this been the case. Since 1954, the same party has controlled the House, Senate, and presidency only 20 percent of the time. This marked change has been accompanied by a marked decline in party voting, and an increase in the number of voters who classify themselves as independents. Split-ticket voting has increased. Insofar as party-based voting on policy issues in Congress is concerned, in 1900 nearly 70 percent of congressional votes reflected majorities of both parties on different sides of the question. By 1984, the figures had declined to 44 percent.[2]

The impact of this on how the national government conducts its policy business has been profound, and it has not developed in a vacuum. The decline in political party influence over executive-legislative relations has occurred in tandem with several other trends which amplify problems introduced by the separation of powers on decision making. Included are the rise of individualized pluralism, the democratization of nominations and elections, a growing impact of television on elections and policy agendas, the rise of candidate-centered campaigns, the virtual entrenchment of legislative incumbency, the growth of the federal bureaucracy as a political force in policymaking, and the tendency for presidents increasingly to seek support for their policy priorities from sources outside the beltway. In essence, the same forces which have triggered these trends have also exacerbated problems of executive-legislative relations. However, since executive-legislative politics reaches its most heated stage near the end of the policy process, public and press criticism of government gridlock is often focused on the impasse between these two institutions, and away from many of the trends cited above.

Separated institutional government as well as divided government has a profound effect on public policy. Separated institutional government has been with us since 1789. It refers to the different constituency- and term-based incentives legislators and presidents bring to their jobs. It affects their ability to cooperate on policy regardless of which party controls each institution. Divided government exacerbates institutional-based conflicts by placing different parties in control of each institution. As the above discussion noted, this has been a more recurrent phenomenon since the 1950s than in the previous forty-year period. It should be stressed that the divided government phenomenon is not an isolated institutional development, but is one that has occurred in tandem with tendencies toward policy fragmentation that have been clearly discernable in government and politics over the past generation or so. This trend has occurred at the very time that political parties have weakened as forces exercising significant discipline over their House and Senate members. This has affected congressional Democrats more than Republicans. For example, President Clinton and House Minority Leader Richard Gephardt were often at odds with each other on such critical policy issues as the NAFTA agreement, designating China as a "most favored nation" trading partner, and welfare reform. Many other House Democrats supported the president on these issues and, in so doing, openly defied the "official" House Democratic party position articulated by Gephardt. After the 1994 Republican congressional sweep, congressional Republicans became more ideologically homogeneous and disciplined than was their party's rank-and-file.

Overall, partisan voting in both houses of Congress has been far more evident since the 1980s than in the previous two decades.[3] Simultaneously, significant power traditionally vested in congressional standing committees has been transferred to committees more concerned with procedural questions, such as the Senate Budget Committee and the House Rules Committee. This shift has allotted House and Senate party leaders more power to mediate and resolve fundamental policy questions than had previously been the case. This institutional partisanship also has affected presidential strategies. The increasing partisanship of OMB, the establishment of the Domestic Council and the Council on Competitiveness, the growing use of fund impoundments, and staff-sponsored efforts to bypass the policy will of Congress in favor of the president's policy perspective (such as the Iran-Contra incident) clearly illustrate this trend.

Of course, partisan voting is very functional to nonincremental policy change and to accountability. However, when partisanship leads to policy gridlock that is encouraged by divided government, then it appears to be the enemy, rather than the ally, of crusades to deal adequately with policy challenges. A brief contrast of the 1993 and 1997 federal budget agreements provides an excellent illustration. Under unified government conditions, President Clinton won the 1993 budget struggle by a very narrow margin, with most Democrats in both houses supporting him. That struggle was noteworthy because the agreement included a significant tax increase. The president made it clear why he thought the tax increase was necessary, and enough Democrats in both houses supported his position to guarantee victory for his plan. Democrats having a majority in both houses, the president's position won.

However, the divided government conditions in 1997 brought about a dramatically different result on the same issue. Faced with strong ideological opposition from the Republican majorities in both houses, the president made major concessions to the Republicans' insistence on spending and tax cuts—matters he wouldn't have to consider so seriously had there been a Democratic majority in Congress. The same year (1997) saw the president strike an agreement with the Republican congressional majority that led to a balanced budget agreement package, to be achieved by the year 2002. Included in the agreement was a capital gains tax cut, an increase in the estate tax exemption, family tax credits for children, an expansion of retirement account privileges, health insurance coverage for children without existing coverage, and tax credits for families with children attending college. It is noteworthy that the balanced budget portion of the agreement was backloaded, so that most of the sacrifices necessary to achieve the goal by 2002 were targeted for the years 2001 and 2002, thereby delaying the painful experience of the austerity necessary to balance the budget by the target date. Fortunately for the president and Congress, as well as the nation, an unprecedented level of economic prosperity, a low interest rate environment, and a unique way of computing available federal revenue that included "borrowable" monies from the Social Security Trust Fund, annual deficits were eliminated for the foreseeable future in 1998. Therefore, the political sacrifice and fiscal austerity that seemed necessary to reach the balanced budget goal by 2002 were not tested. If anything, the campaign against indulgent spending was conveniently postponed until such time that the deficit problem again surfaced. In all likelihood, the new surplus conditions merely postponed the day of reckoning.

The 1997 agreement asked little in the way of sacrifice and yet was portrayed by both President Clinton and the Republican congressional majority as one which would achieve fiscal responsibility, encourage economic growth, take care of the need to help families defray college costs, and provide disadvantaged children with basic health care. A cursory review of the agreement makes it obvious that both the president and Congress were merely postponing difficult long-term policy challenges. It was relatively easy to support legislation that reduced taxes, increased short-term discretionary spending, and asked economic assumptions to do the long-term "heavy lifting." According to economist Robert J. Samuelson, the agreement was reminiscent of what George Orwell defined as "doubletalk" in his novel *1984.* Doubletalk is the act of "holding two contradictory beliefs in one's mind simultaneously, and accepting both of them."[4] According to Samuelson, the agreement's provisions that government spend more and tax less demonstrated "an enormous contempt for the public's intelligence and integrity," offering blatant violations of the "notions of honesty and candor."[5] Samuelson argued that such a law was foolhardy at what, at least in 1997, appeared to be a peak or near peak in the economic cycle. At such a point, the consumer spending triggered by a tax cut poses threats to both deficits and the inflation rate. In sum, sound fiscal policy involves difficult, sacrificial choices between higher taxes and reduced spending. Both President Clinton and the Republican-dominated Congress spurned this inescapable challenge in favor of the "good theater," but bad policy," incorporated into the 1997 agreement.[6] Such a politics was rewarded, at least temporarily, by the favorable economic conditions that prolonged the economic recovery, increased the federal revenue base, and led to a budget surplus in 1998. Samuelson was correct in both his analysis of the risks assumed by the 1997 agreement and the type of politics that led to it. He was wrong in his assessment of how much of an immediate danger such an agreement and such politics posed for the nation.

Moreover, the agreement did little to overcome the influence of pork barrel politics on public policy. Nearly eighty provisions in the agreement provided benefits for fewer than one hundred beneficiaries. Included were tax benefits for draft cider producers in Vermont, a Texas sugar refining company, special business expense deductions for county clerks in Mississippi, special tax privileges for the estate beneficiaries of a deceased Texas business entrepreneur, a provision that permitted American life insurance companies to delay paying taxes on profits accrued from overseas business, and a provision allowing service stations to market gasoline to local governments free of the federal gasoline tax. At the time President Clinton had the option of employing his power under the Line Item Veto Act of 1996 to delete some of these special interest privileges. However, he chose not to do so.

In sum, the divided government conditions during the 1990s encouraged President Clinton to be less rational and more expedient in his approach to policy leadership via the budget. The 1996 election results and the troublesome Lewinsky sex scandal combined to encourage such positioning. With the exception of the public's clear interest in maintaining the solvency of Social Security and Medicare, the president concluded that the electorate itself was rather ambivalent regarding other policy priorities. Lacking the political raw material necessary to succeed in his second term with the same strategy that led to his success with the 1993 budget package, he assumed a "let's make a deal" strategy in 1997 and beyond. Until the Starr report on the Lewinsky episode was made public, Clinton was marginally successful with this approach. A few interbranch agreements were struck. In some fields where agreements were unobtainable, he issued executive orders in an attempt to legitimate part of his programs that were lost due to executive-legislative conflict. He also succeeded in undercutting the political diatribe that had challenged the legitimacy of "big government." While as a candidate he proclaimed that the era of big government was over, the 1996 election showed all too well that the public is very satisfied with a government that is big enough to provide environmental and health protection, work programs, strengthening of family

and community life, and some entitlement programs. Therefore, much of his strategy was to try to refocus the existing resources of government on policy issues that the public had, by its vote, concluded were properly within the purview of government. Of course, such results are not without their costs. Policies tend to be more concessionary and incremental under such conditions, and it is considerably more difficult to hold any one person or party accountable for policy results that are less than adequate. After all, deals struck under these conditions are compromises, and do not represent the original opinion of any party to the issue. Therefore, how can any of them be blamed for a poor decision, since it wasn't their idea in the first place?

When strict divided government prevails, policy impasses popularized as policy gridlock are much more serious than when a president faces a reluctant Congress controlled by his party. In the former case, there is virtually no hope for the party mechanism to bridge the policy gap between the president and Congress because it only links the president to a congressional minority. The congressional majority finds it difficult to accept a president of the other party as its policy leader. This encourages interbranch rivalry and conflict at a time when cooperation is an acknowledged imperative. For the same reason, a Republican president cannot identify with the Democratic congressional majority because that would bolster the Democrats' cause in forthcoming elections. Consequently, all the obstacles to executive-legislative cooperation rooted in constituency and term-length differences mandated by the Constitution that are present during periods of unified government are exacerbated during periods of divided government. The comparatively healthy partisan debates that surface in Congress during periods of unified government tend to escalate into confrontations between the branches of government when party control is divided. Securing the joint consent of the House, Senate, and president to meaningful policies is exceedingly more difficult under these conditions because each party has a stake in discrediting the other, not in cooperating with it. The national policy machine is often immobilized, and neither branch or neither party is solely responsible for it. As a result, the accountability of government to its citizens is lost amid the spectacle of interbranch confrontation.

As discussed, these divided government conditions historically have encouraged pork barrel politics and intensified deficit problems. However, as the nation began its transition to the twenty-first century (1998–1999), the deficit problem was, at least temporarily, decidedly on the wane. In fact, federal government finished Fiscal Year 1998 (September 30, 1998) with the first budgetary surplus in twenty-nine years—a significant $70 billion in the black. Moreover, surpluses were expected to continue for years to come. In his 1999 State of the Union address, President Clinton predicted that surpluses would continue for twenty-five years. Without a doubt, this circumstance was a highly important fiscal watershed, because expanding annual deficits triggered by the Great Society's spending obligations and the Vietnam War had become an annual political expectation for nearly three decades, peaking in 1992 at $290 billion. The deficit problem had become associated with a feared forthcoming decline of the United States as a worldwide economic power. It had forced the national government to borrow heavily and push up interest rates, a condition that affected significantly the ready availability of money for both individuals and corporations. It had augmented the public's skepticism about how able its elected officials were to handle the nation's key policy challenges.

However, the 1998 surplus did not signify a change in the attitudes of politicians about how to represent constituents and how to survive in office. There was no displacement of traditional pork barrel spending politics with a politics of sacrifice. Politicians had not suddenly been won over by a politics of the "rational" that replaced the usual politics of the "expedient." Three factors, two of them related directly to economic prosperity and one related to politics, explain the deficit reprieve of the late 1990s. The first of these can be ascribed to the unprecedented length of the economic recovery that began in the early 1990s. Federal tax revenues increased dramatically as a result of the low-employment and low-inflation environment. Secondly, the Social Security Trust Fund, which collects funds from wage earners and distributes benefits to retirees, began to accumulate more than it was disbursing and, because of that, had developed a $102 billion surplus by late 1998. This development was significant because the federal government, since it borrows from the Trust Fund to support its spending obligations, considers any fund surplus part of its available revenue base. Therefore, the surplus, as welcome as it was, was essentially a mirage. There was no federal bank account containing a $70 billion balance. Had the Social Security figures not been incorporated into the 1998 figures, the federal government would have run a deficit of $32 billion. Therefore, to call such a condition a surplus condition is no doubt good politics, but in essence it was due to the peculiar, although politically advantageous, way the federal government counts its money.

The third contribution to the surplus is a political one. Three key budget agreements between the president and Congress helped considerably. A 1990 budget agreement between President Bush and a Democratic Congress raised some taxes and placed limits on future spending in some key categories. A very controversial 1993 budget agreement between President Clinton and a Democratic Congress raised some taxes and cut spending further. A 1997 budget deal between Clinton and a Republican Congress initiated a plan to maintain a surplus, calculated as just described, for a ten-year period. The 1997 agreement did not involve a tax increase and was struck amidst the prosperous economic conditions noted. Therefore, the expanded revenue base made it relatively easy to agree on a spending plan because few pork barrel projects had to be compromised or sacrificed as a condition for the agreement. The 1990 and 1993 deals were much more controversial because they included tax increases and occurred under much less prosperous economic conditions.

The political landscape between 1969, the last year of a surplus, and 1998 was strewn with a politics of "blame" for growing deficits and a politics of "claim" for the newly enjoyed surplus. As the deficit grew, angry interparty and interbranch arguments over how to corral it became common. In 1984 Democratic presidential candidate Walter Mondale virtually guaranteed his defeat by announcing that he would, if elected, work to increase taxes to help curb the deficit. President George Bush probably destroyed any hope he had for reelection in 1992 by conceding to raise taxes in the 1990 agreement, an agreement that reneged on a pledge he made in 1988 to confront the deficit spending cuts rather than tax increases. A relatively unknown conservative Republican congressman from Georgia, Newt Gingrich, made a name for himself in 1990 by refusing to support the Bush deficit reduction deal because of the tax increase provision. However, when the 1998 surplus arose, the "blame" game was quickly converted to a "claim" game, with each party seeking to claim responsibility for the fiscal turnaround. President Clinton credited the courageous acts of congressional Democrats for the condition, while conservative Republicans, led by House Ways and Means Committee chairman Bill Archer (R–Texas), argued that the fiscally austere attitudes of congres-

sional Republicans were responsible for the welcome reversal of fortune.

Factors encouraging what columnist and author Hedrick Smith has called "blame-game politics" are behind "claim-game politics" as well. According to Smith, divided government offers two options to warring parties operating from two separate institutional perspectives: bipartisan cooperation or partisan confrontations that lead to the blame-game.[7] Bipartisan compromise is difficult to achieve, except during periods of high presidential popularity. When presidents are relatively vulnerable, such as during their second term or when their administrations are impacted by scandal as was President Clinton's second term, partisan divisions grow more acute. This leads to "hardening of the arteries government" whereby parties use the institutional independence of their respective branches as a reason to reject compromise solutions to policy impasses. This was clearly evident during the Reagan years when House Democratic Speaker Tip O'Neill regularly challenged the ideological conservatism of the president when it threatened to undermine policies traditionally supported by congressional Democrats. According to Smith confrontations between the president and Congress during the 100th Congress (1987–1988) were more intense than at any time since the Truman administration.[8] This scenario was repeated during President Clinton's second term when, owing to both his lame duck status and the erosion of his informal authority in the wake of the Lewinsky episode, the congressional Republican majority opposed him at virtually every policy turn, including such issues as how to commit the fiscal windfall growing from the budget surplus, the need for campaign finance reform, and major tobacco reform legislation. According to Smith, "the very fact of divided government invites politicians to play the blame game—to engage in maneuvers which have little chance of implementation but which dramatize their side's virtue and the opposition's villainy. With power politically divided, it is hard for voters to know whom to hold responsible for failure: the president or Congress, Republicans or Democrats. In this situation, the incentives of the power game reward tactical squeeze plays, finger pointing, damage control, and partisan posturing. The temptation is for both sides to protect their sacred cows and gore the other side's oxen."[9] The very same attitudes and strategies go into claim-game posturing, as the political fallout from the 1998 budget surplus suggests.

While the politics of divided government poses serious threats to policy potency, unified government is also plagued by the gridlock syndrome. For that reason, it is advisable to modify, or perhaps broaden, the definition of divided government to incorporate a type of executive-legislative rivalry that is rooted in the separate constitutionally designated missions, terms, and constituencies of each branch. This type of institutional conflict has been present since 1789. The founding fathers had such rivalry in mind when they endorsed the separation of powers–check and balance idea. If different parties control the two branches, this rivalry is certainly aggravated. However, even when control is unified serious rivalries still exist. Consequently, to appreciate the impact of constitutional politics on public policy as manifested by executive-legislative conflict, it is necessary to include the impact not only of divided government as it has been defined traditionally, but also the impact of separate institutional policy perspectives that are rooted in nonparty sources. It is important to do this since the role of the party as a disciplinary force employed to overcome institutional differences has been weakened during the post-Watergate era. President Clinton's struggle to secure the acceptance of the North American Free Trade Agreement (NAFTA) is an excellent illustration of this. In that instance, more

Republicans supported the president than did members of his own party, which controlled both houses of Congress. The national government's response to the major Midwest flood and California earthquake disasters in 1993 and 1994 provide other illustrations. These occurred at the very time the president, as spokesman for both his party and the nation, was stressing the need to cut federal spending to reduce the annual deficit. In the case of the flood relief package congressional Republicans and some conservative Democrats, true to the gridlock politics mentality, argued that the president was just another tax and spend liberal because his assistance package did not propose to fund the relief effort by cutting entitlement programs. In the end, the House and Senate voted overwhelmingly for an amended version of the president's proposal, but not before delaying matters considerably and, in effect, raising doubts in the minds of some Democrats over just how generous the aid package should be in light of the party's commitment to deficit reduction. In the case of the California earthquake, the relief legislation was not subject to as much delay as was the flood relief package, but an almost bizarre act of pork barrel politics had to be appeased before it was formally enacted. In this case, both congressional Republicans and Democrats seized the opportunity to include money for projects in their districts that were totally unrelated to the earthquake disaster. Even states and congressional districts on the East coast received grants for projects that had nothing whatsoever to do with the earthquake. The earthquake's "fiscal tremors" were felt as far east as New York.

President Clinton encountered a similar problem in 1993 with his budget and tax package. All Republicans in both houses announced their opposition to the president's proposal, leaving it up to the Democrats to muster enough party strength to enact it. Since it contained proposals for increased taxes, many Democrats understandably had reservations about how popular it would be with constituents. Facing a very close vote in both houses, especially the Senate, the president complained that gridlock was delaying consideration of his plan. The president's party controlled both houses, but he faced gridlock nonetheless, at least temporarily. It was rooted in a "constituency versus president" dilemma that often confronts congressional Democrats, especially those representing competitive party districts. After making several key concessions, and promising some wavering Democrats generous pork barrel grants, the president prevailed narrowly in both houses. In the Senate, Vice-President Gore had to break a tie vote. In sum, gridlock can be a problem for any president, regardless of which party controls the House and Senate. This is why it is virtually imperative to consider the impact of the separate institution phenomenon as well as the divided government one in examining the impact of executive-legislative relations on public policy.

Institutional Separatism and Divided Government: The Policy Consequences

What are the consequences of the divided government and the separate institutions syndromes on public policy? To what extent is the Constitution at least somewhat responsible? To what degree is constitutional politics responsible for heightening political conflict and impacting heavily on public policy? The following analysis will attempt to shed some light on this trio of questions.

Constrained Government

The Constitution's structure is biased against government activism even under uni-

fied government conditions. Add the more divisive divided government factor and the effect of constitutional structure is amplified. Moreover, it is nearly impossible to register changes in public opinion quickly and accurately within national policymaking institutions because the House, Senate, and president are elected for staggered terms at different times. The House can be captured by a different political party every two years. Since senators serve overlapping six-year terms, and only one-third of the Senate stands for election every two years, it is much more difficult to change party control of the Senate as quickly. Presidents are elected every four years, but because those elections are national in scope, presidential candidates often make different types of appeals to voters than do candidates for House and Senate seats. The result might well be that voters ask different policy pledges from presidential candidates than they (the voters) do from House and Senate contenders. This was the tendency when the Republicans held the presidency and the Democrats both houses of Congress during the 1970s and 1980s. Ronald Reagan, for example, campaigned as a courageous, purposeful helmsman who did not have to be absorbed in policy details, whereas those who ran for Congress at the same time were virtually mandated to be more specific about what they could do for people in their districts or states if elected. In sum, the constitutional requirement for staggered terms of office, plus the constituency differences embodied by each institution, together make it very difficult for all policy actors to experience the same electoral mandates simultaneously.

Given these conditions, it is very difficult for a president and a bicameral legislature to reflect the will of the people accurately at any given time. Even when a president brings party majorities to both houses of Congress through the coat-tail effect, support from his party majority in the House is likely to be temporary and fragile. Even the slightest constituency disenchantment with the president's performance is likely to be registered in party member attitudes, because all House members must stand for reelection every two years. These individuals do not find it difficult to part company with the president if it is in their best political interest to do so. During periods of divided government, there is obviously less partisan incentive for the two branches to cooperate. However, if the public becomes increasingly disenchanted with gridlock, cooperation may well result. However, under these conditions, securing any agreement at all usually is of higher priority than is securing an agreement that adequately addresses the policy issue. There are some exceptions to this tendency. In 1981, President Reagan, a Republican, secured essential support for his tax and spending cut legislation from several members of the Democratic majority in both houses, and this support was secured without the president making many concessions as a prerequisite for Democratic support. However, that support did not continue much beyond Reagan's first year in office, and by the third year the usual divided government interbranch stalemates had become a regular part of the Washington scene, encouraged by a weak economy.

In its 1987 report, the Committee on the Constitutional System (CCS) concluded that the "confrontation, indecision, and deadlock" that are a natural outgrowth of the separation of powers are exacerbated by divided government. Divided government, the Committee observed, leads to "inconsistency, incoherence, and even stagnation in national policy," sometimes even to "nondecisions resulting from frequent deadlocks."[10] The policy gridlock that results from both separate institutional government and divided government does not always result from separate branch and party differences over the generic merits of policy proposals. If that were true, Ameri-

cans would be far more tolerant of gridlock, because it would appear to be a manifestation of the separation of powers–checks and balances principles. However, party rivalries that have affected the relationships between the president and Congress in recent years are rooted in other factors. These separate institutional stages often have been the scene of several "blood and grudge" battles among party partisans over petty, personal issues that have had nothing to do with the intrinsic merits or demerits of policy options. With the media serving as a major catalytic force, consideration of substantive policies are often put on hold while presidents and party factions in Congress fight intensively over whether to confirm Supreme Court nominees such as Robert Bork and Clarence Thomas, whether cabinet nominees should be denied appointment because they did not pay Social Security taxes on wages earned by domestic servants, whether presidential assistants were guilty of criminal acts in sponsoring privately financed aid to anti-Communist forces in Central America, and whether an incumbent president and first lady were guilty of ethical misconduct in a failed real estate venture. To be sure, some of these matters raise serious ethical and legal questions. However, the obsession with them by both the press and ambitious and/or vindictive politicians delays consideration of key policy questions. Furthermore, when presidents are the target of the inquiries, their preoccupation with such issues can undercut their professional reputation, status, ability to use a going public strategy effectively, and, ultimately, their ability to develop meaningful governing policy coalitions. President Reagan experienced such a loss of presidential leverage for an extended period during the Iran-Contra affair. President Clinton often made clear his frustration over how the Whitewater and Lewinsky investigations, and his forced preoccupation with them, had diverted his attention away from such pressing substantive questions as health care and welfare reform. For a time, both presidents, especially Clinton, were seriously diminished in their capacity to pursue their policy agendas as a result of these distracting events.

In Clinton's case, the Starr report on the Lewinsky affair and his subsequent impeachment seriously diminished his ability to apply the moral leverage of the presidency to public affairs. Since the president had not personally lived up to the standards of honesty and sacrifice he had asked from the public to help the nation make the transition to the twenty-first century, any post-Lewinsky efforts to do so were certain to fall on deaf ears. The president's problems were intensified by the divided government conditions he faced in 1998 and 1999. The nation's ultimate fate did not rest on how Congress dealt with the results of the Lewinsky sex and deception scandal, but Clinton's fate most certainly did. However, more important than that are lessons to be drawn from the scandal's effect on the critical role of moral authority for the modern presidency in general and, especially, under conditions of divided government. Presidents can induce others to make sacrifices for national interest in two ways. The first is by applying the constitutional powers of the office vested in it by the country's voters. President Truman could not have removed the popular General Douglas MacArthur from command of the United Nations forces in Korea unless he (the president) had not been constitutionally vested with commander-in-chief authority. However, beyond a president's command responsibilities, his ability to get things done rests on his capability of being influential with others. However, the constitutional blueprint reveals little about what it takes to become an effective president. More important is the ability of presidents to exercise their political skills effectively, have good judgment and a sound

sense of timing, and, perhaps most important, draw on any reservoir of moral authority and trust they are able to build up during the course of their candidacy for, and occupancy of, the office. Abraham Lincoln, Franklin Roosevelt, and Ronald Reagan mastered such a challenge exceedingly well. Bill Clinton did well at times, but sacrificed most of what he had accrued upon the publicity of the Starr report.

The divided government realities Clinton faced in 1998 and 1999 intensified his already weakened leadership position. The Republican leaders in both houses of Congress were quick to criticize his moral behavior. While public opinion polls continually revealed support for him as a president, they also revealed significant doubts about his character. Key congressional Republicans such as then Speaker Newt Gingrich, Trent Lott, Tom Delay, and Orrin Hatch became openly hostile to his legislative initiatives. The support of most of their party members followed. Only months earlier, reacting to Clinton's public popularity and convincing reelection in 1996, these same individuals were noticeably reluctant to openly oppose Clinton on a number of key issues. However, the Lewinsky episode, the Starr report, and his impeachment changed all that. The congressional Republican majority exploited the president's moral leadership vacuum in ways that made many of Clinton's future policy leadership crusades unrewarding ones indeed.

Dependency Politics

Divided and separated government would not impact on policy so greatly were it not for the fact that voters appear to be unable to send Washington a clear message as to what kind of government they want. Voters apply different criteria to presidential and congressional elections and often ask legislators and presidents to support incompatible policy objectives. In a recent treatise on this subject, Harvey C. Mansfield, Jr. argued that elections over the last generation or so have shown voters to be unable to choose between the congressional party (usually the Democrats) and the presidential party (usually a Republican domain).[11] The Democrats in Congress use their positions on key committees and subcommittees to secure incumbency by supporting distributive policies that build up constituent good will. Voters thrive on entitlements, provided each voter gets his or her fair share, and they reward congressional Democrats for it by usually voting to reelect them. Unfortunately, people become accustomed to entitlements, and the result is a culture of dependency of some groups on government entitlement programs. Poor people depend on welfare, workers on Social Security, farmers on price supports and low-interest loans, ethnic minorities on affirmative action programs, and middle-class college-age students on student loans, and so on. This condition undercuts the hope for developing any overall sense of community. This "democratization of dependency" means that the more individuals rely on government for entitlement assistance, the more likely it is that each subsidy recipient will consider the continuance of his or her support to be the most important function of government. Under such conditions, people have little incentive to think of themselves as part of a larger community and act accordingly. They do not forego entitlements for the common good. The reason is eminently logical: Other entitlement dependents don't sacrifice, so why should I/we? To forego assistance unilaterally would handicap a group in the race to claim its "fair" share of the federal largesse.

Historically, Congress has been the institutional bastion of the Democratic Party, and Democrats have used it as a lever to expand force for the systematic, the growth of entitlement policies. Republicans, too, have developed an affinity for entitlements for the same reason. In the past Republicans had the best of both worlds, because they could object to distributive politics as a trend, blame it on the Democratic majority, and profit from the results. Their ascension to majority status in 1994 put a damper on such a strategy. Voters want the president to extricate the country from the very problems created by the politics of dependency. Therefore, recent presidential candidates have preached efficiency, economy, reorganization, the need to rethink and act on new policy priorities, and the need to reduce the burdens of an overly bureaucratic government by restoring individual initiative. These goals are more historically compliant with Republican Party ideology, and that is one reason why Republicans have been more successful in presidential elections in recent decades. However, Democratic presidents, including President Clinton, have been affected by the same imperative. President Clinton's 1992 campaign and many of his budgets had an "incentive" underpinning to them. He focused on a shift from spending more for antipoverty programs to proposals directed at repairing and reinforcing the infrastructure upon which the entire economy depended. Included were an emphasis on economic health and personal security, worker training, technology development, and crime control. The stress was on investments, and programs that would strengthen the family and reduce crime. Republicans complained that the president had invaded their policy turf, and many found it difficult to find differences between themselves and the administration on many key issues, particularly welfare reform and crime control. Clinton was accused of a shrewd political tactic aimed at stealing the other party's "political thunder," and there was undoubtedly some truth to this. However, such a position is also favored by voters, who are simultaneously actuated by both the dependency and nondependency norms.

Consequently, we live with such a contradiction, despite the frustrations that inevitably result from it. Voters like to think, in the abstract, that government's major mission is to encourage individual initiative and protect private rights. They want presidents to champion these causes. However, when politicians make policies, they do so on the assumption that the public interest and the incremental aggregation of entitlements are one and the same. Our historic commitment to a limited government, dedicated to fostering individual initiative, has been replaced by a politics of dependency. It is not surprising that voters as individuals, and political parties as organizations, have developed guilt complexes, unwilling to recognize and/or act on the obvious reality that we can't have it both ways. Until the voters "get it right" and transmit their position unequivocally to both president and Congress, both the separation of powers and its rather devastating stepchild, divided government, will continue to reward the politics of dependency and consequently do battle with a more inclusive notion of the common good.

Demosclerosis

As a condition that seriously threatens to diminish the ability of the political system to respond to the major substantive policy challenges it faces, what journalist Jonathan Rauch has termed "demosclerosis" is not the sole result of executive-legislative conflict in national government.[12] To be sure, the partisanship that has affected, negatively, the ability of the president and Congress to produce effective policies consistently has contributed to demosclerosis. However, in a broader sense executive-legislative conflict serves to register a political malaise that has much deeper roots in the genetic forces of distributive, or dependency, politics.

What is demosclerosis and why is it important? According to Rauch, demosclerosis is a condition which symbolizes government's inability to adapt to changing policy mandates because of its entitlement policy obligations.[13] This results from the institutionalization of dependency politics. Approximately 60 to 75 percent of the federal domestic budget is legally earmarked to support such costly entitlement programs as Social Security, Medicare, welfare, farm price supports, unemployment compensation claims, student loans, and veterans pensions. Two major problems result from this. First, it limits the amount of discretionary money available for new programs. Second, the cost of most of these programs is rapidly escalating. Social Security payments are continually adjusted for inflation. Medicare and Medicaid expenses rise in reaction to the escalating cost of medical care and the inefficient processing of insurance claims.

Demosclerosis is caused by the inability of policymakers to reject the claims of vested interests and constituents who are either responsible for their election for appointment (Congress), or who provide the political support necessary to sustain the policies they administer (bureaucracy). This does not mean that all observers agree on why the political system has allowed demosclerosis to develop. Analysts only agree on the fact that it has developed, that it is the result of the excessive impact of clientism and special interests on government, and that the results are bad. Politicians, like everyone else, are prone to blame other forces or conditions beyond their control to explain policy negatives. In the case of demosclerosis, liberal politicians blame the conservative control of the presidency during the 1980s for the problem, arguing that a marketplace approach to government which eschews the coercion and regulation of the forces of exploitation allows these forces to work their will on public policy. Conservatives counteract with diatribes against liberal political ideology which, they argue, is so dependent on entitlement programs for its sustenance and growth that few, if any, such programs are ever eliminated, irrespective of the obvious need to do so. Some pundits blame the corporate state, with its moneyed elites and effective lobbying campaigns, for the problem. Finally, and most relevant for this discussion, some observers blame the politics of divided and separate institutional government for the condition. These individuals argue that the power devolution that impacted Congress in the mid-1970s encouraged every legislator to use his or her newly found influence to use entitlement programs to build up constituent good will and, hopefully, secure incumbency. The breakdown of political parties as forces of policy discipline accelerated this trend.[14] This development will be discussed in depth later in this chapter.

The Constitution promotes the right of people, acting alone or through groups, to petition the government for policies they believe to be in the public interest, however they define it. The "public interest" is a very subjective concept. It is natural for an individual to equate the public interest with policies that are in his or her best interest. Consequently, if legislators and policy level bureaucrats conclude that distributive policies offer the safest route to securing their careers, they usually support such policies. The vested interests, constituents, and the other targets of entitlement subsidies (such as those on welfare) provide vital political support that helps keep legislators in office and bureaucrats in their jobs. This is why, according to Rauch, demosclerosis may be irreversible. To correct it means that both policymakers and their sources of support must forgo, voluntarily, the advantages and security they have enjoyed due to the politics of dependency.[15]

Ambitious efforts to reverse or stabilize the effects of demosclerosis have been advanced.

Their fate illustrates the depth of the problem. In April 1992 a bipartisan group of senators introduced an alternative budget that placed a cap on many costly entitlement policies. Interest group reaction was instantaneous, negative, and widespread. Groups representing farmers, senior citizens, commodity groups, postal workers, veterans, and education were adamantly opposed, and immediately asked that their programs be exempted from the freeze. The proposal was quickly rejected. This illustrates how influential vested interests have been in converting the law into what might be termed "legalized subsidies" for their causes. Public policies, under such conditions, reward the few at the expense of the many. To adapt Schattschneider's term to the policy process, the bias of the pressure system is backed ultimately by the force of the law. Public policy becomes a "subsidy lock" for well-organized vested interests. Irrelevant and obsolete policies are continued, and new resources are either scarce or unavailable to attack new policy problems. Despite growing citizen dissatisfaction with this state of affairs, that disgust does not translate into a successful assault on the problem of demosclerosis. Voter disenchantment with the system in general does not translate into voting *against* the policymakers who support the politics of dependency and contribute to the demosclerosis problem. Therefore, voters reelect their congressmen and senators because the latter have fulfilled their entitlement obligations to the voter. At the same time, voters complain about the malaise and immobility of the system in general. They can fault the president for a lack of effective leadership, and some can cast protest votes in presidential elections for candidates the likes of John Anderson and Ross Perot. However, such protest candidacies had not, at century's close, garnered much more than 20 percent of the popular vote in any presidential election.

The increasing partisanship of executive-legislative conflict since the 1950s has accelerated the growth of entitlement politics and demosclerosis. As discussed in the previous section, the politics of dependency rises in popularity with a decline in the rewards that accrue from successful efforts of presidents and legislators to share their joint policy obligation responsibly. The ability of policymakers to avoid accountability for the plight of the political system in general, while simultaneously supporting policies that contribute to the demosclerosis problem, is an inevitable by-product of the inability of the president and Congress to overcome the policy malaise rooted in the separation of powers. While constitutional structure has been exploited to further the impact of self-interest government on public policy, it does not, by itself, explain demosclerosis. Structurally fragmented power functions as a catalyst to widen the impact of demosclerosis and to legalize its results. It also makes reform considerably more difficult.

Unsystematic Fiscal Policy

Owing to the unusual, but politically astute, way the federal government keeps its financial books, the existing and projected budget surpluses are, essentially, a mirage. This is because funds borrowed from the Social Security Trust Fund are included in the annual revenue stream. Were this not the case, yearly budget deficits would continue. However, borrowed Social Security funds must be paid back with interest, and that simply adds to the government's debt obligations. Nonetheless, if one accepts such an idiosyncratic accounting strategy, the generation-long annual deficit trend was reversed in 1998 for the foreseeable future. Those facts and projections aside, deficits were a political fact of life for decades preceding the turn of the century. Moreover, they had been far more pronounced during periods of divided government. Furthermore,

there was little indication that the political and institutional facts of life that had encouraged annual deficits had been reversed by the fortunate economic conditions of the 1990s that ultimately led to the surplus. For that reason, a brief examination of the correlation between divided government and budget deficits is in order.

Economists generally agree that annual deficits in excess of 3 percent of the Gross National Product (GNP) are dangerously high.[16] Between the end of World War II and the end of George Bush's presidency, the national government's annual deficits exceeded such a figure on fourteen occasions when different parties controlled the presidency and Congress. During the periods when the same party controlled both institutions, annual deficits fell below the 3 percent figure.

Nobody advocates high deficits in principle. Why, therefore, have they been so common? First, the lock that entitlement policies have on the budget is a major contributing factor. New problems surface constantly and the government must find new sources of funding programs designed to deal with them. If well over half of the budget is obligated to nondiscretionary expenditures, and since raising taxes is very unpopular politically, borrowing money and increasing the national debt is a comparatively painless alternative, at least for the time being. It is relatively painless because the costs of it are passed on to future generations. Second, even in cases where funding for policies is discretionary, the popularity of the politics of dependency makes it highly unlikely that policymakers will have the courage to eliminate or trim popular programs that have helped them build up long-term good will with constituents. Irrespective of the need for new expenditures to address new policy problems, the pork barrel remains an institutionalized part of the political landscape because of its popular distributive character. Third, and most important insofar as the Constitution's contribution is concerned, deficits traditionally have reflected the inability of the president and Congress to fulfill, responsibly, their policy obligations as separate institutions that share the policymaking obligation. Presidents and congresses of the same party have had enough trouble executing this mandate even when divided government is not a factor. When divided government exists, it is much more difficult to build governing coalitions that take budget imbalances seriously. Divided government encourages the opposite. Party rivalry, embellished by divided control of the presidency and Congress, makes executive-legislative consensus on budgets less likely. Furthermore, when divided government puts pressures on deficits, each branch is inclined to blame the other for the problem. Ironically, under these conditions, the more serious the deficit problem, the more fuel it provides for party-based activists to polarize political debates.

Deficits are aggravated by continually increasing revenue and expenditure imbalances and, the 1998 and projected future surpluses aside, history has shown this to be more likely during periods of divided government. Two examples from the Reagan era offer excellent illustrations from both the revenue and expenditure sides. On the revenue side, the Economic Recovery Act of 1981 aggravated the deficit significantly. As usual, the root of the problem was political. Congressional Democrats were very surprised by the conservative gains in the 1980 election. In an attempt to assuage the business community in preparation for the 1982 elections, the Democrats entered into what might be termed a "bidding war" with Congressional Republicans over which party should take credit for the most cuts. The result was a massive tax cut, well beyond what responsible fiscal policy could tolerate. Charles Stewart, in his analysis of the Economic Recovery Act, argues that ap-

proximately 90 percent of federal revenue lost during the 1980s was attributable to revenue shortages introduced by the Act.[17] President Reagan's supply side orientation made it virtually impossible to recoup some of the lost revenue later in the decade, when the serious nature of the law's revenue shortages became apparent. This condition contributed heavily to the near tripling of the national debt during the 1980s.

On the expenditure side, an impasse developed between President Reagan and the Republican congressional minority on the one side, and the congressional Democratic majority on the other, on whether to emphasize defense spending (Reagan) or domestic spending (Democrats). Divided government prevented a victory for either side, defined as one side gaining more expenditures at the expense of the other. According to Matthew McCubbin, the impasse was resolved by employing fundamental game theory. Appropriations for both domestic and defense spending were increased.[18] The impact on the deficit was predictable. It escalated out of control and, coupled with more negative fiscal fallout from the Economic Recovery Act, contributed to tripling the national debt during the 1980s. It is probable that the ideological nature of the conflict between Reagan and the Democrats intensified the effect of divided government on the deficit during this period. However, sometimes it takes an unusual case to illustrate the dangers of a more subtle and corrosive long-term problem.

Due primarily to a peculiar, but politically shrewd, way of computing available revenues, the annual budget deficit was eliminated in 1998. That also was a year of divided government, although institutional control was the reverse of the Reagan years, with Democrats holding the presidency and Republicans the Congress. That year's budget surplus was attributed to increased revenues accruing from a healthy economy, the spending cuts and tax increases produced by the budget agreements of 1993 and 1997, and a long-standing decision to include money borrowed from the Social Security Trust Fund as part of the revenue base. Had the latter not been included as revenue income, the country would still have been incurring a significant annual deficit.

However, although the deficit problem had eased at least temporarily, the divided government and separate institutional politics that have traditionally aggravated the deficit problem remain in place. The type of politics that produced the "game theory" solutions to spending impasses during the Reagan presidency was also illustrated by the 1998 budget agreement (Fiscal Year 1999), approved shortly before the 1998 midterm elections. True to the Reagan experiences, there were no real losers, just winners. President Clinton and the Democrats got major spending commitments for education, a summer jobs program, and a farm relief program. The Republican congressional majority got major commitments for defense, antidrug trafficking, and graduated tax cuts for businesses and the self-employed. The relatively nonpartisan pork barrel was full of constituency-friendly treats that stood to benefit both sides. It was traditional election-year divided government politics. However, the long-term costs could be threatening. Abandoned was the spending ceiling agreed to in the 1997 budget agreement. No existing programs were trimmed back or cut back. The new expenses were to be financed by the new budget surplus, funds the president had originally pledged to commit to refurbishing the Social Security program.

The impact of a large deficit-inflicted national debt on public policy is potentially serious. Large national debts are much like malignancies that go unnoticed for an extended period, only to become of concern after irreparable damage has been done. The most obvious problem is that fiscal red ink handi-

caps government's ability to respond adequately to pressing policy problems. Too much revenue is earmarked to pay interest on money already borrowed. Therefore, despite the fact that the national government began to enjoy an accounting surplus by 1998, it was still plagued by the negative financial fallout of a national debt that then exceeded $4 trillion. The interest payment costs of servicing that amount of debt were projected to remain high for an indeterminate period. Debt-service obligations drain valuable monies from budgets that could best be spent on education, job-training programs, combating poverty and disease, and other pressing problems. In percentage terms, the national budget's debt-service obligations grew from a comparatively acceptable 10 percent in the 1960s to well over 30 percent in the 1990s. This condition severely handicapped the government's ability to address problems such as crime, welfare, poverty, urban infrastructure, medical care, education, and environmental pollution. In sum, the divided government–induced executive-legislative conflict that was so prevalent during the last half of the twentieth century significantly contributed to a staggering national debt that plateaued in 1998. However, even under that comparatively favorable fiscal backdrop, divided government conditions triggered a heated debate between a Democratic president and a Republican congressional majority over how to commit the budget surplus. The politics that helped accelerate the debt problem resurfaced, this time in the form of a "gain" game instead of a "blame" game.

Overboard on Oversight

Legislative oversight includes all congressional efforts to monitor administrative agency decisions to determine how well agencies have complied with both the form and spirit of the law. Officially, oversight efforts seek to make agencies politically accountable and administratively efficient. Unofficially, oversight efforts offer a way for a hostile Congress to embarrass a president, and a way for legislators to ensure that pork barrel largesse or other policy advantages are delivered to constituents and other political beneficiaries with dispatch and without alteration.

Between 1958 and the early 1970s, the height of the institutionalized pluralism era, most oversight efforts involved serious attempts to ensure policy integrity, accountability, and efficiency. Oversight ventures targeted at preserving and expanding consumer rights, exposing possible corporate capture of agency policy missions, problems of the underprivileged, corporate environmental abuses, the cost and availability of health care, and attacks on privacy and civil liberties were led by legislators such as senators William Proxmire, Gaylord Nelson, Warren Magnuson, Philip Hart, and George McGovern and by congressmen such as Henry Waxman, Don Edwards, George Brown, and John Moss. Several of these public interest oversight missions carried over into the 1980s by way of investigations, led by both legislative parties, of the pharmaceutical industry, banking and thrift institutions, and labor unions. During that period several three-member alliances, dedicated to the exposure of citizen interest abuses by corporations, existed between investigative reporters, committee and subcommittee staffs, and several high-profile public interest groups. These alliances helped to uncover malfunctions and abuses and to give them political viability. Investigative journalism and news reporting had not yet been consumed by the scandal fetish.

However, the post-Watergate era's introduction of an individualized pluralism atmosphere to congressional politics also introduced another breed of oversight animal. In contrast to the 1960s oversight focus on making government serve the public better, the approach of the mid-1980s was to use oversight for individual self-promotion, constituency-groveling, and campaign fundraising. Maneuvers to use hearings as a means to attract campaign contributions began in the early 1980s when Democrats had majorities in both houses. It accelerated after the Republicans won control of both chambers in 1994. According to Robert Weissman, by the late 1990s most domestic policy oversight hearings were riveted on partisan-fueled attacks, the harassment of regulatory agencies, and the advancement of a pro-corporate-policy agenda.[19] Since Republicans were in control of both the House and Senate, these were Republican crusades. However, during the early 1990s when a Democratic majority prevailed in both houses, Democratic oversight efforts by no means reflected the "paragon of investigative excellence" that prevailed at mid-century. Owing to the campaign money-raising pressures induced by television-dominated elections, fund-hungry Democrats by that time had noticeably succumbed to corporate special interests.[20] Therefore, the transition from an oversight strategy attempting to ensure that agencies were held accountable to the public interest to one attempting to discredit the role of government when it collides with more restricted political objectives was rooted in fundamental political changes rather than in a shift in congressional party dominance.

Legislative oversight assumes a variety of forms. First, there are hearings on agency budget requests, during which time agencies defend their records and budget requests before the appropriate appropriations subcommittees in both houses. A second type of oversight involves casework. For example, members of Congress regularly ask agencies to investigate and respond to a constituent's complaint about the legitimacy of an action to which he or she, the constituent, has been subjected. Thirdly, there are the more highly publicized, systematic investigations of alleged agency or presidential malfeasances. In these cases, Congress functions much like a grand jury that hears testimony about allegations from both the accusers and the accused. Congressional investigations of Watergate, Iran-Contra, EPA's misuse of "superfund" monies, the HUD scandals, and the Whitewater affair fall generally into this category. In some of these investigations, such as Iran-Contra and Whitewater, parallel inquiries were also conducted by special prosecutors authorized by law to undertake such inquiries. Congress regularly insists on conducting its own inquiries. The official justification for direct legislative intervention is the congressional obligation to hold agencies and presidents accountable. Political motives aside, uncovering the degree to which laws have been, in constitutional terms, "faithfully executed" lends legitimacy to such ventures.

Legislators bring the same political incentives to the oversight challenge as they do to the policymaking challenge. Therefore, the perspectives of different legislators representing different constituencies for differing periods of time all impact on the oversight mandate just as they impact on the legislative mandate. The disaggregated, distributive-based character of American politics, that has been so pronounced since the mid-1970s, has affected not only the ways in which policymakers select and bargain over policy options, but also the ways in which Congress and the bureaucracy interact in oversight transactions. Consequently, the effects of a weak party system and dependency politics have impacted on Congress-bureaucracy relations in much the same way they have on congressional-presidential relations. It is important to remember that the bureaucracy is officially part of the executive branch, but that the existence of specific agencies, their programs, and their budgets is the product of congressional, not presidential, action.

In response to the increasing fragmentation of politics and interbranch mistrust encouraged by divided government, Congress-bureaucracy relations in recent years have been marked by a definitive trend toward congressional "micromanagement" of agency affairs. From the perspective of the president, the executive departments, and the regulatory agencies, Congress has clearly gone overboard on oversight."[21] Congressional micromanagement of the bureaucracy has grown in tandem with the devolution and fragmentation of power in government, the growing weakness of political parties as policy institutions, the appearance of the constant campaign imperative, and the accelerating air of mistrust that has infected executive-legislative relations during the era of divided government. This is by no means a new phenomenon. Nearly a quarter-century before his election to the presidency, the then scholar Woodrow Wilson penned a rather famous essay arguing, in part, that Congress had become too absorbed in the "details of administration."[22] Therefore, while legislative oversight is well rooted in interbranch history, so have been complaints about its tendency to be excessively meddlesome.

Congressional micromanagement of the bureaucracy was a regular irritant to the Clinton administration. The president's ambitious policy agenda and his campaign to "reinvent government" by reforming and reenergizing the bureaucracy produced initiatives that directly threatened to undercut the ties legislators had cultivated with policy-friendly administrators. President Clinton and Vice-President Gore (who directed the reinventing government project) soon discovered that Congress wanted to leave nothing to chance by trusting either the president or his top agency appointees. In contrast to earlier periods of relative executive-legislative harmony and mutual trust, nearly every detail involving the expenditure of appropriated money was being spelled out in the law. Administrators were denied the opportunity to eliminate or delay programs they judged inefficient or ineffective. Administrative innovations were discouraged. As a result, procedural inefficiencies were legislated into nearly every program. For example, when Clinton's Interior Secretary, Bruce Babbitt, assumed office he found a statutory requirement mandating that no fewer than twenty-three Interior Department positions be assigned to the anthracite coal program in Wilkes-Barre, Pennsylvania. Also, the secretary was legally mandated to spend money for projects that were obviously frivolous. An example was a requirement to spend $100,000 in Fiscal Year 1994 to train dogs to sniff out tree snakes.[23] Presumably in reaction to the housing scandals during the Reagan administration, Clinton's HUD Secretary Henry Cisneros found that Congress had disassembled the housing program for the homeless into seven separate programs, each with its own team of congressional watchdogs who were carefully monitoring expenditures in each program area to make sure that money was spent as Congress intended. In addition, during this period it became commonplace for Congress to deny agencies the right to shift money from project to project to improve efficiency. These requirements were mandated by a Democratic Congress during the Bush presidency. President Bush, a Republican, opposed them, but had no choice but to go along. In addition, the growing power of congressional staffs intensified the problem. Since legislators are very dependent upon their staff for advice on how to react to, and vote on, issues that they (the legislators) can't research themselves, committee staffs have filled the vacuum. Very ambitious, and out to make a reputation for themselves quickly, the younger members of some committee staffs have on occasion successfully superimposed their opinions above those of the committee chair on oversight questions.[24]

The public's suspicion of government has become almost cultural. Divided government's policy impact has reinforced this suspicion. Policy success depends as much on sound implementation procedures as it does on the integrity of the theories that underlie them. Administrators are probably just as career conscious as are elected officials. During periods when economy, efficiency, and rational policy planning were not politically as salient as they have been recently, bureaucracies were a low-profile (but nonetheless significant) part of the pluralist culture, and were therefore not prone to work for much more than incremental policy change. However, if presidents such as Reagan and Clinton gain office promising to deal with waste and inefficiency, suddenly these heretofore rather sterile objectives quickly gain momentum as popular political objectives. Administrators are then quick to appreciate the compatibility between working to achieve those objectives and the long-term health of their agencies. However, if they are overburdened by unreasonable legislative micromanagement of their decisions, this can be very difficult to accomplish.

An extended period of unified government would likely help reestablish some of the executive-legislative trust that has become the casualty of the politics of divided government. Micromanagement of the bureaucracy would then likely wane. An increased level of trust is absolutely essential if the president and Congress are to share their joint policy obligations responsibly. By the same token, that trust is very difficult to achieve in an era impacted often by divided government, and one in which politics has moved from a stress on policy issues to a media-encouraged focus on personal character, scandal, and other "newsworthy" subjects.

President Clinton was impacted heavily by this inhospitable environment in 1997 and 1998. He countered with a shrewd use of his executive order powers. He decided to bypass

Congress by issuing executive orders to substitute for many of his stymied legislative proposals. Executive orders are decrees issued by administrators, based on authority granted them by the Constitution or by statute, that have the force of law. President Clinton capitalized on the executive order option as best he could. For example, between 1996 and 1998 he issued executive orders that transformed nearly two million acres of land in Utah into a national monument, established a patient's bill of rights that covered federal employees and individuals covered by Medicare and Medicaid, ordered all federal agencies to develop programs to reduce health and safety risks to children arising from pollution and man-made products, created a program to cross-match federal and state data in an effort to locate deadbeat parents and recover back child support, and ordered federal agencies to cease doing business with companies that had employed nonunion laborers to replace striking workers. The latter order was overturned by federal appellate court.[25] Congress responded in kind by increasing the scope and pace of its micromanagement ventures, beginning with an inquiry into the legality of the president's actions. The result was a series of president-Congress "intimidation wars" that spawned a staggering amount of paperwork as, according to Alexis Simendinger, conservative House Republicans "use(d) their oversight powers to jam the gears of Clinton's bureaucracy."[26] According to Simendinger, a significant negative of these "wars" for government was the "notable degeneration in what is, after all, the fundamental business of government: addressing problems."[27] Nonetheless, this development surprised few, since the 1998 congressional elections were quickly approaching. Each camp needed to make as many precampaign policy points with the public as possible, and they needed to be made straightaway. However, as Thomas E.

Mann noted: "It's a good way for each side to make some headway with the public, but it's the second or third best way of dealing substantively with problems."[28]

Obsession with Scandal

A variation on the oversight theme that has been a regular part of executive-legislative relations during periods of divided government, especially in recent years, has been scandal mongering, or the tendency for the party controlling each branch to invest time and political and financial resources, in an attempt to embarrass the other branch. This is, of course, done at the expense of tending to the country's policy agenda. Watergate, the Iran-Contra affair, the savings and loan scandals, the Whitewater investigation, and the campaign fund-raising inquiry were all illustrative of this trend. Benjamin Ginsberg and Martin Shefter suggest that this is but one variation of "politics by other means" that has affected decision making since the Nixon years, but especially since the Reagan administration.[29] For example, frustrated by their inability to win the presidency, congressional Democrats investigated the activities of Reagan's staff in the Iran-Contra investigation. In a quest to gain control of the House, congressional Republicans brought ethics charges against Speaker Jim Wright and Ways and Means Committee chairman Dan Rostenkowski. Wright resigned his office in wake of the charges against him. Rostenkowski was convicted of misusing House funds and sent to prison.

Other than deflecting legislative attention away from the policy agenda, scandal-mongering has other costs. It increases public pessimism about government, which is already at a historic low. Presidential timidity sets in when it comes to filling key positions in the administration. Afraid of excessive politically motivated scrutiny, talented candidates for appointments sidestep the opportunity to work for a president because some minor indiscretion or poor judgment in their past, might, if exposed, lead to embarrassing investigations that undercut their credibility as public servants. It could be argued that recent nominees for cabinet and staff positions such as John Tower, Anthony Lake, Lany Guanier, and Kimba Wood were rejected or withdrew under political or self-imposed pressure for this reason.

Although cases like this are probably more highly publicized and confrontational during periods of divided government, the separation of powers principle alone can trigger interbranch inquiries during periods of unified government. Majority parties must give credence to minority party causes, because some day party control will shift. Consequently, Mayhew found that there was no major difference in time that Congress spent on investigations of the executive branch during periods of divided government when contrasted with periods of unified government between 1946 and 1990.[30] However, statistics such as these, as well as ones which show that congressional voting along party lines seems to be unaffected by divided or unified government, may not be very meaningful in measuring the impact of party-induced interbranch tension and its impact on policy. This is because statistics do not incorporate a qualitative assessment of how contentious or controversial were the subjects of the investigations or the votes. Unified government does not, of course, do away with factions, and it certainly does not dispense with constitutional factors as causes of executive-legislative conflict.

Scandals occur under conditions of both unified and divided government and, under both conditions, constitutionally mandated conflict between the two branches encourages investigation. The Watergate and Iran-Contra investigations both occurred under divided government conditions and for that reason clearly had political dimensions to them. However, and this cannot be overstressed, each of these inquiries dealt with very profound constitutional questions. When there is a frontal assault on political accountability, or a clear or suspected violation of a constitutional provision or a statute, it is the constitutional obligation of the other branch to respond, politics aside. Consequently, the rate of congressional inquiry into executive affairs remains rather constant irrespective of party-generated interbranch conflict. Factions within parties conflict with each other as easily as do parties with each other. Therefore, legislators who are serious about the constitutional mission of their home branch will dispense with party politics if necessary and defer to the Constitution.[31]

The independent counsel investigation of the Clinton-Lewinsky episode, one that resulted in the president's ultimate impeachment, illustrates just how extensively politics can influence executive-legislative relations in a separated system impacted by divided government. Independent counsel Kenneth Starr's original mandate was to investigate Clinton's possible illegal acts in a scandal-saturated Arkansas land deal while he was serving as governor. Unable to prove illegal presidential involvement in that enterprise, or that the president had used the White House Travel Office for political purposes, or that he was personally involved in his staff's misuse of FBI and CIA personnel files, the investigation finally found what it concluded was creditable evidence that the president had committed perjury and obstructed justice in an attempt to fend off an investigation into his sexual encounters with White House intern Monica Lewinsky. Both Congress and the president were preoccupied with the incident for months and work on major substantive policy issues was virtually put on hold. The reputation of the presidential office as a moral force in American government was compromised significantly. With a scandal-obsessed media serving as a constant catalyst, the Clinton-Lewinsky episode was probably the most glaring example up to that time of the impact of politics on the deterioration of executive-legislative relations during a period of divided government, and it came at what could prove to be a very high price.

Criminalizing Politics

The correlation between divided government and the exploitation of scandal has reached disturbing proportions since the Watergate episode and the passage of the Ethics in Government Act in 1978. That statute authorized the appointment of independent counsels to investigate alleged wrongdoings of executive officials. Officially in pursuit of ethical government through legal action, independent counsels (special prosecutors) have sometimes sponsored investigations that have, in effect, worked against that objective. This trend is so obvious and disturbing that it deserves highlighting as a distinct effect of divided government on politics and, ultimately, on public policy. Briefly stated, divided government in the post-Watergate period has encouraged the criminalizing of politics.[32]

Independent counsels were intended to be engaged as investigatory responses to acknowledged political problems such as the Teapot Dome and Watergate scandals. However, during an era within which campaigns and, ultimately, policy decisions often target the destruction of the political opposition, special investigations by independent counsels can—and have—assumed more of a "search until you find something" mission. In pursuit of a more "ethical" government, the suspicion—or even the possibility—of an illegal act can trigger a prolonged and expensive investigation into suspected illegal behavior. In short, the shortage or absence of evidence to prove an alleged wrongdoing means that

special prosecutors should do all they can to uncover something illegal. In turn, this reality forces the accused into positions in which they must bear up under what at times appear to be enormous financial and psychological pressures. Moreover, the scope of such investigations is not necessarily confined to the original allegation. Special prosecutors can "roam the landscape," so to speak, until they find something that appears to make the accused vulnerable to criminal prosecution. This was clearly the tendency during the Clinton presidency. Clinton appointees such as Richard Holbrooke, Henry Cisneros, Mike Epsy, Alexis Herman, Tony Lake, and Sandy Berger were subjected to investigations over a variety of alleged wrongdoings or conflict-of-interest associations. Of course, the unique target was the president himself who, as the result of a roaming prosecutorial inquiry by independent counsel Kenneth Starr, became only the second president in history to be formally impeached by the House of Representatives. Starr roamed the Clinton political landscape for nearly six years before finding a potentially impeachable Clinton activity. Originally charged with investigating the president and first lady's possible illegal activities in a failed Arkansas land venture (Whitewater), Starr found nothing. He then moved to the Travelgate and Filegate episodes, again finding nothing to implicate the first couple in any wrongdoing. When he discovered that Clinton might have shaded the truth to the point of perjury by concealing the details of a private sexual liaison, Starr dismissed the complete exoneration of Clinton on the charges that originally fueled his six-year investigation of the president as a deck-clearing exercise. The criminalization of politics had, at least to that point in time, reached its zenith.

The Clinton impeachment was the result of the consolidation of a number of post-Watergate political trends and a few developments explainable largely by mere happenstance. The impact of weakened political parties, candidate-centered campaigns almost totally dependent on major corporate contributions, and a media that betrays the public trust by its obsession to make no distinctions between private scandal and political news can have serious political and policy consequences during periods of divided government. Divided government gives warring political factions the opportunity to use the Constitution as a smokescreen to help remake destructive partisanship into a question of constitutional principle, presumably rendering such partisanship more justifiable and therefore more politically acceptable. These adversaries are encouraged to develop strategies and to frame arguments in ways that are clearly compliant with the confessional culture bequeathed to society by television in the post-Watergate period. The media's appetite for real-world soap opera and sensationalism is undeniable. A communications culture that sustains Jerry Springer and Howard Stern is bound to look for offbeat stories in politics and public affairs. While television news shows that featured opinion exchange and argumentation instead of news led the crusade, they were not the only media elements that pounced on the Clinton-Lewinsky story (Monicagate) with all the eagerness of a hunger-ravaged wolf, making it the 1998 version of the O.J. Simpson murder trial. Radio talk shows and newspapers were also active, as were various Internet sites that offered more rumor than confirmed facts.

While the framers expected such questions as impeachment to be affected by politics, their expectation was that such politics would not be triggered by issues involving how judges, administrators, and presidents performed their official governmental responsibilities, not how they conducted their private lives. They also expected that impeachment, while likely to be influenced by partisanship, would not (and should not) be successful unless decisions to impeach incorporated a high degree of bipartisanship. Such assumptions were totally at odds with the politics of personal destruction that dominated American politics at the close of the twentieth century.

The marriage of constitutional politics with the politics of personal destruction reached its most mature and destructive stage with the House of Representatives' impeachment of President Clinton in December of 1998. By the highly partisan floor vote of 228–206 and 221–212, the House approved two articles of impeachment against the president. The first (Article I) alleged that the president provided false and misleading testimony to a grand jury investigating his relationship with White House intern Monica Lewinsky, and the second (officially Article III, since Articles II and IV were not approved) alleged that the president obstructed the administration of justice in Independent Counsel Kenneth Starr's investigation of a sexual harassment suit filed against Clinton by Paula Jones.

With few exceptions, House Republicans concluded that the president was guilty of these offenses and that the nature of the activities under investigation (sexual liaisons and sexual harassment) were of little or no importance to the resolution of the issue. What was important was that the nation's highest law enforcement officer, who had sworn to uphold the Constitution and all public laws enacted in pursuance of it, had in their opinion perjured himself before a grand jury and acted to impede a lawful investigation. These actions, they concluded, met the Constitution's standard of "high crimes and misdemeanors" as a basis for impeachment. All but a few Democrats disagreed, arguing that, while the president's behavior was tawdry and highly offensive, his being devious and perhaps perjurious about sexual liaisons and clearly uncooperative with investigators researching a sexual harassment lawsuit that had already been dismissed (the Jones lawsuit) did not meet the demanding constitutional standards for impeachment. Reacting to what they considered to be the divisive and destructive politics of the era, Democrats argued that the impeachment votes, in effect, amounted to a Republican-sponsored impeachment crusade desperately in search of a "high crime and misdemeanor." The founders, argued the Democrats, intended for impeachment to be considered only in cases involving affairs of state as presidents sought to exercise their official governmental obligations, and not in cases involving the private lives of presidents that had no bearing on the way they performed their official governmental responsibilities.

Therefore, legislators who supported Clinton politically read the Constitution much differently than did his political opponents. It appeared that those who were frustrated by his election and reelection to the presidency sought to undo those elections via the impeachment route. If that was indeed the motivation, the impeachment campaign constituted an assault on the separation of powers principle. It was well known that key House Republicans, including Majority Whip Tom Delay, former Speaker Newt Gingrich, and Majority Floor Leader Richard Army were angry and frustrated with Clinton over not only his deviousness, but also his electoral successes. Many resented his election in 1992 and especially his reelection in 1996. Furthermore, they resented the success the Democrats enjoyed in 1998, an election which saw the presidential party gain House seats (five in 1998) in an off year for the first time in sixty-four years. That Democratic success was such a jolt to the Republican cause that Speaker Newt Gingrich decided to resign not only the House speakership, but also his House seat.

Lending further credibility to the thesis that the impeachment campaign was, first and foremost, a political crusade was the fact that Representative Delay in 1997 had led a campaign to purge, via impeachment, the federal judiciary of three judges who, in his opinion, were too activist on behalf of liberal causes. Legally, judges can be impeached and removed only for cause or being corrupt or negligent in the performance of their official responsibilities. They cannot be removed because their decisions are unpopular. Therefore, it is plausible that the campaign to impeach President Clinton was the next stage of a strategy to employ impeachment or the threat of impeachment to keep officials in rival branches in line with the ideology of the majority congressional party. The ramifications of this trend would, if allowed to continue, likely be serious. If Congress can impose its will on the presidency and judiciary by politically deploying impeachment to temper the impact of the separation of powers on policymaking, it would constitute a direct assault on our system of constitutional government. Impeachment should not be used as a tool to increase the impact of one branch of government on policy and society at the expense of the other two. No doubt conservative Republicans were frustrated by having their agenda blunted by court decisions and splintered by the president. However, to adopt an impeachment strategy as a curative is shortsighted and dangerous. The erosion of the foundation of constitutional government is too great a price to pay for the appeasement of political frustration.

According to the Democrats and many pundits, Republicans were so angry and frustrated over Clinton's electoral and political successes that they reinvigorated the impeachment crusade in retaliation. President Clinton's reckless personal behavior and lack of forthrightness before a grand jury investigating that behavior offered them the opportunity they sought. The president also made himself vulnerable by concluding that the Democrats' success in the 1998 elections would cause Republicans to retreat, rather than to accelerate and intensify the impeachment campaign. Apparently Clinton did not appreciate the fact that House Republicans considered impeachment to be the prerogative of congressional insiders, not an objective that required favorable public opinion to gain legitimacy.

In the more politically polite decades of early- to mid-twentieth-century America, politicians and the media would likely have chosen to ignore or downplay the president's personal indiscretions. However, during the 105th Congress divided government, a scandal-hungry media, an individualized and destructive attitude toward political opponents, and the virtual absence of loyalty to Congress as an institution encouraged Congress's warring factions to use the Constitution as an excuse to leverage their campaigns of inquisition and personal destruction. Suddenly it became politically convenient to make a president's lack of forthrightness before a grand jury over a personal sexual indiscretion qualify as a "high crime and misdemeanor."

In impeaching President Clinton, neither House Republicans nor House Democrats engaged in any serious fact finding. The Republicans merely embraced the prescriptions of Kenneth Starr, and the Democrats challenged both the Starr recommendations and the Republican embracement of them. Debates were often accusatory and comments were frequently cutting. The fact that the public was opposed to impeachment made little difference, especially to Republican zealots, who perceived little political risk in pursuing impeachment. There was good reason for this. While party membership nationwide was rather evenly divided between Republicans and Democrats, House districts had become increasingly less so during the 1980s and 1990s. Regions of the country were becoming

less politically balanced. State legislatures in regions dominated by one of the two major parties were creating more politically safe congressional districts. Campaign appeals to independent voters and moderates of the opposition party were becoming less critical to determining the outcome of House elections. An increasing number of House members were running for reelection without opposition. Fewer middle-of-the-road candidates were running for office, and the political cast of Congress was obviously becoming more polarized. The spirit of bipartisanship that was clearly present during the Nixon impeachment debates twenty-five years earlier was nowhere to be found in the Clinton impeachment debates. Under these conditions, it is not surprising that the punishment hoisted on President Clinton by a sharply divided House did not, to most Americans, seem to fit the crime.

From a historical perspective, the punishment demanded for Clinton was clearly disproportionate to the crime. The president's indiscretions, as offensive as they were, did not involve matters of government. They did not, as did the Watergate incident, involve using the CIA and FBI to destroy political opposition or the payment of hush money to burglars who illegally invaded the opposition party's office. They did not involve, as did the Iran-Contra incident, an effort by members of the president's staff to ignore congressionally imposed restrictions on the president's foreign policy options. They did not involve, as did President Lyndon Johnson's decisions during the Vietnam War, attempts to mislead the American public on bombing strategies and enemy troop strength while simultaneously committing more American troops to combat. In short, Clinton's indiscretions did not involve affairs of state. They were personal and private, not governmental and public. What Clinton did was clearly wrong and he should have been held accountable for his behavior, but it did not justify removing him from office. The president's past sexual indiscretions were well known to the public, and he was elected twice to the presidency in spite of them. The House's attempt to undo those elections over a matter that did not involve Clinton's performance of his official constitutional responsibilities as president was a direct affront to the body politic.

However, during an era of individualized pluralism within which a scandal-hungry media encourages candidates and officeholders to search out the unsavory and use it to politically destroy the opposition, Clinton's attempt to hedge the facts when faced with a special prosecutor's investigation of his private life offered his impeachment hungry opponents the opportunity they sought to pursue the investigation against him. A politics of personal destruction allows no room for the reasoned debate that had traditionally contributed to congressional integrity. Neither Republicans nor Democrats on the House Judiciary Committee deliberated with each other in the classical sense of the term when debating the impeachment issue. Instead, party members on each side accused the other of being either excessively political or too geared toward the political assassination of a president of the opposite party.

President Clinton's impeachment allowed divided government to provide the structural stages upon which the politics of destruction escalated to an unprecedented level in American politics. A president's alleged strategy to cover up the details of his sex life before a grand jury had suddenly become the basis for a successful impeachment crusade. The attack/counterattack tactics of the contemporary political campaign had become an appropriate way to govern. President Clinton's impeachment was one of the most serious examples of the marriage of destructive politics with destructive government. Destructive politics had become prosecutorial politics, and it

had progressed to the highest reaches of national government with yet to be determined, but potentially dangerous, consequences both for the presidency as a policy force and for the separation of powers as an instrument of policy balance.

The Constitution was constantly employed as an ally by those advocating Clinton's impeachment. First, the Constitution became a strategically convenient constituency substitute for public opinion. In effect, impeachment advocates argued it was their constitutional duty to impeach Clinton in light of the criminal acts he had allegedly committed, public opinion to the contrary notwithstanding. According to this rationale, the constitutional constituency obligation is superior to the political constituency obligation. Second, they exploited the fluidity of the Constitution's description of impeachable offenses. The framers did not specifically define "high crimes and misdemeanors" in either the Constitution or the *Federalist Papers*. Most assuredly, however, they meant crimes against the state and not such matters as alleged attempts by presidents to conceal the details of a sexual relationship before a grand jury or to encourage others to do the same. If such allegations could be proved, this behavior might well subject a person to indictment and a possible prosecution in a court of law, but it is not the type of act that should remove a twice-elected president from office. Third, House impeachment advocates exploited bicameralism (two-house legislature) to be more aggressive in their pursuit of Clinton. Presumably, most Republicans expected the Senate to refuse to convict Clinton on the impeachment charges by the required two-thirds majority. Therefore, they could consider the impeachment decision to be the highest level of rebuke short of removal from office. Presumably, since most Republicans did not want Vice-President Al Gore to assume the presidency and then run as an incumbent in the

2000 election, formal impeachment of Clinton without Senate conviction was a reasonable alternative. Fourth, the fact that elections are constitutionally mandated several weeks before a new Congress assumes office, the time lag between the November 1998 elections and the beginning of the 106th Congress in January 1999 allowed the impeachment act to be formalized by a lame duck Congress—one that contained many impeachment supporters who either were not reelected or were retiring. These lame ducks would not be present to vote for impeachment once a more pro-Clinton 106th Congress was sworn in. Finally, by disallowing a vote on censuring the president as a substitute for impeachment, ostensibly because the Constitution did not offer censure as an alternative, the House Republican majority was using it in a most partisan way. The result of such a strategy was to prevent the consideration of an alternative supported by nearly all congressional Democrats, many moderate Republicans, and a clear majority of the American people. In effect, what the Constitution *did not* specifically permit (but also did not prohibit) was employed as a rationale to justify minority rule.

The policy consequences of the Clinton impeachment—indeed the criminalization trend in general—are potentially significant. The Constitution's framers decreed a single executive so that executive accountability could be guaranteed. However, when that individual is subject to a criminal inquiry for actions that have nothing to do with his or her performance as a policy leader and administrator, the presidency's position within the constitutional balance of powers is weakened. Moreover, it is weakened by a legally sanctioned assault on its authority by the efforts of another constitutionally co-equal branch. Justice Antonin Scalia underscored his concern for this possibility as the lone dissenter in a 1988 Supreme Court case that upheld the in-

dependent counsel idea. Politically motivated criminal investigations can debilitate a president. The disposition to relegate difficult issues to independent and unaccountable forces, such as special prosecutors, invites not only the criminalizing of politics, but also the de-democratization of government. The predatory political forces that exploit tabloid journalism to assault the integrity of an independent branch of government can undo what the framers labored so diligently to guarantee.

The costs of such trends are potentially destructive. Converting issue inquiries into criminal investigations diverts the political system from dealing with the causes of and cures for problems into a quest for uncovering evidence to determine just how unethical were the alleged perpetrators of the problem. Congressional treatment of the campaign finance issue during the 105th Congress provided another excellent example of this trend. On another front, the criminalizing of politics compromises the privacy and personal lives of officeholders. It increases public cynicism toward government. It discourages the willing and talented from entering public service. It often victimizes the obviously innocent. Finally, it undermines the role of the necessary loyal opposition in our democracy. The party out of power provides a service to the party in power and to the public in general by being a constructive critic of the majority party's policies. However, when both sides seek to criminalize, instead of constructively criticize, the actions of the opposition (including the private lives of its leaders), the value of the loyal opposition to a healthy, functioning democracy is lost. Free the legal process to find criminals and it will eventually find them. However, this is not what effective democratic government needs. It needs opponents that tell it when its policies are wrong and why they are wrong. The framers response to the democratic challenge was a political structure of balanced, competing forces answerable ultimately to the people. The criminalizing of politics fundamentally undermines that objective.[33]

Micromanagement and the Pork Barrel

The president's managerial capabilities were increased by both statutes and executive orders between 1921 and 1939. Shortly after World War II, under divided government conditions, Congress attempted to recover some of its influence over administrative decisions by passing four laws, each of which, in varying degrees, permitted congressional invasion of administrative affairs on behalf of constituents. The Administrative Procedure Act of 1946 required agencies to publish and circulate the contents of executive orders they proposed to issue for a thirty-day period prior to the official issuance of the orders. This permitted parties affected by the proposed order to inquire as to its specific application and, if deemed necessary, protest the proposed change. The Legislative Reorganization Act of 1946 reorganized and reduced the number of House and Senate standing committees so their jurisdiction would be more closely synchronized with the policy responsibilities of executive agencies, established what is now the Legislative Reference Service of the Library of Congress to conduct policy research for Congress independent of the executive branch, and increased and professionalized congressional staffs in order to make Congress less dependent on administrative agencies for information. The Tort Claims Act of 1946 made executive agencies subject to civil suits instigated by citizens claiming they were unjustifiably harmed by agency decisions. Finally, the Employment Act of 1946 created an executive staff—the Council of Economic Advisors—to advise the president on economic issues, and officially committed the federal government to policies that promoted full employment and economic stability.

Each of these statutes enhanced the potential for legislators to intervene in administrative affairs on behalf of constituents. The Administrative Procedure Act offered legislators and their affected constituents the opportunity to exploit rules procedures for pork barrel purposes. The Legislative Reorganization Act made it possible for legislators to use staff resources to monitor the implementation of pork barrel programs. The Employment Act was used to justify the expenditure of federal funds to create employment opportunities in states and congressional districts. Finally, the Tort Claims Act offered opportunities for legislators to press agencies to address constituent complaints over their alleged unfair treatment. The net effect of these laws was to give Congress the legal right and political clout to intervene in administration to create and monitor the implementation of pork barrel programs.

This right was ritualized over the ensuing half-century, becoming a key ingredient in government efforts to employ public spending to stabilize the economy and encourage economic growth. Opportunities for pork barrel spending have grown in tandem with the expanding obligations of government to provide economic, medical, and physical protection for its citizens. The more money government spends for defense, highways, community facilities, office buildings, and medical facilities, the more opportunities there are for some of those decisions to be motivated primarily by pork barrel considerations. Of course, most of these decisions are a total waste of the taxpayer's money and exist only because they pump money into a legislator's district. Moreover, they are little influenced by political party considerations, being fair game for any legislator who can work the system to his or her constituency's advantage. To be sure, they do reflect presidential-congressional differences, but these differences are rooted in the different institutional perspectives of the two branches mandated by the separation of powers, not in the partisan differences that often divide them during periods of divided government.

Discordant Foreign Policy

Foreign policies and the military policies to support them are most effective if the public and its governing institutions are united behind a single strategy or course of action. This has occasionally been the case, most notably during the two world wars. In contrast, the public, Congress, and the president were sharply divided over how the United States should have responded to the Korean and Vietnam conflicts. Those divisions may well have compromised the ability of the United States to accomplish its military objectives in both conflicts. The end of the Cold War brought with it the problem of how to deal with military and political stabilization problems in countries such as Kosovo, Bosnia, and Somalia. The president's decision to commit U.S. troops in some of these cases was met with more than a little skepticism by both the public and Congress. Similar challenges in the future are a virtual certainty.

Policies, both domestic and foreign, are more likely to address the conditions they seek to change if they are the product of serious debate and discussion. If they become the subject of politically inspired interbranch "grudge matches" or provide individuals or groups the opportunity to avoid responsibility for a decision gone wrong, then they can trigger or reinforce dissension within institutions and augment further the public's growing disenchantment with government. Unfortunately, many post–World War II foreign and military policy ventures have been impacted negatively by such factors. The structural by-products of the Constitution have played no

small role in encouraging such a state of affairs. President Truman's effort to unite the American public behind the allied effort in Korea was hampered by the support by some congressional Republicans of General MacArthur's recommendation to pursue North Korean troops beyond the Yalu River and into Manchuria. Such support encouraged MacArthur to oppose the president publicly, a move that contributed to Truman's dismissing him as commander of the U.N. forces. Negative public reaction to that decision clearly handicapped Truman's ability to coordinate the U.N. effort for the balance of his term in office.

Divided government conditions, with a Democratic president facing a Republican Congress, encouraged all parties to the dispute into rigid, publicly pronounced positions. Although President Lyndon Johnson did not face divided government problems as he attempted to direct American efforts in the Vietnam War, he did face congressional (and public) opposition that was aggravated by the political by-products of the separation of powers. As representatives of a growing number of Americans who were becoming impatient with American frustrations in the war, congressional opponents of the war, both Republican and (especially) Democrat, used their structurally independent institutions (House and Senate) to represent a frustrated public in opposition to the president's continuing commitment of more troops to the conflict. Although it will never be known how much such internal dissent handicapped the president's efforts, there is little question that their awareness of the conflict contributed to the resolve of the North Vietnamese and the Viet Cong. President Reagan experienced the same sort of frustration in Nicaragua in the mid-1980s, but he, unlike Johnson, faced divided government problems. Had the executive-legislative situation been unified, it is likely that the president's staff would have been as prone to sponsor a covert effort to sell arms to Iran and to use the profits to support the Contra rebels in Nicaragua.

Senators holding key positions on congressional committees can use those positions to leverage their cases in support of, and in opposition to, presidential nominations to key ambassadorships and other critical foreign policy positions. President Clinton's nomination of Anthony Lake to be director of the Central Intelligence Agency met with such heated opposition from key Senate Republicans that, rather than face the stress and potential costs to himself and his family of a prolonged altercation, Lake asked the president to withdraw the nomination. Clinton's nomination of Republican William Weld to be ambassador to Mexico was so intensely opposed by Senate Foreign Relations Committee chairman Jesse Helms that he refused to schedule hearings on the nomination. Both these nominations were submitted during divided government conditions, something that can occur only under a separation of powers framework. Had Clinton been favored with unified government conditions, it is likely that neither nomination would have encountered serious difficulty.

The text of the Constitution apportions foreign policy powers to the president and Congress only in general terms. It intermixes responsibilities without specifying precise boundaries. The president is constitutionally endowed with executive responsibilities, but the dimensions and limits of that power are not clearly delineated. The president is specified as commander-in-chief of the armed forces, but Congress has the power to declare war and to appropriate money to support American efforts in all types of conflict, be they declared or undeclared. The president is empowered to negotiate treaties, but only after two-thirds of the senators present and voting on the agreement approve it officially. The president recommends foreign policy

initiatives, but only Congress can legitimate them. The president can veto congressional acts that "regulate commerce with foreign nations," despite the fact that Congress is charged by the Constitution to make those laws. Only the president's power to recognize foreign governments through his authority to "receive ambassadors" stands detached as a constitutional grant of unilateral authority in foreign policy. Add the separation of powers condition to these authority divergences and policy ambiguities and the roots of foreign policy conflict become apparent. As Edward Corwin once observed, the Constitution was (and remains) an "invitation to struggle" for command over foreign policy.[34]

Occasionally these struggles have resulted in each branch employing its constitutional prerogatives in an effort to control the influence of the other in foreign policy. Arguing that it is within their inherent prerogative as the nation's chief executive and chief diplomat, presidents have regularly negotiated executive agreements with foreign governments. Many of these agreements have been treaty-level in significance, but they are not, as are treaties, sent to the Senate for approval. In an attempt to eliminate President Eisenhower's use of executive agreements as a means of bypassing the constitutional requirement for Senate approval of treaties, Senator John Bricker proposed a constitutional amendment that would have invalidated all such agreements that would have been unconstitutional if enacted as ordinary law. The proposal failed to secure the required Senate approval for submission to the states. However, the Case Act of 1972 required that the president transmit to the Senate the text of all executive agreements within sixty days of their negotiation. The Senate was not provided veto authority over the agreements, but the expectation was that the requirement would encourage the president to consider the Senate's position as he negotiated the agreements. Finally, in 1973 and over President Nixon's veto, Congress enacted the War Powers Resolution which attempted to clarify the roles of the president and Congress in the deployment of U.S. troops to combat in situations where war is not declared officially. The president is required in all but the most critical and secretive situations to report his intent to Congress within forty-eight hours of the official commitment. The deployment is to terminate within sixty days unless Congress declares war, specifically authorizes the continued use of the forces, or extends the period of deployment by resolution. If, at any time during the sixty-day period, Congress votes to terminate the deployment, the president must remove the troops. Presidents, regardless of party, argue that the resolution constitutes an unconstitutional invasion into the president's foreign policy prerogatives.

In addition to the foreign policy struggles that have been virtually invited by constitutional ambiguity, the Constitution encourages foreign policy discontinuity by its provisions for fixed, overlapping, calendar elections for the House, Senate, and president. In fact, calendar elections impact heavily on both domestic and foreign policy. On the domestic side, calendar elections feed the constant campaign mentality, they invite money to play an increasingly larger role in determining who wins office, and they significantly influence the ways in which legislators determine issue saliency. However, calendar elections also impact on foreign policy. They provide foreign adversaries the opportunity to annoy us when we are most susceptible. The protracted campaigns that often lead to divided government invite the nation's antagonists, and even our own government, to make hasty and ill-considered decisions. As a presidential candidate in 1960, John F. Kennedy complained that the Eisenhower administration had done little or nothing to support efforts by insurgent Cubans to overthrow Fidel Castro. However, unknown to Kennedy, President Eisenhower had directed the Central Intelligence Agency (CIA) to develop a plan to help the insurgent efforts. Once elected, Kennedy was presented with the CIA plan and ordered it executed, virtually without critical assessment by him or his advisors. The result was the infamous failure at the Bay of Pigs, an event which triggered a public apology by the president. In commenting on the aftermath of the Bay of Pigs humiliation, Peter Wyden observed that "if Kennedy had not been thoroughly defeated by Castro [at the Bay of Pigs] Nikita Khrushchev almost certainly would not have dared to precipitate the Cuban Missile Crisis of 1962," an event which one former CIA director argued brought the world "close to Armageddon."[35] That may be an exaggeration. However, the United States' cooperation in an effort to topple a foreign regime and exterminate its leader should be examined very carefully before its initiation. The Bay of Pigs invasion, with those very objectives, was not such an event. It was planned and advocated by very few individuals during a presidential election campaign during which the candidates, especially Kennedy, made it a political puppet.

It could be argued that the continuation of the U.S. military role in Vietnam after the 1968 presidential election was the result, at least in part, of the efforts of an army general to use a preelection halt in the bombing of North Vietnam to escalate ground conflict in an effort to give the incoming president no alternative but to continue the war by sustaining the U.S. troop commitment. After President Johnson's November 1 decision to suspend the bombing, the U.S. military command in South Vietnam, commanded by General Creighton W. Abrams, inaugurated a policy of "patrolling more aggressively" and "engaging the enemy more frequently than before." CBS News reported on March 7, 1969 that Abrams had capitalized on the period between the election and President Nixon's inauguration to intensify the fighting so that Nixon would have no choice but to sustain the ground effort and, in effect, the war itself.[36]

All policies, including foreign policies, that are advocated and implemented by both the president and Congress are greatly influenced by elections and those forces that control the results of elections. Consequently, the constitutional requirement for periodic calendar elections plays a crucial role in determining both the nature of policies advocated and the timing of their discussion. The types of foreign policies supported by both the president and Congress, and their conflict over them, are heavily influenced by the electoral forces that operate on each of them. This has always been the case, but it has taken on added importance in recent years due to the impact of communications technology on the reporting of foreign events and the American public's reaction to them. Wars, riots, famines, natural disasters, economic happenings, major speeches, and negotiations among world leaders attempting to resolve a variety of problems are all brought directly and virtually instantaneously into our living rooms via television. Americans react and their elected leaders listen. In addition, cross-national differences in the cost of labor and availability of technology to increase production capacity together have created a true international economy from separate national economies whose successes and fortunes formerly rested with forces, both political and economic, within their own borders. Many foreign policies are indeed now intermestic in flavor, in that they impact heavily on the internal health of a nation and its citizens. This growing inseparability of domestic and foreign policy issues means that citizens in general will have personal stakes in the foreign policy positions assumed by their governments. Public opinion and calendar elections will grow as key factors in determining both

the development and implementation of American foreign and military policy.

The Constitution as Solution

One of the more ironic ways in which constitutional politics affects executive-legislative relations is its encouragement of president-Congress debates over the wisdom of formally amending the Constitution to deal with policy deadlock. In recent years, the debates over formal constitutional correctives have been pursued on two major fronts. One of these was a proposal to require annual balanced budgets. The other provided for congressional term limits.

The purpose of the proposed balanced budget amendment was twofold: First, the Constitution would take care of what Congress lacks the courage to do on its own. Second, it would give legislators an excuse for not succumbing entirely to the politics of dependency. Entitlements would have to be sacrificed or curtailed because such action would be necessary to achieve a balanced budget. As unpopular as many policy decisions might be under such a scenario, Congress would not be blamed. The Constitution would become the scapegoat. As formulated during the final months of the Bush administration and the early months of the Clinton administration, the brief, three-hundred-word balanced budget amendment did not actually require any spending cuts nor did it specifically call for a balanced budget. Instead it mandated a three-fifths vote of both houses to approve a deficit budget. It was very popular politically. Public opinion polls showed overwhelming support for the proposal. However, people were much less enthusiastic if it meant an increase in the taxes and/or cuts in their entitlements. Therefore, its main advantage to policymakers was more in what it symbolized than in what it offered.

If a balanced budget amendment were ratified after gaining the approval of two-thirds of both houses of Congress and ratification by three-fourths of the states, its popularity would probably evaporate rather quickly. Politicians could no longer portray themselves as fiscal conservatives by voting for the proposed amendment, expecting it to be rejected by votes of the full House and/or Senate, and then proceed to contribute to the deficit problem by supporting generous fundings for entitlement programs. In sum, the balanced budget proposal is of more value to policymakers as a proposal than it is as a constitutional fact of life.

The amendment's fate in 1994 illustrated this form of constitutional politics very well. The proposal fell four votes short of the necessary two-thirds vote it needed for approval in the Senate. Delighted with the Senate results, House members voted overwhelmingly to approve the amendment, knowing that there was no danger whatsoever of its being submitted to the states for approval in 1994. House party leaders, especially the Democrats, were very concerned about the long-term effects of such overwhelming approval because it might well establish a precedent from which members could not retreat the next time the proposal was introduced in Congress.

Should it ever become a part of the Constitution, a balanced budget amendment would likely foster heated debates between liberals and conservatives over who should pay the price for the policy austerity that would inevitably result. Liberals would argue that it strengthens the case for higher taxes and more defense spending cuts. Conservatives would argue that balance should be achieved through major cuts in entitlement spending. This would likely increase the effects of gridlock on the policy process. Also, it would likely bring the courts increasingly into the policy process, as they would likely be called on to resolve many gridlock disputes by judicial action. This is precisely why presidents and legislators prefer to debate such a proposal more than they want to face up to the policy implications of its ratification.

The proposal for congressional term limits is, for obvious reasons, much less popular in Congress. In contrast to the balanced budget proposal, which seeks a constitutional curative for the unwillingness of legislators to match revenues with expenditures voluntarily, an amendment that would limit House members to six two-year terms and senators to two six-year terms hopes to refocus legislators' incentives away from the pork barrel and toward the common good. The goal is á Congress of "citizen legislators" instead of careerists. If House and Senate members served a maximum of twelve years, so goes the argument, they would be more inclined to govern in the public interest than to concentrate on placating constituents with more and more entitlement monies.

In theory, term limitations can be imposed by statute within states. In several states, voters have approved initiatives which subject state and local officials as well as congresspersons and senators to term limitations. Governors in thirty-seven states, state legislators in sixteen states, and members of Congress in fifteen states were so affected in 1993. More than a few of these actions have been subjected to court challenges. The sponsors argue that it is unconstitutional to impose qualifications for office beyond those of citizenship, age, and state residency as provided in the Constitution. The courts in most states have agreed, and so it appears, that term limitations, if they are to influence legislative decision making in any significant way, will have to be mandated by the constitution.

The term limit movement is a citizen-initiated movement. Voters overwhelmingly favor term limits, and this makes it difficult for legislators to oppose the idea in principle.

Legislators argue that the most effective strike that can be delivered against the repeated re-election of legislators is for voters to reject incumbents at the polls. Voters tend not to do that. Incumbency percentages have reached an all-time high in recent years, with better than 90 percent of all House and Senate members repeatedly returned to office. In short, this is another example of the double standard that voters apply to both policymakers and the policies they produce. Voters reject the policy trends of recent years and the type of politics that produced it. On the other hand, they are rather comfortable with how well their own senators and representatives work for them. Senators and representatives know this and, accordingly, are very content to throw the initiative back into the protestors' ballpark and argue that official voter rejection is the clearest, most flexible, adaptive, and democratic way of dealing with the term limit issue.

There are other practical reasons to oppose term limits. Term limits can compromise outright the role of experience and time perspectives that is very crucial to understanding the long-term implications of many policy proposals. Many legislators with considerable seniority have such a lock on reelection that they can afford to cast votes on policies that are unpopular with their constituents. Term limits might also make legislators more sensitive to short-term political needs than they are under the current system. Since legislators, under such a system, would have a comparatively short time frame within which to make their policy "mark," they would likely show little inclination to rise above short-term political pressures and vote their conscience. The judgment and caution that are often brought to bear on policy issues currently might well be displaced in favor of an even greater tendency for poll-driven government. It is this sort of instantaneous registration of public opinion on public policy that the au-

thors of the Constitution sought to avoid with the check and balance system. If Congress needs anything today, it needs the opportunity to build on systems of trust that have developed between and among legislators, regardless of party, over the years. These sorts of relationships are the foundation for far-sighted public policies that suppress the emotion-laden, intense political pressures and resentments of the moment in favor of policies that might make better sense long term. We do not have nearly enough of this in today's policy process, and we have lost much of it in the past half-century, but it is likely that there would be virtually none if the Constitution were amended to impose term limits on members of Congress.

Another proposed amendment proposal became so popular with congressional Republicans that they, along with many Democrats, in 1996 chose the legislative, instead of the constitutional, route to change. The Line Item Veto Act (P.L. 104–130) for the first time in history gave the president the right to veto specific items in a bill without vetoing the entire bill. Directed specifically at spending items, the president's authority was more constricted than that of governors in forty-three of the fifty states who had state constitutionally endowed authority to veto sections of all types of legislation. The presidential version of the item veto in the 1996 law was, in essence, basically an expansion of his authority to rescind appropriated funds, a power presidents have usually had since the early twentieth century. According to the act, presidents could sign spending bills and then, within five days, veto specific items, including new or expanded entitlement provisions, tax breaks that target one hundred or fewer individuals, discretionary spending authority, and new direct spending.

President Clinton used his new-found statutory prerogative sparingly in the months following its passage, but more regularly in

1997 and 1998, eliminating over $87 million in excess spending in 1997 alone. However, in June 1998 the Supreme Court by a vote of six to three declared the Line Item Veto Act of 1996 unconstitutional. The court majority did not contend that the law was a strict violation of the separation of powers principle. Instead, they argued that it contradicted the specific constitutional procedures for the exercise of the veto power. More specifically, the Constitution did not authorize the president to repeal part of a statute, only the entire statute. To permit the president to veto sections of a law would make the president, not Congress, the primary legislative determinant. Line item veto authority would be acceptable only if the Constitution were amended to permit it. The decision was not unanimous. The three-member court minority, led by Justice Anthony Scalia, argued that the act did not permit the president any more control over financial affairs than that awarded him traditionally in appropriations legislation. Since the early twentieth century, Congress had regularly authorized the president, at his discretion, to refuse to spend funds for certain budgeted items he considered inappropriate. Scalia maintained that there is no actual difference between a president being allowed to cancel spending through a formal item veto and a congressional decision that authorizes him to commit funds at his discretion.

The Supreme Court's 1998 decision to void the Line Item Veto Act rendered speculation on its application obsolete, unless the Constitution is amended to permit it. Should an amendment be proposed and submitted to the states, its chances of confirmation would appear to be reasonable, if for no other reason than because over forty-three state governors had item veto powers in 1998. However, if Democrats continue to hold the presidency with any degree of regularity, Republican-dominated state legislatures might be reluctant to vote confirmation of such an amend-

ment. The line item veto clearly increases presidential bargaining leverage in the budget process, and Republicans might well be unwilling to endow an institution biased toward the Democrats with that kind of political leverage. A constitutional amendment might well offer the president more veto prerogatives than did the 1996 act. More than likely, a constitutional amendment would change the policy power balance between the executive and legislative branches.

Clearly, congressional Republican support of the 1996 Line Item Veto Act was based on the expectation that President Clinton would be defeated in the 1996 election, and that a new Republican president would cooperate with the congressional Republican majority to do battle with the Democrats' pork barrel projects. Pork barrel legislation is constituency-based politics in its most obvious form. What is one legislator's essential program is another's example of unmitigated waste. Since there are party-rooted interbranch differences over how pork barrel matters should be resolved under conditions of divided government, the 1996 act would have been, in all likelihood, an invitation to bargaining and compromise between the branches more than a *de facto* increase in presidential leverage at the expense of Congress.

In contrast to the balanced budget and term limit proposals, a constitutionally endowed item veto would bolster the power of the president at the expense of Congress in the policy process. In recent years, Republicans have championed a line item veto amendment, especially when their party held the presidency. The policy mission of the party in power would be strengthened dramatically if their president had item veto authority. A full-fledged item veto would permit the president to remove a nongermane rider from a bill and, in so doing, he would make it considerably more difficult for Congress to hold significant legislation hostage to special interest, pork barrel programs. In the wake of the Supreme Court's 1998 invalidation of a statute-based line item veto, the president can no longer eliminate wasteful, nongermane, pork barrel provisions in appropriations bills. Wasteful provisions aside, presidents are usually reluctant to veto an entire bill out of concern for the effect of such action on government's continuing policies. Essential programs could suffer a temporary shortage of necessary funding while he and Congress struggled over various types of policy pork that Congress had attached to the legislation.

Therefore, the politics of dependency might well be compromised by a constitutional amendment authorizing a line item veto, and this is not a strictly partisan issue. The politics of dependency thrives under status quo conditions. Members of Congress, particularly senators, regularly exploit the Constitution's lack of flexibility in the exercise of the veto authority to their advantage as they bargain with the president. The House of Representatives has a germaneness rule that prohibits items foreign to a bill's major purpose from being attached to a bill. The Senate has no such rule. Consequently, the effect of an absolute, or all or nothing veto, is to inflate the role of the Senate as initiator of dependency and pork barrel policies, each of which contributes to the fiscal straightjacket that slowly eats away at available discretionary funds. Senators representing thinly populated states can deliver to their constituents more than their equal share of federal largesse. Since all states are represented equally in the Senate, the seventeen smallest states are represented by thirty-four senators, but contain only 7 percent of the country's population.[37] During the 1980s and early 1990s, West Virginia senator Robert Byrd and the late North Dakota senator Quentin Burdick established a reputation for using their seniority and party leverage to gain generous

pork barrel expenditures for their states through the rider strategy.[38]

Of course, all such monies are also spent in some House member's district. Therefore, although House rules prohibit the unilateral inclusion of nongermane items in legislation acted on by that body, House conferees don't usually engage in much prolonged soul-searching before consenting to Senate-initiated pork barrel projects. While powerful senators and (by default) representatives from smaller states have disproportionately high influence under these conditions, the pork barrel impact is felt in all states and most House districts. Reciprocity is the oil that provides such a politics with the fuel and lubrication it needs to sustain its momentum and impact on public policy. The pork barrel fallout incorporated in the 1993 earthquake relief package, discussed earlier, is an excellent example. States and congressional districts far removed from the earthquake site were blessed with pork barrel bonuses tacked onto the relief grants and loans targeted for earthquake victims in the greater Los Angeles area.

The president's influence in public policy, in both substantive policy initiation and in budgeting, has grown markedly over the past half-century. Therefore, should a constitutional amendment providing for a line item veto ever be considered seriously, significant congressional opposition should be expected. According to some legislators, the now disallowed 1996 statute forfeited enough policy leverage to the president. Institutional pride, as well as the spending advantages that accrued to Congress from the traditional all or nothing veto system, might well tip the scales to favor the status quo.

The policy implications of the line item veto debate are profound. Pork barrel and entitlement programs incrementally devour an increasingly larger part of the budget's available discretionary funds at a time when major substantive problems grow increasingly serious from either a lack, or shortage, of policy attention. Voters and legislators in forty-three states have acknowledged by their actions that the item veto is, on balance, a valuable ally in the search for more efficient, rational policy management. House and Senate members are not, of course, oblivious to this advantage. However, national legislators have not traditionally valued increased efficiency, control of waste, and better orchestration of policy priorities as highly as they do securing their congressional careers through pork barrel and dependency politics. The policy leverage offered entitlements and their pork barrel cousins by a constrained item veto authorized by statute, or by none at all, may well be too tempting.

The founding fathers might well find such use of the Constitution disturbing. They hoped that the institutional, constituency, and term duration differences among the House, Senate, and president would force policy compromises that would mitigate the impact of the influence of factions on policy. If they thought a presidential line item veto privilege, constitutional or statutory, would help mitigate the potentially excessive influence of vested interests on policy decisions, they would most likely support either version. The fact that Congress would always retain the right to override any veto, absolute or partial, would provide sufficient deference to the separation of powers principle so that its integrity and policy relevance would not be compromised.

The "constitution solution" as an alternative to legislation (balanced budget, line item veto) or as a way to instill democratic and religious values (school prayer, flag desecration, term limits) as moral standards became more commonplace during the 1980s and 1990s especially following the 1994 midterm elections. Some of these sought to replace laws that had been declared unconstitutional with constitutional provisions, as was the case with flag desecration and term limits. In other cases, especially those involving the control of spending (balanced budget, line item veto) they sought to coerce Congress into abiding by standards that it could not impose itself, namely the political advantages of dependency politics. Let the Constitution impose austerity and responsibility if politicians cannot. Political careers are secured because the Constitution is the villain. In this case the costly political "buck" is passed on to a document, and legislators virtually abdicate any responsibility for what has happened.

The Constitution should not be considered sacred and off-limits to formal alteration via amendment. The formalities of the amendment process exist for good reason. They exist because the framers recognized that time and circumstances would make formal change necessary. On the other hand, the framers felt that formal alteration of the Constitution should be considered very carefully and be subject to multiple reviews and supermajority requirements for approval. Constitutional amendments should not substitute for legislation or as ways to alter, or fine-tune, social values.

The reasons for this are pragmatic more than they are subjective. Kathleen M. Sullivan offers four key reasons for tempering the recent rush to the Constitution as a solution for controversial policy problems.[39] The first cost of such a trend is the forfeiture, or undermining, of government stability. In *Federalist No. 43* Madison argued that constitutional provisions should be changed when experience shows them to be faulty, but cautioned against employing amendments too frequently because it would "render the Constitution too mutable."[40] Constitutional principles stabilize the interaction among political forces, and therefore to amend it too often would likely undermine its contribution to government and political stability, a value revered by the founders, most of whom were conservative democrats. Quick and frequent constitutional change by amendment turns the document into a virtual extension of the legislative process, and undercuts its value as a stabilizing force. Second, the Constitution is valuable because it divorces higher legal authority from the routines of normal politics. As such, it inculcates respect for the higher law which it embodies, thereby encouraging a "compliance with pride" attitude on the part of both citizens and public officials, even though it often demands that each comply with standards that demand sacrifice. For example, the Constitution's standard of political and legal equality of people before the law can force a president from office (Watergate) or dictate that he is not immune from dealing with civil suits, such as sexual harassment, even though he is an incumbent president. The Eighteenth Amendment, providing for prohibition, is an excellent example of how the Constitution can be trivialized, or polluted, by invading a policy area that should be, by its very nature, resolved by legislation. It is the only amendment to have ever been repealed, and for good reason. It was socially very controversial and virtually unenforceable. A balanced budget amendment would be a variation on the same theme. In essence, it seeks to give a debatable macroeconomic policy alternative constitutional status. Such issues should be resolved by elected executives and legislatures, not by the Constitution.

Third, Sullivan argues persuasively that using the Constitution to deal with temporary policy frustrations does battle with the founders' notion of constitutional coherence or how its provisions fit together to produce one coordinated theory of governance. Single amendments deal with particular frustrations or issues that are isolated in history and are not likely to synthesize well with the constitution's overall mission. Again, the balanced budget amendment proposal was an example. The 1995 version asked for super-

majorities in both houses of Congress for both revenue-raising and debt-inducing decisions. This, argues Sullivan, contradicted the founders' intent of requiring simple majorities for such legislation. A supermajority requirement would inflate the role of minorities in fiscal decisions by increasing their bargaining leverage in debates preceding the resolution of such issues. Fourth, the Constitution, as the highest form of law to which a society is subjected, should concern itself with articulating the broad prerequisites of how to engineer democracy both in terms of what values should be sought, and in terms of how to implement those values. It is, by its nature, concerned with the rules of the game and the dimensions of the playing field. If citizens and/or public officials are accused of violating these rules, let the judiciary decide. In other words, regular attempts to amend the Constitution undermine the role of the judiciary as a co-equal branch of government. Courts contribute to public policy by determining the constitutionality of statutes and the meaning of vague statutory language. In sum, the fine-tuning of constitutional doctrine should be left to the courts. They not only keep the Constitution as fundamental law intact, but they also alter it and update it in ways that make change more expeditious and logical.

The popularity of the Constitution as policy solution in recent years illustrates how important the document can be in influencing political and policy discourse. It also illustrates how the individual responsibility that voters expect of their elected official can be compromised, or even avoided, by simplistic gestures that seek structural solutions to pressing policy problems. When the Constitution is advanced as a policy curative, it is likely that political leaders are seeking refuge in a process and an ideology that, in effect, allows them to change the arena of policy conflict by a means that may seem appealing and even principled, to those who elected them. In effect, however, the opposite is the case. Not only is it dangerous, as Kathleen Sullivan indicates, but it also clouds the channels of accountability that connect policymakers with the public.

Executive-Legislative Relations: The Challenge

The deterioration in president-Congress relations over the past half-century has been costly. The centripetal forces of interbranch and interparty bargaining and coalition-building that enabled the system to operate relatively effectively until the 1950s has fallen victim to weakened party structures, the exploitation of modern communication technology to secure incumbency, and the resulting growth of dependency politics. Party-rooted rivalries between presidents and Congress now, more than ever, have individual ego satisfaction, revenge, and ambition, rather than rational public policy, as goals. Distributive policies, in the form of entitlements, thrive under such conditions. In fact, entitlements have become so popular that government has gradually but voluntarily consigned itself to an economic straight-jacket, appropriately termed "demosclerosis."

It will take a persistent and united effort on the part of many groups, individuals, and institutions to extricate the country from these conditions of policy stagnation. Since the president and Congress are both responding to, as well as creating, the conditions which inflate the effects of demosclerosis on public policy, it will take a valiant effort by both institutions to help set the stage for a new era of effective interbranch cooperation. Although the public is growing increasingly annoyed with policy gridlock, the president and Congress will get little direct help from voters in this crusade. One of the causes of gridlock

has been the public's conflicting policy impulses. On the one hand, voters are inclined to reject the idea of widespread government intervention into their lives and the workings of the economy. On the other hand, they have become dependent on various types of entitlement programs to secure their jobs, educate their children, protect their health, and ensure their retirement. This policy dependency has, in turn, encouraged individual policymakers to satisfy voter demands for subsidies while, simultaneously, blaming other individuals and institutions for the inability of government to meet its policy challenges.

Separation of powers and checks and balances can be beneficial to public policy if politicians use their positions as members of institutions, constitutionally separated, to engage in honest, open debate with their policy adversaries over what fundamental theory or theories of government should provide the foundation for public policies. Debates and compromises should be rooted in honest disagreements over what course policies should take and why. Institutional independence can encourage politicians to research their positions and sharpen their arguments, all in the interest of leveraging the significance of that institution, as well as the significance of the members themselves, in policy decisions. However, these same constitutional principles become dysfunctional when institutional differences are employed to provide leverage for ambition, revenge, and personal animosities. Executive-legislative relations since Watergate and Vietnam have reflected too much of the latter and too little of the former.

A brief history of budgeting at the federal level offers an excellent illustration of this. The budget process is fundamentally a policy process, and one that by its very nature requires that the president and Congress cooperate to produce a meaningful, responsible product. Public policy first addressed the policy implications of budgeting in the Budget and Accounting Act of 1921. That law established a federal executive budget. It empowered the president to develop a budget and submit it to Congress for review, amendment, and passage. It also created the Bureau of the Budget to help the president in his development of the budget. The Bureau was originally assigned to the Treasury Department, and was moved to the Executive Office of the President when the latter was created in 1939. The significance of the executive budget for the policy process cannot be overstated: It acknowledged the right of the president to receive spending estimates from all administrative agencies, modify them to accommodate his policy priorities and the demands of fiscal responsibility, and submit final recommendations to Congress. Since fiscal powers are vested by the Constitution in Congress (predominately the House), budgets and policies they support do not become official policy until Congress makes them so by law.

For over half a century the 1921 system (as modified in 1939) worked fairly well. To be sure, the president and Congress had regular differences over the exact ways in which monies should be apportioned. However, by and large, these institutional differences were handled responsibility an with regular dispatch. The Vietnam and Watergate experiences made the public suspicious of government and the president and Congress suspicious of each other. Centrifugal forces replaced centripetal forces as the key dynamic affecting executive-legislative relations. Things haven't been the same since.

The formal manifestation of the political estrangement between the president and Congress came in the form of the Congressional Budget and Impoundment Control Act of 1974. This legislation was passed in the immediate aftermath of the Watergate crisis and was a direct response to President Nixon's liberal interpretation of the presidential authority to impound funds already appropriated by Congress. Existing officially since early in the century, presidential impoundment authority was supposed to be used only in situations in which the president determined that money could not be spent effectively or efficiently. Nixon, however, employed the authority to terminate spending on programs he did not like substantively, irrespective of any cost-benefit criteria.

The Congressional Budget and Impoundment Control Act, enacted in 1974, mandated a major restructuring of the way in which Congress processed the budget. Its goal was to assert Congress's rightful claim to full partnership with the president, in the budget process. Its goals were to control the presidential misuse of impoundments, establish policy priorities through the budget, and authorize Congress to set appropriate annual revenue and expenditure levels. New budget committees were created in both the House and Senate. A new legislative agency, the Congressional Budget Office (CBO), was created to help Congress in much the same way as OMB helps the president with research on the budget. The president irritated Congress further by authorizing the use of funds to bomb and invade Cambodia as part of the Vietnam War effort. In the wake of these events, Congress concluded that it had lost too much policy and budget initiative to the president over the preceding half-century, and took formal action to retrieve some of the power and authority it had delegated to the president. While the formal focus of this effort was on a renewed congressional role in budgeting, its long-term goal was much broader in scope. It was an attempt to restore a more balanced relationship between president, Congress, and the courts in the policy process.

In retrospect, the altercations between Congress and President Nixon in the early 1970s served more as a catalyst, or excuse, for the reassertion of congressional initiative in policy than it did as a root cause for it. Nixon regularly cited the constitution in defense of his actions. He justified the impoundment of funds authorized for rural and urban domestic programs partially on constitutional grounds. Included here were inherent executive powers, implied powers, and precedents established by other presidents. Since his true motive was the elimination of substantive programs to which he objected, the defense of such action on constitutional grounds was far-fetched, but politically shrewd, at least temporarily. New budget congressional processes were adopted, together with a new budget calendar. A new fiscal year (October 1 to September 30) was established to deal more systematically with the timing of the budget cycle. Finally, two new types of impoundments, recisions and deferrals, were authorized. These allowed the president either to stop the expenditure of money, or to defer it until conditions and altered administrative procedures increased the likelihood of its being spent wisely. In both cases, the president was required to submit the proposals to Congress for review.

The Congressional Budget Office (CBO) has been notably helpful in enabling Congress to begin to regain budget parity with the president. It does research for Congress on basic budget data, and analyzes alternative fiscal and budget issues independent of OMB influence. Since partisanship is far more fragmented in Congress than in the White House, its challenge as a spokesperson for a politically diverse body is a much more formidable one than is OMB for the president. While CBO has tended to be more in the good graces of the congressional majority party, it has shown a refreshing degree of objectivity in some of its research. For example, when President Clinton's cost projections for health care reform were announced, CBO director Robert Reichauer (a Democratic Party appointee) announced nonetheless that CBO's research indicated that the president's cost projections were far too optimistic.

CBO has been marginally successful in reintroducing a more healthy, classic type of competition between the president and Congress over policy issues. It has by no means displaced the cancerlike invasion of dependency and pork barrel politics on the discretionary budget. However, the respect it has gained for sober analysis of the advantages, disadvantages, and alternative cost of various policy options offers some hope. Perhaps interbranch debates conditioned by honest differences over the wisdom and costs of policy alternatives will gather additional momentum, and the impact of dependency and pork barrel politics will become somewhat more constrained.

One thing is clear: It is virtually mandatory that Congress and the president be more anticipatory, or proactive, as they jointly confront the conflicting demands that dependency politics and the need for rational, long-term policy planning place on the system. There is no guarantee of it happening even when the same party controls both institutions. Dependency politics needs significant restraint at a minimum, and significant retrenchment if possible. This would restore some flexibility to budgeting and make more discretionary money available for commitment to other areas. Several reforms could be considered. One possibility is to establish a special fund available for use only during emergencies such as floods or earthquakes. Another would be to adopt a "needs test" for all ongoing entitlement programs which would verify, on a regular basis, an individual's or a family's need for continued support. Another might be "sunset" provisions in all authorizing legislation. This would mean a statute would automatically expire after a set period of time, thereby compelling Congress and the president to do a bottom up analysis of its policy results before reauthorizing and funding the program again. Finally, as in the case of the Personal Responsibility and Work Opportunity Act of 1996 (discussed in Chapters 10 and 11), time and benefit limitations could be placed on assistance, virtually compelling recipients and governments to develop plans to return dependent individuals and families to the workforce. Should any or all of these prescriptions edge their way into just a few policies, the success of the CBO experience will have been expanded to set the stage for a more honest and progressive application of the separation of powers principle to presidential-congressional relations.

Executive-legislative relations were not designed to be constantly harmonious. Only on occasion, during periods of crisis, have they been for any extended period of time. The separation of powers virtually guarantees conflict, in part because of constituency differences, and in part because of the different constitutional missions assigned to each branch. Institutional conflict exacerbated by partisanship encourages parties to the struggle to be clear and informed so that the merits of an argument can be leveraged in the debates and discussions that precede compromise.

Divided government exacerbates executive-legislative differences, but does not introduce them. They are sewn into the nature of the constitutional system. Voters create divided government by their votes, and like, at least in principle, what they have done. However, as divided government continues, voter frustration seems to grow. It appears to be both a measure of voter cynicism, and a cause for it. The open, partisan nature of the conflict between the president and Congress under divided government clearly amplifies the impact of the separation of powers on policymaking. When gridlock sets in, and the government is shut down temporarily or an agreement can't be reached on a key issue such as health care reform, cynicism increases. Perhaps the public

reasons that self-serving legislators and presidents will do less damage if they are occasionally deadlocked or forced to make major concessions preceding the compromises that inevitably come. Still, gridlock tends to increase public cynicism.

Given the policy challenges of the late twentieth and early twenty-first centuries, the structural and political constraints on effective decision making may be too burdensome. Compromises are indeed struck, but they may be too incremental and backloaded, i.e., passed onto future generations, to truly represent a courageous effort to deal with policy problems now, with the resources at hand. Public skepticism, weak party structures, the high cost of campaigning, a sensationalist-oriented media, and split-ticket voting all contribute to increased public disaffection which, in turn, leads to more policy paralysis. As a result, the constitutional bias against significant policy change is amplified. Structure becomes more important as an input into policy decisions.

It will take a stronger, more ideologically based politics and an interested, mobilized voting public to overcome the structural constraints that the Constitution places on executive-legislative relations. President Clinton and the Republican-controlled congresses of the late 1990s did reach agreements on many key policy issues. However, most of them were tepid, bipartisan agreements reflecting the politics of the possible, not the rational. In an age where anxiety is high and economic and cultural changes are dramatic, this kind of politics will contribute to cynicism and despair, not alleviate it.

Partisanship needs to become more principled and less personal and petty. Conflicts need to stress different theories of governing and not differences in personality and character. Voters may not realize it, but they crave political-party-based policy guidance. Party leaders today do not organize their members around coherent, principled policy agendas that contrast clearly with the agendas and principles of rival parties. Bipartisanship has become a diversion from the policy questions at hand. The dissipation of the Republican Revolution of 1994 is an excellent illustration. What began as a promise to fundamentally alter the system virtually evaporated in a whirlwind of accommodation. President Clinton's 1993 deficit reduction legislation, won by a razor-thin margin on a highly partisan vote, underscored the ideological distinctions between the two major parties. The 1997 deficit reduction agreement illustrated the opposite—bipartisan concession to the politics of the middle.

Bipartisan solutions to some policy questions are probably the preferred course. Reforming campaign finance is probably one of them. However, to be meaningful, others need solutions that reflect a theory of governing. There is, in all likelihood, no workable policy middle ground when it comes to dealing with problems of poverty, crime, drug addiction, the environment, and education. In these areas, the middle ground is, in all likelihood, the "muddle ground," because most compromises seeking the lowest common policy denominator are likely to offer only marginal alterations to the status quo. Most of the nation's serious policy problems demand more than that. If the president and Congress continue to seek bipartisan solutions to key policy questions on the assumption that any agreement is better than no agreement at all, the Constitution will continue to handicap the search for realistic solutions to policy problems.

Endnotes

1. See Lloyd N. Cutler, "Now Is the Time for All Good Men . . . ," *William and Mary Law Review,* vol. 30, no. 2 (Winter 1989), pp. 387–402.

2. *Ibid.,* p. 392.

3. See Kenneth A. Shepsle, "The Changing Textbook Congress," in John E. Chubb and Paul E. Peterson, *Can the Government Govern?* (Washington, D.C.: The Brookings Institution, 1989), pp. 238–266.

4. Orwell, as quoted in Robert J. Samuelson, "Balancing Act," *Newsweek* (August 11, 1997), p. 24.

5. *Ibid.,* pp. 24–25.

6. *Ibid.,* p. 27.

7. Hedrick Smith, *The Power Game: How Washington Works* (New York: Random House, 1988), p. 656.

8. *Ibid.*

9. *Ibid.,* p. 657.

10. As cited in James L. Sundquist, *Constitutional Reform and Effective Government,* rev. ed. (Washington, D.C.: The Brookings Institution, 1992), p. 97.

11. Harvey C. Mansfield, Jr., *America's Constitutional Soul* (Baltimore, Md.: Johns Hopkins University Press, 1991).

12. Jonathan Rauch, "Demosclerosis," *National Journal,* vol. 24, no. 36 (September 5, 1992), pp. 1998–2000. See also Jonathan Rauch, *Demosclerosis: The Silent Killer of American Government* (New York: Random House, 1994).

13. *Ibid.,* p. 1998.

14. *Ibid.,* pp. 1998–1999.

15. *Ibid.,* p. 1998.

16. See Cutler, *op. cit.,* p. 391.

17. Gary Cox and Samuel Kernell, eds., *The Politics of Divided Government* (Boulder, Colo.: Westview Press, 1991), as referenced in Richard M. Valelly, "Divided They Govern," *The American Prospect,* no. 11 (Fall 1992), pp. 124–136.

18. *Ibid.*

19. Robert Weissman, "Hearings Loss," *The American Prospect,* no. 41 (November–December 1998), p. 50.

20. *Ibid.*

21. David Broder and Stephen Barr, "Going over the Top on Oversight," *Washington Post National Weekly Edition* (August 2–8, 1993), p. 31.

22. Woodrow Wilson, "The Study of Administration," *Political Science Quarterly,* vol. 2 (June 1887).

23. Broder and Barr, *op. cit.,* p. 31.

24. *Ibid.*

25. Alexis Simendinger, "The Paper Wars," *National Journal,* vol. 30, no. 30 (July 25, 1998), p. 1736.

26. *Ibid.,* p. 1732.

27. *Ibid.,* p. 1733.

28. As quoted in *Ibid.,* p. 1733.

29. Benjamin Ginsberg and Martin Shefter, *Politics by Other Means: The Declining Importance of Elections in America* (New York: Basic Books, 1992).

30. Mayhew, David R., *Divided We Govern: Party Control, Lawmaking, and Investigations 1946–1990* (New Haven, Conn.: Yale University Press, 1991).

31. Valelly, *op. cit.*

32. For an excellent analysis of this point of view see Anthony Lewis, "The Prosecutorial State: The Criminalizing of American Politics," *The American Prospect,* no. 42 (January-February 1999), pp. 26–31. The discussion in this section draws heavily from the Lewis essay.

33. *Ibid.,* pp. 30–31.

34. Edward S. Corwin, *The President: Office and Powers, 1787–1957* (New York: New York University Press, 1957), p. 171.

35. Peter Wyden, *Bay of Pigs* (New York: Simon & Schuster, 1979), p. 7., as quoted in Charles M. Hardin, "The Separation of Powers Needs Major Revision," in Robert A. Goldwin and Art Kaufman, eds., *Separation of Powers: Does It Still Work?* (Lanham, Md.: American Enterprise Institute, 1986), p. 98.

36. *Ibid.*

37. Howard E. Shuman, *Politics and the Budget,* 3rd ed. (Englewood Cliffs, N.J.: Prentice Hall, 1992), p. 67.

38. See Brian Kelly, *Adventures in Porkland: How Washington Wastes Your Money and Why They Won't Stop* (New York: Villard Books, 1992), pp. 4–5, 23–25.

39. Kathleen M. Sullivan, "Constitutional Amendmentitis," *The American Prospect,* no. 23 (Fall 1995), pp. 20–27. This theme is pursued by Sullivan and others in Alan Brinkley, Nelson W. Polsby, and Kathleen M. Sullivan, *The New Federalist Papers* (New York: 20th Century Fund, 1997).

40. *The Federalist Papers,* as quoted in *Ibid.,* p. 21.

chapter ten

Federalism

Intergovernmental Politics and Public Policy

Along with the separation of powers principle, federalism represents an attempt by the Constitution's framers to discourage tyranny by officially fragmenting policy responsibilities. Separation of powers accomplished this within the confines of the national government. Federalism accomplished it on an area, or geographical, plane by constitutionally dividing policy responsibilities between a national government and subnational (state) governments. A nation's government is not genuinely federal unless it meets three distinct criteria. First, a written constitution must divide government policy authority between a central government and subnational governments, guaranteeing sovereignty and significant policy responsibilities to each. In the American system, a general division of national-state policy responsibilities was incorporated in the Tenth Amendment. Nation-state powers are distributed as follows: Powers delegated specifically to the national government by the Constitution (foreign affairs, regulation of interstate commerce, coinage of money, regulation of bankruptcy, management of the public debt) are the exclusive responsibility of the national government. The remaining policy responsibilities, sometimes called reserved or residual powers, are left to the states and, in effect, to the people therein. These residual powers are sometimes labeled the "police" powers, or the power to enact policies that affect (and improve) the health, safety, welfare, and morals of the people. While subsequent discussion will show the national government to be significantly involved in state residual power activity (education, health, welfare, roads, housing), this involvement has usually come at the behest of the states. Therefore, although states retain their official sovereignty over residual powers, our policy system has become developed into a *shared* policy system, within which the official constitutional division of policy responsibilities takes a back seat to the acknowledged need for both levels of government to join forces in confronting policy problems that are of concern to both levels.

Second, a constitutional system that is legitimately federal allows both national and subnational levels of government to enact policies that require citizen compliance. This stands in direct contrast to the two alternative ways of constitutionally dividing power geographically. One alternative is a unitary system, within which all constitutional policy power is assigned a national government which can, at its discretion, parcel out policy responsibilities to subnational units as it sees fit, with the understanding that such policy privileges can be withdrawn at any time. The other alternative is a confederation, within which all significant policy powers are assigned to the subnational units which can, at their discretion, assign policy power to the national government. Under a unitary system, only the national government has the authority to determine which policies impact directly on citizens and how they are to be administered. Under a confederation, only subnational governments act directly on citizens. National governments exercise their limited policy authority (if any) directly on the subgovernments, not on the people directly.

Third, in a viable federal system, the distribution of policy powers between national and subnational governments cannot be altered unilaterally by either level of government by statute. It must be done by constitutional amendment. In the American system, the amending process allows states equal representation in part of the deliberations over the content of proposed constitutional amendments and equal representation in the ratification process. Amendments must be proposed by a two-thirds vote of both houses of Congress, and states have equal representation in the Senate. Amendments must be ratified by legislatures or conventions in three-fourths of the states, with all state votes being treated equally. It is very important to underscore the salience of states as sovereign geographic entities in the amendment process. This represents yet another way in which the framers sought to temper the impact of majority rule on government.

The three characteristics discussed above summarize the formal qualities of federalism. They do not address the issue of why some nations prefer federations over confederations or unitary systems. Federated constitutional democracies certainly consider one advantage to be the fragmentation of popular input into government, but not to the point of rendering government impotent. Federalism seeks to blend the need to coordinate some policies on a national scale with the need to keep some policies independent and state centered. In short, federalism is an excellent illustration of how structure affects decision processes and how those processes affect policy. Federalism channels political and policy activity in ways that make policies different, by either insisting on distinct structure-honed preconditions for policy cooperation, or by insisting that some policies be made and administered by jurisdictions independently.

The values or advantages that are traditionally assigned to a federal structure all have policy implications. They include flexibility, pluralism, access, accommodation of diversity, experimentation, citizen choice, and efficiency. Federalism is said to be flexible because it encourages pragmatic policy solutions that accommodate diverse conditions and preferences. It makes a pluralist democracy more viable by providing a way for ethnic, religious, and economic forces to benefit from both community identity and self-government on the one hand, and the benefits of political and economic union on the other. By affording citizens access to multiple points of government decision making, federalism encourages appeals to other jurisdictions when one jurisdiction is unresponsive. Multiple governments also check and balance one another, and thereby limit chances for arbitrary decisions and insensitive treatment of minority groups. By encouraging unity without uniformity, a federal system protects human diversity, which in turn promotes freedom and quality of life. By constitutionally establishing both national and subnational policy laboratories, federalism encourages policy adaptation and innovation. Some experiments succeed, and some fail. Most are tested in subnational arenas before other governments decide to accept or reject them. This is efficient, and it rewards innovation. Federalism gives citizens choices about where they live and work, allowing them to, in a sense, "vote with their feet." If a person or family is dissatisfied with a jurisdiction's tax structure, its civic values, or the equality of its services, he or she can leave or threaten to leave. Such options put pressure on governmental jurisdictions to match available services to citizen preferences. Finally, although federal systems frequently are accused of encouraging inefficiency because services are often duplicated and jurisdictions often too small or too large to deliver cost-effective service, often just the opposite is the case. While subnational jurisdictions are often slow and rather unsystematic in their approach to policymaking and administration, central governments have been, historically, even less efficient.[1]

Federalism and Public Policy: A Historical Perspective

Federalism was designed to discourage the abuse of power, but its political and policy effects are much broader than that. Federalism in the United States has always affected ways in which policies are made and administered. The growing policy imperatives of the past two centuries have mandated that federalism be converted from a negative, preventive force into one serving the needs of a growing, interdependent, and technologically impacted society. That conversion was slow in coming. Americans revere the Constitution, and to convert a structural institution designed to prevent majority tyranny into a positive policy force drawing its legitimacy from the majority principle took considerable time. States vary widely in their ability to meet their constitutional policy obligations.

Federalism's dynamics have been played out on two major policy stages in the two-hundred-year history of the republic. The first was the competitive stage, where the players (national government and states) competed for policy primacy in such areas as the provision of services, the regulation of economic activity, or guaranteeing civil rights. Ambiguous constitutional policy assignments provided the basis for such conflicts. The Constitution delegates to the national government the power to tax and spend for the general welfare and to enact all laws that are "necessary and proper" to fulfill its delegated objectives. The Tenth Amendment reserves all powers not delegated to the national government, nor denied by it (the Constitution), to the states, and their residents. Since the power to tax and spend for the general welfare would likely include components of states' residual powers—health, roads, housing, welfare, education—the states cannot claim exclusive policy rights in these areas. Nevertheless, constitutional doctrine acknowledges that within the reserved or residual policy area, states have an obligation to deal with these policy problems, and should involve the national government only if they need help. States have needed more than a little help on more than a few occasions, and now only infrequent attention is paid to enforcing the Tenth Amendment's power distribution literally. The national government and the states cooperate far more often than they compete.

However, before such a cooperative state of affairs developed, several policy confrontations between the national government and the states did occur, with most of them being resolved by courts. By far the most important court case that affected the nation-state power balance was *McCulloch* v. *Maryland* (1819).[2] In that case, the state of Maryland challenged the constitutionality of a law passed by Congress authorizing the establishment of a second United States Bank on the grounds that the Constitution did not specifically grant the national government that right. Maryland sought a strict, literal interpretation of the delegated powers. Chief Justice John Marshall, speaking for the Court majority, rejected the argument, noting that the right to create a bank was part of Congress's "implied powers." The Constitution did give Congress the right to coin money and borrow on the credit of the United States. Therefore, a bank was a "necessary and proper" (Article I, Section 8) way to administer Congress's delegated policy obligation. In short, the existence of the national bank was "implied" by the Constitution. Marshall argued that it would be illegal for a state to tax a national government activity (in this case a national bank) because that might mean that a state could destroy a legitimate function of the national government by taxing it to death. Furthermore, Marshall argued that when the two levels seemingly have an equal constitutional claim to a policy prerogative, the national government's claim should be honored. This has been labeled the doctrine of "national supremacy."

As the contentiousness of the *McCulloch* case illustrates, federalism's first hundred years was a competitive period—sometimes labeled the "dual federalism" era. This view projects the national government and the states as independent sovereigns with virtually exclusive jurisdiction over their separate constitutional policy assignments. There was very little interaction between the two levels, and when it occurred it was by joint consent. Each level was on guard constantly to ward off direct and subtle intrusions into its policy domain.

However, the *McCulloch* decision did provide a legal framework through which the two levels of government could move from potential and actual confrontation to conditions that favored cooperation. However, court decisions alone do not change attitudes. Americans have always been suspicious of power. Federalism, as a constitutional doctrine, synchronizes with this attitude. The Madison-Jefferson view of federalism was, at least in theory, primarily a dual federalism point of view. As will be explained below, the current operational dimension of federalism in the United States is, by and large, dominated by a cooperative spirit, but this does not mean that politics and policy are free from the policy problems and attitudes rooted historically in the dual federalism doctrine.

The Constitution grants rights to individuals. It also reserves rights of policy primacy to the states by reserving them powers not delegated to the national government. While the Tenth Amendment makes no specific mention of state policy rights, it can be assumed that if national and state policy positions collide, states might well argue that their involuntary compliance with the national government position would constitute, in effect, an improper invasion of their rights. This makes for what has been labeled the "states rights" argument. It escalates policy competition to the constitutional level. States have often claimed that national action is unconstitutional because it deprives them of their Tenth Amendment policy rights. The most formidable example of states rights politics was the withdrawal of the southern states from the

Union, the event which precipitated the Civil War. However, there are more recent examples. Mid-twentieth-century resistance by southern states to civil rights policies, decreed by both Congress and the federal courts, was based on the argument that the national government was interfering with the right of states to determine their own voting eligibility and education policies. Southern governors Strom Thurmond (South Carolina, 1948) and George Wallace (Alabama, 1964, 1968, 1972) mounted presidential campaigns in defense of these prerogatives. This resistance has waned since the early 1970s, but still surfaces sporadically. In recent years, state and local resistance to decisions on nuclear waste disposal sites have been based on this argument, despite the fact that many of these sites are located on federal property within states. Resistance in the mid-1990s by private militias, such as the Montana Freemen, to national grazing and logging policies in national parks and forests was based on the argument that the states had constitutional sovereignty over such properties. In effect, the national government never owned them.

The dual federalism school aside, for most of the twentieth century, the overriding characteristic of American federalism has been one of cooperation, and not competition. This was not borne out of an ideological change of heart, but because of policy imperatives induced by social, economic, and technological change. The fact that the national government and the states now cooperate more than they compete does not mean, however, that public policy doesn't respond to the structural demands of federalism. Rather, it means that federalism has been accommodated in both the policymaking and administration phases of the policy cycle. In effect, positive government continues in spite of obstacles federalism puts in its way. It also means that questions of whether to centralize or decentralize policy power are often resolved in favor of the latter more as a matter of principle than of logic.

The Progressive Legacy

Progressivism is the term applied to a populist-inspired movement of the late 1880s which sought to make government institutions responsive and effective entities as they helped society adapt to the impact of industrialization and urbanization. It had its major impact on government and society between 1890 and 1920. Progressives argued that, in contrast to the concerns of some of the founding fathers and the dual federalists, government could be more of a friend to the public than an adversary. It sought to purify and reengineer theories of government and politics on two fronts. One was the democratization of political parties by allowing the party rank-and-file more responsibilities to govern parties and nominate candidates for office. This was a challenge to the dominance of many state and local party organizations by party machines. The second part of the Progressive crusade was even more important: Concluding that policy problems would not take care of themselves, Progressives sought to improve the ability of government to meet its new policy obligations through structural reform and more businesslike practices. This meant empowering government to do more and, if necessary, centralizing power to make the administration of policy "justice" more comprehensive. Progressives were moralists who believed that professional experts could provide the businesslike "know how" to get government back on an objective or neutral track.

The Progressive movement was responsible for the Pendleton Civil Service Act of 1883, which introduced the merit principle to the national bureaucracy. Progressive objectives were also behind the Interstate Commerce Commission Act of 1887, which created the

Interstate Commerce Commission as the first independent regulatory agency assigned the responsibility of regulating a sector of the economy (railroads) with the interest of the consumer in mind. Both of these laws sought to remove politics from administration by statute. They were to free decision makers of political pressures so their decisions could be more objective and scientific.

Progressivism was by no means a panacea for society's problems, primarily because many of the movement's assumptions were naive. The democratization of political parties permitted active minority factions within parties to seize control of party affairs. In turn, this led to a rise in the power of vested interests in politics and government. The assumption that politics can be legislated out of administrative decision making was far too optimistic. More than removing politics from administrative decision making, the Progressives' faith in experts meant that a larger and more professionally trained bureaucracy was to be vested with policy discretion to regulate the economy, governed constantly by public interest standards, however defined. This invited vested interests to lobby the bureaucracy and, since bureaucrats were appointed on the basis of merit, introduced serious problems of accountability to government.

Nonetheless, the significance of progressivism for the future policy contours of federalism was very real. First, progressivism set the stage for the people's acceptance of government institutions as friends rather than adversaries. A more centralized government concerned with the objective pursuit of the public interest was, to Progressives, the only logical response to the festering policy problems brought on by industrialization and urbanization. Secondly, progressivism stressed pragmatism—that the way to deal with a policy problem is totally dependent on the nature of the problem itself. Structural and ideological barricades that interfered with

government's attempt to deal with a problem in the most scientific, objective, and rational way were nuisances. Democracy, they argued, has nothing whatsoever to do with how strong government is, only with who ultimately gives government cues about what to do. What was important was for government institutions, powerful or not, to work on the public's behalf. Elected executives, governors, and presidents might well be more able than legislators to articulate and work for a composite, inclusive view of the public interest. Legislative constituencies are more exclusive. Executive constituencies are more inclusive. The policy problems introduced by urbanization and industrialization involved, simultaneously, a number of interests that affected most legislative constituencies, and state governments generally. Therefore, stronger national government and stronger executive leadership at all levels were occurrences not to be condemned out of principle.

The gradual public acceptance of the Progressive doctrine slowly undercut the dual federalism position. Government had to be more pragmatic and less fearful of majority tyranny. State policy autonomy should not be pursued in principle. The prescription was relatively simple: Realistically assess the nature of the policy problem, then decide on how to muster government resources in a way that deals with the problem efficiently, effectively, and with dispatch.

Most national legislation enacted during the Progressive era was not targeted directly at nation-state policy relations. However, the results of much of that legislation did change the policy environments in states by relieving states of some policy burdens. Examples include such laws as the Sherman Anti-Trust Act (1890), the Pure Food, Drug, and Cosmetic Act (1906), and the Federal Reserve Act (1914). Another law, the Budget and Accounting Act of 1921, established a national executive budget. Presidents were to be responsible for drafting preliminary spending plans for the entire bureaucracy. Before that time, each agency made its request directly to the congressional committees that were responsible for authorizing and budgeting its programs. There was no overhead force that consolidated all the requests with an eye to eliminating waste, program duplication, and inefficiency. This law was an excellent illustration of how the increasingly complicated natures of policy issues virtually mandated new planning strategies for coping with them. As such, it embodied the pragmatic manifestations of the progressive movement. Many states quickly followed the federal example, and adopted the executive budget as a way to deal with policy challenges more systematically and efficiently.

Therefore, the Progressive movement's major impact on the character of national-state policy relations was to set the cultural stage for the acceptance of more cooperative policy relationships between the two levels when circumstances demanded. Natural disasters such as floods, hurricanes, and earthquakes require government involvement to degrees that could place state and local governments in financial and jurisdictional straightjackets unless they receive help from the national level. Moreover, policy problems do not naturally confine themselves to the geographical confines of a single state. Air and water pollution, poverty, transportation coordination, and the control of the dissemination and sale of illegal drugs are but a few of many policy issues that are, by their nature, interstate in character. As such they demand the coordinative efforts of several states and the supervisory input and financial support of the national government. In sum, the imperative that results in the need for states and their local governments to share policy responsibilities with their sister states and the national government has rendered classical federalism obsolete. To be sure, in theory, states retain their Tenth Amendment policy sovereignty. However, they can no longer opt to exercise that right as a matter of principle.

The Dawn of Cooperative Federalism: The New Deal Era

The Constitution is not a manual containing detailed prescriptions on how to manage government, and that includes the management of policies along national-state-local networks. The Tenth Amendment suggests a nation-state power balance, but Article I, Section 8 ("necessary and proper" clause) and Article VI ("supreme law of the land" clause), reinforced by the *McCulloch* decision, suggest national supremacy. Ambiguity is sometimes said to be the slave of conflict, and this amorphousness is an illustration of that.[3] It is obvious that the framers couldn't resolve the problem and responded with conflicting and ambiguous constitutional phraseology. Furthermore, they said nothing about the powers of cities, counties, and what are now termed special districts. This is because local governments of all types are creatures of their respective states, and therefore do not have any constitutional claim to policy autonomy.

Nevertheless, problems of local governments, especially metropolitan areas, currently are among the country's most serious. Metropolitan areas face deeply rooted issues of poverty, lawlessness, fatherless families, deteriorating public school systems, drug trafficking, and eroding tax bases. Obviously, when the national government and states cooperate in an attempt to deal with policy problems common to both, it goes without saying that much of the focus is on problems of cities as appendages of states. Out of necessity, intergovernmental policy cooperation involves three, not just two, tiers or layers of government.

In sum, the transition from a competitive, dual federalist mentality to a cooperative one did not face significant constitutional obstacles, owing to both the ambiguous treatment afforded federalism in the Constitution and the absence of any consideration of local government powers and policies in the document. Nonetheless, it took a major crisis, and the policy imperatives ensuing from it, to make a serious case for operationalizing intergovernmental policy cooperation. While the Progressive movement helped lay the cultural groundwork for intergovernmental movement policy cooperation, it took the policy imperatives of the Great Depression to make it a reality. Before the New Deal period, the courts often treated the idea underlying cooperative federalism with hostility. During the late nineteenth and early twentieth centuries, the Supreme Court applied the dual federalism rationale in declaring unconstitutional national efforts to establish a national child labor law and a national minimum wage system. The legal climate was not friendly, nor were policy obligations serious enough to warrant carrying progressivism much beyond the theoretical stage. It took the Great Depression to change things dramatically, and create conditions that made intergovernmental policy cooperation a necessity.

The New Deal was President Franklin Roosevelt's response to the Great Depression. The first one hundred days of his first term in office (1933–1937) produced more emergency legislation than any comparable period in history, before or since. During that period, Congress enthusiastically enacted a series of emergency policies authorizing unparalleled degrees of economic regulation. This was the beginning of the "cooperative federalism" period. It was characterized by cooperative, joint policy undertakings by the federal government, states, and localities. The economic crisis was a joint national, state, and local policy problem. Already compromised significantly by Progressive-era legislation, dual federalism was finally laid to rest as a viable theory. While intergovernmental cooperation had occurred sporadically during the preceding century and a half, the New Deal made it much more habitual and quantitatively more significant. After the enormous policy thrust of Roosevelt's first hundred days, more legislation followed providing for highway construction, public housing, and aid to the disabled and to poor families with dependent children. Each of these programs was initiated by the federal government, but was heavily dependent on states and localities for administrative and financial support.

Policies that had been the exclusive responsibility of states and localities, such as welfare, housing, health care, and roads, quickly took on an intergovernmental complexion. There was no unconstitutional intrusion of the national government into state policy prerogatives because states and localities willingly cooperated. The choice was theirs to make, and they found it rather easy in light of the effects of the Great Depression on their tax bases and revenue streams. The federal government's lure, so to speak, was the grant-in-aid. Grants-in-aid are funds made available by Congress to states and localities to be spent for programs that are usually predetermined, and in accordance with prescribed standards and conditions imposed by the federal government. The federal government insists on the right to supervise the expenditure of funds as a condition for the funds' availability. Usually the recipient government is required to match the federal contribution dollar for dollar or with some other legally prescribed formula or ratio.

The grant-in-aid has been used extensively since the New Deal period because it is a way to exploit the federal government's superior revenue-raising resources to help states and localities meet their policy obligations. The cost to the states has been the loss of rights to some policy initiatives, but that has been a small price to pay, especially for the less wealthy states. In less wealthy states, services become available that, without federal assistance, would be available only to residents of the more prosperous states. In addition, states with obsolete administrative practices have been encouraged to modernize their procedures and improve their capacity to spend the influx of federal money more efficiently and effectively. Therefore, while cooperative federalism has resulted in states forfeiting some policy initiation prerogatives to the federal government in return for more financial resources, their roles as administrative entities have taken on added importance. Only the governments at the delivery end of the policy continuum can fine-tune the expenditure of money in ways that suit the particular social, economic, and cultural expectations of individuals, institutions, and groups that ultimately profit from these policies.

A key example of a New Deal policy that converted a state/local policy responsibility into a cooperative one via the grant-in-aid mechanism was the Social Security Act of 1935. One section of the act established a joint federal-state unemployment insurance program. Another created a categorical assistance program providing federal grants (matching) for aid to dependent mothers and children, the physically disabled, the blind, as well as for public health services and pensions for the elderly. Funds were dispensed according to specific category, with federal standards for recipient eligibility and accountability included as a prerequisite for fund availability. The programs subsidizing dependent mothers and children component of the law remained intact for sixty-one years, until it was replaced in 1996 with the Personal Responsibility and Work Opportunity Act. A second example was the Public Housing Act of 1937. This law established a matching grant-in-aid program linking the financial re-

sources of the federal government to those of state and local governments for the purpose of eliminating unsafe and unsanitary housing conditions, eliminating slums, and replacing them with decent, safe, and sanitary residences for low-income families. A secondary objective was to reduce unemployment and stimulate business activity. A distinct three-tiered intergovernmental partnership emerged from the Public Housing Act. The responsibility for overall management of projects was vested in local housing authorities, which issued bonds to raise funds to pay for construction. States were to enact laws authorizing local governments to participate, and could add their own restrictions or qualifications to the projects. The costs of the projects were borne ultimately by the federal government, which reimbursed local governments for the costs of the construction bonds.

Government-sponsored housing projects were new to the American scene. Some considered it genetically alien to the free enterprise spirit. In addition, many interest groups associated with the construction industry feared competition from government. Naturally, homeowners in middle-class neighborhoods in close proximity to the projects were concerned about the effects of the projects on their property values and quality of life. This resistence intensified as it became clear the projects were being used as a way to advance racial and economic integration. Such resistance was often cited as an example of how insensitive the federal government could be when it came to incorporating grass-roots interests into project planning. The federal government became more responsive to these interests as time passed.[4]

The idea of intergovernmentally sponsored public housing was extended by Title I of the Housing Act of 1949 which established grant-in-aid-supported urban renewal programs. Very similar to public housing, urban renewal was a response to a perceived failure of private markets. However, in contrast to public housing which substituted government for private enterprise, the urban renewal program assigned local urban renewal authorities the responsibility of selecting construction sites, acquiring and clearing land, and selecting developers to construct new facilities. These facilities included housing projects, but also other projects targeted at revitalizing central business districts. This, in turn, was expected to increase a city's revenue base and attract middle-class residents to the revitalized areas. Private developers were to be chosen by the urban renewal authorities to do the renewal work and to finance the projects. The federal government was to pay two-thirds of the "write down," or the difference between what the local authority paid to secure and clear the land and the price it received upon its sale to the private developer. The federal government retained the right to disapprove plans it considered poorly conceived, and retained the right to supervise several stages of the implementation process.

The entry of the federal government into the areas of poverty, public housing, and urban renewal were illustrative of the altered tone of federal-state-local relations that emerged from the New Deal period. In succeeding decades the federal government became financially active in policies affecting highways, airports, education, mass transit, and job training. With the exception of education policy, national involvement was well received. States and localities needed financial assistance to help them meet their constitutional responsibilities. It is true that the price of this change was the forfeiture of some state and local prerogatives to initiate policy. This is very significant because dual federalism standards were dominant for most of the nation's first century. However, this change did not mean that states were to become merely passive entities in the intergovernmental network. What states and localities

lost in the way of initiatives, they gained back in administrative responsibilities. In short, states and localities remain critical to policy success. Federalism has simply been adjusted to meet the demands of changing policy imperatives. The purpose of public policy is to link procedures to objectives by means that enhance both policy effectiveness and democracy simultaneously. Cooperative federalism was an attempt to do this. Therefore, and in light of the policy mandates imposed by the New Deal, to transit from dual federalism to intergovernmental federalism was logical.[5]

Cooperative Federalism and "Picket Fence" Politics

Cooperative federalism has not been a policy panacea by any means. Frequently, the cures it offers appear to be worse than the diseases it was intended to arrest or eliminate. The policies discussed above are certainly no exception to that. The stories of how AFDC programs may well have perpetuated poverty rather than helped overcome it are well known. Many public housing efforts, such as the Pruitt-Igoe development in St. Louis in the 1950s, were colossal failures. Some of this was due to the failure of the projects to attract families other than those affected by chronic, not transitory, poverty. Some of it was to development theories that clashed with the purposes and designs of private developers. All these programs have been amended in an attempt to accommodate new theories and adjust to errors, again with mixed success. The extent to which this is due to assumptions underlying cooperative federalism is a major question, and it has been addressed by legislation enacted since the mid-1960s which has sought to recapture some policy initiatives for states and localities. This will be discussed in further detail below.

Cooperative federalism also has impacted

significantly on politics. Most policies affected by cooperative federalism have been distributive or redistributive in character. As such, they attract vested interests with an economic stake in their success or failure. Money on the grant-in-aid "table" means opportunity for economic interests that might convert it to their use. Consequently, local developers that profit from airport construction, public housing, urban renewal, mass transit programs, and highway construction and maintenance have a vested interest in the perpetuation of federal grants supporting these programs. The growing strength of these forces impacts on Congress when questions of program growth and cutbacks are considered. Legislators are reluctant to vote against these interests because they control votes in elections and are the source of financial support in campaigns. Cooperative federalism's contributions to this condition cannot be understated, especially in the case of the Senate. Since states are represented equally in the Senate, and the Senate is a co-equal legislative partner with the House, vested interests in the thinly populated states have more leverage over policy than their numbers could defend. In short, people are not represented equally in the Senate. This increases the odds of legislation being held hostage to the pork barrel.

One of the major problems with intergovernmental fiscal relations over the past half-century has been its specialized, program-by-program focus, which has prevented states and localities from dealing with policy issues on an integrated, coordinated, areawide basis. One-time North Carolina governor and senator Terry Sanford once offered a "picket fence" analogy as an explanation. He argued that most categorical grants-in-aid are administered by an intergovernmental alliance of professionals at all three levels of government with the singular objective of spending funds for specific programs governed exclusively by legal requirements and professional standards that reward clean, surgical, efficient execution of those programs alone. Each policy is likened to the stakes in a picket fence, depicting separate policy stakes, or pipelines extending from the national level, through the states, to the local level.[6] In reality, most policy problems impact on several fields simultaneously. For example, an undereducated populace contributes to joblessness which, in turn, encourages poverty and drug abuse. Poverty and drug abuse impact negatively on schools and add to law enforcement problems. These problems contribute to a flight of the middle class to the suburbs and all the problems that have resulted from the explosive growth of those areas. Categorical grants-in-aid dispensed along picket fence pipelines simply don't address issues in the integrated, synthesized, comprehensive way that the nature of contemporary policy problems demands. Meanwhile, overall social and economic conditions continue to deteriorate. Unable to see the proverbial "forest for the trees," professionals at all three levels of government take pride in how efficient they have been in committing and spending money. This affects metropolitan areas in particular, where casual policy linkages between education, poverty, crime, drug abuse, housing, health, and transportation can rather easily be detected. Cooperative federalism has, all too frequently, dodged the policy challenges posed by this social, political, and economic reality.

Note the earlier observation that intergovernmental antipoverty and public housing policies may have intensified problems they were supposed to solve. Over the past several decades, the nation's once socially diverse and economically prosperous central cities have lost their social and economic vitality to a pattern of sprawling suburban communities. Middle- to upper-middle-class white families have forsaken the central city for the suburbs, while still depending on the central city for jobs, entertainment, and recreation. The automobile, interstate highways, and mass transit systems have made this all possible. If, however, the overall objective of federal money dispensed to metropolitan areas is to revitalize them economically, socially, educationally, and ethnically (and it should be), these policies have been a colossal failure. Impacted by the picket fence syndrome, many of the programs contributed to the problem, not solved it. They have resulted in the "warehousing" of the poor and ethnic minorities (often one and the same) within the central city's decaying neighborhoods, exacerbating the poverty problem, which is the most obvious cause of escalating crime and inferior school performance.[7]

The intergovernmental policy solution to this problem over the past several years has been to help poor ethnic minorities, but leave them isolated. The Clinton administration, for example, committed several billion dollars to urban "enterprise" and "empowerment" zones in spite of the fact that research had shown that such expenditures had done little to change poverty conditions in central cities. At the same time Congress, supported by the president, committed more billions to build and improve interstate highways and beltways leading into and circumventing central cities, while simultaneously slashing funding for rent voucher programs which would help the poor exit the ghettos for more appealing communities.[8]

Acting unilaterally, cities such as Portland (Oregon) have controlled suburban sprawl successfully with the support of a strong state law allowing the establishment of very effective regional government. Others, such as Austin (Texas), Charlotte (North Carolina), and Columbus (Ohio), have fought the dysfunctions of sprawl by capturing a piece of the growth through annexation of suburban areas.[9] While some federal grant money has been used to help these cities deal with problems on an areawide basis, the pattern of intergovernmental fiscal aid has not shifted in that direction. Where potentially beneficial long-term progress has been made, it has been due to the initiatives, creative instincts, and foresight of state and local leaders and not to the federal government's ability to adapt.

There are two major reasons for such a policy "drift." One resides in the overly technical administrative definition of progress. True to the picket fence analogy, these officials are inclined to define policy success as the efficient dispensation of monies for family assistance, highway construction and maintenance, and the like without considering the relationship of that specific program to overall goals of a long-term decline in levels of poverty, neighborhood racial balance, property values, quality education, crime control, and so on. Second, and perhaps most important, politicians who endorse these fragmented policy patterns do so not out of ignorance, but because it is politically advantageous to do so. They want to secure their political careers as best they can, and it is unpopular to enact programs which would, in effect, redistribute revenues in ways that lower property values and increase taxes in suburban areas that would be impacted by increases in racial balance in both schools and neighborhoods. Campaigns are expensive and votes are precious, and the high turnout rates and contribution potential of suburban residents make it unlikely that politicians will want to invite controversy by shifting wealth (through revenues) from wealthy communities to poorer communities.[10]

Consequently, politics and government in the past generation have been asked to reexamine the assumptions underlying the conventional cooperative federalism. Intergovernmental fiscal and administrative relationships should, so goes the argument, stress state and local, not national, policy initiatives. Grant money should be decategorized and dispensed to states and localities in block form so that recipient governments can apply their own initiatives and experiences as they address problems that are unique to them, and that only they understand. In short, cooperative federalism has been asked to incorporate a new or creative spin. This crusade has enjoyed increased momentum over the past several years, and will be discussed at length later in this chapter.

Cooperative Federalism and Administrative Politics

In order to implement policy successfully, the federal government must solicit cooperation from organizations and individuals who do not share the same administrative orientation and policy perspectives. Since most of these entities are located in, or employed by, state and local government jurisdictions, the influence of national administrators has most often relied on their ability to achieve cooperation by persuasion. Unless it is under the unlikely threat of withdrawing grant support, command is not usually an option. The ostensible purpose of policy administration is instrumental—it matches implementation procedures with goals. Once independent state and local counterparts to federal administrators realize how vital to project success is their cooperation, they can assume an adversarial pose until the federal officials concede on standards, timetables, and even on the constitution of the policies themselves. Of course, it can be argued that this represents a contemporary spin on the founding fathers' effort to deliberately complicate, even disable, government. If one of the major purposes of constitutional politics is to handicap, or disable, policy, then intergovernmental competition between administrative officials is desirable. The fragmentation of administrative authority checks the potential coercive power of government in policy administra-

tion in ways similar to what fragmented institutional power does in policy development. Policy must accommodate fragmented power continually, but that fragmented power should not be so formidable that effective governance is precluded. In the case of intergovernmental policy administration, these conditions mean that policy implementation is often slow, irregular, and sometimes not very efficient. The challenge is for policy to be effective despite the diffusion of authority imposed on it by the federal system. The problem is compounded by the fact that Americans generally equate fragmentation and independence with democracy and political virtue.

The impact of federalism on policy administration is illustrated by Martha Derthick's study of President Johnson's "new towns" innovation in public housing. Attempting to dissipate local complaints against regular housing programs, which often displaced many residents to make way for the housing projects, the president proposed that new towns be built on surplus federal land. This would avoid displacing businesses and residents, a major source of political friction that had regularly plagued low-income housing and urban renewal programs. Furthermore, the president concluded that if federal property could be sold to developers at a below-the-market price, the economic feasibility of the programs would increase. In spite of this, local governments were still unenthusiastic about the new towns program. According to Derthick, the results of the new town projects were, at best, uneven because federal officials failed to generate sufficient local cooperation. Local governments objected to the continuation of stringent restrictions on how money could be spent and to federal requirements for citizen participation. In addition, many jurisdictions thought the projects were too ambitious to yield the results the president expected. Consequently, many local officials balked when HUD officials asked that they do things that only they (local officials) could do to make the developments attractive to potential residents. Included were such exclusively local policy decisions as changing building codes, changing the location and programs offered by schools, and the alteration of transit facilities and routes.[11] Housing policies, by nature, impact on other policies that are completely under the jurisdiction of state and local officials. In sum, shared authority invites uncertainty. States and localities may respond to federal initiatives in ways that circumvent, or even undermine, federal policy goals.

Even in cases in which states and localities are not asked to provide resources and change policies to accommodate federal initiatives, federalism encourages resistance to programs that are incompatible with local interests, or that threaten the ability of a state to protect the welfare of its residents. The nuclear waste disposal site issue is an excellent illustration. Even though most of the federal government's proposed locations for waste sites are on federally owned land, it makes little or no difference to governors of constitutionally independent states. They complain nonetheless. The location is in their state, and the project poses a potential danger and health threat to citizens of their state. Without a doubt, sites need to be selected, but they should "not be in my (state's) backyard" (NIMBY).

Intergovernmental administrative conflict is encouraged by federalism, especially if the policies in question are regulatory in nature, or ask policy concessions that states and local governments are unwilling to make. However, there are also distinctive cooperative dimensions to intergovernmental administrative relations. Usually the lure of the dollar overcomes potential conflict. Cooperation is encouraged by fiscal reality, politics, and the character of policies themselves. While coop-

eration is preponderant, most cooperative intergovernmental policy ventures embody the "vertical policy separatism" of the picket fence, both in how they are legislated and how they are implemented. Asking how federalism influences the policy position of administrative agencies is asking, in part, how federalism affects the structure and deliberations of Congress. Most of the major policies affecting states and localities are legislated first by Congress, and Congress has a distinctive distributive policy bias. Legislators want to please constituents, and can best do that by distributing advantages rather than by demanding sacrifices.

The Senate is constitutionally co-equal with the House under our bicameral legislative system. Since states are represented equally in the Senate, and since they (or their like in other nations) are essential to federalism, how significant is state representational equality to both the character and implementation of public policy? There is a definite cause-effect policy linkage between states as distinct, politically sovereign geographical units, and the role administrative agencies, as creatures of Congress, play in both policymaking and administration.

However, a word of caution is necessary. It should not be assumed that administrative agencies always parrot the wishes of a Congress with a distributive policy bias. What it does assume is that administrative agencies take Congress and its committees and subcommittees into account when they shape and implement policy. It means that agencies will introduce programs knowing that they will have to overcome some opposition to them within Congress. It does not assume that, because states are separate geographic entities, there is usually a homogeneous "state" point of view. States contain many factions motivated by different policy objectives. States as representational and administrative entities carry considerable policy clout because of the political sovereignty and policy authority extended them by the Constitution. This has its behavioral impact. Interest groups clash within states, and state representatives in both the House and Senate reflect the results of such clashes. Nearly all the effects of federalism on administrative behavior can be traced to the fact that states represent formal, constitutionally grounded decision levers that must be accommodated to mold policy alternatives and to implement programs. It means working with different cultures, economic forces, ethnic groups, and general demographic traits that recognize the need to cooperate, but also that tend to hold steadfastly to certain goals and norms without fear of reprisals from "superiors." In short, the manifestations of federalism for the policy process tend to make administrative agencies play accommodational and coordinating roles at the expense of policy leadership roles.

As a result, one of the most significant effects of federalism on public policy is to make politicians of administrators. It does this because it compels federal agencies to seek accommodations between their own interests and those of state and local agencies, most of which have close ties to vested interests within their jurisdictions. As noted above, these state and local counterpart units drive hard policy bargains because their existence and character is not dependent upon the national agency. It makes politicians of administrators because congressional committee and subcommittee biases are slanted to magnify constitutionally secure state and local interests. As the late Morton Grodzins once observed: "The politics of administration is a process of making peace with the legislators who for the most part consider themselves the guardians of local interests. The political role of administrators therefore contributes to the power of states and localities in national programs."[12]

State political autonomy amplifies the role and impact of what Daniel Elazar has called the three dominant patterns of political culture, which virtually compel federal administrators to deal with three different historically nurtured sets of moral standards when they deal with their state and local counterparts. Elazar cites three major U.S. cultural traditions—the individualistic, moralistic, and traditionalistic—each of which pushes its own distinct character in policy development.[13] Elazar's cultural typology is more hypothetical than some scholars want to accept. Although it is based on extensive research, its critics argue that the significance of the cultural patterns for decision making within and among states is minimal. For one thing, the influence of one cultural strain will vary according to subregions within states—cities, rural areas, pockets of ethnic groups. For another, even though it is possible to depict three cultural patterns, some observers argue that this does not help explain differences in state policy patterns and governmental organization. However, a study by Ira Sharkansky confirmed the general validity of the cultural typology and that the various cultures do promote certain policies and attitudes toward government that can be correlated with cultural as well as socioeconomic factors.[14] Therefore, the cultural strains within states and regions of the country do impact on administrative behavior.

States dominated by the individualist culture use government for principally "utilitarian reasons." Governments should do only what they are directed to do by the body politic. This means that efficiency and the regulation of government activities is rewarded. Characterized by a distaste for comprehensive policy planning, it "eschews ideology" in its devotion to businesslike principles. The moralistic culture, present largely in the midwestern and plains states, stresses the use of public policy as a way to alleviate human suffering by employing government to work for the common good. Politics is first and foremost a way to extend man's humanitarianism into public arenas. The traditionalistic culture, dominant in the southern states, equates good policy and good government with maintenance of the existent social and political order. It resembles the moralistic order in viewing government's social mission as a positive one, although this latter role is questioned if it goes beyond maintaining the existent social and economic order. The traditionalistic culture is cast heavily in elitism, with certain families and leaders unofficially endowed with the right to hold public office.

The effects of these cultural strata on public policy are varied. Part of their impact lies in the way that each order views its role in politics and policy development and the bureaucracy's role in each. States where the individualistic strain predominates have what Elazar terms an "ambivalent" view of the bureaucracy's role in society. On the one hand, it is undesirable because the merit system limits the impact of patronage and favoritism as a means to reward and extend the influence of dominant interests within the state. On the other hand, bureaucracy is viewed as functional to the utilitarian underpinnings of the individualistic culture by stressing efficiency. Moralistic states have a positive, functional attitude toward administration because the merit system and neutrality facilitate a "commonweal" view of government as a mechanism to further the common good. In contrast, traditionalistic states react negatively to administration and especially neutrality because neutrality brings about "depersonalized government" and insulates political leadership from the community.[15]

Considering federal-state administrative relations, each cultural perspective is expressed through state administrative and legislative institutions, each of which is legally, politically, and administratively independent of its federal counterpart. Therefore, federal administrators face multiple, well-entrenched,

constitutionally reinforced opposition to policy proposals that must be compromised in seeking consensus on policy. Certainly no single culture completely saturates any one state. However, the dominant strain within a state tends to dominate its politics. Federalism affords culture added leverage by encouraging federal administrators to adapt to it as a precondition for achieving the cooperation that can often seem quite elusive.

In addition, population migration triggered by such matters as urbanization, the industrialization of the economy, and retirement has created pockets of political liberalism and conservatism that have leveraged, through politics, the impact of political culture on both policy content and policy administration. In his analysis of voting trends in the 1996 presidential and congressional elections, Michael Barone noted a distinct tendency for migrating industries, workers, and retirees to "seek out their own kind" when making decisions about where to relocate.[16] This has introduced a sectional, or regional, dimension to U.S. government and politics that is nourished by forms of *cultural* conservatism and liberalism, instead of the more traditional individualist and materialist forms. Cultural conservatives and liberals tend to judge the merit of policies by the degrees to which government in involved or, if a government role is inevitable, the *level* of government which is assigned the most power. Population and industrial migration have accentuated the impact of such attitudes on politics and administration. Population migration creates more cultural homogeneity, and this is having an increasing impact on the types of candidates that are elected to office from the various regions, and in the ways in which policies incorporate cultural attitudes. Voters are increasingly inclined to cast votes for or against parties or candidates on the basis of their commitment in principle to either rugged individualism or government paternalism, with some variations in between. Barone concluded that some regions, most notably New England and the interior regions (Rocky Mountain, southwest, and plains states), are becoming more "monopartisan."[17] New England is becoming more culturally liberal, and the interior region more culturally conservative. The federal system allows these attitudes about the role of government to be leveraged to the point where, potentially, they could pose major roadblocks to the enactment of rational solutions to contemporary policy problems, most of which are notably interstate and interregional in character. Pragmatic solutions to policy problems should not have, indeed cannot have, an exclusive or near exclusive state or regional focus. Unfortunately, at the very time in our nation's history when policy issues are assuming a clear multistate and multiregion quality, voters in some regions are demanding just the opposite—more state sovereignty and independence both from one another and from the federal government.

Cooperative Federalism and Policy Management

The tendency for federalism to establish rather independent fiefdoms of legal authority means that federalism, like the separation of powers doctrine, encourages the formation of agencies dedicated to coordinating policy formation and administration through a varied and constantly changing system of policy "superstructures." Probably the most institutionalized manifestation of such pluralization on policy development and program incrementalism is the interstate board, agency, or commission. Such agencies are established because changing conditions and policy necessities have made them critical to developing area and regional points of view to help overcome the segmented perspectives of

single government units and policy specialists. Organizations such as the national Governors Conference, the Council of State Governments, the American Municipal Association, the National Association of County Officials, and the United States Conference of Mayors are but a few examples of organizations of officials who meet regularly to discuss problems that are regional rather than state in character. In addition to these institutions, several special intergovernmental commissions or boards have been created to develop policy and oversee the administration of programs that exist in response to the acceptance of regionalism and federal-state cooperation.

Therefore, federalism complicates the task of policy management on a number of fronts. It has contributed to what Leonard D. White termed a "loose jointed, easy going, somewhat irresponsible system of administration."[18] The growing pressure to produce programs in response to evolving problems has led to nursing microscopic, uncoordinated, and unequally applied grants of money to states and localities. Governor Sanford considered this one of the most serious problems confronting states in the last half of the twentieth century. President Johnson echoed this sentiment in his 1968 budget message to Congress, noting that "the problem of managing many of our important new programs is intensified by their intergovernmental character."[19] In asking Congress for legislation to consolidate several categorical grants-in-aid in 1969, President Nixon complained that "under our present fragmented system, each one of a group of closely related categorical grants is encumbered with its own individual array of administrative and technical requirements. This unnecessarily complicates the planning process; it discourages comprehensive planning; it requires multiple applications, and multiple bookkeeping, both by the Federal agencies and by state and local governments."[20] The late Stephen K. Bailey, in commenting on how policy management problems were aggravated by the introduction of programs attendant to President Johnson's Great Society, remarked that the "barriers" to effective administration seem nearly insurmountable in Washington, and they grow even more so away from Washington. Between the nation's capital and the 90 percent of federal employees who work in other parts of the country, there is a lack of cooperation and an absence of effective coordination that threatens the very base of program effectiveness.[21]

It would, of course, be foolhardy to blame such a state of affairs on federalism alone. The nature of administration in a pluralistic political system, regardless of the constitutional distribution of geographic authority, is an important causal force. Federalism does, however, tend to encourage policy parochialism on the part of state and local politicians and administrators. The political autonomy of states and their representational subdivisions inflates the importance of these localized perspectives as policymakers seek politically realistic solutions to both policy development and implementation. Much recent federal legislation has emphasized the need to involve states, localities, and citizens generally in policymaking and administration.

Bailey and Mosher, in their study of the implementation of the Elementary and Secondary Education Act of 1965, acknowledged that states and localities have recognized the inevitability of a major federal role in financing education, but also that "acceptance of the federal government's new role in education is bound to be hesitant and grudging among those who have strong interests in maintaining traditional state, local, and professional autonomies."[22] Officials in the United States Department of Education, responsible for administration of the act, were forced to "work out the frictions of partnership with its state, local, professional clients,"

and therefore saw advantages to "keeping boat rocking to a minimum."

The Community Action Programs (CAPs) were excellent examples of how local power structures coopted the antipoverty program to serve group ends rather than the program's goals.[23] Some officials were concerned that the Air Quality Act of 1967 would fail if states were given discretion to set standards beyond those set by the Department of Health, Education and Welfare (DHEW) because competition between the states to attract industry might make those states with the lowest antipollution standards the most appealing to industry. Accordingly, the DHEW secretary would find it difficult to "resist political pressures arising from cries of lost jobs or bankruptcy if industries move elsewhere."[24] In sum, the more policy discretion allotted states and localities by federal grants, the less likely the substantive purpose of the program as expressed in national enabling legislation will be accomplished. Of course, if state and local policy discretion is a goal unto itself, then changes in the substantive intent of legislation during the administrative phase of the policy cycle is more tolerable.

Policy administrators must deal with states as geographical, administrative subdivisions, even though they do not contribute rationalism to either policy planning or implementation. Policy problems transcend state boundaries. Metropolitan areas transcend state lines and reflect problems that, although common to citizens and special districts within the area, are not afforded the same priority in the statehouses. Federal administrators are placed in a position of having to bargain and to organize advisory committees and regional commissions to cultivate policy perspectives that, hopefully, will subdue the illogical, atomized divisiveness expressed by interest dominant within states. To placate these interests to secure any solution means that the development of strategies to achieve cooperation and consensus are paramount.

Cooperative Federalism in Transition: The Policy Implications

The affinity of Americans for *ad hoc*, uncentralized patterns of cultural development, economic growth, and religious and social diversity affects the way government institutions are structured and the way they are reformed. Federalism as a constitutional principle was designed to accommodate these conditions. Governments at all levels reflect a bias against centralized authority. As a result, proposals to decentralize, or devolve, power within and among institutions usually encounter little, if any resistance. Cooperative federalism is no exception. Instead of reevaluating the theories underlying failed programs, reformers are inclined to seek procedural correctives. Sometimes these correctives are hierarchical in cast, but decentralization, or devolution, is the preferred alternative.

Cooperative federalism has been subjected to two devolutionary movements since the mid-1960s. One of these was called "creative" federalism, and it extended from the Johnson administration through the Carter administration. It called for the decentralization of policymaking authority from the federal level to states and localities, usually within the structure of the categorical grant network. The second was labeled the "new" federalism. It began with the Reagan administration and continued through the 1990s. It called for a general reorientation of grants from categories to a "block" format, wherein monies were allocated to states and localities by policy field or area, not by category, thereby increasing the policy discretion potential for the recipient governments.

After impacting a few Great Society programs, in the mid-1960s, the creative federalism movement (and its new federalism derivative) gained increased momentum as the nation approached the twenty-first century. The speed of the movement has been inconsistent, but the direction has been clear. Its assumption is that if the *processes* of decision making are altered to accommodate state and local diversity, the ability to achieve policy *goals* will be improved. The assumption is that policies do not self-implement, and the processes should not be considered ends or goals unto themselves. In theory, the movement has a good deal of policy integrity. Experience has shown that too much centralization of both policy initiatives and policy administration can be inefficient and counterproductive. On the other hand, there may be danger in decentralizing decision making as a matter of principle without keeping the means-ends linkage constantly in mind.

States are constitutionally independent. The Constitution guarantees their territorial and jurisdictional integrity. However, this means that the different policy challenges they face are not always met with the same level of legislative will, financial resources, and administrative competence in each state. There is nothing the federal government or, for that matter, the states and localities, can do about it except to work to overcome the results of such conditions without tampering with their jurisdictional causes. Consequently, standards of equality and fairness often are compromised in the interest of accommodating the legislative and administrative independence of constitutionally sovereign states. People who need assistance are either advantaged or disadvantaged by chance of birth and/or migration. Too often, the chances of whether a program will be of measurable help to an individual, a family, or a school rest almost exclusively on what state and/or locality the people or schools are located. Such conditions intensify problems of inequality in a nation whose constitution is committed to the opposite.

Since the mid-1960s, the cooperative federalism movement has had three distinct objectives, all of them procedural in nature, and each beginning with the letter "D": decentralization, decategorization, and democratization. Each trend involves the devolution of both policymaking and administrative power. Recipient governments decide, within limits, what should be done as well as how to do it. This can be accomplished within the traditional categorical grant framework—by insisting that recipient government spend money for specific categories within those fields. Local discretion is obviously enhanced under such conditions. Also, it has been assumed that citizen or client input, especially from people and organizations directly affected by the program, will enhance a program's chance for success. Some legislation, such as that authorizing Community Action Programs (CAPs), required this. However, usually participatory decisions are made by on-line administrators who understand the advantages of grass-roots inputs to a specific policy's success or failure.

These objectives have been incorporated in laws in several ways. It is important to bear in mind that the alleged advantages of creative federalism are advantages in theory, not necessarily in fact. Sometimes they may improve programs. Other times they may not. Occasionally they may even be counterproductive. Moreover, these trends are not comprehensive, wholesale trends. Most federal grant-in-aid programs have been sustained in their old-school, categorical form. Finally, the nature of the program in question often determines whether grass-roots inputs are necessary and helpful. For example, highway construction and maintenance and hospital construction programs do not, by their nature, invite much citizen input, whereas antipoverty, crime control, and education policies most likely do, at least when they are first introduced, sometimes as experiments.

Community Action Programs

Community Action Programs (CAPs) were created by the Economic Opportunity Act of 1964 which was part of President Johnson's Great Society package of social, economic, and education reforms. The Great Society programs as a package were not the embodiment of creative federalism. Quite to the contrary, they mostly represented an attempt to reinvigorate and expand the federal government's role in social end economic reform in ways clearly consistent with the Progressive and New Deal traditions.

However, the Community Action Programs were an exception to this. Their purpose was to stimulate communities to organize and direct their resources toward the alleviation and ultimate elimination of poverty. Federal grants were made available to local agencies, both public and private, to pioneer antipoverty policies that involved the poor directly in program administration. Illustrative programs included job training, vocational rehabilitation, health services, job development, literacy training, family counseling, recreation activities, and homemaker services. Local agencies were required to secure the "maximum feasible participation" of individuals affected by the programs into their administration. The law didn't insist on a strict participatory percentage of the poor on governing boards or commissions. As a result, frequently local administrators offered the poor only token representation. Some CAPs did indeed introduce innovative approaches to the poverty problem. Others were victimized by political patronage and did not take the participation mandate very seriously.[25]

Housing and Community Development Act

The Housing and Community Development Act of 1974 was one of a series of laws enacted to supplement the objectives of the Public Housing Act of 1937. It was notable for its embodiment of creative federalism. While both public housing and urban renewal programs had incorporated local participation, President Nixon concluded that it was at too modest a level. The 1974 law decentralized the administration of housing programs substantially more than had earlier policies.

The 1974 act consolidated previously legislated categorical grants for neighborhood development, housing rehabilitation, community open spaces, public facilities loans, and water and sewer projects into a single block grant system called Community Development Block Grants (CDBGs). Instead of competing for grants, as they had in the past, communities with populations of at least 50,000 were allotted funds automatically, although they still had to apply officially to the Department of Housing and Urban Development (HUD) for the money. HUD could (and did) ask that certain conditions and priorities be met before funds were disbursed, but the overall effect of CDBGs was to allow local administrators much more discretion than they had previously. Priority was to be given to projects that affected low-income groups, but most projects did not have that as their first priority. CDBGs were used for such diverse projects as street repaving, traffic lights, senior citizen centers, day-care services, commercial development, industrial parks, parks and recreation facilities, health care, urban renewal,

and its policy sister, the model cities program, as separate and distinct federal programs.

Evidence suggests that localities did not use CDBGs to help people and conditions in distressed neighborhoods as much as was originally intended.[26] The earlier categorical grant system seemed to benefit the poor in distressed sections of cities more than did CDBGs. Some cities concluded that it was more cost-effective, and therefore more productive, to invest money in transitional neighborhoods as opposed to those that were the most distressed. Perhaps more important than this was the pressure put on public officials to invest in more middle-class and moderate income neighborhoods which needed projects, and which were more politically alert and active than were residents of the more depressed areas. Concerned about this trend, President Carter issued a series of executive orders requiring HUD to dispense at least 75 percent of money to low to moderate income neighborhoods. HUD complied, but relaxed its application of the standard in response to local and congressional political pressure.[27] When Ronald Reagan assumed the presidency, HUD dispensed with the standard entirely.

CDBGs were designed in part to encourage increased citizen participation in development projects. However, because local discretion was emphasized, neither the law or executive orders issued by HUD dictated a particular structure or formula specifying how participation was to be integrated into decision processes. With a few exceptions, it was not. Usually the poor and minorities were not given official roles in decisions, and inputs from citizen advisory committees were usually not considered seriously. Nor did the flexibility afforded local officials inspire a tidal wave of innovative local projects. Most new projects were based on successful experiments attempted elsewhere or were the result of federal government recommendations. To be sure, local officials enjoyed their new-found empowerment, but the key question was to what forces, ideas, traditions, norms, and so on did they respond when they applied the discretion? It was common for these officials to spend the funds comfortably—that is, in ways that did not offend the balance of local political forces.[28] In conclusion, CDBGs hoped that the decategorization, decentralization, and (expected) democratization of development project decision making would improve both decision-making processes and policy results. Instead, the grants accomplished only one objective: the decentralization, democratization, and decategorization of procedures, and not decisions that consciously integrated those procedures with meaningful results. Making procedures ends unto themselves turns policy and administrative decisions into, as one observer commented, a "crap game," the results of which are almost totally dependent on the mosaic of politics that dominates the recipient government's arena.[29]

President Reagan's "Decentralization as Abdication"

Presidents Nixon and Reagan were considerably more concerned with decentralizing policy authority and financial responsibility than were the early proponents of creative federalism, who assumed that the federal government would dominate in substantive decisions, and states and localities in administration. Comparing the two presidents, Reagan was more concerned with policy decentralization in principle than was Nixon. Most of Nixon's proposals and successes were designed to retain the federal-state cooperative state of affairs, but to adjust them to the realities of changing times. By way of contrast, Rea-

gan sought to regain a state of affairs that he thought had been insidiously destroyed by the growth of big government. Nixon was more the pragmatist, and Reagan the idealist. Reagan entered office with a classic dual federalism mentality. He introduced a sweeping consolidation of block grants, the core of which still survives. However, he will best be remembered for what he attempted, but failed, to accomplish. In an attempt to harness the federal budget while simultaneously seeking a restoration of state and local power, Reagan proposed a major "turnback" or transfer of grant responsibilities to the states (not localities) and a "swap" of responsibilities with the states. In sum, Reagan offered a new federalism spin to the creative federalism trend.

Both Reagan proposals were part of the Omnibus Budget and Reconciliation Act of 1981. Some fifty-seven federal block grants were consolidated into nine categories, and it was proposed that the federal government's role in the distribution of funds in the new categories be reduced and assigned to state, not local, governments. The purpose was to return to literal, constitutional federalism, which makes states, not localities, co-equal partners (or protagonists) with the federal government. Reagan's Fiscal Year 1983 budget sought to engineer this plan by introducing the most sweeping reform of federalism in the twentieth century. These were proposed changes only, appearing in the president's budget plan, and were not accepted by Congress or state officials. However, they are important because of how they illustrate politically how appealing an argument for constitutional literalism can be, and how an affinity for such an appeal clouds real issues in politics and government.

Beginning in Fiscal Year 1984, Reagan proposed a major swap of federal and state policy responsibilities. States were to assume complete responsibility for the Food Stamp and AFDC programs. In return, the federal government would take total control of Medicaid, a medical assistance program for the poor which was a joint federal-state responsibility. Furthermore, Reagan proposed that a total of forty-four existing grant-in-aid programs be returned to the states, accompanied by federal financial support, but at significantly reduced levels. Had this proposal been accepted, the national government's role in social policy would have been confined to matters of health and income security. All other existing federal-state cooperative policy efforts would have been reassigned to the states. The proposals were quickly rejected by Congress and state officials. The results would have been too unpredictable, and program budget cuts would have been too severe ($45 billion) for financially strapped states facing a recession and mounting pressures to raise taxes. Furthermore, the president did not discuss the proposal with state governors in advance, encouraging some observers to conclude that one of the proposal's major objectives was, in reality, to cut federal spending.[30]

In conclusion, although the Reagan reforms amounted to too much too soon, the political and cultural mindset behind them was to continue and manifest itself more dramatically more than a decade later during the Clinton administration.

President Clinton's "New Age" Federalism

President Clinton was elected during a relatively tranquil period in our nation's history. There was no crisis to offer him the political and economic raw material to initiate major policy reforms, and he understood this. The direction in federalism was that of devolution and the president was in no position to reverse that momentum were he so inclined, and he wasn't. In keeping with the creative federalism spirit, his preference was for what has been termed "New Age Federalism," or an arrangement under which the federal government would continue to support what can be labeled a "devolution solution" to the presumed federal-state policy imbalance. However, since federal grant-in-aid funds would continue to be channeled to states and localities to help them introduce innovative programs, the federal government would continue to insist on performing a general oversight function, and step in to help states when they were in obvious need of financial or administrative assistance. The most high-profile example of New Age Federalism and the devolution of power within the federal system was the Personal Responsibility and Work Opportunity Act of 1996. The following discussion is devoted to the description and analysis of that legislation, and its policy significance.

Although President Reagan's "swap" and "turnback" proposals were defeated, the theory behind them survived, and helped pave the way for the elections to the presidency of George Bush in 1988 and Bill Clinton in 1992. Devolution had been popular with conservative movements since the 1960s. Bush found it necessary to assuage the conservative, or right, wing of the Republican Party to secure the presidential nomination. The same forces were critical to his election. Republican conservatives had become increasingly ideological in cast since Reagan's election, focusing on fiscal austerity and power devolution as major reform crusades. Bush could not ignore these trends either as a candidate or as an incumbent president. However, since he faced a Democratically controlled Congress that was, by and large, hostile to power devolution in principle, there were no significant changes in the federal-state power pattern during the Bush presidency.

Bill Clinton's presidency was another story, however, flavored with a good deal of irony on a number of fronts. Federal-state relations was certainly one of them. Clinton did not campaign for the presidency as an old-line, New Deal liberal with a commitment to Roosevelt's and Johnson's centralized version of cooperative federalism. Although his political opponents attempted to label Clinton as a traditional tax and spend liberal, such was not in fact the case. Clinton may in fact have been spiritually committed to traditional Democratic Party values and government's role in their achievement but, as a practical political matter, it was not good politics to be a professed and practicing New Deal liberal in the mid-1990s. Accordingly, Clinton politically was more of a pragmatist than an ideologue. He knew well that his election did not represent a Democratic counterrevolution to the emerging conservatism of the 1980s. He had campaigned as a "new Democrat," committed to cutting government waste and inefficiency, to prioritizing policy objectives very carefully, and to reinvigorating the federal system.

Clinton was well aware of public cynicism about government, and how that could be translated easily into a frontal assault on the national government as a "top heavy" policy force. The 1994 election results dramatically underscored this reality. Although the elections brought Republicans to majority status in both houses of Congress for the first time since 1954, this represented more of an antigovernment, antisystem revolt than it did a pro-Republican statement. Nonetheless, Clinton knew that the public's antisystem mindset was congruous, at least symbolically, with devolution as a route to policy reform. Since Clinton faced divided government conditions from 1995 on, he decided that a variation on the theme "if you can't beat 'em, join 'em" was the only practical route to social policy reform during his presidency. He attempted to draw from the devolution idea changes that would simultaneously both decentralize policy administration and improve its effect. This provides the rationale behind Clinton's support of the Personal Responsibility and Work Opportunity Act of 1996, a law hailed as a groundbreaking moment in the nation's history because of its dramatic impact on traditional nation-state relations in social programs. Reagan's turnback idea had finally become a fact, at least in one critical policy area.

With the Personal Responsibility and Work Opportunity Act, the nation began an experiment in decentralization the results of which will take years to assess. The most significant part of the law replaced national responsibility for establishing basic eligibility standards for Aid to Families with Dependent Children (AFDC), and a national agreement to match state spending for low-family-income assistance, with a fixed block grant of funds to states that was to be used for the same policy objectives. Standards of eligibility for support were to be determined by the states. Instead of categorical AFDC assistance, the states were to receive lump-sum grant payment computed on the basis of how much AFDC assistance they had received between 1992 and 1994. Although the Department of Health and Human Services (HHS) was to certify states' plans formally, this was just a pro-forma matter. States were, in effect, free to deal with family poverty on their own. After two years of receiving assistance, recipients would be required to find employment on their own, or participate in state-certified work programs. Half the recipients were required to have achieved work status by the year 2002. States were permitted to use block grant money to fund employer incentive programs, and to establish community service employment programs. A lifetime limit of five years was established for recipient families with dependent children. Families without dependents were limited to two years' assistance, although states were permitted to exempt up to 20 percent of their family caseloads from these requirements.

To say that the 1996 welfare changes were a bold experiment would be an understatement. They were based on the conclusion, supported by both experience with traditional AFDC practices and a bit of political opportunism, that the traditional categorical assistance approach to the poverty problem had failed. Recipients had not become self-sufficient as a rule. Costs had gotten out of hand. The federal government had become too large, inflexible, rigid, and heavily mired in bureaucracy. The hope was—and it will remain a hope for the foreseeable future—that a reduction in the national role in entitlements policies will spur state policy creativity and adaptiveness.

Traditional assumptions that underlay New Deal and Great Society reforms were repealed by the 1996 act. The federal government was no longer to bear responsibility for providing minimum family income support. The law also put an end to the assumption that the federal government bears the responsibility for family income security, regardless of the family's state of residence. Since 1996 states have borne the responsibility of designing more effective and efficient welfare support systems, appropriately tuned to local conditions and local goals.

The 1996 reforms were premised on the view that procedural changes almost automatically yield better results. Although the law does link procedures to results generally, it does not do so specifically. In effect, it decentralizes decision making with the expectation that things will improve. There is, of course, no guarantee of that. The poor are not well organized and have little political clout. Their satisfaction yields little political advantage to policymakers. Of course, if poverty problems are exacerbated in some states in the wake of these changes, the resultant policy spillovers, or externalities, will affect everyone by increasing crime, aggravating problems in schools, exacerbating the drug problem, and

impact negatively the overall quality of life. However, such possibilities are not likely to impress public officials with a short-term orientation directed at assuaging interests with money and political clout. This is why President Clinton was roundly criticized by some members of his own party for supporting reforms. Prominent Democratic figures such as Daniel Moynihan and Richard Gephardt voiced concern that the reforms might well intensify the problems of poor families (especially children) in states that were unwilling to commit the effort to dealing with poverty problems creatively and systematically. Some states, including Wisconsin, Maryland, and Virginia, had exploited the "policy laboratory" opportunity offered by a federal structure and made significant strides in the state-initiated reform, even in advance of the 1996 law's passage. However, other states with a tradition of low-level financial support for entitlement and education programs entitlement had done little, if anything, in anticipation of welfare reform.

In addition to the elimination of AFDC, the 1996 reforms reduced the federal government's financial obligation for the Food Stamp Program by 13 percent, and relaxed standards on how states were to disburse Medicaid funds. Critics of this new strategy argued that the momentum to both decentralize and downsize grossly overestimated the value of the old system to the poor and vulnerable while, at the same time, it overestimated the ability of states, as a group, to develop improved alternative ways of combating the problems. While nearly everyone agreed that the problems need attention, they argued that combining cost reduction and decentralization simultaneously was a recipe for disaster. It would, so went the argument, destroy the national "safety net" and not replace it with anything that the poor could count on. The federal government's role in these areas was introduced because states were either unable or unwilling to address the problems of their poor. Even if the changes make for success in some states, the problems of the poor could well be intensified in others.

The pessimists' fears were certainly not manifest after welfare reform's first year which, by virtually any measure, was a noteworthy success. By mid-summer, 1997, welfare rolls had dropped by nearly two million since the law's passage a year earlier. Employment opportunities produced by a strong economy were partly responsible for the reduction, but probably not for most of it. Even during earlier periods of economic prosperity, a caseload drop of 250,000 was considered excellent. Most of the improvement should be credited to the "dole to payroll" spirit of the reforms themselves. Welfare applicants were being processed as preemployment applicants and not as welfare check recipients. In most states, the "climate of expectations" had changed from one of applicant dependency to one of applicant potential. In one Michigan county, all of the previous year's 413 welfare families were off the dole by mid-1997.[31] Tempering such optimistic results was the fact that the most difficult challenges lay ahead. People employed during the law's first year were clearly the most employable. Any major future successes will depend heavily on the ability of governments to encourage the private sector to develop innovative ways to both employ and have patience with the less employable. However, if economic prosperity continues and corporations do their part, according to Jonathan Alter, we may be "on the threshold of the greatest social policy achievement in a generation."[32]

The Devolution Solution: A Critique

Federalism, as a constitutional principle, is a symbolic ally of devolution as a reform strategy.

It encourages reformers to think of decentralization as intrinsically good in principle. However, this is not always the case. States and localities do not always succeed where the national government fails. To unshackle the states from nationally imposed policy standards does not mean that the quality of policymaking and administration will improve because of that procedural change alone. For example, states are said to outshine the national government in matters of financial management. Many states regularly balance their budgets, most often because their constitutions require it. Devolution advocates argue that if the federal government would impose the same austerity standard on itself, it would not be in the debt-ridden financial bind in which it finds itself today. This explains why proposals to amend the Constitution to require a balanced budget are often advanced. However, a closer look at comparative finance strategies (national government and the states) reveals that states have two key advantages over the federal government that help them balance their budgets, at least officially. First, all states that are required to balance their budgets also have a capital budgeting option. Capital budgets permit governments to finance long-term capital development projects such as roads and buildings by borrowing money to finance the projects. These debt obligations, financed through general obligation and revenue bonds, are not incorporated as expenditure obligations in regular state budgets. However, the federal budget is not divided into capital and current spending obligations. Therefore, the cost to the federal government of servicing the national debt is incorporated into its current budget obligations. Second, federal government spending obligations include smoothing out the business cycle by borrowing and spending strategies. If successful, this strategy eases the impact of recessions by stimulating growth when the economy is depressed. Therefore, spending beyond the government's means benefits nearly everyone, but it is at odds with the classical notion of fiscal responsibility. States' spending rarely has economic stability as a primary goal. Therefore, such spending strategies that would likely increase state debt are not part of state policy scripts. States have situational advantages when it comes to financial management that have little to do with better financial savvy or more ability to impose fiscal self-discipline.

Other myths support a devolution solution that may mean it promises more than it can deliver. For one, many devolution gurus assume that states and (especially) localities are able to deal with their policy challenges in comprehensive, rational ways. On close examination, there is little evidence to support this, at least if all, or nearly all, state and local government experiences are considered. As noted earlier in this chapter, most metropolitan areas include scores of special districts, many of which do not make unusual efforts to orchestrate their activities with those of other jurisdictions. The federal government expects a fusion, or integration, of energy that may well not come to pass.

Most policy problems are areawide, or regional in dimension, not local. Confronting them on a piecemeal basis is doomed to failure because problems such as poverty, economic development, pollution control, transportation planning, education, and job training do not naturally fall under the jurisdiction of one government. This fundamental conflict between the nature of policy problems and the fragmentation of local governments could, in fact, make the devolution solution worse than the diseases with which it was supposed to deal. Vast sums of money could be spent to little or no avail, while problems fester and public funding becomes scarce. Local governments, including special districts, jealously guard their fiefdoms. However, the policy problems that the devolution revolution asks them to address cannot be re-

solved by these governments acting on their own. Of course, the decentralization crusade could well trigger reorganization and regionalization movements in some areas. If it does, then devolution harbors much potential for those areas.

Despite some notable successes, the overall record of states as sources of creative policy initiation and successful experimentation has not been promising. Once the devolution "genie" has been freed from the bottle, it may be very difficult to undo the resulting damages accruing from the unwillingness or inability of states and localities to respond with the creativity and enthusiasm assumed by the crusade. John Donahue, a former top executive in the Labor Department, argues that states, newly endowed with more policy discretion, could well respond by actually lowering both entitlement spending levels and taxes in an effort to attract corporations and wealthy citizens to relocate within their confines. South Carolina and Ohio did just that in the 1980s to lure automobile manufacturers to their states. If this becomes a trend, then public spending for schools, parks, and entitlements may well be sacrificed in favor of industrial profits. To lure high-income residents, states could increase their more regressive consumption taxes, which harm those on modest incomes disproportionately, and lower property and income taxes, which advantage the wealthy. In sum, state "bidding wars" encourage regressive policies which, in turn, make the rich richer, the poor more desperate, and the middle class increasingly discouraged. Furthermore, argues Donahue, assuming that states function well as creative laboratories is a myth. The record shows that states are slow to learn and adapt from their own successes and failures, let alone from those of others.[33]

Another myth affecting the devolution crusade is the assumption that advocates support the movement because they believe it is sound policy theory. In some cases, that may well be true. However, in many cases it is surely not. President Reagan no doubt advanced his swap and turnback proposals in part to reinstitute classical federalism. However, Reagan was also interested in finding ways to reduce federal spending. What better way is there to relieve federal spending pressures than to transfer costly obligations to other jurisdictions with reduced levels of support? President Nixon attempted the same thing with some entitlement programs in 1974. Nixon sought not only to reduce spending, but also to fragment the administration of some programs so badly that the case for their continuance would be weakened.[34] In sum, decentralization strategies can serve as convenient smokescreens for political and administrative "hot potatoes." Devolution can lend legitimacy to buck passing. If you can't cope, delegate. If the policy then fails, blame those who actually have the new responsibility. If this strategy can be cloaked with the symbolic honor of a constitutional principle such as federalism, so much the better.

Finally, devolution strategies may be based somewhat on the belief that states and localities can keep policy objectives in focus and in line better than can the federal government. In other words, states and localities can better resist the efforts of vested interests and professionals to convert policies to their own use and away from their original public objectives than can the federal government. Vested interests spend much time and money in presidential and congressional elections, and on lobbying, in efforts to keep government servile to them. However, state and local governments are by no means immune from such pressures. Politicians and administrative professionals at these levels are no less career conscious than are their national counterparts. Therefore, pressures on state and local decision makers to forgo efforts to deal with poverty, employment, education, and housing problems rationally and with major financial

commitments can be significant. Many beneficiaries of decentralized policies are weak politically. Recipients of welfare entitlements are a good example. Therefore local authorities may opt for the safe and secure track, and appease the forces of cooptation rather than resist them. If this becomes the case, then the only thing that devolution has actually accomplished has been to transfer policy authority and the politics that accompanies it to other arenas, inviting the same play to be acted out on different stages. The political rhetoric which underlies the devolution issue reveals, in effect, what may indeed be the true incentive behind it. In all likelihood, a major (if not the major) incentive behind proposals to route policies to the states is not a belief that the states can do better than the federal government, but a cynical determination that both the talk and actuality of devolution is an effective smokescreen for a crusade to downsize government.

Federalism: The Policy Potential

Cooperative federalism and its most recent devolutionary derivatives can improve policy effectiveness. As discussed earlier in this chapter, the experiences of cities such as Austin, Texas and Portland, Oregon with the regionalization of infrastructures to deal with economic development, racial relations, and housing are testimony to that. Wisconsin's experience with a workfare-based welfare reform policy that was in place before the revolutionary 1996 reform legislation lends further support to the notion. Federalism can be rejuvenated and policies can be improved simultaneously.

However, the road to the realization of those joint objectives is full of policy and political land mines. The federal system has often been criticized for discouraging change because it requires many actors in many arenas to agree on policy actions. Effective top down coordination of policies is difficult. However, meaningful policy change is not impossible in a federal system. In a sense, federalism encourages policy changes by offering opportunities for subnational policy experimentation. Disputes over the best way to deal with a policy problem can encourage the introduction and careful examination of policy options that would not have been introduced if the system had been unified instead of fragmented.

Policymakers can muster the courage to resist the pressures of vested interests to drain the vitality out of new ideas. The states can serve as essential experimentation laboratories. Procedural changes, such as devolution, can inspire new governments to resist the drift toward policy stagnation, incrementalism, and financial waste. To succeed takes commitment and courage and, above all, a constant attempt to develop realistic ways to reach predetermined policy objectives.

However, the challenge is formidable. The political and policy by-products of federalism are not easily overcome or compromised. Education policy, of concern to most Americans, offers an excellent example. Perhaps more than any other policy area, local control of education has been a tradition. Suggestions of wholesale national intervention into local control of school curricula or faculty affairs are rejected almost out of principle. However, concern over the conditions within our schools is high priority to most public officials at any level of government including the federal government. The reasons for this are clear: If government is intent on dealing with the root causes of drug abuse, poverty, crime, family stability, disease prevention and treatment, teenage pregnancies, and job training it has to deal with conditions in the schools. Students having family problems, nutrition problems, and poverty problems take these with them when they attend school, and this

compromises their ability, and the ability of their classmates, to learn. Weapons are brought to the classroom. Drugs are sometimes sold on, or near, school property. Hostile student attitudes rooted in an unstable family situation affect student attitudes toward their classes, classmates, and teacher. In sum, the schools reflect and embody a composite of society's problems in microcosm. Therefore, it is logical for the federal government to be interested in what happens within schools and the effect of that on society in general.

However, the principle of local control over school policy interferes with national attempts to deal with education problems systematically. The most comprehensive law ever enacted by the federal government to deal with problems in the public schools was the Elementary and Secondary Education Act of 1965, part of President Johnson's "war on poverty" crusade. Despite the fact that the president had overwhelming Democratic Party majorities in both houses of Congress, he had to construct and frame his education policy proposals to conform to objectives of the antipoverty crusade. He could not make it a broad across-the-board attempt to subsidize schools and students generally. Instead, monies were to go to help children in schools with poor financial bases in economically disadvantaged sections of the country, such as Appalachia. Without such a strategy, any federal intervention into local school affairs probably would have been rejected in principle.

If the need to deal with education problems systematically was evident in 1965, it is most certainly so as the nation enters the twenty-first century. Nonetheless, reform proposals proposed by federal or state officials are often resisted in principle, and fought tooth-and-nail by forces that realize full well that the "local control over local affairs" strategy works to their own economic and professional advantage. The quality of education offered students is the casualty. The role of teachers unions as barriers to school reform offers an excellent illustration. Unions are routes to economic and job security for their members. However, when the strength of teachers unions means that incompetent teachers cannot be dismissed, or that school districts can't modify the tenure principle in favor of multiyear, renewable merit-based contracts, the union movement becomes dysfunctional to the school mission. It can take years and hundreds of thousands of dollars for a school district to defend in court its decision to dismiss an incompetent teacher, and the efforts usually fail.[35] Proposals introduced in state legislatures to replace teacher tenure with performance-based renewable contracts are met with heavy resistance from the American Federation of Teachers (AFT), the National Education Association (NEA), and their state and local affiliates. Union pressure usually results in burying reform bills in state legislative committees. Union campaign support is very critical to the political careers of state legislators when they seek reelection. Confrontation with teachers unions may well be tantamount to political suicide for career-conscious politicians, and most of them cannot afford to take the chance.[36]

In the meantime, meaningful reform of education policy is the casualty. In response to growing public pressure, at its 1997 national convention, the NEA passed a controversial resolution endorsing a peer review system of teacher evaluation. In essence, this means that teachers with solid teaching records are appointed to panels that evaluate those with questionable teaching records. The aim is to help those in question improve their performances. Should that fail, then dismissal decisions presumably would encounter less opposition because the union position would be represented on the panels that make the decisions. Such a change may well result in improved teaching competence. However, the

NEA resolution also illustrates how groups often pacify their opponents by offering proforma concessions to altered procedures that may or may not affect policy content or, in this case, teaching performance. Integrating the NEA concession into teacher evaluation procedures is still a state and local responsibility. Therefore, it is virtually guaranteed that successes with the plan will vary from state to state and from community to community. Federalism not only makes it relatively easy for groups to resist change, it also places formidable obstacles in the way of implementing change once it has been accepted.

As a candidate for president in 1996, Republican Robert Dole raised the teachers union issue. His party had been considerably more supportive of jurisdictional devolution than had been the Democrats. His decision to introduce the union issue as one of national concern was somewhat ironic. Since the unions had entrenched themselves at the state and local levels, Dole probably could have done little about their influence if he had been elected president. Dole was being strategically opportunistic in his quest for votes, and that was not surprising. However, his position ran counter to the Republicans' commitment to devolution in principle, and he quickly abandoned it. This was done, despite the obvious fact that the union problem was, and remains, a problem that is national in scope.

Intransigent commitment to principle is almost invariably the enemy of pragmatism. Facts support the notion that the problem with teachers unions is that they have exploited the cultural affinity for local control of local affairs to their advantage. However, the acknowledged need for teacher law reform has been resisted by the unions employing strategies that exploit the nation's affinity for "local control of (historically) local affairs." The results have been negative, and could well be repeated on other policy stages if the "devolution as principle" crusade remains popular. Dante Chinni's commentary on the success of unions in resisting meaningful teacher law reform changes seems appropriate. According to Chinni, the message is, essentially, that organized minorities can defeat disorganized majorities with regularity, and that an organized lobby has "an easier time running over a small money-hungry governmental body than it does a large one."[37] Unions can control results more effectively if jurisdiction over schools remains exclusively state and local in scope. To centralize it would mean the dilution of union interests with reform interests. From the union point of view, that should be resisted at all cost. If these conditions continue on this and other policy fronts, federalism will continue to be the enemy, not ally, of necessary policy reform. The history of teachers union resistance to teacher law reform makes a case against, not for, policy devolution.

This is not to say that all is lost. However, it is to say that obstacles to changes, nourished by federalism, can indeed be formidable. The commitment to meaningful reform can become a viable option to place before voters, and people committed to overcoming structurally nourished obstacles to meaningful change can be elected, and they can make a difference. Democracy tends to play itself out reactively, in that problems tend to fester longer than they should before voters and federalism can be the ally, rather than the opponent, of constructive policy change.

The Telecommunications Act of 1996 represents how a law providing for meaningful reform can surface from a fragmented governmental system in a way that puts fragmentation of power, particularly federalism, to good use. The act changed existing telecommunications policy in two major ways that affected the provider of telecommunications products and facilities as well as the consuming public. First, it mandated that service providers coordinate their efforts when marketing their services. Second, it permitted companies other than the conventional providers of telephone service, usually the regional bell operating companies, to compete in local telephone markets with the established players. The established companies, of course, fought the proposal, and mounted a major lobbying effort to defeat it. In this case, the previous experience of states (as policy laboratories) had resulted in trial regulatory efforts that freed free market forces to determine local services and pricing policies. Furthermore, these experiments helped identify crucial regulatory issues unique to the competitive telecommunications environment that became invaluable to Congress when it considered instituting national standards in the 1996 act. In this case, state experiences were used to make the case for, not against, federal policy intervention.

The history of the Telecommunications Act shows how pragmatic and effective federalism can be if conditions encourage politicians to look at policy problems pragmatically instead of ideologically. Of course, the nation's affinity for capitalist, or marketplace, solutions to policy problems was well served in this case, and it was a critical ally to the reform efforts. Nonetheless, it had to be exploited in a way that permitted policymakers to merge pragmatism with good politics while simultaneously exploiting federalism's favorable side. Policy jurisdiction was centralized in this case for good reason: Local telephone markets needed to be open to competition, and the only practical way to do this was to permit the national government to intervene and mandate similar competitive environments in all fifty states. Although some states had done well on their own in this regard, it was impossible to expect this from all states. Fighting the issue on a company-by-company, state-by-state basis would have been lengthy and taxing, and the results would have been unsystematically timed and substantively un-even. It might well have taken decades to achieve on a state-by-state basis what the 1996 act achieved with the stroke of the presidential pen. In short, there was really no realistic substitute for federal intervention in this case, and Congress and the president, despite the polarity often introduced by divided government, knew it. In this instance, fragmented constitutional power was the servant, not the opponent, of meaningful change.[38]

It should be noted that the consuming telecommunications public is more interested and activist than are entitlement recipients. This made it more convenient for policymakers to, in effect, legislate a competitive environment. The means—federal intervention—worked to their advantage in this case. Furthermore, the law didn't cost taxpayers anything, so the public had far more to gain than they had to lose. It is rare indeed to find a policy decision that isn't actuated, at least in part, by political opportunism, and the Telecommunications Act is no exception. However, in this instance self-interest was focused in ways that enabled both federalism and divided government to work for, rather than against, the public interest.

One of the most apparent trends in late-twentieth-century politics has been the popularity of the new federalism in its various forms. The Telecommunications Act is but one example. Nearly all politicians pay at least passing attention to the proposition that states and localities are best suited to addressing peoples' needs rather than are the more distant and removed federal bureaucrats. The apex of the movement may well have been the 1996 move to end welfare as a New Deal and post–New Deal federal entitlement program, and transferring more authority to the states to develop "welfare-to-work" programs on their own. However, even before the enactment of welfare reform, states such as Wisconsin and New Jersey had experimented success-

fully with their own versions of such programs. Other states, such as Minnesota and Hawaii, were experimenting with health care reforms at the very time President Clinton's comprehensive proposal was being trashed by Congress. While Congress was contesting the future of the Department of Education, Florida and Michigan sponsored programs to sell inflation-proof college savings bonds to financially strapped families. Acting on their own, California voters approved initiatives changing the state's programs on affirmative action, criminal rights, illegal immigration, and the medicinal use of marijuana. Indeed, President Clinton's successful 1996 reelection campaign stressed the role of the federal government as an overseer of state and local initiatives in many key policy areas. In short, the Telecommunications Act was not an isolated incident. Without tutoring or financial assistance from the federal government, states were functioning as effective policy laboratories on a number of policy fronts in the late 1990s.

The Telecommunications Act also illustrated how federalism encourages legislators, especially senators, to recognize the political advantages of supporting policies that benefit the citizen as consumer. There are more consumers than there are producers and providers. This means there are more voters among the consuming public than within, for instance, Wall Street boardrooms. Because of federalism, states are represented equally in the Senate. Therefore, serving and placating consumers in Idaho and Wyoming are just as vital to Senate support of legislation as is favoring consumer interests in highly populated states such as New York and California. The broader the political base served by legislation, especially if that base is active or potentially so, the more servile politicians will be to it. For example, in the early 1980s former Navy Secretary John Lehman inaugurated a "home porting" strategy that increased the number of states within which carrier and destroyer bases were located. Ostensibly, this was to reduce the nation's military vulnerability to attack in the event of a nuclear war. In fact, the actual purpose was to spread the economic pie among several states as a way to broaden the support base for the Navy's budget in Congress, especially in the Senate. More people were affected by jobs and commercial trade in more states as a result of Lehman's action. If the public becomes increasingly concerned about the effects of smoking on public health, policymakers will side with the public against the tobacco companies. If automobile owners become concerned over the pricing and servicing of automobiles, or over the cost and reliability of safety features in automobiles, policymakers will usually side with the public and against the automobile producers and dealers. This explains why the military services like to get into the employment and real estate business by locating bases, employment opportunities, and weapons contracts with companies in as many states as possible. This reduces the Defense Department's vulnerability to budget cuts and base closings. Of course, it has little, if anything to do with its policy mission to "provide for the common defense" as efficiently and economically as possible. Self-interest is the common denominator behind all these strategies. Federalism helps to accentuate both the advantages and disadvantages of self-interest as it impacts on public policy.

Frustrations with Federalism: The Policy Alternatives

Policy frustration triggered by federalism, the separation of powers, and divided government has encouraged both scholars and practitioners to explore alternative ways of dealing with the nation's policy problems. By and large, these alternatives focus on ways to assist states and localities to meet their policy responsibilities under the Tenth Amendment. In essence, they call on nonpublic resources in an effort to realize public policy goals. Two such alternatives, social capital and privatization, will be explored here.

Social Capital

Writing in the 1830s, Alexis de Tocqueville concluded that a key element in explaining democracy's success in the United States was the citizenry's participation in civic associations. Sometimes called the "civil society" culture, it contributes to democracy and policy vitality by encouraging community participation in religious, artistic, cultural, and political associations. The cultural result of such experiences is an attitude of "civility," or one that stresses tolerance, compassion, understanding, and the value of self-sacrifice for the common good. This idea has recently experienced a resurgence in the United States. Its devotees argue that big government solutions to pressing policy problems have, by and large, been a failure, and a return to the civil society culture of the 1830s is necessary.

The civil society's most well-known scholar-advocate has been Robert Putnam, who advocates its rejuvenation as a way to direct what he terms "social capital" in ways that will help society address problems effectively.[39] He has been joined by other scholars, as well as by several former public servants, including William Bennett, Patricia Schroeder, Bill Bradley, Sam Nunn, Lamar Alexander, Colin Powell, and presidents Bill Clinton, George Bush, and Jimmy Carter. The movement is clearly a bipartisan one.

America has always involved private energies in the development and administration of policy, but the civil society movement is attempting to do this on a systematic, volunteer plane. The movement's major goal is to develop an appropriate balance between government and volunteer energies, as both camps seek alleviation of major social problems. They question whether traditional governmental solutions are the most appropriate and efficient. If not, then individuals and volunteer organizations are encouraged to join in, hopefully with new ideas and levels of energy that will transform both policy content and administration. The focus is on state and (especially) local governments, making the move a procedural ally of devolution. Social capital organizers search for common denominators that unite both public officials and volunteer forces, thereby encouraging a spirit of civility and pragmatism. The public's growing cynicism about government ineffectiveness also bolsters the movement.

Social capitalists assume that civic institutions have been weakened by an obvious decline in self-imposed moral standards over the past several decades. Social pathologies such as the abandonment of children, drug dealer infestation of housing complexes, teenage pregnancies, and various forms of white collar crime suggest to the social capitalists that civic moralism needs renewal. Volunteerism, they argue, helps people gain an appreciation and empathy for the problems of others, and offers fresh ideas to those who are married to administrative routines. Some movement champions hope that it will lessen the impact of partisanship among political factions and redirect that energy more productively to policy problems. With that in mind, former Chief of Staff Colin Powell organized a "volunteer summit" in Philadelphia in May 1997 to the bipartisan nature of the crusade. Attending were former presidents Jimmy Carter and George Bush, as well as the incumbent president, Bill Clinton.

Volunteerism should be encouraged as a supplement to government's efforts to address policy problems effectively. However, it is certainly not a panacea. The drive and intensity of the commitment will vary from locale to locale. The movement may well be the weakest where it is needed the most—in localities affected by noticeably high levels of crime, poverty, and family instability. Nevertheless, it should be encouraged both as a way to provide help to the needy and as a way to help restore the Jeffersonian notion of commitment to the public purpose.

Most important, from the standpoint of public policy as essentially a means-ends challenge, volunteerism offers hope to governments that are bogged down in partisan-based stalemates and faced with constraints of financial resources. President Clinton's enthusiasm for the movement most certainly was based, at least in part, on this realization. Anxious for a creditable niche in political history and faced with limited funds and divided government, it was not at all surprising that he called on his bully pulpit skills in an attempt to boost volunteerism in his 1996 campaign as well as in speeches early in his second term.

Many public policies, especially in the entitlement area, have become political hot potatoes. To some, devolution has become a convenient constitutionally defensible way to deal with the problem. This is a compelling reason to revitalize the notion of civic culture, or social capital. It needed revitalizing anyway. Now there is more of a practical imperative to do it. If the decentralization of policy responsibility in our governmental system is partly due to political opportunism, and it most surely is, then that opportunism may well help do for the social capital movement what it could not do for itself. The political buck eventually stops somewhere. Whether the civic culture is able to accept and respond effectively to the challenge remains to be seen. The opportunity is most certainly there.

Privatization

The civic culture movement seeks to reenergize and refocus the efforts of state and local governments by encouraging volunteerism. It emphasizes joint, collaborate efforts between public and civic elements to address problems with a new sense of determination and flexibility. The official distinction between government and civic inputs is blurred because the focus is on policy effectiveness, and not on a firm division of labor between government and volunteer forces. In a sense, government's cooperation with charities, foundations, philanthropic institutions, and individual volunteers incorporates the spirit of the assumptions of cooperative federalism in that efforts are joint, flexible, and goal oriented.

Another movement—the movement to privatize both the development and administration of public policies—is an alternative with the same objectives in mind, but one which prescribes a wholly different means to achieve those goals. In contrast to volunteerism, the privatization alternative prescribes a strict division of roles for governmental and nongovernmental forces. This line is prescribed, in many cases, by a legal document—a contract—which specifies what the private firm will do for the government, what it will cost, how long it will take, and what results are to be expected. It assumes that marketplace incentives can deliver results that government often cannot—service delivery or project completion with more dispatch and efficiency at less cost. Most policies subject to privatization are primarily state and local responsibilities. Included are health care delivery, road construction and maintenance, refuse collection, ambulance services, welfare, public transportation services, janitorial and maintenance services, park and recreation services, and recycling programs. In addition, the privatization syndrome underlies the school choice movement, with proposals that would provide students with vouchers to help them defray the cost of attending private schools or public schools outside their residential school

district. The privatization movement, like the civic culture movement, is a response to growing public cynicism over the ability of public institutions to deliver what they promise. Like devolution and volunteerism, it is culturally compatible with the country's individualistic, capitalistic, nonhierarchical political culture.

Some governmental functions can be, and have been, privatized with success, if efficiency is the major criterion for success. Wisconsin's early successes with welfare reform relied substantially on the privatization strategy in key programs.[40] Therefore, in a policy environment where pilot projects and experimentation are frequently rewarded, as with the Telecommunications Act of 1996, the privatization of some policy functions (mostly administration) is a viable option. However, as with devolution, it is naive to conclude that privatization in principle is the solution for all, or even most, policy problems.

There are several reasons for this. However, one is perhaps more significant than the rest. All levels in the United States have had more experience with privatization in fact than is commonly acknowledged. The results of these experiences have been mixed at best. Many reputable scholars/observers have argued persuasively that the results have been dysfunctional, if not devastating. At issue here are official government responsibilities that have been contracted out, as is the case with defense contracts and research on environmental hazards and drug safety. In addition, many more policies have been affected by the *de facto* privatization of decision making. This is a more subtle, insidious type of privatization, because it is integrated with, and has become a part of, conventional decision-making processes.

An explanation for this is found in the impact of pluralism on government and politics. Pluralism has been examined in previous chapters as both a theory of politics and as an explanation for institutional behavior. The relationship between pluralism and privatization begins with James Madison. Madison argued that liberty encourages the creation and growth of factions, most of which have material or economic gain as an objective. The constitutional fragmentation of institutional power helps control the excessive impact of factions on policy. It accomplishes this by establishing many decision-making arenas and structuring decision making within those arenas in ways that foster compromises among factions. Schattschneider and Lowi have noted, however, that the interest group universe doesn't provide all individuals equal leverage in policy decisions. The wealthiest groups, the ones with better leadership, and the ones whose members are the most active fare better when it comes to influencing policy decisions. Some individuals, in obvious need of routes to potential policy influence, are not well represented by factions. According to Schattschneider, the interest group network is biased in favor of groups representing society's economic elites.

How does this translate into the impact of the privatization syndrome on the policy process? Reflect briefly on the impact of iron triangles on policy. They allow vested interests to collude with congressional subcommittees and administrative agencies to advance mutually advantageous policies. Reference also the public bureaucracies, whose professional experts develop alliances with what Gerald Garvey calls "shadow" bureaucrats representing private firms, and who provide administrators with valuable data which they use as the basis for policy decisions, especially regulatory decisions.[41] It surfaces any time the Defense Department makes a decision, based on competitive bidding, to award a contract to a company to supply the armed services with weapons, ships, or aircrafts. It surfaces each time agencies, such as the Food and Drug Administration, accept the results of industry-sponsored research as a basis for authorizing the distribution and sale of medicines, food additives, preservatives, and insecticides. The effects of the private sector are felt on political campaigns which can be run effectively only by purchasing costly television advertising time, virtually compelling candidates to turn to corporate sources for financial support. Finally, the privatization syndrome surfaces each time a local housing or public facilities authority reviews and accepts bids for the construction of public housing facilities, mass transit systems, roads and highways, office buildings, airports, and so on. In sum, public policies have been, in fact, already privatized a great deal by the natural course of politics in our capitalist democracy.

Privatization, whether by politics or by contract, increases problems of accountability, or the ability of the public to hold government responsible for policy decisions. In effect the "buck" has been passed to private-sector forces and they, not government, are responsible for mistakes that are made. Privatization of public policy can undercut the ability of public institutions to sustain and improve the quality of service they offer their client. For example, consider the school choice issue. Providing students with vouchers to attend nonneighborhood schools, public or private, sounds inviting at first blush. However, it can undercut the ability of those neighborhood schools to offer the students who must remain, or choose to remain, in those schools a high-quality faculty and a selection of courses and special programs that they desperately need. School choice, offering the private sector as an option, may well be the enemy of the traditional, and vital, public school system. This is why school administrators, especially in large cities, firmly resist the school choice alternative.

Privatization as the New Feudalism

Both decentralization and privatization have assumed "chic" proportions in political rhetoric over the past several years. As noted above, any procedural corrective pursued as a matter of "principle" probably harbors more disadvantages than advantages. Privatization as a crusade is potentially more dangerous than is decentralization. Decentralization advocates the devolution of power within and between arenas of government. There is no extragovernmental authority challenge to governmental authority. On the other hand, privatization poses a significant potential threat to the policy parameters of government—not those outlined in the body of the Constitution, but in the Preamble. Strictly speaking, the Preamble is not a part of the Constitution. It states the Constitution's mandate, or purpose, in very general terms. However, in the search for the founders' interpretation of the Constitution's mandate, the Preamble is essential reading. It states, in its entirety: "We the people of the United States, in order to form a more perfect Union, establish justice, insure domestic Tranquility, provide for the common defense, promote the general Welfare, and secure the Blessings of Liberty to ourselves and our Posterity do ordain and establish this Constitution for the United States of America." Naturally, unending arguments can be held over how these challenges translate into specific policy mandates, e.g., whether support of a National Endowment of the Arts is included under the mandate to promote the general welfare. In addition, the Bill of Rights restricts governmental power over individual behavior in several key fields. Nonetheless, the Preamble does offer a loose definition of the founders' interpretation of the proper scope of government authority.

The privatization movement, as a theory of how and where power should be assigned in society, is prepared to compromise that view of governmental policy legitimacy. In sum, it threatens to produce a condition that Jay M. Shafritz, E.W. Russell, and Michael Lind have termed a "new feudalism" in American society.[42] This tendency, in and of itself, may not necessarily be bad if it would advance other objectives of our constitutional democracy. However, it may well undermine them. Take, for example, the issue of school choice, discussed above, and the potential threat that the voucher idea poses for the goal of equality of opportunity. Not only does the voucher idea threaten to deny students remaining in the abandoned schools equal opportunity for a good education, it also permits society's elites to buy their way out of public concerns. The wealthy have always been able to finance a private education for their children, and the privatization idea permits them to do it without bearing their fair share of the cost for a sound public education system. The privatization spirit, which is clearly the driving force behind the voucher idea, would ultimately lessen the tax burden on every taxpayer, including the wealthy, to support a system of public education. It is inconceivable to think that the founders didn't include public education in their challenge to government to "provide for the general welfare."

The new feudalists willingly accept the socialization of their activities within their residential enclaves. They support their own private police, streets, and parks. As residential homeowners within their own private residential citadels, they accept and support regulations on the admission of visitors to their communities, pay special user fees for refuse collection, accept lawn care regulations, and accept homeowner association regulations on the exterior maintenance and remodeling of their homes. However, by and large, they oppose the increased application of such a theory of governance to society in general. They oppose increases in tax levies to support public schools, parks, roads, and highways. In short, they have abdicated their civic responsibilities for what their privileged status can buy them privately. This is an ominous condition and trend. Over four million people live in such walled enclaves presently, and that number is expected to double within the next decade or so.[43] Journalist Michael Lind has noted that this propensity "reverses the trend of the past thousand years toward the government's provision of basic public goods like policing, public roads, transportation networks, and public schools," concluding that "in the United States—to a degree unmatched in any other industrial democracy—these public goods are once again becoming private luxuries."[44]

If some people can afford private country clubs, golf courses, tennis clubs, and ski resorts for recreation and entertainment, what happens to their obligation as taxpaying citizens to help provide parks and other public spaces for people who cannot afford to buy access to private facilities? What happens to the Preamble's mandate to "insure domestic tranquility" if residents in some communities can afford to enclose themselves in gated housing developments with their own privately financed guard and security systems? If privatization spreads to the point of borderlessness, it can pose a serious threat to the legitimacy of government to deal directly with policy problems and offer services that only the public sector can provide.

Ironically, many of the individuals and groups that advocate privatization and withdrawal of government from its "Preamblenourished" obligations use the Constitution to justify their actions. In all probability, most of them do not understand the Constitution, nor have many made an attempt to do so. Timothy McVeigh, convicted for the 1995 Oklahoma City bombing tragedy, allegedly committed the act in retaliation for the federal government's "unconstitutional" actions at the Branch Davidian compound in Texas a year earlier. The Constitution's First Amendment, in effect, separates church and state by defining what public authorities cannot do by way of regulating religious practice. However, to some individuals, because the Constitution

does not literally separate church and state (in those terms), the door is open to integrate religious activities and practices with regular school activities. The local insurgent movements (including militias) that surfaced in the 1980s and 1990s often claimed that they were organizing to defend the country and themselves from government policies that were not specifically assigned government by the Constitution. These actions are, in effect, a variation on the privatization theme. They are justified and pursued in behalf of the Constitution. Their effect, however, is just the opposite. The Constitution's quest to "form a more perfect Union" is brought into question. Instead of using policy challenges to discover ways that governments at all levels can do their jobs better, the legitimacy of government authority itself is being undermined.

Policy problems are becoming increasingly serious and their solutions more complex. The federal system offers much potential help in this regard. It also harbors some dangers if misused in deference to blind ideology or principle. This is why the regeneration of civic culture is much preferable to privatization as an alternative way to help government out of its policy bind. Volunteerism supplements public authority; it does not challenge it. It is spiritually optimistic, not grounded in cynicism. It offers the opportunity for public and private forces at all levels of government to experiment, adapt, and learn. It discards ideology as a fetish and replaces it with an opportunity to renew the cultural spirit of democracy while, at the same time, focusing on policy challenges from a realistic, means-ends perspective.

Federalism and Public Policy: The Opportunity

Federalism can be an impediment to effective policy change, or it can provide an opportunity.

Its main asset is its potential for flexibility and adaptation to local and regional demographics. Its main liability is that it doesn't compel governments and special districts to think in collaborative or regional terms until problems have been allowed to fester to a point of crisis. Devolution, social capital, and even privatization have roles to play in enhancing the ability of governments to meet their policy challenges head on. However, they will only if they synchronize with effective state and local regional planning. None of these options will be very effective if inspired only by a perceived need to find a symbolic alternative to assuage frustrations over the apparent inability of government to deal with a problem. All governments at all levels need to start thinking and acting collaboratively.

Federalism as a constitutional principle deliberately divides governmental policy authority between two tiers of government. Originally, its purpose was to discourage tyranny by fragmenting authority. However, in an era where a positive role for government is unavoidable, it can be an impediment. The nation has long passed the point in history when federalism could be used as an excuse for confronting policy challenges. It must now be considered an opportunity to do things adaptively, creatively, and collaboratively. Federalism now carries with it an obligation on the part of all governments to be practical, proactive, and flexible. In the case of metropolitan areas, unless governments start to collaborate and adapt, urban rot will become increasingly cancerous, and creep beyond the bounds of the central and begin to swallow the older suburban communities. Uncontrolled urban sprawl does not come without cost. It decimates inner city property values. It destroys economic growth. It allows poverty and economic decline to invade once prosperous suburban communities. It is extremely difficult to persuade local governments and special districts, with their jurisdictional autonomy and

separate tax bases, to "go regional" and forfeit autonomy in the interest of policy cohesion. However, it is an imperative that cannot be ignored. Although historically unnatural, collaboration must become a state of mind before the costs of mandating it become prohibitive. That is the challenge to federalism as a policy and political force as the nation enters the twenty-first century.

Endnotes

1. Taken from John Kincaid, The Relevance of the Federal Idea in the Contemporary World, presentation made to the Salzburg Seminar "Perspectives on Federalism," May 22–28, 1993, Salzburg, Austria.

2. 4 Wheaton 316 (1819).

3. Jeffrey R. Henig, *Public Policy and Federalism: Issues in State and Local Politics* (New York: St. Martin's Press, 1985), p. 13.

4. *Ibid.*, pp. 162–175.

5. Christopher Hamilton and Donald T. Wells, *Federalism, Power, and Political Economy* (Englewood Cliffs, N.J.; Prentice Hall, 1990), p. 40.

6. Terry Sanford, *Storm over the States* (New York: McGraw-Hill, 1966), p. 80.

7. David Rush, "Policies That Promote Poverty," *Washington Post Weekly*, vol. 14, no. 30 (May 26, 1997), p. 21.

8. *Ibid.*

9. *Ibid.*

10. *Ibid.*

11. Martha Derthick, *New Towns in Town: Why a Federal Program Failed* (Washington, D.C.: Urban Institute, 1972).

12. Morton Grodzins, *The American System: A New View of Government in the United States* (Chicago: Rand-McNally, 1966), p. 273.

13. Daniel J. Elazar, *American Federalism: A View from the States*, 2nd ed. (New York: Crowell, 1972), pp. 84–127.

14. Ira Sharkansky, "The Utility of Elazar's Political Culture: A Research Note," *Polity*, vol. 2 (Fall 1969), pp. 66–83.

15. Elazar, *op. cit.*, pp. 100–101.

16. Michael Barone, "Divide and Rule," *National Journal*, vol. 29, no. 28 (July 12, 1997), pp. 1408–1412.

17. *Ibid.*, p. 1409.

18. Leonard D. White, *Introduction to the Study of Public Administration* (New York: Macmillan, 1955), p. xii.

19. Federal Budget Message to Congress, January 29, 1968.

20. As quoted in *Congressional Record*, 115: H221, April 30, 1969.

21. Stephen K. Bailey and Edith K. Mosher, *ESEA: The Office of Education Administers a Law* (Syracuse, N.Y.: Syracuse University Press, 1968), p. 228.

22. *Ibid.*, p. 229.

23. John C. Donovan, *The Politics of Poverty*, 2nd ed. (New York: Pegasus, 1973), pp. 49–80.

24. Bryce Nelson, "Air Quality Act of 1967: A Step Forward, But Don't Expect Immediate Improvement of Your Air," *Science*, 158 (October 20, 1967); and Elinor Langer, "Water Pollution: Federal Law Is Strengthened by Law Authorizing New Agency and Quality Standards," *Science*, 150 (October 8, 1965), as reprinted in Michael D. Reagan, ed., *The Administration of Public Policy* (Glenview, Ill.: Scott, Foresman, 1969), p. 187.

25. Henig, *op. cit.*, pp. 184–187.

26. *Ibid.*, p. 186.

27. *Ibid.*, p. 185.

28. *Ibid.*, p. 186.

29. *Ibid.*, p. 187.

30. Thomas J. Anton, *American Federalism and Public Policy: How the System Works* (New York: Random House, 1989), pp. 217–222.

31. Jonathan Alter, "A Real Piece of Work," *Newsweek* (August 25, 1997), p. 32.

32. *Ibid.*

33. John D. Donahue, *Disunited States* (New York: Basic Books, 1997).

34. Richard P. Nathan, *The Plot That Failed: Nixon and the Administrative Presidency* (New York: Wiley, 1975).

35. Dante Chinni, "Teacher's Pet," *The Washington Monthly*, vol. 29, nos. 1 & 2 (January/February 1997), pp. 22–25.

36. *Ibid.*, p. 23.

37. *Ibid.*, p. 25.

38. Royce J. Holland, "Proof That Government Can, in Fact, Work," *Christian Science Monitor*, vol. 88 (March 22, 1996), p. 18.

39. Robert D. Putnam, "Bowling Alone: America's Declining Social Capital," *Journal of Democracy*, vol. 6, no. 1 (January 1995), pp. 65–78.

40. Adam Cohen, "The Great American Welfare Lab," *Time* (April 21, 1997).

41. Gerald A. Garvey, *Facing the Bureaucracy: Living and Dying in a Public Agency* (San Francisco: Jossey-Bass, 1993), pp. 52–55.

42. Jay M. Shafritz and E. W. Russell, *Introducing Public Administration* (New York: Longman, 1997), p. 88.

43. *Ibid.*, p. 89.

44. *Ibid.*, p. 88.

chapter eleven

The Bureaucracy

Constitutional Politics and the Unelected Branch

The public bureaucracy consists of all offices or bureaus that comprise the executive branch of government. Their core responsibility is to administer or implement public policies. Their existence is implied in the Constitution, but they are not directly empowered by it. The traditional view of the public bureaucracy was that it should consist of people professionally trained to implement legislative policy directives by the most efficient and expeditious means. The job of the administrator was a scientific one. Administrators were not to incorporate politics or their personal judgments into their implementation decisions. Their work was endemically neutral, scientific, and objective in nature. If the bureaucracy's neutrality could be guaranteed, so went the assumption, then administrators would function mainly as policy "transmission belts" and affect policy only by the efficient way they implemented it, not in the way it was decided. Probably the most famous American champion of this point of view as a prescription for the public bureaucracy was Woodrow Wilson, who once challenged public administrators to become "civil servants prepared by special schooling and drilled, after appointment, into a perfected organization."[1]

These were the assumptions of the classical school, or model, of administration. They were parleyed very effectively by the Progressives during the late nineteenth and early twentieth centuries. These individuals did not believe that public servants were naturally value neutral or that self-interest was not an issue with the public bureaucracy. Quite to the contrary. Their crusade for a neutral bureaucracy was sparked by their repulsion over the excessive politicalization of the public bureaucracy at all levels of government. They were disgusted with how the Jacksonian spoils system had made civil servants a plebeian group whose loyalties had been patronized by corrupt politicians and their interest group allies. To the Progressives, the politics of self-interest and self-service should play no role in public administration, and they created laws and founded institutions that would encourage administrative agencies to embody neutrality as a performance standard.

Few public-sector administrative enterprises have ever successfully embodied and applied the norms of the classical model. As early as 1936 Pendleton Herring noted that, once legislatures vested administrative agencies with substantial policy discretion, the agencies began to serve basically as forums within which interest groups and citizens competed for policy advantages.[2] This "window" was later popularized as the "bureaucratic coalition-building" or "bureaucratic politics" model of bureaucracy. Other attributes of constitutional democracy also encouraged digressions from the classical model. Democracy requires that administrative agencies be accountable to the public, and that this accountability be expressed through several government institutions, each of which has its own definition of accountability. The separation of powers principle means that most agencies work for at least two institutionally separate masters—the president and Congress—each of which has its own politically honed definition of the public interest. In short, public-sector administrative agencies are cast into political arenas by the inevitabilities of their mission challenge. The following analysis is based on the assumption that the role of administrative agencies in public policy can best be understood and appreciated by contrasting the traditional, classical mission of agencies with the roles they have assumed due to the politicization of that mission. The focus will be on the causes for, and the policy effects of, that politicization. Finally, the analysis will examine the extent to which constitutional politics is responsible for agencies' roles in both politics and policy.

The Public Bureaucracy and the Classical Model

The classical mission of administration is the implementation of policy by the most efficient means. Administrators are expected to be professionals, dedicated to determining the best means or procedures to use to implement a decision made by a policymaking body. According to this model, the selection of the most efficient way to implement policies is fundamentally a scientific enterprise, or should strive to be as scientific as possible. Therefore, administration is removed from the mainstream of politics by the very definition of its mission. In pursuit of this goal, administrators should be appointed on the basis of merit, not politics. On the job, they apply their knowledge and experience enthusiastically to the policy task at hand, irrespective of its content.

The classical model of administration had its genesis in the writings of such figures as Max Weber and Frederick W. Taylor. Weber argued that sound administration is the foundation for societal success, because it is deliberately rational, and makes sense out of conditions and circumstances that would otherwise be chaotic. Without a reliable and professional cadre of administrators dedicated to neutrality, no organization, private or public, should expect to achieve its policy objectives. Taylor focused on the ways in which administrators could determine, scientifically, how to implement a goal in the shortest amount of time with the least expenditure of energy. His approach, sometimes known as the school of "scientific management" or "Taylorism," focused on how to apply the Weberian mandate to specific administrative challenges.

The early literature on public administration relied heavily on the assumptions and conclusions of writers such as Weber and Taylor.

The most celebrated example of this was Woodrow Wilson's famous essay, "The Study of Administration," published in 1887.[3] In this essay, Wilson introduced what has come to be known as the "politics-administration" dichotomy. He argued that politics and policy-making are the proper concerns of legislatures, elected executives, and other entities that have legally vested policy responsibilities. Administration is the responsibility of professional administrators, trained to be such, who implement policies in a neutral, passionless fashion, regardless of their (the policies') substantive content. The Wilsonian dichotomy served as a normative backdrop for the most significant law in the history of public personnel administration—the Civil Service Act of 1883. Authored and introduced by Senator George H. Pendleton, this law introduced the national bureaucracy to the merit system, or the notion that bureaucrats should be selected on the basis of what they know about the science of administration rather than because of their political connections.

Neutrality and objectivity continue to be the norms or standards by which the performance and integrity of the public bureaucracy are judged. Rarely are these objectives realized, and this undoubtedly explains why the public bureaucracy is held in such low regard by so many Americans. Bureaucrats are often considered to be incompetent, apathetic, self-serving, "briefcase-toting rogues" who care little, if anything, about the classical mission. It would be easy and, to some, very satisfying to explain such a reputation by the genetic defectiveness of the animal. In other words, administrators who work for government do so because they do not have the ability or incentive to face up to the challenges of private-sector administration. However, this conclusion is wrong. It is wrong because it fails to consider the impact of the democratization of the bureaucracy on its role obligations, and because it fails to appreciate how democratization has made it impossible for administrative agencies to avoid playing key roles in politics and policymaking. Under such conditions efficiency as a goal is often sacrificed, or at least subject to some compromise.

Neutrality is an unrealistic standard for judging the performance and credibility of the public bureaucracy for several reasons. First, agencies are vested by law with significant discretionary policy power to fill in the details of very broadly construed statutes. More often than not, administrative action gives meaning to laws that often, standing alone, are merely loosely phrased statements of policy intent. The Commodity Credit Corporation (CCC), located in the Department of Agriculture, is required by law to decide on price support levels for each agricultural crop based on its (the agency's) judgment as to the amount of a crop's projected harvest. The Food and Drug Administration (FDA) is required by statute to supervise contracted research designed to uncover possible dangers to humans of new drugs that pharmaceutical firms want to market commercially. The Environmental Protection Agency (EPA) is legally mandated to determine what factories must do to reduce the amount of toxic waste dumped into rivers and lakes and toxic gasses allowed to escape into the atmosphere. When agencies act on these statutory mandates, they issue executive orders to force industries, farmers, or consumers to comply with their decisions. These orders are, for all intents and purposes, the law. Therefore, when industries, farmers, or consumers seek changes in the policies that affect them, they lobby the bureaucracy as well as Congress.

Second, the bureaucracy is populated with individuals who, due to their training, experience, and work assignments, have developed considerable expertise in their professional specialties. Consequently, they are called on for advice as to the feasibility of various policy options, and are often asked to generate fresh policy recommendations that draw on their knowledge and experience. They often testify before congressional committees. They answer media inquiries, and sometimes deliver speeches on the subject. As the official servants of Congress, which has authorized their existence and funded their activities, they provide legislators with data that they use to augment their arguments in committee and subcommittee discussions, and in floor debates.

Third, the concept of neutrality, ironically, exists as an evaluative standard because the functions of the bureaucracy are intrinsically political, and Americans are uncomfortable with such a state of affairs. Americans like to think that administrative agencies ought to be guided by Weberian and Wilsonian standards, but this has never been the case for any extended period of time. The merit system was nonexistent for the first century of the republic's existence. Appointments to administrative ranks were based on party affiliation and, beginning with Andrew Jackson's administration, assumed a spoils system cast, whereby key jobs went to individuals who had worked diligently to elect the president. Competence was secondary to politics as a prerequisite for office. Jackson championed the cause of the common man throughout government, and felt that democracy was best served by choosing party loyalists for administrative positions and rotating them regularly from position to position. Jackson assumed that job rotation was critical to keeping government in touch with the people. If a person served too long in one position, he might grow increasingly desensitized to changes in public opinion. Besides, since government was to be "of the people" as well as "by the people," someone else deserved his turn at public service. Job rotation also occurred when the incumbent party lost the presidency. When voters tired of one political

party, they voted out not only its president, but also the multitude of party loyalists that staffed the bureaucracy. This was another way to ensure job rotation. In fact, job rotation induced by a change in party control of the government was, according to Jackson, a key contributing force to representative democracy.

A representative bureaucracy supported by the spoils principle was undercut, ultimately, by its own excesses. Political appointees became increasingly unable to handle the growing technical responsibilities of their jobs. In addition, corruption gradually infiltrated the far reaches of the bureaucracy, with many appointees accepting bribes in return for policy concessions. Public sentiment turned against these dysfunctional manifestations of Jacksonian democracy. The result was the Pendleton Civil Service Act of 1883. With a neutral bureaucracy as an objective, the Pendleton Act established a merit standard for administrative appointments. The neutrality crusade was soon reinforced by another law—the Interstate Commerce Act of 1887—which created the nation's first independent regulatory commission, the Interstate Commerce Commission (ICC). Recently reorganized and reassigned to the Department of the Treasury as the Office of Motor Carriers, the ICC, like all independent regulatory commissions established since 1887, made policy by issuing regulations, overseeing the implementation of those regulations, and adjudicating any disputes that arose from the rules or their administration. Commission members served for set, overlapping terms. Later, the ICC regulated services, rates, and the overall business activities of interstate carriers, including railroads, trucks, buses, oil pipelines, and inland waterway carriers. Since it was officially independent, and its members served for fixed terms, presumably its decisions were to reflect objectivity rather than partisanship. However, its jurisdiction over vital areas of the economy, the fact that its regulatory jurisdiction and budgets were set by Congress, and the fact that its members frequently had distinguished careers within the industries over which the Commission had jurisdiction made it very susceptible to political pressure. Its official "neutral" mission was meaningless. It operated in the real world of pluralist politics and responded accordingly. The same can be said of other regulatory agencies such as the Environmental Protection Agency, the Federal Trade Commission, the Federal Communications Commission, and the Securities and Exchange Commission. Ironically, legislation designed to encourage a neutral bureaucracy has encouraged the opposite result. Appointing employees on the basis of merit and guaranteeing them tenured, career status after a probationary period offers them the opportunity to unobtrusively and subtly defy their hierarchical superiors, including the president and cabinet secretaries, if those superiors advance new programs or suggest changes in existing programs to which the bureaucrats object. Placing regulatory agencies outside the regular administrative hierarchy, mandating that they make decisions based exclusively on the facts of each case, and immunizing their members from dismissal for political reasons make them more, not less, vulnerable to pressures for vested interests. After all, Congress is subject to pressures from those same interests, and Congress controls the agencies' policy jurisdiction and budget allotment.

The point of all this is clear: Any attempt to legislate administrative neutrality in the public bureaucracy is severely handicapped from the beginning. Such action is a tacit admission that the public bureaucracy is inherently a political institution. Although the mythology of the neutral bureaucrat is still very much alive, especially in academic and reform circles, it is its very status as a myth that sustains it. In this context, a myth is an idea or goal to which the public subscribes without insisting on proof of its inherent validity. It may be true or it may be

false, but we believe in it regardless. The facts of political life in America have always groomed the bureaucracy to be responsive to political inputs, regardless of the neutrality norm. Therefore, to condemn the public bureaucracy for its embroilment in politics is eminently unfair. More will be said about this later in the chapter.

Therefore, the classical model of administration is of value to students of public policy and bureaucracy primarily as a standard against which the actual political activities of agencies can be compared. In short, if a major gap exists between the theoretical ideal and the real world of administrative decision making, being able to appreciate the inevitable reasons for the divorce makes the acceptance of the results more tolerable.

Bureaucracy as the Mobilization of Bias

The classic model of bureaucracy stresses the role of administrators as rational technocrats. A more descriptive model offers, by definition, a more realistic alternative that is based on a description of what administrators in the public service actually do and, more important, why they do it. This can be termed a "politics" or "policy" model. It is based on the conclusion, derived from research and observation, that public administrative agencies and their leaders are actively engaged in what the late E. E. Schattschneider once labeled the "mobilization of bias."[4] Schattschneider's expression surfaced in his analysis of interest groups in American politics, arguing that the most effective groups were those which, among other things, were the best at mobilizing the bias or value commitments of their members, and strategically translating and transmitting those values to policymakers in ways that maximized the groups' influence over policy decisions. Adapting the "mobilization of bias" standard to the public bureaucracy is not difficult. It requires only that one accept the inevitable connection between what agencies do as organizations that recommend and administer policies, and the interest of legislators and interest groups in those activities. Since agencies with both distributive and regulatory policy obligations are vested with the discretion to fill in the details of broadly construed statutes, agency actions that operationalize these very broad mandates are of great concern to interest groups and congressional committees.

The bottom line is that the public bureaucracy, by and large, is not expected to be overly efficient. Efficiency is not a high-priority item with the forces that empower agencies with policy responsibilities, budget them, and support them politically. Agencies respond accordingly. While efficiency and effectiveness will never be permanently shelved as objectives, they will be given high priority only in times when it is politically advantageous to work for such ends. Legislators sometimes endorse efficiency and effectiveness in principle, especially during periods of high deficits, declining revenues, and when waste and conflict of interest have become high-profile news items, as they did when the HUD scandal and the EPA Superfund controversies surfaced during the Reagan administration. Even during times when administrative reform becomes politically popular, legislators are inclined to endorse classical administrative principles as a general objective only, and fiercely support the maintenance of policies that are critical to their constituencies, and therefore their reelection. With a distinctively more homogeneous client base, interest groups are decidedly more tenacious than are legislators in clinging to programs that support their causes. Issues of administrative waste and inefficiency are only a regular part of the crusades of public-interest-oriented interest groups such as Common Cause, Public Citizen, and the Concord Coalition. However, embers of these organizations are so widely dispersed among congressional districts that they have very little leverage over votes by individual legislators on specific policies. In sum, public agencies exist because of politics, and how they are organized and managed reflects the strategies and interests of those who hold and exercise political power.

Therefore, when legislators and interest groups try to impact on the structure and activities of administrative agencies, they do not do so because of a selfless concern for the public interest. To be sure, the official defense of what agencies do, and how generously they are funded, is often couched in national interest terminology. However, that is meaningful only if it translates into policies that are futuristic in focus and ask individuals and groups to repress their appetites for distributive and favorable regulatory policies. This rarely occurs. Those with the power to influence public policy are more interested in assuaging farmers, autoworkers, trade associations, the maritime industry, truckers, civil rights groups, and so on. They exercise their policy leverage in ways that are servile to such interests. Choices about administrative structure, program assignments, and budgets are not immune from such concerns. When legislators, under pressure from vested interests, make choices about administrative structure and budgets, they are making implicit choices about policy, and they know it. Any suggestion that political actors should turn choices about how agencies are organized, financed, and audited over to professional administrators, actuated by the norms of efficiency and effectiveness through neutrality, defies political reality. In politics, organization is rarely an activity designed to implement a predetermined policy by the most efficient, professional, and neutral means available. In politics, organization is meaningful only as an effective way to mobilize and extend the impact of biases or values that are critical to the careers and economic well-being of those forces that have the power to determine the course of public policy.

Another factor, endemic to administration and bureaucracy, reinforces the impact of politics on the public bureaucracy. It owes its origin to the individual's basic instinct for survival and security. Madison's concern for the impact of self-interest on the politics of factions is relevant to understanding this, largely because Madison was speaking to a universal trait of humans as social and political animals. An individual's quest for survival and security, once accomplished, grows to express itself in the form of ego-satisfaction, status, and the expansion of one's influence and recognition. Although this is rooted in an individual's psychological needs, it gains more leverage and influence if expressed collectively by groups or organizations. This was why Madison was so concerned about the impact of factions on politics and government. Factions were natural ways to inflate the impact of ego and selfishness on policy by collective, rather than individual, action. Consequently, government should be structured to control the excessive influence of such claims on public policy. Schattschneider was concerned about the same phenomenon in his analysis of the impact of group politics on public policy, especially because some groups tend to develop more policy leverage than others due to their wealth, leadership, and historical access to the formal arenas of power.

The objectives of people who hold positions in the public bureaucracy are no different from those who work elsewhere. They want security, status, and recognition. Like most others, as economic security becomes less and less of an issue, recognition and status take on added importance. Therefore, if these objectives of security and status are best served by identifying with the political powers

that be, so be it. Furthermore, if these objectives are served by actively promoting the growth and expansion of their statutorily assigned policy responsibilities by expanding the base of political support for them, so be it. In sum, administrative agencies, as collectivities of individuals actuated by the quest for security, recognition, and status, will naturally adopt strategies designed to solidify and expand the impact of their agencies' policies on politics and government. Responding to political pressures is a route not only to survival, but to agency and individual "prosperity" in several senses of the term. Therefore, agencies are part of the bias mobilization phenomenon for both political and psychological reasons.

An agency's quest for survival and growth can be explained in part by forces endemic to the needs of bureaucrats as individuals. This is manifested through what Robert Kharasch once labeled the "institutional imperative." According to Kharasch, administrative agencies are prime examples of simultaneous institutional adaptation to the needs of their members and the political environment. Agencies qualify as institutions because they consist of groups of individuals working together, and abide by the prescribed routines of their work assignments as they, the workers, interpret them. Furthermore, the organizational presence of any one individual, or group of individuals, is not necessary to the survival of the institution. Employees come and go, but the institution continues. Therefore, all administrative agencies, all legislative committees and subcommittees, as well as the presidency, are institutions. The employee work patterns that develop within institutions constitute what Kharasch labeled their (the agencies') "internal machinery."[5] Since employees make the internal machinery function, and since employees as individuals are influenced by the psychological need for security, status, and (sometimes) power, it is natural for them to equate their job responsibilities with the essential mission of the institution. This led Kharasch to conclude that whatever results from the workings of an agency's internal machinery is considered by the employees to be the institution's purpose.[6] This led him to a definition of the "institutional imperative," which he defined as the understood imperative for employees to make decisions or take actions that will "keep the institutional machinery working."[7] Kharasch considered the institutional imperative to be an absolute norm that conditions all employee behavior. It is never violated in practice. It is an attitude felt "bone and gut" by all individuals working within institutions.[8]

In a more recent and more theoretical exploration of the same phenomenon, John Ralston Saul connects this problem to the tendency of all institutions, public and private, to atrophy in the face of what he calls the "dictatorship of reason."[9] Focusing his study on the role elites have played in government and nongovernment institutions over the past four centuries, Saul argues that leaders eagerly promise major substantive policy reforms only to become preoccupied with their own procedures and intra-organizational routines. Gradually, this preoccupation displaces any serious concern for substantive progress or change. Leaders in administration, legislation, philanthropy, religion, journalism, science, finance, art, and academia have all fallen victim to the same tendency. Although elites in all these sectors will deny it, their appeal to reason and rationalism as a way to deal with social and political issues amounts to nothing more than an appeal to constituents to accept administrative methods as the *de facto* goals of their organizations. These methods are, in effect, the equivalent of the "internal machinery" described by Kharasch. According to Saul, as a result of the dominance of process and technique over substance, over the past four centuries the Western world's social, economic, and political institutions have been turned into disjointed and directionless machines run by process-minded experts. These experts, or elites, are so enamored with the techniques of scientific management and related administrative procedures that their decisions are devoid of any sense of morality or judgment about what kinds of decisions are qualitatively "good" for society.

Saul explains the arms race, inflation, government waste, and the increasing irrelevance of many policies that administrative agencies and legislatures support for reasons of habit, economic advantage, and political survival by efforts of institutions to rationalize some form of substantive good out of their tendency to mistake "method for content" and "structure for morality."[10] In short, if the people who staff organizations believe in the organization's purpose, then they will uncover what appears to them to be a sensible way to execute that mission. If the organization's commitment evolves into a preoccupation with structure and method, then the organization loses its sense of direction. Means become ends unto themselves. Democratic governments, over time, succumb to technology and technique, and their policy obligations to their people are abandoned. Rational administration, with its near-total commitment to method, undermines democracy by estranging the government from the needs and wants of its citizens.[11]

Political scientist Michael Nelson once offered an excellent example of how this problem has affected the far reaches of the federal bureaucracy.[12] Some years ago in the Atlanta office of the Department of Health, Education, and Welfare (DHEW, now HHS), an elderly woman was one of many who submitted an application for Supplemental Security Assistance program benefits. DHEW regulations at the time specified precisely the qualifications for SSA. The DHEW claims processor, positioned authoritatively behind his desk, concluded that the woman had savings which were $500 over the DHEW regulation limit, and therefore could not qualify for the money unless she liquidated assets that totaled at least that amount. His suggestion was to "blow" the $500 on a color television set and then resubmit an application. When she told the processor that her savings were earmarked for her funeral expenses, and that it would be irresponsible to spend the money that way, she was told in no uncertain terms that she was ineligible for Supplemental Security Assistance. In effect, the claims processor had used the inflexibility of DHEW regulations to make what he considered to be a rational decision, but which was clearly not qualitatively appropriate for the case at hand. The applicant clearly needed the assistance, but either the rules and methods of the claims process did not permit it or the claims processor did not think it in his best interest to exercise any discretionary options he may have had. The processor received credit for processing the application and, to him, that was his job. To the claims processor, the organization's processes had become the organization's goals. However, the theory underlying DHEW's existence as a presumably rational policy institution, democratically established, and dedicated to serving the underprivileged had been clearly undermined. In all likelihood, the claims processor was both unaware and unconcerned about this.

The existence of the institutional imperative and its role in encouraging technique to overcome reason provides added incentives for public servants to cultivate policy alliances using all available sources. Legislators and interest group leaders are not nearly as concerned over how efficiently and effectively monies are spent, so long as they are spent in ways which help them secure their political careers (legislators) and gain economic advantages for their members (interest groups). The same can be said for administrators. It is

more important to keep agencies funded at respectable levels and to keep the internal machinery running than it is to relate administrative routines and processes to substantive policy accomplishments. The institutional imperative serves to reinforce and extend the impact of administrative agencies as political institutions on public policy. It does so by encouraging bureaucrats, in their exercise of policy discretion, to concentrate on procedures and "safe" incremental changes in existing policy. Sometimes doing the safe thing in a procedurally efficient fashion is often at odds with what is necessary. The institutional imperative encourages institutions, both executive and legislative, to dodge consideration of substantive policy options that are necessary adaptations to changing social and economic conditions in society and, for that matter, the world. Its perpetrators are not genetically defective or unintelligent people. They are simply part of an institutional culture that assumes that every action taken by the institution is inherently correct. This is why administrative agencies and legislatures do not appear able to absorb and act on facts that appear clearly obvious to forces outside the institution, including the general public. In commenting on how this condition can threaten presidential policy leadership, historian Arthur Schlesinger, Jr., once noted that the career bureaucracy can often be a "bulwark against change . . . a force against innovation with an inexhaustible capacity to dilute, delay, and obstruct the presidential purpose."[13] Such a predicament works against the ability of a democratic system to adapt its policies to changing conditions.

Constitutional Politics and Administrative Power

Administrative agencies have policy power because they are agents of institutions that have constitutionally vested policy responsibilities. If the demands made on agencies were exclusively those requiring efficient policy administration, the standards for judging the degree of agency success or failure would be universally accepted. However, the delegation of policy power to agencies complicates the scenario considerably. The ability for any institution to make policy or to recommend policy subjects it to pressures rooted in pluralist politics. The national bureaucracy is no exception.

Four types of agencies comprise, collectively, the national administrative universe, and each of them incorporates missions that reflect policy values, or biases. Executive departments and their subordinate units (sometimes called "bureau-tier" agencies) are, in general, responsible for administering distributive policies. With the partial exception of those departments and bureaus dealing with foreign policy (State and Defense), these agencies have close ties with those sectors of the economy that receive various types of government subsidies or other types of support, including grants, loans, tax credits, and contracts to do research or provide government with a service or physical facility. For example, the Department of Commerce has close ties with the business community, Agriculture the farming community, Housing and Urban Development the construction industry, Interior the conservation movement and those seeking rights to use resources found on federal land, Health and Human Services the social service, education, and health professions, and so on. Each of these agencies, and especially their subordinate "bureau-tier" components, has built up a rather cozy relationship with these policy clients. The relationship is usually an amiable one because the agencies and the client groups share the same policy objectives. They both prosper if government funding for the programs they jointly support steadily increases. They are both somewhat threatened if that support dwindles by any significant amount.

Regulatory agencies or commissions, discussed briefly above, are concerned primarily with regulatory policy and are organizationally independent of the regular executive department hierarchy. Presumably, each is given independent status and regulatory power so that it can apply its experience and judgment to regulate key sectors of the economy in ways that reflect a reasonable balance between business and consumer interests. The Federal Energy Regulatory Commission, the Federal Communications Commission, the Federal Trade Commission, and the Securities and Exchange Commission are prime examples of such agencies. Each is subject to the laws empowering it to act, and is therefore not independent of the government. However, while each is assumed to be immune from presidential and congressional pressures, in fact, threats from either to restrict a commission's policy jurisdiction or to trim its budget can result in the agency's being far more servile to the president and Congress than the law would imply. Since regulatory commissions are mandated to regulate economic behavior, their decisions are bound to please some economic forces and displease others. Regulatory decisions are therefore usually much more controversial than are distributive ones, and consequently attract the interest and lobby efforts of various policy forces that do not share the same policy objectives.

In contrast to independent regulatory agencies, agencies that are strictly independent are headed by single administrators and are organizationally responsible to the president. Their directors are appointed by him and can be removed by him at any time. Their hierarchical relationship to the president is similar to that of the executive departments. The decision to position them outside the executive department hierarchy is usually based on a desire by both the president and Congress to give their policy missions a high public profile, and to help them to avoid at least some of the red tape that could be imposed on them by a preexisting parent agency. Examples of independent executive agencies include the General Services Administration, the Environmental Protection Agency, the Small Business Administration, and the Smithsonian Institution.

A fourth component of the national administrative system is the presidential staff system. As discussed earlier, this complex consists of the various components of the Executive Office of the President (EOP). Included are such high-profile operations as the Office of Management and Budget, the White House Office, the Domestic Council and its subsequent derivatives, the Council of Economic Advisors, and the National Security Council. The policy bias of these agencies is reflective of the president's national constituency. They are more inclusive, or integrative, in their approach to policy analysis. They approach policy questions in ways that bring the more distended and atomized forces that dominate the decisions of "bureau-tier" agencies in the executive departments and in congressional subcommittees into conflict with one another.

The common denominator that affects the role system of agencies in all four categories is that they operate within, and therefore respond to, political influences. Their official mandates require that they administer the public's business as reflected by the Constitution and by statute. They soon realize, however, that these mandates are meaningful to the forces that empower them to act (Congress and the president) only if they incorporate or reflect inputs rooted in their respective constituencies. Since public agencies do not respond exclusively to market forces, as do their counterparts in the private sector, their markets (or consumers) are usually the clientele that benefit from their programs, the political elites which empower them to act, or organized interest groups. They nego-

tiate with, and respond to, these forces in order to attain the legitimacy they need to continue their activities and sustain the budgetary support so essential to that continuance. In sum, a public agency's transactions with forces in its political environment is dominated by politics, and therefore its outputs are inevitably political.

These outputs differ, depending on an agency's official legal mandate. Official mandates incorporate policy missions that ask the agency to distribute advantages (distributive policy), regulate a sector or sectors of the economy (regulatory policy), or redistribute advantages or opportunities among classes of people or income groups (redistributive policy). As discussed in Chapter 3, each of these policy outputs reflects different patterns of interest group inputs that reflect the sacrifices and/or advantages that groups are asked to make by the policies themselves. In distributive arenas the political environment usually offers consensus that supports an agency's distributive policy mission. In regulatory arenas, conflict between the agency and interest groups is encouraged because regulatory decisions ask some forces to forgo advantages in the interest of more policy equity for others. This is especially true during the early, postnatal years of a regulatory agency's existence, before it begins to accommodate to intense interest groups as a matter of course. Agencies administering redistributive policies are subject to pressures from broadly based social and economic classes of people. Accordingly, they tend to develop rather intricate rules and internal procedures to help them explain and defend their decisions by the formalities of bureaucracy and the law, as opposed to their judgment of what is intrinsically "right" or "moral."

The issue of how an administrative agency responds to its political environment would not be so paramount were it not for the fact the public bureaucracy is expected to be the public's servant. The major question is that of accountability, or the need to respond to the will of the people as interpreted by legislatures and elected executives. The founding fathers did not empower agencies to do anything directly. They did empower Congress and the president to share the policymaking obligation, restrained continually by the impact of the separation of powers, checks and balances, and constituency differences fostered and nourished by the principle of federalism. Their purpose was to constrain the impact of selfishness and greed on policy by ways and means mandated by the Constitution. Power was diffused to control the negative effects of self-interest on policy, yet institutions were mandated to cooperate to produce policies by transcending the structural "obstacle course" introduced by the Constitution. The concern of the founders was for accountability in the exercise of policy authority by the president, Congress, and the judiciary, but not the bureaucracy. The potential threat that administrative power might harbor for democratic government was not debated during the Constitutional Convention. The founders never considered the impact of a large, expert-based public bureaucracy on public policy and, most important, the need to make it accountable to the people.

Ironically, it was the desire of the founders to fragment policy authority among Congress, the president, and the courts as a means for ensuring policy accountability that has encouraged the growth of the public bureaucracy as a formidable policy force. The fragmented system of policy authority resulting from both the formal separation and operational "blending" of powers establishes sources of empowerment and lines of authority over the bureaucracy that are notable for their overlapping and diverse character. In contrast to their private-sector counterparts, public agencies do not have a singular boss and one overriding policy mission. Article II, Section 1 of the Constitu-

tion does vest the "executive power" of government in the president but does not define that power. The president, as the nation's *de facto* chief legislator, does recommend policies to Congress, but it is Congress that has the power to legitimize policies, fund them, and establish and empower agencies to administer them. Top administrators are nominated by the president, but cannot assume office until confirmed by the Senate. Both Congress and the president have a stake in overseeing what agencies do with their discretionary policy power. The courts are often asked to rule on whether an agency has exceeded its statutory power when it issues a particular rule or regulation, or whether its decision-making procedures are fair and equitable. In sum, it is not easy for agencies to satisfy the expectations of accountability in our political system because the different political forces which make legitimate claims to agency loyalties do not agree on the norms or values to which agencies should respond. More often than not, these forces are in conflict with one another over policy priorities. Furthermore, all of them have some power to control what agencies do, but none has exclusive power over them. Agencies cannot escape being drawn into the conflicts between presidents and Congress as each seeks to persuade the public that its view of the public interest is inherently right. Both the president and Congress, and the plethora of factions acting within and upon each, are lured into the persuasion game because, due to the shared powers principle, each needs the support of the other before policy can be legitimized. Policy agreement in our political system results from intense confrontations, bargaining, negotiation, and compromises. Administrative agencies are of use to all parties to these conflicts and compromises because they can provide information and justification to support the cases each party tenders both to its governmental adversaries and to the public in general.

The situation is perhaps even more complicated at the state and local level. In some states, the governor's control over state bureaucracy is even less than that of the president at the national level. The heads of the major departments and commissions in some states are elected rather than appointed. In some states and localities, independent boards and commissions are even more prevalent than they are at the national level. Furthermore, some agencies at the state and local level are granted varying degrees of fiscal autonomy from executives and legislatures because they can levy fees for services rendered or because funds for their operations are earmarked for their activities alone. In sum, at all levels of government, administrative accountability is complicated by the constitutional fragmentation of institutional power and by the statutory fragmentation of fiscal support. Add to this the implications for policy autonomy of the institutional imperative, discussed above, and the result is a public-sector administrative mechanism that has significant policy responsibilities but which is deprived of agreed-on ways to ensure its accountability to the public.

The Constitution, and how it is used politically by forces seeking to influence public policy, plays a major role in both encouraging and securing the policy roles of administrative agencies. The fragmentation of institutional power decreed by the Constitution results in what Norton Long has described as a "who is boss?" dilemma for administrative agencies.[14] Neither Congress, with its ability to create and fund agencies, nor the president with his pro-forma supervisory role over the bureaucracy has plenary power over agency activities and decisions. The merit system, with its official goal of a neutral bureaucracy, provides most bureaucrats with tenure and career status after serving a brief probationary period in office. This further immunizes agencies from complying directly with presidential and congressional demands that may undercut agencies' historical claims to their policy turf. Therefore, actuated by the institutional imperative, agencies seek support and security by establishing power bases outside the institutional framework of government. The "transitory amateurs" that occupy and direct these institutions—the president, cabinet officers, and members of congressional committees and subcommittees—do not offer agencies the long-term security they seek. Interest groups that support and profit from the policies the agencies administer can offer such support. Therefore, according to Long, if the "lifeblood of administration is power," then that power is best secured from political forces outside the government which employ their money, access, and leadership savvy to influence government institutions to support the policies that nourish the policy missions and career aspirations of agencies and their personnel.[15] This, of course, makes agencies key contributors to the impact of pluralist politics on public policy. It also explains why the iron triangle or subgovernment phenomenon has had such an impact on the course of public policy.

The repercussions of the "who is boss?" issue impact on both the processes and character of public policy in the United States. The separation of powers principle, accentuated by institutional constituency differences, makes the "boss" issue far more salient in our political system than it would be in a parliamentary system. The impact of this condition on the role of the public bureaucracy in politics and public policy will be analyzed from four different perspectives.

Contradictory Empowerment

Administrative agencies are empowered to do the business of government by developing and issuing regulations based on statutory authority and by implementing policy decisions as efficiently as possible. Our presidential system, as opposed to a parliamentary system, does not provide the policy solidity and continuity necessary to enable the bureaucracy to pursue such goals in an orchestrated, cohesive, and coordinated fashion. As discussed above, the separation of powers principle fragments the political inputs to which the president and Congress respond. Neither branch can claim the bureaucracy as its own. In parliamentary systems, both executive and legislative power is fused in a cabinet whose members work diligently to develop policy cohesion to keep the support of the legislature. Among other things, this involves appeasing would-be policy opponents so that the current majority party's control of government can be sustained. In the United States, the constitutionally independent legislative, executive, and judicial branches produce politically rooted incompatible policy norms. These norms do battle with the classical administrative norms of efficiency and effectiveness, and insist that the classical missions be abandoned or compromised in favor of political responsiveness, the pursuit of social justice, or the economic and/or civil rights of client groups.

Moreover, and perhaps more important insofar as public policy is concerned, this condition encourages the bureaucracy to adopt policy goals that are mutually incompatible with one another. Take public policy toward tobacco as an example. Agencies with public health as part of their mission—such as the Food and Drug Administration, the Public Health Service, and the Federal Trade Commission—work to discourage and, in some cases, outlaw the public use of tobacco products. At the same time the Department of Agriculture spends money on programs and subsidies to encourage tobacco farmers to grow and harvest tobacco at levels that guarantee them a decent market price and standard of living. Some federal agencies such as

the Department of Housing and Urban Development and the Department of Commerce subsidize activities that encourage the redevelopment of central cities and surrounding neighborhoods. At the same time, the Department of Transportation sponsors highway and bridge construction projects that make it relatively easy for white collar workers to live in the suburbs and commute to their jobs in the central city. In sum, administrators are placed in "catch-22" situations, facing condemnation regardless of their policy choice. The Constitution does not place direct policy constraints on the bureaucracy, but in presidential systems where policy responsibilities are deliberately fragmented, that is the inevitable result. The president, as the constitutionally designated chief executive, finds himself unable to direct and coordinate the bureaucracy. Furthermore, his ability to oversee the administration of policies is also compromised. From the president's point of view this is a serious handicap because agencies are vested by law with significant rule-making authority and the presidential impact on those rules (policies) is consequently limited. In some countries, popular frustration with such a situation can trigger armed protests, revolutions, and military coups. In the United States it has the ironic result of encouraging agencies to act on their own to seek out policy allies and pursue policies that augment their claims on the budget.

The absence of unified supervision and direction from a single hierarchical source permits administrative agencies to search for, and solidify, relations with policy allies that have no interest whatsoever in the planning and coordination of policies to serve the public interest. To be sure, the "public interest" is a very elusive concept. However, that is immaterial. Agencies and their policy bedfellows, both outside government, are so accustomed to equating the public interest with their own interests that a more selfless, inclusive definition of the term would be unacceptable to them. Therefore, agencies struggle with one another for policy advantage in much the same way as do interest groups outside the formal channels of government. Policy struggles that affect the bureaucracy involve not only competition among interest groups for administrative allies, but also competition among agencies for new programs, generous budgetary support, and abundant policy discretion. For example, the decision as to whether to sacrifice or modify an environmental clean-up effort in order to uncover new and cheaper sources of energy involves several administrative agencies—the Departments of Energy, Interior, and Labor and the Environmental Protection Agency. Each wants to claim the program as its own. The question of how to deal with the problem of chronic poverty is addressed in about as many ways as there are agencies that have concern for policies that affect the lives and incomes of those living in poverty. Consequently, to the Department of Housing and Urban Development the poverty problem is fundamentally a housing problem, to the Food and Drug Administration it is fundamentally a nutrition and drug addiction problem, to the National Institutes of Health it is a preventive medicine and health problem, to the Department of Commerce it is a jobs or employment problem, and to the Department of Labor it is a wage and fringe benefit problem.

Under such unstructured conditions, it is no wonder that many agencies cultivate their political roots so effectively that they and their policies live well beyond their usefulness. In his study of agency longevity, Herbert Kaufman observed that agencies are usually established to deal with a policy problem that surfaces rather suddenly, and they tend to be established in clusters. Agriculture agencies were created in the late nineteenth century, regulatory agencies in the early part of the twentieth century, and welfare agencies during the mid-twentieth century. Lacking confidence in the standing bureaucracy to absorb and administer new policy challenges effectively, public officials and interest groups usually prefer to establish new agencies in the hope that they will provide the necessary spark and thrust that will give the new programs a chance to succeed.[16]

The institutional imperative takes on added significance as an administrative norm because the president and Congress are the constitutionally designated comanagers of the bureaucracy. The absence of definitive, unified hierarchical directives encourages agencies to defend their policies as ones critical to the public good. If it becomes clear that policy momentum is against them, they often demonstrate an uncanny ability to replace unpopular policies with ones that attract more political support. The strategies of the Federal Energy Administration (FEA) from its creation as an independent agency in 1974 to its absorption into the Department of Energy in 1977 provide an excellent example of how naturally the institutional imperative locks into the mindset of agency leaders, and how such a mindset helps agencies deal with an institutional adaptation crisis. Established to deal with the energy shortage created by the energy crisis of 1974, FEA was originally mandated to serve as an administrative "militia" to help ease the short-term inconveniences caused by the Arab oil embargo. When the embargo ended, FEA feared for its organizational life. Agency leaders were quick to respond. Immediately the agency policy focus changed from one concerned with the effects of the embargo to one stressing the need for the United States to secure energy independence from the rest of the world. In effect, this strategy converted a temporary mission into a more long-term, if not permanent, one. If FEA were mandated to uncover additional sources of energy and to supervise the stockpiling of reserves in anticipation of another crisis, then the energy problem, and therefore the need for the agency, could be prolonged virtually indefinitely. FEA officials pursued agency permanency on yet another front. By identifying the energy problem as a national problem, as opposed to the oil industry's alone, it recruited many allies for its cause by expanding its base of political support. Former agency adversaries could now see some benefit to them in the remodeled agency with the new assignment. Attempts by the president, Congress, the business community, and the press to appease their various constituencies with promises of cheap and plentiful sources of energy turned them into allies of FEA and its programs virtually overnight. FEA's characterization of the energy problem as everyone's problem made such action quite natural. FEA provided all interested groups and individuals with information that would help make the case for FEA as a permanent agency. The fact that FEA was elevated to departmental status (Department of Energy) in 1977 gives testimony to how successful was such a strategy. The irony of such a strategy is that, by naturally responding to the institutional imperative, agencies actually profit by making policy problems worse instead of better. According to Nicholas Lemann, many administrative agencies "depend on a bad situation continuing to exist, and they are themselves the chief judge of how bad the situation really is."[17]

Therefore, the contradictory empowerment phenomenon encourages the "who is boss?" dilemma to affect the strategies of policy executives in the bureaucracy. Executive and legislative comanagement of the bureaucracy, a by-product of the separation of powers principle, places agencies in a supervisory "no man's land." As a result, there is little agreement among presidents, the houses of Congress, congressional committees and subcommittees, and the public in general as to what administrative agencies should be doing. Con-

sequently, agencies are encouraged to act on their own preferences, and the long-term effects of this on both the policy process and policy substance can be profound indeed.

Agencies seek security by cultivating allies from sources inside and outside government. The iron triangle is the most obvious and easily understood example of this strategy. However, the increased decentralization and fragmentation of power within Congress, on line since the late 1960s, has weakened the influence of iron triangles because power, once quite centralized, has become increasingly proliferated. This means that administrative agencies confront a "multiple master" problem from within Congress in addition to the most traditional "who is boss?" issue directly resulting from the separation of powers principle. According to David C. King, "public managers in Washington fear jurisdictional fragmentation because their multiple masters occasionally give conflicting demands."[18] Jurisdictional fragmentation does harbor advantages for democracy by providing multiple points of access within Congress for individuals and factions, and by virtually mandating more interjurisdictional communication and coalition-building within Congress in advance of votes on legislation. However, for administrative agencies it undermines their quest to maximize their security as expeditiously as possible. Their leaders have to work harder at the challenge and, of course, it makes their jobs inevitably more political.

Dispersion of Policy Accountability

The institutions to which administrative agencies respond are actuated by different incentives. Presidents want agencies to cooperate with them as they attempt to orchestrate policy priorities to meet the demands of a widely diverse national constituency. Assisted by the Office of Management and Budget (OMB) in this effort, presidents usually ask some agencies to curtail or sacrifice some of their programs to meet the changing policy priorities of the nation in general. This means that presidents hope, and expect, agencies to cooperate with them in this effort. Presidents' policy incentives are planning incentives. This is not because presidents are necessarily more public spirited or public interest oriented than other elected officials, but because the diverse character of presidential constituencies encourages such a stance. On the other hand, legislators assess the worth of agency programs by criteria that are more appropriate for their more restricted constituency bases. They serve states and subdivisions thereof. Consequently, they are inclined to support policies (and the agencies that administer them) that subsidize, or otherwise support, key groups in their constituencies. In sum, the president's perception of the public interest is more macroscopic in character, while those of legislators are more microscopic.

The degree to which an individual or institution is accountable for his, her, or its actions is the degree to which such actions satisfy the hierarchical superiors of each entity. Presumably, most superiors apply standards imposed on them by both the law and, in some cases, their interpretation of the law when they make judgments about the quality and integrity of decisions by subordinates. Elected officials are accountable to the general public, which is politically sovereign. In the case of appointed officials, such as those that staff the bureaucracy, accountability efforts are directed toward organizational superiors. If a single hierarchical superior exists, then agencies have no difficulty in identifying to whom they must be accountable. However, in the public sector the "who is boss?" issue surfaces to complicate matters measurably. Agencies have two bosses, both "superior" to them in the sense that each can make legal claims (sometimes constitutional) on agency policy

loyalties and priorities. They have additional bosses, both actual and potential, within the interest group complex. These entities are busy lobbying the president and Congress, as well as agencies, to adopt the groups' policy positions.

However, agencies find the conflicting claims of the president and legislators to be the most troublesome, not only because these claims have constitutional roots, but also because the failure to satisfy them can threaten an agency's future. This is especially true regarding the bureaucracy's relationship with Congress. Congress controls an agency's budget and jurisdictional authority. Agencies are inclined to be very obedient to legislative demands as a result. Therefore, the often-heard accusation that the bureaucracy is unaccountable, or "out of control," is inaccurate. In reality, it means that the public is frustrated over the bureaucracy's response to the political facts of life. Agencies' identification with the congressional bias toward distributive policies that help legislators solidify their relationships with their constituents is understandable in light of the fiscal and jurisdictional control Congress has over agency affairs. In sum, Congress has given the country the kind of bureaucracy that Congress wants. Agencies find themselves the target of waves of public ridicule for not earnestly pursuing the classic administration goals of efficiency and economy. However, from agencies' perspectives, to do this in the face of pressures from their budget and jurisdiction "bosses" would amount to outwardly defying their benefactors. The risk is too great.

Presidents have a constituency-based incentive to want to make the bureaucracy more accountable to standards that most people accept as being appropriate for administrative agencies. These include efficiency, economy, and effective long-term planning. For reasons discussed above, legislators do not seek such outputs from agencies. Consequently, when it comes to securing more accountability of the bureaucracy to the classical objectives of administration, Congress and the president demonstrate a clear mismatch of incentives and capabilities. Morris Fiorina described it very accurately when he noted that "Congress has the power but not the incentive for coordinated control of the bureaucracy, while the president has the incentive but not the power."[19] When agencies spend money to nurture a congressional constituency, it is not an agency that is out of control, but one that is, according to Fiorina, "paying of the Congressmen who nurture it."[20]

Legislators seek to extend their constituencies into the ranks of the bureaucracy so that agencies employ their policy discretion in ways that help legislators cement good relations with their constituents. An agency's instinct for survival and growth (institutional imperative) encourages it to identify with the cause of any institution or individual that can help it satisfy its self-preservation instinct. Since Congress exercises so much control, both actual and potential, over agencies through both the budget and policy empowerment, it would be very unusual if agencies did not support the policy crusades of legislators and subcommittees which are so critical to their future. Add to this network the vested interests that profit from these same policies and the iron triangle or triple alliance is complete.

While, the term "constituency" is usually applied to the relationship between elected officials and those who elected them, it is equally appropriate to apply it to administrative agencies. Constituencies impact on politics and policy in two ways. They reinforce the power base of those they elected and/or direct, and they limit, simultaneously, the policy discretion of those same entities. When administrative agencies search for ways to enhance their power they usually find they have much in common with legislators, for reasons noted above. Legislators know this and, as a result, want a bureaucracy that is large, fragmented, and inefficient. Congressmen gain constituent support by creating new agencies to deal with problems important to their constituents, and build even more constituent support by helping voters who have been victimized by these same agencies' mistakes. According to Fiorina legislators "take credit coming and going . . . they are the alpha and omega."[21]

The political party allegiance of House and Senate members is of little consequence when it comes to evaluating the utility of the national bureaucracy. To be sure, there are frequent rhetorical exchanges between Democrats and Republicans over the value of government as an intervening force in social and economic affairs. However, when it comes to policy and spending decisions, the differences between the two parties usually involve which agencies (and their policies) to emphasize and which to deemphasize. Debates between the two parties usually involve differences over which parts of the bureaucracy should be larger and which should be smaller, but not over whether a large bureaucracy is good or bad. Republicans tend to favor policies that support what has been termed a "military" or "defense" pork barrel, and Democrats support entitlement-type policies that nourish a "social" pork barrel. When spending cuts are debated, arguments usually develop over which type of pork barrel should be sacrificed in the interest of fiscal integrity. Invariably, to the protagonists it is the opposition's policy indulgences that should be eliminated or, at minimum, significantly harnessed. Unable to agree on the priorities of fiscal and policy austerity, Congress allows spending to continue on virtually all fronts and "both barrels overflow."[22]

The president's perspective on the issue of managing the bureaucracy is different from that of Congress, but certainly not devoid of constituency-based incentives. Fiorina's observation that presidents have more of an incentive to hold the bureaucracy accountable is certainly true, but only because the presidential constituency naturally encourages such a stance. Delegates to the Constitutional Convention of 1787 were concerned about how the bureaucracy in the newly constituted government should be managed. Under the Articles of Confederation, legislative committees oversaw administrative affairs, usually on a part-time basis. The result was gross administrative inefficiency. The Convention's solution was to endow the president with the power to appoint department heads (cabinet secretaries) with the approval of the Senate. Presumably, this would establish a clear hierarchical relationship of command and accountability between the president and the departments. This may seem naive today, but it appeared to be eminently practical to the founders. Departments were small in size and policy missions were comparatively simple and clear-cut. However, two centuries of bureaucratic growth in response to the escalating policy missions of government have changed things dramatically. Agencies are now staffed by hundreds of thousands of career specialists, immune from being dismissed for political reasons, who have exploited the "who is boss?" condition by cultivating alliances with legislators and interest groups to perpetuate policies that often have little to do with the nation's policy priorities as presidents interpret them.

Upon assuming office, new presidents quickly realize that the bureaucracy is, in Walter Shapiro's terms, "intractable."[23] Reforms aimed at making it more compliant with the president's policy perspectives have invariably failed, largely because career bureaucrats and their legislative allies conspire to protect existing programs from encroachment by any force unsympathetic to the sanctity of their mission as they define it.

Presidents try diligently to bring the bureaucracy to heel before surrendering out of frustration. President Nixon proposed a "supercabinet" whereby the eleven existing cabinet-level departments were to be consolidated into five "superdepartments," each having an organizational focus more synchronized to the actual compass of policy problems. Nixon proposed consolidating the existing departments into new departments of Community Development, Natural Resources, Human Resources, Economic Affairs, and Foreign Affairs. As discussed above, organization in public affairs reflects, in effect, a clear mobilization of policy bias. The proposed departments did not synchronize with the assorted policy biases of congresspersons and their allies in the bureaucracy. Consequently, Congress did not acquiesce to the proposal. Nixon responded by reorganizing his Executive Office to develop advisory councils headed by policy "czars" who were to provide policy advice to reflect the policy perspectives of the would-be cabinet secretaries under the proposed reorganization. Key members of Congress complained about the elitist overtones of such a move. Moving on yet another front, Nixon sought to infiltrate the regular bureaucracy by what Richard Nathan labeled an "administrative presidency" strategy.[24] This plan involved the use of a policy decentralization and job rotation strategy to discourage and demoralize careerists committed to programs which the president opposed, encourage them to resign or request transfers, and then appoint Nixon political loyalists to the vacant positions. Former Senator James Abourezk (D–South Dakota) labeled such a strategy "operation mangle," because its purpose was to decentralize and fragment programs to the point of ineffectiveness, and then to use such disarray as a justification to cut back or eliminate some programs which the president opposed.[25]

Nixon's plans for Executive Office policy

"czars" and for an "administrative presidency" were abandoned in the face of the developing Watergate scandal in 1973. Nonetheless, his frustration over unsympathetic and embedded bureaucracy provides an excellent illustration of the issues that surface when presidents attempt to make the national bureaucracy more accountable to the national interest as perceived by its only elected spokesperson—the president. Nixon's White House coordinator for the assault on the bureaucracy, Frederick V. Malek, once called the merit system "a device by which the bureaucrats operate their own patronage system while telling politicians to 'keep their hands off.'"[26] Those who openly opposed the move, such as Senator Abourezk and Congressman Chet Holifield (D–California), called it a direct affront to the balance bred into politics and policymaking by the separation of powers. Malek, however, defended it as a way to increase the accountability of government to the people. Ironically, career employees in one agency defended their resistance to the Nixon strategy on grounds that it undermined democratic government, arguing that the people supported the policies that Nixon was attempting to dismantle. Therefore, drawing on their experiences and career status to fight the plan made them, not the president and Malek, the conduits of policy accountability. Arguing against the administration's attempt to "usurp official duties of career bureaucrats . . . and make all acts political in nature," one local AFL-CIO affiliate defended the career bureaucracy as the savior of substantive democracy under such circumstances by posing the following question: "Are employees ultimately loyal to the Administration, or are they ultimately loyal to the Constitution, the laws, and the people when the two are not compatible?"[27] Such an attitude illustrates the key role that a career bureaucracy plays in a democracy impacted by constitutionally fragmented power. This is illustrative

of how the Constitution can serve as a smokescreen for an agency in its attempt to fend off assaults on its policies, and perhaps on its own existence and future. Under such conditions career administrators can exploit their career status and fragmented institutional power to justify resistance to doctrines alien to their own interpretation of the public interest, conditioned, of course, by the institutional imperative.

Regarding the presidency, the problem of bureaucratic intransigence is an institutional problem faced by all presidents, and not a partisan one facing only Democrats or Republicans. Presidents Carter, Reagan, Bush, and Clinton all experienced the same sort of frustration as did Nixon. Carter had plans for his own "superdepartments" that were dashed by Congress. He introduced plans for a zero-based budgeting system (ZBB) which would have required all agencies to prioritize their programs annually and (in all probability) face cutbacks in those programs that were rated as low priority. Introduced officially as a system of guidelines for the development of agency budgets, agencies found ways to exempt some programs from consideration because of their alleged indispensable character as they, the agencies, defined them. The idea was abandoned rather quickly as a strategy before it achieved significant administrative reform.

Undoubtedly President Carter's major contribution to the effort to make the bureaucracy more efficient and accountable was his championing of the Civil Service Reform Act of 1978 (CSRA). Facing considerable opposition from federal employee unions which thought the proposal assigned too much power to managers, Carter's proposal was enacted nearly intact within six months of its introduction. Directed at reducing delay and red tape, and at increasing accountability for decisions, CSRA established the Office of Personnel Management (OPM) and the Merit

Systems Protection Board (MSPB) to serve as the president's personnel arm (OPM) and to function as a recourse forum for aggrieved employees (MSPB). It established the Federal Labor Relations Authority (FLRA) to supervise federal labor-management policies and a Senior Executive Service (SES) staffed by approximately 9,000 top management personnel, who worked for increased efficiency and effectiveness in policy management, for which they could receive salary bonuses if their work was exceptional. The overall purpose of CSRA was to increase administrative accountability to the president by calling on the classical values and practices of administrative management. It sought administrative accountability through hierarchy. This was particularly true of the Senior Executive Service (SES). The president was authorized to appoint some SES members on the basis of their loyalty to his policies, thereby reintroducing some vestiges of the spoils principle that had been officially rejected by the Pentleton Act in 1883. However, it is important to understand exactly what neutrality means to policy executives in an administrative system anchored in the hierarchical principle. It means, in essence, that administrators pledge themselves, presumably enthusiastically, to the administration of the legitimized policies of their political superiors, regardless of the nature of those policies. Carter, like all recent presidents, considered a neutral bureaucracy to be one dedicated to being accountable to the policies of the president who, in turn, is the policy spokesperson for the entire body politic. Such a mission collides with legislative incentives as congressional committees and subcommittees "micromanage" the bureaucracy. It also collides with the policy implications of the institutional imperative, as well as with agency strategies to establish power bases outside the formal institutions of government.

Although they did not sponsor any major changes in the laws affecting administrative accountability, presidents Reagan and Bush worked diligently to make CSRA an effective accountability mechanism. This was especially true in the case of Reagan who, in an adaptation of the spoils principle to personnel governance, succeeded in grooming OPM and SES to become institutions that worked aggressively for the success of his policy agenda. Conservatives pledged to Reagan's supply side policy reforms were named to fill key positions in both OPM and SES.[28] Although Carter may not have expected the reintroduction of the spoils idea to extend quite as far as Reagan extended it, the intent of both presidents was to use both administrative structure and personnel policy to foster administrative accountability to the dominant political ideology of the times as articulated by the president.

As a presidential candidate, Bill Clinton pledged to continue the crusade for administrative accountability. Shortly after assuming office, he introduced plans to "reinvent government" by tapping the talents of the private sector in an attempt to establish a more efficient bureaucracy. Influenced by the arguments of journalist David Osborne and former city manager Ted Gaebler in their book *Reinventing Government: How the Entrepreneurial Spirit Is Transforming the Public Sector*, the president in 1993 organized the National Performance Review to determine how the Osborne and Gaebler thesis could be applied successfully to alleviate problems of waste, inefficiency, and (policy) ineffectiveness at the federal level.[29] Vice-President Al Gore directed the study. In September 1993, the Gore task force issued a report recommending ways to save billions of budget dollars by reducing, simultaneously, the cost of government while improving policy performance. Clinton and Gore pursued the reinventing crusade with resolve, and tens of billions of dollars were trimmed from the federal budget over the next several years, mostly from inefficient program operations. In a sense, the

Clinton assault on administrative inefficiency was less ambitious than those of Nixon, Carter, and Reagan. The latter were more clearly concerned about eliminating substantive policies that had outlived their usefulness, but were nonetheless still alive because of the impact of demosclerosis on the policy system. Clinton was less inclined than either Carter, Nixon, or Reagan to challenge the beneficiaries of distributive policies, even though many of those policies were of benefit to no one other than the direct beneficiaries themselves. The reinventing crusade carefully avoided questioning the benefit of particular policies, and concentrated instead on more procedural and opaque issues such as personnel and procurement programs where there was general agreement that the federal government could operate more efficiently.

In short, the Clinton reforms did not confront the key cause of an unaccountable bureaucracy—a political system that had defaulted in its obligation to govern in the interest of the many, not the few. This is much more than simply a victory of iron triangle politics over the politics of substantive policy reform. A more fundamental cause for government timidity on such questions is the public's attitude, which is notably contradictory. Despite all the rhetoric about waste and inefficiency in government, most Americans still view government primarily as a vehicle that should support their quest for economic security and prosperity. In short, government policies have a distributive bias because the public has a distributive policy bias. Most Americans believe that, once a policy benefit has been bestowed on them, they have a "right" to its continuance and it should not be withdrawn. Revoking policies upon which people depend would be "unjust" or "unfair." Iron triangles have the significant effect they do on public policy because they are not faced with effective countervailing forces. The evaluative standard that is lost amidst the

public's contorted, although understandable, reasoning is whether public policies serve anybody but their direct beneficiaries.

As Rauch noted in his explanation of demosclerosis, the policy system no longer debates the sweaty and controversial question of whether claims on policy content serve the national interest or just those of specific beneficiaries. Understandably, virtually all beneficiaries argue that their pet policies simultaneously serve the common good. It is therefore up to the policy system to determine which of these claims have more linkage to the common good, and which do not. The policy system, including the president if the Clinton attitude becomes the norm, has succumbed to the easy way out, and defaulted on this most critical challenge.

In contrast to the nineteenth century when few organized interest groups engaged in politics and electioneering, interest groups during the twentieth century (especially since the New Deal period) have articulated policy demands that involve the services of administrative agencies. Accordingly, members of Congress concluded rather quickly that their chances for reelection would be greatly enhanced by meeting the demands of groups prominent in their constituencies. This meant that a professional, efficient bureaucracy that would be capable of delivering these services would be a political plus for legislators. As a result, legislators strongly supported the transition from a spoils-based bureaucracy to one selected and managed on the basis of merit. Administrators quickly realized that administrative neutrality as a performance standard would work to their advantage if agencies provided efficient, specific services to organized interest group forces. The grants-in-aid idea, endorsed overwhelmingly by virtually all public officials during the New Deal period, represented, in part, a government response to the impact of organized interests on the resources and talents of government as it—the government—wrestled with the problems of the depression. Grants came in the form of cash allocations to states and localities and were conditional on the recipient governments' willingness to administer them with professional bureaucracies of their own. Consequently, grants for such programs as highways, housing, and welfare were awarded with the understanding that the states and localities would create their own professional planning cadres of highway engineers, construction specialists, and social workers. Authority in these bureaucracies was vested in these professional administrative elites. The benefits to both legislators and bureaucrats were obvious. Professional, neutral bureaucracies served the political needs of the politicians and the career aspirations of professional bureaucrats.

Therefore, in theory legislators and bureaucrats agree on the policy roles of the bureaucracy for reasons rooted in the career aspirations of each. The reasons for the prominence and strength of iron triangles, or subsystems, in the policy process are clear. While the relationship among all three parties to these alliances has been, by and large, a cooperative one, strains have developed on occasion. These tensions are not rooted in any change in the circumstances which brought about the marriage in the first place, but rather in policy problems caused by the growing bureaucratization of administrative agencies. As agencies become increasingly bureaucratized, they become absorbed in routine, red tape, and making decisions according to the rules instead of according to the unique circumstances governing each individual policy decision they are asked to make. Nelson's allegory of "the desk" discussed earlier is an illustration of this, as is Saul's thesis that the bureaucratization of Western societies has resulted in a dictatorship of reason based on science, procedures, and technique as opposed to judgment.

Cathy Marie Johnson has examined the causes for conflict between legislators and agencies within the iron triangle networks, and has concluded that what she calls the "self-interest decision model" does not always explain the relationship between the two entities. If both legislators and agency personnel shared constantly the same self-interest-based policy objectives, then there would be little reason for conflict between the two entities. However, Johnson argues that mutual policy-grounded self-interest does not always explain the relationship. Instead, she offers a "policy model" as a substitute model to explain why relationships between legislators and administrators are often less than harmonious.[30] In examining the history of policy tensions between four administrative agencies—the Bureau of Reclamation, the Bureau of Indian Affairs, the Food and Drug Administration, and the Social and Rehabilitation Service—and their parent congressional authorization committees, she found numerous instances of agency reluctance to assume new policy responsibilities, change the routines by which they dealt with existing policies, and alter the character of the policies for which they had responsibility. Agencies took this position despite the fact Congress had already authorized changes. Johnson argues that policy differences divide legislators and administrators because, in contrast to the "received" opinion, legislators are more interested in good policies than they are in cementing ties with voters to secure reelection when they ask agencies to change both their policies and their routines. This conclusion is somewhat suspect because it challenges a spate of research that makes clear linkages between legislators' committee assignments, their desire to serve their constituencies, and their quest for reelection.[31]

Therefore, it is highly likely that the conflict between congressional committees and agencies noted by Johnson is rooted, at least somewhat, in the growing tendency for agencies to be overly absorbed in policy procedures at the expense of policy substance. A bureaucratic environment, especially in the public sector where there is no profit motive, encourages administrators to adopt procedures or processes as the primary goals of their work lives. It becomes politically advantageous for legislators to try to change this because it may interfere with the efficient dispatch of monies and privileges to constituents. Therefore, the aberrations of the merit system brought on by such a "means as ends" administrative mentality makes it politically shrewd for legislators to champion the cause of putting merit back into the merit system. Good administration becomes allied with good politics. This is a problem encountered by both the president and Congress as they seek to make the bureaucracy accountable to their conflicting, constituency-rooted policy standards. Administrative procedures and routines that compromise policy substance and permit agencies to be accountable to their own internally generated standards are of concern to both the president and Congress.

Despite occasional conflict between legislators and committees, the separation of powers as a constitutional principle has encouraged most administrative agencies to prefer the iron triangle spin on accountability. This is more acceptable to Congress than to the president. Still, as the Clinton example illustrates, most presidents are inclined to abandon or deemphasize the quest for major substantive policy sacrifices and, albeit reluctantly, accept the hold of beneficiary government on the policy system. Even their own political appointees to the bureaucracy often end up supporting the agencies' causes in opposition to those of the president. Instead of being representatives of the president's point of view to the agencies, they often become the representatives of the agencies' causes to the president. This is because they come quickly to realize that they must identify with the history and policy crusades of the agencies (and their career policy executives) in order to maintain any semblance of creditability as the agencies' leaders. While the separation of powers and its "who is boss?" operational derivative does not dictate the incentives of policy actors, fragmented government allows beneficiary government, or the politics of dependency, to dominate the strategies of administrative agencies as they seek to satisfy the demands of the institutional imperative, encouraged by a system of atomized constitutional power.

Interest Group Liberalism

A third effect of constitutional politics on the public bureaucracy's role in public policy is rooted in the Constitution's role in encouraging a condition Theodore Lowi has labeled interest group liberalism.[32] In effect, interest group liberalism is the institutionalized result of the marriage of administrative agency and interest group policy missions discussed earlier. Fundamentally, it is a theory of policy-making which argues that the net effect (even the purpose) of public policy is to parcel out public authority (via the law) to interest groups which, in turn, use this authority to further their organizational objectives. The result is a government that is unable to plan ahead because so much of its resources have been invested in appeasing group demands. Consequently, government assumes the role of a "holding company" for vested interests, thereby forfeiting its mandate to make difficult policy choices among competing political values.

Before interest groups can gain a lock on public policy, they must get the consent, active or passive, of government's policy institutions to do so. Since the policy system has a distributive, beneficiary policy bias, this is not difficult to accomplish. Components of iron triangles (subcommittees, bureaus, interest groups) all profit from nourishing the seeds and results of interest group liberalism. Although the public is quick to condemn the results of interest group liberalism, the cultural roots of the theory find much public acceptance. Ironically, Americans generally have little argument with the notion that interest groups should be a major source of policy options. This is due to the public's cultural affinity for individualism, capitalism, competition, and the Protestant ethic. The Constitution's suspicion of centralized power and its endorsement of civil rights illustrate such cultural norms. Interest groups compete with each other for the rewards of public policy, most of which involve actual or potential economic advantages for group members.

Capitalism has been especially important in nourishing the public's acceptance of the transition of group competition from private, economic arenas to government institutions. Our cultural affinity for capitalism as an economic system that expects firms and groups to compete for markets and economic advantage makes the transformation of such dynamics to government arenas largely a matter of "changing the scene" rather than one of accepting an entirely new political dynamic. Consequently, competition among group allies in government—administrative bureaus, committees, subcommittees—for favorable policy advantages represents, by and large, a transplantation of the competitive spirit from extra-government arenas to intra-government arenas. The transplantation has been so successful, argues Lowi, that Americans and their elected policy agents have come to consider group-based policy options as the most dependable, safe, and legitimate source of policy inputs.

It is impossible to analyze the impact of a subcommittee or an administrative agency on public policy without incorporating the impact of its group affiliates, or groups that challenge those affiliates, on its policy stance. The Forest Service in the Department of Agriculture (DOA) supervises competition among conservation forces seeking to preserve forests and those who want to use them as a source of timber for construction and paper products. Other DOA bureaus bargain with farmers over what quantity of crops to grow, the price of commodities, and acceptable poison levels of weed killers. Bureaus in the Department of Transportation (DOT) negotiate with automobile manufacturers over the safety features of newly manufactured automobiles. The Environmental Protection Agency (EPA) bargains with manufacturers over acceptable levels of toxic fumes and surface pollutants that can be discharged into the atmosphere, lakes, rivers, and streams. Mayors and directors of big city housing authorities strike deals with the Department of Housing and Urban Development (HUD) for public housing and sewer grants. Smaller communities in rural areas get the same from DOA. Indian tribes secure support for similar projects from the Interior Department. Regulatory agencies, with their legally empowered right to issue regulations controlling excessive exploitation of consumers by industry, have seen their policy mission compromised, and sometimes cooptated, by an onslaught of lawyers, lobbyists, trade associations, public relations experts, consultants, and countless corporate representatives who come to Washington to compete with one another over the content of agency regulations. Between the 1960s and the 1980s, as the consumer protection and environmental protection movements gained political momentum, the regulatory policy mission of government took on added significance. Nearly two hundred major regulatory laws were enacted during this period. The result of this, according to William Greider, was to bring the Fortune 500 to Washington, accompanied by thousands of lawyers to argue their respective cases before congressional subcommittees and regulatory agencies.[33]

Greider has compared modern government to a "bazaar" or "marketplace" condition wherein merchants bargain with customers for the best deal. Ideally, to govern effectively means that public policy acts to suppress strong private interests for the common good. However, the "bazaar" analogy rejects public interest government, and substitutes a system within which policy rewards are dispensed by administrative agencies to vested interests that make the most mutually advantageous offers. Agencies reciprocate with generous subsidies or, in the case of regulatory policies, often with decisions that require little in the way of corporate sacrifice. Money and legal privilege dispensed by bureaus as a result of their policy discretion become the subjects of a bargaining game, and any concern for effective long-term planning in the public interest is abandoned.

So much for the interest group component of interest group liberalism. The question might well be asked: In what way is the model "liberal"? Schattschneider argued that the most wealthy and well-led interest groups dominate their weaker competitors in politics. Interest group liberalism theory asserts that groups impact the bureaucracy the same way. These privileged groups are also the most conservative ones politically.

Therefore, what is "liberal" about interest group liberalism? The answer is, in essence, that interest group liberalism is liberal only in a procedural sense, but not in a substantive one. Groups exploit big government to their advantage, and big government is a product of the "liberal" New Deal era. The substantive policy results of interest group liberalism tend to be conservative, in that they are biased toward maintaining existing economic and social structures as advocated by most of the groups that have gained "inside track" access to the bureaucracy and Congress. What

makes interest group liberalism liberal is the fact that the more conservative interest group forces have tapped the *growth* of government, and the growth of bureaucracy that has accompanied it, and used it for their own benefit. Americans generally have been suspicious of the accretion of policy power from states and localities to Washington, and from legislatures to bureaucracies at all levels of government. They equate such an aggregation of power with liberal politics because centralization advocates such as the Progressives and New Dealers sought to centralize power and use it to help society's exploited and underprivileged. In short, stronger and more centralized government could be used to "liberate" the disadvantaged. This can be explained by the impact of the Progressive movement and its most famous policy manifestation, the New Deal, on American public opinion. In sum, the politics of the Progressive and New Deal eras made government intervention on behalf of both democracy and more equitable public policies more culturally acceptable to a citizenry that was culturally suspicious of government power.

Administrative agencies were the prime beneficiaries of this change. Recognizing this, interest groups began to target agencies as potential policy allies. Generally receptive to these advances, agencies began to depend on interest groups for data to support their budget requests. It became increasingly difficult to separate the policy priorities of agencies from those of their interest group allies. Many agencies became within-government lobbies for interest group causes, making the distinction between interest group policy positions and administrative agency policy positions largely an academic one. The liberating objective of government empowerment and expanded administrative policy discretion succumbed to the natural forces of politics.

However, in general the substantive policy results of this phenomenon have been conservative, not liberal, in cast. The fusion of group and administrative expertise is difficult to challenge and has, in many instances, created an almost impenetrable obstacle to change. Instead of striking balanced compromises from among interest group claimants with some notion of the common good in mind, centralized interventionist government has allowed the newly endowed powers of government to be inordinately influenced, and sometimes consumed by the very forces it was supposed to repress and control. According to Lowi, the acceptance of a group's right to claim parcels of government authority as its own via the law and use it has, in effect, made conflict of interest a principle of government. In many cases, what government does cannot be distinguished from what the major interest groups want it to do. Group policy positions become part of the law. The result is the corruption, demoralization, and impotence of democratic government in the United States. It is corrupt because long-term policy rationalism is sacrificed by permitting agencies to use their policy discretion to accommodate vested interests. It is demoralized because the search for social and economic justice has all but been abandoned in the face of such an onslaught. It is impotent because it considers accommodation of vested interests as the *de facto* goal of the policy process.

The Constitution, and its political exploitation by both interest groups and agencies with official jurisdiction over policies that concern them, has played a major role in both encouraging and reinforcing the impact of interest group liberalism on public policy. Much of this can be traced to the political repercussions of the "who is boss?" issue. Administrative agencies simply have more leeway to search out and solidify extragovernmental support for their policy causes under a government of officially separated powers than is the case when powers are concentrated. Furthermore, the Constitution, as

a document embracing the notion of fragmented power as a principle of government, has contributed to a cultural acceptance of the "right" of factions to compete among themselves for any advantages they might gain from government's effort to distribute and redistribute resources and wealth, and regulate industry on behalf of workers, consumers, and the general public. Of course, the public is quick to complain about some of the most obvious inequities and injustices that result from such a process, but it is far less likely to complain about the political and legal environment that encourages the development of such a condition.

According to Herbert Kaufman, over the past two centuries the public bureaucracy has been subjected to three politically induced performance norms or standards—those of representativeness, neutrality, and executive leadership.[34] The preceding analysis has shown how each of these standards is exploited by interested parties, both public and private, in an attempt to encourage agencies to march to their policy beat. Each of these norms has tended to gain popularity at times when public policies seem unable to cope effectively with the challenges facing society. The tendency to carry representativeness to the point of saturating bureaucracy with incompetence and corruption led to the Progressive movement and legislation establishing neutrality as the most appropriate administrative standard. However, seeking to legislate neutrality by establishing a merit system, and establishing independent boards, commissions, and regulatory agencies, begot accountability problems. Both the president and Congress had much less control over what bureaucrats did (they were neutral and immune from dismissal) and over policies issued by the new "independent" agencies. These frustrations led to the enthronement of increased executive power as a way to bring prodigal government to heel. Beginning in the early 1900s, this crusade reached its zenith during the New Deal and post–World War II period. Presidential efforts to reorganize the bureaucracy and adopt new management strategies, discussed above, are examples of the application of the executive leadership norm to the national bureaucracy.

Ironically, while all three of these norms appear, by themselves, to be compatible with both democratic theory and sound management practices, as a package of standards they are contradictory. A bureaucracy cannot be neutral and representative at the same time, nor can it identify with and attempt to sell the policy program of an elected chief executive and lay claim to objectivity.

Interest group liberalism as a condition affecting the bureaucracy and policy can possibly lay claim to some policy legitimacy via the norm of representation. Not all citizens are represented by Congress, interest groups, and the president. As an institution of government, the public bureaucracy *potentially* has a valid claim to being as representative of the people in a sociological sense as are, say, judges who are appointed for life, or a senator from a small state elected by a narrow margin in a three- or four-way race for the seat. Administrative agencies are created by statutes by the people's elected representatives, and their day-to-day work is supervised by other electees, namely presidents, governors, and mayors. The Constitution gives no single branch of government or other political entity complete sovereignty over the bureaucracy. Consequently, it could be argued that the bureaucracy potentially represents them all, and since the others have more direct ties to the people, is potentially a force that consolidates the representation of people as voiced through those other institutions. It could have, in John Rohr's terms, a mandate to preserve the *constitutional* order as a force that consolidates other institutional representation of the popular will.[35]

The problem with interest group liberalism as a facilitator of the constitutional order under such conditions is that the theory makes no distinction between interest group politics and public interest politics. Therefore much of the balanced representation of public opinion that could emanate from a diversified bureaucracy is lost amid the tendency for agencies to identify with the strong, well-financed, and cohesively organized interest groups to the disadvantage of the relatively unorganized and underfinanced groups that, collectively, represent a much larger segment of the public.

An excellent illustration of this phenomenon developed in the wake of the enactment of the Personal Responsibility and Work Opportunity Act of 1996. The act transferred major policy and finance responsibilities for entitlement programs from the federal government to the states and (especially) localities. The stress was on the conversion of traditional "welfare" programs to what were termed "workfare" programs, or ones requiring welfare recipients to accrue valuable work experience through work programs sponsored either by governments or nonprofit organizations, but only for as long as it took participants to gain employment in the regular workforce.

Since its establishment, and in line with the political patterns that produce interest group liberalism, the Department of Labor had gradually absorbed the policy missions of organized labor and made them the *de facto* mission of the department itself. In the wake of the enactment of welfare reform, and in response to pressures from labor unions, especially public employee unions, the Labor Department quickly issued policy regulations that required (as a prerequisite for receiving essential federal financial support for workfare programs) all state and local workfare programs to consider program participants regular employees. This meant that state and local sponsoring agencies would have to guarantee participants the federal hourly minimum wage; allow them to join labor unions, sue employers, and file discrimination suits; and perhaps make special workplace accommodations for disabled participants. The minimum wage requirement proved to be especially troublesome, so much so that it threatened to undermine the purpose of the reform legislation. The act required that states have at least 25 percent of their welfare recipients working at least twenty hours per week or face cuts in the federal government's subsidy of the programs. If sponsors were willing to pay workforce participants (who remained on welfare during their participation in the program) the federal minimum wage, it was feared that participants would be increasingly reluctant to enter the regular workforce where compensation was often less than the minimum wage. Workfare was not intended to be a regular source of employment, but only a way to offer participants valuable work experience as a route to regular employment.[36]

Although they had cooperated in the development and enactment of welfare reform, President Clinton and congressional Republicans were divided on this issue. In the immediate aftermath of the decision, the president concluded it was too much of a political risk to oppose the unions on the issue, and threatened to veto any law or rider that sought to exempt workforce participants from labor laws. On the other hand, congressional Republicans and many state governors, including some Democrats, were avidly opposed, vowing not to let the president "turn back the clock" on welfare reform. This opinion was shared by a senior policy analyst at the Heritage Foundation, who argued that the application of labor laws to workfare would make the goal of regular employment "impractical on any scale."[37] In sum, the forces of interest group liberalism, this time the labor unions

aligned with the Labor Department, threatened to undermine a key part of one of the most revolutionary entitlement laws enacted since the New Deal era.

Policy Counterbureaucracies

Policy counterbureaucracies are administrative agencies created to coordinate policy planning, develop budget priorities, reduce jurisdictional redundancy, and promote increased management efficiency within the public bureaucracy. They are organizational superstructures that respond to the comparatively narrow, specialized policy orientation of most bureaus. Such an orientation is rooted, first and foremost, in the legislation that grants agencies policy authority. Legislators want to keep a close watch over policies that are of benefit to their constituencies. Consequently, a large number of agencies with relatively narrow policy responsibilities are a boon to the legislative notion of accountability, but a bane to the presidential notion of the same. Again, the explanation for such a condition is rooted in the different constituencies and different policy roles assigned the presidency and Congress by the Constitution.

From the standpoint of numbers alone, the complex of administrative agencies at all levels of government offers opportunities for individuals and groups to gain access to decision centers that would be denied them in a constitutional system with a more hierarchical power pattern. With the exception of agencies dealing directly with foreign and military policy, most national agencies must deal with state and local "counterpart" agencies when they seek uniform and systematic compliance with national policy standards. These counterpart units are established by state governments as a matter of right because the constitutional principle of federalism allows states to organize and structure their governments as they please. Therefore, the fact that national agencies can do very little legally in the way of coercing lower-level counterpart agencies to cooperate with them, relations between entities at the two levels is dominated by a bargaining and negotiation atmosphere. Frequently, federal agencies can secure the cooperation of state and local units by attaching conditions to their acceptance of federal grants-in-aid money. Sometimes federal law requires that state and local counterpart agencies hire their personnel on the basis of merit, and that they agree to spend grant money only for programs specifically targeted by federal funds. Therefore, in part for reasons of political expediency, the relationship between national bureaus and their state and local counterparts is usually a cooperative one.

However, interlevel cooperation among policy professionals by no means suggests that programs are coordinated at either the planning or execution stages. If anything, vertical coordination discourages essential interprogram coordination on a horizontal plane. Often grants-in-aid are funneled through rather small policy pipelines that do not cooperate well with one another to deal with urban or rural problems systematically. As a result, the organizational landscape is proliferated, or pluralized, even further by counterbureaucracies.

Counterbureaucracies have developed to assist in the coordination of national, state, and local efforts to deal with policy problems within subnational arenas. The movement toward regionalism is an excellent example. Regionalism represents a redistribution of agency authority downward from the federal government to interstate regional councils and commissions, and often from the states and localities outward. The goal is to cooperate in the administration of policies that were previously solely under the jurisdiction of the states. Regionalism has broken down state policy resistance to nationally instituted changes for the past few decades. The federal government has sought to bring new order, effi-

ciency, and better evaluations to programs heavily subsidized by grants-in-aid, and regionalization strategies help reduce localized resistance to national supervision of their implementation. Regionalism has manifested itself in the form of Federal Regional Councils consisting of officials from the Departments of Health and Human Services, Housing and Urban Development, Transportation, Labor, and the Environmental Protection Agency, and in the form of numerous federal special districts to administer multipurpose programs in the areas of transportation, solid waste, rural development, and environmental protection. In addition the Advisory Commission on Intergovernmental Relations (ACIR), consisting of representatives of national, state, and local governments, and several Councils of Government (COGs) have been generated to discuss problems of intergovernmental policy management in virtually every key policy area.

With the national government, the counterbureaucracy cause has been championed mostly by presidents who have a vested interest in more effective policy planning and policy administration because, as representatives of the entire body politic, establishing policy priorities and working for more efficient policy administration is more constituency-effective for presidents than for legislators. Only by stressing efficiency and planning can the president appeal to the long-term interest of everyone. To be sure, such a position asks sacrifice of some individuals and groups. However, in contrast to the standards by which voters evaluate legislators, people have come to expect such challenges from presidents. This is the way in which voters deal with the contradictory impulses of the desire to indulge on the one hand, and the need to compromise on indulgences for the common good. Voters know it is their civic duty to, on occasion, forgo their indulgences for the common good, but are unwilling to ask individual candidates for office to deal with both impulses simultaneously. As a result, voters are more inclined to support presidents who preach sacrifice and legislators who promise to appease their perceived need for immediate benefits. This is the way voters live with the contradictions between the two impulses. Rather than deal with the contradiction, voters tend to ask different institutional leaders elected for different political reasons to deal with the contradiction as they clash over policy priorities.

Since the policy incentives of presidents and legislators are so different, it is not surprising to discover that presidents have introduced many counterbureaucracies to the policy system, especially since the New Deal period. The creation and growth of the Executive Office of the President embodies this trend. Established officially to help the president manage his time and manage policy administration more efficiently, EOP has developed into an institution that has major responsibilities for the development of policy alternatives that incorporate national, as contrasted to state and local, policy perspectives. The Office of Management and Budget (OMB), the Council of Economic Advisors (CEA), the Office of Policy Development (OPD) and its organizational derivatives, and the National Security Council (NSC) have all functioned to provide the president with policy advice reflecting an integrated, synthesized perspective that is not reflected by individual legislators or administrative departments and bureaus, each of which has a constituency that is decidedly more parochial in policy orientation.

Problems of interagency policy coordination are, therefore, often handled by creating new organizations, superimposed over existent ones, in the hope that the new ones will overcome the structured policy biases incorporated within the older units. Interest groups, administrative agencies, and legislators like such fractionalized policy power. Presidents do not. The clashes between these two perspectives are rooted in the constitutionally decreed constituency differences between the president and Congress. A pluralized bureaucracy offers legislators more access to, and control over, administrative officials who can direct money and other advantages to legislative constituencies. The more agencies that are created to accomplish this, the more the bureaucracy becomes pluralized and difficult to coordinate. Counter-bureaucracies then become necessary to coordinate matters, because the pluralization of administration increases the incidence of conflict within the policy system over scarce budgetary resources. Any increase in the number of agencies with partial jurisdiction over a field of public policy increases, commensurately, the need to create commissions, staff agencies, and intergovernmental and interagency task forces to attempt to placate the vested interests that have a stake in the policy outcomes and which, in all probability, have secured the allegiance of one or more of the agencies to help in such a quest. The process of developing ways to achieve coordination can make coordination an end unto itself, and interfere with the obvious need to develop quality substantive policies. A preoccupation with the means of policy administration can displace the overriding objectives of the coordination efforts themselves.

Democratic Accountability: Roadblock to Rationality

The above discussion highlights how our institutionally fragmented democracy contributes to the inevitable integration of administration and politics. Each of the factors examined affects the ways in which public agencies and their employees go about their daily responsibilities. Under these conditions, realizing the goals of the classical model is merely a pipe dream. Public administrators confront several conditions in their daily work that detract directly from their ability to achieve the administrative rationalism advocated by the classical school. None of these conditions have to do with the quality of persons employed by the public sector, nor with their degree of commitment to their responsibilities. The "roadblocks to rationalism" are rooted in matters beyond their control. What are they and how do they, collectively, make public agency decision making inevitably a nonrational enterprise?

The classical model assumes that administrators are accountable to the norms of their profession as they work to implement policies efficiently. There is no incongruity between that expectation and the expectations written in the laws *provided that* those laws deal with relatively simple policy challenges whose objectives are described clearly in the laws. Under such conditions, the challenge to administrators is to select the most appropriate way, or means, to achieve those objectives. Administrators focus exclusively on the means. They have nothing whatsoever to do with selecting or altering the objectives of the laws themselves.

Unfortunately, today's public administrators are not presented with such a clear-cut policy administration dichotomy. Laws often contain objectives that are quite general in tone, asking administrators to fill in the details by making decisions, often in the form of administrative orders or rules that apply those general objectives to specific situations in the real world. This asks administrators to become policymakers of sorts, and subjects their decision processes to scrutiny by the public directly or by institutions that act on behalf of the public, usually legislatures and courts. Insofar as agencies are concerned, these "watchdog" responsibilities, although legitimate, mean that they (the agencies) must make every effort to respond to every inquiry as completely as possible. Therefore, they must establish and follow legally prescribed or ac-

ceptable decision procedures, keep thorough records, and respond quickly and completely to both formal and informal questions posed to them by legislatures and courts. In short, vesting agencies with policy discretion means that they must establish machinery and devote time to explaining why that discretion has been employed in ways that make the agencies the loyal servants of the body politic. Under these conditions, democracy is not an option. It is part of an agency's mandate and its employees' job descriptions. Accountability issues surface more regularly with respect to the bureaucracy's activities precisely because administrators are not popularly elected. Therefore, institutions whose members are popularly elected (legislatures, elected executives) or which serve as guardians of the popular sovereignty principle (courts) insist on agencies' subservience to the accountability norm.

Administrators know this, and respond accordingly. The result is an adaptation of classical "principal-agent" theory to meet the demands of democracy on administrative activities. The principal-agent model describes a cooperative relationship between two entities—a principal who gives orders and an agent who implements them—that works because both parties are ethically or morally committed to the success of the enterprise as a whole. Principals and agents do not have to know one another because each needs the other for the venture to succeed. Therefore, the understood obligations of agency (principal-agent theory) mean that parties to the enterprise can, in effect, depend on strangers to help them without fear of exploitation. Modern organization theorists have adapted the model to fuse the activities of specialized public bureaucracies to the demands of democracy. In theory, all public administrators are obligated to obey both their organizational and nonorganizational political superiors because these superiors are agents of the people. The entire chain of command within an agency becomes a cooperative venture between superiors and subordinates that has, as its ultimate objective, accountability to the people through their elected representatives. Therefore, public agencies can employ the classical principle of hierarchy to integrate administrative decisions with the principle of democracy.[38] Unfortunately, the execution of this theory within public bureaucracies is often less than perfect. The major impediment is the inclination for career-status functionaries located organizationally beneath the levels of elected representatives in legislatures and politically appointed executives in agencies to resist directives that may threaten their jobs or status. Save for extraordinary circumstances, these agency careerists cannot be dismissed. Therefore, they can call on their expertise, their experiences, and the procedural requirements of their jobs to suppress, delay, and defeat innovative proposals.

The result of all this are administrative agencies that are "rule bound" in cast. Rules of proper procedure are established and administrators are encouraged to follow them to the letter. Records are meticulously kept. Adaptations to changing conditions are discouraged out of fear of violating the rules or the anticipated expectations of auditors or inquiring legislators or judges. Responsiveness to the changing needs of agency target groups or institutions can be slighted in the interest of being responsive to organizational and political superiors. Red tape conditions can develop and quickly become institutionalized. With respect to regulatory policies, where administrators often have the discretion to introduce very innovative policies, there is often a reluctance to do so for fear of legislative and judicial reprisal. Agencies can appear to be slothy and unresponsive when, in fact, they are just playing it safe by abiding by the rules and documenting decisions in case their actions are questioned by their political, and democratic, superiors.

These conditions stand in stark contrast to the assumptions of the Progressives, who assumed that professional administrators could be vested with significant amounts of policy discretion, and trusted to make democratically correct decisions on their own without being subjected to constant oversight by intra-agency and extra-agency forces. The public's values could be internalized by professional training at the best schools and cultivated further by on-the-job experiences. If administrators grew accustomed to making ethical decisions, so went the assumption, those decisions would embody the democratic ethic. Therefore, administrative decision making and democratic accountability were one and the same. Much legislation, such as the Interstate Commerce Commission Act of 1887, embodied that philosophy. Agencies were vested with broad discretionary authority with the expectation that administrative expertise would be applied in an objective, and therefore democratic, way. However, this assumption was too optimistic. The possession of expertise did not mean that administrators possessing it would find it easy, or even natural, to employ it objectively. Interest groups began to pressure administrators to interpret vaguely phrased legislation in ways that advantaged them. While the conclusion that interest groups regularly captured agencies and converted them to dependable allies is probably an exaggeration, it is definitely true that agencies often became more friendly with their private-sector counterparts than they should have, especially in light of the Progressives' hopes and expectations.

The fear that administrative policy discretion could be abused led to efforts by legislatures, courts, and politically appointed senior administrators to impose a web of rules and legislative restrictions on agencies' use of discretion. Much of the rule boundedness and red tape that impact on administrative decision making today can be traced to efforts to harness the application of the very discretion that Progressives wanted agencies to apply in a relatively rule-free environment. More than in the past, legislatures and courts today write and interpret laws in ways that restrict agencies' ability to apply expertise to changing conditions. According to Gerald Garvey, judges and legislators often "prescribe in meticulous detail what administrators must do to whom—and, often, exactly how they may do it. The result has an externally imposed regime of details that crimp appointive officials' freedom of action."[39]

The Administrative Procedure Act of 1946 (APA) ushered in the new era of legislative and judicial micromanagement of administrative affairs. It outlined specific due process procedures that federal administrative agencies must follow before legitimating their executive orders. In compliance with APA's stress on procedural due process, courts have imposed requirements on agencies that have expanded the access of interested parties to their decision processes by giving potentially affected parties legal standing before the agencies. Martin Shapiro has labeled this trend "superpluralism" because it represents an attempt to extend pluralist democracy to its limit.[40] In theory, a healthy pluralist system represents all groups equally, or nearly so. If some groups or, for that matter, individuals, can't gain their just share of the policy action in everyday politics, the courts have decided they should get it within administrative arenas. According to Gerald Garvey, this judicial superpluralism unlocked the gates of administrative regulation "to almost every conceivable directly affected, secondarily affected, indirectly affected, and even possibly affected group within sight, earshot, or mail service of a federal decision maker."[41]

Appeals to administrative agency rulings are heard in federal courts. Court rulings, in turn, mean that agencies have to comply with uncountable "judge-made" rules that are sandwiched on top of innumerable legislative and APA-imposed rules. Since the early 1960s, Congress has imposed its micromanagement strategy in basic legislation that establishes policies and empowers agencies to implement them. Laws such as the Occupational Safety and Health Act (1970), the Employees Retirement Income and Security Act (1974), the Federal Land Policy and Management Act (1976), the Natural Gas Policy Act (1978), and the Clean Air Acts of 1970, 1977, and 1990 all prescribe administrative decision procedures in minute detail for policies that are by nature already hypertechnical in character.[42] The micromanagement crusade is just as apparent in state legislation as well. James Q. Wilson has observed that elementary schools in California "are governed by the better part of five volumes of the state's education code, 2,846 pages in all (including commentary). And this is just the legislature's contribution to defining a good education . . ."[43]

The rule boundedness, delays, and red tape introduced by the norm of democratic accountability are only a few of the constraints that prevent administrative agencies from seriously pursuing the goals of the classical, rational model of administration. Most public agencies offer services to target groups or the public in general. It is difficult to measure scientifically just exactly how well service-oriented agencies perform the implementation challenge. Service-based policies such as law enforcement, education, antipoverty programs, parks and recreation facilities, fire protection, housing, natural resources management, environmental protection, crime control, sanitation, health care, and economic security programs all have a service flavor to their missions. As such, it is often difficult, if not impossible, to employ quantitative standards to assess just how well they are doing. Thorough evaluations must necessarily be judgmental. For example, social service workers judge their successes by the number of individuals or families they transfer from the public dole to economic self-support. However, the road to that goal may be a very rough one that takes a prolonged period to negotiate. Therefore, from a social service perspective, it is much better to equate success with a long-term successful rehabilitation effort than merely count the number of individuals or families counseled. Brief counseling experiences usually do little to rehabilitate an individual or family. Therefore, equating agency success with the number of contacts made, regardless of how brief, may yield impressive numbers but very little mission accomplishment. By the same token, it is misleading to measure the success of a forest management program solely by the amount of tree acreage that has been logged or harvested. One objective of forest management is resource conservation, and logging activities should be balanced with reforestation or other conservation programs. On another front, it is misleading to measure the success of public schools by the number of graduates or by the number of students who complete specialized training programs. The true measure of success is a qualitative one—how well prepared are the students to meet future professional, social, and civic challenges? Finally, it is wrong to judge the success of law enforcement and antidrug programs by the number of arrests made. The most successful law enforcement programs are those stressing the prevention of crime, not the apprehension of suspected criminals.

How does the service mission of most public agencies compromise the quest for rationalism in administration? In part it is because services are often targeted at clients, such as the poor and the handicapped, that have little political clout with both politicians and the public. Therefore, during periods of austerity or high deficit levels politicians find it comparatively easy to cut budgets for such programs. Second, in light of the difficulty of evaluating the long-term results of investing in these programs, administrators responsible for them often can appear slothlike and uninspired in their approach to their jobs. Public policymaking and administration is, in essence, a search for "proximate solutions to insoluble problems," and the relative success or failure of investments in these areas may not be evident for years. There are no quick fix solutions to any of these problems, yet both politicians and the public expect them. In response, agencies will often search for symbolic signs of progress to pacify inquiring forces. Consequently, often they will turn to quantitative measures as a defensive strategy, focusing on the number of arrests made, the acres of trees harvested, or acres leased for grazing rights. Such strategies undermine agencies' long-term goals and, when it becomes clear that agencies have drifted away from their long-term objectives, public frustration increases.

Another barrier to rationalism in public service agencies is what Garvey describes as the problem of overdetermination.[44] Overdetermined conditions are rooted in the multiple, often inconsistent, inputs or criteria that agencies must consider when making both policy and administrative decisions. Often several interest groups have a stake in the decision. Frequently administrators have honest disagreements over the appropriate techniques to employ. When it comes to policies supported by intergovernmental grants-in-aid, federal officials have to cope with a variety of viewpoints nourished by different state and local conditions as they (federal officials) attempt to develop as much cohesion and cooperation as possible among those jurisdictions. When questions of regulatory policy are at issue, the views of industry must be considered along with the needs of the consumer, worker, or the public in general. Occasionally, as did Environmental Protection Agency director William Ruckelshaus in an air-pollution-control versus jobs issue, administrators will convene together those representing disparate points of view so that they can come to appreciate what a difficult task it is to protect the environment effectively in such a heated political environment.[45] Under such conditions, the value of administrative expertise to decisions is often limited because, as inconsistent criteria enter the decision spectrum, political compromises among them become the only realistic alternative. Often it is necessary to sacrifice some criteria entirely. Once agencies are vested with policy discretion they become targets of political pressure. As the public's agents it behooves agencies to be as representative and accountable as possible. Conditions of overdetermination are an inevitable result of this, and the agency response is to listen, deliberate, explain, absorb, and balance inconsistent criteria. This is a time-consuming and complicated process, and one that helps to permanently separate public agency behavior from the goals of the classical model.

As many public administrative problems are overdetermined, so are some of them underdetermined, and these also serve to estrange public agencies from administrative rationalism. Underdetermined conditions exist when there is either a lack of sufficient data or information upon which to base a decision, or (most often) when decision makers are unable to control the behavior of players from whom they need cooperation to make a decision work. The position of employee unions on personnel or cutback decisions is an example. Unions always resist changes that threaten the economic security of their members, and they can threaten or instigate walkouts or strikes to prove their point. Attempts by federal agencies to gain state and local support for their (federal agencies') view of how grants-in-aid funds should be committed are the result of negotiation and bargaining, not command. Knowing that their cooperation is

a necessary prerequisite to program success, state and local agencies are inclined to resist cooperating until they believe they have optimized their leverage on decisions. Again, the unique views of administrative and policy professionals often have to be compromised before any agreement can be struck. On occasion, administrators fail to identify and work with forces that are essential to the success of a program. A classic case study by Pressman and Wildavsky of a failed Economic Development Administration (EDA) employment and public works project in Oakland, California provides an excellent illustration of such a problem. EDA failed to enlist the support of and gain input from several key local agencies for a new docking, loading, and transportation complex in Oakland. The project could employ mostly skilled workers, not the area's hard-core unemployed, who were the target of the project. EDA failed to consult and bargain with the forces necessary to make realistic manpower decisions. According to Pressman and Wildavsky, EDA failed to gain input and approval from interested autonomous stakeholders (labor, business, politicians, community organizations) for the nearly seventy different agreements that had to be struck for the project to succeed.[46] The Oakland case was a classic example of how underdetermined conditions can impact heavily on policy implementation unless agencies identify them and deal with them in an orderly way.

The above items are a few of the key determinants and conditions that the mandate of democratic accountability begets for decision making within public administrative agencies. Agencies must be faithful to the expectations of democratic government, and this mandate necessitates many compromises to the rational administrative model. Occasionally, agencies with fresh policy assignments that are supported by a clear public majority do enjoy a temporary merger of democratic politics and rational administration. The

National Aeronautic and Space Administration (NASA) experience with the moon landing and exploration program is a good example. However, that represents the proverbial exception that proves the rule. Usually democratic accountability means extended deliberations and delays in decision making and decisions that, out of necessity, reflect compromise rather than rational comprehensive design.

Bureaucracy and Public Policy: The Challenge

As institutions responsible for the implementation of the public's will as articulated by its elected representatives, administrative agencies should be, first and foremost, conduits of accountability in the American political system. This is not because the framers of the Constitution dealt directly with the issue of administrative accountability. Clearly, they did not. It does mean that, at least in theory, agencies should respond to appeals from institutions whose policies and practices are subject to public approval, and which have been subjected to the institutional competition that the founders considered so essential to ensuring the accountability of government to the people. These institutions—the president and Congress—have been directly affected by the Constitution's requirements for a diffusion of policy authority and divergence of constituencies. The framers' decision to deal with the potential problem of excessive self-interest in public policy was to separate authority among the various levels and institutions of government. Different institutions, staffed by self-interest-motivated politicians, had to share the policymaking power so that the odds would favor policies that would incorporate acceptable policy compromises from among the various expressions of self-interest emanating from individual legisla-

tors, congressional committees, and, eventually, from elected presidents.

The Constitution provided mechanisms for encouraging policy accountability from the president, Congress, and the judiciary, but not for the bureaucracy. That fact in no way detracts from the significance of a system of diffused policy power for a public bureaucracy that wields vast policy powers. In what ways and to whom is the public bureaucracy expected to be accountable in a constitutional system that separates and divides power within and between levels of government, as does our Constitution? In contrast to the lines of authority that affect private bureaucracies, most of which are internal to the agencies and hierarchical in nature, the lines of authority (and hence accountability) that affect public agencies are both internal and external to the respective organizations and are often frustratingly unclear, frequently contradictory.

The Constitution vests executive power in the president, but leaves the particulars of that power undefined. Congress legitimates policies and creates agencies to administer them. Congress appropriates money to support agency continuance, usually at the recommendation of the president. Top administrators are appointed by the president but confirmed by the Senate. Both branches oversee administrative activity. A "who is boss?" issue, and how to deal with it, surfaces regularly as agencies decide how to apply their policy discretion in ways that both conform to the law and are servile to the psychological and institutional demands of the institutional imperative. Administrative accountability in our system of constitutionally fragmented power means that the uncertainties of external control are complicated by institutional conflict between the forces that exercise that external control. All external forces have some claim to agency policy loyalty, but none has exclusive claim.

Such conditions invite agencies to seek political support and policy continuity from extra-governmental sources, primarily the interest group community. This means, more often than not, that the public bureaucracy embodies what is both good and bad about the pluralist model of democracy and how it has been operationalized in the United States. Too often agencies adopt policy postures and administrative procedures that accommodate society's more powerful vested interests, thereby reflecting the "bias of pluralism" phenomenon, as explained by Schattschneider. Reform proposals to rid the system of such a problem, or at least ameliorate it, have traditionally involved strengthening the policy and administrative hand of the presidency over the national bureaucracy. This is the classical solution to problems of ineffective policy planning and administrative inefficiency. In the case of national administrative reform, such proposals usually encounter reluctance on the part of both Congress and the agencies themselves. Congress does not want to see its control over the activities of agencies challenged by a president whose policy incentives are more universal in cast. Agency personnel do not want to forgo the security of the merit system for a system that permits the president to appoint more of his political loyalists to key policy positions. In sum, reforms that are fundamentally sound when judged by principles of classical organization and management clash with the realities of politics and psychology. Organization and management in the public sector are indeed the mobilization of a variety of policy and individual biases that have nothing to do with the classical objectives of administration and management. Until the public and its elected representatives decide that the long-term costs of the policy impasses that have plagued the political system in the past generation or so are too great, the policy impact of the bureaucracy will be to continue to contribute to, if not exacerbate, the conditions that have led to the impasses.

Endnotes

1. Woodrow Wilson, "The Study of Administration," *Political Science Quarterly*, vol. 2 (June 1887), p. 216.

2. E. Pendleton Herring, *Public Administration and the Public Interest* (New York: McGraw-Hill, 1936).

3. Wilson, *op. cit.*

4. E. E. Schattschneider, *The Semi-Sovereign People* (New York: Holt, Rinehart & Winston, 1960), p. 40.

5. Robert N. Kharasch, *The Institutional Imperative: How to Understand the United States Government and Other Bulky Objects* (New York: Charterhouse Books, 1973), p. 12.

6. *Ibid.*

7. *Ibid.*, p. 24.

8. *Ibid.*

9. John Ralston Saul, *Voltaire's Bastards: The Dictatorship of Reason in the West* (New York: Free Press, 1992).

10. *Ibid.*, p. 238.

11. *Ibid.*, p. 235.

12. Michael Nelson, "The Desk," *Newsweek* (September 11, 1978), p. 17.

13. Gerald A. Garvey, *Facing the Bureaucracy: Living and Dying in a Public Agency* (San Francisco: Jossey-Bass, 1993), p. 71.

14. Norton Long, "Power and Administration," *Public Administration Review*, vol. 9, no. 4 (1949), pp. 257–264.

15. *Ibid.*

16. Herbert Kaufman, *Are Government Organizations Immortal?* (Washington, D.C.: The Brookings Institution, 1976), p. 6.

17. Nicholas Lemann, "Why the Sun Will Never Set on the Federal Empire," *The Washington Monthly*, 8 (September 1976), p. 36.

18. David C. King, *Turf Wars: How Congressional Committees Claim Jurisdiction* (Chicago: University of Chicago Press, 1997), p. 142.

19. Morris P. Fiorina, "Control of the Bureaucracy: A Mismatch of Incentives and Capabilities," in William S. Livingston, Lawrence C. Dodd, and Richard L. Schott, *The Presidency and the Congress: A Shifting Balance of Power* (Austin, Tex.: The Lyndon B. Johnson School of Public Affairs, 1979), p. 127.

20. *Ibid.*, p. 129.

21. Morris P. Fiorina, "Big Government: A Congressman's Best Friend," in Charles Peters and Michael Nelson, *The Culture of Bureaucracy* (New York: Holt, Rinehart & Winston, 1979), p. 139.

22. Walter Shapiro, "The Two Party Pork Barrel," in *Ibid.*, pp. 140–145.

23. Walter Shapiro, "The Intractables," in *Ibid.*, p. 56.

24. See Richard P. Nathan, *The Plot That Failed: Nixon and the Administrative Presidency* (New York: John Wiley, 1975); and Richard P. Nathan, "The Administrative Presidency," *The Public Interest*, no. 44 (Summer 1976), pp. 40–54.

25. *Congressional Record*, vol. 120, no. 14, pp. S1638–S1645.

26. Nathan, "The Administrative Presidency," *op. cit.*, p. 42.

27. Quote excerpted from a flyer circulated by AFL-CIO Affiliate Local 41 to Social and Rehabilitation Service employees in January 1974.

28. Chester A. Newland, "The Reagan Presidency: Limited Government and Political Administration," *Public Administration Review*, vol. 43, no. 1 (January/February 1983), pp. 1–21.

29. David Osborne and Ted Gaebler, *Reinventing Government: How the Entrepreneural Spirit Is Transforming the Public Sector* (Reading, Mass.: Addison-Wesley, 1992).

30. Cathy M. Johnson, *The Dynamics of Conflict Between Bureaucrats and Legislators* (Armonk, N.Y.: M. E. Sharpe, 1992).

31. See Glen R. Parker and Roger Davidson, "Why Do Americans Love Their Congressman So Much More Than Their Congress?" *Legislative Studies Quarterly*, vol. 4 (1979), pp. 53–62.

32. See Theodore J. Lowi, *The End of Liberalism: The Second Republic of the United States*, 2nd ed. (New York: W. W. Norton, 1979), Chapter 3.

33. William Greider, *Who Will Tell the People?* (New York: Simon & Schuster, 1992), p. 107.

34. Herbert Kaufman, "Administrative Decentralization and Political Power," *Public Administration Review*, vol. 29, no. 1 (January/February 1969), pp. 3–15.

35. John A. Rohr, "Professionalism, Legitimacy and the Constitution," *Public Administration Quarterly*, vol. 8 (Winter 1985), pp. 401–418.

36. Marilyn Weber Serafini, "Wimping Out," *National Journal*, vol. 29, no. 42 (October 18, 1997), pp. 2072–2075.

37. *Ibid.*, p. 2073.

38. Henry D. Kass, "Stewardship as a Fundamental Element in Images of Public Administration," in Henry Kass and Bayard Catron, *Images and Identities in Public Administration* (Newbury Park, Calif.: Sage Publications, 1990), pp. 115–116.

39. Gerald Garvey, *Public Administration: The Profession and the Practice* (New York: St. Martin's Press, 1997), p. 129.

40. Martin Shapiro, *Who Guards the Guardians?* (Athens: University of Georgia Press, 1988).

41. Gerald A. Garvey, *Facing the Bureaucracy* (San Francisco: Jossey-Bass, 1993), pp. 194–195.

42. *Ibid.*

43. James Q. Wilson, "Can the Bureaucracy Be Deregulated?: Lessons from Government Agencies," in John J. Dilulio, ed., *Deregulating the Public Service* (Washington, D.C.: The Brookings Institution, 1994), p. 44, as quoted in *Ibid.*, p. 129.

44. James Q. Wilson, "The Bureaucracy Problem," *The Public Interest*, vol. 6 (Winter 1967), p. 3, and James Q. Wilson, *Bureaucracy: What Government Agencies Do and Why They Do It* (New York: Basic Books, 1991), Chapter 7.

45. See "Managing Environmental Risk: The Case of Asarco," in Robert B. Reich, *Public Management in a Democratic Society* (Englewood Cliffs, N.J.: Prentice Hall, 1990), pp. 161–175.

46. See Jeffrey Pressman and Aaron Wildavsky, *Implementation*, 2nd ed. (Berkeley: University of California Press, 1979).

chapter twelve

The Judiciary

Procedural Democracy and Policy Justice

The role of U.S. courts in government and politics has been determined by four basic constitutional realities. The first is the separation of powers, which guarantees the judiciary's independence from and power equivalence with the legislative and executive branches. On the other hand, it means that courts cannot exercise legislative and executive responsibilities. The judiciary's independence from the other branches is ensured by three other constitutional provisions. Article III of the Constitution requires the courts to perform only judicial responsibilities. This means that the federal courts, once petitioned to do so, apply the Constitution's mandates, statutes enacted by legislatures (usually Congress), and rules and regulations issued by administrative agencies to both the public and private sectors. In addition, Article III stipulates that judges "hold their Offices during good Behavior." This means they serve as long as they wish, and can be removed against their will only if convicted of "Treason, Bribery, or other high Crimes and Misdemeanors." Finally, the Constitution states that judges' salaries "shall not be diminished during their Continuance in Office." If either Congress or the president had the right to do so, presumably it would give them undue leverage over judicial decisions which, in theory, are presumed to be objective—i.e., totally impartial and based only on facts pertaining to the cases they decide. In theory, these three constitutional provisos—judicial responsibilities only, the right to hold office during good behavior, and the prohibition against diminished compensation—secure judicial independence from the other branches and, therefore, impartial decision making.

Such a surgical apportionment of powers among the three branches may seem unduly simplistic, and it is. This is not because the powers of the three branches—legislative, executive, and judicial—can't be distinguished by definition, because they can. It is because, in order for policies to be made and implemented in ways that affect individuals, groups, and institutions in ways intended by the law, often all three branches of government are involved in the process. Legislation determines policy goals, and can prescribe or suggest implementation procedures. However, more often than not, legislation delegates policy discretion to administrative agencies, mandating them to fill in the details of laws that are very vague in construct. Some laws are essentially expressions of moral intent, and very little else. For example, the National Environmental Policy Act of 1969 and the Environmental Protection Act of 1970 essentially endorsed the idea of a clean environment and the federal government's role in securing it, and established and budgeted an agency—the Environmental Protection Agency (EPA)—to work to achieve it. In essence, this made EPA the policy kingpin. Congress simply brought public honor and support to the idea. Congressional delegation of policy responsibility to administrative agencies is the rule, not the exception. Often courts are asked to rule on the legitimacy of the delegation act itself, as well as on how faithfully agencies have employed their policy discretion. When the courts rule, it is their decision that stands and they, not Congress or the president, have final determination over how laws and administrative action affect the lives of individuals, groups, and institutions. Therefore, the making and administration of policy often become the joint responsibility of all three branches of government. Under such circumstances, it could be argued that it is the judicial branch, not the legislative or executive branch, that gives policy its exact meaning.

While the Supreme Court has not regularly relished the role of policy caretaker, the impact of the Industrial Revolution on American society, and the subsequent intervention by government into social and economic ac-

tivity that it spawned, has made such a role inevitable at times. That role cannot be comprehensive and systematically applied because the Court's power to give meaning to statutes and administrative rules does not permit it to select the cases it wants to hear. Often cases that come to the court do so primarily because of the saliency of the issues in question rather than merits of the cases. Nonetheless, on matters of statute interpretation, the Court does have some latitude to pick and choose what cases it will hear. For that reason, David O'Brien has portrayed the Supreme Court as a "super legislature" that serves as a "roving commission, selecting and deciding issues of national importance for the governmental process."[1] Frequently such cases involve effort by interest groups, especially (but not exclusively) those representing minorities and the underprivileged, to undo policy grievances on behalf of a category or class of people. According to Chief Justice Fred M. Vinson, the Court is inclined to select cases that "present questions whose resolution will have immediate importance far beyond the particular facts and parties involved," and he emphasized to attorneys representing these "class action" cases that "you represent your clients, but (more crucially) tremendously important principles, upon which are based the plans, hopes, and aspirations of a great many people throughout the country."[2] By way of referencing the Supreme Court's role in adjudicating such cases, Justice Lewis Powell noted that " the judiciary may be the most important instrument for social, economic and political change."[3] Class action lawsuits instigated by liberal public interest groups such as Common Cause, the American Civil Liberties Union (ACLU), Public Citizen, the Sierra Club, the Natural Resources Defense Council, and the Environmental Defense Fund, as well as by conservative public interest law firms such as the Pacific Legal Foundation and the

Mountain States Legal Foundation have resulted in what Justice Robert Jackson termed "government by lawsuit," or the "stuff of power politics in America."[4]

The Judiciary and Policy Balance: An Overview

An eminent scholar of government and politics once observed that, if the three branches of national government were assigned "success ratings" that reflected how effectively they had accomplished their constitutional mandates, the Supreme Court would rank first, the president second, and Congress third. Of course, that is only one observer's opinion, but it seems to be the result of good judgment rooted in fact. The founding fathers did not intend for either the judiciary or the presidency to be instruments of popular opinion. The president has become one because of the *de facto* democratization of the Electoral College. The Supreme Court has not, yet its decisions affect how democracy registered in the other two branches impacts on society. Therefore, the significance of such an observation lies in its acknowledgment that the judiciary, especially the Supreme Court, has a policy role that was never envisioned by the founders. In other words, the Supreme Court has acquired more policy power informally relative to where it began than has the president. Since the gap between original intent and contemporary fact is wider in the case of the Supreme Court when compared to the other branches, the Court has been the most successful of the three.

This raises an issue of policy balance that can be phrased in the form of a few questions. Has the federal judiciary gone too far and upset the balance of power envisioned by the framers? Is it troubling that the branch with the least direct association with the voting public can have a very profound effect on the character of public policy? Does the job of refereeing how the Constitution and statutes affect society mean, in effect, that ours is a system of "judicial supremacy" and not one of branch equality?

Before exploring issues that will help provide at least tentative answers to these questions, a brief summary of how the federal judiciary came to enjoy the potential of being such a significant policy force is in order. One reason was noted above—the tendency for statutes to be vague in structure and for them to vest significant amounts of policy discretion in the hands of administrators. These conditions often require the courts to decide what vague statutory phraseology means and if administrative agencies are filling in the policy details within the compass of the law as the courts define it. However, in addition to the obligation to give meaning to statutes and administrative orders, the federal courts have the power of *judicial review,* or the right, if not the obligation, to declare an action of Congress, administrative agency, or any state or local legislature or court contrary to the provisions of the U.S. Constitution.

This very significant power was not assigned to the federal judiciary by the Constitution. The Supreme Court, in effect, declared it in the case of *Marbury* v. *Madison* (1803).[5] The Court ruled that an effort by Congress to alter the jurisdiction of the Supreme Court by statute was unconstitutional because it attempted to accomplish by statute what had to be done by constitutional amendment. Chief Justice John Marshall defended the decision, and the Court's "seizure" of the significant new power, on the grounds that the Constitution would be meaningless as a charter, or rule book, unless some institution of government could function as referee and determine when its provisions had been violated. This power is significant because of the nation's acceptance of constitutionalism as a force which constrains the activities of individuals and governments. Constitutionalism exists if those governed accept the existence of, and agree to abide by, the terms of a constitution. They realize it will occasionally limit their freedom and cost them money, but that is the price paid in the hope that society will be more civil and stable as a result. Constitutionalism accepts the "rule of law" as preferable to the "rule of men."

Marshall's decision in the *Marbury* case was controversial, mostly because it raised the possibility of a policy imbalance developing among the three branches of government. While the founders accepted the need for a judiciary, they were not at all certain about how to endow it. The language in Article III is among the Constitution's most elusive, stating that the "judicial power of the United States shall be vested in one supreme Court, and such inferior courts as the Congress may from time to time ordain and establish." While Article III enumerates the types of cases over which federal courts have jurisdiction, it does not define the term "judicial power." Undoubtedly that reflects an inability of the founders to agree on a definition of how far the reach of the judiciary should extend. The gradual public acceptance of the *Marbury* decision does not mean that it was the dominant one at the Constitutional Convention of 1787, or in the *Federalist Papers*. Only one of the three authors of the *Federalist Papers*, Alexander Hamilton, argued the position eventually assumed by Marshall in the *Marbury* decision.

Hamilton subscribed to what Robert Burt has termed the "indivisible sovereign authority" interpretation of the judiciary's role in government.[6] Hamilton believed this authority was vested in the national government as opposed to the states and, within the national level, in the Supreme Court instead of with Congress or the president. Hamilton articulated this position clearly in *Federalist No. 78*. Scholars and students of the judiciary have come to accept this position as the one endorsed by a majority of the founders. However, Burt argues that this was Hamilton's own individual view, but not the one favored by a majority of delegates to the Constitutional Convention.

Burt argues that James Madison's view of judicial power, dramatically different from Hamilton's, was favored by most Convention delegates.[7] Madison's views do not appear in a single *Federalist* essay, but are dispersed throughout *Federalist Nos. 47* through *51*, his correspondence, the Virginia Resolution, and elsewhere. Extracting Madison's opinion regarding judicial power from all these sources, Burt organizes it into four rather clear principles. First, policy sovereignty should be dispersed throughout government. Second, the federal judiciary is supreme over actions of state governments, but deserves only co-equality with other branches at the national level. Third, the interpretation of the Constitution's meaning is a linear process, in that it occurs over time. The judgment of any single institution or individual at a specific time about the constitutionality of a law is not the test of its constitutionality. Finally, government institutions should compete for the right to give meaning to the Constitution, but this competition should be conducted with the understanding that no one opinion is supreme over others. Consequently, branches of government should accommodate one another's point of view in deciding on the constitutionality of any law or action taken by an individual.[8] Therefore, Madison's view was a balanced one, incorporating the same assumptions as did his defense of separation of powers, checks and balances, and federalism. In effect, the more power was evenly dispersed the better it would be for society, because such a condition would mandate that separate institutions compromise their positions to reach policy decisions. This would make government more stable, less radical, and more representative.

According to Burt, it was unfortunate for the country that the Hamiltonian point of view prevailed between 1789 and the Civil War period. The idea that every government must have a supreme sovereign authority encouraged the North-South split over the slavery issue, ultimately resulting in the secession of the South and, of course, the Civil War. This may not have occurred had both factions attempted to appreciate each other's point of view, and not insisted on a separate, unitary, uncompromisable locus of sovereign authority.[9] Consequently, the Supreme Court's attempt, in the *Dred Scott* case, to terminate slavery unilaterally by judicial decree, and the South's effort to end the same dispute by secession, violated the Madisonian principles of power equivalence and mutual respect. Unilateral coercion of any type is an inappropriate way to settle disputes, and therefore the judiciary should not have such an option.

One of the most significant and celebrated cases in Supreme Court history was, according to Burt, successful because it incorporated Madisonian principles. In *Brown* v. *Board of Education* the Supreme Court ruled that the very existence of a racially separated school system implies racial subjugation and is therefore unconstitutional.[10] However, the Court realized it could not erase the impression that decades of social and cultural segregation had made on people's minds and attitudes. It could not impose new attitudes by decree. All it could do was to officially negate state and local laws prescribing school segregation and then ask that school integration proceed with "all deliberate speed." The Court expected, and received, cooperation from Congress, lower federal courts, and some state and local legislative bodies. For example, although it took a decade, Congress responded with the Civil Rights Act of 1964, which officially integrated most businesses and public facilities. Although the *Brown* ruling was necessary to legitimize school integration, and in that sense it embraced the Hamilton position, the Supreme Court's overall role in the implementation of the ruling was essentially Madisonian. The Court realized that school districts, with the help of the law, would have to work it out on their own.[11]

On the other hand, the Supreme Court's decisions involving the Nixon tapes (Watergate), the death penalty cases, and the abortion cases incorporated the Hamilton theory. In all three instances, the Court took firm positions that discouraged the type of dialogue advocated by Madison. In the case of the death penalty and abortion, the Court decisions were not unanimous, a condition that discourages opinions suggesting conciliation. It is, of course, unrealistic to suggest that universal consent can be achieved on critical policy issues, whether they are contested in legislatures, in courts, or both. On the other hand, if a conciliatory "state of mind" can be both reflected in and suggested by court decisions, disputations can be handled more democratically and more effectively in the long term. In Burt's opinion, the notion of judicial supremacy subverts this ideal.[12]

It should be noted that the role of the judiciary in public policy is, by force of circumstances, both a selective and a reactive role. Courts cannot anticipate forthcoming problems and deal with them proactively. A statute or action must first be challenged in court before courts can render decisions that may have policy implications. This means that judicial rulings will not ever deal with policies with any scale of priority in mind. Some interests are more able than others to bring lawsuits that may end up in the Supreme Court. The assets of large corporations give them an inside track in this regard. By way of contrast, minorities who have been victimized by what they consider to be illegal or unconstitutional practices sometimes can get a fair airing of a grievance that has been denied them by the normal routines of politics. Judges are often expected to be judicial spokespersons for those who appoint and confirm them. This has the potential to reduce their policy independence, but that is tempered somewhat by the fact that lifetime tenure for judges means that presidents can't do anything about judges who disappoint them politically.

Judicial Activism and Constitutional Politics

Judicial activism is an attitude, or state of mind, that affects how judges use the law. Activist judges are those who, in the course of ruling on cases, do not hesitate to substitute their opinions for those of legislatures. If they think their opinions are more consistent with the Constitution than are legislative opinions contained in the law, these judges do not hesitate to declare the relevant laws, or sections thereof, unconstitutional. They are more Hamiltonian than Madisonian in attitude. They do not think their role as judges should constrain their efforts to bring about policy justice through judicial means, even if they will often collide with legislatures in the process. Chief Justice John Marshall introduced judicial activism in the *Marbury* decision, and reinforced its relevance in the case of *McCulloch* v. *Maryland*.[13] More recent decisions incorporating the activist theory are the *Brown* case and the decision in *Roe* v. *Wade* in which the Supreme Court overturned state laws preventing abortion in the first trimester of pregnancy.[14] The principal argument against judicial activism is its tendency to usurp legislative and executive authority. The counterargument is that, because legislation on contentious issues is often made deliberately vague, courts are virtually compelled to render decisions that appear to be activist, especially to those who object to the decisions.

The judicial activist school can be contrasted with that of judicial self-restraint which holds that, unless judges consider a legislative act to be clearly in violation of a specific provision of the Constitution, they should restrain themselves and let legislative decisions stand. These judges favor a very constricted interpretation of the law as it emanates from both legislative and administrative arenas. Supporting self-restraint as a judicial norm, Justice Harlan Fiske Stone noted in *U.S.* v. *Butler* that "while unconstitutional exercise by the executive and legislative branches is subject to judicial restraint, the only check on our own exercise of power is our own sense of self-restraint."[15] Judges committed to self-restraint theory often employ the doctrine of the "political question" as a rationale for letting legislative and executive actions stand. In this case, judges argue that some issues are genetically political in nature and should therefore best be left to the political branches to decide. For example in *Colegrove* v. *Green* the Supreme Court ruled that courts had no jurisdiction over cases involving legislative district malapportionment because such issues are political and therefore should be resolved by legislatures.[16] That position was later reversed in *Baker* v. *Carr* in which the Court ordered that state legislative districts should be reapportioned to contain approximately the same number of people.[17]

If a judge or court backs away from a case because of its political nature, it means that judge or court subscribes to the doctrine of "original intent." These judges believe that no court has the right to alter the constitutionally prescribed separation of powers boundaries, the federal division of policy responsibilities between the national government and the states, or long-recognized standards that specify the extent of constitutional rights. Justice Felix Frankfurter, writing for the Supreme Court majority in the *Colegrove* case, argued that only if a law is clearly unconstitutional should a court nullify it. In uncertain cases courts should yield to the elected branches of government by giving them the benefit of the doubt, and assume that the law in question is constitutional. Frankfurter, who served on the Supreme Court between 1939 and 1962, found his position to be clearly the minority one after Earl Warren was appointed chief justice in 1953 and the Court began to assume an activist posture on civil rights cases. The "original intent" position has been mainly out of favor since that time. However, it does surface occasionally because some nominees for judgeships cling tenaciously to its tenets. One such nominee was Robert Bork, whom President Reagan nominated for a Supreme Court appointment in 1987. Bork believed that the only way to lend any semblance of objectivity to the interpretation of the vague clauses of the Constitution or statutes is to research and discover the intent of those who authored those clauses. There are several ways to accomplish this, the most favored being the examination of Constitutional Convention and congressional debates that produced the constitutional or statutory phraseology. Only by such a method, argued Bork, can judges secure their opinions in something objective. Otherwise, they are prone to incorporate their political positions or their feelings in their decisions.

Bork failed to win Senate confirmation to the Court, essentially because his philosophy was out of favor with key groups and movements that had profited from the generation-long activist profile of the Supreme Court. Pro-choice feminist organizations feared that he would, if confirmed, vote to overturn *Roe* v. *Wade* (1973), a decision that legalized abortion on the assumption that a "right to privacy" was implied by the Constitution's Ninth Amendment. Bork suspected the framers had no such right in mind when they formulated the Bill of Rights. Civil rights groups also feared Bork, reasoning that his "originalist" approach might result in a restricting of the existing interpretation of the Fourteenth Amendment's "equal protection" clause.

These forces, along with their Senate allies, generated a major publicity campaign against Bork's nomination, and his nomination was defeated. The story of the defeat illustrates how deeply embroiled in politics are judges and the institutions from which they render supposedly objective interpretations of the law, both constitutional and statutory.[18]

Judicial activists argue that the "original intent" idea is based on the false assumption that the framers intended the Constitution to be a fixed document and that judges were expected to perform essentially mechanistic functions. They maintain that the Constitution was not formulated for the deep freeze, but was intended to be an evolutionary document. In essence, judges are the facilitators of that evolutionary expectation. For most of the past half-century, the Supreme Court has maintained an activist profile, and its decisions have served the causes of both liberals and conservatives who have sought to undo legislative decisions that are dysfunctional to their missions. Undoubtedly some judges seek to be activists as a matter of principle, and want to use the judicial platform to advance a political cause. Owing to the vague nature of controversial legislation, others subscribe to it out of necessity, considering it the only practical alternative to statute ambiguity.

Regardless of the incentives that underlie it, judicial activism has positioned courts, especially the U.S. Supreme Court, in the center of the public policy drama. However, such a role was not accepted overnight. The notion of original intent has always been popular in key political circles, and by no means the least significant of these was the antistatist position of the Jeffersonians during the founding period. In order to gain legitimacy over time, judicial activism had to be utilized in ways that served the policy requirements of both the governors and the governed. Its record since the late nineteenth century has helped the courts accomplish that goal.

The growth and acceptance of judicial activism can be traced in part to the Constitution, especially to the principle of constitutionalism (discussed above and in Chapter 2), but its success also depended on the ability of the Supreme Court to employ constitutionalism with a good deal of political skill.[19] During the post–Civil War period it began to apply its referee role carefully and selectively, thereby limiting confrontations with the executive and legislative branches. By being both careful and selective, what might have produced discontent with the Court's role instead produced what Lawrence Baum has termed "widespread acceptance of the Court's position as a significant policy maker."[20] In ruling against major government efforts to regulate economic activity, the Court developed a *de facto* alliance with the corporate community which, in turn, provided it with political support for continuing the activist role. The Progressive and New Deal periods introduced more government activism which, in turn, made for challenges to government policies. The ensuing court litigations, especially on civil liberties issues, offered the Court more opportunity to decide policy through judicial intervention. Constitutionalism offered the means, but events and clever Supreme Court political strategies provided the momentum. Executives, legislatures, and the public in general grew to accept judicial activism as a functional complement to the separation of powers principle. Clever political strategy had enabled judges to defeat serious assaults against the growing activist role. Had judges not been so astute, the chance to elevate activism to policy prominence may well have been lost.[21]

Courts, Public Policy, and the Politics of Ambiguity

Opportunities for judicial activism derive from three conditions—the obligation for courts to interpret statutes, their right to judge the constitutionality of executive and legislative actions (judicial review), and the ambiguous quality of both constitutional principles and statute content. The existence of the third has helped make the other two exigencies more significant to public policy. Ambiguity is the servant of issue conflict, and issue conflicts must be resolved before meaningful policies can be produced and administered. The history of policy development and administration over the past half-century has been the history not only of government's expanding policy responsibilities, but also the history of the decreasing clarity of policy statutes. As problems become more complicated and their solutions require more specialized, technical competence, the government must rely more on administrative experts and courts to fill in the details so that government power and services are directed to the appropriate targets. Statute ambiguity can also be sound political strategy. If the policy deals with a sensitive, controversial issue, it is often advantageous for legislators to transfer generous amounts of policy discretion to administrators so that the latter can be held to blame for public dissatisfaction with the results. This is but one of the subtle impacts of the Constitution on public policy. In this case legislators use the Constitution to abdicate responsibility for potential negative policy fallout.

However, there is yet another reason for statutory obscurity. If legislatures decide that the true intent of a policy objective can only be realized if its administration is tailor made to fit a wide variety of target group situations, then often the only realistic option is to endow administrative agencies and, ultimately, the courts with the authority to make those determinations. In other instances, the solution may be to make legislation very straightforward and specific. Both scenarios harbor the potential for courts to interpret statutes creatively. Many reformers seeking to democratize the House and Senate in the 1960s and 1970s had that very objective in mind when they produced legislation that was either deliberately ambiguous, as were portions of the 1964 Civil Rights Act, or deliberately specific in ordering administrative procedures and in mandating certain results. Much of this legislation dealt with rights questions—either constitutional rights or the newly emerging quest for economic rights. Because of the rights backdrop to many of these questions, the judiciary was bound to be involved very quickly in their application to specific situations.

Given its activist inclinations, the Supreme Court welcomed such a development. The objectives of the renovated Congress and the Supreme Court became one and the same. In fact, the civil rights role of the judiciary had been firmly reoriented since the 1954 *Brown* decision. That decision was the first stage in a Supreme Court–sponsored effort to uproot racial segregation and institute a new system of race relations in the United States. Soon the crusade impacted the lower federal courts. That crusade has occasionally been placed on hold, as during part of the Burger era, but it has never been challenged seriously. The policy ambiguity that flavored civil rights legislation during the congressional reform era synchronized well with the Court's new civil rights policy mission, creating what R. Shep Melnick has termed an "institutional marriage of convenience."[22] From the congressional perspective, the power of full committees gave way to a strengthened subcommittee system which offered newly elected liberal legislators the opportunity to enact new policies, refocus existing ones, and vie with the president for legislative preeminence. Ambiguous legislation was discarded in favor of legislation that directed specific provisions in specific policies to specific groups with the expectation of specific policy results. The courts responded by interpreting these directives very flexibly, especially if

specificity would result in split decisions. Often both liberal and conservative factions on courts could agree on casting legislative specifics broadly, whereas efforts to be more exacting might result in split votes.[23] Thus, the interests of Congress and the courts merged. Judges would interpret legislative subcommittee directives very broadly, making their application to state and local governments all the more likely. This pleased Congress because it enabled the policy effects of the legislative revolution to be applied more universally and more expeditiously. It pleased the federal courts because it brought state and local institutions, including courts, more directly under their influence.

Melnick offers the policy history of the Education for All Handicapped Act as an illustration of the Congress and court marriage of convenience. Congressional subcommittees had been insisting for years that handicapped children had a right to special educational opportunities that required the learning experience to accommodate their handicaps. Both the Nixon and Ford administrations defeated efforts to accomplish this. Then, in 1975, two lower federal courts ordered the District of Columbia and the state of Pennsylvania to provide such children with special educational opportunities. Local school districts then demanded that Congress support these efforts with money and specific performance guidelines. That appeal, being congruent with the dominant congressional mindset, resulted in the subcommittees claiming that handicapped children had a right to special educational opportunities and programs. Wary of past state and local successes in sabotaging such efforts, Congress responded with legislation (the Education for All Handicapped Children Act) that required extensive hearing and appeals processes in the hope of ensuring that all qualified children were offered the opportunity to take advantage of the new law. Furthermore, the law required that the courts review these plans and make judgments about their adequacy. Over the next decade, the judiciary's supervision of state and local special education programs resulted in the establishment of a well-accepted series of common law principles that govern the administration of funds and education programs for handicapped children. Despite this, only a small fraction of the funding for these programs is supplied by the federal government.[24]

The marriage of legislative and judicial incentives was also served by provisions of laws which were made deliberately cryptic, necessitating eventual court intervention to determine how they were to apply to specific situations. The Civil Rights Act of 1964 offers an excellent illustration of how both legislatures and courts can profit from the "politics of ambiguity." The Civil Rights Act was the first attempt by Congress to apply the spirit of the *Brown* decision comprehensively to all sectors of society and the economy. The *Brown* decision had brought the "equal protection" clause of the Fourteenth Amendment to life, after having been virtually dormant for nearly half a century. It inaugurated the federal government's concern for the systematic application of nondiscrimination rights to all sectors of society, public and private.[25] Discrimination because of both race and gender was prevented in hotels, restaurants, theaters, auditoriums, and service facilities. It directed that a newly established agency—the Equal Employment Opportunity Commission (EEOC)—cooperate with the Department of Health, Education, and Welfare (HEW) to engineer a dual enforcement system which proved to be very effective, especially in overseeing school integration programs.

The 1964 act was significant, not only because of its broad compass, but also because of its ambiguity. It outlawed *discrimination* but did not define it. The bill's sponsors assumed that past and future judicial decisions had

provided and would provide definitions appropriate to conditions, which would vary. Congress did not mean to infer that "nonproportional" conditions of race and gender in employment or in use of facilities necessarily meant deliberate discrimination. Still, it didn't assume that proof of overt discrimination had to be established for a firm to be, in fact, guilty of discrimination. On the other hand, it concluded that racial and gender quota programs were too strict.[26] Congress couldn't decide on middle ground standards, and so they chose to delegate the responsibility to the courts. It was politically advantageous to delegate the responsibility because the trend of federal government involvement in nondiscrimination efforts was already on line. Therefore, it was politically perilous to oppose the idea in general. On the other hand, the application of the nondiscrimination principle to specific cases of alleged discrimination could well be perilous, and so that was best left to the courts. If judges make unpopular decisions, their hold on their jobs is not threatened. That cannot be said for Congress. Insofar as the implications for the courts' role in policy are concerned, these conditions invited a new level of judicial activism, and most court rulings reflected that. In many instances, the courts have not called on the Equal Protection clause to determine the definition of discrimination, but on their judgment of what the stewards of the Civil Rights Act specifically had in mind.[27]

The net effect of the trend toward both legislative detail and ambiguity was to challenge the "do it by the book" policy legacy of the New Deal, which dominated the policymaking and administration scene between the mid-1930s and the late 1960s. According to Martin Shapiro, the overriding norm of that period could be condensed into one word—deference. The courts were to defer to Congress, and Congress to the president. This meant, in effect, that the courts were to defer to the president.[28] However, the subsequent dispersion of responsibility for policymaking and administration from the president and bureaucracy to congressional subcommittees and the courts represented, in effect, an alteration of the means utilized to reach the goals of the New Deal policy reforms. It did not change the commitment of government to a positivist role in the search for social and economic justice. In fact, one of the policy legacies of both the New Deal and Great Society periods was to alter and, in effect, elevate the status of some policies from that of rather gratuitous government distributions of money and privileges to target groups to a position within which elements in both society and government were prepared to offer these rewards to individuals as a matter of right rather than privilege. When policies are, in effect, promoted to a rights status, courts are bound to be involved in the adjudication of their application, thereby involving judges more systemically in the policy drama. As the following discussion will illustrate, the politicalization of rights in the wake of the New Deal reforms was certainly no exception.

Judicial Activism and the Politics of Rights

Rights guaranteed to individuals by the Constitution, mostly within the Bill of Rights, were not intended to be exclusive. The Ninth Amendment states: "The enumeration in the Constitution, of certain rights, shall not be construed to deny or disparage others retained by the people." Impacted by an individualist culture and a capitalistic economy, Americans were quick to jump on the rights bandwagon, offering their own interpretation of just how far the notion of rights should extend. Americans are devoted to asserting their right to a number of conditions, opportunities, and benefits. Many of the most con-

tested public policy controversies involve disputations between individuals and groups that claim to have the right to secure a benefit or privilege against the right of others to deny them those same benefits and privileges. Corporations claim a right to exploit natural resources in quest of profits. Conservationists argue their right to deny them that opportunity. Pro-choice advocates defend a woman's right to an abortion. Their opponents argue that a fetus has a right to life. Some religious groups argue that their right to the free practice of religion includes the right to solicit converts by going door-to-door. Some homeowners object, claiming they have the right to privacy. Labor unions claim the right to strike, but businesses claim they have the right to replace striking workers with nonunion employees. Rhetoric spawned by individuals and groups arguing their right to do or get something is a major component of political colloquy in the United States.[29]

Rights are central to our political culture. Our affinity for rights is closely connected to our belief in democracy and allegiance to the Constitution. Surveys note that the public's major attachment to the Constitution comes through the Bill of Rights. Young people associate democracy with its guarantee of individual rights.[30] The notion of rights is central to democratic theory. The more rights that are extended to individuals, the more leverage they have over policy decisions, and therefore the more democratic the society. Therefore, when minorities and women are extended the right to organize and to vote they become a part of the democratic community, and the system is healthier because of it. The rhetoric and pursuit of rights can be, and has been, an effective way to enlarge the participatory base of a democratic society, and that is all to the good.

Unfortunately, in recent years the democratic community conception of rights has been displaced by a growing tendency to "privatize" the concept.[31] Americans are increasingly defining rights in ways that have no relationship to their significance to the democratic community. We want good schools, but we don't attend school board or parent-teachers meetings regularly. We want fire protection, but don't want to join volunteer fire departments. We want effective police protection and crime control policies, but are relatively uninvolved in "neighborhood watch" programs. We want jury trials, but try to avoid serving on juries. Since ours is such a culturally individualistic society, it is difficult for us to appreciate the connection between rights as a claim and democracy as a process, and the latter has been compromised as a result. People are inclined to consider their goals as individuals and their rights as one and the same. Some claim the right to smoke, others the right to drive at any speed, and still others the right to carry concealed weapons at any time in any place. These alleged rights have no relationship whatsoever to the traditional democratic rights of speech, religion, press, and assembly. The tendency to frame policy debates in terms of rights usually means we slight consideration of pragmatic solutions to problems, and focus instead on the question of whether or not a claim deserves classification as a right. In short, the privatization and trivialization rights divorce our policy objectives (rights) from the sacrifices we are willing to make to attain them. No right can exist in fact unless people are willing to assume the responsibility for attaining it.

A "rights without obligation" frame of mind influences the relationship between people and their government. It encourages citizens to adopt a distributive policy or dependency relationship between themselves and their government. Therefore, people connect with their government mostly by demanding from it services and privileges to which their rights entitle them. There is virtually no spiritual linkage between the citizen and his or her government that promotes any serious concern for the long-term betterment of society in general. The link between participation and responsibility has been obliterated, as illustrated by the comment from a talk show guest who, in commenting on the savings-and-loan crisis, argued forcefully that the people shouldn't have to pay for the industry's bailout, because that was the responsibility of the government.[32] This illustrates how difficult it is to get both citizens and public officials to focus on the public interest as a policy standard. If government exists primarily to service our rights as we define them, then there is no other definition of the public interest. According to William Hudson, much of the success the National Rifle Association (NRA) has enjoyed rests on its ability to persuade legislators, and some citizens, that the Constitution's guarantee of the right to bear arms should have priority over any counterargument that public safety, and therefore the public interest, may be endangered by such weapons possession permissiveness.[33] In short, public concern for the common good becomes secondary to self-interest when what Mary Ann Glendon has termed "rights talk" becomes pervasive. Most important, such discourse undermines institutions of social capital. According to Professor Glendon, "rights talk" encourages individuals to "place the self at the center of our moral universe. . . . Saturated with rights, political language can no longer perform the important function of facilitating public discussion of the right ordering of our lives together. . . . It captures our devotion to individualism and liberty, but omits our traditions of hospitality and care for the community."[34]

The rights fetish is encouraged further by the economic incentives of the legal profession. Lawyers have an economic interest in encouraging and extending conflict. They do this by encouraging clients to bring lawsuits based on the quest for, or deprivation of, their (the clients') rights, however defined. This places them at odds with the objectives of the legal system, which presumably exists to offer rapid and fair resolution to disputations that arise over the interpretation of rules (laws) that society establishes for itself. However, to the legal profession the more ambiguous and cumbersome are laws, the better off are lawyers. Since the law is often the dominant profession in legislatures, laws are structured to encourage disputants to seek legal solutions to problems that could often be handled by conciliation or not introduced at all. For example, most American lawyers scorn the "English Rule" for handling civil disputes, and statutes at all levels of government do not allow for it. Briefly stated, the English Rule holds that the losing litigant in a civil suit must pay the winning litigant's attorneys' fees. Such a rule discourages weak and petty suits. It also encourages defendants in strong suits to agree to out of court settlements.

Lawyers encourage people to seek legal resolutions to conflicts, and to do so often as a matter of right. Court dockets are becoming increasingly congested with claims for private damages that stem from an alleged deprivation of an individual's or group's rights. These involve such matters as contract violations, personal injury, product liability, medical malpractice, fraud, libel, and employment discrimination whether of the race, age, or sexual variety. As governments' policy responsibilities have expanded, new statutes create new rights. In addition, lawyers have argued successfully that legal doctrine should be expanded to include protection against such matters as wrongful termination, or the right not to be fired from a job for indefensible reasons.

In one sense, such a trend can be defended as a way to protect individuals from arbitrary treatment by bureaucracies. The threat of being taken to court can restrain employers from treating employees arbitrarily. On the other hand, resorting to a legal solution to relatively minor disputes can impose heavy costs on the judicial system and on society in general. Such is the case today. Lawyers abhor such things as the English Rule because it virtually forces them and their clients to evaluate the merits of cases before litigating them. It is in their economic self-interest to "game" the system and encourage lawsuits. However, this is very costly and psychologically draining on clients, regardless of who ultimately wins. The increasing possibility of lawsuits nourishes distrust and encourages more elaborate and protective contracting. This, in turn, encourages physicians and drug companies to practice and to research new products defensively for fear of provoking lawsuits. In sum, often in the name of rights expansion, a profession that, in theory, its supposed to expedite justice and render its application more effective and efficient, seeks instead to accommodate itself economically at the expense of those goals.

Even in cases where lawyers' interest in litigation is not primarily economic, seeking legal recourse to problems that are primarily social in nature can do battle with the objectives of a policy crusade. Journalist Jim Sleeper has argued that the early to mid-twentieth century crusade of social and political liberals to reduce the impact of racism on society was compromised when, during the latter part of the century, they switched from a social capital, "common culture building" approach to the problem to one that emphasized recourse through rights-based challenges in the courts. Claiming that minorities have the right to court-decreed equal status, argues Sleeper, only serves to remind Caucasians and minority groups of the existence of, and reasons for, racial discrimination. This results in an institutionalization of ethnically based double standards which, in turn, maintains existing patterns of discrimination rather than reducing them.[35]

Since issues are becoming increasingly influenced by rights arguments and claims, and since these claims have root in the Constitution's concern for preserving individual rights, the judiciary cannot escape involvement. Since parties to policy disputes regularly launch their arguments from a rights position, the inclination is to take it to the courts for resolution rather than talk it out. Therefore, the nature of such disputes makes judges the most critical participants in their resolution. Judges are not constitutionally endowed policy participants, nor are they popularly elected. Nonetheless, they become the final arbiters of an increasing number of policy disputes owing to the privatization of the Constitution's concern for individual rights.

Effective self-government rests on the assumption that citizens' loyalty to their community and country—as opposed to their self-interest—produced a politics that encourages the development of a consensus that incorporates the common good into public policy. According to some observers, such a quest is compromised, if not defeated, if citizen responsibilities to their communities and country are undercut by the political and judicial acceptance of a system of "distributive justice" that accepts the privatization of rights as inherently constructive. For example, Michael J. Sandel argues that sound republican political theory, with its emphasis on the development of citizen capacity for self-government through honest discussion and deliberation, has been repressed by the liberals' view of government as a positive force in society, which distributes rewards and opportunities to individuals based on standards of equity and objectivity. Historically, the courts have accepted and legitimized this trend, largely because of its presumed roots in the Constitution's stress on political equality and equal opportunity. According to Sandel, the courts' tendency to approve of a wide range of political and cultural opinions has created a "pro-

cedural republic," or one that emphasizes the inherent equality of ideas toward religion, obscenity, and (especially) the communications freedoms of speech, press, and petition. Taking advantage of these freedoms, applied objectively by the courts, individuals soon become more aware of the economic, ethnic, religious, and political differences that divide rather than unite them. The "neutral state" that has resulted from this trend has encouraged competition among individuals and groups, and both sanctioned and rewarded these perceived differences. In turn, this has done battle with the quest for the common good via consensus because it has divided, not united, people and groups. In sum, the trend has "deflated American ideals" and "disempowered" the public philosophy.[36] Therefore, supported first and foremost by the Constitution, courts have legitimized the privatization of rights and encouraged political division rather than consensus. Americans now argue regularly about what rights, if guaranteed, will help them pursue their own interests. According to Sandel, this is an inappropriate, if not debilitating, substitute for the cultivation of a more responsible, community-based sense of citizenship prescribed by more communitarian-oriented theorists.[37]

The Privatization of Rights: Entitlements and Collective Action

The judiciary's involvement in disputes over discriminatory and procedural rights was discussed above, with case illustrations from the Civil Rights Act and the Education for All Handicapped Children Act offered as illustrations of each. However, the privatization of constitutional rights has involved the courts in other rights disputes that have had even more policy significance for the courts than have discriminatory and procedural rights disputes. Relevant here are rights-based issues involving entitlements and collective action.

In the late 1960s, the federal courts began to alter the traditional "rights-privilege" dichotomy that had been historically applied to entitlement disputes. Before that time, welfare benefits were considered privileges, not rights. However, in a 1970 case, *Goldberg* v. *Kelly,* the Supreme Court ruled that welfare benefits were "property rights" and not "privileges" parceled out by magnanimous legislatures and bureaucrats.[38] In order for anyone to be deprived of his or her entitlement property, hearings would have to be held to determine just cause for the proposed action. The Constitution's guarantee against depriving anyone of property without "due process of law" would then be applicable. This interpretation ran contrary to legislative intent but, beginning with the Warren era, the Supreme Court began to milk such an interpretation from the Fourteenth Amendment's equal protection guarantee. They also drew what they could from assessments of legislative intent. However, to most observers, it was clear that they were pursuing an entitlement policy crusade on their own, perhaps not as a way to boost the weight of the courts in policymaking as much as it was a way to take advantage of the judiciary's special constitutional position and push for changes they thought were fundamentally important to society. Most legislators rejected this "need only" criterion for welfare eligibility, but the federal courts pursued it nonetheless.[39] In some instances where the courts drew on statutes to justify decisions, Congress rescinded the authority by amending the law, and the Berger Court (1980s) was, in principle, somewhat less activist in this respect. In addition, the budget and debt crises of the 1990s resulted in sweeping alterations to federal dominance of entitlement policy, culminating in a major welfare reform act in 1996. In addition, the Supreme Court of the 1990s was far more conservative

than was the Court of the 1960s and 1970s. While these more conservative judges were very activist as a rule, many of them were philosophically opposed to the notion of welfare as a right. Therefore, things changed, but they changed not because of the Court's turn to self-restraint as a role guideline, but because a majority of the justices didn't want the Court's policy impact to include a crusade to maintain entitlements as rights.

Nonetheless, congressional liberals of the 1960s and 1970s welcomed the Supreme Court's liberal interpretation of both the Constitution and the statutes because the goals of the legislators and the Court were the same. Reactions to judicial activism are subjective. If judges' and legislators' interests coincide, then the judges are simply reaffirming popular will. If they clash, then the courts are exploiting their constitutional independence to thrust unpopular, and therefore undemocratic, policies on society.

In addition, courts have had to deal increasingly with collective action rights issues. Collective benefits are benefits that cannot be withheld or granted to one individual or group without other individuals and groups being affected by the action. Environmental protection, worker safety, and resource conservation policies are three good examples. At first blush, this concept may appear alien to the notion of individual rights. Nonetheless, the judiciary is being petitioned regularly to rule favorably on petitions to preserve collective rights. Judges have often responded favorably, believing that groups of people are, in essence, assemblies of individuals each of which has a private interest in the policy. When ruling favorably on collective rights petitions, judges argue that the courts have the obligation to see that administrative agencies administer programs according to congressional intent. For example, Congress intends for environmental protection and worker safety laws to affect all individuals and workers equally. However, often the bureaucracy does not implement statutes that way. Therefore it is up to the courts to oversee policy implementation to maintain some semblance of benefit equality. The federal courts began questioning administrative competence in the collective benefit field in the late 1960s, and began to intervene on behalf of disappointed citizens and workers. Judge Skelley Wright, a District of Columbia circuit judge, once commented that the courts' responsibility "is to see that the legislative purposes heralded in the halls of Congress, are not lost in the vast halls of the federal bureaucracy."[40] In addition to the matter of legislative intent, some judges consider health, safety, and environmental protection to be constitutional rights. Federal Judge David Bazelon once remarked that "courts are increasingly asked to review administrative action that touches on fundamental personal interests in life, health, and liberty. These interests have always had a special claim to judicial protection."[41] Such an interpretation waned in face of the conservative revolution of the 1980s and 1990s. Judges assumed the bench who did not share Bazelon's aggressive stance toward the preservation of environmental, health, and worker protection rights. Nonetheless, the federal courts' activist crusade on behalf of legislative intent in the area of collective rights illustrates how little interested are judicial activists in strictly interpreting the separation of powers when they have public opinion and an equally activist congressional majority on their side.

Bashing the Bench: Activism and Constitutional Politics

The Constitution advantages courts in the struggle for policy prominence for two basic reasons. First, judges' claims to their positions do not hinge on public approval of their decisions. Second, court decisions are backed by the "rule of law," which citizens respect and honor, regardless of the popularity of a court decision. As a result, judges can allow government "for the people" to dominate concerns for government "by the people" when they render decisions. The Constitution does not always endorse the most popular course of action, but presumably it endorses the most intrinsically correct course of action. For example, it is important to protect free speech rights and a free press under most conditions, regardless of the popularity of the messages conveyed as a result of the existence of those rights. The same is true for individuals accused of crimes. They have a right to counsel, to not being compelled to be a witness against themselves, not to fear cruel and unusual punishment, and in many cases a jury trial. In sum, the Constitution is antimajoritarian both in structure and in its concern for substantive and procedural rights.

Therefore, the Constitution mandates the judiciary to do the right thing more than it mandates it to do the popular thing. Consequently, if judges have the Constitution, or a reasonable interpretation thereof, in mind when they render decisions, often those decisions are going to be unpopular. For example, consider the Court's unanimous decision in *Brown* v. *Board of Education,* thought by some to be the pinnacle of judicial activism. Few would argue that the decision to declare racially segregated schools inherently unconstitutional was inconsistent with either the language of the Fourteenth Amendment or the intent of those who introduced it. Nevertheless, it was an unpopular decision. School integration certainly would not have proceeded on the scale that it did and with the speed that it did had it been left to school boards across the country to do it voluntarily. Indeed, more than a few school systems would still be strictly segregated. This is perhaps the best example of the Supreme Court's "going to bat" for a minority to instate its constitutional rights. The Court did not have to negotiate or compromise the idea of racial equality in the course of considering the decision. Legislatures, including school boards, would most certainly have had to make concessions, had the idea made its way to their agendas. As in Schattschneider's "schoolyard analogy," where the mistreated student takes his or her case to the school principal or superintendent, so too can minorities without much political clout find friends in the court system. They are far more likely to apply constitutional and statutory standards of justice to minority petitions than are institutions whose members are popularly elected.

Of course, if judges want to be political as a matter of priority, then that quest for justice can serve as a smokescreen to mask those purposes. Should he or she desire, nearly every decision can be rationalized to meet a judge's definition of constitutional rights or legislative intent. Opponents of decisions very often accuse judges of doing that very thing. Supporters of the same decisions hail them as examples of how the Constitution works, even amid heated political controversy.

It is important not to conclude that, because judges are not elected and they have lifetime tenure, judicial review is therefore undemocratic. However, to accomplish this it is necessary to analyze the results of judicial review rather than the institutional conditions through which it is practiced. First, the Court's decisions can be overruled by Congress and the states via the constitutional amendment process. The Thirteenth, Fourteenth, and Fifteenth Amendments, ratified shortly after the Civil War, accomplished that very objective regarding slavery and the citizenship of blacks. The Eleventh Amendment (prohibiting lawsuits against states by citizens of another state), the Sixteenth Amendment (providing for the federal income tax), and the Twenty-Sixth Amendment (authorizing the eighteen-year-old vote) are other amendments which, in effect, overruled Supreme Court decisions. Second, the argument that the Supreme Court's independence enables it to make judgments in the public interest over the head of Congress has some merit. Courts can insert relevant constitutional factors into decisions that would otherwise be ignored by Congress. Third, as shown in the above discussion of the *Brown* case, courts represent some minority interests better than do Congress and the president. The two political branches are genetically attuned to making "politically appropriate" decisions. If placating some minority groups doesn't seem to be politically cost-effective to the president and Congress, their cause is unlikely to be high priority to the political branches. Federal courts don't have that problem, and frequently have used both judicial review and statute interpretation to advance the causes of minority groups. Therefore, when courts do unpopular things they are not necessarily doing undemocratic things. However, when they are making unpopular decisions they are also making political decisions. Judicial activism works in both political directions. Politically conservative judges can make decisions that frustrate liberal politicians, and politically liberal judges can do the same for conservatives. When court decisions establish a trend in either direction, it is common for political opponents of the decisions to accuse judges of not only making political decisions, but also of violating the separation of powers principle by intruding on the turf of the political branches.

President Franklin Roosevelt's unsuccessful attempt in 1937 to "pack" the Supreme Court in reaction to its activist-based negation of some of his New Deal policy reforms is probably the best historical example of an assault on the Supreme Court by a political branch. Roosevelt sought congressional approval to name a new Supreme Court justice for each sitting judge over the age of seventy. In 1937, this would have permitted Roosevelt to appoint six additional justices to the Court, making a total of fifteen. Had it succeeded, the Court's decisions would have turned in favor of the New Deal reforms. Congress rejected the idea on the grounds that Roosevelt's proposal constituted an unwarranted political invasion by one branch on the structure and decision processes of another, thereby violating the spirit of the separation of powers. In reality, the proposal proved to be unnecessary because, shortly after the proposal was made, the existing court began approving New Deal legislation. Sometimes called the "switch in time that saved nine," this reversal was explained largely by the fact that the existing justices, although conservative in orientation, realized that the Supreme Court could not maintain its status as a coequal branch of government unless its decisions were more congruent with public opinion.[42] This reality makes judges, in effect, ultimately accountable to the public despite the fact that they aren't elected and can't be removed for political reasons.

This accountability can be registered in a number of ways, both procedurally and substantively. Courts are mandated to respect the integrity of constitutionally decreed procedures, whether those involve protecting the rights of citizens or maintaining the integrity of the separation of powers, checks and balances, and federal principles. However, activist-oriented courts also have had the opportunity to define and work for what might be termed the public's substantive rights—to broaden the application of the rule of law to provide, for the powerless, access to educational, economic, and political opportunities.

During the 1950s and 1960s the Warren Court worked consistently toward these goals, enlisting the Kennedy and Johnson administrations in the crusade. Chief Justice Warren argued that the Constitution, as a document

in total, presupposed the existence of a set of ethical policy imperatives that would, if pursued, produce a more decent, moral, and civil society. The task of the Warren Court was to uncover these imperatives and apply them rigorously to the social and economic circumstances of the times, even at the expense of uprooting accepted values and the policies that embodied them. On the basis of these assumptions, the Warren Court established new policy directions in such fields as the integration of schools and public facilities, legislative apportionment and voting rights, a rigorous due process orientation in the criminal justice system, the exercise of communications and religious freedoms, and church-state relations. The Court sanctioned statutes and executive orders that, in the interest of social and economic justice, revised the meaning of equal protection of the laws, the commerce clause, the due process clause, and the nature of nation-state relations. The Court mandated the national government to aggressively protect individual rights from intrusions by states, groups, and individual citizens. The result of this policy revolution, especially the Court's view of the Fourteenth Amendment's equal protection guarantee, triggered major changes in federal policies affecting employment practices and public education. This was the policy legacy of an activist Court in a liberal era, during which Congress, the president, and the public were willing to accept an interpretation of judicial activism that mandated government to become more activist in the pursuit of social and economic justice.

Congress and the Courts

Constitutional politics is manifested in several ways, especially when germinated by the separation of powers which, almost by definition, invites tension and open conflict among the three branches of government. A constitutional framework that established three separate, self-reliant, co-equal branches of government and authorized each to impact on policy is going to produce its share of tension among those branches. The Congress-court relationship perhaps invites a high level of tension because Congress is constitutionally authorized to establish the size, budget, jurisdiction, and some of the procedural rules the courts must apply. Therefore, when the drift of court decisions goes against the politics of key congressional elements, tension can surface very quickly. The Roosevelt attack on the Supreme Court was a presidential attack against a conservative court. However, in the late 1990s a Republican-dominated Congress launched a like-minded assault against liberal-minded federal judges who were, in the legislators' opinion, negating too many voter-approved state and local policy initiatives. The terms "judicial activism" and "judicial imperialism" frequently were employed by congressional conservatives to explain these judges' efforts to, in their opinion, make laws rather than to interpret them. Most of the targeted judges had been appointed by Democratic presidents. Some of the court decisions that angered congressional conservatives included decisions that overruled local school board decisions on school curricula, overruled police search and seizure practices against suspected drug dealers, mandated local tax increases to support racial integration programs (especially in the schools), overruled state policies that banned racial preferences in employment, defeated a state term limits proposition, overruled a popular vote to make English the official language with which to conduct a state's business, and blocked imposition of the death penalty in capital cases. Each of these policies had been supported decisively by voters in the affected jurisdictions. Nevertheless, in what the congressional conservatives considered a power grab, the targeted judges substituted their opinion for that of the majority.

Conservative opposition to these conditions was heated in both the House and Senate. Senate Judiciary Committee chair Orrin Hatch (R–Utah) complained about the judges' tendency to twist the "text, history and structure of the Constitution beyond any intelligible meaning . . ." so that they (the judges) could decide issues "in the way they prefer." Senator John Ashcroft (R–Missouri), chair of the Judiciary Subcommittee on Constitution, Federalism, and Property Rights, argued that the courts "have made liars of Hamilton and Madison . . . for what the Framers intended to be the weakest branch of government has become the most powerful."[43]

Since the Democrats controlled the presidency, it was impossible for the hostile legislators to revert to a court-packing strategy. Some favored impeachment, because impeachment charges and decisions are initiated by Congress. Supporting such an option, House Majority Whip Tom DeLay (R–Texas) noted that "it is within the precedent of this country and the precedent of Congress to impeach them for making political decisions."[44] Other suggestions at reform were more modest. An amendment limiting the lifetime tenure of judges was introduced and considered. One senator sent a detailed questionnaire to federal judges asking about their workloads, the work assignments of their law clerks, and the amount of time they spent on the lecture circuit and in writing articles for law reviews. In an effort to prevent President Clinton from securing Senate confirmation of his appellate court nominees, some Republican senators suggested proposals that would have compromised the role of the Judiciary Committee, chaired by Senator Hatch, to review the nominations. Another proposal would have referred referendum challenges to a three-judge panel, instead of to a single judge, and required that appeals to that panel's rulings be heard by the appellate courts, not the district courts that were asked to rule in the first instance. That same proposal also recommended that judges not be allowed to raise taxes to enforce their rulings.[45] Another proposal sought to create an inspector general within the Administrative Office of the United States Courts. The Administrative Office was created in 1939 to provide auxiliary services to federal courts, including such matters as office space, the review of pending legislation to determine its potential impact on judicial proceedings, and researching ways to make the courts operate more efficiently. Although there was no evidence to substantiate it, several congressional conservatives thought the office had become a political arm of court activists, and wanted to institute a system of in-house oversight with the inspector general proposal. Others complained that it was a violation of the separation of powers principle for Congress to establish such an office to uproot waste, scandal, and conflict of interest when there was no evidence of any of these. Such an office could well amount to congressionally sponsored, in-house harassment.[46]

It is clear that this assault by congressional conservatives was based less on their concern about judicial activism in principle, and more on their frustration over the content of the decisions themselves, and their search for a way to deal with the problem. It should be noted that, concurrent with the liberal activism of district judges, the Supreme Court was being activist in directions that were, on balance, conservative. The fight was with activism that was presumed to be activated by liberal, not conservative, objectives. Congressional conservatives that were actively opposed to liberal-instilled activism had virtually no problem with conservative-instilled activism.

The separation of powers was central to this conflict, and it is noteworthy how the conservative offensive was countered by arguments employing the separation of powers, either in defense of the judges' actions, or

simply to maintain the independence of the judiciary in principle. The latter point was even stressed by some conservatives, including Senator Hatch, chair of the Senate Judiciary Committee, and Supreme Court Chief Justice William Rehnquist, who noted that some of the congressional moves could constitute "an unwarranted and ill-considered effort to micromanage" the federal judiciary.[47] Chief Judge Gilbert S. Merritt of the U.S. Court of Appeals for the 6th Circuit argued that the idea of the judiciary as the strongest branch was "absurd," that the Constitution's granting of the powers of the purse and sword to Congress and the president, together with their public opinion support base, obviously made them the strongest branches.[48] He went on to observe that ambiguous legislation is a major cause of the problem of judicial overreaching. He blamed that on the unwillingness of Congress to take firm positions on controversial issues, preferring instead to enact ambiguous legislation that inevitably draws the courts into the process to apply the legislation to specific circumstances. His position was supported by a Cato Institute constitutional scholar, Roger Pilon, who argued that when laws are ambiguous it is very difficult to establish a standard by which to measure judicial responsibility, making judicial activism "inevitable."[49]

As discussed above, the "politics of ambiguity," albeit a selective strategy, enhanced legislative-judicial cooperation during the Supreme Court's Warren and early post-Warren years. During the waning years of the century, this same legislative bias toward ambiguity helped to estrange the two branches from one another. The common denominator that seems to underlie all interbranch conflict involving the judiciary is not that judges are aggressive politicians seeking to work their will on society from institutional positions that are not directly accountable to the people. Instead, it is the fact that politicians often disagree with what judges say the Constitution and statutes mean, and they (the politicians) cite the separation of powers principle as a way to both explain and correct the problem. However, the problem is politics, not the courts. If legislators or, for that matter, presidents think the courts are too activist, they often have only themselves to blame, especially when the courts act to clarify ambiguous legislation and administrative rules. Ambiguity invites conflict, and constitutional politics only serves to make that conflict more intense and its resolution more difficult.

Ambiguity in legislation is often deliberate. Often, Congress is able to be more policy-specific, but chooses not to do so. Knowing that the courts can be asked to determine what Congress probably meant by ambiguous language, legislators find it easy to dodge responsibility for controversial laws if the negative effects of laws on society can be traced directly to court, not congressional, decisions. Such a "pass the buck" strategy thrives under a system of constitutionally mandated separated institutional powers. However, this congressional timidity makes judicial activism an inevitability. Because Congress is strategically shy about policy specifics, the courts often have no choice other than to become activist. It is inevitable when they give ambiguous legislation the focus it needs to become meaningful. Consequently, it is inappropriate for Congress to blame the Supreme Court for being too activist by "making law" because legislatively instituted policy obscurity leaves them (the courts) no realistic alternative.

The Supreme Court's 1998 term illustrates this circumstance very well. Had Congress been specific in designating the exact applications of the Americans with Disabilities Act, the Court could not have rendered it applicable to the reproductively handicapped, more specifically the carriers of the AIDS virus. Had Congress resolved the question of whether or not employers could be held accountable for

unreported sexual discrimination practices, the Court would not have been compelled to decide that they were. Had Congress been specific with respect to the schools' responsibility for sexual harassment under the same conditions, the Court would not have been compelled to say that they (the schools) were not responsible. In commenting on this trend during the Supreme Court's 1998 term, legal scholar Robert A. Katzmann noted: "You look at a number of these cases and say that the essential problem is that Congress has been deliberately vague and knew full well that they would want the courts to step in and resolve the issue. The pattern is that Congress doesn't want to face up to its responsibilities and then blames the court afterward for its decisions. Essentially, in these cases, what you've got is the Congress, through deliberate ambiguity, presenting the court with choices and the court doing exactly what it should be doing—trying to make sense of them."[50]

Such a trend may be inevitable. It is perfectly understandable why Congress has chosen not to confront, for example, the social, political, and economic policy ramifications of affording disability status to people infected with the AIDS virus. Legislators have chosen to leave such sensitive decisions to the courts. Some observers have concluded that these conditions have created a "conversation" or "dance" atmosphere between Congress and the courts. If so, notes Fred Barbash, "it's become seriously one-sided, [with] unelected judges and justices doing most of the talking." If the "dance" analogy is preferred, then "one partner is leading."[51]

Due Process and Public Policy: The Case of Adversarial Legalism

Conflict encouraged by policy ambiguity is often exacerbated because parties to policy conflicts often employ court-sanctioned due process strategies to gain policy advantages over their opponents. While due process guarantees are an essential component of a procedural democracy, the concept itself is an ambiguous one, gaining meaning only when applied to specific circumstances. Usually these strategies are introduced to thwart change, not to expedite it. As government has become more activist in makeup, these procedural tactics become increasingly significant to the procedural course and substantive character of public policy.

Since the New Deal period, government at all levels has become more significant to the lives and activities of individuals, groups, and corporations. Periodically, crusades are launched to reduce the impact of government on society, but these efforts usually fail, due in large part to the fact that society has grown comfortable with the protection and support offered by this positivist state. If the New Deal period established the positivist state, the due process revolution in criminal procedures of the 1960s transplanted positivism to the courts and administrative agencies. Contemptuous police practices in the segregated southern states and in large, crime-infested northern cities stirred egalitarian-oriented citizen activists into action. Congress and the Department of Justice did not have the constitutional authority to impose national equal opportunity or due process standards on local police departments. As the institution of last resort, the Warren Court intervened and filled the vacuum by issuing a series of decisions that guaranteed procedural rights to those accused of crimes and, most important, prescribed adversarial instruments for implementing the newly established rules. The result was an effective, but cumbersome, expensive, and politically controversial manner of regulating local criminal justice systems. Occurring simultaneously were the egalitarian-triggered and politically inspired social and political revolutions in civil rights, environmental protection, consumer protection, and anti-poverty policy. Each of these policy crusades demanded a more activist role for the federal government, often to the point of overriding hostile state and local laws. Ironically, many of the leaders who sponsored these campaigns were also somewhat leery of the increased centralized government power they produced. They believed both Congress and administrative agencies to be overly conservative and too susceptible to corporate pressures. Therefore, they worked to encourage the increased fragmentation of government authority. They demanded that national policymaking, implementation, and judicial procedures accommodate the principles of political pluralism. To be sure, each of these public interest crusades sought major policy changes, but only if they were managed through what Michael McCann labeled a "judicial model of the state."[52]

The effect of these high-profile policy campaigns was to fragment authority centers in Congress and within the Democratic Party. Within Congress the seniority system was enfeebled, and much of the power of committee chairs assigned to a plethora of subcommittees, many of which were chaired by liberal advocates of the policy revolutions. Seeking to defend their crusades from the more hostile Nixon administration, the reformers worked to expand the rights of citizens and advocacy organizations to seek judicial review of unfriendly administrative decisions, arguing that these decisions should be based on facts produced by research and not on the judgment of administrators. They worked to legally constrict administrative discretionary authority. To expedite citizen oversight of administrative activity, they pressured Congress to create special oversight agencies and appeal boards, thereby increasing opportunities for legal challenges to official decisions. To discourage subjectivity in the administration of welfare policy, the Supreme Court required states and localities to guarantee due process hearings before terminating welfare benefits, and awarded citizens and advocacy groups the right to sue states and localities for poor administration of federal legislation.[53]

Therefore, activist government has produced notably transformative, if not revolutionary, policies, many of which were decreed by activist courts such as the Warren Court. However, this policy activism has been consummated within a constitutionally dictated structural environment that was designed to thwart these very trends. In short, government structure and guarantees of due process, both constitutional and statutory in origin, embrace a suspicion of government authority. They demand that policy proposals find ways to either bypass, accommodate, or adjust to complicated procedures that exist to ensure fair and responsible public policies.

As a result of legally mandated due process requirements and the possibility of judicial review, policy processes in the United States have become notably permeated, in some cases even swamped, by what Robert A. Kagan has labeled a framework of "adversarial legalism."[54] Since both the Constitution and statutes guarantee parties to a conflict the right to be heard, to appeal decisions, and to be treated objectively by policymakers, policy processes have assumed a due process cast that proffers inordinate delays in decision making and can significantly increase costs to all parties. The United States, in contrast to other advanced democracies, has been notably overwhelmed by an adversarial legal culture. This is because the policy objectives of an activist government must contend with, and ultimately overcome, a legal environment that favors procedural due process over substantive policy content. Affected stakeholders to a policy have rights that must be accommodated before policy decisions are finalized.

Policy issues involving compensation of the injured, regulating industry to ensure a safe environment, guaranteeing equal educational opportunities, and averting malpractice by physicians and law enforcement officials are all impacted heavily by adversarial legalism.

According to Kagan, policy processes, such as those in the United States, exhibit adversarial legalism if they (1) embody complex legal rules, (2) require adversarial procedures to resolve squabbles among political and scientific forces, (3) allow for legal contestation of decisions and processes, (4) invite judicial review of administrative decisions, and (5) provide for serious legal sanctions against those who transgress due process guarantees.[55] As a result, policy and dispute resolution processes embody high degrees of (1) formal legal contestation, whereby parties to a dispute regularly insist on being guaranteed their legal rights and that decision procedures be fair, (2) litigant activism, whereby lawyers are engaged to gather evidence and articulate and dispute claims, and (3) substantive legal uncertainty, or conditions under which decisions are expected to be "variable, unpredictable, and reversible."[56]

Adversarial legalism is part of our constitutionally conditioned legal culture. We revere the rule of law and the right of all citizens to seek legal redress from anyone, including public officials. By the same token, we are proud to proclaim that no one, even a president, should be above the law. There are several advantages to this. People can challenge laws and executive orders that they feel have been misconceived or misdirected. The politically and economically disadvantaged can demand their just due or rights from government, as was the case in the civil rights movement. It has led to more equitably apportioned electoral districts, to more humanitarian conditions in mental institutions and prisons, to determining the constitutional limits of religious practice, and to more sensitive administration of welfare policies. The benefits of court-endorsed litigiousness have, and can be, numerous. They should not be understated.

However, adversarial legalism also has negative implications for both policies and the processes that produce them. As an equal opportunity sword, it can also be used to frustrate the very groups it is designed to assist. Opponents to equal opportunity can use it to delay the consideration of proposals, increase litigation costs, and ultimately elicit key concessions from its advocates. By increasing liability and malpractice insurance costs, it increases the consumer's tab for health care, education, law enforcement, and environmental engineering by forcing potentially vulnerable professionals in these and other fields to spend countless hours producing "defensive paperwork" to protect themselves while they neglect or slight their job responsibilities. It can undermine the value of pluralist democracy by converting meaningful debates between stakeholders into due-process-inspired face-offs that often spiral so far out of control that policy objectives are either abandoned or compromised to the point of impotency. In regulatory policy, where the well-being of relatively unorganized groups (consumers and underprivileged) are the focus of the regulatory effort, serious attempts to protect these interests are frequently lost amidst an environment of a repetitive, prolonged series of regulatory and judicial proceedings. If verifiable scientific findings are a necessary prerequisite to a regulatory decision, potential losers can challenge, procedurally, the accuracy and integrity of the research that produced the findings. In assessing the effect of adversarial legalism on attempts by proenvironment forces to integrate environmental concerns with industrial objectives regarding a harbor-dredging project in Oakland, California, Kagan concluded that procedurally induced delays in considering the complaints of environmental forces in some cases amounted to an endorsement of the status quo. At other times the port authority was so concerned over potential litigation costs of challenging the environmentalists that it immediately conceded to "any plausible claim of (potential) environmental harm."[57] The Oakland case offers an excellent example of a process that a National Research Council committee once described as "complex, cumbersome, unpredictable and fragmented," and one which Kagan calls "chilling" in its effect on both the cost of decision making and, of course, on the input balance that is necessary for rational decision making.[58]

The history of the Environmental Protection Agency's administration of Superfund monies offers another excellent example of the impact of adversarial legalism on policy. Congress created Superfund by way of the Comprehensive Environmental Response, Compensation, and Liability Act of 1980 (CERCLA) to provide EPA with resources to decontaminate hazardous waste sites, and amended the act six years later in an effort to improve a program that had been criticized because of its cumbersomeness and overall ineffectiveness. The law's ineffectiveness may well have been an inevitable result of the impact of the litigiousness it invited. Virtually each project targeted by Superfund efforts was welcomed with an extended series of multiparty court confrontations. Businesses in polluted areas could be deemed liable for clean-up costs, even if they hadn't contributed to the contamination problem. Therefore, polluting forces sought to spread both the blame for contamination and the costs for eradicating it to as many firms as possible. Blame was dispersed so widely, triggering so many lawsuits, that any hope for expeditious resolutions to the problems became swamped in obstructing tactics and lawsuits. Many were third-party lawsuits from property owners whose property values had declined due to the contamination. Realists with a cyn-ical bent often referred to the Superfund law as the "Lawyers' Full Employment Act of 1980." One city recounted that a $30 million clean-up project triggered a projected $700 million in lawsuits. Research sponsored by the American Insurance Association projected that decontaminating the 1,800 sites targeted by Superfund would propagate approxi-mately $8 billion in legal costs.[59] It was also es-timated that, of the average ten-year time span it takes to shepherd a Superfund project from start to finish, seven of those years are involved with project studies, legal proceed-ings, and solution development in advance of the actual beginning of clean-up efforts.[60]

Such an environment usually favors the sta-tus quo over the forces of change. Opponents of change can thwart change merely by im-posing due process burdens on the decision chain. Whether their position is defensible or not is often irrelevant. The purpose is to delay or nullify any change in the status quo. The agribusiness industry is well known for its abil-ity to utilize such a strategy when the poten-tial safety of pesticides applied to growing crops is brought into question. While the level of chemically imposed toxicity is being researched and run through the procedural gamuts of the regulatory process, the suspect chemicals remain in use. The procedural due process guarantees of our antiauthority spin democracy can, and often do, affect the sub-stance of policy in significant ways. Govern-ment "by the people" can make effective gov-ernment "for the people" much more of a challenge.

The Constitution, and laws enacted to fa-cilitate its objectives, embody the American cultural distrust of government authority. The constitutionally prescribed practice of dispersing policy authority among mutually restraining institutions, the practice of sub-jecting administrative agency decisions to ju-dicial review, and legally affirming the rights

of citizens to challenge administrative deci-sions in court collectively nourish conditions under which adversarial legalism can thrive. Government has become more centralized and activist because the public has demanded it. However, it has had to do so within a legal environment that rewards efforts to fragment, not centralize, that very power. Attempts to pursue transformative policies within this re-vised institutional framework clash directly with a legal structure that is notably reactive, uncentralized, and nonhierarchical in cast. Adversarial legalism prospers under such con-ditions, and the results for both the policy process and the quality of policies themselves are far more negative than they are positive. Kagan compliments the American political system for its agenda-setting efficiency in not-ing that it has "become highly responsive to political demands (and) . . . quickly generates knowledge and public policies reflecting new insights and values." However, he concludes that that ability is frequently wasted because adversarial legalism often "results in enor-mously costly, time consuming, and erratic policy implementation and dispute resolu-tion, conducted in courts or in the forbidding shadow of judicial review." The result is that "good policy ideas are thus transmuted into bad case-level outcomes."[61]

Courts, Public Policy, and Microgovernment

Endorsement by courts of case-level solutions to policy problems has impacted society nega-tively on yet another front in recent years. Courts have extended individual and group due process claims to the point of establishing what Jonathan Rauch has called a state of "mi-crogovernment" in the United States. In Rauch's opinion, to complain about judicial procedures being too litigious, too concerned with rights as a route to private betterment, or too activist in purpose and effect, is to miss perhaps the most contemporary negative impact of courts on public policy. He maintains that courts, because they have responded favorably to rights-based lawsuits over the years, have introduced Americans to a new brand of regulatory policies, a brand "based on the premise that each individual is entitled to a safe, clean or, especially, fair personal environment."[62] Rauch argues that microgovernment is not synonymous with small government. In fact, it is a notably extensive type of government. However, its extensiveness "takes the peculiar form of an infinity of microdecisions, each building upon, yet separate from, all others."[63] Microgovernment is the result of a continuous shower of court decisions that permeate the everyday lives of people in numerous ways. Regulatory agencies are not the source of these regulations, but usually are plaintiffs seeking redress for clients through lawyers, judges, and juries, all of which work separately to "spin, in the fashion of a mass of caterpillars, a cocoon of intricate social regulation that enfolds even the most minute details of everyday life."[64]

In effect, microgovernment literally means millions of decisions that affect millions of people regularly in significant but uncoordinated ways. There is no big picture or theory within which they "fit" to tell a means-ends policy story. Examples abound. Recent court decisions have compelled the Professional Golfers Association to allow a disabled person to use a golf cart while competing in tournaments, forced the New York State Board of Law Examiners to grant a person with a reading disability more time to take a bar examination, obligated a television producer to pay a multimillion-dollar judgment to a pregnant woman for refusing to cast her as a seductive hussy, determined under what conditions it is appropriate or inappropriate for a coach to slap a football player on the backside, and compelled a fast-food chain to pay a $2.7 mil-

lion punitive judgment to a woman who was seriously burned when she spilled some of the chain's hot coffee on herself.[65]

Some of these judgments were necessary and some were comparatively frivolous. However, their significance lies in the ominous trend they represent. They are unlike any other kind of regulatory enterprise. Historically, regulatory policy in the United States has followed two general tracts. The first was an economic regulatory crusade introduced by the Progressives in the late nineteenth century. That movement was designed to control the price exploitive and monopolistic practices of big business. The policy solution to this problem was to establish regulatory agencies to control prices and to supervise entry into markets. Largely achieved, that campaign was mostly dissipated by the time of the New Deal. The second crusade was social regulatory in construct. It began in the 1960s, and sought to prevent corporations from imposing social, economic, and physical harms on people who were unorganized and unable to safeguard themselves from such occurrences. This time the solution was to establish regulatory agencies to regulate worker safety, the environment, food and drug purity and safety, and consumer rights. These two movements had different objectives, but were united in their reliance on administrative agencies to organize and orchestrate comprehensive efforts to deal with policy issues by area.

The third regulatory tract, that of microgovernment, like the other two owes its reality to the unjust and damaging effects of the market economy on innocent people. However, it breaks with the other two in the way it answers the problem. It rejects bureaucracy as a management solution and, under pressure from political activists, substitutes a system that asks agencies to seek remedies in court on behalf of harmed individuals. Instead of a group of afflicted individuals seeking an administrative ruling that will apply a single compensatory standard to indemnify them all, each member of the group hires a lawyer and seeks redress only for himself or herself. Courts have responded favorably. Since the 1960s and 1970s, courts have widened their interpretation of tort laws to permit people to claim more damages from more organizations for more reasons. The result has been a random, unsystematic, case-by-case concoction of "personal safety" decisions that are costly, confusing, omnipresent, and totally devoid of any theoretical policy consistency. A major consulting firm has reported that between the mid-1960s and mid-1980s, tort case costs, as a percentage of the economy, more than doubled, with plaintiffs receiving less than half those funds whereas lawyers collected approximately 30 percent.[66] The social and economic manifestations of microgovernment are reported daily, and they affect an increasingly larger number of individuals. They come in the form of sexual harassment litigation, product safety lawsuits, workplace harassment disputes, and court-instigated quests to articulate and guarantee patient and consumer rights. It is not necessary to ask administrative agencies to improve matters by executive orders or to ask legislatures to make these bothersome decisions. Regulation by litigation is self-financing or, according to Pietro Nivola, it marks a "shift to off-budget governance."[67]

Therein lies the problem. Policies that are "off-budget" and "off-government" also tend to be, in Rauch's terms, "off-accountability." Good regulatory practice presupposes that an overall policy plan or map is developed before rule-making begins, that results rather than procedures are the goals of any regulatory enterprise, that rule-making enterprises should be constantly affected by cost-benefit assessments of the propriety of taking a particular regulatory route, that proposed administrative rules be publicized in advance to invite interested party comment, that rules should be clearly written so that all affected parties know where they stand, that rule makers should not benefit economically from their efforts, and that rules can (and should) be reviewed by legislators and elected executives so that the regulators can be held accountable for their actions. Microgovernment conditions offer none of these protections to individuals or to society in general. Administrators are not involved systematically, costs are of no concern to courts responding to individual requests for singular justice on a singular problem, politicians are bystanders, and agendas are actuated by angry individuals and by lawyers who are rewarded for finding more and more punishable offenses. On top of it all, juries are notoriously unpredictable and largely unconcerned with fairness and consistency from one case to another. Successful regulatory ventures do not turn government over to private-sector lawyers. They focus on measurable results and on the systematic use of feedback to make mid-course policy corrections. Microgovernment provides for none of that. The scene is not unlike that of a headless octopus with tentacles flaying randomly in all directions but lacking the essential control center to make the expenditure of such energy meaningful. According to Rauch, "all microgovernment sees is *each* job, and *each* disabled person, and *each* person's right to accommodation. Microgovernment is one-eyed."[68] If agencies were mostly at fault, they could be punished by restricting their jurisdictions or cutting their budgets. That is not a realistic option when courts are the provocateurs.

Microgovernment also undermines trust and privacy. Subjecting jobs, schools, workplaces, relationships, and even innocent attempts at humor to legal "strip searches" can rigidify and formalize the work environment and interfere with productivity. It can humiliate and overwhelm organizations and communities that depend on trust. It can be staggeringly unfair in its definition and dispensation of "justice." One restaurant chain was ordered to pay a $3.75 million settlement to three men and their lawyers after the men were turned down for waiting jobs because it was the chain's practice to hire only sparingly clad females for such positions. According to Rauch, if an administrative agency had investigated the problem, it probably would have concluded that, of the 370,000 restaurants in the United States, allowing a few to hire only meagerly clad females would probably not be all that unjust. However, microgovernment notices "only the unfairness in each particular case. Discrimination in allocating even one serving job is too much."[69]

Another problem with microgovernment is that it is insidiously incremental and offers no single target to which the disabused can protest. It doesn't overwhelm with a frontal attack, but rather gnaws away at privacy and trust from a myriad of sources. It doesn't come from legislatures, from elected executives, or from bureaucracies that are going about their official business. It offers those concerned about its costs, both economic and personal, no place to demonstrate, petition, testify, or picket. Finally, just as the presumed intemperances of regulatory activity in the 1960s and 1970s made the public suspicious of government bureaucracy, the microgovernment culture will likely reinforce that suspicion by extending it to include suspicion of the courts as effective governing mechanisms. Microgovernment is, in essence, regulation devoid of regulators, and for courts to let it run amuck under the pretense of being faithful to the mandate to preserve individual rights is to invite upon the judicial system the same sort of public protests that have undermined both the prestige and effectiveness of legislative and executive institutions in recent years.

Eventually, microgovernment's excesses will be brought to heel. The only question is how far it will go and what individual and social prices will have to be paid before that happens.

The Supreme Court, the Constitution, and the Decline of Political Parties

Political parties are essential representation vehicles in a democratic system. In America's two-party system, parties are essentially assemblages of interest groups whose policy positions are often compromised in the interest of party unity. The disproportionate representation of one or a few factions runs counter to the role of the party as a unifying agent. In sum, strong political parties make the representation of people and the groups with which they are affiliated more balanced.

However, if political parties are weak because they are dominated by a few high-profile and financially well-heeled factions, that advantage is lost or compromised significantly. Individuals elected to office under such conditions are more beholden to those factions and public policy is impacted substantially. Court decisions during the past quarter-century, especially those of the Supreme Court, have advanced the causes of factions at the expense of parties in ways that have dramatically affected representational balance in American politics and, ultimately, public policy. Many of these decisions have been activist in effect, replacing laws with court decrees on such critical matters as campaign finance, congressional districting, ballot access, patronage, and the administration of party primaries. In effect, the courts have exerted a very powerful influence over policy inputs. This has usually been accomplished by applying the Constitution's First Amendment guarantees of free speech, press, and petition in ways that overrule legislative intent.

The Supreme Court case that gave factions

the opportunity to suppress political parties as effective intermediaries in American politics was the 1974 decision in *Buckley* v. *Valeo*.[70] In this decision, the Court held that the Federal Election Campaign Act of 1972, which established strict reporting requirements for candidates seeking federal office, their campaign committees, and all other individuals and organizations contributing to campaigns, was, with one major exception, constitutional. That exception concerned limitations on overall campaign spending and on what an individual candidate could spend on his or her campaign. Those limitations were declared unconstitutional because they violated the First Amendment's free speech guarantee. Defending this interpretation, the court majority stated: "In the free society ordained by our Constitution, it is not the government but the people . . . who must retain control over the quantity and range of debate . . . in a political campaign."[71] Therefore, while the full disclosure of campaign contributions was legitimate, Congress could not curtail speech by placing limits on overall spending.

The *Buckley* decision had far-reaching effects on the ways campaigns were subsequently financed and, ultimately, on the effectiveness of parties as intermediary institutions in American politics. Some of those results were expected, while others were not. The most obvious effect of the decision was a dramatic increase in the cost of campaigning for office. The lack of overall limits on expenditures allowed Diane Feinstein and Michael Huffington to spend upwards of $44 million in their 1994 contest for a U.S. Senate seat from California, allowing the wealthy Mr. Huffington to fund his entire campaign at a cost of $29 million.[72] An unintended consequence of the *Buckley* decision was the dramatic increase in the number of Political Action Committees (PACs) as group campaign "front" organizations, established for the sole purpose of contributing money to political campaigns. The

Federal Election Campaign Act limited organization campaign contributions to $5,000 per candidate, but did not place a limit on the number of organizations (PACs) that could be established by groups to make such contributions. Since all candidates, rich or poor, had to find funds to challenge each other, group contributions through their PACs became critical to campaign success. No limits were placed on a group's soft money contributions to parties and candidates. Soft money is money that supports a campaign staff, pays printing and advertising costs, pays the costs of transporting candidates and their staffs, and pays rent and utility costs for the rental of buildings used during campaigns.

According to David K. Ryden, the effect of the Supreme Court's decision in *Buckley* and later cases is to introduce a "crisis of representation" into American politics.[73] The effectiveness of political parties as intermediary institutions providing balance to the representation system has given way to the domination of representation by vested interests. It rewards candidates and organizations that are well heeled and well connected and, in effect, denies the same opportunity to those of lesser economic and political status. This undermines democracy, especially the notion of equality of opportunity. In addition, it means that courts have not dealt effectively with the contradictions inherent in the pluralist theory of democracy. Pluralism presupposes that individuals need, and should get, equal representation in the political process. The political system needs that also so that public policy can reflect balanced group inputs. However, all groups are not represented equally in politics for several reasons—money, access, reputation, quality of leadership, degree of member interest, and geographical dispersion of membership. If courts examined group politics through an equality of opportunity lens they would work to overcome the bias of pluralism in the representative world. They have chosen not to do that. Instead, the *Buckley* decision, as well as others, accepts group inequality as an inevitable by-product of the free speech guarantee and, most important, condones the reality. According to Ryden, "political parties provide a set of structures that are integral to the attainment of effective representation. Nevertheless, they are consistently overlooked or disparaged by the Court."[74] Party-engineered campaign financing is far more equal and fair than has been the practice since *Buckley*.

Judicial activism triggered by the Supreme Court's loyalty to the First Amendment in principle has had significant consequences for both procedural and substantive democracy in the United States since 1974. The Supreme Court has been the "trigger" institution for the introduction of the candidate-centered campaign and, the (apparent) imperatives of the First Amendment aside, should be held at least partly accountable for the impact of it on both the nature of representation and the public policy bias that has followed. Privileged business interests have had the policy "inside track" since the advent of the candidate-centered campaign. This poses a threat to American democracy on a number of fronts. First, it is both genetically and operationally incompatible with the notion of political equality. Second, as a result of the first point, it means that interests are not represented equally in the political process. Third, it discourages and even alienates people in general from their government. Finally, public policies biased toward the corporate sector are very often contrary to the interest of the public in general.

Judicial Activism and Presidential Leadership

Presidents have the most inclusive constituency in American politics. They represent everybody, and are therefore more concerned about court decisions that do battle with representational balance. Presidents that actively respond to their national constituency will consistently pursue policies that stress equality of opportunity, and are apt to become impatient with court decisions affording constitutional sanction to conditions leading to the opposite. Franklin Roosevelt was one such president. Bill Clinton was another. Roosevelt was fortunate enough to serve during an era when the nation welcomed activist government as a force working for both political and economic equality. Therefore, the trouble he received from a conservatively oriented activist Supreme Court was temporary. Bill Clinton was not so fortunate. He served during a conservative era marked by a clear public suspicion of big government. Furthermore, he faced a moderate-to-conservative Supreme Court that was very willing to play an activist role, provided, of course, that constitutional "principle" was at stake.

Historically speaking, the last quarter of the twentieth century found the Supreme Court in perhaps its most activist mode. Under chief justices Warren Burger and William Rehnquist, the rejection rate of legislative and administrative actions rose dramatically. The New Deal court activists, controversial as they were, struck down only thirteen New Deal reform laws. By way of contrast, the Court invalidated thirty-two laws during Chief Justice Burger's seventeen-year reign, and eighteen between 1986 and 1997, under Chief Justice Rehnquist. While few, if any, activist-inspired decisions will ever rival the *Brown* decision in social significance, the Burger and Rehnquist courts did render controversial decisions that had a major impact on society and on public policy. For example, the Burger Court's decision in *Roe* v. *Wade* legalized abortions in the United States, stating that governments did not have the power to forbid them during the first trimester of a pregnancy.[75] Also during the Burger reign, the Court invalidated the legislative veto, which had been in existence since 1932. The legislative veto allowed the president to propose a policy change and permit Congress to consider it for sixty to ninety days. If neither house of Congress disapproved of the proposal within that time frame, the proposal became law. If either house voted disapproval, the proposal was defeated. Between 1932 and 1983, several hundred statutes were enacted under such conditions, most of them dealing with executive branch reorganization issues. The War Powers Resolution of 1973 carried the veto strategy to a new dimension. It permitted Congress to reject presidential foreign policy initiatives, most of which involved the commitment of troops, within sixty days of the commitment. In 1983, the Berger Court invalidated the legislative veto as authorized by the Economy Act of 1932 and subsequent statutes. Since the War Powers Resolution was not under challenge, the legislative veto's role under that law remained intact. The Court argued that an "either house" veto of a presidential proposal was unconstitutional because it allowed Congress to bypass the president and enact a law without giving the president a chance to sign or veto the measure.[76]

The Rehnquist Court, especially during the Clinton administration, rendered decisions that were perhaps even more significant because they dealt with matters that affect all people sooner or later. Included were decisions on the use of the Internet to transmit material that is allegedly pornographic in content (sanctioned), the right to a physician-assisted suicide (denied, finding no constitutional right to die), the right for a teacher to use private school facilities to seek remedial help for students (sanctioned), and a state law that relaxed weapons registration requirements that were first introduced by the Brady Act (sanctioned). Of the above cases, only the right to die ruling was unanimous. Some, such as the ruling that compromised the Brady Act, were decided by narrow 5–4 votes. The Internet ruling offers a good illustration of how an activist Supreme Court can use the Constitution to overturn a policy that was overwhelmingly supported by both the president and Congress. The law itself was rather broadly cast, but its intent was to deny minors access to cyberspace-transmitted pornographic materials. Its bipartisan popularity was due, in part, to the popularity of the promotion of family values as a policy standard. However, the Court ruled that to deny minors access to such material also means that adults are deprived of their First Amendment rights to free speech.

The Supreme Court's 1996–1997 term was a good illustration of how judicial activism can interfere with a president's policy agenda and, in Clinton's case, force him and his family to deal with personal civil suits that diverted him from his presidential responsibilities. In addition to the laws on use of the Internet, the Brady Act, and a law intended to enhance religious freedom, all of which the president had signed into law and which the Court subsequently invalidated, the Court also ruled that Clinton's presidential status did not make him immune to having to defend himself against a sexual harassment suit filed by Paula Jones, and that White House lawyers had to surrender to investigators notes of conversations they had with Mrs. Clinton relative to the Whitewater incident. In 1998 the Court invalidated the Line Item Veto Act of 1996, a law that provided the president an opportunity to strike wasteful expenditures from appropriations legislation.

The Rehnquist Court was, for the most part, more literal in its interpretation of the Constitution's provisos than the politics of both the president and many members of Congress found comfortable. Both the president and Congress often support legislation of questionable constitutionality in order to soothe voters. Legislation designed to support family values that allows victims of family violence to instigate federal court action against alleged offenders, as did the Violence Against Women Act, may well be invalidated because such cases have traditionally been tried in state, not federal, courts. Nonetheless, the political branches often find it profitable symbolic politics to try to escalate the judicial arena, irrespective of the move's constitutionality. The political rewards of impressing constituents are usually worth the risk of being rejected by the judiciary. Therefore, the resurgence of constitutionalism in court decisions is not always due to the Constitution's renaissance in the minds of judges. It can also be the result of presidents and legislators being somewhat cavalier about the constitutionality of laws that are, first and foremost, strategies of political posturing.

The Supreme Court has been active in constraining presidential discretion and privileges since the Watergate incident, an event that triggered an antiestablishment mindset among the citizenry and within legislatures. In a sense, limits placed on the presidency by the Court since Watergate reflect the Court's ability to absorb public opinion and reflect it in its decisions. In this sense, the Court offers a venue other than the legislative and executive, for the representation of the public in policy decisions.

While the Watergate incident and the Paula Jones sexual harassment suit cannot be equated in either scope or significance, they did share one key principle in common. Both cases underscored the fact that the Supreme Court considers the president to be, first and foremost, an ordinary citizen when it comes to the law. In the Watergate incident, President Nixon argued that Oval Office tape recordings of presidential business, including Watergate, should not be made public because of their "executive privilege" status. The president argued that the recordings contained critical discussions of highly sensitive issues that would be contrary to U.S. interests both at home and abroad if they were made public. Therefore, he alone should be the judge of whether they should be made public. The Supreme Court, with many of Nixon's own appointees voting against him, voted unanimously that the executive privilege claim was without merit and that the tapes should be made available. The president of the United States, said the Court in *United States* v. *Nixon,* is not beyond the reach of the law.[77] In *Clinton* v. *Jones* (1997), the president's lawyers argued that a 1982 case that found the president to be exempt from civil suits should cover suits dealing with his personal behavior as well. With Justice John Paul Stevens citing the Watergate ruling as precedent, the Court (including two Clinton appointees) unanimously rejected the argument, holding that, in "appropriate circumstances . . . the president is subject to judicial process."[78] Although a president's basic powers and prerogatives were not compromised by either the Watergate or Jones decisions, they did serve to put the president on notice that there are limits to a president's claim to inherent or circumstantial powers or privileges. Still, it was not the Court's intention in the Jones case to compromise the true significance of presidential stewardship to both the Constitution and the American people. To remind President Clinton of this, in the Jones case the justices resurrected Justice Robert Jackson's commentary on presidential power in the 1952 steel seizure case, a case in which the Court ruled that President Truman's seizure of steel mills impacted by a workers' strike was unconstitutional. Jackson noted that executive power is vested "in a single head in whose choice the whole nation has a part, making him the focus of public hopes and expectations."[79]

Judicial Federalism: Devolution, Minorities, and the Rehnquist Court

The Rehnquist Court's window on federalism perhaps has been its most enduring activist legacy for both the Constitution and public policy. Beginning in 1994 the Rehnquist Court, by close split decisions (usually 5–4), began to reexamine nation-state relations across the entire compass of the Constitution, and began gradually to limit federal power and assign increased policy discretion to the states. This was accomplished in policy areas that had for generations, due to the widespread acceptance of both concurrent jurisdiction rights and the practical need for co-operative federalism, been considered to be the joint responsibility of both the federal government and the states. Furthermore, the Court's decisions may well have handicapped the ability of governments at all levels to deal with problems that potentially can affect nearly every citizen and the ability of minorities to secure equal opportunities on a number of fronts.

For example, in 1996 a Supreme Court ruling limited the ability of Congress to deal with the problem of lethal weapons in and around schools. In another decision the Court limited the ability of the federal government to take a state to court to mandate that it enforce the provisions of a federal law. In another it ruled that states have the right to make decisions about the disposal of nuclear waste unilaterally, without considering federal input. In one of the 1997 term's most highly publicized decisions the Court, in a 5–4 decision, ruled that the Brady Act's requirement that states make background checks of would-be gun purchasers was unconstitutional. Most of these invalidated practices were, in the opinion of most observers, logical adaptations of the Constitution's inherent flexibility. Consequently, it appeared to some that the Court majority was pursuing devolution in principle, rather than examining the practical intergovernmental aspects of administering policies supported by decided popular majorities. Three justices—Rehnquist, O'Connor, and Scalia—were the most decidedly states rights

in principle. States rights is frequently viewed as a contemporary conservative political trend, being rooted in the proslavery Confederacy movement that led to the Civil War. It was compromised by the war's results, as well as by the Fourteenth Amendment, which the Supreme Court employed to enforce civil rights legislation, the most noteworthy example being the 1954 *Brown* decision.

The dissenters in the above cases consistently alluded to the practical need for cooperation and flexibility in federal-state relations. These justices, led by Justices John Paul Stevens and David Souter, profoundly disagreed with the narrow court majority. In their dissents, they frequently argued that the new trend—which has major implications for federal policies regulating the environment, business, and minority rights—leaves states unaccountable for power abuses, be they intentional or not. For example, in a 1996 ruling that reversed a famous 1989 decision that required the state of Pennsylvania to assume part of the cost of cleaning up a river that it had helped pollute, the Rehnquist Court determined that the state could claim immunity from such an obligation under the Constitution's Eleventh Amendment, which prohibits citizens of one state from suing the government of another. In this case, an Indian tribe located mostly outside Pennsylvania was economically dependent on the waters of the stream that had been polluted by out-of-state forces. Court moderates felt that decisions such as this were regressive, amounting to a return to the relaxed legislative climate of the 1890s. During that period, Congress and the courts rolled back many post–Civil War Reconstruction laws, thereby permitting states to claim state sovereignty, or states rights, as a justification for their continued support of racial segregation. In essence, the argument is that the federal government's delegated powers imply that it, the federal government, has an obligation to enact legislation to make states accountable for the enforcement of rights the federal government guarantees to its citizens.

Advocates of judicial federalism invariably argue that states and localities have the unique ability to identify their own problems and make their own decisions about how to deal with those problems. States should not, so goes the argument, be mere administrative subcontractors for the federal government's edicts. The constitutional base for such a position is a literal interpretation of the Tenth Amendment. However, if the matter of equality, especially as it impacts on the rights of minorities, is employed as a standard to judge the integrity of a policy, then such an approach is wrought with hazards. Not only does it undercut the federal government's responsibility to enforce the administration of rights it (the federal government) must guarantee, but it also is at odds with the practical need to ensure equality of policy administration for all people in all states.

This is why judicial federalism has serious long-term implications for public policy. It could be argued that, in assuming such a crusade, the Supreme Court is merely following a contour in public opinion that has been notably discernable since Watergate and Vietnam. There is a good deal of merit in this position. However, it is also true that justices can use their lifetime tenure status to leverage policies and procedures to which they are committed by virtue of their background and experiences. This is why Edward Lazarus's analysis of the Rehnquist Court's bias toward judicial federalism is so interesting and timely.[80] A former law clerk to Justice Harry Blackmun, Lazarus argues that what herein has been termed "judicial federalism" is rooted in the state and regional orientation of the justices themselves. Justice Souter's liberalism on the question of federal-state relations, according to Lazarus, was rooted in New Hampshire's Civil War era–rooted New

England Republicanism, which avidly opposed the Confederacy, and therefore a post-war acceptance of a states rights argument. The tradition of frontier individualism and self-reliance, and therefore a healthy respect for states rights, affected the attitude of Justices O'Connor (Arizona), Kennedy (California), and Chief Justice Rehnquist (Arizona) when they sided with the states on most federalism issues that faced the Rehnquist Court. Justices Scalia and Thomas, the other two devolution advocates, were so more because of ideology than of regional influence. Lazarus notes that the above five justices, constituting a narrow court majority, pay little heed to judicial self-restraint when it comes to questions of nation-state relations. Rather, they pursue activist-inspired policy devolution with zeal when it comes to questions of federal-state power. Ironically, the sectional tensions that led to the Civil War, expanded and adapted to the conservatism of the frontier, continue to impact on politics and government, and their impact is leveraged significantly if court votes on nation-state relations reflect such regional orientations. Lazarus maintains that they do.

To a degree, the Court's orientation is reflective of what might be termed a discernable trend toward "cultural regionalism" in the United States. Urbanization, industrialization, and the ease of migration have encouraged individuals of like-minded attitudes about the role of government in their lives to gravitate to regions populated by people of similar persuasions. They tend to cast votes for or against parties and candidates on the basis of their commitment in principle to either rugged individualism or government paternalism, and possibly some variation in between. According to Michael Barone, voting in the 1996 elections reflected such a trend. In analyzing the 1996 vote, Barone divided the country into five regions—New England, South Atlantic, Mississippi Valley, Interior, and Pacific Rim. He concluded that some regions, notably New England and the Interior (Rocky Mountain and plains states), are becoming more "monopartisan." New England was becoming more liberal and Democratic, and the Interior region was becoming more conservative and Republican. Barone also noted an increased tendency for straight-ticket voting in 1996, a trend consistent with the trend toward cultural regionalism.[81] The Rehnquist Court's bias toward judicial federalism reinforces the cultural overtones to the 1996 vote. However, that does not harbor good things for effective policy coordination between and among states, or between states and the federal government. Very few policy problems are exclusively state or regional in character. Therefore, adequate solutions to these problems cannot focus exclusively on states or regions as separate geographic entities. Consequently, at the very time policy problems and their possible solutions are assuming an increasingly multistate and multiregion compass, voters and the Supreme Court are promoting just the opposite—a mindset nourishing state sovereignty and political independence from one another and from the federal government.

Finally, the Supreme Court's docket incorporates a healthy slice of the nation's policy agenda. The social, political, and economic interests of minorities underlie much of that agenda. As cases reach the Supreme Court, asking it to rule on the equity quality of federally imposed restrictions on state discretion, minorities will have much at stake, because it is they who have historically suffered the most from variations in state commitments to their interests. If Lazarus is correct, and regionalism continues to influence Court decisions on federal-state relations, and split decisions continue to give narrow victories to the idea of renewing state powers in principle, such a procedural fetish could well undermine the equity objectives that nationally imposed policy standards have, for over half a century, sought and often attained.

The Rehnquist Court and Cautious Activism

While the Rehnquist Court, through 1997, did issue judgments that altered well-accepted policy traditions and administrative procedures, with the exception of Justices Scalia, Thomas, and occasionally Kennedy and Rehnquist, the court majority frequently was very conscious of the need to incorporate public opinion and both national and state legislative judgment into policy questions on which they ruled. In most of the decisions mentioned above, the court was very careful not to issue definitive decisions that did not leave room for legislatures and administrators to supplement the decisions with actions of their own that might well be constitutional.[82] Take, for example, the decision that invalidated parts of the Brady Act. Although the court did rule, by a 5–4 vote, that Congress could not mandate registration and investigation procedures affecting purchasers of firearms, only Scalia and Thomas insisted on negating any federally imposed procedures entirely. Although she sided with the majority in the case, Justice O'Connor wrote a separate opinion arguing that the decision was not as profound as it may appear, because there were ways other than prepurchase investigations to achieve the act's objectives. The same was true for the assisted suicide ruling. Some of the justices, including Scalia, Thomas, and Chief Justice Rehnquist, argued for an absolute ban against any claim for physician-assisted suicide. However, O'Connor, again siding with the majority on the decision, in a separate opinion noted that the ruling only meant that the Ninth Amendment should not be interpreted to include the right to commit suicide. She noted that the Court did not say that a competent person faced with a terminal illness could not arrange for a physician-assisted suicide. That issue may well be resolved in another case, but it was not in the 1997 ruling. Justice O'Connor was often joined by Justices Breyer, Ginsburg, Stevens, and Souter in assuming such a position on questions involving claimed fundamental rights by way of the Ninth Amendment and the due process clauses contained in the Fifth and Fourteenth Amendments. This group of justices had, in 1997 and in previous terms, written similar opinions in noting the limited applications of the rulings on Internet pornography, the constitutionality of drawing congressional districts to accommodate racial minorities, the application of affirmative action standards, the rights of homosexuals, and the application of punitive damage awards in civil cases.

With the exception of Justices Scalia, Thomas, and sometimes Justice Kennedy and the Chief Justice himself, the Rehnquist Court was inclined to back away from issuing clear, definitive, absolute rulings on the constitutionality of rights questions. In effect, this showed a deference for the deliberative processes within Congress, the state legislatures, and bureaucracies. It was certainly true that the court's ideologically conservative "bloc" was able to organize split-vote majorities on most of the key constitutional issues that came before them. On the other hand, the decisions had select, not universal, application. The Court backed away from broad, absolute, universal rulings like that of the *Brown* decision. While this attitude certainly would not qualify the Rehnquist court as one dominated by a self-restraint attitude, it certainly means that its judicial activism was, at least through 1997, more cautious and constrained than some observers were willing to acknowledge. In sum, the Court majority acknowledged that, in Professor Cass Sunstein's terms, "judgments about basic principle are a political as well as a judicial responsibility."[83]

Courts, Democracy, and Public Policy: A Critique

Judicial activism has become an institutionalized part of the policy drama. Its source is the Constitution. The separation of powers, reinforced by judges' lifetime tenure status, enables courts to be bold with policy initiatives when circumstances suit an activist position. Circumstances are becoming more and more appropriate, both politically and institutionally. Legislation is often ambiguous for political reasons, and the courts are often asked to intervene to clarify ambiguous statutes. Rights have been privatized, encouraging individuals and groups to seek economic gain through a rights strategy. Courts must often rule on the legitimacy of such claims, and that makes their role central to determining how resources are distributed in society and the economy.

Public policies are becoming more technically complicated, and many of them are being subjected to major devolutionary pressures. All these trends invite judicial involvement. It is impossible to expect courts to be neutral on policy issues, because however issues are resolved, there will be both winners and losers. By and large, courts render decisions that are humane, and therefore democratic in a substantive sense. However, this should not detract from the fact that, from a procedural point of view, courts are oligarchic and undemocratic. They become more democratic in fact because their success rests on the acceptance of both their roles and rulings by the public and members of governmental institutions selected by the public. Most of the policy questions decided by courts are not momentous ones. However, some are highly significant. When major policies are determined by the courts, especially the Supreme Court, the fact that they are rendered within the context of the Constitution affords them considerable legitimacy. Because of this, the Supreme Court occasionally renders decisions that are clearly antimajoritarian. The Court's constitutional position as a separate, independent branch, relieved of electoral politics, enables it to have an impact on policy that would be impractical if it were fused more formally with electoral politics.

The major challenge to the courts as policy instruments, therefore, is to maintain a loyalty to a Constitution that is strong because of its adaptability, and not be imprisoned by doctrinaire commitment to pursue any substantive policy or government procedure as an end unto itself. More than anything, it is the responsibility of judges in a democratic society, in the course of making decisions, to make as few "points" and as much "sense" as possible.

Endnotes

1. David M. O'Brien, *Storm Center: The Supreme Court in American Politics*, 2nd ed. (New York: W. W. Norton, 1990), pp. 245–247.

2. As quoted in *Ibid.*, p. 247.

3. *Ibid.*

4. *Ibid.*, p. 248.

5. 1 Cranch 137 (1803).

6. Robert A. Burt, *The Constitution in Conflict* (Cambridge, Mass.: The Belknap Press of Harvard University Press, 1992), p. 52.

7. *Ibid.*, pp. 68–69.

8. *Ibid.*, pp. 68–73.

9. *Ibid.*, p. 78.

10. 347 U.S. 483 (1954).

11. Robert A. Burt, *op. cit.*, p. 303.

12. *Ibid.*, p. 374.

13. 4 Wheaton 316 (1819).

14. 410 U.S. 113 (1973).

15. 297 U.S. 1 (1936). See also John P. Roche, "Judicial Self-Restraint," *American Political Science Review*, vol. 49 (September 1955).

16. 328 U.S. 549 (1946).

17. 369 U.S. 186 (1962).

18. See Mark Gittenstein, *Matters of Principle: An Insider's Account of America's Rejection of Robert Bork's Nomination to the Supreme Court* (New York: Simon & Schuster, 1992).

19. Lawrence Baum, "Supreme Court Activism and the Constitution," in Peter F. Narduli, ed., *The Constitution and American Political Development* (Urbana: University of Illinois Press, 1992), p. 157.

20. *Ibid.*

21. *Ibid.*, p. 159.

22. R. Shep Melnick, "The Courts, Congress, and Programmatic Rights," in Richard A. Harris and Sidney M. Milkis, eds., *Remaking American Politics* (Boulder, Colo.: Westview Press, 1989), p. 190.

23. *Ibid.*, p. 191.

24. *Ibid.*, pp. 191–192.

25. *Ibid.*, p. 193.

26. See Alexander M. Bickel, "The Civil Rights Act of 1964," *Commentary*, vol. 33 (August 1964), p. 30; Nathan Glazer, *Affirmative Discrimination: Ethnic Inequality and Public Policy* (New York: Basic Books, 1978); and Gary Bryner, "Congress, Courts, and Agencies: Equal Employment and the Limits of Policy Implementation," *Political Science Quarterly*, vol. 93 (1981), p. 411.

27. Melnick, *op. cit.*, p. 194.

28. Martin Shapiro, "APA: Past, Present, and Future," *Virginia Law Review*, vol. 72 (1986), p. 451., as cited in *Ibid.*, p. 207.

29. Mary Ann Glendon, *Rights Talk: The Impoverishment of Political Discourse* (New York: Free Press, 1991).

30. *Ibid.*, p. 12.

31. See Benjamin R. Barber, "The Reconstruction of Rights," *The American Prospect* (Spring 1991), p. 44.

32. Amitai Etzioni, *The Spirit of Community: Rights, Responsibilities, and the Communitarian Agenda* (New York: Crown, 1993), p. 253, as quoted in William E. Hudson, *American Democracy in Peril*, 2nd ed. (New York: Chatham House, 1998), p. 318. Hudson's discussion of the "pathologies of rights" (pp. 98–108) is exemplary.

33. Hudson, *op. cit.*, p. 106.

34. Glendon, *op. cit.*, pp. xi–iii.

35. Jim Sleeper, *Liberal Racism* (New York: Viking Press, 1997).

36. Michael J. Sandel, *Democracy's Discontent: America in Search of a Public Philosophy* (Cambridge, Mass.: The Belknap Press of Harvard University Press, 1996), pp. 274–275.

37. *Ibid.*, p. 346.

38. 397 U.S. 254 (1970).

39. R. Shep Melnick, *op. cit.*, pp. 198–199.

40. *Calvert Cliffs Coordinating Committee* v. *AEC* (449 F. 2d) at 1111, as quoted in *Ibid.*, p. 200.

41. *EDF* v. *Ruckelshaus* (439 F.2d 584 (1971) at 598, as quoted in *Ibid.*, p. 201.

42. See William E. Leuchtenburg, "The Origins of Franklin D. Roosevelt's "Court-Packing" Plan," *The Supreme Court Review* (1966), ed. Philip B. Kurland (Chicago: University of Chicago Press, 1966).

43. As quoted in "Bashing the Bench," *National Journal*, vol. 29, no. 22 (May 31, 1997), pp. 1078–1079.

44. As quoted in *Ibid.*, p. 1079.

45. *Ibid.*, p. 1081.

46. Kirk Victor, "Judgement Day," *National Journal*, vol. 29, no. 21 (May 25, 1996), p. 1141.

47. *Ibid.*, p. 1143.

48. Victor, "Bashing the Bench," p. 1079.

49. *Ibid.*, p. 1081.

50. As quoted in Fred Barbash, "Congress Didn't, So the Supreme Court Did," *Washington Post National Weekly Edition* (July 13, 1998), p. 21. The above examples were drawn from this essay.

51. *Ibid.*

52. As quoted in Robert A. Kagan, "Adversarial Legalism and American Government," *Journal of Policy Analysis and Management*, vol. 10, no. 3 (1991), p. 395.

53. *Ibid.*, p. 396.

54. *Ibid.*, pp. 369–406.

55. *Ibid.*, p. 372.

56. *Ibid.*

57. *Ibid.*, pp. 381–384.

58. *Ibid.*, p. 386.

59. Marc K. Landy and Mary Hague, "Private Interests and Superfund," *The Public Interest*, no. 108 (Summer 1992), as quoted and referenced in Susan Rosegrant, "Wichita Confronts Contamination," Case Program, John F. Kennedy School of Government, Harvard University, 1992. Excerpts reprinted in Richard J. Stillman, *Public Administration: Concepts and Cases*, 6th ed. (Boston: Houghton Mifflin, 1996), p. 151.

60. *Ibid.*

61. Kagan, *op. cit.*, p. 370.

62. Jonathan Rauch, "Tunnel Vision," *National Journal*, vol. 30, no. 38 (September 19, 1998), p. 2148.

63. *Ibid.*, p. 2149.

64. *Ibid.*

65. *Ibid.*, pp. 2149–2150.

66. *Ibid.*

67. *Ibid.*, p. 2150.

68. *Ibid.*, p. 2152.

69. *Ibid.*, p. 2153.

70. 424 U.S. 1 (1974).

71. *Ibid.*

72. David K. Ryden, *Representation in Crisis: The Constitution, Interest Groups, and Political Parties* (Albany: State University of New York Press, 1996), p. 1.

73. *Ibid.*, pp. 1–3, 179–192.

74. *Ibid.*, p. 2.

75. 410 U.S. 113 (1973).

76. *Immigration and Naturalization Service* v. *Chadha*, 454 U.S. 812 (1983).

77. 418 U.S. 683 (1974).

78. As quoted in Joan Biskupic, "Gaveling Back the Imperial Presidency," *Washington Post National Weekly Edition* (June 9, 1997), p. 21.

79. As quoted in *Ibid.*, p. 21.

80. Edward Lazarus, "The Geography of Justice," *U.S. News and World Report* (July 7, 1997).

81. Michael Barone, "Divide and Rule," *National Journal*, vol. 29, no. 28 (July 12, 1997), pp. 1408–1412. This article was adapted from the introduction to the *Almanac of American Politics 1998*, authored by Barone and Grant Ujifusa, and published by the *National Journal*.

82. Cass R. Sunstein, "In the Court of Cautious Opinions," *Washington Post National Weekly Edition*, vol. 14, no. 37 (July 14, 1997), pp. 22–23.

83. *Ibid.*, p. 23.

chapter thirteen

Constitutional Politics and Public Policy

Problems, Possibilities, and Prospects

A fear of the dangerous policy potential of mob rule, especially its possible threat to property rights, directed the founding fathers toward a representative democracy, or republic. They concluded that a republican government, held at bay by the possible imposition of official restraints imposed by nonrepublican institutions, was the most practical solution to problems introduced by the colonies' experiences with the British Crown before the Revolutionary War and by the Articles of Confederation. Supposedly representative government would help protect people from their own passions and provide the stability necessary to govern the country effectively while preserving individual liberties. John Adams once warned: "Remember, democracy never lasts long. It soon wastes, exhausts, and murders itself. There never was a democracy that did not commit suicide." Pure democracy, a condition under which citizens of small communities govern themselves directly, is theoretically possible only in very small communities. However, the idea can be transposed and modified to apply to larger societies by incorporating the representative mechanism as the vehicle whereby public opinion is translated into public policy. However, even the representative principle can be misdirected and therefore, according to the framers, it was necessary to place several constitutionally rooted structural "filters" between the public's agents and ultimate policy decisions. The U.S. Constitution, both originally and as modified, both officially and by custom, does just that.

In fact, these filters inhibit pure democracy. However, because they are an integral and historically accepted part of our system, most Americans do not bother to distinguish between our system and systems with more direct linkages between the public and policy outcomes. However, when these very structural forces help prevent government from offering coherent policy remedies to pressing problems, Americans become discouraged and cynical. We still believe in our constitutionally filtered system of self-government, but what it produces all too often doesn't seem to fit current policy realities. Often the obvious gap between truth and trust is so apparent and, in fact, so painful that we turn away from its obvious implications. Government by the people as a measure of our democracy's health seems ineffective in the face of a policy system that increasingly caters to economically privileged interests at the expense of the public in general. Ironically, these were the types of interests the framers sought to control through the Constitution-based structural fragmentation of governmental power. Now these forces exploit that fragmented power to embed their values in public policy while, all too often, responding to public necessities with solutions that are more symbolic than real. This is not because these forces are congenitally bad. Rather, it is because they are far too isolated from the values of rank-and-file America to advance coherent policy agendas that address the nation's long-term policy needs.

The Constitution is a document that, by its assignment of policy power to separate institutions that must share policymaking responsibilities, and by its guarantee of communications rights, encourages the political balance so prized by the framers. The framers assumed that a healthy balance among contending political forces ultimately leads to self-correction when unpopular and unrealistic values temporarily become popular. Democracy assumes that government adjusts to the realities and demands of change only after listening to what the public says is necessary. The public as a whole usually speaks the language of pragmatism, not that of the extremes. It is no accident that, over the past two centuries, public policy has usually reflected pragmatism and balance. The Constitution, either directly or through extra-constitutional institutions and practices that have been conditioned by it, has played a key role in encouraging policy to reflect the balance the framers thought to be essential. These balancing and self-correcting features have been so commonplace that we often forget to associate them with the founders' design.

For decades America has been beset with policy problems that demand government intervention into the affairs of individuals and corporations. Given such conditions, a constitution originally designed to prevent arbitrary action can be put to its best use only if those powers deliberately fragmented to enhance safety can be employed to encourage a healthy competition of ideas and policy experimentation. In theory, this alternative holds potential. Competition for power between the two major parties and among interest groups is framed, in fact, by the constitutional fragmentation of power and its guarantee of communications freedoms. The probe of government activity by the press is rooted in the same rights guarantees. The organic tension among three constitutionally co-equal branches of government and the natural competition among issue networks that surfaces when policy imperatives take a regulatory or redistributive turn are all illustrative of the political and policy balance encouraged by the Constitution.

Unfortunately, while the formalities of balance are still very much a part of the official political and policy scenes, their beneficial impact on policy appears to be waning. Elections are still held according to the Constitution's prescribed timetable. The two major political parties still exist very much in form and, as always, usually offer the only realistic way for aspirants to office to gain ballot respectability. The president and both houses of Congress, as always, must cooperate to produce legislation. The media is probably more involved than ever in covering public affairs and public figures. However, these institutions and processes are losing their ability to provide the political balance and policy pragmatism that they usually have in the past. Elections are dominated by privileged contributors and a sensationalist-oriented press. Political parties do not have much policy or financial influence in elections, and have thereby lost much of their ability to rally their candidates and rank-and-file members around meaningful policy principles. The president and Congress often strike agreements that reflect institutional and political deadlock, and therefore are often far too incremental, symbolic, or back-loaded to be very meaningful. The media are often too enamored with the sensationalist and newsworthy story to offer citizens the opportunity to examine and debate the intricacies of policy options. Instead of creating a bureaucracy dedicated to the efficient, objective administration of public policy, the separation of powers condition has encouraged administrative agencies to be patently political in their search for sources of support that can provide them with the security and longevity they seek. In short, the historical advantages that the Constitution has harbored for representational and institutional balance, policy pragmatism, and procedural self-correction have degenerated and offer little hope for a quick recovery. Some possible reasons for this condition, together with some proposals that may help the Constitution and the political system regain some of their lost vitality, are discussed in the sections that follow.

The Constitution as Creed

Americans' reverence for the Constitution and the mission of the framers has, in a sense, blinded them to a fundamental cause for the current policy crisis. Our tendency to condemn a politics and policy scenario significantly influenced by the Constitution on the one hand, together with the corresponding tendency to increasingly cherish the document and the framers' incentives on the other, encourages two negative results. First, it causes us to look for other causes for the current policy predicament and blame those elements more than we should. If the framers cannot possibly be blamed, their heirs must be responsible. Ambitious politicians, the media, vested interests, and minority groups have, collectively, thrown the Constitution "off course." Second, it escalates the level of public pessimism, even cynicism, about politics and government.

Daniel Lazare calls this timeless and extraordinary faith in the founders' assumed wisdom our "civic religion," and concludes that such a frame of mind is very dangerous. It is dangerous because we do not realize that our unfettered faith in the framers' judgment is irrational. Because the Constitution is our civic religion, to question its germaneness to the policy needs of the twenty-first century is, for want of a better term, sacrilegious. However, according to Lazare, we should recognize that the founders drafted the Constitution for different political conditions at a very, very different time in our political history. To consider the Constitution the model of civic and democratic perfection is collective self-delusion, and such a mindset underlies the excruciating gap between our expectations and what the current system actually delivers.[1] In fact, current policy problems are not the blemished manifestations of a perfect constitutional design. Instead, they are the result of a defective master plan designed to structurally frustrate the expression of popular sovereignty at a time when it was politically acceptable to do so, and may well have been necessary.

However, according to Lazare, this is not the case today. This is one of those eras, faced by all governments from time to time, when a nation needs to cast aside old presumptions and develop new standards of civic action. America cannot afford to be constrained by immutable reverence to the notion of constitutionally decreed institutional power balance or, for that matter, by an immutable worship of the document itself. Neither the public or its elected representatives should suffocate themselves in the rush to keep the "Faith" or the "Word" that is, to most of us, synonymous with the Constitution. To do so can only exacerbate the problems of urban areas, housing, education, environmental pollution, race relations, and so on. The framers' governmental system was deliberately unresponsive. Responsiveness should be the highest priority in today's political world. Most important, citizens must shoulder this responsibility themselves. Neither they, nor the country, can afford to damn the government and the politicians that have, presumably, lost the Faith. In short, rather than looking to the founders for help, the public must resolve to help itself.[2]

The framers wanted the Constitution to thwart majority rule. Now it needs to be encouraged. Because of a culturally nurtured reverence for the Constitution, citizens fail to appreciate the connection between it and the formation of meaningful majorities. Although more than two centuries have passed since the Constitution's ratification, it is still popular to advance an act on the notion that it is good to distrust majority rule. The results of such an attitude have been profound. We believe both in democracy and in the antimajoritarian pitch of the Constitution, blinding ourselves to the inherent contradiction between the two assumptions. Most Americans would very likely consider separation of powers, checks and balances, federalism, and judicial review as prerequisites of democracy when, in fact, they usually work to impede it. Nearly a century ago, J. Allen Smith commented on this irony with words that are as relevant today as they were when he first penned them. He noted that constitutional literature "has been too much preoccupied with the thought of defending and glorifying the work of the fathers and not enough interested in disclosing its true relation to present day thought and tendencies. . . . It is this contradiction in our thinking that has been one of our chief sources of difficulty in dealing with political problems. . . . While honestly believing that we have been endeavoring to make democracy a success, we have at the same time tenaciously held on to the essential features of a political system designed for the purpose of defeating the ends of popular government."[3]

Popular government assumes the existence of a majority and a minority that is constructively critical of the majority's actions. Both Smith and Lazare suggest that the registration of majority will has been thwarted by the public's unwillingness to sever its culturally embedded reverence of the Constitution and update it to make it more majoritarian. This assumes the existence of a majority, albeit a frustrated one. However, there is no solid evidence to suggest that this is the case. To the contrary, some scholars have argued that it is unrealistic to expect a nation so culturally, ethnically, economically, and socially diverse as is the United States to produce a majority actuated by policy goals that unite its members. Voters want periodic opportunities to choose parties and leaders that will make decisions on their behalf, and subsequent opportunities to reject and remove these individuals from office if the policies they enact are judged by the voters to be inappropriate. Voters in general do not want the responsibility of choosing a set of comprehensive policies themselves because they, the voters, do not exist as a single public. They are torn among many contradictions and prefer not to resolve the problem themselves. They do not know what policies are theoretically sound and administratively workable. In general, voters would rather pass the buck to elected officials and then react to what they do.

Such an argument has considerable merit. The United States has always been more accurately described as a nation of varied minorities than one with clear policy demarcations dividing a single majority and a single minority. Nonetheless, often these minorities coalesce in unmistakable support of major policy changes that privileged factions exploiting the current constitutional system are able to defeat. Recent examples include comprehensive health care reform, meaningful campaign finance reform, and significant gun control legislation. In each case, cohesive, well-financed, well-organized, and well-connected vested interests were able to thwart the majority will. Consequently, constitutional, statutory, and administrative reforms directed at correcting this condition should be considered seriously.

Constitutional Politics and Public Policy: The Condition

The American Constitution is a multipurpose document. First, it serves as a measure of ethical judgment, or gauge of legitimacy, by which the actions of individuals, their elected representatives, and administrative officials can be judged. Second, through the principle of constitutionalism, or the rule of law, it prescribes that public behavior be governed by constitutional or statutory edicts. Third, it assigns power to governing institutions, and prescribes conditions under which those powers can be applied. Finally, it guarantees citizens certain fundamental rights—both substantive and procedural—that cannot be denied them by government in the course of their daily lives, or under conditions in which their lives, liberties, or property are threatened by governmental action.

The American Constitution surfaced as a practical solution to problems faced by a na-

tion newly exonerated from unitary control by a noncontinental power. Its natural reaction was to produce a government whose powers were too meager and uncentralized to meet the basic challenges of governing. The Constitution surfaced as a pragmatic solution to the impotency of the Articles of Confederation. Part of that solution was for the new Constitution to mandate government to do more than it could under the Articles. However, in so doing, the Constitution became the center of a power struggle over exactly how those new powers were to be employed. What has herein been labeled "constitutional politics" is, in essence, an idea that studies and evaluates the efforts made by individuals, groups, politicians, and judges to apply the Constitution's original faith to the real world in ways that help them personally or politically, or help them perform more effectively as public servants. The result of these efforts has been the *de facto* conversion of the Constitution into a document that, very frequently, leverages the ability of these forces to work their will in the policy processes. The Constitution is employed as an ally in crusades to advance some policy causes, and deter others.

Society and its policy challenges have changed dramatically in the past two centuries. The Constitution sought to prevent the arbitrary rule of hasty majorities. Now the challenge is to alert majorities to the need to employ politics, statutes, and the Constitution in ways that allow majorities to govern themselves effectively. In sum, a document that was conceived largely to prevent bad decisions must now be utilized in ways that help government make good policy decisions. That challenge is compounded by at least three factors. First, the challenge to make good policy decisions in today's world means making decisions that affect several sectors of society simultaneously. Second, most of those policies are going to demand that many individuals and groups sacrifice their indulgences for the common good, as elusive as that concept may be. Third, although today's policy problems virtually mandate that governments at all levels be involved in their solution, a morality-based preventive political culture is still very much a part of the contemporary political and governmental scene. The last factor is very significant, because if governments in general, or a level of government in particular, attempt(s) to do things that people conclude are beyond the moral scope of that jurisdiction, it is very difficult to overcome those positions by the normal routines of politics. Samuel Huntington once observed that, in the United States, "polarization occurs over moral issues rather than economic ones. . . ." It is Americans' "moral passions" that distinguish our politics from that of our sister democracies.[4]

This is a major challenge. The following discussion and analysis will examine its prospects. The assumption, indeed the hope, is that the public will allow the Constitution to meet the challenges while still preserving its (the Constitution's) integrity as a document which mixes the need to guarantee individual liberties on the one hand, and the need to govern effectively on the other. Ultimately, it is the public that allows the document to be used as it is used. That is why the discussion's emphasis will not be on the need to reform or amend the Constitution. That is very difficult to accomplish, especially on matters as fundamental as altering the principles of separation of powers, checks and balances, and federalism. More important, it is the public and its elected representatives that give meaning to any democratic government, regardless of its official structure. If an overwhelming majority of people want significant policy changes, they will transpire, regardless of governmental structure. Historian Arthur Schlesinger, Jr., once observed that "agitation about constitutional reform is a form of escapism. . . .

Fascinating as constitution-tinkering may be, like the Rubic cube, let it not divert us from the real task of statecraft. Let us never forget that politics is the higher and serious art of solving substantive problems."[5]

On the other hand, if the public is divided and uncertain about the future course of public policy, then the constitutional proliferation of power among institutions and levels of government accentuates that uncertainty and ambivalence, thereby encouraging drift, delay, and conflict-of-interest politics. It discourages statecraft in the search for solutions to policy problems. Politics and policy stress the accommodation of vested interests at the expense of the more serious, and arduous, task of dealing with problems comprehensively and for the long term.

Therefore, structure is highly significant to explaining both policy impasses and ways to extricate ourselves from them. This book would not have been written were structure not critical to policy in both an input and catalytic sense. Structure and institutional design can expedite or impede the capability of governments to respond to policy challenges. Hopefully, the discussion below will highlight just how important structural factors are to policy. However, it is to say that the right set of political circumstances can overcome impediments imposed by structure on the ability of governments to produce meaningful public policies. Therefore, as out of date as the Constitution may appear to some who seek meaningful policy changes, those changes can occur in spite of the procedural barriers offered by the Constitution to impede them. In fact, it could be argued that, if the Constitution's rights guarantees and procedural attributes were employed to channel public opinion in a direction more attuned to the public's long-term needs, the document could actually facilitate, rather than impede, meaningful policy reform.

Naturally, the questions of what is the right

direction and what are those long-term needs quickly surface. The first can be answered efficiently. Policies need to be more proactive, as opposed to reactive, in cast. They should incorporate current policy trends in an effort to prevent their worsening in the future. Sound, responsible policies stress ways to prevent problems from developing or, if they exist, prevent their future escalation. They need to be developed by leaders who can read and interpret social and economic trends, articulate goals, connect the realization of those goals with logical ways of attaining them, and convince the public that patience and sacrifice will pay off in the long run. Austerity and patience can become viable political options, especially in an era marked by growing public pessimism about a government that cannot seem to free itself from the chains of conflict-of-interest politics.

The question of how to judge the public interest quality of policies is as old as government itself, and this effort will offer no special insight. Such an effort involves value judgments, and no method has ever been discovered that enables one to determine the inherent superiority of one value over another by any objective measure. It is much easier for an individual to judge what policies are bad than it is for him or her to determine what ones are good. We tend to consider those policies that affect us negatively as bad, and those that affect us favorably as good. It is common for politicians to cloak the policies they favor with a public interest label, using the well-being of those to whom the policy is directed as the sole criterion for such a classification.

Therefore, a defendable way to develop a standard for judging a policy's long-term integrity, and therefore its public interest quality, is to relate it to values that most Americans would like to see incorporated into policies focused on the long term. These values should be articulated clearly in advance of specific proposals geared toward achieving them. This is because individuals are more likely to be tolerant of sacrifice and develop patience with specific policies if they think it likely they will help achieve long-term policies embodying their shared values. One of these values is the long-term improvement in the quality of life for all, especially today's underprivileged. This, of course, impacts on policies in a number of areas, including education, housing, race relations, health care, recreation, and transportation. We will be divided on how exactly to achieve such a state, but we are more likely to be patient with policy decisions that are linked consistently by their supporters to the long-term realization of those values. Second, most Americans are likely to support most measures that show promise of making their participation in politics and community affairs more meaningful. This includes elections and other political party activities, as well as engaging and interacting with others through social capital networks. Policies that invite more direct public participation in policy decisions should be stressed. Efforts by any public official that explain carefully how difficult it is to make rational decisions when confronted with competing values and group pressures could trigger levels of public tolerance and patience that might well surprise even the most optimistic of persons.

The framers didn't anticipate a society, an economy, or, for that matter, a world that would demand so much of the constitution they produced. Therefore these changes will have to be realized in spite of, not because of, the barriers posed by the Constitution to decisions of the kind necessary to meet the challenges of the twenty-first century. On the other hand, the Constitution doesn't prevent such a policy course. In fact, it may provide opportunities not available to citizens and their governments in democracies with more homogeneous structures. Constitutionally separate institutions could become competitive forums of open debate that force advocates of certain policies to clarify and improve the "means-ends" linkages in the policies they champion.

Democratic governments must be both responsive and effective. Democracy involves government both "by the people" and "for the people." This is a very difficult challenge because there is not just one public, but many, and they want different, even incompatible things. While most individuals know what they want for themselves and their immediate family, they are less aware of the needs of those in their community, state, and nation. Their opinions on issues affecting those beyond their immediate circle are by no means fixed, but highly changeable, depending on how issues arise, how they are debated, and how individuals understand the alternatives. The public has a short policy memory, and is notably unable to connect current issues to past problems and how they were resolved.

To function effectively, democracy needs both an interested and informed public and leaders who inform them and keep them interested. Without both, it will either seriously underperform or even fail. The challenge to leaders in both intermediary and policymaking institutions is to offer the public alternative interpretations of what is both desirable and possible. If leaders are too responsive, the difficult questions are avoided. If they are too manipulative, they show disrespect for the very foundation of democratic government itself—the public. Citizens then begin to question the value of self-government, and often withdraw from their civic responsibilities. A healthy democracy obligates leaders to interact with citizens to stimulate discussion of policy issues and to encourage them to reexamine their values and assumptions. This is difficult, painstaking work that demands more than the usual amount of energy and patience. Furthermore, there is no guarantee

that a policy consensus will result. Social learning can breed tolerance, but it could also sharpen, not ameliorate, differences within the public, making consensus development even more difficult in the future. Often citizens will surrender in frustration and mandate leaders to make the decisions on their behalf. However, that is not what democracy is all about. It involves a joint, reflective, social learning experience between leaders and citizens.

The Constitution's fragmentation of policy power and governing obligations among institutions and levels of government has the potential to enhance this notion of "reflective democracy." Fragmented power encourages politicians to reflect on their thoughts, make their policy more relevant to the challenges at hand, and sharpen their policy arguments as they seek to increase the leverage of their parent institution, and therefore themselves, on policy decisions. Federalism fragments power geographically, but it also encourages states and communities to experiment with policy options. In short, the Constitution offers some hope for the policy challenges of the twenty-first century. However, it will take commitment, tenacity, and the desire to make constitutional politics an ally, not a foe, of effective democratic government.

Constitutional Politics and Public Policy: The Bond

Before offering a few options for improving both procedural and substantive democracy in the United States within the compass of the Constitution, it is advisable to summarize and highlight the impact of constitutional politics on public policy. With that goal in mind, the discussion turns first to a brief assessment of the effects of the Constitution, and how it has been used politically, on three critical public policy tracts—the effect on policy processes, the effect on the power and political profile of government institutions, and the effect on policy content. They are listed in no order of assessed importance.

1. *The Constitution's deliberate structural fragmentation of power increases the leverage of factions, or groups, in the policy process and ultimately in the content of public policy.* This is accomplished in two ways. First, it offers groups that want to defeat legislation multiple points of access to policy deliberation, any one of which can result in the defeat of a legislative proposal. If groups can get either house of Congress, the president, or the Supreme Court to say no to a policy proposal or, in the case of the Supreme Court, to a recently enacted policy, the policy is very likely dead. Second, because legislative and executive powers are separately composed under the Constitution, thereby encouraging institutional conflicts over public policy, iron triangle alliances that unite groups with congressional subcommittees and administrative bureaus to advance mutual policy goals become critical sources of the cooperation necessary to enact policy. The more inclusive-focused institutions—the presidency, cabinet departments, and the full committees in Congress—very often accept policies produced by these alliances because they are based on the "expert" analysis of legislative staffs and policy specialists in the bureaucracy, and because they very often involve the expenditure of money in ways that help endear politicians to their constituencies.

Furthermore, the group universe is not represented equally in government. The pressure system, in Schattschneider's terms, is biased toward the well-heeled groups representing corporations, labor unions, professional associations, trade associations, and some retirees. Not only does this introduce an equality of representation problem into the representative system, but it also encourages

members of these groups to buy their way out of any concern for society's underprivileged groups. They focus on recreation and educational opportunities they can finance for themselves, and are little concerned with using public policies to provide the same opportunities for the lesser privileged.

2. *Encouraged by the Constitution's allocation of policy powers to separate institutions, institutions seek to secure their own power base through political strategies favoring policies that are distributive in content.* Politicians find it rather painless and very politically rewarding to distribute advantages to constituents in the form of grants, entitlements, licenses, and many types of subsidies. This is, in essence, the politics of the pork barrel. Interest groups, administrative bureaus, and congressional subcommittees—the iron triangle components—are potent mostly because of their distributive policy orientation. Legislators of all political persuasions all agree that the mutual support of policies that serve the career aspirations of as many fellow legislators as possible is, simply put, painless and basically good politics. It is a way to develop cohesion out of a fragmented structure that encourages conflict rather than conciliation. Furthermore, because distributive policies often distribute rewards to members of well-organized and financially strong interest groups, such an orientation helps produce needed financial resources to run election campaigns that are becoming expensive because of their candidate-centered quality.

Perhaps the most significant problem with a government built on distributive, or service, policies is that it encourages individuals and organizations to expect more and more of the same. However, the distributive well is bound to run dry sooner or later, thereby dashing such hopes and expectations. Despite this inevitable fact of life, elected policymakers compete constantly for the public's favor with an assortment of distributive policies aimed at, to borrow an idea from economics, the highest level of marginal satisfaction for the most people. The trouble is that, in an effort to gain voter favor, politicians promise more return on investment than they can deliver. This has been a constant problem for presidents, and it is probably the most important reason behind the rapid turnover in that office during the twentieth century, a century during which very few presidents enjoyed two elected terms of incumbency. Of the nineteenth-century presidents (including McKinley), only five completed two or more elected terms of office. In addition, the national government's bias toward distributive policies has increased its obligations and dependencies to the point of sapping its ability to meet new challenges with vigor and meaningful financial support.

3. *The Constitution's fragmentation of institutional power introduces problems of policy responsiveness and accountability to government.* Politicians can have the best of both worlds if they can find ways to enjoy the rewards of public office and dodge many of the responsibilities. Under these conditions, discovering ways to escape the responsibility for policies gone bad is just good politics. If the president and both the House and Senate agree on a policy, and it doesn't produce the intended results, often none of the three is willing to accept responsibility for the failure. Each can argue that the policy would have been better had its position been the dominant one. Unfortunately, because constitutionally fragmented power makes separate institutions share the policy burden, compromises are necessary. Often lost or modified beyond significance in the compromise processes are the "creative" ideas produced by policy entrepreneurs within the individual branches. In short, there is a tendency for the shared policy responsibilities induced by the separation of powers to necessi-

tate interbranch and interhouse compromises that offer only marginal or incremental changes from the status quo. These can be very modest or bland in nature. If they fail, no person, party, or institution is willing to accept the responsibility for the result because their ideas were negotiated to impotency by the bargaining process itself. As will be noted below, divided government conditions exacerbate this problem.

The separation of powers was supposed to reduce government's responsiveness. It was a way to chill democracy's passions by filtering them through several constitutionally separate government institutions. The notion of limited government, by offering ways for minorities to thwart majorities, served the same objective. The defense of this rather comprehensive strategy of frustrating majorities was that, if majority ideas were intrinsically sound, they would ultimately defeat attempts to defeat them procedurally. The constitutional system would frustrate transient, passionate majorities, but not those with sound ideas produced by careful thought and debate. The integrity of the separation of powers was, therefore, based on the assumption that unwise majorities would be stifled, but that wise majorities would succeed.

Although it is clearly a matter of judgment, over the past two centuries the separation of powers often appears to have impeded what many would consider responsible policies backed by popular majorities. This structurally nourished bias against policy innovation finds illustration in the fact that the United States is the only industrialized democracy that does not provide all its citizens access to health care, either in the form of subsidized health care services or universal health insurance. This is the case despite the fact that public opinion polls have shown overwhelming support for such programs.[6] Other illustrations can be found in the successful efforts of a cohesive legislative minority of southern congressmen to block congressional consideration of civil rights proposals in the 1940s and 1950s. The National Rifle Association has been very successful in thwarting overwhelming popular majorities supporting gun control legislation. If citizen majorities strongly support reasonable legislation that is thwarted by minorities employing the separation of powers as their ally, not only is the system being unresponsive but also citizens grow cynical about the ability of government to respond to their claims. This, in turn, increases apathy and offers organized minorities more opportunities to fill the void and make government and its policies even more beholden to their interests.

The same can be said of accountability. The separation of powers tends to botch the ability of citizens to hold their elected representative accountable for his or her actions. Because of the shared powers reality, the president and Congress must cooperate to create and administer policy. However, voters are asked to hold them accountable in isolation from one another. Come election time, voters are asked to make qualitative judgments about how well things are going. If they find matters totally or partially unsatisfactory, then they (the voters) are shouldered with the responsibility of determining to what extent the president, the House, and the Senate are responsible. This becomes a virtual impossibility, because candidates seeking reelection deliberately misrepresent the record and their responsibility for it in an attempt to convince voters to reelect them. This problem is particularly acute during periods of divided government when one branch blames the other for policy failures. Even when there is clear bipartisan support for a policy that eventually goes bad, the public finds it exceedingly difficult to hold specific legislators in specific congressional positions accountable. The failure of the decision to deregulate the savings-and-loan industry offers an excellent illustration.

That fiasco cost taxpayers well over half a trillion dollars. Nonetheless, when it was revealed in 1988 (well before the elections), each branch of government and each political party immediately blamed the other. Politicians were so careful to cover their role in supporting the idea that it never surfaced as a key issue in the 1988 presidential campaign, nor in many House and Senate campaigns. Politicians knew very well that voters would not be able to hold either branch or either party responsible because all were, in fact, responsible.[7]

In addition, in an effort to avoid accountability for unpopular decisions, many politicians also exploit the delegation of vast amounts of policy discretion to the bureaucracy to this end. If a policy fails for whatever reason, then the bureaucracy can be blamed, not the well-intentioned politicians who were deferring to administrative experts to give meaning to programs by filling in the (policy) details.

4. *Because fragmented constitutional power introduces a "dual boss" environment (president and Congress) to the federal bureaucracy, administrators assume more of a political (and policy) role than they would under a unified, or parliamentary, system of government.* Congress creates administrative agencies, assigns them administrative and policy responsibilities, and budgets them. On the other hand, the president, as chief executive, supervises their day-to-day activities, makes recommendations for changes in their policy priorities, and often oversees their rule-making (policy) activities. Like legislators, administrators want as much career security as possible. They often can't find it within a system which often places the president and Congress at odds with each other. Therefore, especially if the agencies have distributive policy responsibilities, agencies seek support for their policy causes from the political arena. They find welcome allies in the interest group complex and the congressional subcommittee system. This explains the agencies' willing association with these forces to form iron triangles. Add to this condition their (the agencies') possession of abundant Congress-endowed policy discretion, and the potential political clout of the bureaucracy is increased accordingly.

The bureaucracy's response to interest groups is a development unforeseen by the Constitution's founders, and no doubt they would hold it in disdain. The founders expected factions to impact on the legislative, not the executive, process. They expected administration to be scientific and energetic, thereby functioning as a unified, objective counterbalance to the partisanship that inevitably would surface with Congress. This, they assumed, would be one way in which the separation of powers would be operationalized in day-to-day government. The executive branch, headed by the president, would offer a way for the public as a whole to be represented effectively because of the president's broad, inclusive constituency. In addition, such constituency inclusiveness provided one of several ways to mitigate the potentially excessive effect of one, or a few, factions on policy decisions.

Unfortunately, the impact of factions on congressional deliberations has been transplanted to the executive branch. Granting administrative agencies substantial amounts of policy discretion has made them the target of interest group pressures. Through the budgetary process, legislative investigations, and oversight hearings, bonds are forged between congressional subcommittees, administrative bureaus, and the corporate sector, usually in an effort to advance policy causes that are mutually advantageous to each. Each of these policy subgroups, or iron triangles, is not monitored regularly and, unless faced with major proposed budget cuts or a scandal, is left to bore its own policy "comfort zone" within government.

From a constitutional point of view, these alliances operate in a world virtually unimpacted by the separation of powers. Their decisions are dominated by the same policy incentives, or norms. Administrative agencies are impacted by the same forces that impact Congress. The framers wanted the bureaucracy to be objective, inclusive, and decisive. Its politicalization has made it partisan, exclusive, and incremental. Both the spirit and operational reality of the separation of powers is working in ways contrary to the founders' intentions.

5. *Fragmented constitutional power often results in divided government which, in turn, exacerbates some problems of governance, especially the ability to establish and maintain loyalty to a set of long-term policy priorities.* Divided government lowers elite cohesion and increases the importance of the veto points (discussed above) to the policy process. It encourages short-term electoral pressures on both the president and Congress to increase their usage of the accountability blame game as a way to assuage constituents, at least temporarily. Policy deadlocks often encourage politicians to give all groups more than they deserve in the face of the negative impact of interbranch policy impasses on government's ability to plan. This often exacerbates the problem of government deficits.

6. *Accordingly, the realities of divided government, or even unified government under weak party conditions, often result in incremental, bipartisan "solutions" to policy problems that desperately need long-term, comprehensive attention.* Sometimes the bipartisan middle can become the "bipartisan muddle," giving public policies a marginal, incremental, accommodative flavor that does little more than buy time for electoral-conscious politicians while the policy problems themselves continue to compound. Sometimes, the political middle is the only realistic solution to a policy problem. Campaign finance reform is probably one such problem. However, more often than not, adequate policy solutions are not centrist solutions. They are innovative ideas produced either by reasoned debate among politicians and citizens, or by the commitment of a well-disciplined majority party and (especially) its leadership to the cause. The relatively short-term electoral horizons of national politicians reinforces the preference for the bipartisan solution. Any decision is preferable to none, or the more rational alternative that requires sacrifice.

Madison argued in *Federalist No. 51* that the intricacies of governmental structure would, and should, make significant policy changes difficult. It was better to be safe than sorry, and so major innovations would have to await the development of a very broad base of political support. The framers thought it unwise for government to be overly ambitious, and so ambitious proposals would have to be subjected to careful, deliberate, and prolonged constructive criticism that offered skeptics the opportunity to uncover flaws in the proposals. In this sense, the tendency for divided government to produce bipartisan, often incremental, solutions is congruent with the framers' design.

However, this structurally induced bias toward safety and incrementalism now works to protect and expand policies established, at least in part, as a result of its design. It was very difficult to enact policies such as Medicare and Medicaid. Now it appears to be virtually impossible to pass legislation that will control the cost of operating them. Enacting legislation to support a depressed farm economy and, in effect, family-type farmers through price supports and acreage allotment policies was very difficult. Now it is very difficult to control the cost of subsidizing farmers with the same programs, despite the fact that the farming industry is now dominated by corporate, not family-type, farming. It was very difficult to muster public and congressional enthusiasm for our military efforts in World War II and the Cold War. Now, although the nation is not faced with either type of challenge, it is very difficult to enforce any meaningful cost-containment model or strategy on defense spending. Divided government encourages bipartisanship, bipartisanship encourages incrementalism, incrementalism favors the status quo because it is both organizationally and politically safe.

The divided government conditions contributing to President Clinton's second term bipartisan posture illustrate the potential hazards of a policy middle ground to the quest for rational, long-term solutions to policy problems. Policy gridlock breeds public cynicism. This encourages policy leaders to "go bipartisan" to show the public that adversaries whose positions are reinforced by their constitutionally separate institutional affiliations can indeed produce policies. However, questions of policy sufficiency quickly surface under such conditions. Faced with a Republican Congress, Clinton endorsed policies that were clearly at variance with the Democratic Party's traditional approach to such issues. Included were agreements that supported tax cuts for the wealthy as a condition for a projected balanced budget, a major welfare reform law, proposals to extend the NAFTA agreement to Latin America and Asia, and stop-gap measures that guaranteed the short-term integrity of Medicare and Social Security. Because Clinton made major concessions to congressional Republicans to accomplish these matters, it appeared that long-term agendas were sacrificed in favor of short-term efforts to appease political adversaries and comfort a skeptical public. In sum, it was good tactically but bad strategically. In addition, some traditional Democrats argued that Clinton's strategy threatened to alienate the groups from which the party had traditionally drawn its strength—the underprivileged, dependent, and disaffected.[8] Bipartisanship harbors dangers for rational policymaking if its major objective is to accommodate partisan adversaries instead of to elicit and integrate the views of individuals with honest differences over how best to formulate and administer new policies to meet new challenges. Moreover, the extent to which the accommodated adversaries are unrepresentative of the public in general is the extent to which such a strategy raises questions of accountability, and therefore of democracy itself. Finally, a search for the pragmatic political center in principle damages the potential for political parties to function as effective intermediary institutions. Under conditions that encourage a search for the most inoffensive policy products it is often difficult to find major policy differences between the two major political parties. The effectiveness of parties as intermediaries rests on the existence of healthy policy differences, not accommodational similarities, between the two major parties.

7. *The Constitution's distribution of power among the three national branches (separation of powers) and between two levels of government (federalism) encourages a two-party system, and gives political parties a "confederal" power cast which weakens their ability to function as effective policy intermediaries.* Representative democracies are served well by strong, disciplined political parties whose members, candidates, and officeholders are committed to a set of party policy principles. Such a condition encourages more serious consideration and debates over the intrinsic merits and demerits of policy alternatives. It ensures that the winning alternative will be enacted without major compromises. This, in turn, enables voters and the minority party to hold politicians accountable for policy decisions. However, the Constitution's provisions for a presidential executive system and a federal system discourage such conditions

with the two major U.S. parties. The Constitution's guarantee of state political sovereignty means that state and local party organizations can define party principles in ways that enhance their candidates' appeal to voters. If that is at variance with national party officials, so be it. Since the president is chosen independent of Congress, by an Electoral College that requires a majority to win, third-party challenges are discouraged. Furthermore the president, as both candidate and officeholder, is the only politician who must appeal to a national constituency with strategies that enhance his appeal to that constituency. This can be accomplished without asking the party for much financial support or for any policy leadership. It is his candidacy or presidency appealing to his constituents in his own way. In fact, the costs of using television as the communication centerpiece for both electoral and governmental politics has made candidates for all offices at all levels must less dependent on party organizations and more dependent on themselves for their political survival. The potential for political parties to serve as effective policy vehicles is eroded further by such conditions.

8. *The Constitution's guarantee of communication freedoms (First Amendment) often encourages strategies by politicians and the media that debase both the quality of representation and the quality of policy dialogue.* The First Amendment allows the major intermediary institutions—political parties, interest groups, and the media—to conduct their business in ways that are dysfunctional to a healthy, representative democracy. The party problem was summarized above. In the case of interest groups, in the name of free expression, the Constitution permits the strong to dominate the weak in terms of access to decision centers. It permits the same dominant corporate forces to dominate campaigns through the use of PACs and soft money contributions. In turn, this inclines elected officials to favor distributive policies that cater to the same group demands. Public policy regularly reflects such a bias, resulting in public policies that reflect these same groups' claims. In essence, there is often little distinction between what these "inside track" groups want and what public policy provides.

The inside track syndrome increasingly restricts the availability of public office to the very rich. Supported by a Supreme Court decision that, in effect, allows money to buy free speech, most national and many subnational offices are available only to the well connected and the very wealthy. For some reason, while such things as poll taxes are wrong because they make voting easier for the wealthy than for the poor, there appears to be nothing wrong with making it easier for the rich to seek office. Somehow, while it is unfair to buy voters, it is all right to buy elections. For some reason, in the age of electronic journalism, those who are born economically privileged and use their wealth to serve themselves have easier access to elections than those who were born poor and have spent their lives serving others. Because of the high costs of television advertising, in 1996 it took upwards of $20 million to make a serious run at a party's presidential nomination. Candidates such as Steve Forbes and Ross Perot can buy the publicity they need. Those who can't spend years in a constant campaign mode raising the necessary funds, usually from corporate sources which expect policy reciprocity from those who are elected. This is an extremely odd condition for a government that, at least symbolically, stresses equality of opportunity at virtually every turn. According to the Supreme Court, the Constitution says you are free to speak your mind, but money speaks louder than words during elections. Therefore, the more money you have, the more free speech you can purchase. This insensible standard makes a laughing stock of the one person–one vote principle.

In the case of the media, competition not only between the major television networks but also between the networks and local television stations has encouraged news selection, reporting, and analysis to focus on scandals, hard-copy-like stories, and other events with a sensationalist twist. The public's dependence on television as a major source of entertainment has encouraged the development of an entertainment "culture" which, in turn, encourages citizens to be passive and reactive, as opposed to innovative and proactive, in their response to policy challenges. While these results can be defended in the name of free expression, they are counterproductive to the mission of a free press as a provider of vital information for use by citizens as they pass judgment on how to best confront and deal with society's major problems. A visual culture has significant implications for government and public policy. So far most of them have been negative. It is one thing for politicians to employ television to inspire. Media coverage is drawn to politicians that do it effectively. However, it is quite another matter to convert these abilities into political strategies that offer the public what it needs in terms of a realistic policy agenda and the commitment to arduously achieve it.

Another very significant impact of the Constitution on political dialogue, and ultimately on policy, is its tendency to encourage politicians and activist citizens to frame debates in ideological rather than in pragmatic terms. Although it is usually overly simplistic and misleading to do so, groups and individuals often approach the solution to policy problems in terms of which level of government should be responsible, or if government at any level has the legitimate right to compromise an individual's freedom by regulating his or her behavior. Most often, these questions have already been resolved, and to cling to such arguments while problems continue to fester serves mostly to distract the nation from the real policy issues, inflame attitudes, and delay the ability of government to devote its full energy to the real policy problems at hand.

Usually these problems are implementation, or "how" problems, not ideological or "should" problems. For example, while the Constitution definitely has an individualistic bias, it also has moral, or ethical, dimensions. Therefore, it is folly to argue that some of life's risks shouldn't be socialized. They have been for nearly a century through such things as government-sponsored pension programs and assistance to the handicapped and disabled. To preach that this ethic is, in effect, "unethical" does not speak to the policy issue. The key policy issue is how can government structure its entitlement policies to minimize the dependency of some on the prosperity of others. When simplistic, often mindless, statements of opposition to the exercise of government power become the centerpiece of policy debates, everybody loses, including those who stick to their ideological arguments in principle. Although it is indeed true that government power needs to be curtailed, even eliminated in some policy areas, in most areas it is an inevitability and a necessity. In most policy areas, government power definitely needs to be continually subjected to constructive criticism, fine-tuning, refocusing, and being made more efficient.

Constitutional structure has a negative impact on political dialogue on yet another plane. Fragmented government, especially divided government, usually handicaps legislators and (especially) presidents in their postelection attempts to fulfill campaign promises. Fragmented government often mandates compromises that bargain away the core objectives of many campaign pledges. Aware of their inability to deliver on their promises, and yet anxious for reelection and/or an honorable niche in history, presidents adjust their rhetoric, alter their objec-

tives, and redefine policy solutions in ways that put the most favorable spin on what government under their leadership has been able to accomplish. For example, when advantaged by unified government President Clinton worked rather consistently for partisan solutions to major policy problems such as health care and the budget deficit, considering the bipartisan alternatives inadequate. However, when faced with divided government conditions, Clinton quickly became the champion of bipartisanship in both rhetoric and strategy. The extent to which such a turn to the possible and away from the necessary misleads the public and cultivates a false sense of security is difficult to determine and, of course, will vary from case to case and president to president. However, the trend is corruptive and the results potentially very erosive of the public's confidence in government once the gap between heralded successes and reality becomes apparent.

9. *Federalism, with its emphasis on the political sovereignty of states, undermines the notion of equality in both the development and administration of public policy.* States are represented equally in the Senate, regardless of population. Both the House and Senate must agree on legislation before it is sent to the president. Therefore, citizens and vested interests in the thinly populated states have much more leverage in policy decisions than do their counterparts in highly populated states. Furthermore states, as geographic entities, are not convenient administrative "districts" for the administration of policies that have multistate causes and need multistate cooperation to be administered effectively. States vary in their financial and administrative capacity to administer federally instigated policies, and to cope effectively with the policy and administrative challenges of new responsibilities sent them via devolution from the federal government.

Federalism introduces complexities into the development of cohesive policies in the fields of social regulation (civil liberties, crime, education), economic regulation (business practices), and economic justice (welfare, job programs, health), and complicates problems of implementing policies in these areas. Regulating individuals and corporations in the pursuit of equal application of policy and implementation goals in each of these areas is a herculean task. Regulatory agencies in many states are often heavily influenced by economic elites. Debates about the roles of various levels of government are highly visible and very contentious, in part because these elites are cognizant of the political advantages that state and local control over these policies holds for them. Federal patterns often make it difficult for the downtrodden and socially unpopular groups to secure redress. In many ways, the recent devolutionary trends in federalism introduce a policy paradox—allowing circumstances of inequality to be confronted effectively if states and localities are so inclined, yet permitting injustice to worsen if no such inclination exists. Usually a high-priority policy item at the national level, the implementation of equality and justice policies is, because they are at the mercy of changing economic conditions, often found near the bottom of state and local policy-priority ladders.

10. *Since the Supreme Court, by way of applying the First Amendment's free speech guarantee, has refused to place limits on total campaign expenditures, and because those costs are escalating rapidly, both the campaign challenge and the governing challenge have assumed a synthetic quality. Serious policy dialogues in both undertakings have diminished in favor of strategies and discourses targeted at discrediting and destroying the opposition.* Instead of focusing on the best way to govern, both the campaign challenge and the governing challenge now focus on how to win and retain office. In a healthy democracy, con-

tentions over how best to govern should dominate both enterprises. The American political system currently embraces the opposite. It is becoming increasingly difficult to distinguish between strategies and values that are incorporated into campaigning and those incorporated into governing.

The strong ties that have existed between electoral politics and governing have been seriously eroded by the failure of intermediate institutions, especially political parties and the media. The high cost of campaigning drives candidates to cash-rich interest groups. This undercuts the loyalties of politicians to their parties. The governing challenge has been eroded further by candidates' dependence on marketing experts to develop strategies for winning elections. Image experts manufacture and test-market issues to suit the audience at hand for the sole purpose of winning elections. They pay little or no attention to either articulating governing challenges or how to accomplish them in the postelection period. Governing behavior increasingly mirrors campaign behavior. The result is the constant campaign and all its negative policy manifestations. Regardless of how rapidly the nation's problems escalate in both number and intensity, officeseekers become increasingly absorbed in developing financial and (ultimately) policy linkages with interest groups. The cost is the virtual forfeiture of the governing challenge along with the development of leaders and the commitment to sacrifice it takes to govern adeptly.

11. *Organized minorities can and have employed some provisions of the Constitution to undermine the intent of other provisions.* Substantive policy justice can be compromised by forces employing due process rights to delay and defeat policy innovations, as with the case of legal adversarialism and microgovernment. In an attempt to undo a presidential election and despite the existence of strong public opinion to the contrary, congressional parties can initiate impeachment proceedings against presidents for behavior that has nothing to do with the presidents' performance of their constitutional responsibilities. The impeachment of President Clinton was the most conspicuous example of this in our constitutional history. Such actions have potentially serious implications both for the ability of government to tend to its policy challenges and for the institutional balance of power among the three branches of government as prescribed by the Constitution.

12. *While the democratization of the Constitution potentially can overcome the policy manifestations of fragmented government, during the post-Watergate period its effect has been the opposite.* If democratization occurs through the channels of a strong party system, then the contribution of fragmented government to policy incrementalism can be overcome by uniting the executive and legislative branches behind a party's policy missions. However, if party discipline wanes and the public grows increasingly cynical about institutional power and the ability of government to perform effectively, government policy performance can be compromised often to the point of impotence. Such conditions encourage divided government, candidate-centered campaigns, and a media inclined to define scandal as news and, as a consequence, blur the distinction between the politics of winning elections and the politics of governing the nation. This has been the inclination since the Watergate incident.

13. *Many of the public's "moral imperatives," although dysfunctional to efforts to lend more cohesion to both policymaking and administration, gain both legitimacy and political clout because they have roots in the Constitution.* Moral imperatives are goals individuals seek from policies because, in their opinion, they (the goals) are

genetically good, or moral. Many are cultural in origin, and therefore are not often subjected to constructively critical evaluations. One obvious example is the policy decentralization, or devolution, fetish, which has its roots in the principle of federalism. Federalism lends support to the notion that government is best if policies are made and administered close to home. The movements to liquidate government regulatory responsibilities altogether, or to privatize policy administration, are extensions of this attitude. Furthermore, the proliferation of policy power lessens the danger of hasty majorities enacting irresponsible policies. The tendency to privatize the notion of individual rights is another example. Instead of using the constitutionally guaranteed communications freedoms to discuss and debate public issues that affect all for the long term, many individuals and factions now claim the right to a job, a subsidy, a promotion, or economic security. These claims are afforded at least some legitimacy because they are made as a matter of right rather than privilege or advantage. Interest groups are more bold in their approach to politicians because they have the right to be under the First Amendment. After all, they are petitioning government for the right to acquire and use property in the form of real or financial assets. Of course, the right to property, along with the right to life and liberty, is protected by the Constitution. Historically, the states rights argument often was employed as a constitutional defense for a state's unwillingness to cooperate with a nationally mandated policy. In short, individuals and groups gain some symbolic leverage for their policy crusades if they can implant them in the moral vale of the Constitution.

The success of such strategies is dependent on the degree of reverence Americans have for the Constitution, and that is quite high. However, its implications for both policy content and administration are mixed at best.

Often these crusades are pursued as a matter of principle, and that is usually dysfunctional to both policy content and administration. Policy benefits are rarely maximized if they are, for example, totally decentralized. Constitutionally guaranteed rights lose much of their meaning if they are expanded and, in effect, privatized to include the economic indulgences of individuals and groups. An otherwise healthy, and democratic, dedication to the common good is replaced by a manifestation of rugged individualism that considers self-interest the one and only objective of politics and government. Such attitudes and trends are counterproductive for a nation that now, more than ever, needs the commitment of a dedicated public to work for long-term solutions to problems that are rapidly escalating out of control.

14. *Because both the public and the courts tend to enshrine democratic procedures as ends unto themselves, the capacity of the political system to deal effectively with the challenges of substantive democracy is severely constricted.* Procedural democracy stresses the ways or means by which policies are developed and administered. Substantive democracy focuses on how well policies themselves serve the public's needs. If we stress government "by the people" to the point that it significantly compromises the ability of the system to do constructive things "for the people" then some sort of rebalance is imperative. Healthy democracies embody a healthy balance of both.

As these pages have shown, opportunities for the people to govern themselves effectively through the electoral, legislative, and administrative processes often provide opportunities for wealthy elites to convert those processes to their own ends. The founders' fear of majority tyranny was unfounded. The very thing the framers feared most—the democratization of the Constitution and political processes—has served to further increase and cement the impact of wealthy elites on politics and policy. Ironically, the reforms that the founders feared would challenge elitist influence on government and encourage majority tyranny have been the very reforms that have corroborated the ability of elites to thwart that tyranny. These government "by the people" inconsistencies are played out daily in the way electronic journalism selects and reports the news, in the conditions that have virtually institutionalized the constant campaign as a permanent fixture on the political scene, and in the way dependency politics impacts on elections and deranges the ability of officeholders to deal with the complex policy issues of the times.

A relatively recent aberration of procedural democracy can be found in the impact of adversarial legalism and its first-generation descendant, microgovernment, on policymaking and on society generally. For most of the twentieth century, Americans have asked their governments to do more for them. However, under the pretext of guaranteeing parties affected by potential administrative rulings their constitutional due process rights, procedural democracy has defeated or compromised the ability of institutions to confront and manage many key policy problems effectively. Because of constitutionally nourished and court-sanctioned due process guarantees, the transaction costs of policy effectiveness are often prohibitively high. The result is an increasing demoralization of decision-making processes, and growing public skepticism about the ability of government to deliver what it promises. At the very time in history when the public is demanding more and more effective substantive policy from government, the contentiousness of the processes that should deliver those policies often makes those processes a roadblock to, rather than a facilitator of, necessary policy reform. The costs of adversarial legalism are difficult to determine, and that has become a major part of the problem. Not only do agencies have to cope with an implementation environment that is becoming progressively formal, adversarial, and complex, but they also find that efforts to anticipate the costs of implementation are insurmountable. Lawsuits breed more lawsuits, and often the most rational response is to forgo attempts to do anything rather than cope with the costs and policy sacrifices that are likely to result from a series of seemingly endless legal confrontations.

15. *Many attempts to invoke constitutional principles to improve policymaking and policy implementation estrange, or threaten to estrange, much of what government does from traditional channels of political accountability.* The more activist and involved government becomes, the more the policies it produces necessitate an interaction between the public and private sectors. The more private forces are impacted by public policy, the more interest they have in influencing the character of that policy. That character can be influenced by "representing" private causes by contributing to campaigns, by arguing that guarantees of communications freedoms translate into using television in ways that allow the economically privileged to gain communication advantages over those who are unable to buy such freedoms, by gaining more direct access to decision centers by working to decentralize power within legislatures and within the federal system, by privatizing the concept of rights and going to court to gain those rights, by forming policy alliances with administrators, and by urging governments to privatize functions in order to streamline their implementation. Each of these strategies is considered legitimate because each offers a different spin on how to represent people and factions in a democracy impacted by the constitutional fragmentation of institutional power.

The problem is that each, in its own distinctive way, can encourage government to go "off accountability." The deliberate decentralization and privatization of power make it difficult to hold a single individual, institution, or process responsible for policy successes or mistakes. Indeed, power may become so fragmented that the overall thrust or purpose of a policy may go undefined. To cite constitutionally guaranteed communications freedoms as the justification for buying disproportionate access to voters during election campaigns or to define news as scandal shows flagrant disdain for the principle of majority rule. Public opinion is denigrated by the very forces and processes designed to make it meaningful. The policy choices supported by most Americans are stable, consistent, pragmatic, principled and, most important, at odds with the views of most key national leaders. Confronted with these obvious "disconnects" on issue after issue, Congress and (especially) its leaders, presidents, and the mainstream media simply turn away. They seem uninterested in what are the reasonable policy preferences of public supermajorities. Policymakers support and enact the desires of special interests, and ignore the concerns of the many.

Governing correctly, and therefore accountably, is not easy. It requires courage and a sober consideration of the long-term implications of current decisions. It requires placing the public's unfinished business stage center on the policy agenda. Moreover, it disdains the politics of the "artful dodge." It should not, for example, permit the political obsession with a presidential sex scandal to overrun valuable time that could be spent on securing the future of Social Security, making available adequate and attainable health care, attempting to protect society's youth from the dangers of tobacco and addictive drugs, or legislating a sense of fair play into democracy's lifeline—the election process—that is being slowly strangulated by contributions bent on overpowering elections for their own purposes. Elections are designed to hold those who govern accountable for what they do. If they do not intend to govern, they should be held accountable for that.

Keeping the Republic

Some Proposals

Sustaining the integrity of Dr. Franklin's republic under the weight of the policy challenges of the twenty-first century will be a difficult task. It is not a question of the Constitution's sustenance, for it will endure. The challenge is to make it a significant document of higher law that helps, rather than hinders, the nation in its quest to deal effectively with its policy challenges. This is a big order, primarily because the Constitution's original purpose was to thwart policy responsiveness in the interest of caution and stability. Today, the challenge of government is to muster the energy and courage to deal with policy problems in a proactive, rational way. In light of such a challenge, it could well be argued that the very last thing the nation needs is a constitution that impedes, rather than serves, these ends.

One possible route to effective policy reform is constitutional reform, or what is herein termed the "constitution solution." Structural change can have significant effects on system outputs, but it is important not to overemphasize that potential. Structure can either mitigate or amplify the impact of individual and group claims on policy decisions. The original Constitution focused on the former. After more than two hundred years of evolution, it now does more of the latter than the former, at least in a select sense. The very group excesses the founders wanted to repress now find refuge in constitutional procedures and rights guarantees, and use those advantages to leverage their influence over public policy. Madison was correct in his as-

sumptions about the self-interest incentives that underlie both individual and group participation in politics. However, his assumption that the natural development of the faction universe would result in conditions that allowed all individuals and causes to be represented equally, or virtually so, was in error. Communications freedoms have not resulted in a natural equilibrium among groups, but rather the domination of politics and policy by groups that are comparatively well endowed, well organized, and well led, and which have developed close political connections to major political actors. On another plane, the separation of powers, and its concomitant mandate that separately endowed institutions share the obligation to develop policy, encourages policy outputs that are usually quite moderate and incremental in tone. Such policies rarely reflect the public's enthusiasm for innovative change. In short, the assumption is that if procedures are changed to make the policy system more responsive, policies will be more responsive and less incremental. Therefore, amending the Constitution to expedite this objective is often raised as an option.

Would a restructuring of the procedural (and therefore power) relationships between and among national policy institutions help make government more majoritarian, and therefore more responsive? The answer is yes, in all probability. The *degree* to which this would be true is open to speculation. If structure can be employed to defeat or mitigate, it can be used to overcome and enhance. Therefore, a brief glance at some reform possibilities is probably advisable for two reasons. First, such a focus helps the reader to appreciate the importance of constitutional politics to the current state of policy affairs. Second, it may well be possible that acquiring an appreciation for the potential that structural reform might harbor for policy reform could increase the odds for the former.

However, before any intellectual enthusiasm for reform's potential escalates too far, three caveats need to be introduced. First, achieving structural change through the amendment process is very slow and very unlikely because it requires the approval of supermajorities in both Congress (two-thirds vote of both houses), and the states (three-fourths vote of state legislatures). Second, structural change does not alter basic human incentives. It can only channel them in ways that encourage long-term thinking and interinstitutional cooperation. Third, all major structural changes need widespread public support. History has shown that such support is offered only under what might be termed "crisis" conditions. During such conditions, such as the Civil War and the New Deal periods, structural impediments to the efficient expression of majoritarianism are not very effective. When the public clearly demands dramatic change, it is inclined to get it irrespective of any constitutionally imposed impediments to majority rule. The beginning of the twenty-first century is not a crisis period, at least in the immediate sense of the term. However, it is entirely possible that domestic and world events, coupled with the existing reactive and incremental approach to dealing with policy issues, might well present the nation and the world with a major crisis in the not-too-distant future. For the time being, despite widespread public cynicism about the ability of government to perform effectively, voters are disinclined to carry that cynicism to the point of "cleaning house" come election time. As political parties have weakened and the power of electronic journalism over campaigns and government has increased, voters usually react with overwhelming endorsements of incumbency and divided government.

With all the above listed caveats and realities in mind, a brief examination of some reforms that might enhance government responsiveness and efficiency is in order.

Some of these would involve constitutional amendments. Others would most likely involve legislation only. One—the strengthening of political parties—involves a combination of both, together with a definitive cooperative nudge from party members themselves. All are interdependent, meaning that the impact of the enactment of the entire package would likely be greater than the sum of the parts.

1. *Lengthen and harmonize terms of office.* This would require a constitutional amendment or amendments, and therefore be difficult to accomplish. The current election scenario makes both the House of Representatives, the president, and a third of the Senate hyperattendant to actual or perceived fluctuations in constituency opinion. In effect, the constant campaign becomes part of the job of governing. At a minimum House terms could be extended to four years, with the president and the House being elected simultaneously. Senate terms might be extended to eight years. The purpose of all these options is to free politicians to contemplate and debate policy issues seriously without fear of near term voter rejection. Unpopular short-term policies could be enacted that might prove effective for the long term. The election of presidents and the entire House simultaneously should reduce chances for divided government significantly.

2. *Consider joint executive-legislative office holding.* These changes would not officially alter the separation of powers, but would help cultivate interbranch communication and tolerance, and would help encourage the development of a common state of mind. They would also require constitutional amendments. Having cabinet members hold nonvoting membership in Congress and, if practical, having key committee and subcommittee chairs hold positions in agencies over which their legislative units have jurisdiction has some appeal, but a reduced workload is certainly not one of them. This would add a parliamentary flavor to policy discussions. The assumption is that such interbranch membership overlap would help the president, the cabinet and other key administrators, and Congress develop a sense of mutual appreciation for each other's policy positions. This might well reduce executive-legislative rancor and encourage serious debates over policy issues, and could lessen the political impact of a bureaucracy currently impacted by the dual boss condition discussed above and in Chapter 11.

3. *A line item or limited item veto.* A version of this was enacted by statute in 1996. President Clinton used it numerous times until the Supreme Court declared it unconstitutional in 1998. While some of its advocates think it is possible to structure a new line item veto statute that the Court would find satisfactory, the only realistic alternative seems to be a constitutional amendment. This would be very time consuming and difficult to achieve. However, the advantages of a line item veto, if exercised strictly to eliminate waste, would well be worth the effort. By permitting the president to veto items in bills that he considers wasteful and/or irrelevant, a line item veto has the potential to reduce waste, limit the impact of pork barrel politics on public policy, and prohibit vested interests from slowly undermining critical public interest programs by attaching riders to appropriations legislation. The dangerous potential of the latter on environmental policy was illustrated in late 1998, several months after the Supreme Court declared the 1996 law unconstitutional. Attempting to assuage fat cat campaign donors, many congressional Republicans and a few Democrats used must-pass appropriations bills as a camouflage for assaults on federal environmental laws. This marriage of environmental policy and the

"purse strings" involved such items as the prohibition of funding projects to reduce carbon dioxide levels (a major contributor to global warming), delays in efforts to regulate mercury emissions from coal-fired power plants, requiring the Forest Service to sell more timber on federal property to private companies, and preventing the Environmental Protection Agency from requiring a major corporation to dredge its toxic pollutants from one of the nation's major rivers.

Of course, a line item veto could also be used by presidents to increase their bargaining leverage with Congress on pork barrel issues, with the president agreeing not to veto legislative pork if Congress will endorse presidential pork. Showing deference to reciprocity, in such cases the president likely would agree not to exercise the veto and eliminate the waste and pork that would otherwise be on the veto table. Strict majoritarian veto override possibilities could discourage this. To maintain a healthy executive-legislative power balance, the best line item veto override option would be one that permits a presidential action to be overridden by simple majorities in both houses of Congress.[9]

4. *Curb the constant campaign.* The constant campaign should be curbed because it makes running for office more important than governing and because it results in equating what governing there is with policies that assuage the forces that are financially dominant during campaigns. Legislators and, increasingly, presidents are far too beholden to corporate America, largely because they depend heavily on large campaign contributions from corporations to finance their campaigns for office. It is impossible to have responsible government "for the people" in general when the "by the people" processes are so dependent on economic elites to function. By a decisive margin, the public supports significant campaign finance reform. However, at the same time the public is willing to tolerate an election system that functions without it. This is because people have become sluggish and indifferent about their ability to change matters, and most legislators know it. Legislative majorities have concluded that a public that is growing increasingly inanimate about its civic responsibilities is unlikely to seriously protest an inequitable campaign finance system. It's a vicious circle: Democracy does not work unless citizens participate, but they fail to participate because they know the system isn't working on their behalf. However, such fatalism must be dislodged. It is nothing short of heresy to permit constitutional guarantees of communications freedoms to be transposed this way. The public should not permit the processes of American democracy to be subcontracted out to special interest peddlers.

Democracy works best when policymakers make policies that combine responsiveness to voters with judgments that oblige society's future needs. There are both "by the people" and "for the people" components to a representative democracy. Elected legislators and executives cannot possibly do well with either challenge if effective campaigns for office are dependent on large contributions from society's privileged interests. Campaign funding needs to be reduced and democratized. Campaign contributions from sources outside the contested districts should be prohibited. Soft money contributions should be eliminated. Candidates need to be guaranteed generous, publicly funded free and equal access to television for both advertising and debate purposes. The degree to which campaign reform efforts move along these lines is the degree to which those elected will be more prone to examine the premises, contents, and implications of policy changes for their constituencies in composite and, indeed, for society in general.

If campaign finance reform should place overall limits on campaign spending, it would likely require a constitutional amendment that confines the guarantees of the First Amendment to speech, press, and petition rights, but not to campaign finance. If it focused on limiting or eliminating soft money contributions and the sponsorship of limited but free access to television by the candidates, it most likely would not require a constitutional amendment. Any serious effort to reduce the impact of money, and therefore society's well-heeled individuals and corporations, on campaigns and (ultimately) on governing is long overdue. The constant campaign imperative desperately needs to be restrained. The nation needs policymakers who spend their time legislating instead of soothing the privileged as a prelude to the next campaign.

Despite the fact that citizens overwhelmingly support meaningful campaign finance reform, Congress has been slow to respond and notably parochial in its definition of the problem. In 1998, an election year, a significant reform bill did pass the House, only to be rejected by the Senate. Too many senators concluded it was too risky to undercut key sources of campaign revenue, especially in an election year. In part, this is due to the virtual lock on campaign revenue that incumbents have secured under the current system. It has been reinforced by citizen unwillingness to insist on congressional legislative follow-through despite the fact that the public overwhelmingly supports the idea. Finally, although most public interest groups, such as Common Cause and Public Citizen, have campaign reform as a high-priority item, these organizations have been unable to cooperate with one another and pool their energies and resources in ways that would enhance the potential for meaningful reform.[10]

What would constitute meaningful reform is open to debate, but it certainly must deal with legislating major changes in what is legal under the current system, and not concentrate on outlawing practices that are currently *illegal*. By focusing on matters such as questionable foreign contributions and on where and by whom campaign funds are solicited, legislators are diverted from the major problem—what the laws currently permit and how that often results in nothing short of legalized bribery. This is not a partisan issue. Both major parties have become obsessed with abandoning principle in search of funds to support campaigns that they think must be won at virtually any cost. Democracy abandons its claim to integrity under such conditions. What should be done? Although several necessary changes would likely involve amending the Constitution, nevertheless here are a few possibilities. Make soft money contributions illegal. Place rigid limitations on campaign contributions and spending. Provide for public financing of campaigns via a "check-off" system on income tax forms. Mandate that the major television networks and their local counterparts donate free time for political debates. Mandate that campaign advertising meet rigorous issue-focused standards, and require that all contributions to campaigns come from sources within the candidates' districts. Many of these regulations work well in other democracies, and even in some states.

Finally, Congress could eliminate the current limitations on campaign contributions. As it stands, candidates who do not finance their own campaigns are faced with laws restricting individual and corporate contributions, save for soft money contributions. In presidential campaigns, if candidates accept federal matching funds, they also face contribution limitations. Those who finance their own campaigns face no limitations whatsoever. Therefore, why not make it fair for all? Should a candidate support his or her campaign to a level that exceeds what others may raise, then all limits for all candidates would be eliminated. The wealthy would, of course, spend their own money at will; others could raise and spend as much as they could. This would mean that personal wealth would no longer allow the rich to be above laws that others must observe.

One of the major obstacles to campaign finance reform is the prevailing view that it will not happen. That is flawed reasoning. If the public wants significant campaign reforms, they will come, irrespective of the legal and political obstacles that have suppressed them in the past.

On what might appear to be a more suspect venture because of its possible antidemocracy overtones, negative television campaign advertising should be carefully regulated. Television advertising rewards a "small sound bite" advertising strategy that stresses short attacks against the opponent, not the positives for sponsoring a candidate. Democracy trade-offs are seemingly involved here. Such action appears to violate the free speech principle and, of course, it does if considered only in the matter-of-fact sense of the term. However, all freedoms are relative, and free speech is no exception. In fact, both free speech and an improved political process can be enhanced by the elimination of attack campaign advertising. First, these ads are the antithesis of the issue-based debates that are necessary for a healthy democracy. They undermine the type of free speech intended by the framers. Second, they alienate voters and discourage voter turnout. Voters hear the "don't vote for" a candidate so often that they frequently conclude that, in effect, there is no candidate to support. Third, they impair the development of an essential sense of civility in politics, further alienating voters. Fourth, such advertising further erodes the impact of political parties on politics by making the candidate, his or her money, and his or her political consultant the only keys to electoral success. The party becomes less useful to both candidates and elected office holders as a source of policy direction, and is converted into an organized service center for consultant pursuits and fund-raising. Consultants are concerned only with winning, and therefore emphasize a politics of the "wedge" rather than a politics stressing principled debates over policy issues.

5. *Strengthen political parties.* The late V. O. Key once remarked: "For government to function, the obstruction of the constitutional mechanism must be overcome, and it is the party that casts a web, at times weak, at times strong, over the dispersed organs of government and gives them a semblance of unity."[11] As discussed in Chapter 5, the current weaknesses of national party organizations are rooted in the strengths of state and local party organizations, and in the increasing costs of campaigning by television which forces party candidates to finance campaigns through their own, not the party's, efforts. This new party stress on the efforts of individual candidates, with organizations styled by themselves, and with fund-raising strategies tuned to their own talents as politicians has replaced the more traditional hierarchical parties that relied more on elites, loyalty, and patronage for their strength. Party weakness has strengthened the impact of interest groups in both elections and policy. Interest groups have developed into what might be termed "protoparties." They have entered the political marketplace by employing top-ranking polling organizations and public relations experts that develop ads, do field research, and coordinate their efforts with the electoral strategies of candidates from whom they solicit, and receive, favors.

Significant campaign reform legislation would help correct this condition, as would the harmonization of executive and legislative elections. A reduction in the reliance on primaries as the source of party nominees would also help significantly by increasing the role of party hierarchy in party affairs, both in terms of molding party policy positions and in

the selection of party candidates for office. One alternative, easily accomplished by legislation, is for parties who have incumbents running for reelection not to hold primaries unless large numbers of the party's rank-and-file, by petition, choose to hold them. In other words, there would be major support within the party to oust the incumbent. Otherwise, that party would hold no primary for that election. This would foreclose the possibility of candidacies from "hobby" candidates who, for the experience and (perhaps) attention, enter races and trigger costly and time-consuming efforts by incumbents to oppose them, even though they (the hobby candidates) have virtually no chance of winning.

However, none of these changes will occur unless voters see advantages to stronger parties. They continue to show little interest. If citizens had shown interest, many centralizing changes would already have transpired. Partly because of the public's inherent distrust of centralized authority, and partly because of the legacy of Progressivism, the public has for well over a century displayed an inherent distrust of strong parties and has seized virtually every opportunity to democratize and therefore weaken them.

6. *Digital democracy.* Technology has impacted television in ways that are mostly dysfunctional to reasoned participation in politics and government. The introduction of the personal computer to an ever increasing number of homes has, in one sense, contributed further to individual and family isolation from an already weakened civic culture. However, the personal computer, if utilized to potential, offers an opportunity to extricate people from the simplistic and sensationalist-oriented political menus proffered by commercial television. In its place could come Web sites offering in-depth analyses of policy questions, together with opportunities for on-line discussions and debates. Web sites offer

many opportunities for this. Issues on most sites are discussed in depth, and people may indeed find it to be invigorating to bypass commercial television's market-driven fetish for drama. Better informed and more enthusiastic citizens harbor the potential of effectively countering the negative policy effects of factions and candidate-centered campaigns. In addition, voter turnout might well increase, with elections possibly even being conducted by computer. National referendums might become a distinct possibility. The idea of the town meeting, as the procedural centerpiece of pure democratic theory, might conceivably be transposed to the national stage via technology. To be sure, this is only potential at this time. However, technology's impact on politics and policy has been a mixed bag at best up to this point. The opportunity to exploit it for the net benefit of democracy and policy improvement should not be ignored or slighted.

However, opportunities are not without their potential hazards and, in the case of digital democracy, there are many. A key problem for American democracy is the decline and degeneration of the intermediary institutions, especially political parties and televised network news and analysis programs. Unless digital democracy encourages patrons to think in terms of what unites them politically, it could virtually kill the party as an intermediary vehicle. Web transmissions mean that users have access to any data they choose, regardless of their accuracy. They encourage people to interact with others of their own mindset obsessions. This would fragment political discourse, not focus it around alternative theories of governing. Cyberspace technology could become the enemy of the common political and policy perspectives cultivated by a healthy political party system. Principles don't derive naturally from the use of optics for political discourse. However, they are a necessary prerequisite for the critical examination of policy issues.

Finally, unless employed in ways that encourage people to systematically organize and debate policy issues, cyberspace technology could undermine political leadership as we have come to know it. Effective leaders are those who both embody our opinions and find ways to represent and defend them effectively in decision arenas. If cyberspace undermines further the ability of intermediary institutions to encourage us to think and organize our political thoughts, then leaders are likely to represent, as best they can, the sum total of our thoughts, whims, idiosyncrasies, and (unfortunately) our misinformation. This would constitute hyperdemocracy at its worst. Leaders would become mere conduits or "weigh stations" for public opinion, and their value as innovators, judges, and crusaders would be lost.

7. *Civic education.* The concept of government implies the existence of moral standards that can be applied only by government in an effort to control the more egoistic, even predatory, incentives of individuals and factions. Madison didn't believe that policymakers, however chosen, would be vested with a special sense of policy morality. However, he did think that compromises among factions mandated by constitutional structure would result in a policy middle ground. This would encourage policy decisions that were both accommodative of all interested factions and much less dangerous than if they reflected the position of just one, or a few factions. A major purpose of constitutional power fragmentation was to avoid either the tyranny of the majority or the tyranny of one or a few factions. That being the standard, any process that enhanced safety and stability in the face of such dangerous potential was, in effect, a process that advanced policy morality. In Madison's view, policies were moral (relatively) if they avoided the dangers of factional or majority tyranny.

The potential for majority tyranny has never been a real one for the United States. However, a policy landscape that embodies the values of privileged interests against those of the rank-and-file has become a serious problem. Frequently it is difficult to determine the difference between official public policy and the values of private interests affected, or served, by those policies. Such a state of affairs corrupts government because there is no distinct public standard incorporated in those policies that gives them a value cast different from the private interests that the policies themselves should, in theory, keep in tow.

The framers dealt with this corruption potential not by any exhortation to the goodness of people or by any hope or expectation that the good would ascend to govern. They sought the solution in constitutional structure. The objective was to establish and conserve some relationship between the ideal and the practical, or between form and reality. They did not think their solution was a panacea, nor was it the product of any special insight bestowed on them. The one result they hoped for was that constitutional structure would resist attempts by factions and elites to manipulate it for their own good. That has not been the case. That which was intended to control factional excess often is employed to leverage the impact of the more privileged interest on public policy.

We need to recognize the problem and, through education and a renewed sense of purpose, reinstitute the distinction between private and public morality. Morality is a very subjective term and we should not be under the illusion that a majoritarian interpretation of it will surface spontaneously once we begin the search. However, not knowing exactly what it is or might become should not deter us from recognizing what it is not. It is not what we have. We can safely say that it is something more than the willing acceptance of

government as a force in our lives and the absence of insurrection. Also, we can say that it has something to do with the public's acceptance of, and expectation that, public policy should reflect a set of values that cannot be exploited for momentary advantage. Finally, and closely related to this, we can say that it has something to do with giving the policy expectations of the many priority over the claims of the select few. If, by educating ourselves and interacting with one another within and through schools, civic forums, television, newspapers, and the Internet, we can challenge government to articulate a standard or several standards of policy legitimacy and defend what it is doing by those standards, change will not be long in coming. Compelling policymakers to do this could well mean that the public doesn't have to initiate standards of legitimacy. Policymakers can initiate them and citizens can react.

Civic education does not necessarily mean that citizens have to give themselves lessons in policy morality. However, it does mean that they should be taught to resist accepting anything government does simply because government does it. Citizens have the obligation to insist that government defend its actions according to a principle or set of principles that the public finds acceptable. We need to be more politically active and interested in what government does on our behalf. Consent should not be automatic. A healthy skepticism should be a regular part of civic life.

8. *Reinvent government the right way.* The implementation of public policy is perhaps more critical to its success than the ideas that inspire its creation. The separation of powers encourages agencies to stray from the classic objective of administration—the efficient, objective implementation of public policies. President Clinton's commitment to "reinvent" government was an attempt to adapt private-sector successes in administration and planning to the public sector. The early stress of the crusade was on the reduction of waste and inefficiency in agency operations, not on whether the policies themselves were necessary. This is understandable. It is safe, sound politics. Nearly everyone wants government's machinery to operate more efficiently. As an issue, it is genetically nonpartisan.

However, the questions of an agency's policy responsibilities are considerably more controversial. Decisions to eliminate, reorient, or combine programs are far more disputable than are decisions to reorganize, reduce, and downsize. Organization, according to Schattschneider, is the "mobilization of bias," and the extent to which reinvention wants to disassemble the old machine and construct a new one is the extent to which these decisions are going to spark controversy. It is good politics to streamline and refocus procedures, and potentially bad politics to advocate the liquidation of substantive policies themselves. Nonetheless, some of the latter is necessary if government is to remain accountable to its citizens and a meaningful assault on budget deficits is to be made. The challenge would be relatively easy if the choice was between making government either work better or cost less. We do not have the advantage of such a choice. We must do both. We need both a smaller and leaner and a better focused workforce. Otherwise both policy and administrative mismanagement will reign, costs will escalate further, and citizen cynicism will increase. Determining how to do this and mustering the will and tenacity to accomplish it is no small order. We are going to have to both "reinvent" government overall and "uninvent" some parts of it.

In addition, it is mandatory that continued reinvention efforts take into account the differences between public-sector and private-sector administration. There are vast differences in the types of policies that preoccupy each sector. The private sector, for the most part, seeks profits. Most public-sector agencies provide services. It is relatively easy to determine the former, but comparatively difficult to determine how well agencies do with the latter challenge. Assessments of the quality of provided services are often very qualitative, or subjective, and often the best results can be achieved only at relatively high cost. Reinvention efforts should take into account the fact that most government services are popular with key segments of the body politic, and that most of the cost of government is not administrative costs, but the costs of the substantive programs themselves.

It is difficult to underestimate the ability of administrative agencies to survive and grow, even during periods of fiscal austerity. The permanent government is the most embedded and determined interest group in Washington. Most bureaucrats are tenured. They work their associations with iron triangles with shrewdness and sophistication. They are intensely committed to their careers and their job security. History has shown that they can either defeat or force major compromises in even the most popular of reform efforts. Their professional existence and way of life depends on the maintenance and augmentation of an already bloated, extravagant, and redundant bureaucratic machine. They do not share the views of most Americans about them and their work. They consider themselves a benevolent group of people empowered to do good things for an unappreciative public.

Presidents Carter, Reagan, and Clinton all made serious efforts to bring the permanent government to heel in ways that would constrain its growth and prioritize its functions. There were significant accomplishments in selected areas, but each president fell far short of the necessary overhaul. That can only be accomplished by a strong will, the expenditure of serious political capital, consistency, patience, a long attention span, and a dedication to systematic monitoring and follow-through. There is widespread public support for such a crusade, but policymakers will have to persist even when this support doesn't appear to be of high voter priority. Although the realization of these objectives will be difficult, the objectives themselves are the conventional ones. Agencies should be leaner. Functions should be examined for their relevance, both in terms of their reason to exist and in terms of what administrative sector—national, state, community, or private—should have jurisdictional responsibility. Agency policy objectives should be clarified as best they can. Agency successes should be determined by how well they achieve their objectives, and not by how well they oil and operate their processes or procedures. Agencies and their employees need to be rewarded for improvements they make in their routines and in their ability to accomplish their policy objectives, not just with salary increases, but with public acclaim. Workers' perceptions of their own value are driven as much by what the public thinks of their work as by the demands of their jobs. The public, assisted by the media, needs to show continued interest in the value of policy implementation to policy success. It is impossible to measure the impact of pride and civic appreciation on the quality of work, but it is profound indeed. Cooperation between the federal, state, and local governments was so effective in slicing through the traditional red tape barriers that usually stifle efficiency that the Santa Monica Freeway, heavily damaged by the devastating 1994 southern California earthquake, was completely reconstructed in 66 days instead of the 140 that was anticipated. In commenting on this remarkable achievement, Michelle Cottle and Sherri Eisenberg noted that the workers made special efforts to complete the project early because they were aware of not only how critical the project was, but also of the fact that their work was constantly in the public eye. They

noted that when the public's welfare is at stake and workers are under close public scrutiny, "bureaucrats and politicians are loathe to risk public embarrassment and outrage by dragging their feet or behaving in their own narrow self-interests. . . . It also decreases the need for time-consuming, mind numbing bureaucratic procedures. . . . "[12] Until administrators begin to realize that they will be given what they deserve and credit for good work, the nation is unlikely to get it on any systematic basis. Those who make policy operate regularly under public scrutiny. Now it is time to give administrators some carefully focused and regular attention. Only under those conditions, argue Cottle and Eisenberg, will agencies be goaded into "jettisoning the dead weight, rooting out the inefficiencies, and working to show the public exactly what they can accomplish."[13]

Finally, the question of whether the national government's power should be devolved, or decentralized, instead of reinvented deserves a special word. The movement to decentralize policy and administrative authority is rooted in the constitutional principle of federalism. In recent years, the advocacy of devolution in principle has been politically popular, both as a way to absolve the federal government of intractable problems (welfare), and as a way to assuage the public's affinity for strong community government and only essential central government. However, many of the imperatives favoring devolution are rooted in real-world exigencies that are far less sentimental than that. Economies throughout the world are becoming increasingly decentralized and, given the rapid globalization of economics in general, it may make a good deal of sense to let states and localities work to link the well-being of industries within their confines to the trade and market strategies of comparable industries in other countries. The idea of monolithic trade and research policies operated by a central government makes less and less sense under such conditions.

9. *Beware of the bandwagon.* If only a few of the reform alternatives cited above were adopted as suggested, government structure and operations would be recast and both political and policy power would be redistributed substantially. Most of the suggestions are populist in spirit, in that they would empower citizens to reestablish their claim on government and the policies it produces. Populist-based reforms have grown increasingly popular with think tanks, editorialists, television talk shows, and scholars. Most of the proposals, some of which were examined above, are framed in terms of eliminating the harmful influences of special interests on politics and policy. Such a mission resonates forcefully with a public seeking to liberate and refurbish a political system overrun with insider influence, careerism, financial deceitfulness, waste, and conflict of interest. There is little doubt that the system needs significant reform.

However, an element of caution is in order. Before endorsing neopopulism in principle as a panacea, we need to be reminded that often cures can be worse than the diseases they seek to correct or alleviate unless they are implemented and monitored in ways that keep them on course. The momentum of the reform "bandwagon" often can blind reformers to the need to link means to ends consistently. Procedural reforms such as devolution and democratization often can introduce policies that are more politically and administratively fragmented than they were when under the influence of hierarchical forces. According to the advocates of term limits, career legislators have virtually ruined Congress and the state legislatures. They spend most of their time finding and using ways to secure their careers and spend the public's money. They shake down interest groups and their lobbyists for campaign support in return for policy favors.

The result has been the successful imposition of the interests' policy agendas on government. The term limit advocates want to replace this system with one in which "good citizens" volunteer a few years of their professional time for legislative service after which they return to their professions. However, those most able to do this effectively may not want to do it because a legislative career would no longer be a possibility. When you remove a career as an option for holding political office you most likely change the motivation for people to seek office in the first place. The objectives of reinventing government and privatizing some policies are salutary. However, if carried too far as a matter of principle they may well introduce significant problems of accountability to government. Campaign finance reform is long overdue. If it results in reducing the correspondingly close relationships that legislators and president have with their financial supporters it is bound to be advantageous. However, the soft money that is likely to be a key target of any meaningful reform effort has regularly been used by parties for voter registration and voter turnout efforts. To reduce significantly or eliminate such contributions might well further weaken a party system that is already very fragile.

Finally, it should be noted that the mere pro-forma replacement of economic elites with civic elites as key players in politics and policy does not remove elitism as a factor in government. Civic reformers tend to have an uncritical view of their own moral judgments, and that alone can make them unsympathetic with the procedures of democracy. Prescribing a system of reforms that, under an election system conducted under very rigid and intricate rules, brings to office individuals who believe their sense of policy morality immunizes them from the claims of interest groups may well introduce an elite problem of another sort.

At issue here are two interpretations of democracy. One is the marketplace view that pictures democracy in a large and complex society as naturally playing itself out through rather disorderly brawls among interest groups, issue networks, ambitious politicians with inflated egos, and a fragmented Congress and bureaucracy. Constitutional rules intercede regularly in the marketplace to keep conflict from becoming completely indecorous. The other view is that of a "temple" democracy. Currently the most popular, it advocates a political system run by public-spirited, selfless individuals whose role as the moral "guardians" of the system enables them to resist the corrupting influence of favor seekers. Today, both the public and reformists find the second interpretation far more appealing.

This is not to say that any of these reforms shouldn't be attempted. All should be considered seriously. However, it is to say that a wholesale commitment to populist-based reforms could leave some populist demagoguery in its wake. Therefore, reforms should not be accepted wholesale as part of a reform bandwagon or "chic" without careful, critical examination. The healthy skepticism that could result from a commitment to a new civic education, noted above, could serve the public well in this regard. The assumption that the theoretical spirit underlying them will cause them to self-execute in ways totally functional to their official mission is probably naive. It must be remembered that democracy can be easily corrupted if citizens fail to take their obligations seriously. All too often there is not effective citizen follow-through to the formal democratization of institutions. If the success measure applied to procedural reforms is how well they improve an institution's ability to focus on effective solutions to policy problems in the long term, then many recent populist-inspired reforms have had mixed results at best. The decentralization and democratization trends of the 1970s and 1980s that impacted on political parties, Congress, the presidency, and the media are excellent examples. Reforms need consistent, energetic commitment to their purpose and need to be constantly monitored to keep them on track. In short, constitutional democracy carries with it a great deal of responsibility.

The Devolution Dilemma

"Neither time nor tide waits for any man," so goes the saying. A variation on that theme may well make the case for meaningful policy reform occurring within the Constitution's existing procedural boundaries. Because the Constitution apportions power among several policy institutions, there exists the possibility of adjusting the policy dynamics between or among two or more institutions to achieve meaningful policy reform. While the document is not procedurally streamlined to accommodate the obvious need for policy reform, the weight of policy responsibilities can be reapportioned among institutions in an effort to achieve the same end. A common way to do this has been to transfer significant amounts of policy discretion to administrators. As discussed in Chapter 11, this has its advantages and disadvantages, both as a legislator-induced political strategy and as a way to make policy content and administration more meaningful.

However, the most recent "within the structure" strategy has involved the reassignment of significant amounts of policy responsibilities from the national level to states and localities, a trend that has been herein described as the devolution solution. To be sure, an underlying incentive for such a strategy is partly political, or a way for Congress and the president to deal with the deficit problem by transferring costly policy responsibilities to other levels of government. On the other hand, through political opportunism may well lie policy opportunity. Moreover, since the die has already been cast, both politicians and administrators at all three levels of government have little option other than to try to make the best of it.

Policy reform trends tend to follow a power centralization–power decentralization cycle and, since the late 1960s, the trend in the United States has been clearly biased toward the latter. In a sense, our experiences with Vietnam and Watergate cost the public its sense of proportion, or pragmatism, when it comes to deciding on the best way to deal with complicated policy challenges. We find it comforting to think that both the devolution and privatization of power in principle may well be the procedural solutions to the policy quagmires of the times. Devolution harbors the potential to rekindle the sinews of civic interaction that have been eroded by the impact of technology, especially television, on our social selves. The policy responsibilities that flow from policy devolution can pay off through increased levels of education, understanding, and tolerance. By fostering cooperative policy efforts between government and volunteer organizations, it can ease government's workload, contribute to increased levels of civic pride, and increase the chances for policies to be administered and services delivered in a more efficient, realistic way. Indeed, there is potential here.

That potential is reinforced by the current facts of political life. By way of fact, many of the serious problems that concern voters are not the primary responsibility of the federal government anyway. In other words, many of the nation's most serious policy problems are ones that the federal government can do the least to solve. Problems attendant to the education crisis, the AIDS epidemic, crime, society's alleged decaying moral fabric, welfare, and drug use are problems that, by way of tra-

dition, are the primary responsibilities of state and local governments. Dealing effectively with the crime problem involves sound preventive measures and, while the federal government can help with research and financial assistance, the significant strides are made in the schools, within families, and through state and local government sponsorship of youth activities. The same can be said for policies targeted at drug use. The federal government can spend funds to try to control smuggling and to support research on effective treatment of drug abusers. However, the best way to deal with the problem on a long-term basis is to prevent its development and fight its spread. That is best done within families, schools, and other community organizations—all of which are affected continually by state and local, not federal, policies. The federal government's role in combating AIDS is consigned to supporting research on potential cures for the disease. However, it is up to states and localities to sponsor programs which stop behavior which leads to its spread, with schools, churches, and other grass-roots organizations being the most critical players. The concern about the quality of education in public schools is well founded. However, public education is definitively under the policy control of states and localities. The federal government can do little more than act as cheerleader and occasionally offer a few suggestions. Most Americans worry about the cost and long-term results of welfare spending, and when the federal government had jurisdiction over family-based welfare programs, it was only normal to expect public skepticism to be focused on the federal government. However, the Personal Responsibility and Work Opportunity Act of 1996 essentially terminated federal programs that had established a safety net for the country's indigent. Welfare reform is now definitely a state and local policy responsibility. In sum, the best way to deal with all these problems is to prevent them or to control their spread. Organizations and activities that can provide preventive leadership are mostly under the control of state and local governments, not the federal government.

As the nation approached the turn of the twenty-first century, the national government had a lower policy profile relative to the states than at any time since the period immediately preceding the New Deal. The aura of public expectation that the federal government could act swiftly and effectively to combat problems, very much a part of our political culture during the New Deal and Great Society periods, had virtually disappeared. There were several reasons for this. First, there was a global cause. The end of the Cold War meant that the fate of the free world was no longer in America's hands. Second, there was the agreement between President Clinton and Congress to erase budget deficits early in the new century. That agreement, at least temporarily, virtually eliminated tax and spending debates between the Democrats and Republicans. Third, as discussed above, prompted by the Republican takeover of Congress in 1994, the devolution "chic" infiltrated many public policies, most notably the 1996 welfare reform legislation. Fourth, the trends toward divided government encouraged bipartisan, as opposed to party-engendered, policy outputs. The public found such a "compromise and appease" atmosphere notably undynamic and, in effect, uninteresting. Fifth, the Twenty-Second Amendment, limiting a president to two terms in office, played a role. President Clinton was a second-term, lame duck president during the twentieth century's final years, and such terms historically have been generally uninspiring. Finally, and perhaps most important, the public had lost confidence in the federal government's ability to produce effective policy change. The 1996 nominating conventions

and televised presidential candidate debates were the most unwatched of the television era. An increasing number of Americans had decided that the before-camera posturing by Washington politicians had little connection with the problems that they faced in their communities.[14]

In all probability, citizen identification with the anti-Washington political culture of the late 1990s was not born out of a conviction that states and localities had all the policy answers. However, it was born out of a conviction that the federal government definitely did not. The Constitution became an ally to this crusade. The principles of limited government and (especially) federalism lend "higher-law" support to the notion that people can be governed more effectively, responsibly, and efficiently by governments that are close to home. The Constitution can serve as a haven for nostalgia, and much of this was apparent during this period. It was a period of high social anxiety brought on society and the economy by what economists and other social scientists called "postindustrial" economic trends. Technology had replaced the production of machinery and durable goods as the major growth sector of the economy. Companies reorganized, merged with one another, and downsized their workforces. It was little wonder that the appeal of procedural decentralization of public policies became popular. People who were losing control over their social and economic well-being found comfort in a trend that promised to reinvigorate government and policy in ways endorsed by the founding fathers two centuries earlier. If they were losing control over their economic lives due to trends beyond their control, they could compensate by reasserting it over their political lives through devolution.

Devolution offers both opportunities and potential pitfalls. It is dangerous to advance either centralization or decentralization in principle as a policy curative. It is much more prudent to be flexible, even opportunistic. In other words, it pays to be pragmatic. For example, the "ready, fire, aim" approach (as opposed to "ready, aim, fire") might well prove profitable as a pragmatic strategy to minimize the problems that could accrue from an overemphasis of devolution in principle. States and localities, as policy laboratories, could experiment with pilot projects in a number of policy areas. Some will succeed and some will fail. The successes could become models for other states and communities. The failures could be discarded or, if all experiments relating to the development and administration of essential policies fail, then perhaps the national government or regional governments could take up the slack. In addition, "backward mapping" as an administrative strategy might well prove useful in many policy areas. In contrast to "forward mapping," a strategy that orchestrates the administration of a policy from the top of the organizational pyramid, a backward mapping strategy asks that field managers analyze the unique nature of the administrative challenge very carefully and then determine what combination of human, political, and physical resources are necessary to implement the policy successfully. In many cases these resources will be almost exclusively state and local in root. However, in other cases, they may well demand the investment and time of federal agencies and officials. In such circumstances, the reality that devolution is the most popular current administrative trend should not prevent pragmatism from prevailing and making the solution truly intergovernmental in nature.

Both the devolution of power and the democratization of decision making as procedural correctives to policy processes were constructively criticized at various points in previous chapters, most notably in the analysis of political parties and federalism. At other times they have been championed as potential correctives for a political system that has become too beholden to vested interests at the expense of the masses. This may appear contradictory, but it is not, and the reason is rather rudimentary. Structural change provides the impetus and potential for change, *if those who are newly empowered as the result of the change energize their efforts in ways that steer structural reform in the intended direction.* Otherwise the remedy may nurture results that are worse than the original condition. *Unless newly empowered citizens and state and local governments work tenaciously to fulfill the objectives of devolution and democratization, these reforms will merely offer subnational-level legislatures and bureaucrats and the vested interests that support them the opportunity to fill policy and administrative "vacuums" created by the reforms themselves.* Most efforts at devolution are accompanied by cuts in federal support for programs newly assigned to states and localities. In an attempt to secure their positions and maintain their policy responsibilities, subnational bureaucrats will very likely become strong lobbies for state and local budgets to replace the financial losses. If subnational legislatures resist, the bureaucrats will likely enlist the support of their unions and other group beneficiaries that had been subsidized by federal funds. Many of these groups, such as teachers unions, represent large, congruous blocks of votes in state and local elections. Therefore, it is important to provide subnational bureaucrats with considerable discretion over how lost national support should be replaced. While this would not reduce the overall level of spending, it would encourage administrators to use their familiarity with subnational problems in ways that make the administration of policies to combat them more efficient. This would advance the goals of devolution in ways intended by its advocates.

The potential for both the devolution and democratization of policy processes presumes an improvement in the nation's democratic health, which has been on the decline. Jurisdictional, structural, and administrative changes can be worthwhile if legislators, administrators, and citizens are willing to assume the responsibility to make it work. On the other hand these reforms can be major impediments to meaningful policy reform if indifference, withdrawal, and uncertainty reign.

Effective government in an era increasingly impacted by technology, global economic expansion, urbanization, and population growth should combine both hierarchy and democracy in ways that allow the direction of policy reform to be developed and overseen from the top, but to be engineered and energized by public officials and citizens in regional, state, and local jurisdictions. Governments and citizens should not be against either the centralization or the decentralization of power in principle. Each should be available as a tool to be used, as conditions demand, by those attempting to improve the foundation and policy products of government. The Constitution bestows both options and presents few barriers to their being harmonized in the day-to-day policy operations of government.

The Challenge

The policy problems faced by the United States as it enters the twenty-first century are, to one degree or another, shared by all industrial democracies. Because they are democracies, they tend to promise much more than they can deliver. When citizens become aware of this, they become frustrated and gradually lose faith in their governments. Therefore, it would be inappropriate to blame all the policy faults of the United States on the Constitution's guarantee of communication rights or on its structural by-products. Undoubtedly, some observers, in search of easily understood scapegoats, are more than willing to do this. However, such a view is somewhat simplistic. Constitutionally prescribed decision structures and power assignments alone cannot determine the fate of a democratic government.

However, the Constitution's attributes can be employed by political forces to accentuate both the positives and negatives of self-government. If the public's interest is high and optimistic, and political parties are strong and unified, government by the people can overcome procedural obstacles introduced by a Constitution made for a different time and different policy challenges. However, if the public is pessimistic and its interest and participation are waning, then those same procedural obstacles to policy responsiveness can become major roadblocks to a society's efforts to address its policy challenges effectively and efficiently. Therefore, the challenge is to convert the Constitution's negatives into positive, or neutral, forces in an effort to meet the policy challenges of the twenty-first century. The most important ingredient in such a quest is public insistence, with persistence, that this be done. Once that happens, the other necessary prerequisites will, sooner or later, fall into line. If a firm, resolute, and patient public insists on more public service–oriented television programming, it will get it. If a firm, resolute, and patient public insists that both separated and divided government be launching platforms for serious institutionally grounded debates over the content and administration of public policies, it will get it. Most important, once the public conveys to its elected politicians that austerity and sacrifice are creditable policy options, politicians will begin to think, and, most important, act, more seriously about the long term. As Anthony King has noted: "There is no special virtue in a system that requires large numbers of politicians to run the risk of martyrdom in order to ensure that tough decisions can be taken in a timely manner in the national interest."[15] The public must let its leaders know, in no uncertain terms, that political extinction is not the cost of policy courage. The Constitution need not be an impediment to rational government. It can become an asset. However, to make it so will require patience, dedication, and cooperation. Democracy is a major responsibility that the public and its leaders must shoulder together.

Edmund Burke once observed that "man is entitled to freedom only to the extent that he can place chains on his own appetite." Such is the case with our constitutional republic. It can only survive if we make the most of it, despite its imperfections. However, a fundamental prerequisite for the Republic's survival is not to use the Constitution as a way to justify or rationalize indulgences and political opportunism. Rather, it should be used as a way to remind us that our long-term survival as a democracy and as a society depends on our willingness to recognize that the United States as a society is no stronger than its weakest part. This is the most formidable of challenges. It is also a fact of life. Benjamin Franklin recognized and appreciated the close ties that exist between citizenship and civic responsibility in a constitutional democracy. He also knew that it would take diligence and hard work to make both function productively. In all likelihood, that is precisely what he had in mind when he posed that demanding challenge to Mrs. Powell and the

new nation on a Philadelphia street on a quiet evening in the fall of 1787.

Endnotes

1. See Daniel Lazare, *The Frozen Republic: How the Constitution Is Paralyzing Democracy* (Fort Worth, Tex.: Harcourt Brace Jovanovich, 1996).

2. *Ibid.*

3. J. Allen Smith, *The Spirit of American Government,* ed. Cushing Strout (Cambridge, Mass.: The Belknap Press of Harvard University Press, 1965), as quoted in John F. Manley and Kenneth M. Dolbeare, eds., *The Case Against the Constitution: From the Antifederalists to the Present* (Armonk, N.Y.: M. E. Sharpe, 1987), p. 19.

4. Samuel P. Huntington, *American Politics: The Promise of Disharmony* (Cambridge, Mass.: Harvard University Press, 1981), p. 11.

5. Arthur Schlesinger, Jr., "Time for Constitutional Change?" *Wall Street Journal* (December 24, 1982).

6. See Eric Eckholm, "Rescuing Health Care," *New York Times* (May 2, 1991), p. B12.

7. William E. Hudson, *American Democracy in Peril,* 2nd ed. (Chatham, N.J.: Chatham House, 1998), pp. 54–55.

8. See Robert B. Reich, "Up from Bipartisanship," *The American Prospect,* no. 32 (May/June 1997), pp. 26–32.

9. James L. Sundquist, *Constitutional Reform and Effective Government,* rev. ed. (Washington, D.C.: The Brookings Institution, 1992), p. 324.

10. See Michelle Cottle, "Where Are the Good Guys When We Need Them?" *The Washington Monthly,* vol. 29, no. 9 (September 1997), pp. 20–25.

11. V. O. Key, Jr., *Politics, Parties, and Pressure Groups,* 5th ed. (New York: Crowell, 1964), p. 656.

12. Michelle Cottle and Sherri Eisenberg, "Government Can Work," *The Washington Monthly,* vol. 29, no. 5 (May 1997), p. 10.

13. *Ibid.*

14. See Howard Kurtz, "Dullsville USA," *Washington Post National Weekly Edition* (July 14, 1997), pp. 6–7.

15. Anthony King, "Running Scared," *The Atlantic Monthly,* vol. 279, no. 1 (January 1997), p. 60.

We The People of the United States, in Order to form a more perfect Union, establish justice, insure domestic Tranquility, provide for the common defence, promote the general Welfare, and secure the Blessings of Liberty to ourselves and our Posterity, do ordain and establish this Constitution for the United States of America.

The Constitution of the United States

Article I

Section 1. All legislative Powers herein granted shall be vested in a Congress of the United States, which shall consist of a Senate and House of Representatives.

Section 2. The House of Representatives shall be composed of Members chosen every second Year by the People of the several States, and the Electors in each State shall have the Qualifications requisite for Electors of the most numerous Branch of the State Legislature.

No Person shall be a Representative who shall not have attained to the Age of twenty five Years, and been seven Years a Citizen of the United States, and who shall not, when elected, be an inhabitant of that State in which he shall be chosen.

Representatives and direct Taxes shall be apportioned among the several States which may be included within this Union, according to their respective Numbers, which shall be determined by adding to the whole Number of free Persons, including those bound to Service for a Term of Years, and excluding Indians not taxed, three fifths of all other Persons. The actual Enumeration shall be made within three Years after the first Meeting of the Congress of the United States, and within every subsequent Term of ten Years, in such Manner as they shall by Law direct. The Number of Representatives shall not exceed one for every thirty Thousand, but each State shall have at Least one Representative; and until such enumerations shall be made, the State of New Hampshire shall be entitled to chuse three, Massachusetts eight, Rhode-island and Providence Plantations one, Connecticut five, New-York six, New Jersey four, Pennsylvania eight, Delaware one, Maryland six, Virginia ten, North Carolina five, South Carolina five, and Georgia three.

When vacancies happen in the Representation from any State, the Executive Authority thereof shall issue Writs of Election to fill such Vacancies.

The House of Representatives shall chuse their speaker and other Officers; and shall have the sole Power of impeachment.

Section 3. The Senate of the United States shall be composed of two Senators from each State, chosen by the Legislature thereof, for six Years; and each Senator shall have one vote.

Immediately after they shall be assembled in Consequence of the first Election, they shall be divided as equally as may be into three Classes. The Seats of the Senators of the first Class shall be vacated at the Expiration of the second Year, of the second Class at the Expiration of the fourth Year, and of the third Class at the Expiration of the sixth Year, so that one third may be chosen every second Year; and if Vacancies happen by Resignation, or otherwise, during the Recess of the Legislature of any State, the Executive thereof may make temporary Appointments until the next Meeting of the Legislature, which shall then fill such Vacancies.

No Person shall be a Senator who shall not have attained to the Age of thirty Years, and been nine Years a Citizen of the United States, and who shall not, when elected, be an Inhabitant of that State for which he shall be chosen.

The Vice President of the United States shall be President of the Senate, but shall have no Vote, unless they be equally divided.

The Senate shall chuse their other Officers, and also a President pro tempore, in the Absence of the Vice President, or when he shall exercise the Office of President of the United States.

The Senate shall have the sole Power to try all Impeachments. When sitting for that Purpose, they shall be on Oath or Affirmation. When the President of the United States is tried, the Chief Justice shall preside: And no Person shall be convicted without the concurrence of two thirds of the Members present. Judgment in Cases of Impeachment shall not extend further than to removal from Office, and disqualification to hold and enjoy any Office of honor, Trust or Profit under the United States: but the Party convicted shall nevertheless be liable and subject to Indictment, Trial, Judgment and Punishment, according to law.

Section 4. The Times, Places and Manner of holding Elections for Senators and Representatives, shall be prescribed in each State by the Legislature thereof; but the Congress may at any time by Law make or alter such Regulations, except as to the Places of chusing Senators.

The Congress shall assemble at least once in every Year, and such Meeting shall be on the first Monday in December, unless they shall by Law appoint a different Day.

Section 5. Each House shall be the Judge of the Elections, Returns and Qualifications of its own Members, and a Majority of each shall constitute a Quorum to do business; but a smaller Number may adjourn from day to day, and may be authorized to compel the Attendance of absent Members, in such Manner, and under such Penalties as each House may provide.

Each House may determine the Rules of its Proceedings, punish its Members for disorderly Behaviour, and, with the Concurrence of two thirds, expel a Member.

Each House shall keep a journal of its Proceedings, and from time to time publish the same, excepting such Parts as may in their judgment require Secrecy; and the yeas and Nays of the Members of either House on any question shall, at the Desire of one fifth of those Present, be entered on the journal.

Neither House, during the Session of Congress, shall, without the Consent of the other, adjourn for more than three days, nor to any other place than that in which the two Houses shall be sitting.

Section 6. The Senators and Representatives shall receive a Compensation for their Services, to be ascertained by Law, and paid out of the Treasury of the United States. They shall in all Cases, except Treason, Felony and Breach of the Peace, be privileged from Arrest during their Attendance at the Session of their respective Houses, and in going to and returning from the same; and for any Speech or Debate in either House, they shall not be questioned in any other Place.

No Senator or Representative shall, during the

Time for which he was elected, be appointed to any civil Office under the Authority of the United States, which shall have been created, or the Emoluments whereof shall have been encreased during such time; and no Person holding any Office under the United States, shall be a Member of either House during his Continuance in Office.

Section 7. All Bills for raising Revenue shall originate in the House of Representatives; but the Senate may propose or concur with Amendments as on other Bills.

Every Bill which shall have passed the House of Representatives and the Senate, shall, before it become a Law, be presented to the President of the United States; if he approve he shall sign it, but if not he shall return it, with his Objections to that House in which it shall have originated, who shall enter the Objections at large on their journal, and proceed to reconsider it. If after such Reconsideration two thirds of that House shall agree to pass the Bill, it shall be sent, together with the Objections, to the other House, by which it shall likewise be reconsidered, and if approved by two thirds of that House, it shall become a Law. But in all such Cases the Votes of both Houses shall be determined by yeas and Nays, and the Names of the Persons voting for and against the Bill shall be entered on the Journal of each House respectively. If any Bill shall not be returned by the President within ten Days (Sundays excepted) after it shall have been presented to him, the Same shall be a Law, in like Manner as if he had signed it, unless the Congress by their Adjournment prevent its Return, in which Case it shall not be a Law.

Every Order, Resolution, or Vote to which the Concurrence of the Senate and House of Representatives may be necessary (except on a question of Adjournment) shall be presented to the President of the United States; and before the Same shall take Effect, shall be approved by him, or being disapproved by him, shall be repassed by two thirds of the Senate and House of Representatives, according to the Rules and Limitations prescribed in the Case of a Bill.

Section 8. The Congress shall have Power To lay and collect Taxes, Duties, Imposts and Excises, to pay the Debts and provide for the common Defence and general Welfare of the United States; but all duties, Imposts and Excises shall be uniform throughout the United States;

To borrow Money on the Credit of the United States;

To regulate Commerce with foreign Nations, and among the several States, and with the Indian Tribes;

To establish an uniform Rule of Naturalization, and uniform Laws on the subject of Bankruptcies throughout the United States;

To coin Money, regulate the Value thereof, and of foreign Coin, and fix the Standard of Weights and Measures;

To provide for the Punishment of counterfeiting the Securities and current Coin of the United States;

To establish Post Offices and post Roads;

To promote the Progress of Science and useful Arts, by securing for limited Times to Authors and Inventors exclusive Right to their respective Writings and Discoveries;

To constitute Tribunals inferior to the supreme Court;

To define and punish Piracies and Felonies committed on the high Seas, and Offences against the Law of Nations;

To declare War, grant Letters of Marque and Reprisal, and make rules concerning Captures on Land and Water;

To raise and support Armies, but no Appropriation of Money to that Use shall be for a longer Term than two Years;

To provide and maintain a Navy;

To make rules for Government and Regulation of the land and naval Forces;

To provide for calling forth the Militia to execute the Laws of the Union, suppress Insurrections and repel Invasions;

To provide for organizing, arming, and disciplining, the Militia, and for governing such Part of them as may be employed in the Service of the United States, reserving to the States respectively, the Appointment of the Officers, and the Authority of training the Militia according to the discipline prescribed by Congress;

To exercise exclusive Legislation in all Cases whatsoever, over such District (not exceeding ten

Miles square), as may, by Cession of particular States, and the Acceptance of Congress, become the Seat of the Government of the United States, and to exercise like Authority over all Places purchased by the Consent of the Legislature of the State in which the Same shall be for the Erection of Forts, Magazines, Arsenals, dock-Yards, and other needful Buildings;-And

To make all Laws which shall be necessary and proper for carrying into Execution the foregoing Powers, and all other Powers vested by this Constitution in the Government of the United States, or in any Department or Officer thereof.

Section 9. The Migration or Importation of such Persons as any of the States now existing shall think proper to admit, shall not be prohibited by the Congress prior to the Year one thousand eight hundred and eight, but a Tax or duty may be imposed on such Importation, not exceeding ten dollars for each Person.

The Privilege of the Writ of Habeas Corpus shall not be suspended, unless when in Cases of Rebellion or Invasion the public Safety may require it.

No Bill of Attainder or ex post facto Law shall be passed.

No Capitation, or other direct, Tax shall be laid, unless in Proportion to the Census or Enumeration herein before directed to be taken.

No Tax or Duty shall be laid on Articles exported from any State.

No Preference shall be given by any Regulation of Commerce or Revenue to the Ports of one State over those of another: nor shall Vessels bound to, or from, one State, be obliged to enter, clear, or pay Duties in another.

No money shall be drawn from the Treasury, but in Consequence of Appropriations made by Law; and a regular Statement and Account of the Receipts and Expenditures of all public Money shall be published from time to time.

No Title of Nobility shall be granted by the United States: And no Person holding any Office of Profit or Trust under them, shall, without the Consent of the Congress, accept of any present, Emolument, Office, or Title, of any kind whatever, from any King, Prince, or foreign State.

Section 10. No State shall enter into any Treaty, Alliance, or Confederation; grant Letters of Marque and Reprisal; coin Money; emit Bills of Credit; make any Thing but gold and silver Coin a Tender in Payment of Debts; pass any Bill of Attainder, ex post facto Law, or Law impairing the Obligation of Contracts, or grant any Title of Nobility.

No State shall, without the Consent of the Congress, lay any Imposts or Duties on Imports or Exports, except what may be absolutely necessary for executing its inspection Laws: and the net Produce of all Duties and Imposts, laid by any State on Imports or Exports, shall be for the Use of the Treasury of the United States; and all such Laws shall be subject to the Revision and Controul of the Congress.

No State shall, without the Consent of Congress, lay any Duty of Tonnage, keep Troops, or Ships of War in time of Peace, enter into any Agreement or Compact with another State, or with a foreign Power, or engage in War, unless actually invaded, or in such imminent Danger as will not admit of delay.

Article II

Section 1. The executive Power shall be vested in a President of the United States of America. He shall hold his Office during the Term of four Years, and, together with the Vice President, chosen for the same term, be elected, as follows

Each State shall appoint, in such Manner as the Legislature thereof may direct, a Number of Electors, equal to the whole Number of Senators and Representatives to which the State may be entitled in the Congress: but no Senator or Representative, or Person holding an Office of Trust or Profit under the United States, shall be appointed an Elector.

The Electors shall meet in their respective States, and vote by Ballot for two Persons, of whom one at least shall not be an Inhabitant of the same State with themselves. And they shall make a List of all the Persons voted for, and of the Number of Votes for each; which List they shall sign and certify, and transmit sealed to the Seat of the Government of the United States, directed to the President of the Senate. The President of the Senate shall, in the Presence of the Senate and House of Representatives, open all the Certificates, and the Votes shall then be counted. The Person having the greatest Number of Votes shall be the

President, if such Number be a Majority of the whole Number of Electors appointed; and if there be more than one who have such Majority, and have an equal Number of Votes, then the House of Representatives shall immediately chuse by Ballot one of them for President: and if no Person have a Majority, then from the five highest on the List the said House shall in like Manner chuse the President. But in chusing the President, the Votes shall be taken by States, the Representation from each State having one Vote; A quorum for this Purpose shall consist of a Member or Members from two thirds of the States, and a Majority of all the States shall be necessary to a Choice. In every Case, after the Choice of the President, the Person having the greatest Number of Votes of the Electors shall be the Vice President. But if there should remain two or more who have equal Votes, the Senate shall chuse from them by Ballot the Vice President.

The Congress may determine the Time of chusing the Electors, and the Day on which they shall give their Votes; which Day shall be the same throughout the United States.

No Person except a natural born Citizen, or a Citizen of the United States, at the time of the Adoption of this Constitution, shall be eligible to the office of President; neither shall any Person be eligible to that Office who shall not have attained to the Age of thirty five Years, and been fourteen Years a Resident within the United States.

In Case of the Removal of the President from Office, or of his Death, Resignation, or Inability to discharge the Powers and Duties of the said Office, the Same shall devolve on the Vice President, and the Congress may by Law provide for the Case of Removal, Death, Resignation or Inability, both of the President and Vice President, declaring what Officer shall then act as President, and such Officer shall act accordingly, until the Disability be removed, or a President shall be elected.

The President shall, at stated Times, receive for his Services, a Compensation, which shall neither be encreased nor diminished during the Period for which he shall have been elected, and he shall not receive within that Period any other Emolument from the United States, or any of them.

Before he enter on the Execution of his Office, he shall take the following Oath or Affirmation:-"I do solemnly swear (or affirm) that I will faithfully execute the Office of President of the United States, and will to the best of my Ability, preserve, protect and defend the Constitution of the United States."

Section 2. The President shall be Commander in Chief of the Army and Navy of the United States, and of the Militia of the several States, when called into the actual Service of the United States, he may require the Opinion, in writing, of the principal Officer in each of the executive Departments, upon any Subject relating to the Duties of their respective Offices, and he shall have the Power to grant Reprieves and Pardons for Offences against the United States, except in Cases of Impeachment.

He shall have Power, by and with the Advice and Consent of the Senate to make Treaties, provided two thirds of the Senators present concur; and he shall nominate, and by and with the Advice and Consent of the Senate, shall appoint Ambassadors, other public Ministers and Consuls, Judges of the supreme Court, and all other Officers of the United States, whose Appointments are not herein otherwise provided for, and which shall be established by Law: but the Congress may by Law vest the Appointment of such inferior Officers, as they think proper, in the President alone, in the Courts of Law, or in the Heads of Departments.

The President shall have Power to fill up all Vacancies that may happen during the Recess of the Senate, by granting Commissions which shall expire at the End of their next Session.

Section 3. He shall from time to time give to the Congress Information of the State of the Union, and recommend to their Consideration such Measures as he shall judge necessary and expedient; he may, on extraordinary Occasions, convene both Houses, or either of them, and in Case of Disagreement between them, with Respect to the Time of Adjournment, he may adjourn them to such Time as he shall think proper; he shall receive Ambassadors and other public Ministers; he shall take Care that the Laws be faithfully executed, and shall Commission all the Officers of the United States.

Section 4. The President, Vice President and all civil Officers of the United States, shall be removed from Office on Impeachment for, and Conviction of, Treason, Bribery, or other High Crimes and Misdemeanors.

Article III

Section 1. The judicial Power of the United States, shall be vested in one supreme Court, and in such inferior Courts as the Congress may from time to time ordain and establish. The Judges, both the supreme and inferior Courts, shall hold their Offices during good Behaviour, and shall, at stated Times, receive for their Services, a Compensation, which shall not be diminished during their Continuance in Office.

Section 2. The judicial Power shall extend to all Cases, in Law and Equity, arising under this Constitution, the Laws of the United States, and Treaties made, or which shall be made, under their Authority;-to all Cases affecting Ambassadors, other public Ministers and Consuls;-to all Cases of admiralty and maritime Jurisdiction;-to Controversies to which the United States shall be a Party;-to Controversies between two or more States; between a State and Citizens of another State;-between Citizens of different States;-between Citizens of the same State claiming Lands under Grants of different States, and between a State, or the Citizens thereof, and foreign States, Citizens, or Subjects.

In all Cases affecting Ambassadors, other public Ministers and Consuls, and those in which a State shall be Party, the supreme Court shall have original Jurisdiction. In all the other Cases before mentioned, the supreme Court shall have appellate Jurisdiction, both as to Law and Fact, with such Exceptions, and under such Regulations as Congress shall make.

The Trial of all Crimes, except in Cases of Impeachment, shall be by Jury; and such Trial shall be held in the State where the said Crimes shall have been committed; but when not committed within any State, the Trial shall be at such Place or Places as the Congress may by Law have directed.

Section 3. Treason against the United States, shall consist only in levying War against them, or in adhering to their Enemies, giving them Aid and Comfort. No Person shall be convicted of Treason unless on the Testimony of two Witnesses to the same overt Act, or on Confession in open Court.

The Congress shall have Power to declare the Punishment of Treason, but no Attainder of Treason shall work Corruption of Blood, or Forfeiture except during the Life of the Person attainted.

Article IV

Section 1. Full Faith and Credit shall be given in each State to the public Acts, Records, and judicial Proceedings of every other State. And the Congress may by general Laws prescribe the Manner in which such Acts, Records and Proceedings shall be proved, and the Effect thereof.

Section 2. The Citizens of each State shall be entitled to all Privileges and Immunities of Citizens in the several States.

A Person charged in any State with Treason, Felony, or other Crime, who shall flee from justice, and be found in another State, shall on Demand of the executive Authority of the State from which he fled, be delivered up, to be removed to the State having jurisdiction of the Crime.

No person held to Service or Labour in one State, under the Laws thereof, escaping into another, shall, in Consequence of any Law or Regulation therein, be discharged from such Service or Labour, but shall be delivered up on Claim of the Party to whom such Service or Labour may be due.

Section 3. New States may be admitted by the Congress into this Union; but no new State shall be formed or erected within the jurisdiction of any other State; nor any State be formed by the junction of two or more States, or Parts of States, without the Consent of the Legislatures of the States concerned as well as of the Congress.

The Congress shall have Power to dispose of and make all needful Rules and Regulations respecting the Territory or other Property belonging to the United States; and nothing in this Constitution shall be so construed as to Prejudice any Claims of the United States, or of any particular State.

Section 4. The United States shall guarantee to every State in this Union a Republican Form of Government, and shall protect each of them against Invasion; and on Application of the Legislature, or of the Executive (when the Legislature cannot be convened) against domestic Violence.

Article V

The Congress, whenever two thirds of both Houses shall deem it necessary, shall propose Amendments to this Constitution, or, on the Application of the Legislatures of two thirds of the several States, shall call a Convention for proposing Amendments, which, in either Case, shall be valid to all Intents and Purposes, as Part of this Constitution, when ratified by the Legislatures of three fourths of the several States, or by Conventions in three fourths thereof, as the one or the other Mode of Ratification may be proposed by the Congress; Provided that no Amendment which may be made prior to the Year One thousand eight hundred and eight shall in any Manner affect the first and fourth Clauses in the Ninth Section of the first Article; and that no State, without its Consent, shall be deprived of its equal Suffrage In the Senate.

Article VI

All Debts contracted and Engagements entered into, before the Adoption of this Constitution, shall be as valid against the United States under this Constitution, as under the Confederation.

This Constitution, and the Laws of the United States which shall be made in Pursuance thereof, and all Treaties made, or which shall be made, under the Authority of the United States, shall be the supreme Law of the Land; and the Judges In every State shall be bound thereby, any Thing In the Constitution or Laws of any State to the Contrary notwithstanding.

The Senators and Representatives before mentioned, and the Members of the several State Legislatures, and all executive and judicial Officers, both of the United States and of the several States, shall be bound by Oath or Affirmation, to support this Constitution; but no religious Test shall ever be required as a Qualification to any Office or public Trust under the United States.

Article VII

The Ratification of the Conventions of nine States, shall be sufficient for the Establishment of this Constitution between the States so ratifying the Same.

done in Convention by the Unanimous Consent of the States present the Seventeenth Day of September in the Year of our Lord one thousand seven hundred and Eighty seven and of the Independence of the United States of America the Twelfth In witness whereof We have hereunto subscribed our Names,

	G, Washington-Presid^t and deputy from Virginia
New Hampshire	John Langdon
	Nicholas Gilman
Massachusetts	Nathaniel Gorham
	Rufus King
Connecticut	Wm Sam! Johnson
	Roger Sherman
New York	Alexander Hamilton
New Jersey	Wil: Livingston
	David Brearley.
	Wm Paterson.
	Jona: Dayton
Pennsylvania[1]	B Franklin
	Thomas Miff lin
	Robt Morris
	Geo. Clymer
	Thom FitzSimons
	Jared Ingersoll
	James Wilson
	Gouv Morris
Delaware	Geo Read
	Gunning Bedford jun
	John Dickinson
	Richard Bassett
	Jaco: Broom
Maryland	James McHenry
	Dan of St Tho! Jenifer
	Danl Carroll
Virginia	John Blair-
	James Madison Jr.

[1] Spelled with one n on the original document.

North Carolina	W<u>m</u> Blount
	Rich<u>d</u> Dobbs Spaight.
	Hu Williamson
South Carolina	J. Rutledge
	Charles Cotesworth Pinckney
	Charles Pinckney
	Pierce Butler.
Georgia	William Few
	Abr Baldwin

Amendments

[The first ten amendments were ratified December 15, 1791, and form what is known as the Bill of Rights.]

Amendment 1

Congress shall make no law respecting an establishment of religion, or prohibiting the free exercise thereof, or abridging the freedom of speech, or of the press; or the right of the people peaceably to assemble, and to petition the Government for a redress of grievances.

Amendment 2

A well regulated Militia, being necessary to the security of a free State, the right of the people to keep and bear Arms, shall not be infringed.

Amendment 3

No Soldier shall, in time of peace be quartered in any house, without the consent of the Owner, nor in time of war, but in a manner to be prescribed by law.

Amendment 4

The right of the people to be secure in their persons, houses, papers, and effects, against unreasonable searches and seizures, shall not be violated, and no Warrants shall issue, but upon probable cause, supported by Oath or affirmation, and particularly describing the place to be searched, and the persons or things to be seized.

Amendment 5

No person shall be held to answer for a capital, or otherwise infamous crime, unless on a presentment or indictment of a Grand Jury, except in cases arising in the land or naval forces, or in the Militia, when in actual service in time of War or public danger; nor shall any person be subject for the same offence to be twice put in jeopardy of life or limb; nor shall be compelled in any criminal case to be a witness against himself, nor be deprived of life, liberty, or property, without due process of law; nor shall private property be taken for public use, without just compensation.

Amendment 6

In all criminal prosecutions, the accused shall enjoy the right to a speedy and public trial, by an impartial jury of the State and district wherein the crime shall have been committed, which district shall have been previously ascertained by law, and to be informed of the nature and cause of the accusation; to be confronted with the witnesses against him; to have compulsory process for obtaining witnesses in his favor, and to have the Assistance of Counsel for his defence.

Amendment 7

In Suits at common law, where the value in controversy shall exceed twenty dollars, the right of trial by jury shall be preserved, and no fact tried by a jury, shall be otherwise re-examined in any Court of the United States, than according to the rules of the common law.

Amendment 8

Excessive bail shall not be required, nor excessive fines imposed, nor cruel and unusual punishments inflicted.

Amendment 9

The enumeration in the Constitution, of certain rights, shall not be construed to deny or disparage others retained by the people.

Amendment 10

The powers not delegated to the United States by the Constitution, nor prohibited by it to the States, are reserved to the States respectively, or to the people.

Amendment 11
(ratified February 7, 1795)

The Judicial power of the United States shall not be construed to extend to any suit in law or equity, commenced or prosecuted against one of the United States by Citizens of another State, or by Citizens or Subjects of any Foreign State.

Amendment 12
(ratified July 27, 1804)

The Electors shall meet in their respective states, and vote by ballot for President and Vice-President, one of whom, at least, shall not be an inhabitant of the same state with themselves; they shall name in their ballots the person voted for as President, and in distinct ballots the person voted for as Vice-President, and they shall make distinct lists of all persons voted for as President, and of all persons voted for as Vice-President, and of the number of votes for each, which lists they shall sign and certify, and transmit sealed to the seat of the government of the United States, directed to the President of the Senate;-The President of the senate shall, in the presence of the Senate and House of Representatives, open all the certificates and the votes shall then be counted;-The person having the greatest number of votes for President, shall be the President, if such number be a majority of the whole number of Electors appointed; and if no person have such majority, then from the persons having the highest numbers not exceeding three on the list of those voted for as President, the House of Representatives shall choose immediately, by ballot, the President. But in choosing the President, the votes shall be taken by states, the representation from each state having one vote; a quorum for this purpose shall consist of a member or members from two-thirds of the states, and a majority of all the states shall be necessary to a choice. And if the House of Representatives, shall

not choose a President whenever the right of choice shall devolve upon them, before the fourth day of March next following, then the Vice-President shall act as President, as in the case of the death or other constitutional disability of the President.-The person having the greatest number of votes as Vice-President, shall be the Vice-President, if such number be a majority of the whole number of Electors appointed, and if no person have a majority, then from the two highest numbers on the list, the Senate shall choose the Vice-President; a quorum for the purpose shall consist of two-thirds of the whole number of Senators, and a majority of the whole number shall be necessary to a choice. But no person constitutionally ineligible to the office of President shall be eligible to that of Vice-President of the United States.

Amendment 13
(ratified December 6, 1865)

Section 1. Neither slavery nor involuntary servitude, except as a punishment for crime whereof the party shall have been duly convicted, shall exist within the United States, or any place subject to their jurisdiction.

Section 2. Congress shall have power to enforce this article by appropriate legislation.

Amendment 14
(ratified July 9, 1868)

Section 1. All persons born or naturalized in the United States, and subject to the jurisdiction thereof, are citizens of the United States and of the State wherein they reside. No State shall make or enforce any law which shall abridge the privileges or immunities of citizens of the United States; nor shall any State deprive any person of life, liberty, or property, without due process of law; nor deny to any person within its jurisdiction the equal protection of the laws.

Section 2. Representatives shall be apportioned among the several States according to their respective numbers, counting the whole number of persons in each State, excluding Indians not taxed.

But when the right to vote at any election for the choice of electors for President and Vice President of the United States, Representatives in Congress, the Executive and judicial officers of a State, or the members of the Legislature thereof, is denied to any of the male inhabitants of such State, being twenty-one years of age, and citizens of the United States, or in any way abridged, except for participation in rebellion, or other crime, the basis of representation therein shall be reduced in the proportion which the number of such male citizens shall bear to the whole number of male citizens twenty-one years of age in such State.

Section 3. No person shall be a Senator or Representative in Congress, or elector of President and Vice President, or hold any office, civil or military, under the United States, or under any State, who, having previously taken an oath, as a member of Congress, or as an officer of the United States, or as a member of any State legislature, or as an executive or judicial officer of any State, to support the Constitution of the United States, shall have engaged in insurrection or rebellion against the same, or given aid or comfort to the enemies thereof. But Congress may by a vote of two-thirds of each House, remove such disability.

Section 4. The validity of the public debt of the United States, authorized by law, including debts incurred for payment of pensions and bounties for services in suppressing insurrection or rebellion, shall not be questioned. But neither the United States nor any State shall assume or pay any debt or obligation incurred in aid of insurrection or rebellion against the United States, or any claim for the loss or emancipation of any slave; but all such debts, obligations and claims shall be held illegal and void.

Section 5. The Congress shall have power to enforce, by appropriate legislation, the provisions of this article.

Amendment 15
(ratified February 3, 1870)

Section 1. The right of citizens of the United States to vote shall not be denied or abridged by the United States or by any State on account of race, color, or previous condition of servitude.

Section 2. The Congress shall have power to enforce this article by appropriate legislation.

Amendment 16
(ratified February 3, 1913)

The Congress shall have power to lay and collect taxes on incomes, from whatever source derived, without apportionment among the several States, and without regard to any census or enumeration.

Amendment 17
(ratified April 8, 1913)

The Senate of the United States shall be composed of two Senators from each State, elected by the people thereof for six years; and each Senator shall have one vote. The electors in each State shall have the qualifications requisite for electors of the most numerous branch of the State legislatures.

When vacancies happen in the representation of any State in the Senate, the executive authority of such State shall issue writs of election to fill such vacancies: Provided, That the legislature of any State may empower the executive thereof to make temporary appointments until the people fill the vacancies by election as the legislature may direct.

This amendment shall not be so construed as to affect the election or term of any Senator chosen before it becomes valid as part of the Constitution.

Amendment 18
(ratified January 16, 1919. repealed December 5, 1933 by Amendment 21)

Section 1. After one year from the ratification of this article the manufacture, sale, or transportation of intoxicating liquors within, the importation thereof into, or the exportation thereof from the United States and all territory subject to the jurisdiction thereof for beverage purposes is hereby prohibited.

Section 2. The Congress and the several States shall have concurrent power to enforce this article by appropriate legislation.

Section 3. This article shall be inoperative unless it shall have been ratified as an amendment to the Constitution by the legislatures of the several States as provided in the Constitution, within seven years from the date of the submission hereof to the States by the Congress.

Amendment 19
(ratified August 18, 1920)

The right of citizens of the United States to vote shall not be denied or abridged by the United States or by any State on account of sex.

Congress shall have power to enforce this article by appropriate legislation.

Amendment 20
(ratified January 23, 1933)

Section 1. The terms of the President and Vice President shall end at noon on the 20th day of January, and the terms of Senators and Representatives at noon on the 3d day of January, of the years in which such terms would have ended if this article had not been ratified; and the terms of their successors shall then begin.

Section 2. The Congress shall assemble at least once in every year, and such meeting shall begin at noon on the 3d day of January, unless they shall by law appoint a different day.

Section 3. If, at the time fixed for the beginning of the term of the President, the President elect shall have died, the Vice President elect shall become President. If a President shall not have been chosen before the time fixed for the beginning of his term, or if the President elect shall have failed to qualify, then the Vice President elect shall act as President until a President shall have qualified; and the Congress may by law provide for the case wherein neither a President elect nor a Vice President elect shall have qualified, declaring who shall then act as President, or the manner in which one who is to act shall be elected, and such person shall act accord-ingly until a President or Vice President shall have qualified.

Section 4. The Congress may by law provide for the case of the death of any of the persons from whom the House of Representatives may choose a President whenever the right of choice shall have devolved upon them, and for the case of the death of any of the persons from whom the Senate may choose a Vice President whenever the right of choice shall have devolved upon them.

Section 5. Sections 1 and 2 shall take effect on the 15th day of October following the ratification of this article.

Section 6. This article shall be inoperative unless it shall have been ratified as an amendment to the Constitution by the legislatures of three-fourths of the several States within seven years from the date of its submission.

Amendment 21
(ratified December 5, 1933)

Section 1. The eighteenth article of amendment to the Constitution of the United States is hereby repealed.

Section 2. The transportation or importation into any State, Territory, or possession of the United States for delivery or use therein of intoxicating liquors, in violation of the laws thereof, is hereby prohibited.

Amendment 22
(ratified February 27, 1951)

Section 1. No person shall be elected to the office of the President more than twice, and no person who has held the office of President, or acted as President, for more than two years of a term to which some other person was elected President shall be elected to the office of the President more than once. But this Article shall not apply to any person holding the office of President when this Article was proposed by the Congress, and shall not prevent any person who may be holding the office of President, or acting as President, during the term within which this Article becomes operative from holding the office of President or acting as President during the remainder of such term.

Section 2. This article shall be inoperative unless it shall have been ratified as an amendment to the Constitution by the legislatures of three-fourths of the several States within seven years from the date of its submission to the States by the Congress.

Amendment 23
(ratified March 29, 1961)

Section 1. The District constituting the seat of Government of the United States shall appoint in such manner as the Congress may direct:

A number of electors of President and Vice President equal to the whole number of Senators and Representatives in Congress to which the District would be entitled if it were a State, but in no event more than the least populous State; they shall be in addition to those appointed by the States, but they shall be considered, for the purposes of the election of President and Vice President, to be electors appointed by a State; and they shall meet in the District and perform such duties as provided by the twelfth article of amendment.

Section 2. The Congress shall have power to enforce this article by appropriate legislation.

Amendment 24
(ratified January 23, 1964)

Section 1. The right of citizens of the United States to vote in any primary or other election for President or Vice President, for electors for President or Vice President, or for Senator or Representative in Congress, shall not be denied or abridged by the United States or any State by reason of failure to pay any poll tax or other tax.

Section 2. The Congress shall have power to enforce this article by appropriate legislation.

Amendment 25
(ratified February 10, 1967)

Section 1. In case of the removal of the President from office or of his death or resignation, the Vice President shall become President.

Section 2. Whenever there is a vacancy in the office of the Vice President, the President shall nominate a Vice President who shall take office upon confirmation by a majority vote of both Houses of Congress.

Section 3. Whenever the President transmits to the President pro tempore of the Senate and the Speaker of the House of Representatives his written declaration that he is unable to discharge the powers and duties of his office, and until he transmits to them a written declaration to the contrary, such powers and duties shall be discharged by the Vice President as Acting President.

Section 4. Whenever the Vice President and a majority of either the principal officers of the executive departments or of such other body as Congress may by law provide, transmit to the President pro tempore of the Senate and the Speaker of the House of Representatives their written declaration that the President is unable to discharge the powers and duties of his office, the Vice President shall immediately assume the powers and duties of the office as Acting President.

Thereafter, when the President transmits to the President pro tempore of the Senate and the Speaker of the House of Representatives his written declaration that no inability exists, he shall resume the powers and duties of his office unless the Vice President and a majority of either the principal officers of the executive department or of such other body as Congress may by law provide, transmit within four days to the President pro tempore of the Senate and the Speaker of the House of Representatives their written declaration that the President is unable to discharge the powers and duties of his office. Thereupon Congress shall decide the issue, assembling within forty-eight hours for that purpose if not in session. If the Congress, within twenty-one days after receipt of the latter written declaration, or, if Congress is not in session, within twenty-one days after Congress is required to assemble, determines by two-thirds vote of both Houses that the President is unable to discharge the powers and duties of his office, the Vice President shall continue to discharge the same as Acting President; otherwise, the President shall resume the powers and duties of his office.

Amendment 26
(ratified July 1, 1971)

Section 1. The right of citizens of the United States, who are eighteen years of age or older, to vote shall not be denied or abridged by the United States or by any State on account of age.

Section 2. The Congress shall have the power to enforce this article by appropriate legislation.

Amendment 27
(ratified May 7, 1992)

No law, varying the compensation for the services of the Senators and Representatives, shall take effect, until an election of Representatives shall have intervened.

Bibliography

Abraham, Henry J., *Justices and Presidents*, 3rd ed. (New York: Oxford University Press, 1992).

———, *The Judicial Process*, 7th ed. (New York: Oxford University Press, 1998).

Adler, Mortimer, *We Hold These Truths: Understanding the Ideals and Ideas of the Constitution* (New York: Macmillan, 1987).

Agabin, Pacifico A., *Unconstitutional Essays* (Honolulu: University of Hawaii Press, 1997).

Alexander, Herbert E., *Financing Politics: Money, Elections, and Political Reform*, 4th ed. (Washington D.C.: CQ Press, 1992).

Anton, Thomas J., *American Federalism and Public Policy: How the System Works* (New York: Random House, 1989).

Armor, David J., *Forced Justice: School Desegregation and the Law* (New York: Oxford University Press, 1995).

Arnold, Peri, *Making the Managerial Presidency* (Princeton, N.J.: Princeton University Press, 1986).

Arnold, R. Douglas, *Congress and the Bureaucracy* (New Haven, Conn.: Yale University Press, 1979).

Bailey, Stephen K., and Edith K. Mosher, *ESEA: The Office of Education Administers a Law* (Syracuse, N.Y.: Syracuse University Press, 1968).

Baker, Ross K., *House and Senate* (New York: W. W. Norton, 1989).

Barber, Benjamin, *Strong Democracy: Participatory Politics for a New Age* (Berkeley: University of California Press, 1984).

———, and Patrick Watson, *The Struggle for Democracy* (Boston: Little, Brown, 1988).

———, *An Aristocracy of Everyone: The Politics of Education and the Future America* (New York: Ballantine, 1992).

Barber, James D., *The Presidential Character: Predicting Performance in the White House*, 3rd ed. (Englewood Cliffs, N.J.: Prentice Hall, 1985).

Barber, Sotirios A., *On What the Constitution Means* (Baltimore, Md.: Johns Hopkins University Press, 1986).

Bardach, Eugene, *The Implementation Game* (Cambridge, Mass.: MIT Press, 1977).

Barger, Harold M., *The Impossible Presidency* (Glenview, Ill.: Scott, Foresman, 1984).

Barlett, Donald L., and James B. Steele, *America: What Went Wrong?* (Kansas City, Mo.: Andrews and McMeel, 1992).

Barnet, Randy, *The Structure of Liberty: Justice and the Rule of Law* (New York: Oxford University Press, 1998).

Barone, Michael, *Our Country: The Shaping of America from Roosevelt to Reagan* (New York: Free Press, 1990).

Baumgartner, Frank R., and Bryan D. Jones, *Agendas and Instability in American Politics* (Chicago: University of Chicago Press, 1993).

Beard, Charles A., *An Economic Interpretation of the Constitution of the United States* (New York: Macmillan, 1913).

———, *The Economic Origins of Jeffersonian Democracy* (New York: Free Press, 1943, 1965).

Bellah, Robert N., Richard Madsen, William M. Sullivan, Ann Swidler, and Steven M. Tipton, *Habits of the Heart: Individualism and Commitment in American Life* (Berkeley: University of California Press, 1985).

Bennett, W. Lance, *News: The Politics of Illusion* (New York: Longman, 1988).

———, *The Governing Crisis: Media, Money, and Marketing in American Elections,* 2nd ed. (New York: St. Martin's Press, 1996).

Benson, Lee, *The Concept of Jacksonian Democracy* (Princeton, N.J.: Princeton University Press, 1961).

Berger, Raoul, *Government by Judiciary* (Cambridge, Mass.: Harvard University Press, 1977).

———, *Federalism: The Founders' Design* (Norman, Ok.: University of Oklahoma Press, 1987).

Berns, Walter, *Taking the Constitution Seriously* (New York: Simon & Schuster, 1987).

Berry, Jeffrey M., *The Interest Group Society* (Boston: Little, Brown, 1984).

Bessette, Joseph M., *The Mild Voice of Reason: Deliberative Democracy and American National Government* (Chicago: University of Chicago Press, 1994).

Bibby, John, *Politics, Parties, and Elections in America* (Chicago: Nelson-Hall, 1996).

———, and Sandy Maisel, *Two Parties—or More?: The American Party System* (Boulder, Colo.: Westview Press, 1998).

Binder, Sarah A., and Stephen S. Smith, *Politics or Principle?: Filibustering in the United States Senate,* Washington, D.C: The Brookings Institution, 1996).

Blakely, Edward J., and Mary Gail Snyder, *Fortress America: Gated Communities in the United States* (Washington, D.C.: The Brookings Institution, 1997).

Blasi, Vincent, *The Burger Court: The Counter-Revolution That Wasn't* (New Haven, Conn.: Yale University Press, 1983).

Bowen, Catherine Drinker, *Miracle at Philadelphia: The Story of the Constitutional Convention, May to September 1787* (Boston: Little, Brown, 1966, 1987).

Bowman, Ann O. M., and Richard C. Kearney, *The Resurgence of the States* (Englewood Cliffs, N.J.: Prentice Hall, 1986).

Brandt, Irving, *James Madison* (Indianapolis, Ind.: Bobbs-Merrill, 1961).

Brinkley, Alan, Nelson W. Polsby, and Kathleen M. Sullivan, *The New Federalist Papers* (New York: 20th Century Fund, 1997).

Brown, Robert E., *Charles Beard and the Constitution* (Princeton, N.J.: Princeton University Press, 1956).

Bryce, James, *The American Commonwealth,* ed. Louis Hacker (New York: G. P. Putnam's Sons, [1889]1959).

Burnham, Walter Dean, *Critical Elections and the Mainsprings of American Politics* (New York: W. W. Norton, 1970).

Burns, James MacGregor, *The Deadlock of Democracy; Four Party Politics in America* (Englewood Cliffs, N.J.: Prentice Hall, 1962).

———, *Presidential Government: The Crucible of Leadership* (Boston: Houghton Mifflin, 1965).

———, and Stewart Burns, *The People's Charter: The Pursuit of Rights in America* (New York: Knopf, 1991).

Burt, Robert A., *The Constitution in Conflict* (Cambridge, Mass.: The Belknap Press of Harvard University Press, 1992).

Callan, Eamonn, *Creating Citizens: Political Education and Liberal Democracy* (New York: Oxford University Press, 1997).

Campbell, Colin, *The U.S. Presidency in Crisis: A Comparative Perspective* (New York: Oxford University Press, 1998).

Canon, Bradley C., "A Framework for the Analysis of Judicial Activism," in *Supreme Court Activism and Restraint,* ed. Stephen C. Halpern and Charles M. Lamb (Lexington, Mass.: Lexington Books, 1982).

Caplan, Russell L., *Constitutional Brinksmanship* (New York: Oxford University Press, 1988).

Cappella, Joseph N., and Kathleen Hall Jamieson, *Spiral of Cynicism: The Press and the Public Good* (New York: Oxford University Press, 1997).

Chemerinsky, Erwin, *Interpreting the Constitution* (New York: Praeger, 1987).

Chopper, Jesse H., *Judicial Review and the National Political Process* (Chicago: University of Chicago Press, 1980).

Chubb, John E., and Paul E. Peterson, *New Direction in American Politics* (Washington, D.C.: The Brookings Institution, 1985).

———, *Can the Government Govern?* (Washington, D.C.: The Brookings Institution, 1989).

Cigler, Allan J., and Burdett A. Loomis, eds., *Interest Group Politics,* 2nd ed. (Washington, D.C.: Congressional Quarterly, 1986).

Clausen, Aage, *How Congressmen Decide: A Policy Focus* (New York: St. Martin's Press, 1973).

Clauson, Dan, et al., *Money Talks: Corporate PACs and Political Influence* (New York: Basic Books, 1992).

Clifford, Clark, *Counsel to the President: A Memoir* (New York: Random House, 1991).

Clinard, Marshall, and Peter Yeagar, *Corporate Crime* (New York: Free Press, 1980).

Cohen, Richard E., *Washington at Work: Back Rooms and Clean Air* (New York: Macmillan, 1992).

Conlan, Timothy, *The New Federalism* (Washington, D.C.: The Brookings Institution, 1988).

———, *From New Federalism to Devolution: Twenty-Five Years of Intergovernmental Reform* (Washington, D.C.: The Brookings Institution, 1998).

Cook, Timothy E., *Making Laws and Making News: Media Strategies in the U.S. House of Representatives* (Washington, D.C.: The Brookings Institution, 1989).

———, *Governing with the News: The News Media as a Political Institution* (Chicago: University of Chicago Press, 1997).

Cooke, Edward F., *A Detailed Analysis of the Constitution,* 6th ed. (Lanham, Md.: Rowman and Littlefield, 1994).

Cooper, Joseph, *The Origins of the Standing Committees and the Development of the Modern House* (Houston, Tex.: Rice University Studies, 1970).

Cooper, Phillip J., *Battles on the Bench: Conflict Inside the Supreme Court* (Lawrence: University of Kansas Press, 1995).

Corrado, Anthony, Thomas E. Mann, Dan Ortiz, Trevor Potter, and Frank Sorauf, *Campaign Finance Reform: A Sourcebook* (Washington, D.C.: The Brookings Institution, 1997).

Cox, Gary W., and Samuel Kernell, eds., *The Politics of Divided Government* (Boulder, Colo.: Westview Press, 1991).

Coyne, James K., and John H. Fund, *Cleaning House: America's Campaign for Term Limits* (Washington, D.C.: Regnery Gateway, 1992).

Craig, Barbara, *Chadha: The Story of an Epic Constitutional Struggle* (New York: Oxford University Press, 1988).

Cronin, Thomas E., *The State of the Presidency,* 2nd ed. (Boston: Little, Brown, 1980).

———, *Direct Democracy* (Cambridge, Mass.: Harvard University Press, 1989).

———, and Michael A. Genovese, *The Paradoxes of the American Presidency* (New York: Oxford University Press, 1998).

Crozier, Michel, Samuel Huntington, and Joji Watanuki, *The Crisis of Democracy* (New York: New York University Press, 1975).

Currie, David P., *The Constitution in the Supreme Court: The Second Century, 1888–1986* (Chicago: University of Chicago Press, 1990).

Cushman, Barry, *Rethinking the New Deal Court: The Structure of a Constitutional Revolution* (New York: Oxford University Press, 1998).

Dagger, Richard, *Dilemmas of Pluralist Democracy* (New Haven, Conn.: Yale University Press, 1982).

———, *Democracy and Its Critics* (New Haven, Conn.: Yale University Press, 1990).

———, *Civic Virtues: Rights, Citizenship, and Repub-*

lican Liberalism (New York: Oxford University Press, 1997).

Davidson, Roger, ed., *The Postreform Congress* (New York: St. Martin's Press, 1992).

Davis, Abraham L., and Barbara Luck Graham, *The Supreme Court, Race, and Civil Rights* (Thousand Oaks, Calif.: Sage Publications, 1995).

Davis, David, *American Environmental Politics* (Chicago: Nelson-Hall, 1998).

Davis, Richard, *Decisions and Images: The Supreme Court and the Press* (Englewood Cliffs, N.J.: Prentice Hall, 1994).

———, *The Web of Politics: The Internet's Impact on the American Political System* (New York: Oxford University Press, 1998).

Derthick, Martha, *New Towns in Town: Why a Federal Program Failed* (Washington, D.C.: Urban Institute, 1972).

———, *Uncontrollable Spending for Social Service Grants* (Washington, D.C.: The Brookings Institution, 1975).

———, and Paul J. Quirk, *The Politics of Deregulation* (Washington, D.C.: The Brookings Institution, 1985).

Devins, Neal, and Douglas Davison, eds., *Redefining Equality* (New York: Oxford University Press, 1998).

Dionne, E. J., ed., "Civil Society: What It Is and Why Everyone Is Talking About It," *The Brookings Review* (Fall 1997).

Dodd, Lawrence C., *Studies of Congress* (Washington, D.C.: CQ Press, 1985).

———, and Bruce I. Oppenheimer, eds., *Congress Reconsidered,* 3rd ed. (Washington, D.C.: CQ Press, 1985).

Domhoff, William, *The Power Elite and the State* (New York: de Gruyter, 1990).

Donahue, John D., *The Privatization Decision: Public Ends, Private Means* (New York: Basic Books, 1991).

———, *Disunited States: What's at Stake as Washington Fades and the States Take the Lead* (New York: Basic Books, 1997).

———, *Confronting Equality in an Era of Devolution* (Washington, D.C.: The Brookings Institution, 1998).

Donovan, John C., *The Politics of Poverty,* 2nd ed. (New York: Pegasus, 1973).

Draper, Theodore, *A Very Thin Line: The Iran-Contra Affair* (New York: Hill and Wang, 1991).

Drier, Peter, *Housing Policy and Devolution: A Delicate Balancing Act* (Washington, D.C.: The Brookings Institution, 1998).

Dummett, Michael, *Principles of Electoral Reform* (New York: Oxford University Press, 1997).

Dworkin, Ronald, *Freedom's Law: The Moral Reading of the American Constitution* (Cambridge, Mass.: Harvard University Press, 1997).

Dye, Thomas R., and Harmon Zeigler, *American Politics in the Media Age,* 2nd ed. (Monterey, Calif.: Brooks/Cole, 1986).

Eberly, Don E., ed., *The Content of America's Character: Recovering Civic Virtue* (Lanham, Md.: University Press of America, 1995).

Edelman, Murray, *Constructing the Political Spectacle* (Chicago: University of Chicago Press, 1988).

Edsall, Thomas Byrne, and Mary D. Edsall, *Chain Reaction: The Impact of Race, Rights, and Taxes on American Politics* (New York: W. W. Norton, 1991).

Edwards, George C. I. III, *The Public Presidency: The Pursuit of Popular Support* (New York: St. Martin's Press, 1983).

Eksterowicz, Anthony J., and Glenn P. Hastedt, eds., *The Post–Cold War Presidency* (Boston: Rowman and Littlefield, 1998).

Elazar, Daniel J., *American Federalism: A View from the States,* 2nd ed. (New York: Crowell, 1972).

———, "The Principles and Traditions Underlying American State Constitutions," *Publius 12* (Winter 1982).

———, "Our Thoroughly Federal Constitution," in *How Federal Is the Constitution?* ed. Robert A. Goldwin and William A. Shambra (Washington, D.C.: American Enterprise Institute, 1987).

Elkin, Stephen L., and Karol Edward Soltan, eds., *A New Constitutionalism: Designing Political Institutions for a Good Society* (Chicago: University of Chicago Press, 1993).

Ellis, Richard, *American Political Cultures* (New York: Oxford University Press, 1996).

Ellul, Jacques, *The Technological Society* (New York: Vintage Books, 1964).

———, *Propaganda* (New York: Vintage Books, 1965).

———, *The Political Illusion* (New York: Vintage Books, 1967).

Entman, R. M., *Democracy Without Citizens* (New York: Oxford University Press, 1990).

Etzioni, Amitai, *The Spirit of Community: Rights, Responsibilities, and the Communitarian Agenda* (New York: Crown, 1993).

Evans, C. Lawrence, and Walter J. Oleszek, *Congress Under Fire: Reform Politics and the Republican Majority* (Boston: Houghton Mifflin, 1997).

Fallows, James, *Breaking the News: How the Media Undermine American Democracy* (New York: Pantheon, 1996).

Farrand, Max, ed., *The Records of the Federal Convention of 1787* (New Haven, Conn.: Yale University Press, 1987).

Fausold, Martin L., and Alan Shank, eds., *The Constitution and the American Presidency* (Albany, N.Y.: SUNY Press, 1991).

Fellman, David, *The Constitutional Right of Association* (Chicago: University of Chicago Press, 1963).

Fenno, Richard, *The President's Cabinet* (New York: Vintage Books, 1959).

———, *Congressmen in Committees* (Boston: Little, Brown, 1973).

———, *Learning to Govern: an Institutional View of the 104th Congress* (Washington, D.C.: The Brookings Institution, 1997).

Feresia, Jerry, *Toward an American Revolution: Exposing the Constitution and Other Illusions* (Boston: South End Press, 1988).

Fiorina, Morris, *Divided Government* (New York: Macmillan, 1991).

Fischer, William, David Gerber, Jorge Guitart, and Maxine Seller, *Identity, Community and Pluralism in American Life* (New York: Oxford University Press, 1997).

Fisher, Louis, *The Constitution Between Friends* (New York: St. Martin's Press, 1978).

———, *Constitutional Conflicts Between Congress and the President* (Princeton, N.J.: Princeton University Press, 1985a).

———, *Does Separation of Powers Still Work?* (Washington, D.C.: American Enterprise Institute, 1985b).

Fishkin, James S., *Democracy and Deliberation: New Directions for Political Reform* (New Haven, Conn.: Yale University Press, 1991).

Fiss, Owen M., *The Irony of Free Speech* (Cambridge, Mass.: Harvard University Press, 1996).

Frederickson, H. George, *The Spirit of Public Administration* (San Francisco: Jossey-Bass, 1997).

Freeman, J. Leiper, *The Political Process: Executive Bureau-Legislative Committee Relations* (New York: Random House, 1965).

Fritschler, A. Lee, *Smoking and Politics: Policymaking and the Federal Bureaucracy,* 4th ed. (Englewood Cliffs, N.J.: Prentice Hall, 1989).

Gais, Thomas L., and Michael J. Malbin, *The Day After Reform: Sobering Campaign Finance Lessons from the American States* (Washington, D.C.: Rockefeller Institute Press, 1997).

Garrity, John A., ed., *Quarrels That Have Shaped the Constitution* (New York: Harper & Row, 1987).

Garvey, Gerald R., *Facing the Bureaucracy: Living and Dying in a Public Agency* (San Francisco: Jossey-Bass, 1993).

Garvey, John H., and T. Alexander Aleinikoff, *Modern Constitutional Theory: A Reader,* 2nd ed. (St. Paul, Minn.: West, 1991).

Gawthrop, Louis C., *Bureaucratic Behavior in the Executive Branch: An Analysis of Organizational Change* (New York: Free Press, 1969).

Germond, Jack W., and Jules Witcover, *Mad as Hell: Revolt at the Ballot Box 1992* (New York: Warner Books, 1993).

Gilmore, John B., *Strategic Disagreement: Stalemate in American Politics* (Pittsburgh, Pa.: University of Pittsburgh Press, 1995).

Ginsberg, Benjamin, and Martin Shefter, *Politics by Other Means: The Declining Importance of Elections in America* (New York: Basic Books, 1990).

Glendon, Mary Ann, *Rights Talk: The Impoverishment of Political Discourse* (New York: Free Press, 1991).

———, *A Nation Under Lawyers: How the Crisis in the Legal Profession Is Transforming American Society* (New York: Farrar, Straus & Giroux, 1994).

Goldfarb, Jeffrey C., *The Cynical Society: The Culture of Politics and the Politics of Culture in American*

Life (Chicago: University of Chicago Press, 1991).

Goldstein, Joseph, *The Intelligible Constitution: The Supreme Court's Obligation to Maintain the Constitution as Something We the People Can Understand* (New York: Oxford University Press, 1992).

Goldstein, Leslie Friedman, *In Defense of the Text: Democracy and Constitutional Theory* (Lanham, Md.: Rowman and Littlefield, 1991).

Goldwin, Robert A., and Art Kaufman, eds., *Separation of Powers: Does It Still Work?* (Washington, D.C.: American Enterprise Institute, 1986).

———, and William Schambra, *How Democratic Is the Constitution?* (Washington, D.C.: American Enterprise Institute, 1981).

———, *How Federal Is the Constitution?* (Washington, D.C.: American Enterprise Institute, 1987).

Goodwin, Charles Stewart, *A Resurrection of the Republican Ideal* (Lanham, Md.: University Press of America, 1995).

Green, John C., and Daniel M. Shea, eds., *The State of the Parties: The Changing Role of Contemporary American Parties*, 3rd ed. (Boston: Rowman and Littlefield, 1998).

Green, Phillip, *The Pursuit of Inequality* (New York: Pantheon, 1981).

Greider, William, *The Education of David Stockman and Other Americans* (New York: New American Library, 1986).

———, *Who Will Tell the People?: The Betrayal of American Democracy* (New York: Simon & Schuster, 1992).

Grodzins, Morton, *The American System: A New View of Government in the United States*, ed. Daniel Elazar (Chicago: Rand McNally, 1966).

Grofman, Bernard, and Donald Wittman, eds., *The Federalist Papers and the New Institutionalism* (New York: Agathon Press, 1989).

Gutmann, Amy, and Dennis Thompson, *Democracy and Disagreement* (Cambridge, Mass.: The Belknap Press of Harvard University Press, 1996).

Haider, Donald H., *When Governments Come to Washington: Governors, Mayors, and Intergovernmental Lobbying* (New York: Free Press, 1974).

Haines, Charles G., *The American Doctrine of Judicial Supremacy*, 2nd ed. (Berkeley: University of California Press, 1932).

Hall, Kermit L., *The Supreme Court and Judicial Review in American History* (Washington, D.C.: American Historical Association, 1985).

Haltom, William, *Courting the Press* (Chicago: Nelson-Hall, 1998).

Hamilton, Alexander, James Madison, and John Jay, *The Federalist Papers* (Des Plaines, Ill.: Bantam, 1988).

Hamilton, Christopher, and Donald T. Wells, *Federalism, Power, and Political Economy* (Englewood Cliffs, N.J.: Prentice Hall, 1990).

Hardin, Charles M., *Constitutional Reform in America* (Ames: Iowa State University Press, 1989).

Harris, Richard A., and Sidney M. Milkis, eds., *Remaking American Politics* (Boulder, Colo.: Westview Press, 1989).

Hart, John, *The Presidential Branch: From Washington to Clinton*, 2nd ed. (New York: Pergamon Press, 1995).

Hayes, Michael T., *Lobbyists and Legislators* (New Brunswick, N.J.: Rutgers University Press, 1981).

Heclo, Hugh, *A Government of Strangers: Executive Politics in Washington* (Washington, D.C.: The Brookings Institution, 1977).

———, "Issue Networks and the Executive Establishment," in *The New American Political System*, ed. Anthony King (Washington, D.C.: American Enterprise Institute, 1978).

Held, David, *Models of Democracy* (Stanford, Calif.: Stanford University Press, 1987).

Henig, Jeffrey R., *Public Policy and Federalism: Issues in State and Local Politics* (New York: St. Martin's Press, 1985).

Henkin, Louis, *Foreign Affairs and the United States Constitution*, 2nd ed. (New York: Oxford University Press, 1997).

Henry, Nicholas, and John Hall, *Reconsidering American Politics* (Needham Heights, Mass.: Allyn & Bacon, 1985).

Herrnson, Paul S., and John C. Green, eds., *Multiparty Politics in America* (Boston: Rowman and Littlefield, 1997).

Hess, Stephen, *Organizing the Presidency* (Washington, D.C.: The Brookings Institution, 1976).

———, *News and Newsmaking* (Washington, D.C.: The Brookings Institution, 1996).

Hickok, Eugene W., Jr., Gary L. McDowell, and Philip J. Costopoulos, *Our Peculiar Security: The Written Constitution and Limited Government* (Lanham, Md.: Rowman and Littlefield, 1993).

Higginbotham, A. Leon, *Shades of Freedom: Racial Politics and Presumptions of the American Legal Process* (New York: Oxford University Press, 1996).

Hightower, Jim, *There's Nothing in the Middle of the Road but Yellow Stripes and Dead Armadillos* (New York: HarperCollins, 1997).

Hoffman, Daniel M., *Our Elusive Constitution: Silences, Paradoxes, and Priorities* (Albany, N.Y.: SUNY Press, 1997).

Holbrook, Thomas M., *Do Campaigns Matter?* (Thousand Oaks, Calif.: Sage Publications, 1996).

Hovey, Harold A. *Can the States Afford Devolution?* (Washington, D.C.: The Brookings Institution, 1998).

Howard, A. E. Dick, *The Road from Runnymede: Magna Carta and Constitutionalism in America* (Charlottesville: University of Virginia Press, 1968).

Hudson, William E., *American Democracy in Peril: Seven Challenges to America's Future*, 2nd ed. (Chatham, N.J.: Chatham House, 1998).

Hummel, Ralph, *The Bureaucratic Experience*, 3rd ed. (New York: St. Martin's Press, 1987).

Huntington, Samuel P., *American Politics: The Promise of Disharmony* (Cambridge, Mass.: Harvard University Press, 1981).

Hyneman, Charles S., *Bureaucracy in a Democracy* (New York: Harper & Row, 1950).

Iyengar, Shanto, *Is Anyone Responsible?: How Television Frames Political Issues* (Chicago: University of Chicago Press, 1987).

———, and Richard Reeves, eds., *Do the Media Govern?: Politicians, Voters, and Reporters in America* (Thousand Oaks, Calif.: Sage Publications, 1997).

Jackson, Brooks, *Honest Graft: Big Money and the American Political Process* (New York: Knopf, 1988).

Jacobson, Gary C., *The Politics of Congressional Elections* (New York: HarperCollins, 1992).

Jamieson, Kathleen Hall, *Eloquence in an Electronic Age: The Transformation of American Political Speechmaking* (New York: Oxford University Press, 1988).

———, *Dirty Politics: Deception, Distraction, and Democracy* (New York: Oxford University Press, 1992).

———, *Packaging the Presidency: A History of Presidential Campaign Advertising* (New York: Oxford University Press, 1996).

———, and D. Birdsell, *Presidential Debates: The Challenge of Creating an Informed Electorate* (New York: Oxford University Press, 1988).

Janis, Irving L., *Victims of Groupthink* (Boston: Houghton Mifflin, 1982).

Jillson, Calvin C., and Cecil L. Eubanks, "The Political Structure of Constitution Making: The Federal Convention of 1787," *American Journal of Political Science*, 28 (August 1984).

Joe, Tom, and Cheryl Rogers, *By the Few, for the Few: The Reagan Welfare Legacy* (Lexington, Mass.: Lexington Books, 1985).

Johnson, Cathy M., *The Dynamics of Conflict Between Bureaucrats and Legislators* (Armonk, N.Y.: M. E. Sharpe, 1992).

Johnson, Haynes, and David Broder, *The System: The American Way of Politics at the Breaking Point* (Boston: Little, Brown, 1996).

Johnson, Thomas J., Carol E. Hays and Scott P. Hays, eds., *Engaging the Public: How Government and the Media Can Reinvigorate American Democracy* (Lanham, Md.: Rowman and Littlefield, 1998).

Jones, Charles R., *The Presidency in a Separated System* (Washington, D.C.: The Brookings Institution, 1994).

———, *Separate but Equal Branches: Congress and the Presidency* (Chatham, N.J.: Chatham House, 1995).

———, *Passages to the Presidency* (Washington, D.C.: The Brookings Institution Press, 1998).

Jones, Megan, David Guston, and Lewis M. Branscomb, *Informed Legislatures: Coping with Science in a Democracy* (Lanham, Md.: University Press of America, 1996).

Kamber, Victor, *Giving Up Democracy: Why Term Limits Are Bad for America* (Washington, D.C.: Regnery Gateway, 1995).

Kammen, Michael, *A Machine That Would Go of Itself: The Constitution in American Culture* (New York: Knopf, 1986).

Katzmann, Robert A., *Judges and Legislators: Toward Institutional Comity* (Washington, D.C.: The Brookings Institution, 1988).

———, *Courts and Congress* (Washington, D.C.: The Brookings Institution, 1997).

Kellerman, Barbara, *The Political Presidency: Practice of Leadership from Kennedy Through Reagan* (New York: Oxford University Press, 1984).

———, and Ryan J. Barilleaux, *The President as World Leader* (New York: St. Martin's Press, 1991).

Kelly, Alfred H., Winfred A. Harbison, and Herman J. Belz, *The American Constitution: Its Origins and Development*, 6th ed. (New York: W. W. Norton, 1983).

Kelly, Brian, *Adventures in Porkland: How Washington Wastes Your Money and Why They Won't Stop* (New York: Villard Books, 1992).

Kerbo, Harold, *Social Stratification and Inequality* (New York: McGraw-Hill, 1983).

Kernell, Samuel J., *Going Public: New Strategies of Presidential Leadership*, 3rd ed. (Washington, D.C.: CQ Press, 1997).

Kertzer, David I., *Ritual, Politics, and Power* (New Haven, Conn.: Yale University Press, 1988).

Ketchum, Ralph, *The Anti-Federalist Papers and the Constitutional Convention Debates* (Denver, Colo.: Mentor Books, 1986).

Kettl, Donald F., *Reinventing Government: A Fifth Year Report Card* (Washington, D.C.: The Brookings Institution, 1998).

———, Patricia W. Ingraham, Ronald P. Sanders, and Constance Horner, *Civil Service Reform: Building a Government That Works* (Washington, D.C.: The Brookings Institution, 1996).

Key, V. O., Jr., *Politics, Parties, and Pressure Groups*, 6th ed. (New York: Crowell, 1966).

Kharasch, Robert N., *The Institutional Imperative: How to Understand the United States Government and Other Bulky Objects* (New York: Charterhouse Books, 1973).

Kiewiet, D. Roderick, and Mathew D. McCubbins, *The Logic of Delegation: Congressional Parties and the Appropriations Process* (Chicago: University of Chicago Press, 1991).

King, Anthony, ed., *The New American Political System* (Washington, D.C.: American Enterprise Institute, 1978).

King, David C., *Turf Wars: How Congressional Committees Claim Jurisdiction* (Chicago: University of Chicago Press, 1997).

King, Desmond, *Separate and Unequal: Black Americans and the U.S. Federal Government* (New York: Oxford University Press, 1995).

Klusmeyer, Douglas B., *Between Consent and Descent: Concepts of Democratic Citizenship* (Washington, D.C.: The Brookings Institution, 1996).

Krislov, Samuel, and David H. Rosenbloom, *Representative Bureaucracy and the American Political System* (New York: Praeger, 1981).

Krugman, Paul, *The Age of Diminished Expectations* (Cambridge, Mass.: MIT Press, 1992).

Krusch, Barry, *The 21st Century Constitution: A New America for a New Millennium* (New York: Stanhope Press, 1992).

Kurland, Philip, and Ralph Lerner, eds., *The Founders' Constitution* (Chicago: University of Chicago Press, 1987).

Kurtz, Howard, *Hot Air: All Talk, All the Time* (New York: Times Books, 1996).

Ladanyi, Thomas, *The 1987 Constitution* (New York: Tribonian Press, 1987).

Lamare, James W., *What Rules America?* (St. Paul, Minn.: West, 1988).

Lammers, Bernard, *Fragmented Government* (Lanham, Md.: University Press of America, 1997).

Lasch, Christopher, *The Revolt of the Elites and the Betrayal of Democracy* (New York: W. W. Norton, 1995).

Laver, Michael, *Private Desires, Political Action: An Invitation to the Politics of Rational Choice* (Thousand Oaks, Calif.: Sage Publications, 1997).

Lazare, Daniel, *The Frozen Republic: How the Constitution Is Paralyzing American Democracy* (Fort Worth, Tex.: Harcourt Brace Jovanovich, 1996).

Leach, Richard H., *American Federalism: A View from the States*, 2nd ed. (New York: Crowell, 1972).

———, ed., *Intergovernmental Relations in the 1980s* (New York: Dekker, 1983).

Leonard, Herman B., *Checks Unbalanced: The Quiet Side of Public Spending* (New York: Basic Books, 1992).

Leuchtenburg, William E., *The Supreme Court Reborn: The Constitutional Revolution in the Age of Roosevelt* (New York: Oxford University Press, 1995).

Levine, Herbert M., et al., *What If the American Political System Were Different?* (Armonk, N.Y.: M. E. Sharpe, 1992).

Levy, Leonard W., ed., *Encyclopedia of the American Constitution,* 4 vols. (New York: Macmillan, 1986).

Lindblom, Charles E., *The Policymaking Process* (Englewood Cliffs, N.J.: Prentice Hall, 1968).

Lipset, Seymour Martin, *The First New Nation: The United States in Historical and Comparative Perspective* (New York: W. W. Norton, 1979).

Livingston, William S., Lawrence C. Dodd, and Richard L. Schott, *The Presidency and the Congress: A Shifting Balance of Power* (Austin, Tex.: The Lyndon B. Johnson School of Public Affairs, 1979).

Lord, Carnes, *The Presidency and the Management of National Security* (New York: Free Press, 1988).

Lowi, Theodore, ed., *Private Life and Public Order* (New York: W. W. Norton, 1968).

———, *The Politics of Disorder* (New York: Basic Books, 1971).

———, *The End of Liberalism: The Second Republic of the United States,* 2nd ed. (New York: W. W. Norton, 1979).

———, *The Personal President: Power Invested, Promise Unfulfilled* (Ithaca, N.Y.: Cornell University Press, 1985).

———, and Joseph Romance, *A Republic of Parties?: Debating the Two-Party System* (Boston: Rowman and Littlefield, 1998).

Lyons, Gene, et al., *Fools for Scandal: How the Media Invented Whitewater* (New York: Franklin Square Press, 1996).

Mackenzie, G. Calvin, and Saranna Thronton, *Bucking the Deficit: Economic Policymaking in America* (Boulder, Colo.: Westview Press, 1996).

Macpherson, C. B., *The Life and Times of Liberal Democracy* (Oxford, England: Oxford University Press, 1977).

Madison, James, *Notes of Debates in the Federal Convention of 1787* (New York: W. W. Norton, 1987).

Maidment, Richard, and John Zsvesper, eds., *Reflections on the Constitution: The American Constitution After Two Hundred Years* (Manchester, England: Manchester University Press, 1989).

Main, Jackson Turner, *The Anti-Federalists* (New York: W. W. Norton, 1974).

Malbin, Michael J., *Unelected Representatives* (New York: Basic Books, 1980).

Malbin, Michael J., and Thomas L. Gais, *The Day After Reform: Sobering Campaign Finance Reform Lessons from the American States* (Washington, D.C.: The Brookings Institution, 1998).

Manley, John F., and Kenneth M. Dolbeare, eds., *The Case Against the Constitution: From the Antifederalists to the Present* (Armonk, N.Y.: M. E. Sharpe, 1987).

Mansfield, Harvey C., Jr., *America's Constitutional Soul* (Baltimore, Md.: Johns Hopkins University Press, 1991).

Manuel, Paul Christopher, and Anne Marie Cammisa, *Checks and Balances: How a Parliamentary System Could Change American Politics* (Boulder, Colo.: Westview Press, 1998).

Margolis, Michael, *Viable Democracy* (London: Penguin Books, 1979).

Marshall, Burke, *A Workable Government?: The Constitution After 200 Years* (New York: W. W. Norton, 1987).

Martin, Rex, *A System of Rights* (New York: Oxford University Press, 1993).

Matthew, Robert Kerbel, *Remote and Controlled: Media Politics in a Cynical Age,* 2nd ed. (Boulder, Colo: Westview Press, 1998).

Mayhew, David, *Congress: The Electoral Connection* (New Haven, Conn.: Yale University Press, 1974).

———, *Divided We Govern: Party Control, Lawmaking, and Investigations 1946–1990* (New Haven, Conn.: Yale University Press, 1991).

Mazmanian, Daniel A., and Paul A. Sabatier, *Implementation and Public Policy* (Glenview, Ill.: Scott, Foresman, 1983).

McCleskey, Clifton, *Political Power and American Democracy* (Pacific Grove, Calif.: Brooks/Cole, 1989).

McCloskey, Robert G., *The American Supreme Court* (Chicago: University of Chicago Press, 1960).

McConnell, Grant, *Private Power and American Democracy* (New York: Knopf, 1966).

McDonald, Forrest, *We the People: The Economic Origin of the Constitution* (Chicago: University of Chicago Press, 1963).

———, *The American Presidency: An Intellectual History* (Lawrence: University of Kansas Press, 1994).

McIlwain, Charles H., *Constitutionalism and the Changing World* (New York: Cambridge University Press, 1969).

McLuhan, Marshall, *Understanding Media* (New York: Signet Books, 1964).

Melusky, Joseph A., *The Constitution: Our Written Legacy* (Malabar, Fla.: Krieger Publishing Company, 1991).

———, and Whitman H. Ridgway, *The Bill of Rights: Our Written Legacy* (Malabar, Fla.: Krieger Publishing Company, 1992).

Meyers, Marvin, *The Jacksonian Persuasion: Politics and Belief* (Stanford, Calif.: Stanford University Press, 1957).

Mill, John Stuart, *Considerations on Representative Government* (Indianapolis, Ind.: Bobbs-Merrill, 1958).

Miller, Arthur Selwyn, *The Supreme Court and American Capitalism* (New York: Free Press, 1968).

Miller, James E., *Democracy Is in the Streets* (New York: Simon & Schuster, 1987).

Miller, John, *Alexander Hamilton* (New York: Harper & Brothers, 1969).

Miller, Warren E., and J. Merrill Shanks, *The New American Voter* (Cambridge, Mass.: Harvard University Press, 1996).

Mills, C. Wright, *The Power Elite* (New York: Oxford University Press, 1956).

Morris, Richard B., *The Forging of the Union, 1781–1789* (New York: Harper & Row, 1987).

Morrow, William L., *Congressional Committees* (New York: Scribner's, 1969).

———, *Public Administration: Politics, Policy and the Political System,* 2nd ed. (New York: Random House, 1980).

Mosher, Frederick, *Democracy and the Public Service,* 2nd ed. (New York: Oxford University Press, 1982).

Moyers, Bill, "The Public Mind." Four-part television series, Public Broadcasting System, WNET, Boston, 1989.

Mueller, Dennis C., *Constitutional Democracy* (New York: Oxford University Press, 1996).

Murphy, Walter F., *Congress and the Court* (Chicago: University of Chicago Press, 1962).

Narduli, Peter F., *The Constitution and American Political Development* (Urbana: University of Illinois Press, 1992).

Nathan, Richard P., *The Administrative Presidency* (New York: Wiley, 1983).

———, "The Untold Story of Reagan's 'New Federalism,'" *Public Interest* 77 (Fall 1984).

———, and Fred C. Doolittle, *Reagan and the States* (Princeton, N.J.: Princeton University Press, 1987).

Nedelsky, Jennifer, *Private Property and the Limits of American Constitutionalism* (Chicago: University of Chicago Press, 1990).

Negrine, Ralph, *The Communication of Politics* (Thousand Oaks, Calif.: Sage Publications, 1996).

Nelson, Michael, ed., *The Presidency and the Political System,* 5th ed. (Washington, D.C.: CQ Press, 1998).

Nelson, William E., *The Roots of American Bureaucracy, 1830–1900* (Cambridge, Mass.: Harvard University Press, 1947).

Neuman, W. Russell, Marion R. Just, and Ann N. Crigler, *Common Knowledge: News and the Construction of Political Meaning* (Chicago: University of Chicago Press, 1992).

Neustadt, Richard, *Presidential Power and the Modern Presidents: The Politics of Leadership from Roosevelt to Reagan* (New York: Free Press, 1990).

Nimmo, Daniel, and James Combs, *Mediated Political Realities* (New York: Longman, 1990).

Novak, Michael, *The Spirit of Democratic Capitalism* (New York: Touchstone, 1982).

Nye, Joseph S., Philip D. Zelikow, and David C. King, *Why People Don't Trust Government* (Cambridge, Mass.: Harvard University Press, 1997).

O'Brien, David M., *Storm Center: The Supreme Court*

in American Politics, 2nd ed. (New York: W. W. Norton, 1990).

O'Conner, Karen, *No Neutral Ground: Abortion Politics in an Age of Absolutes* (Boulder, Colo.: Westview Press, 1996).

Offner, Paul, *Medicaid and the States* (Washington, D.C.: The Brookings Institution, 1998).

Oleszek, Walter, *Congressional Procedures and the Policy Process,* 3rd ed. (Washington, D.C.: Congressional Quarterly Press, 1988).

Ollman, Bertell, and Jonathon Birnbaum, eds., *The United States Constitution* (New York: New York University Press, 1990).

O'Neill, Michael J., *The Roar of the Crowd: How Television and People Power Are Changing the World* (New York: Times Books, 1993).

Ontiveros, Suzanne Robitaille, ed., *The Dynamic Constitution: A Historical Bibliography* (Santa Barbara, Calif.: ABC-CLIO, 1986).

Ostrom, Vincent, *The Political Theory of a Compound Republic: Designing the American Experiment* (Lincoln: University of Nebraska Press, 1987).

O'Toole, Lawrence J., Jr., ed., *American Intergovernmental Relations: Foundations, Perspectives, and Issues,* 2nd ed. (Washington, D.C.: CQ Press, 1993).

Padover, Saul K., *The Living U.S. Constitution,* rev. ed. (New York: World, 1968).

Page, Benjamin I., and Robert Y. Shapiro, *The Rational Public: Fifty Years of Trends in Americans' Policy Preferences* (Chicago: University of Chicago Press, 1992).

Parenti, Michael, *Inventing Reality: The Politics of the Mass Media* (New York: St. Martin's Press, 1986).

Pascall, Glenn, *The Trillion Dollar Budget: How to Stop the Bankrupting of America* (Seattle: University of Washington Press, 1985).

Pateman, Carole, *Participation and Democratic Theory* (Cambridge, England: Cambridge University Press, 1970).

Patterson, Thomas E., *Out of Order: How the Decline of Political Parties and the Growing Power of the News Media Undermine the American Way of Electing Presidents* (New York: Random House, 1993).

Penny, Timothy J., and Steven E. Schier, *Payment Due: A Nation in Debt, A Generation in Trouble* (Boulder, Colo.: Westview Press, 1996).

Percy, Stephen L., *Disability, Civil Rights, and Public Policy: The Politics of Implementation* (Tuscaloosa: University of Alabama Press, 1989).

Perry, Michael J., *The Constitution in the Courts: Law or Politics?* (New York: Oxford University Press, 1994).

———, *Religion in Politics: Constitutional and Moral Perspectives* (New York: Oxford University Press, 1997).

Peterson, George E., and Carol W. Lewis, *Reagan and the Cities* (Washington, D.C.: Urban Institute, 1986).

Peterson, Paul E., *The Price of Federalism* (Washington, D.C.: The Brookings Institution, 1995).

———, Barry G. Rabe, and Kenneth K. Wong, *When Federalism Works* (Washington, D.C.: The Brookings Institution, 1986).

Pettit, Philip, *Republicanism: A Theory of Freedom and Government* (New York: Oxford University Press, 1997).

Pfiffner, James P., *The Managerial Presidency* (Pacific Grove, Calif.: Brooks/Cole, 1991).

———, and Roger H. Davidson, eds., *Understanding the Presidency* (New York: Longman, 1997).

Phillips, Anne, *The Politics of Presence* (New York: Oxford University Press, 1995).

Phillips, Kevin, *Arrogant Capital* (Boston: Little, Brown, 1996).

Polsby, Nelson W., *Political Innovation in America: The Politics of Policy Initiation* (New Haven, Conn.: Yale University Press, 1984).

———, and Aaron Wildavsky, *Presidential Elections,* 8th ed. (New York: Free Press, 1991).

Popkin, Samuel L., *The Reasoning Voter: Communication and Persuasion in Presidential Campaigns* (Chicago: University of Chicago Press, 1991).

Postman, Neil, *Amusing Ourselves to Death* (New York: Penguin, 1986).

Powell, Janet, *The United States Constitution and the Supreme Court* (Bronx, N.Y.: H. W. Wilson, 1988).

Price, David, *Who Makes the Laws?: Creativity and Power in Senate Committees* (Cambridge, Mass.: Schenkman, 1972).

Price, David E., *Bringing Back the Parties* (Washington, D.C.: Congressional Quarterly Press, 1984).

Price, Don K., *The Unwritten Constitution* (Baton Rouge: Louisiana State University Press, 1983).

Price, Douglas H., "The Congressional Career— Then and Now," in *Congressional Behavior*, ed. Nelson W. Polsby (New York: Random House, 1971).

Pritchett, Herman C., *The Roosevelt Court* (New York: Macmillan, 1948).

———, *The American Constitution* (New York: McGraw-Hill, 1977).

Proctor, Robert N., *Cancer Wars: How Politics Shapes What We Know and Don't Know About Cancer* (New York: Basic Books, 1995).

Pyle, Christopher H., and Richard M. Pious, *The President, Congress, and the Constitution* (New York: Free Press, 1984).

———, *The Politics of Rich and Poor: Wealth and the American Electorate in the Reagan Aftermath* (New York: Random House, 1992).

Radin, Beryl A., and Willis D. Hawley, *The Politics of Federal Reorganization: Creating the U.S. Department of Education* (New York: Pergamon Press, 1988).

Ragsdale, Lyn, *Presidential Politics* (Boston: Houghton Mifflin, 1993).

Rauch, Jonathan, *Demosclerosis: The Silent Killer of American Government* (New York: Random House, 1994).

Reagan, Michael D., *The New Federalism* (New York: Oxford University Press, 1972).

Redford, Emmette, *Democracy in the Administrative State* (New York: Oxford University Press, 1969).

Reedy, George, *The Twilight of the Presidency* (Cleveland: World Press, 1970).

Reich, Robert, *The Work of Nations* (New York: Vintage Books, 1992).

Reith, Jean Schroedel, *Congress, the President, and Policymaking: A Historical Analysis* (Armonk, N.Y.: M. E. Sharpe, 1994).

Resnick, Philip, *Twenty-First Century Democracy* (Toronto, Canada: McGill-Queens University Press, 1997).

Revel, Jean-Francois, *How Democracies Perish* (New York: Harper & Row, 1985).

Reynolds, David, *Democracy Unbound: Progressive Challenges to the Two-Party System* (East Haven, Conn.: South End Press, 1997).

Ricci, David, *Community Power and Democratic Theory: The Logic of Political Analysis* (New York: Touchstone, 1982).

Richardson, Shula P., *Term Limits for Federal and State Legislators: Recent Proposals in the States (1991–1992)* (Washington, D.C.: Congressional Research Service, 1992).

Rieselbach, Leroy, *Congressional Reform* (Washington, D.C.: Congressional Quarterly Press, 1986).

Rimmerman, Craig A., *The New Citizenship: Unconventional Politics, Activism, and Service* (Boulder, Colo.: Westview Press, 1997).

Ripley, Randall B., and Grace A. Franklin, *Policy Implementation and Bureaucracy*, 2nd ed. (Chicago: Dorsey Press, 1986).

———, *Congress, the Bureaucracy, and Public Policy*, 5th ed. (Pacific Grove, Calif.: Brooks/Cole, 1991).

Robinson, Donald L., ed., *Reforming American Government: The Bicentennial Papers of the Committee on the Constitutional System* (Boulder, Colo.: Westview Press, 1985).

———, *Government for the Third American Century* (Boulder, Colo.: Westview Press, 1989).

Rockman, Bert A., *The Leadership Question: The Presidency and the American System* (New York: Praeger, 1985).

Roelofs, Joan, "Judicial Activism as Social Engineering: A Marxist Interpretation of the Warren Court," in *Supreme Court Activism and Restraint*, ed. Stephen C. Halpern and Charles M. Lamb (Lexington, Mass.: Lexington Books, 1982).

Rohde, David, *Party Leaders in the Post Reform House* (Chicago: University of Chicago Press, 1991).

———, and Harold J. Spaeth, *Supreme Court Decision Making* (San Francisco: Freeman, 1976).

Rose, Gary L., *The American Presidency Under Siege* (Albany, N.Y.: SUNY Press, 1997).

Rosen, Bernard, *Holding Government Bureaucracies Accountable*, 2nd ed. (New York: Praeger, 1989).

Rosen, Jay, *Getting the Connections Right: Public Journalism and Its Message to the Press* (Washington, D.C.: The Brookings Institution, 1996).

Rosenbloom, David H., *Federal Service and the Constitution* (Ithaca, N.Y.: Cornell University Press, 1971).

Rosenkranz, Joseph, *Buckley Stops Here: Loosening the Judicial Stranglehold on Campaign Finance Reform* (Washington, D.C.: The Brookings Institution, 1998).

Rosner, Jeremy D., *The New Tug-of-War: Congress, the Executive Branch, and National Security* (Washington, DC: The Brookings Institution, 1995).

Rossiter, Clinton, *Seedtime of the Republic* (New York: Harcourt, Brace, 1953).

———, *The American Presidency* (New York, Harcourt, Brace, 1956).

———, *The Federalist Papers* (New York: Mentor, 1961).

———, *1787: The Grand Convention* (New York: Macmillan, 1976).

Rourke, Francis E., ed., *Bureaucratic Power in National Policy Making*, 4th ed. (Boston: Little, Brown, 1986).

Rubin, Irene S., *The Politics of Public Budgeting: Getting and Spending, Borrowing and Balancing* (Chatham, N.J.: Chatham House, 1990).

Rush, Mark E., and Robert D. Ritchie, *Fair and Effective Representation: Debating Voting Reform and Minority Rights* (Boston: Rowman and Littlefield, 1998).

Ryden, David K., *Representation in Crisis: The Constitution, Interest Groups, and Political Parties* (Albany, N.Y.: SUNY Press, 1996).

Sabato, Larry J., *The Rise of Political Consultants: New Ways of Winning Elections* (New York: Basic Books, 1981).

———, *PAC Power: Inside the World of Political Action Committees* (New York: W. W. Norton, 1985).

———, *The Party's Just Begun* (Glenview, Ill.: Scott, Foresman, 1988).

———, *Feeding Frenzy: How Attack Journalism Has Transformed American Politics* (New York: Free Press, 1991).

Sandel, Michael J., *Liberalism and the Limits of Justice* (New York: Cambridge University Press, 1982).

———, *Democracy's Discontent: America in Search of a Public Philosophy* (Cambridge, Mass.: The Belknap Press of Harvard University Press, 1996).

Sanford, Terry, *Storm over the States* (New York: McGraw-Hill, 1966).

Sarat, Austin, ed., *Race. Law, and Culture: Reflections on* Brown v. Board of Education (New York: Oxford University Press, 1997).

Schattschneider, E. E., *Party Government* (New York: Henry Holt, 1942).

———, *The Semi-Sovereign People: A Realist's View of Democracy in America* (New York: Random House, 1971).

Schick, Allen, *The Federal Budget: Politics, Policy, Process* (Washington, D.C.: The Brookings Institution, 1995).

Schier, Steven E., *A Decade of Deficits: Congressional Thought and Fiscal Action* (Albany, N.Y.: SUNY Press, 1992).

Schlesinger, Arthur M., Jr., *The Age of Jackson* (Boston: Little, Brown, 1945).

———, *The Cycles of American History* (Boston: Houghton Mifflin, 1986).

Schlozman, Kay L., and John T. Tierney, *Organized Interests and American Democracy* (New York: Harper & Row, 1986).

Schneier, Edward V., and Bertram Gross, *Legislative Strategy: Shaping Public Policy* (New York: St. Martin's Press, 1993).

Schramm, Peter W., and Bradford P. Wilson, *American Political Parties and Constitutional Politics* (Lanham, Md.: Rowman and Littlefield, 1993).

Schwartz, Bernard, *Decision: How the Supreme Court Decides Cases* (New York: Oxford University Press, 1996a).

———, ed., *The Warren Court: A Retrospective* (New York: Oxford University Press, 1996b).

Scigliano, Robert, *The Supreme Court and the Presidency* (New York: Free Press, 1971).

Seidman, Harold, *Politics, Position, and Power: The Dynamics of Federal Organization,* 5th ed. (New York: Oxford University Press, 1997).

Seligman, Lester G., and Cary R. Covington, *The Coalitional Presidency* (Chicago: Dorsey Press, 1989).

Shapiro, Martin, *The Supreme Court and Administrative Agencies* (New York: Free Press, 1968).

Shepsle, Kenneth, *The Giant Jigsaw Puzzle* (Chicago: University of Chicago Press, 1978).

————, "Institutional Equilibrium and Equilibrium Institutions," in *Political Science: The Science of Politics,* ed. Herbert F. Weisberg (New York: Agathon, 1986).

Sherlock, Richard, Kent E. Robson, and Charles W. Johnson, eds., *The Normative Constitution: Essays for the Third Century* (Lanham, Md.: Rowman and Littlefield, 1995).

Siegan, Bernard, *The Supreme Court's Constitution* (New Brunswick, N.J.: Transaction Publishers, 1987).

Silverstein, Gordon, *The Imbalance of Powers: Constitutional Interpretation and the Making of American Foreign Policy* (New York: Oxford University Press, 1996).

Simon, James F., *The Center Holds: The Power Struggle Inside the Rehnquist Court* (New York: Simon & Schuster, 1995).

Skowronek, Stephen, *The Politics Presidents Make: Leadership from John Adams to Bill Clinton* (Cambridge, Mass.: The Belknap Press of Harvard University Press, 1997).

Slater, Phillip, *The Pursuit of Loneliness* (Boston: Beacon Press, 1990).

Smith, J. Allen, *The Spirit of American Government, a Study of the Constitution: Its Origin, Influence and Relation to Democracy* (New York: Macmillan, 1907).

Smith, Stephen D., *The Constitution and the Pride of Reason* (New York: Oxford University Press, 1997).

Sorenson, Leonard R., *Madison on the "General Welfare" of America: His Consistent Constitutional Vision* (Lanham, Md.: Rowman and Littlefield, 1995).

Spitzer, Robert J., *The Presidential Veto: Touchstone of the American Presidency* (Albany, N.Y.: SUNY Press, 1988).

Staeheli, Lynn, Janet E. Kodras, and Flint Colin, *State Devolution in America: Implications for a Diverse Society* (Thousand Oaks, Calif.: Sage Publications, 1997).

Stern, Philip, *The Rape of the Taxpayer* (New York: Random House, 1973).

————, *The Best Congress Money Can Buy* (New York: Pantheon, 1988).

Steuerle, C. Eugene, Edward M. Gramlich, Hugh Heclo, and Demetra M. Nightengale, *On Common Ground: America's Domestic Challenges and Opportunities* (Lanham, Md.: University Press of America, 1997).

Stockman, David, *The Triumph of Politics: Why the Reagan Revolution Failed* (New York: Harper & Row, 1986).

Stone, Geoffrey R., Richard A. Epstein, and Cass R. Sunstein, *The Bill of Rights in the Modern State* (Chicago: University of Chicago Press, 1992).

Storing, Herbert, ed., *The Anti-Federalist* (Chicago: University of Chicago Press, 1985).

Strick, Anne, *Injustice for All* (New York: Penguin, 1977).

Stuckey, Mary E., *The President and Interpreter-in-Chief* (Chatham, N.J.: Chatham House, 1991).

Sundquist, James L., *Politics and Policy* (Washington, D.C.: The Brookings Institution, 1968).

————, *Constitutional Reform and Effective Government* (Washington, D.C.: The Brookings Institution, 1991).

Sussman, Gerald, *Communication, Technology, and Politics in the Information Age* (Thousand Oaks, Calif.: Sage Publications, 1997).

Thomas, Norman C., and Joseph A. Pika, *The Politics of the Presidency,* 4th ed. (Washington, D.C.: CQ Press, 1997).

Thompson, Kenneth, ed., *The Budget Deficit and the National Debt—Volume I* (Lanham, Md.: University Press of America, 1997).

Tocqueville, Alexis de, *Democracy in America* (New York: Random House, [1835] 1981).

Tolchin, Susan J., *The Angry American: How Voter Rage Is Changing the Nation,* 2nd ed. (Boulder, Colo.: Westview Press, 1998).

Troy, Gil, *See How They Ran: The Changing Role of the Presidential Candidate* (Chicago: Dorsey Press, 1991).

Truman, David B., *The Governmental Process* (New York: Knopf, 1951).

Tugwell, Rexford G., *The Emerging Constitution* (New York: Harper's Magazine Press, 1974).

————, *The Compromising of the Constitution* (South Bend, Ind.: University of Notre Dame Press, 1976).

Tulis, Jeffrey K., *The Rhetorical Presidency* (Princeton, N.J.: Princeton University Press, 1987).

Tushnet, Mark, *Making Constitutional Law: Thurgood Marshall and the Supreme Court, 1961–1991* (New York: Oxford University Press, 1997).

Ultey, Robert L., Jr., ed., *The Promise of American Politics: Principles and Practice After Two Hundred Years* (Lanham, Ind.: University Press of America, 1989).

Van Horn, Carl E., Donald C. Baumer, and William T. Gormley, Jr., *Politics and Public Policy* (Washington, D.C.: CQ Press, 1989).

Verba, Sidney, Kay L. Schlozman, and Henry E. Brady, *Voice and Equality: Civic Voluntarism in American Politics* (Cambridge, Mass.: Harvard University Press, 1995).

Vile, John R., *Rewriting the United States Constitution: An Examination of Proposals from Reconstruction to the Present* (New York: Praeger, 1991).

———, *The Constitutional Amending Process in American Political Thought* (New York: Praeger, 1992).

———, *A Companion to the U.S. Constitution* (New York: Praeger, 1993a).

———, *Contemporary Questions Surrounding the Constitutional Amending Process* (New York: Praeger, 1993b).

Vogel, David, *Fluctuating Fortunes: The Political Power of Business in America* (New York: Basic Books, 1989).

Walker, David B., *Toward a Functioning Federalism* (Cambridge, Mass.: Winthrop, 1981).

Ware, Alan, *The Breakdown of Democratic Party Organization, 1940–1980* (New York: Oxford University Press, 1985).

Warshaw, Shirley A., *Powersharing: White House–Cabinet Relations in the Modern Presidency* (Albany, N.Y.: SUNY Press, 1996).

Wasby, Stephen L., "Interest Groups in Court: Race Relations Litigation," in *Interest Group Politics*, ed. Allan Cigler and Loomis Burdett (Washington, D.C.: CQ Press, 1983).

Waterman, Richard W., ed., *The Presidency Reconsidered* (Itasca, Ill.: Peacock Publishers, 1993).

Wattenberg, Martin P., *The Decline of American Political Parties, 1952–1994* (Cambridge, Mass.: Harvard University Press, 1996).

Wayne, Stephen, *The Legislative Presidency* (New York: Harper & Row, 1978).

Weaver, R. Kent, and Bert A. Rockman, *Do Institutions Matter?: Government Capabilities in the United States and Abroad* (Washington, D.C.: The Brookings Institution, 1993).

Weber, Paul, and Barbara Perry, *Unfounded Fears* (Westport, Conn.: Greenwood Press, 1989).

Whicker, Marcia, Ruth Strickland, and Raymond Moore, *The Constitution Under Pressure* (New York: Praeger, 1987).

White, Leonard D., *The Jacksonians* (New York: Macmillan, 1954).

Wiebe, Robert H., *Self-Rule: A Cultural History of American Democracy* (Chicago: University of Chicago Press, 1995).

Wiecek, William M., *The Guarantee Clause of the U.S. Constitution* (Ithaca, N.Y.: Cornell University, 1972).

Wilcox, Clyde, *Onward Christian Soldiers?: The Religious Right in American Politics* (Boulder, Colo.: Westview Press, 1996).

Wildavsky, Aaron, *The Beleaguered Presidency* (New Brunswick, N.J.: Transaction Publishers, 1991).

Will, George F., *Restoration: Congress, Term Limits, and the Recovery of Deliberative Democracy* (New York: Free Press, 1992).

Wilson, Bradford, and Peter W. Schramm, eds., *Separation of Powers and Good Government* (Lanham, Md.: Rowman and Littlefield, 1994).

Wilson, James Q., *Bureaucracy: What Government Agencies Do and Why They Do It* (New York: Basic Books, 1991).

Wilson, Woodrow, *Congressional Government* (Boston: Houghton Mifflin, 1885).

———, *Constitutional Government in the United States* (New York: Columbia University Press, [1908] 1917).

Wiltse, Charles M., *The Jeffersonian Tradition in American Democracy* (New York: Hill and Wang, 1960).

Wolfe, Christopher, *How to Read the Constitution: Originalism, Constitutional Interpretation, and Judicial Power* (Lanham, Md.: Rowman and Littlefield, 1994a).

———, *The Rise of Modern Judicial Review: From Constitutional Interpretation to Judge-Made Law,* rev. ed. (Lanham, Md.: Rowman and Littlefield, 1994b).

Wolpe, Bruce C., and Bertram J. Levine, *Lobbying Congress: How the System Works* (Washington, D.C.: CQ Press, 1996).

Wood, Gordon, *The Creation of the American Republic* (Chapel Hill: University of North Carolina Press, 1969).

Woodward, Gary C., *Perspectives on American Political Media* (Boston: Allyn & Bacon, 1997).

Wormuth, Francis D., *The Origins of Modern Constitutionalism* (New York: Harper & Row, 1949).

Wright, Deil S., *Understanding Intergovernmental Relations* (Belmont, Calif.: Duxburg, 1979).

————,*Understanding Intergovernmental Relations,* 2nd ed. (Monterey, Calif.: Brooks/Cole, 1982).

————, and Harvey L. White, eds., *Federalism and Intergovernmental Relations* (Washington, D.C.: American Society for Public Administration, 1984).

Zinn, Howard, *Declarations of Independence: Cross-Examining American Ideology* (New York: Harper & Row, 1991).

Index